Rome

"All you've got to do is decide to go and the hardest part is over.

So go!"

TONY WHEELER, COFOUNDER – LONELY PLANET

Duncan Garwood, Alexis Averbuck, Virginia Maxwell

Contents

Plan Your Trip 4

Explore Rome 52

Understand Rome 251

Survival Guide 291

Rome Maps 321

KIEVVICTOR / SHUTTERSTOCK ©

COVID-19

We have re-checked every business in this book before publication to ensure that it is still open after the COVID-19 outbreak. However, the economic and social impacts of COVID-19 will continue to be felt long after the outbreak has been contained, and many businesses, services and events referenced in this guide may experience ongoing restrictions. Some businesses may be temporarily closed, have changed their opening hours and services, or require bookings; some unfortunately could have closed permanently. We suggest you check with venues before visiting for the latest information.

(left) **Terme di Caracalla p191** Awe-inspiring ruins of an ancient bathing complex.

(right) **Coffee p40** Drink it standing at the bar, Italian style.

EKATERINA SMIRNOVA / GETTY IMAGES ©

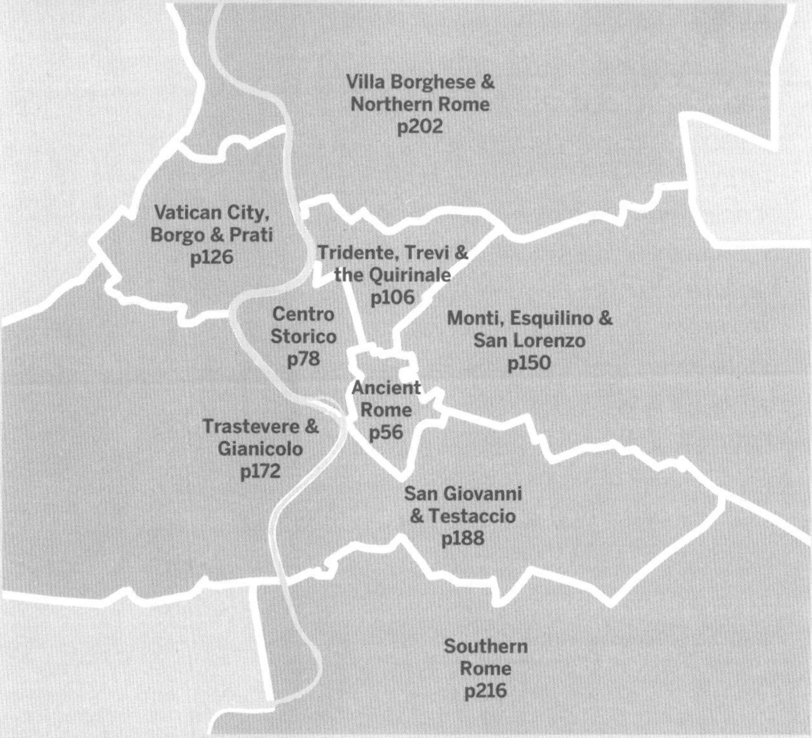

Right:
Trastevere (p172)

PHOTO BETO / GETTY IMAGES ©

WELCOME TO

Rome

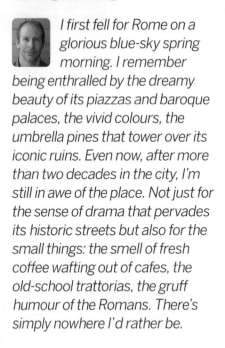

I first fell for Rome on a glorious blue-sky spring morning. I remember being enthralled by the dreamy beauty of its piazzas and baroque palaces, the vivid colours, the umbrella pines that tower over its iconic ruins. Even now, after more than two decades in the city, I'm still in awe of the place. Not just for the sense of drama that pervades its historic streets but also for the small things: the smell of fresh coffee wafting out of cafes, the old-school trattorias, the gruff humour of the Romans. There's simply nowhere I'd rather be.

By Duncan Garwood, Writer
For more about our writers, see p352

RUGANTINO
...AO...
Se EntRa
DA QuA!!!
Se stai a dieta
Perdi solo n'sacco
De Tempo..
mettete a sede
e magna
vedrai che starai
mejo!!!
RUGANTINO
RUGANTINO

Rome's Top Experiences

1 MONUMENTAL RUINS

Rome's tumultuous past is writ large on its historic streets. From iconic monuments such as the Colosseum and Pantheon to the tumbledown remnants of the forums, the city's muscular ruins recall its ancient heyday as *caput mundi* (world capital). More than two thousand years on and it remains an exhilarating experience to explore these sites and retrace the footsteps of Rome's legendary heroes.

Roman Forum

Give your imagination a workout as you explore the ruins of the Roman Forum (pictured right), once a busy district of temples, basilicas, shops and streets. Above, the remnants of the vast imperial palace lie strewn across the Palatino hill. p64

Colosseum

No photograph can prepare you for the thrill of seeing the Colosseum (pictured above and left) for the first time. More than any other monument, this fearsome amphitheatre encapsulates the blood and thunder of ancient Rome, and it's still an electrifying sight today. p58

Pantheon

The best preserved of Rome's ancient monuments, the Pantheon (pictured above) is a truly extraordinary building. Its columned portico and thick-set walls impress, but it's only when you get inside and see the dome soaring above you that you get the full measure of the place. p80

2 A VATICAN PILGRIMAGE

You don't have to be a believer to be bowled over by the Vatican. Centred on St Peter's Basilica, the tiny sovereign state is home to an unbelievable treasure trove of artistic and architectural riches. These include several of Michelangelo's most revered masterpieces, frescoes by the Renaissance artist Raphael, and a stunning series of ancient statuary in the Vatican Museums.

Vatican Museums

Michelangelo's kaleidoscopic Sistine Chapel frescoes provide the grand finale to the Vatican Museums (below), Rome's largest and most sumptuous art museum. Housed in the lavishly appointed Palazzo Apostolico Vaticano, the complex showcases the Vatican's immense collection of classical sculptures, Old Masters, frescoes, modern art and much more besides. p133

GRAFALEX/SHUTTERSTOCK ©

St Peter's Basilica

Even in a city of churches, St Peter's (above) stands head and shoulders above the rest. Everything about it is astonishing: the sweeping piazza, grandiose facade, opulent interior and, crowning it all, Michelangelo's dome, an architectural masterpiece. p128

Vatican Gardens

To complete your visit to the Vatican take a tour of the Vatican Gardens (right). The pope's private estate is a serene wonderland of grottoes, fountains, monuments and fortifications. p141

3 DIVINE ART

EVGENII IAROSHEVSKII/SHUTTERSTOCK ©

Few cities can rival Rome's artistic heritage. Throughout history, the city has attracted the top artists of the day and inspired them to push the boundaries of creative achievement. The result is a city awash with masterworks by the titans of European art – sculptures by Michelangelo, paintings by Caravaggio, frescoes by Raphael, fountains by Bernini.

Museo e Galleria Borghese

The greatest gallery you've never heard of, the Museo e Galleria Borghese (pictured above) houses some of Rome's most spectacular artworks. Chief among them are a series of sensational sculptures by Bernini and a celebrated statue by Canova. p204

Capitoline Museums

On one of Rome's most beautiful squares, the Capitoline Museums features amazing classical statuary, including Rome's iconic *Lupa Capitolina* (Capitoline Wolf), and a gallery of paintings by big-name baroque artists. p69

Museo Nazionale Romano: Palazzo Massimo alle Terme

Fabulous Roman frescoes and wall mosaics star at the Museo Nazionale Romano: Palazzo Massimo alle Terme, an oft-overlooked gem near Termini station. p152

4 LIVING THE DOLCE VITA

A trip to Rome is as much about enjoying the *dolce vita* lifestyle as gorging on art and culture. Browsing chic designer boutiques, sipping cappuccinos at streetside cafes, people-watching on pretty piazzas – these are all quintessential city experiences. So do as the Romans do and take time to enjoy the simple pleasures of life.

BELENOS/SHUTTERSTOCK ©

ANIBAL TREJO/SHUTTERSTOCK ©

BELENOS/SHUTTERSTOCK ©

Piazza Navona

With its ornamental fountains, showy church and baroque *palazzi*, Piazza Navona (pictured above left) is the elegant poster child of Rome's great piazzas. Adding to the spectacle are its ringside cafes and ever-present street artists. p82

Trevi Fountain

Join the crowds for your compulsory coin-throwing stop at the Trevi Fountain (pictured top right), Rome's most celebrated water feature. Local lore holds that you'll return to the city if you throw a coin into the water. p110

Spanish Steps

Sashay down the Spanish Steps (pictured bottom right) en route to the designer boutiques and flagship fashion stores on Via dei Condotti, Rome's premier shopping strip. p108

5 GOING UNDERGROUND

Hidden beneath Rome's spectacular cityscape is a thrilling underworld of pagan temples, creepy catacombs and underground ruins. This subterranean wonderland grew over the centuries as successive rulers rebuilt the city, piling their new palaces and churches atop existing buildings. Nowadays, modern construction projects regularly unearth archaeological finds in the city's fertile *sottosuolo* (underground).

VALERIOMEI/SHUTTERSTOCK ©

TROTALO/SHUTTERSTOCK ©

Catacombs

Rome's most famous catacombs (pictured top left) lie beneath Via Appia Antica in the city's south. Built as burial grounds by the early Christians, they extend for kilometres and hold thousands of bodies. p214

Domus Aurea

Go deep to discover the underground remains of the Domus Aurea (pictured bottom left), a colossal palace complex Nero built for himself. p155

Basilica di San Clemente

Beneath this medieval basilica (pictured above) lies the city's stratification: remains of an earlier basilica, a pagan temple and a 1st-century house. p192

6 GREEN OASES

VALERIOMEI/GETTY IMAGES ©

DIEGO FIORE/SHUTTERSTOCK ©

Rome's parks and gardens provide welcome sanctuary from the city's relentless noise and heat. Ranging from elegant, landscaped estates to hilltop hideaways and former hunting reserves, they vary in look and size. Some boast blistering museums and romantic views while others simply offer space and the peace to recharge your batteries.

Villa Borghese

Rome's Central Park, Villa Borghese (left) is the best known of the capital's main parks. Much frequented by tourists and Romans alike, it features several superlative museums, leafy lanes, and heavenly views from the Pincio Hill. p204

Giardino degli Aranci

For yet more panoramas, head to the Giardino degli Aranci (Parco Savello; pictured left), a hilltop garden on the Aventino. Nearby, you can admire an altogether different view through the keyhole of the Villa del Priorato di Malta. p194

Orto Botanico

A top place to unwind, Rome's 12-hectare botanic garden cloaks the steep slopes of the Gianicolo hill above Trastevere. p177

7 ROMAN FEASTING

Eating out is one of the great pleasures of a trip to Rome and the combination of romantic alfresco settings and fantastic food is a guarantee of good times. For contemporary fine dining, there are any number of refined restaurants, but for a truly Roman experience try one of the capital's convivial trattorias or boisterous pizzerias.

Cucina Romana

For a taste of authentic nose-to-tail Roman cuisine, head to Testaccio. The area's trattorias are renowned for their traditional vibe and classic old-school cooking. p196

An Evening in Trastevere

The Instagram-friendly Trastevere neighbourhood (pictured above) is a top spot for a night's dining. Its medieval lanes and animated piazzas harbour hundreds of bars, cafes, trattorias and restaurants catering to Romans and besotted visitors. p182

Street Food

Street food fans can fill up on world-beating *pizza al taglio* (sliced pizza) – try Bonci Pizzarium – as well as gelato, *supplì* (fried rice balls) and *trapizzini* (stuffed cones of pizza-like dough). p143

Right: Claudio Torcè, of gelato house Torcè (p197)

8 EPIC VIEWS

Rome's historic monuments and hills provide stunning vantage points for enjoying views over the city's rooftops, domes and spires. Some perches require serious legwork to get to; others can be accessed by lift. But however you reach them, you'll be rewarded with panoramas that have been entrancing visitors for centuries.

Vittoriano

Not recommended for vertigo sufferers, the summit of the Vittoriano towers over the rest of Rome, providing sweeping 360-degree views of the city and distant hills. p75

Gianicolo

A short but steep walk up from Trastevere, the Gianicolo hill commands classic views over Rome's skyline (pictured above). Look out for the Pantheon's concrete dome and Michelangelo's *cupola* atop St Peter's Basilica. p182

Piazza del Quirinale

The piazza fronting Italy's Presidential palace sets a suitably grand setting for mellowing out to romantic sunset views. p113

What's New

After more than a year of COVID lockdowns and semi-deserted streets, Rome is back in business. In recent months, the ever-resilient Romans have voted for a new mayor, applauded a number of restorations at historic monuments and welcomed several new street murals.

Green Pass

A digital Green Pass has become the latest must-have in Rome. The COVID vaccination certificate is now required for a number of activities, including eating indoors in restaurants and visiting museums, monuments, and cultural sites. Visits to most sites must also now be pre-booked online.

Electric Scooters

Electric scooters have invaded Rome's streets. Scooter sharing schemes were introduced in mid-2020 and have proved very popular, particularly among the city's young.

Not all Romans are fans, though, and critics have highlighted the illegal carrying of passengers, speeding on sidewalks, and badly parked scooters blocking pavements.

Ancient Openings

Several high-profile monuments have opened their doors to visitors after major restoration projects. At the Colosseum, large swathes of the hypogeum (underground backstage area) were made accessible to the public after extensive renovations. These came as the second phase in a three-part project at the amphitheatre. The final part, expected to be completed in 2024, will see the construction of a new visitor centre.

Elsewhere, the Mausoleo di Augusto opened to visitors for the first time in decades, and the Casa delle Vestali reopened on the Roman Forum.

Near Piazza Navona, restoration continues at the Chiesa di Sant'Ivo alla Sapienza after the Borromini-designed church suffered damage in a 2016 earthquake.

LOCAL KNOWLEDGE

WHAT'S HAPPENING IN ROME

Duncan Garwood, Lonely Planet writer

Italy was hit hard by COVID-19. Rome shut down in March 2020 when Italy became the first European country to impose a nationwide lockdown. The rules were strict and an eerie silence descended on the city. To keep morale high Romans sang from the rooftops, bellowing out the national anthem and *Bella ciao* from their balconies. More than a year on and it's not quite business as usual – some COVID restrictions remain – but the streets are busy, shops and offices are open, and the gossips are back in the bars. With coffee in hand, they debate hot topics such as the city's perennial struggle with waste collection and the state of *degrado* (degradation) afflicting many streets and parks. So far, so usual. What's not so usual is the lack of tourists. Tourism was thriving before the pandemic when the talk was of ever-increasing numbers, even overtourism. Now, the challenge is to find a way of encouraging visitors back to the city in a way that's both sustainable and environmentally viable.

Boars in the 'Burbs

Wild boars have become a political hot potato in Rome. Sightings of boars waddling around the suburbs have become increasingly common in recent times, prompting a bitter blame game between mayor Raggi and her critics.

This came to a head in the run-up to the 2021 mayoral election when Raggi sued Lazio's regional government for failing to control the boar population in the surrounding countryside.

On social media, wits called for the installation of *piste cinghiabili* (wild boar lanes) alongside *piste ciclabili* (cycle lanes).

Caravaggio's Coins

September 2021 marked the 450th anniversary of the birth of Caravaggio, the great baroque painter whose masterpieces adorn several of Rome's museums and galleries.

To mark the occasion, the Vatican issued a commemorative €2 coin depicting a detail from the artist's *Ragazzo col Canestro di Frutta* (Boy with a Basket of Fruit), the original of which hangs in the Museo e Galleria Borghese.

Street Art

Three of Rome's favourite actors have been immortalised in a trio of giant murals by street artist Lucamaleonte.

Alberto Sordi is depicted as one of his best-loved characters, the Marquis of Grillo, in the Garbatella neighbourhood. To the northeast, the much-loved Anna Magnani looks down on the Tiburtino III district, while in the northern Tufello neighbourhood, Gigi Proietti gazes down on his old stomping ground.

New Mayor

It's all change at City Hall after Virginia Raggi of the Five Star Movement was voted out of office in the 2021 mayoral elections.

Raggi made headlines when she became Rome's first woman mayor in 2016 but during her time in office she never managed to win over her vociferous critics who accused her of failing to clean up the city's streets and improve public transport.

In late 2021, her successor was decided: centre-left candidate Roberto Gualtieri beat out his right-wing opponent, Enrico Michetti in a runoff.

LISTEN, WATCH & FOLLOW

For inspiration and up-to-date news: www.lonelyplanet.com/rome

Wanted in Rome (www.wantedinrome.com) News, listings and ideas from in-the-know expat magazine.

Katie Parla (www.katieparla.com) Roman cuisine and all the latest on the city's food scene.

Rachel Eats (www.racheleats.wordpress.com) Tales from the Roman kitchen of British food writer Rachel Roddy.

Romeing (www.romeing.it) For features, whats-on and insights into the city's cultural scene.

FAST FACTS

Food trend Farmer's markets

Obelisks Rome boasts more ancient obelisks than any other city; the first were brought from Egypt by the emperor Augustus.

Euros The celebrations that greeted Italy's victory in the Euro 2020 football championship were so loud they were picked up by seismologists monitoring for earthquake activity.

Pop 2.8 million

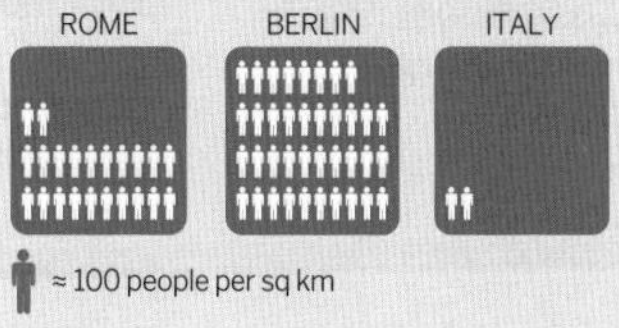

Need to Know

For more information, see Survival Guide (p291)

Currency
Euro (€)

Language
Italian

Visas
Not required by EU citizens. Not required by nationals of Australia, Canada, New Zealand, USA and UK for stays of up to 90 days.

Money
ATMs are widespread. Major credit cards are widely accepted but some smaller shops, trattorias and hotels might not take them.

Mobile Phones
Local SIM cards can be used in European, Australian and unlocked US phones. Other phones must be set to roaming.

Time
Western European Time (GMT/UTC plus one hour)

Tourist Information
There are tourist information points at Fiumicino (Fiumicino Airport; International Arrivals, Terminal 3; ⌚8am-8.45pm) and Ciampino (Arrivals Hall; ⌚8.30am-6pm) airports, as well as locations across the city. Each can provide city maps and sell the Roma Pass.

Daily Costs

Budget: Less than €110

- Dorm bed: €15–45
- Double room in a budget hotel: €60–130
- Pizza plus beer: €15

Midrange: €110–250

- Double room in a hotel: €100–200
- Local restaurant meal: €25–45
- Admission to Vatican Museums: €17
- Roma Pass, a 72-hour card covering museum entry and public transport: €38.50

Top end: More than €250

- Double room in a four- or five-star hotel: €200 plus
- Top restaurant dinner: €45–160
- Opera ticket: €17–150
- City-centre taxi ride: €10–15
- Auditorium concert tickets: €20–90

Advance Planning

Two months before Book high-season accommodation.

One month before Check for concerts at www.auditorium.com. Book tickets for Colosseum tours and visits to the Museo e Galleria Borghese and Palazzo Farnese.

One to two weeks before Reserve tickets for the pope's weekly audience at St Peter's.

Few days before Reserve tables at top restaurants. Book Vatican Museums and Colosseum tickets (advisable to avoid queues).

Useful Websites

060608 (www.060608.it) For practical details on sights, transport and upcoming events.

Coopculture (www.coopculture.it) Ticket booking for Rome's monuments.

Lonely Planet (www.lonelyplanet.com/rome) Destination information, hotel reviews, traveller forum and more.

Romeing (www.romeing.it) English-language site with events listings, thematic sections and features.

Turismo Roma (www.turismoroma.it) Rome's official tourist website.

Vatican Museums (www.museivaticani.va) Book tickets and tours to the museums and Vatican sites.

WHEN TO GO

Spring (April to June) and autumn (September and October) are the best times – the weather's good and there are many festivals and outdoor events on.

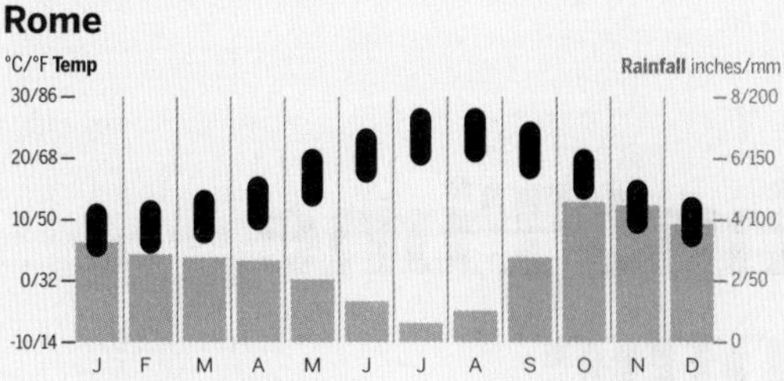

Arriving in Rome

Leonardo da Vinci (Fiumicino) Airport Leonardo Express trains to Stazione Termini 6.08am to 11.23pm, €14; slower FL1 trains to Trastevere, Ostiense and Tiburtina stations 5.57am to 10.42pm, €8; buses to Stazione Termini 6.05am to 12.40am, €6 to €6.90; airport-to-hotel shuttles from €22 per person; taxis €50 (fixed fare to within the Aurelian walls).

Ciampino Airport Buses to Stazione Termini 4am to 12.15am, €6; airport-to-hotel shuttles €25 per person; taxis €30 (fixed fare to within the Aurelian walls).

Stazione Termini Airport buses and trains, and international trains, arrive at Stazione Termini. From there, continue by bus, metro or taxi.

For much more on **arrival** see p292

Getting Around

Public transport includes buses, trams, metro and a suburban train network. The main hub is Stazione Termini. Tickets, which come in various forms, are valid for all forms of transport. Children under 10 years travel free.

➡ **Metro** The metro is quicker than surface transport, but the network is limited. Two main lines serve the centre, A (orange) and B (blue), crossing at Stazione Termini. Trains run between 5.30am and 11.30pm (to 1.30am on Fridays and Saturdays).

➡ **Buses** Most routes pass through Stazione Termini. Buses run from approximately 5.30am until midnight, with limited services throughout the night.

➡ **Foot** Walking is the best way of getting around the *centro storico* (historic centre).

For much more on **getting around** see p294

Sleeping

Rome is expensive and busy; book ahead to secure the best deal. Accommodation ranges from palatial five-star hotels to hostels, B&Bs, *pensioni* (guesthouses) and private rooms; there's also a growing number of boutique suite and apartment hotels. Hostels are the cheapest option, and many offer both dorm beds and private rooms; most *pensioni* are in the budget range, too. B&Bs and hotels cover every style and price range.

Useful Websites

➡ **Lonely Planet** (www.lonelyplanet.com/italy/rome) Author-reviewed accommodation options.

➡ **Cross Pollinate** (☎06 9936 9799; www.cross-pollinate.com) Personally vetted rooms and apartments by the team behind Rome's Beehive (p247) hostel.

➡ **Bed & Breakfast Italia** (☎06 8837 3407; www.bbitalia.it) Italian B&B network listing many Rome options.

For much more on **sleeping** see p240

First Time Rome

For more information, see Survival Guide (p291)

Checklist

- Check your passport is valid.
- Organise travel insurance.
- Inform your credit-/debit-card company of your travels.
- Check that you can use your mobile phone.
- Book accommodation and tickets for sights like the Vatican Museums, Colosseum and Museo e Galleria Borghese.
- If coming at Christmas or Easter, check details of services at St Peter's Basilica and other churches.

What to Pack

- Trainers or comfy walking shoes – cobbled streets can be murder on the feet.
- Smart-casual evening clothes – Romans dress up to go out.
- Purse with strap – petty theft can be a problem.
- Water bottle – refill it at drinking fountains.
- Electrical adaptor and phone charger.

Top Tips for Your Trip

- Don't try to cover everything. Focus on a few sights/areas and leave the rest for next time.
- Rome's historic centre is made for leisurely strolling, so allow time for mapless wandering. Half the fun of Rome is discovering what's around the corner.
- When choosing where to eat, never judge a place by its appearance. You'll often have your most enjoyable meals in modest-looking trattorias.
- Expect queues at major sights such as the Colosseum, St Peter's Basilica and Vatican Museums. Pre-booking tickets costs extra but reduces queuing time.
- To deal with summer heat, adjust to the local rhythm: go out in the morning, rest after lunch and head out again in the late afternoon.
- August is Italy's main holiday period. Romans desert the city in droves, and many shops and eateries close for a week or two around 15 August.

What to Wear

Appearances matter in Rome. That said, you'll need to dress comfortably because you'll be walking a lot. Suitable wear for men is generally trousers (pants) and shirts or polo shirts, and for women, skirts, trousers or dresses. Shorts, T-shirts and sandals are fine in summer, but bear in mind that strict dress codes are enforced at St Peter's Basilica and the Vatican Museums. For evening wear, smart casual is the norm. A light sweater or waterproof jacket is useful in spring and autumn.

Be Forewarned

- Rome is a safe city, but petty theft can be a problem and pickpockets are active in touristy areas, around Stazione Termini and on crowded public transport – the 64 Vatican bus is notorious.
- In case of theft or loss, always report the incident to the police within 24 hours and ask for a statement.

Money

ATMs (*bancomat* in Italian) are widespread. Major credit cards are widely accepted but some smaller shops, trattorias and hotels might not take them.

Save money by drinking coffee standing at the bar rather than taking a seat.

State-run museums are free every first Sunday of the month between October and March. The Vatican Museums are *gratis* every last Sunday of the month.

For more information, see p302.

Taxes & Refunds

A value-added tax known as IVA *(Imposta sul Valore Aggiunta)* is included in the price of most goods and services. It currently ranges from 4% to 25%. Tax-free shopping is available at some shops.

All overnight stays in the city are subject to an accommodation tax (p241) – the exact sum depends on the length of your sojourn and type of accommodation.

Tipping

Romans are not big tippers:

Taxis Optional, but most people round up to the nearest euro.

Restaurants Service *(servizio)* is generally included; if it's not, a euro or two is fine in pizzerias and trattorias, no more than five to 10% in smart restaurants.

Bars Not necessary, although many people leave small change if drinking at the bar.

Hotels Tip porters about €5 at A-list hotels.

Language

You can get by with English, but you'll improve your experience no end by mastering a few basic words and expressions in Italian. This is particularly true in restaurants where menus don't always have English translations and some places rely on waiters to explain what's on. For more on language, see p306.

1 What's the local speciality?
Qual'è la specialità di questa regione?
kwa·*le* la spe·cha·lee·*ta* dee *kwes*·ta re·*jo*·ne

A bit like the rivalry between medieval Italian city-states, these days the country's regions compete in speciality foods and wines.

2 Which combined tickets do you have?
Quali biglietti cumulativi avete?
kwa·lee bee·*lye*·tee koo·moo·la·*tee*·vee a·*ve*·te

Make the most of your euro by getting combined tickets to various sights; they are available in all major Italian cities.

3 Where can I buy discount designer items?
C'è un outlet in zona? che oon *owt*·let in *zo*·na

Discount fashion outlets are big business in major cities – get bargain-priced seconds, samples and cast-offs for *la bella figura*.

4 I'm here with my husband/boyfriend.
Sono qui con il mio marito/ragazzo.
so·no kwee kon eel *mee*·o ma·*ree*·to/ra·*ga*·tso

Solo women travellers may receive unwanted attention in some parts of Italy; if ignoring fails have a polite rejection ready.

5 Let's meet at 6pm for pre-dinner drinks.
Ci vediamo alle sei per un aperitivo.
chee ve·*dya*·mo *a*·le say per oon a·pe·ree·*tee*·vo

At dusk, watch the main piazza get crowded with people sipping colourful cocktails and snacking the evening away: join your new friends for this authentic Italian ritual!

Etiquette

Italy is quite a formal society, and the niceties of social interaction are observed.

Greetings Greet people in bars, shops, trattorias etc with a *buongiorno* (good morning) or *buonasera* (good evening).

Asking for help Say *mi scusi* (excuse me) to attract attention; use *permesso* (permission) to pass someone in a crowded space.

Dress Cover up at churches and go smart when eating out.

Roma Pass

This useful pass is available online, from participating museums, tourist info points and metro ticket offices.

72 hours (€38.50) Provides free admission to two museums or sites, unlimited transport and reduced admission to extra sites.

48 hours (€28) Gives free admission to one museum or site, then as per the 72-hour pass.

Perfect Days

Day One

Ancient Rome (p56)

Start the day at the **Colosseum**, Rome's huge gladiatorial arena – try to get there early to avoid the queues. Then head over to the **Palatino** to poke around crumbling ruins and admire sweeping views. From the Palatino, follow on to the **Roman Forum**, an evocative area of tumbledown temples, sprouting columns and ruined basilicas.

Lunch Sample regional specialities at Terre e Domus (p77).

Ancient Rome (p56)

After lunch, climb up to **Piazza del Campidoglio** and the **Capitoline Museums**, where you'll find some sensational ancient sculpture. Done there, enjoy great views from the **Vittoriano** before pushing on to the *centro storico* (historic centre) to explore its labyrinthine lanes and headline sights such as the **Pantheon** and **Piazza Navona**.

Dinner Dine on modern Italian cuisine at La Ciambella (p91).

Centro Storico (p78)

In the evening get a taste of *dolce vita* bar life. Depending on what you're after, you could chat over coffee at **Caffè Sant'Eustachio**, or sip brilliantly executed G&Ts at the **Gin Corner**.

Day Two

Vatican City, Borgo & Prati (p126)

On day two, hit the Vatican. First up are the **Vatican Museums**. Once you've blown your mind on the Sistine Chapel and the myriad other masterpieces, complete your tour at **St Peter's Basilica**. If you have the energy, climb its Michelangelo-designed dome for fantastic views over St Peter's Square and the nearby Castel Sant'Angelo. But if the queues are bad or you're suffering art overload, stop first for an early lunch.

Lunch Savour Rome's best sliced pizza at Bonci Pizzarium (p143).

Tridente, Trevi & the Quirinale (p106)

Recharged, jump on the metro and head over the river to check out **Piazza di Spagna** and the **Spanish Steps**, then push on to the **Trevi Fountain** where tradition dictates you throw a coin into the water to ensure you'll return to Rome. Next, head up the hill to catch the sunset on **Piazza del Quirinale** in front of the presidential palace, Palazzo del Quirinale.

Dinner Dine on creative cuisine at hip Pianostrada (p95).

Centro Storico (p78)

Spend the evening in the buzzing area around **Campo de' Fiori**. Try **Roscioli Caffè** for an aperitif, **Open Baladin** for craft beers or **Barnum Cafe** for chilled cocktails.

RUDYBALASKO/GETTY IMAGES ©

St Peter's Basilica (p128)

Day Three

Villa Borghese & Northern Rome (p202)

Day three starts with a trip to the **Museo e Galleria Borghese** – remember to book tickets – to marvel at amazing baroque sculpture and Renaissance masterpieces. Afterwards, wander through **Villa Borghese** to the **Pincio Hill Gardens** for some romantic rooftop views.

Lunch Fill up on the vegetarian buffet at Il Margutta (p116).

Tridente, Trevi & the Quirinale (p106)

In the afternoon, check out arty **Via Margutta** before heading over to **Piazza del Popolo** where you can catch a couple of Caravaggios at the **Basilica di Santa Maria del Popolo**. Next, dedicate some time to browsing the flagship stores and designer boutiques in the upscale streets off Via del Corso.

Dinner Book at Dal Cavalier Gino (p97) for an authentic trattoria experience.

Trastevere & Gianicolo (p172)

Over the river, the picture-perfect Trastevere neighbourhood bursts with life in the evening as locals and tourists flock to its many cafes and bars. Hotspots include **Terra Satis**, a laid-back neighbourhood wine bar, and mellow **Niji Roma**, a stylish spot for cool cocktails.

Day Four

Southern Rome (p216)

On day four it's time to venture out to **Via Appia Antica**. The main attractions here are the catacombs, and it's a wonderfully creepy sensation to duck down into these sinister pitch-black tunnels. Back above ground, you'll find the remains of an ancient racetrack at the nearby **Villa di Massenzio**.

Lunch Eat on the Appia, at Qui Nun se More Mai (p224).

Monti, Esquilino & San Lorenzo (p150)

Once you've eaten, head north to Stazione Termini and the nearby **Museo Nazionale Romano: Palazzo Massimo alle Terme**, a superb museum full of classical sculpture and stunning mosaics. Then, drop by the monumental **Basilica di Santa Maria Maggiore**, famous for its mosaics, and the **Basilica di San Pietro in Vincoli**, home to Michelangelo's muscular *Moses* sculpture. Finish up with some shopping in the fashionable boutiques of the **Monti** district.

Dinner Enjoy great wine over dinner at La Barrique (p160).

Monti, Esquilino & San Lorenzo (p150)

Stay put in Monti, where there's plenty of late-night action. Pick a wine bar or cafe from which to see out the day. **Ai Tre Scalini** is an ever-popular hang-out.

Month By Month

TOP EVENTS

Natale di Roma, April

Estate Romana, June to September

Lungo il Tevere, June to September

Festa de' Noantri, July

La Festa di Roma, December

January

As New Year celebrations fade, the winter cold digs in. It's a quiet time of year, but the winter sales are a welcome diversion.

Shopping Sales

Running from early January, typically the first Saturday of the month, to mid-February, the winter fashion sales offer savings of between 20% and 50%.

February

Rome's winter quiet is disrupted by weekend invasions by cheerful rugby fans in town for the annual Six Nations rugby tournament.

Carnevale

Roman children traditionally don fancy dress and throw *coriandoli* (coloured confetti) over each other during carnival. Costumed parades are also sometimes held around Piazza del Popolo, Via del Corso, Piazza di Spagna and Piazza Navona.

April

April is a great month in Rome, with lovely, sunny weather, fervent Easter celebrations, azaleas on the Spanish Steps and Rome's birthday festivities. Expect high-season prices.

Easter

Easter is a big deal in Rome. On Good Friday the pope leads a candlelit procession around the Colosseum, and there are other smaller parades around the city. At noon on Easter Sunday the pope blesses the crowds in St Peter's Square.

Mostra delle Azalee

From early April to mid-May, the Spanish Steps are decorated with hundreds of vases of blooming, brightly coloured azaleas).

Natale di Roma

Rome celebrates its birthday on 21 April with music, processions, historical re-creations and fireworks. Action is centred on Via dei Fori Imperiali and the Circo Massimo.

May

May is a busy, high-season month. The weather's perfect – usually warm enough to eat outside – and the city is looking gorgeous with blue skies and spring flowers.

Primo Maggio

Thousands of fans troop to Piazza di San Giovanni in Laterano for Rome's free May Day rock concert. It's a mostly Italian affair with big-name local performers, but you might catch the occasional foreign guest star.

June

Summer has arrived and with it hot weather and the Italian school holidays. The city's festival season breaks into full stride with many outdoor events.

Festa dei Santi Pietro e Paolo

On 29 June Rome celebrates its two patron saints, Peter and Paul, with flower displays on St Peter's Square and festivities near the Basilica di San Paolo Fuori le Mura.

Lungo il Tevere

Nightly crowds converge on the River Tiber for this popular summer-long event. Stalls, clubs, bars, restaurants, cinemas, even dance floors line the river bank as Rome's nightlife goes al fresco.

Roma Incontra il Mondo

From late June to August, Villa Ada is transformed into a colourful multi-ethnic village for this popular annual event. There's a laid-back party vibe and an excellent program of gigs ranging from reggae to jazz and world music.

Estate Romana

From June to September Rome's big summer festival involves everything from concerts and dance performances to book fairs, puppet shows and late-night museum openings.

July

Hot summer temperatures make sightseeing a physical endeavour, but come the cool of evening, the city's streets burst into life as locals come out to enjoy the summer festivities.

Festa de' Noantri

Trastevere celebrates its roots with a raucous street party in the last two weeks of the month. Events kick off with a religious procession and continue with much eating, drinking, dancing and praying.

August

Rome melts in the heat as locals flee the city for their summer holidays. Many businesses shut down around 15 August, but hoteliers offer discounts and there are loads of summer events to enjoy.

Festa della Madonna della Neve

Rose petals are showered on celebrants in the Basilica di Santa Maria Maggiore to commemorate a miraculous 4th-century snowfall.

September

Life returns to the city after the August torpor. The kids go back to school and locals return to work, but there's still a relaxed summer vibe and the weather's perfect. High-season rates apply.

Romaeuropa

Established international performers join emerging stars at Rome's autumn festival of theatre, opera and dance. Events staged across town from mid-September to mid-November range from avant-garde dance to installations, multimedia shows and recitals.

October

Autumn is a good time to visit – the warm weather is holding, Romaeuropa ensures plenty of cultural action and, with the schools back, there are far fewer tourists around.

Festa del Cinema di Roma

At the Auditorium Parco della Musica in late October, Rome's film festival rolls out the red carpet for Hollywood hot shots and bigwigs from Italian cinema.

December

The build-up to Christmas is a festive time – the Christmas lights go on, shopping takes on a new urgency and *presepi* (nativity scenes) appear across town, most spectacularly in St Peter's Square.

Piazza Navona Christmas Fair

Rome's showpiece baroque piazza becomes a festive market with stalls selling everything from stuffed toys to teeth-cracking *torrone* (nougat). Tradition dictates that the *befana* (witch) appears on Epiphany (6 January) to hand out sweets to children.

Under the Radar

Seeing Rome's headline acts means crowds and the risk of overtourism, particularly in peak periods. To avoid the queues and discover another side of Rome, set your sights on the city's lesser-known gems and neighbourhoods.

Alternative Neighbourhoods

Garbatella

Built in the 1920s and '30s as a garden suburb for city workers, Garbatella (p223) is a colourful neighbourhood known for its eclectic architecture, lush courtyards and eye-catching street murals.

EUR

In Rome's southern reaches, EUR (p226) is a world apart with its wide spaces and muscular modern architecture. A highlight is the Palazzo della Civiltà del Lavoro, a masterpiece of Italian rationalism known locally as the Square Colosseum.

Quartiere Coppedè

The pocket-size Coppedè (p209) district, designed in the 1920s and hidden away northeast of Villa Borghese, is a fairy-tale mishmash of turreted villas, towers, gargoyles, arches and graceful palm trees.

Sites Minus the Masses

Museo Nazionale Etrusco di Villa Giulia

This elegantly housed museum (p208) provides a fascinating introduction to Italy's mysterious pre-Roman civilisation with its superb collection of Etruscan treasures.

Centrale Montemartini

Ancient sculptures sidle up to heavy industrial machinery at the Centrale Montemartini (p223), a de-commissioned power station turned classical art museum in Ostiense.

Cimitero Acattolico per gli Stranieri

Overlooked by an ancient pyramid, Rome's serene Protestant cemetery (p194) is a verdant oasis of peace in Testaccio. Look for the graves of poets John Keats and Percy Shelley.

Palazzo Spada

This ornate Mannerist palace (p86) near Campo de' Fiori harbours one of Rome's most famous architectural follies, the Prospettiva del Borromini (Borromini's Perspective).

Crowd-Free Churches

Chiesa di Santo Stefano Rotondo

Few people make it to this secluded Celio church (p193), but those who do rarely forget its chilling cycle of 16th-century frescoes depicted the appalling horrors suffered by many early Christian saints.

Basilica di Santa Prassede

From the outside this small, easy-to-miss basilica (p154) looks nothing special, but go inside and you'll come face to face with some of Rome's most dazzling Byzantine mosaics.

Chiesa di San Francesco d'Assisi a Ripa Grande

In a quiet corner of Trastevere, this seemingly unremarkable church (p176) is home to one of Rome's great baroque masterpieces: Bernini's sensual sculpture of Beata Ludovica Albertoni.

With Kids

Despite a reputation as a highbrow cultural destination, Rome has a lot to offer kids. Child-specific sights might be thin on the ground, but if you know where to go, there's plenty to keep the little 'uns occupied and parents happy.

TRAVNIKOVSTUDIO / SHUTTERSTOCK ©

Trevi Fountain (p108)

History for Kids

Colosseum

Everyone wants to see the Colosseum (p58) and it doesn't disappoint, especially if accompanied by tales of bloodthirsty gladiators and hungry lions. For maximum effect prep your kids beforehand with a Rome-based film.

Terme di Caracalla

Virtual reality brings the Terme di Caracalla (p191) back to life courtesy of headsets that recreate the massive baths as they looked in their heyday.

Le Domus Romane di Palazzo Valentini

Parents and older kids will enjoy the multimedia tour of Roman excavations beneath Palazzo Valentini (p114).

Museums for Kids

Explora

Near Piazza del Popolo, Explora – Museo dei Bambini di Roma (p208) is a hands-on museum for kids under 12, with interactive displays and a free play park.

Museo delle Cere

Go face to face with popes, rock stars and footy players at Rome's cheesy wax museum, the **Museo delle Cere** (Map p332, D8; ☎06 679 64 82; www.museodellecereroma.com; Piazza dei Santissimi Apostoli 68a; adult/reduced €10/8; ⏲9am-9pm summer, to 8pm winter; 👪).

Museo delle Mura

Walk along a stretch of the Aurelian Wall at the Museo delle Mura (p218), a small museum housed in one of Rome's ancient city gates.

Hands-on Activities

Trevi Fountain

Join the crowds and throw a coin into the Trevi Fountain (p110). And if the kids ask, you can tell them that about €3000 is thrown in on an average day.

CITY TRAILS

For an insight into Rome aimed directly at kids, pick up a copy of Lonely Planet's *City Trails: Rome*. Perfect for children aged eight and up, it opens up a world of intriguing stories and fascinating facts about Rome's people, places, history and culture.

Bocca della Verità

Put your hand in the Bocca della Verità (Mouth of Truth; p76). Just don't tell a fib; legend says the mouth will bite it off.

Creepy Sights

Catacombs

Spook your teens with a trip to the catacombs on Via Appia Antica (p218). These creepy tunnels, full of tombs and ancient burial chambers, are fascinating, but not suitable for children under about seven years old.

Convento dei Cappuccini

One for older kids, the crypt under the Convento dei Cappuccini (p115) is a decidedly weird place where everything is made from human bones.

Food for Kids

Pizza

Pizza al taglio (pizza by the slice) is a godsend for parents. It's cheap (about €1 buys two small slices of pizza *bianca* – with salt and olive oil), easy to get hold of (there are hundreds of takeaways around town) and works wonders on flagging spirits.

Gelato

Ice cream is another manna from heaven, served in *coppette* (tubs) or *coni* (cones). Child-friendly flavours include *fragola* (strawberry), *cioccolato* (chocolate) and *bacio* (with hazelnuts).

NEED TO KNOW

Getting around Cobbled streets make getting around with a pram or pushchair difficult.

Eating out In a restaurant ask for a *mezza porzione* (child's portion) and *seggiolone* (highchair).

Admission prices Under-18s get in free at state-run museums, while city-run museums are free for under-sixes and discounted for six to 25 year olds.

Transport Under-10s travel free on all public transport in the city.

Run in the Park

To let the kids off the leash, head to Villa Borghese (p207), the most central of Rome's main parks. There's plenty of space to run around in – though it's not absolutely car-free – and you can hire family bikes. Other parks are Villa Celimontana (p193) and Villa Torlonia (p209).

Animal Spotting

Animal Sculptures

Try to spot as many animal sculptures as you can. There are hundreds around town, including an elephant (outside the Basilica di Santa Maria Sopra Minerva), lions (at the the Cordonata staircase), bees (on Bernini's fountain just off Piazza Barberini), horses, eagles and, of course, Rome's trademark wolf in the Capitoline Museums (p69).

Cats

Cats have had the run of Rome's streets for centuries. These days they hang out in the ruins on the Largo di Torre Argentina (p813).

Zoo

After all those churches and museums, the **Bioparco** (Map p348, E5; ☎06 360 82 11; www.bioparco.it; Viale del Giardino Zoologico 1; adult/reduced €16/13; ⏰9.30am-6pm summer, to 5pm winter; 🚌Bioparco) in Villa Borghese offers some light relief.

Like a Local

Gregarious and convivial, Romans enjoy their city. They love hanging out in its piazzas and speeding around in small cars; they like to dress up and adore going out. They know theirs is a beautiful city, but they're not jealous and everyone is welcome.

Drink Like a Local

Coffee

Prendere un caffè (having a coffee) is one of the great rituals of Roman life. As a rule, locals will stop at a bar for a coffee in the morning before work, and then again after lunch. To fit in with the crowd, ask for *un caffè* (the term espresso is rarely used) and drink standing at the bar. Also, never order a cappuccino after lunch.

For a taste of Rome's finest, head to Caffè Sant'Eustachio (p99) in the *centro storico* (historic centre) or Sciascia Caffè (p146) in Prati.

Cocktails

Romans have discovered craft cocktails in a big way, and underground speakeasies are a big thing right now. Hotspots include Keyhole (p183), a model underground bar in Trastevere, and Club Derrière (p99), a hidden hang-out in the heart of the *centro storico.*

Cool Neighbourhoods

Trastevere

A picturesque district full of bars, cafes and trattorias, Trastevere (p172) has long been a foreigners' favourite. But Romans love it too, and amid the tourist bustle you'll find some characteristic city haunts.

Ostiense

With its disused factories, authentic trattorias and university campus, Ostiense (p223) is home to hot clubs and hip bars, as well as several cultural gems.

San Lorenzo

San Lorenzo (p150), a grungy, graffiti-daubed district, is one of the most energetic after-dark 'hoods. Students, fun-seekers and left-leaning urbanites pack its craft-beer bars, gritty clubs and basement venues.

Testaccio

Down by the Tiber, once-proletarian Testaccio (p188) is a local foodie hotspot with its market stalls and ever-popular Roman trattorias such as Flavio al Velavevodetto (p196).

Passeggiata on Via del Corso

The *passeggiata* (traditional evening stroll) is a quintessential Roman experience. It's particularly colourful at weekends when families, friends and lovers take to the streets to strut up and down, slurp on gelato and window-shop.

To join in, head to Via del Corso around 6pm. Alternatively, descend the Spanish Steps and watch the theatrics unfold on Piazza di Spagna (p108).

Football at Stadio Olimpico

Football is a Roman passion, with support divided between the two local teams: Roma and Lazio. Both play their home games at the Stadio Olimpico (p213), Rome's impressive Olympic stadium. If you go to a game, make sure you get it right – Roma play in red and yellow and their supporters stand in the *Curva Sud* (South Stand); Lazio play in sky blue and their fans fill the *Curva Nord* (North Stand).

For Free

Rome is an expensive city, but you don't have to break the bank to enjoy it. A surprising number of its big sights are free, and it costs nothing to stroll the historic streets, piazzas and parks, basking in their extraordinary beauty.

Need to Know

Transport Holders of the Roma Pass (p21) are entitled to free public transport.

Wi-Fi Free wi-fi is available in most hostels and hotels, as well as bars and cafes.

Tours To take a free tour check out www.newromefreetour.com.

Art & Museums

Churches

Feast on fine art in the city's churches. They're all free and many contain priceless treasures by big-name artists such as Michelangelo, Raphael, Bernini and Caravaggio. Major art churches include St Peter's Basilica (p128), Basilica di San Pietro in Vincoli (p154), Chiesa di San Luigi dei Francesi (p86) and Basilica di Santa Maria del Popolo (p109).

Vatican Museums

Home to the Sistine Chapel and kilometres of awesome art, the Vatican Museums (p133) are free on the last Sunday of the month.

State Museums

Eight of Rome's municipal museums are free, including **Museo Carlo Bilotti** (Map p348, D6; 06 06 08; www.museocarlobilotti.it; Viale Fiorello La Guardia; 1-7pm Tue-Fri, 10am-7pm Sat & Sun summer, 10am-4pm Tue-Fri, to 7pm Sat & Sun winter; Via Pinciana) FREE and **Museo Barracco di Scultura Antica** (Map p328, D6; www.museobarracco.it; Corso Vittorio Emanuele II 166; 10am-4pm Tue-Sun winter, 1-7pm Tue-Sun summer; Corso Vittorio Emanuele II) FREE. All state-run museums are *gratis* on the first Sunday of the month between October and March.

Monuments

Pantheon

A pagan temple turned church, the Pantheon (p80) is a staggering work of architecture and an astonishing sight with its cavernous interior and soaring dome.

Trevi Fountain

You don't have to spend a penny to admire the Trevi Fountain (p110), although most people throw a coin in to ensure they'll return to Rome.

Vittoriano

Rome's most high-vis monument, the Vittoriano (p75) towers over the forums, affording stunning city views from its vast terraces.

Piazzas & Parks

Piazzas

Hanging out and people-watching on Rome's piazzas is a signature Roman experience. Top spots include Piazza Navona (p82), Campo de' Fiori (p86), Piazza di Spagna (p108) and Piazza del Popolo (p112).

Parks

It doesn't cost a thing to enjoy Rome's parks. The most famous is Villa Borghese (p207), but also worth searching out are Villa Torlonia (p209), Villa Celimontana (p193) the Gianicolo (p182), and Via Appia Antica (p218).

MAGNAGO / SHUTTERSTOCK ©

Saltimbocca alla Romana (pan-fried veal escalopes wrapped with prosciutto and sage and finished in white wine)

Dining Out

This is a city that lives to eat. Food feeds the Roman soul, and a social occasion would be nothing without it. Over recent decades the restaurant scene has become increasingly sophisticated, but traditional no-frills trattorias still provide Rome's most memorable gastronomic experiences. And everywhere, cooking with local, seasonal ingredients remains the norm, as it has been for millennia.

Roman Cuisine

Like most Italian cuisines, the *cucina romana* (Roman cooking) was born of careful use of local ingredients – making use of the cheaper cuts of meat, like *guanciale* (pig's cheek), and greens that could be gathered wild from the fields.

There are a few classic Roman pasta dishes that almost every trattoria and restaurant in Rome serves. These carb-laden comfort foods are seemingly simple, yet notoriously difficult to prepare well. Iconic Roman dishes include carbonara (pasta with *guanciale,* egg and salty *pecorino romano;* sheep's milk cheese), *alla gricia* (with *guanciale* and onions), *amatriciana* (invented when a chef from Amatrice added tomatoes to *alla gricia*) and *cacio e pepe* (with *pecorino romano* and black pepper).

Other Roman specialities include *baccalà con i ceci* (salted cod with chickpeas), *trippa alla Romana* (tripe stewed in tomato sauce and topped with *pecorino*), *saltimbocca alla Romana* (pan-fried veal escalopes wrapped with prosciutto and sage and finished in white wine) and *coda alla vaccinara* (oxtail stew, cooked with tomato sauce, celery, clove and bitter chocolate).

NEED TO KNOW

Opening Hours

- Most restaurants open noon to 3pm and 7.30pm to 11pm, usually closing one day per week (often Sunday or Monday).
- In August most eateries close for at least a week; some close for the entire month. Ring first to check that everyone hasn't gone to the beach.

Price Ranges

The pricing here refers to the average cost of a meal that includes an *antipasto* or *primo* (first course), a *secondo* (second course), a glass of house wine and *coperto* (cover charge). Don't be surprised to see *pane e coperto* (bread and cover charge; €1 to €5 per person) added to your bill.

€ less than €25

€€ €25–45

€€€ more than €45

Etiquette

- Dress up to dine out.
- Bite through hanging spaghetti – no slurping it up please.
- Pasta is eaten with a fork (no spoon).
- It's OK to eat pizza with your hands.
- In Italian homes, *fare la scarpetta* (make a little shoe) with your bread to wipe plates clean.

Tipping

Although service is almost always included, leave a tip: anything from 5% in a pizzeria to 10% in a more upmarket place. Or at least round up the bill.

NEIGHBOURHOOD SPECIALITIES

Most entrenched in culinary tradition is the Jewish Ghetto area, with its hearty Roman-Jewish cuisine. Deep-frying is a staple of *cucina ebraico-romanesca* (Roman-Jewish cooking), which developed between the 16th and 19th centuries when the Jews were confined to the city's ghetto. To add flavour to their limited ingredients – those spurned by the rich, such as courgette (zucchini) flowers – they began to fry everything from mozzarella to *baccalà*. Particularly addictive are the locally grown artichokes, which are flattened out to form a kind of flower shape and then deep-fried to a golden crisp and salted to become *carciofo alla giudia*. By contrast, *carciofo alla romana* (Roman-style artichokes) are stuffed with parsley, mint and garlic, then braised in an aromatic mix of broth and white wine until soft.

For the heart (and liver and brains) of the *cucina romana*, head to Testaccio, a traditional working-class district clustered around the city's former slaughterhouse. In the past, butchers who worked in the city abattoir were often paid in cheap cuts of meat as well as money. The Roman staple *coda alla vaccinara* translates as 'oxtail cooked butcher's style'. This is cooked for hours to create a rich sauce with tender slivers of meat. A famous Roman dish that's not for the faint-hearted is pasta with *pajata*, made with the entrails of young veal calves, considered a delicacy since they contain the mother's congealed milk. If you see the word *coratella* in a dish, it means you'll be eating *lights* (lungs), kidneys and hearts.

Seasonal Calendar

As is the case all over Italy, Romans eat according to what's in season. Fresh, often sun-ripened ingredients zing with flavour, and the best food is *zero-kilometri* – the less distance it has had to travel, the better.

SPRING

Spring is prime time for lamb, usually roasted with potatoes – *agnello al forno con patate*. Sometimes it's described as *abbacchio* (Roman dialect for lamb) *scottadito* (hot enough to burn fingers).

March is the best month for *carciofo alla giudia*, when the big round artichokes from Cerveteri appear on the table (smaller varieties are from Sardinia), but you can continue eating this delicious dish until June. Other artichoke varieties are available throughout the year.

May and June are favourable fishing months, and thus good for cuttlefish and octopus, as well as other seafood.

Grass-green *fave* (broad beans) are eaten after meals and are an essential element in the countryside picnics that Roman workers traditionally enjoy on 1 May, the May Day public holiday. The *fave* are usually accompanied by some salty *pecorino*.

The lighter green, fluted *zucchine romanesche* (Roman courgette) appear

Eating by Neighbourhood

Villa Borghese & Northern Rome
Fashionable restaurants, pasticcerie (pastry shops) for those with a sweet tooth (p210)
Vatican City, Borgo & Prati
Sophisticated restaurants, delicious takeaways, heavenly gelaterie (p142)
Tridente, Trevi & the Quirinale
A mix of old-school restaurants, reliable trattorias and chic cafes (p116)
Centro Storico
Romantic hideaways, old-school trattorias, top pizzerias (p91)
Monti, Esquilino & San Lorenzo
Ethnic options, wine bars, and cheap eats (p159)
Ancient Rome
Slim pickings, with few compelling options (p76)
Trastevere & Gianicolo
Touristy but terrific trattorias, gelaterie, bars and pizzerias (p177)
San Giovanni & Testaccio
Traditional Roman cuisine and top street food (p195)
Southern Rome
Cheap eats, a flash food emporium and a few neighbourhood trattorias (p224)
0 1 km
0 0.5 miles

on market stalls, usually with the flowers still attached – these orange petals, deep-fried, are a delectable feature of Roman cooking.

SUMMER

Tonno (tuna) comes fresh from the seas around Sardinia; *linguine ai frutti di mare* and *risotto alla pescatora* are good light summer dishes.

Summertime is *melanzane* (aubergine or eggplant) time: tuck into them grilled as antipasti or fried and layered with rich tomato sauce in *melanzane alla parmagiana*. It's also time for leafy greens, and Rome even has its own lettuce, the sturdy, flavourful *lattuga romana*.

Tomatoes are at their full-bodied finest, and seductive heaps of *pesche* (peaches), *albicocche* (apricots), *fichi* (figs) and *meloni* (melons) dominate market stalls.

AUTUMN

Alla cacciatora (hunter-style) dishes are sourced from Lazio's hills, with meats such as *cinghiale* (boar) and *lepre* (hare).

Fish is also good in autumn; you could try fried fish from Fiumicino, such as *triglia* (red mullet), or mixed small fish, such as *alici* (anchovies).

Autumn equals mushrooms – the meaty porcini, *galletti* and *ovuli*. Heaping the markets are *broccoletti* (also called *broccolini*), a cross between broccoli and asparagus, *uve* (grapes), *pere* (pears) and nuts.

WINTER

Winter is the ideal time to eat cockle-warming dishes with *ceci* (chickpeas) and vegetable-rich minestrone, as well as herb-roasted *porchetta di Ariccia* (pork from Ariccia).

Puntarelle ('little points' – Catalonian chicory), found only in Lazio, is a delicious, faintly bitter winter green usually served as a salad with anchovy sauce.

Markets are piled high with *broccoli romaneschi* (Roman broccoli), *arance* (oranges) and *mandarini* (mandarins).

In February, look out for *frappé* (strips of fried dough sprinkled with sugar), eaten at carnival time.

When to Eat

For *colazione* (breakfast), most Romans head to a bar for a cappuccino and *cornetto* (croissant); there are various types of *cornetti,* including *semplice* (plain), *marmellata* (filled with jam), *integrale* (wholewheat), *cioccolato* (filled with chocolate) or *crema pasticcera* (filled with custard).

The main meal of the day is *pranzo* (lunch), eaten at about 1.30pm. Many shops and businesses close for one to three hours every afternoon to accommodate the meal and siesta that follows. On Sundays *pranzo* is particularly important.

Many restaurants offer 'brunch' at weekends, but this isn't the breakfast-lunch combination featuring pancakes and eggs that English and American visitors might expect. Brunch in Rome tends to mean a buffet, available from around noon to 3pm.

Aperitivo is a buffet of snacks to accompany evening drinks, usually from around 6pm till 9pm, and costing around €10 for a drink and unlimited platefuls.

Cena (dinner), eaten any time from about 8.30pm, is usually simple, although this is changing as fewer people make it home for the big lunchtime feast.

A full Italian meal consists of an *antipasto* (starter), a *primo piatto* (first course), a *secondo piatto* (second course) with an *insalata* (salad) or *contorno* (vegetable side dish), *dolci* (sweet), fruit, coffee and *digestivo* (liqueur). Few Italians eat meals this large, though. When eating out, you can do as most Romans do, and mix and match: order, say, an *antipasto, insalata* or *contorno* followed by a *primo.*

Where to Eat

Take your pick according to your mood and your pocket, from the frenetic energy of a Roman pizzeria to the warm familiarity of a third-generation-run, centuries-old trattoria, from chic bars laden with a sumptuous *apertivi* banquets to modern bistros and destination restaurants where both presentation and flavours are works of art.

ENOTECHE

Romans rarely drink without eating, and you can eat well at *enoteche,* wine bars that usually serve snacks such as bruschette (grilled bread topped with tomatoes), *crostini* (toasts with toppings) and platters of cheeses or cold meats), salads and hot dishes.

TRATTORIA, OSTERIA OR RESTAURANT

Traditionally, trattorias are family-run places that offer a basic, affordable local menu, while *osterie* usually specialise in one dish and *vino della casa* (house wine). There are still lots of these around. *Ristoranti* offer more choices and smarter service, and are more expensive.

PIZZERIAS

Remarkably, pizza was only introduced to Rome post-WWII, by southern immigrants. Needless to say, it quickly caught on. Every Roman's favourite casual (and cheap) meal is the gloriously simple pizza, with Rome's

FOOD BLOGGERS

Katie Parla (http://katieparla.com) Finger-on-the-pulse restaurant reviews and culinary insights by food-and-beverage journalist Katie, a Rome-based New Jersey native and author of the highly recommended *Tasting Rome* (2017).

Elizabeth Minchilli in Rome (www.elizabethminchilliinrome.com) Reliable dining recommendations by the author of *Eating Rome,* an American food writer at home in Italy.

Heart Rome (www.heartrome.com) Food and lifestyle in the eternal city seen through the smart eyes of Australian Maria Pasquale.

An American in Rome (http://anamericaninrome.com) Bar and restaurant reviews by freelance writer Natalie Kennedy who arrived in Rome, fresh from California, in 2010.

Romeing Guide (www.romeing.it) Guide to Rome's cultural life, events and food hotspots written for tourists and expats visiting or living in Rome.

signature wafer-thin bases covered in fresh, bubbling toppings, slapped down on tables by harried waiters. Pizzerias often only open in the evening, as their wood-fired ovens take a while to get going.

Most Romans will precede their pizza with a starter of *bruschette* or *fritti* (mixed fried foods, such as zucchini flowers, potato, *baccalà,* olives etc) and wash it all down with beer – only craft beer in the case of the city's trendiest new pizzerias. Pizza menus are traditionally divided into *pizza rosso* ('red' pizza meaning with tomato sauce) and *pizza bianco* ('white' pizza with no tomato sauce, traditionally simply sprinkled with rosemary, salt and olive oil, but available with a variety of optional toppings today). Some places in Rome serve pizza with a thicker, fluffier base that is more Neapolitan in style.

For a snack on the run, Rome's *pizza al taglio* (by the slice) places are hard to beat, with toppings loaded onto thin, crispy, light-as-air, slow-risen bread that verges on the divine. The best *pizza al taglio* joint is generally acknowledged to be Bonci Pizzarium (p143) near the Vatican. Bonci also has a second outlet in the Mercato Centrale (p160) at Termini Station.

FAST FOOD

Fast food is a long-standing Roman tradition, with plenty of street-food favourites.

A *tavola calda* (hot table) offers cheap, pre-prepared pasta, meat and vegetable dishes, while a *rosticceria* sells mainly cooked meats.

Another favourite on the run are *arancini,* fried risotto balls that have fillings such as mozzarella and ham. These originate from Sicily, but are much loved in Rome too, where they're known as *supplì*.

Fast food is the latest Roman tradition to be reinvented, with a new-fangled offering of gourmet snacks that riff on family favourites. These days you'll find hip new places serving *supplì* or *fritti* with a twist. And these are no victory of style over substance – the new guard takes their gastronomy just as seriously as the old.

GELATERIE

Eating gelato is as much a part of Roman life as morning coffee – try it and you'll understand why. The city has some of the world's finest ice-cream shops, which use only the finest seasonal ingredients, sourced from the finest locations. In these artisan gelaterie, flavours are strictly seasonal and ingredients are sourced from the best locations (pistachios from Bronte, almonds from Avola, and so on). It's all come a long way since Nero snacked on snow mixed with fruit pulp and honey. A rule of thumb is to check the colour of the pistachio flavour: ochre-green means 'good', bright-green means 'bad'. In the height of summer Romans love to eat *grattachecca* (literally 'scratched ice'), with kiosks selling crushed ice topped with fruit and syrup along the riverside open from May to September. It's a great way to cool down.

Most places open from noon to 1am, with shorter hours in winter. Prices range from around €2.50 to €5.50 for a *cona* (cone) or *coppetta* (tub or cup).

DELIS & MARKETS

Rome's well-stocked delis and fresh-produce markets are a fabulous feature of the city's foodscape. Most neighbourhoods have a few local delis and their own daily food market. Markets operate from around 7am to 1.30pm, Monday to Saturday. There are also some excellent farmers markets, mostly taking place at the weekends.

Rome's most famous markets:

Mercato di Campo de' Fiori (p95) The most picturesque, but also the most expensive. Prices are graded according to the shopper's accent – tourists pay top dollar.

Nuovo Mercato Esquilino (p170) Cheap and the best place to find exotic herbs and spices.

Mercato di Piazza San Cosimato (p180) Trastevere's neighbourhood market, at least a century old and still the biz for fresh, locally sourced foodstuffs.

Nuovo Mercato di Testaccio (p196) A purpose-built covered market hall that's home to some enticing stalls, including some selling gourmet fast food to go.

Vegetarians, Vegans & Allergies

Vegetarians eat exceedingly well in Rome, with a wide choice of bountiful antipasti, pasta dishes, *insalate* (salads), *contorni* (side dishes) and pizzas. Many high-end restaurants serve vegetarian menus, and slowly but surely, exclusively vegetarian and/or vegan eateries and cafes are cropping up: Monti and Tridente are areas where vegetarian and vegan eateries are proliferating.

FOOD & WINE TOURS

Casa Mia (www.italyfoodandwinetours.com) Food and wine tours for serious foodies with tastings and behind-the-scene meetings with local shop keepers, producers, chefs and restaurateurs. Bespoke tours, dining itineraries and reservations too.

Local Aromas (www.localaromas.com) Food- and wine-tasting tours in neighbourhoods including Trastevere and Campo de' Fiori.

Katie Parla (https://katieparla.com) Now a Roman resident, New Jersey native Katie Parla writes the city's best-known English-language food blog and also conducts private walking tours for small groups. These cover Testaccio, the *centro storico* (historic centre), Prati, Trionfale and Esquilino.

GT Food & Travel (www.gtfoodandtravel.com) Small, themed food-lover tours, including market tours and a 'Cucina Povera & Roman Cuisine' tour in Monteverdi.

The Tour Guy (p297) Foodie tours in Trastevere with this fun tour company.

Eating Italy Food Tours (www.eatingitalyfoodtours.com) Informative four-hour tours around Testaccio, Trastevere and the Jewish Ghetto, tasting different delicacies along the way; maximum 12 people per tour.

A Friend in Rome (p297) Street-food walks in off-the-beaten-track Rome with private-tour specialists.

Elizabeth Minchilli (www.elizabethminchilliinrome.com) Small food tours, with tastings, of Campo de' Fiori and the Jewish Ghetto, Testaccio and Monti, plus custom-made tours and an insider 'Gelato Stroll' with American food blogger Elizabeth Minchilli or her daughter Sophie.

Be mindful of hidden ingredients not mentioned on the menu – for example, steer clear of anything that's been stuffed (like zucchini flowers, often spiced up with anchovies) or check that it's *senza carne o pesce* (without meat or fish). To many Italians, vegetarian means you don't eat red meat.

Vegans are in for a tougher time. Cheese is used universally, so you must specify that you want something *senza formaggio* (without cheese). Remember that *pasta fresca*, which may also turn up in soups, is made with eggs. The safest bet is to self-cater or try a dedicated vegetarian restaurant, which will always have some vegan options.

Most restaurants offer gluten-free options, as there is a good awareness of coeliac disease here: one of the city's top restaurants, Aroma (p195), has a four-course, gluten-free menu (€120). Just say *Io sono celiaco* or *senza glutine* when you sit down, and usually the waiters will be able to recommend suitable dishes.

EU laws specify that restaurant menus should flag dishes that contain substances or products causing allergies or intolerances. This is done using letters (A signifies dishes including cereals containing gluten, C eggs, E peanuts, G milk and lactose etc). Not all Roman menus include these codes, but many do.

Courses & Workshops

With food and wine classes and workshops being much on trend, new venues are opening in Rome all the time. Recommended courses include the following:

Vino Roma (www.vinoroma.com) Serious wine-tasting classes in a tasting studio in Monti.

GT Food & Travel (www.gtfoodandtravel.com) Cooking classes and in-home dining experiences.

Eataly (p224) Imaginative cooking classes, show cooking, demonstrations and wine tastings in the city's trendiest, most gargantuan food mall in southern Rome.

Pasta Chef (www.pastachefroma.it) Informal, pasta-making classes with contemporary kings of gourmet pasta-to-go, Mauro and Leopoldo, at their kitchen in Monti.

Città di Gusto (www.gamberorosso.it) Demonstrations, workshops, lessons and courses in the headquarters of Italian food organisation Gambero Rosso, in the Monteverdi neighbourhood west of Testaccio.

Latteria Studio (https://latteriastudio.com Highly personalised market tours and cooking classes in a stylish, food-photography studio in backstreet Trastevere.

Lonely Planet's Top Choices

La Ciambella (p91) Dine on modern Roman cuisine at this tranquil backstreet restaurant.

Colline Emiliane (p120) The Latini family's elegant eatery serves sensational regional cuisine from Emilia-Romagna.

La Tavernaccia (p178) Delicious food makes this simple trattoria one of the city's most sought-after tables.

Flavio al Velavevodetto (p1946) A model Roman trattoria in Testaccio serving classic *cucina romana*.

Trattoria Da Cesare al Casaletto (p181) Heavy on taste and light on attitude, this may be Rome's best trattoria.

Salumeria Roscioli (p96) Deli-restaurant hybrid serving top-notch food and wine.

Best by Budget

€

Bonci Pizzarium (p143) Top-of-the-range *pizza al taglio* (pizza by the slice).

Panella (p161) Historic bakery serving fresh-baked food all day.

Supplì (p179) Wonderful Trastevere *tavola calda* serving reliable, bargain-priced meals.

Sbanco (p195) New-school pizzeria known for its sumptuous fried morsels and creative pizza toppings.

€€

Pianostrada (p95) Creative modern cuisine and a fashionable bistro vibe.

Piccolo Arancio (p118) Trevi trattoria specialising in seafood.

Da Enzo (p178) Quality local produce and arguably the city's best *pasta cacio e pepe.*

La Buca di Ripetta (p116) Modern Roman cuisine near the Spanish Steps.

€€€

Metamorfosi (p212) Roy Caceres' stupendously good fusion dishes never fail to impress.

Enoteca La Torre (p145) Sophisticated contemporary cuisine in glamorous surrounds.

Aroma (p197) The rooftop restaurant of the Palazzo Manfredi hotel has 'marry-me' views over the Colosseum.

Zia Restaurant (p180) Up-and-coming chef and a good-value lunch menu.

Best by Cuisine

Traditional Roman

Flavio al Velavevodetto (p196) Classic *cucina romana* in a popular neighbourhood trattoria.

La Tavernaccia (p178) Family-run trattoria sticking solidly to the classics.

Trattoria Da Cesare al Casaletto (p181) Fantastic trattoria beloved by both local regulars and visiting foodies.

Da Enzo (p178) Hugely popular Trastevere address, known for quality sourced ingredients.

Trattoria Da Teo (p178) So traditional that it still cooks gnocchi on a Thursday only; honest and delicious food.

Modern Roman

L'Arcangelo (p145) Updated takes on classic Roman dishes at this Prati favourite.

Pianostrada (p95) Modern Roman dining with a strong emphasis on vegetables.

La Ciambella (p91) The surrounds include ruins of the ancient Terme di Agrippa, but the cuisine is unabashedly modern.

Salumeria Roscioli (p96) Deli-restaurant hybrid serving traditional food prepared with a contemporary sensibility.

VyTA Enoteca Regionale del Lazio (p118) Specialities from the Lazio region given a sophisticated contemporary twist.

Regional

Colline Emiliane (p120) Sensational antipasti, pastas and desserts from Emilia-Romagna.

Seacook (p227) Chic seafood fresh from Salento in southern Italy.

Casa Coppelle (p91) Theatrical restaurant serving refined French cuisine.

Piccolo Arancio (p118) Huge choice of seafood dishes paying homage to Italy's south.

Il Chianti (p119) Tuscan classics that can be enjoyed on a gorgeous terrace near the Trevi Fountain.

Best Pizzerias

Sbanco (p195) Creative pizzas and craft beer served in a casual bar-like setting.

Emma Pizzeria (p95) Smart outfit dishing up excellent wood-fired pizzas in the historic centre.

Pizzeria Da Remo (p198) Spartan but stunning: a frenetic Roman pizzeria experience in Testaccio.

Pizzeria Ai Marmi (p178) Streetside tables and fabulous pizza haul in the hoards to Trastevere's *'l'obitorio'* (the morgue).

Alle Carrette (p159) Top-notch *baccalà* and down-to-earth pizza, super-thin and mighty tasty.

Best Gelaterie

Fatamorgana (p143) Rome's finest artisanal gelato flavours, now in multiple central locations.

Gelateria del Teatro (p95) Around 40 choices of delicious ice cream, all made on-site.

Otaleg (p182) Classic and experimental flavours.

Fior di Luna (p179) Great artisan ice cream in Trastevere.

Gelateria Dei Gracchi (p116) A taste of heaven in several locations across Rome.

Best Fast Food

Trapizzino (p198) Home of the *trapizzino*, a cone of doughy bread with fillers like *polpette al sugo* (meatballs in tomato sauce).

Mercato Centrale (p160) Gourmet fast-food stalls galore at this food hall in Rome's main train station.

Supplì (p179) Gourmet versions of Rome's favourite fried risotto-ball snacks, as well as great pizza by the slice.

Fa-Bìo (p142) Popular organic takeaway near the Vatican.

Panificio Bonci (p142) Bakery near the Vatican serving tasty pizzas and *panini* (sandwiches) to go.

Antica Norcineria Iacozzilli (p179) Delicious *panini* stuffed with rosemary-scented *porchetta* (suckling pig).

Best Local Dining

Da Felice (p199) Traditional local cooking in Testaccio, the heartland of Roman cuisine.

Panella (p161) Hugely popular bakery and *tavola calda* in Esquilino; go for lunch.

Trattoria Da Teo (p178) Reservations essential at this much-liked trattoria, with terrace seating on a pretty Trastevere piazza.

Pizzeria Ostiense (p225) Fabulous thin-crust pizza in Rome's ex-industrial, hip neighbourhood of Ostiense.

Hostaria Romana (p119) Buzzing trattoria dining footsteps from the Trevi Fountain.

Best Sliced Pizza

Bonci Pizzarium (p143) Pizza slices created by the master, Gabriele Bonci.

Forno Roscioli (p94) Thin and crispy, this is some of the best *pizza rossa* (with tomato and oregano) in Rome, if not the world.

La Renella (p179) Historic bakery known for its bread, biscuits and pizza slices.

Antico Forno Urbani (p96) A kosher bakery in the Ghetto with incredible *pizza bianca* (with olive oil and rosemary).

Best Vegetarian Menus

Verde Pistacchio (p225) Veggie and vegan treats, including a bargain lunchtime deal.

Il Margutta (p116) All-vegetarian menu with lots of vegan choices and a popular lunch/brunch buffet.

100% Bio (p198) Organic lunch buffet with 30 vegetarian and vegan dishes to choose from.

Il Pagliaccio (p96) Rome's only restaurant with two Michelin stars offers a dedicated vegetarian tasting menu.

Best Food Shops

Eataly (p224) Mall-size, state-of-the-art food emporium, with produce from all over Italy, and multiple restaurants.

Salumeria Roscioli (p102) The rich scents of fine Italian produce, cured meats and cheeses intermingle in this superlative deli.

Antica Caciara Trasteverina (p185) Century-old deli with fresh ricotta and to-die-for *ricotta infornata* (oven-baked ricotta), among other delicacies.

Volpetti (p201) This super-stocked deli is a treasure trove of gourmet delicacies and helpful staff.

Confetteria Moriondo & Gariglio (p103) Source magical chocolate creations at this historic confectioner.

Best Wine Lists

La Barrique (p160) Interesting list of wines from small producers, including natural wines.

Casa Bleve (p94) High-end restaurant with one of the largest and most interesting wine lists in the city.

Salumeria Roscioli (p96) Sensational list by the glass and bottle.

Litro (p181) Vintage-styled bistro-bar with extensive list of natural and organic wines.

Trattoria Da Cesare al Casaletto (p181) Serves one of the best house wines in town.

L'Arcangelo (p145) Well-curated wine list to complement creative contemporary bistro food.

Bar, Trastevere (p181)

Bar Open

There's simply no city with better backdrops for a coffee or drink than Rome: you can sip espresso in historic cafes, claim piazza seating for an aperitivo (pre-dinner drink and snacks) or wander from wine bar to restaurant to late-night drinking den, getting happily lost down picturesque cobbled streets in the process.

Rome After Dark

Night-owl Romans tend to eat late, then drink at bars before heading off to a club at around 1am. Like most cities, Rome is a collection of districts, each with its own character, which is often completely different after dark. The *centro storico* (historic centre) and Trastevere pull in a mix of locals and tourists as night falls. Ostiense and Testaccio are the grittier clubbing districts, with clusters of clubs in a couple of locations – Testaccio has a parade of crowd-pleasing clubs running over the hill of Monte Testaccio. There are also subtle political divisions. San Lorenzo and Pigneto, to the east of central Rome, are popular with a left-leaning, alternative crowd, while areas to the north (such as Ponte Milvio and Parioli) attract a more right-wing, bourgeois milieu.

The *bella figura* (loosely translated as 'looking good') is important. The majority of locals spend evenings checking each other out, partaking in gelato, and not drinking too much. However, this is changing and certain areas – those popular with a younger crowd – can get rowdy with drunk teens and tourists (for example, Campo de' Fiori, San Lorenzo and parts of Trastevere).

NEED TO KNOW

Opening Hours

- Most cafes: 7.30am to 8pm
- Traditional bars: 7.30am to 1am or 2am
- Most bars, pubs and *enoteche* (wine bars): lunchtime or 6pm to 2am
- Nightclubs: 10pm to 4am

Dress Codes

Romans tend to dress up to go out, and most people will be looking pretty sharp in the smarter clubs and bars in the *centro storico* (historic centre) and Testaccio. However, over in Pigneto and San Lorenzo or at the *centri sociali* (social centres), the style is much more alternative.

Online Resources

- Romeing (www.romeing.it) Webzine covering Rome nightlife and cultural happenings.
- 2night. (http://2night.it) Nightlife listings, in Italian only.

Rome in Summer (& Winter)

From around mid-June to mid-September, many nightclubs and live-music venues close, some moving to EUR or the beaches at Fregene or Ostia. The area around the Isola Tiberina throngs with life nightly during the Lungo il Tevere (p25), a summer festival along the riverbank, which sprouts bars, stalls and an open-air cinema. Pop-up bars stretch the length of the riverside footpaths between Ponte Palatino and Ponte Mazzini, and open nightly from around 5pm to 2am. Attempts are made to limit excessive alcohol consumption – water-edge bars are not allowed to serve double shots, for example.

Be aware that in winter, bars often close earlier in the evening, particularly in areas where the norm is to drink outside. This said, an increasing number of bars have heated pavement terraces in winter, ensuring year-round al fresco drinking.

Where to Drink

ENOTECHE

The *enoteca* (wine bar) was where the old boys from the neighbourhood used to drink rough local wine poured straight from the barrel. Times have changed: nowadays they tend to be sophisticated but still atmospheric places, offering Italian and international vintages, delicious cheeses and cold cuts.

BARS & PUBS

Bars range from regular Italian cafe-bars that have seemingly remained the same for centuries, to chic cocktail bars serving esoteric cocktails to the glitterati. There are also laid-back, perennially popular haunts – such as Freni e Frizioni (p182) in Trastevere and Ai Tre Scalini (p164) in Monti – that have a longevity rarely seen in other cities. Pubs are also popular, with several long-running Irish-style pubs in the Esquilino area filled with chattering Romans. Pub-like bars are opening on the back of the artisanal beer trend, too – head to San Lorenzo to check out some of the best.

NIGHTCLUBS

Rome has a range of nightclubs, mostly in Ostiense and Testaccio, with music policies ranging from lounge and jazz to dancehall and hip-hop. Clubs tend to get busy after midnight, or even after 2am. Often admission is free, but drinks are expensive. Cocktails usually cost between €10 and €20, but you can drink much more cheaply in the studenty clubs of San Lorenzo, Pigneto and the *centri sociali* (social centres).

CENTRI SOCIALI

Rome's flip side is a surprising alternative underbelly, centred on left-wing *centri sociali:* grungy squatter arts centres that host live music and contemporary-arts events. They offer Rome's most unusual, cheap and alternative nightlife options. These include Brancaleone (p213) and Esc Atelier (p169).

What to Drink

COFFEE

For an espresso (a shot of strong black coffee), ask for *un caffè;* if you want it with a drop of hot or cold milk, order *un caffè macchiato* ('stained' coffee) *caldo/freddo.* Long black coffee (as in a watered-down version) is known as *caffè lungo* (an espresso with more water) or *caffè all'american* (a filter coffee). If you fancy a coffee but one more shot will catapult you through the ceiling, you can drink *orzo,* made from roasted barley but served like coffee.

Then, of course, there's the cappuccino (coffee with frothy milk, served warm rather than hot so as to treat the milk respectfully). If you want it without froth, ask for a *cappuccino senza schiuma;* if you want it extra hot, ask for it *ben caldo*. Italians drink cappuccino only during the morning and never after meals, and they are deeply disapproving of those who request theirs *ben caldo*.

In summer, *cappuccino freddo* (iced coffee with milk, usually already sugared), *caffè freddo* (iced espresso) and *granita di caffè* (frozen coffee, usually with cream) top the charts.

A *caffè latte* is a milkier version of the cappuccino with less froth; a *latte macchiato* is even milkier (warmed milk 'stained' with a spot of coffee). Few Italian adults drink these, but Italian children sometimes do. A *caffè corretto* is an espresso 'corrected' with a dash of grappa or something similar.

There are two ways to drink coffee in a Roman bar-cafe: either standing at the bar, in which case you pay first at the till and then, with your receipt, order at the counter; or you can sit down at a table and enjoy waiter service. In the latter case you'll pay at least double what you'd pay at the bar. In both scenarios, a complimentary glass of tap water is often served with your coffee – if it isn't, don't be shy to ask for one.

LAZIO WINES

Lazio wines may not be household names, but it's well worth trying some local wines while you're here. Although whites dominate Lazio's production – 95% of the region's Denominazione di Origine Controllata (DOC; the second of Italy's four quality classifications) wines are white – there are a few notable reds as well. To sample Lazio wines, VyTA Enoteca Regionale del Lazio (p118) and Terre e Domus (p77) are the best places to go. For biodynamic and natural vintages, head for Litro (p181) in Monteverdi or La Barrique (p160) in Monti.

CRAFT BEER

In recent years a spate of specialised bars offering microbrewed beers have opened. Most offer a range of Italian and global choices. Local beers reflect the seasonality that's so important in Rome – for example, look for winter beers made from chestnuts.

COCKTAILS & DIGESTIVES

There's a thriving cocktail scene in Rome, with basement speakeasies serving expertly mixed cocktails alongside craft beers being a hot trend; some of these require patrons to pay a small membership fee (usually €5). Many long-standing cocktail bars double as laid-back cafes by day – Trastevere has plenty of examples.

Popular *aperitivi* are based on bitter alcoholic liqueurs, such as Campari Soda or spritz, which mixes Aperol with prosecco. Crodino is a herbal, medicinal-tasting non-alcoholic *aperitivo*. Italians love to finish off a meal with a *digestif*. The best of these aren't shop bought, so if it's *fatta in casa* (made at home), give it a try.

LGBTIQ+ Rome

There is only a smattering of dedicated gay and lesbian clubs and bars in Rome, but the Colosseum end of Via di San Giovanni in Laterano is a favourite hangout and many clubs host regular gay and lesbian nights. The Circolo Mario Mieli di Cultura Omosessuale (p301) organises social functions. Its website has info and listings of forthcoming events.

Most gay venues (bars, clubs and saunas) require you to have an Arcigay (p301) membership card. These cost €10 and are available from the Arcigay headquarters in Testaccio or at any venue that requires one.

The biggest LGBTIQ+ event of the year is Gay Village (p301), which runs from June to early September. It attracts crowds of partygoers and an exuberant cast of DJs, musicians and entertainers to Testaccio's bars, cafes and clubs.

Drinking & Nightlife by Neighbourhood

Centro Storico (p99) Loads of great cafes, and plenty of bars and *enoteche* too.

Trastevere & Giancolo (p181) Cafe action by day, a vibrant drinking scene by night.

Monti, Esquilino & San Lorenzo (p164) Busy bar scenes in Monti, San Lorenzo and nearby Pigneto.

San Giovanni & Testaccio (p199) Testaccio is a clubbing and bar hub with an alternative vibe.

Southern Rome (p228) Ostiense is home to Rome's cooler nightclubs, housed in ex-industrial venues.

Tridente, Trevi & the Quirinale (p120) Chic cafes galore, along with a few glam bars.

Vatican City, Borgo & Prati (p146) A scattering of cafes and bars with a local feel.

Villa Borghese & Northern Rome (p212) Fashionable clubbing district.

Lonely Planet's Top Choices

Ai Tre Scalini (p164) Monti stalwart, with a lively student vibe, reasonable prices and good food.

Terra Satis (p181) Trastevere favourite serving great coffee during the day and quality tipples at night.

Barnum Cafe (p100) Urban retro cool goes hand-in-hand with coffees and cocktails.

Roscioli Caffè (p100) *Dolci* become miniature works of art at this smart *centro storico* cafe.

Sciascia Caffè (p146) Serving exceptional coffee since 1919.

Best Cafes

Sciascia Caffè (p146) Delicious coffee in an elegant interior.

Caffè Sant'Eustachio (p99) Historic *centro storico* cafe serving exceptional coffee.

La Bottega del Caffè (p164) Terrace seating overlooking Monti's prettiest piazza; great coffee, too.

Barnum Cafe (p100) Laid-back *Friends*-style cafe with shabby-chic furniture and good coffee.

Antico Caffè Greco (p122) Located near the Spanish Steps, this 1760 charmer is Rome's oldest cafe.

Best Terraces & Gardens

Zuma Bar (p120) Possibly the most glamorous rooftop bar in Rome.

Stravinskij Bar (p120) Hotel de Russie's elegant bar, with courtyard garden backed by Borghese gardens.

Il Palazzetto (p122) Terrace with five-star views over the comings and goings on the Spanish Steps.

Caffè Ciampini (p122) Graceful summer cafe with vintage garden-party vibe and tables beneath orange trees.

Necci dal 1924 (p167) One of Rome's best summer terraces; a perfect stop for coffee and a gelato.

Best Enoteche

Rimessa Roscioli (p99) Gourmet wine bar offering wine tastings and delicious food.

Wine Concept (p199) Run by expert sommeliers, with an extensive selection of Italian regional labels and European vintages.

Ai Tre Scalini (p164) Buzzing *enoteca* that feels as convivial as a pub.

Cavour 313 (p77) This historic choice located near the Colosseum stocks hundreds of Italian wines.

Best Aperitivi

Freni e Frizioni (p182) Perennially cool bar with lavish nightly buffet of snacks.

Doppiozeroo (p224) Popular Ostiense address with impressive buffet choice.

Momart (p212) Students and local professionals love the expansive array of pizza and other snacks.

Rec 23 (p200) Hip New York–inspired venue offering Testaccio's best *aperitivo* spread.

Lettere Caffè (p184) The *aperitivo* selection at this inclusive Trastevere cafe is all-vegetarian.

Best Cocktail Bars

Zuma Bar (p120) Swish cocktail bar on the rooftop terrace of Palazzo Fendi.

Salotto 42 (p100) Sitting-room-style cocktail bar facing the ancient Roman Stock Exchange.

Co.So (p168) Craft cocktails in Pigneto.

Pimm's Good (p183) Head here to watch serious mixologists at work.

Niji Roma (p183) Mellow Trastevere choice offering exquisitely poured and presented cocktails.

Best Clubs

Circolo Degli Illuminati (p228) Ostiense club on the international DJ circuit, with underground vibe and star-topped courtyard garden.

Vinile (p228) Food, music, dancing and party happenings on the southern fringe of Ostiense.

Goa (p228) Rome's serious superclub, at home in a former motorbike repair shop in industrial-styled Ostiense.

Lanificio 159 (p213) Cool underground venue hosting live gigs and club nights.

Best LGBTIQ+ Venues

Coming Out (p200) A friendly gay bar near the Colosseum, open all day, with gigs, drag shows and karaoke later on.

L'Alibi (p201) Kitsch shows and house, techno and dance pumping up a mixed gay and straight crowd.

My Bar (p200) A mixed crowd by day, and gayer by night, in the shadow of the Colosseum.

Aldo Caputo performing at the Auditorium Parco della Musica (p213)

Showtime

Watching the world go by in Rome is often entertainment enough, but there are plenty of organised events to capture your attention too. As well as gigs and concerts in every genre, there are some excellent arts festivals (especially in summer), opera performances with Roman ruins as a backdrop, and football games that bring the city to a standstill.

Music & Dance

CLASSICAL MUSIC

Music in Rome is not just about catching Rome's world-class Orchestra dell'Accademia Nazionale di Santa Cecilia (www.santacecilia.it) at the Auditorium Parco della Musica (p213). There are concerts by the Accademia Filarmonica Romana at Teatro Olimpico (p213); the Auditorium Conciliazione (p147), Rome's premier classical-music venue before the newer auditorium was opened, is still a force to be reckoned with; and the Istituzione Universitaria dei Concerti (p169) holds concerts in the Aula Magna of La Sapienza University.

Free classical concerts are held in many of Rome's churches, especially at Easter and around Christmas and New Year; look out for information at Rome's tourist kiosks. Rome's second-largest church after St Peter's, the Basilica di San Paolo Fuori le Mura (p223), hosts an important choral mass on 25 January and the hymn 'Te Deum' is sung at the Chiesa del Gesù (p88) on 31 December.

NEED TO KNOW

Tickets

Tickets for concerts, live music and theatrical performances are widely available across the city. Prices range enormously depending on the venue and artist. Hotels can often reserve tickets for guests, or you can contact the venue or organisation directly – check listings publications for booking details. Otherwise you can try the following:

Vivaticket (www.vivaticket.it)

Orbis Servizi (www.boxofficelazio.it)

Internet Resources

Comune di Roma (www.060608.it)

Romeing (www.romeing.it)

In Rome Now (www.inromenow.com)

Rome Opera Omnia (www.romaopera omnia.com)

Eventful (http://rome.eventful.com)

OPERA & DANCE

Rome's opera house, the Teatro dell'Opera di Roma (p169), is a grandiose venue but its productions can be a bit hit and miss. It's also home to Rome's official Corps de Ballet and has a ballet season running in tandem with its opera performances. Both ballet and opera move outdoors for the summer season at the ancient Roman baths Terme di Caracalla (p201), which is an even more spectacular setting.

You can also see opera in various other outdoor locations; check listings or at the tourist information kiosks for details.

Rome's Auditorium Parco della Musica (p213) hosts classical and contemporary dance performances, as well as the Equilibrio Festival of new dance in February and March. The Auditorium Conciliazione (p147) is another good place to catch contemporary-dance companies.

JAZZ, ROCK & POP

Besides the Auditorium Parco della Musica, large concerts also take place at sports stadiums, including Stadio Olimpico (p213) and the racetrack on the Appia Nuova, the Ippodromo La Capannelle.

The *centri sociali,* alternative arts centres set up in venues around Rome, are also good places to catch a gig. One of the best of these is Brancaleone (p213) in northern Rome, which programs hip-hop, electro, dubstep, reggae and dancehall.

Theatre

Rome has a thriving local theatre scene, with theatres including both traditional places and smaller experimental venues. Performances are usually in Italian.

Particularly wonderful are the summer festivals that make use of Rome's archaeological scenery. Performances take place in settings such as Villa Adriana in Tivoli, Ostia Antica's Roman theatre and the Teatro di Marcello (p89).

Outdoor Cinema

There are various atmospheric outdoor summer film festivals; check festival websites for program and ticketing details. The Isola del Cinema (p101) shows independent films in the romantic setting of the Isola Tiberina annually from mid-June to September. This runs in conjunction with the riverside Lungo il Tevere (p25) festival.

Spectator Sports

FOOTBALL

In Rome you're either for AS Roma (*giallorossi* – yellow and reds) or Lazio (*biancazzuri* – white and blues), with both teams playing in Serie A (Italy's premier league). A striking new 52,500-seat stadium – a contemporary glass-and-steel structure inspired by the Colosseum – is planned for Roma at Tor di Valle in southwest Rome, but construction is yet to commence and the development process has been mired in allegations of corruption; current estimates have it opening in 2023 at the earliest. Both sets of supporters have an unfortunate controversial minority who have been known to cause trouble at matches.

September to May there's a game at home for Roma or Lazio almost every weekend, and a trip to Rome's football stadium, the Stadio Olimpico (p213), is an unforgettable experience. Note that ticket-purchase regulations are strict. Tickets have to bear the holder's name and passport or ID number, and you must present a photo ID at the turnstiles when entering the stadium. Two tickets are permitted per purchase for Serie A, Coppa Italia and UEFA Champions League games. Tickets cost from €10 to €750. You can buy them online at the AS

Roma website (www.asroma.com), from **TicketOne** (www.ticketone.it; 892101), at authorised TicketOne sales points (check its website) or one of the AS Roma or Lazio stores around the city. To get to the stadium, take metro line A to Ottaviano-San Pietro, then bus 32.

BASKETBALL

Basketball is a popular spectator sport in Rome, though it inspires nothing like the fervour of football. Rome's team, Virtus Roma (www.virtusroma.it), plays throughout the winter months at the Palalottomatica (p229) in EUR.

RUGBY UNION

Italy's rugby team, the Azzurri (the Blues), entered the Six Nations tournament in 2000, although success has been scarce. The team currently plays home international games at the Stadio Olimpico.

TENNIS

Italy's premier tennis tournament, the Internazionali BNL d'Italia (www.internazionalibnlditalia.com) is one of the most important events on the European tennis circuit. Every May the world's top players meet on the clay courts at the monumental, Fascist-era Foro Italico (p208). Tickets can usually be bought at the Foro Italico each day of the tournament, except for the final days, which are sold out weeks in advance.

EQUESTRIAN EVENTS

Rome's top equestrian event is the Piazza di Siena showjumping competition (www.piazzadisiena.org), an annual international event held in May, gorgeously set in Villa Borghese.

MARIANO MONTELLA / SHUTTERSTOCK ©

Performer at Stadio Olimpico (p213)

Entertainment by Neighbourhood

➡ **Centro Storico** (p101) Great for concerts in churches or theatres (usually in Italian).

➡ **Trastevere & Gianicolo** (p184) A few blues and jazz live-music venues.

➡ **Monti, Esquilino & San Lorenzo** (p169) Live-music venues and Rome's major opera house in Monti; alternative cultural venues in San Lorenzo.

➡ **San Giovanni & Testaccio** (p201) Regular live gigs in the district's clubs and summertime opera in the Terme di Caracalla.

➡ **Southern Rome** (p229) A scattering of theatres and live-music venues.

➡ **Villa Borghese & Northern Rome** (p213) Home to the great Auditorium Parco della Musica, as well as Rome's major sporting venues.

ROMA VS LAZIO

The Rome derby is one of the football season's highest-profile games. The rivalry between Roma and Lazio is fierce, and little love is lost between the fans. If you go to the Stadio Olimpico, make sure you get it right – Roma fans flock to the Curva Sud (southern stand), while Lazio supporters stand in the Curva Nord (northern stand). If you want to sit on the fence, head to the Tribuna Tevere or Tribuna Monte Mario.

For more details on the clubs, check out www.asroma.it and www.sslazio.it.

Lonely Planet's Top Choices

Auditorium Parco della Musica (p213) An incredible venue hosting an eclectic, must-see program of music, art and more.

Terme di Caracalla (p191) Opera and ballet performed against the amazing backdrop of the ruined Roman Baths of Caracalla.

Teatro dell'Opera di Roma (p169) Rome's premier opera house.

Roma Incontra il Mondo (p25) Summer-long world-music festival in the parklands of Villa Ada.

Caffè Letterario (p229) Entertaining post-industrial all-rounder, in a former garage in southern Rome, offering fantastic live performances.

Nuovo Cinema Palazzo (p169) Alternative film, theatre, live music and DJ sets in an old cinema.

Best Classical Venues

Auditorium Parco della Musica (p213) Great acoustics, top international classical musicians and multiple concert halls.

Teatro dell'Opera di Roma (p169) Red velvet and gilt interior for Rome's opera and dance companies.

Terme di Caracalla (p201) Wonderful outdoor setting for summer opera and ballet.

Chiesa di Sant'Agnese in Agone (p82) Chamber music in a baroque church overlooking Piazza Navona.

Best For Live Gigs

Nuovo Cinema Palazzo (p169) Exciting creative happenings in San Lorenzo's former Palace Cinema.

Blackmarket Hall (p164) Two bars filled with vintage sofas and armchairs, great for eclectic, mainly acoustic, live music.

Caffè Letterario (p229) Live gigs in a post-industrial space: designer looks, gallery, co-working space, stage and lounge bar.

Lanificio 159 (p213) Ex-wool factory hosting underground live gigs alongside club nights.

ConteStaccio (p201) Free live music on the Testaccio clubbing strip.

Fonclea (p146) Prati pub with live gigs featuring everything from rock to doo-wop.

Best For Jazz

Alexanderplatz (p146) Rome's foremost jazz club, with a mix of international and local musicians.

Auditorium Parco della Musica (p213) Stages, among other things, the Roma Jazz Festival.

Charity Café (p169) Spindly tables and chairs, in an intimate space, hosting regular live gigs.

Big Mama (p183) An atmospheric Trastevere venue for jazz, blues, funk, soul and R&B.

Gregory's Jazz Club (p122) This smooth venue near the Spanish Steps is popular with local musicians.

Best Festivals

Natale di Roma (p24) The city celebrates its birthday on 21 April with music, processions, historical re-enactments and fireworks.

Roma Incontra il Mondo (p25) World-music acts play close to the lake in Villa Ada.

Lungo il Tevere (p25) Open-air cinema and stalls line the Tiber riverbank and Tiberina island.

Romaeuropa (p25) Autumn celebration of theatre, opera and dance.

Festa de' Noantri (p25) Trastevere's raucous street party in July.

Gianicolo in Musica (p184) Annual music festival staged atop the Gianicolo hill from July to September.

Best Theatres

Area Archeologica di Ostia Antica (p232) Wonderful summer theatre in the ancient amphitheatre built by Agrippa.

Teatro Argentina (p101) Rome's premier theatre with a wide-ranging program of plays, performances and concerts.

Silvano Toti Globe Theatre (p213) Open-air theatre, like London's Globe, but with better weather (plays in Italian).

Teatro India (p230) The alternative home of the Teatro di Roma.

Best Sporting Venues

Foro Italico (p208) Magnificent Fascist-era sports complex.

Stadio Olimpico (p213) Rome's 70,000-seat football stadium, part of Foro Italico.

Piazza di Siena (p207) Lovely equestrian venue in the middle of the Villa Borghese park.

Palazzo dello Sport (p226) Circular stadium near to EUR in Southern Rome.

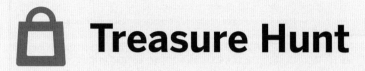

Treasure Hunt

Rome has a huge and diverse array of specialist shops, fashion boutiques and artisans' workshops, with a particularly impressive portfolio of food, clothing and accessory boutiques. Many of these businesses are family owned, having been passed down through the generations. Others have grown from their modest origins into global brands known for their classic designs and quality craftwork.

Fashion

Big-name designer boutiques hawk their covetable wares in the grid of streets between Piazza di Spagna and Via del Corso in Tridente. All the great Italian and international names are here, as well as many lesser-known designers, all selling highly fashionable clothes, shoes, accessories and dreams for men, women and children. The immaculately clad designer-fashion spine is Via dei Condotti, but plenty of haute-couture boutiques pepper Via Borgognona, Via Frattina, Via della Borghese, Via della Vite, Via del Babuino and Via dei Due Macelli too.

For chic, independent boutiques stocking pieces by lesser-known or young rising designers, try Via dell'Oca and Via della Penna near Piazza del Popolo, or head to Via del Boschetto in Monti and Via del Governo Vecchio in the *centro storico* (historic centre).

Downsizing more than a few euros, midrange stores line Via del Corso, Via Nazionale in Monti, Via dei Giubbonari in the *centro storico* and Via Cola di Rienzo in Prati, with some enticing small boutiques set amid the high-street chains.

Antiques

For antiques, Via dei Coronari, Via Giulia and Via dei Banchi Vecchi in the *centro storico* and Via Margutta in Tridente are the best places to look – quality is high, as are the prices.

Artisans

Rome's shopping scene has a surprising number of artists and artisans who create their goods on the spot in hidden workshops. There are good options in Tridente (try Via Margutta, Via dell'Oca and Via della Penna) and Monti (try Via del Boschetto and Via Panisperna).

Food & Markets

Rome is deli heaven, of course – try Salumeria Roscioli (p102) in the centre or Volpetti (p201) in Testaccio. Also worth a visit are Rome's wonderful food markets where you can buy cheese, salami and other delicious stuff. There are also various weekend farmers markets around town.

Shopping by Neighbourhood

- **Centro Storico** (p101) Boutiques, one-off designers, antiques, vintage and jewellery, as well as some swoon-worthy delicatessens.
- **Tridente, Trevi & the Quirinale** (p123) From high-fashion designer stores around Via dei Condotti to affordable chains on busy Via del Corso.
- **Monti, Esquilino & San Lorenzo** (p169) Centre for independent and vintage boutiques.
- **Trastevere & Gianicolo** (p184) Gifts and one-off shops in one of Rome's prettiest neighbourhoods.
- **San Giovanni & Testaccio** (p201) Browse a colourful food market and glorious delis.
- **Southern Rome** (p224) Home of mall-like food emporium Eataly.

NEED TO KNOW

- Most city-centre shops open from 9am to 7.30pm (or 10am to 8pm) Monday to Saturday; some close Monday morning. Smaller shops open 9am to 1pm and 3.30pm to 7.30pm (or 4pm to 8pm) Monday to Saturday.
- Winter sales run from early January to mid-February, and summer sales from July to early September.
- Non-EU residents who spend over €155 on any one given day in a shop offering 'Tax Free for Tourists' shopping (www.taxrefund.it) are entitled to a tax refund of up to 22%. You'll need to show your passport, get a form and have it stamped by customs as you leave Italy.

Lonely Planet's Top Choices

Calzoleria Petrocchi (p102) Historic store handcrafting shoes from the finest leather.

Chez Dede (p102) Ultra-chic boutique selling hand-crafted accessories, fashions, homeware and books.

Confetteria Moriondo & Gariglio (p103) Historic chocolate shop selling handmade chocolates made from 19th-century recipes.

Marta Ray (p101) A Roman-born brand specialising in women's ballerina flats.

Mercato di Porta Portese (p185) Mammoth Sunday-morning flea market.

Best Fashion

Bomba (p123) Family-operated boutique selling gorgeous women's and men's clothing.

Chiara Baschieri (p123) Elegant, beautifully tailored womenswear created by a young Roman designer.

Gente (p124) An emporium-style, multi-label boutique; essential stop for Roman fashionistas.

Tina Sondergaard (p170) Retro-inspired dresses, adjusted to fit, in bijou Monti and *centro storico* boutiques.

Best Artisanal

Artisanal Cornucopia (p123) Chic concept store showcasing artisan pieces by Italian designers.

Federico Buccellati (p124) Prestigious store run by the third generation of a family famous for smithing silver and gold.

Ibiz – Artigianato in Cuoio (p102) Father-and-daughter workshop producing leather wallets, bags and sandals.

Il Sellaio (p147) Beautifully crafted leather bags, belts and accessories.

Perlei (p170) Artisan-made jewellery that will appeal to those with a modernist aesthetic.

Best Homewares

Bialetti (p213) The place to go for cool Italian kitchenware.

Mercato Monti Urban Market (p170) Vintage homeware finds cram this weekend market.

c.u.c.i.n.a. (p125) Gastronomic gadgets to enhance your culinary life.

Best Italian Global Brands

Borsalino (p123) Famous hat shop known for its classic straw and felt models.

Fendi (p124) Long-standing prestige Roman brand producing top-quality fashion accessories and clothing, especially leather and fur.

Mandarina Duck (p125) Handbags, wallets and suitcases with a distinctive contemporary design and affordable prices.

Tod's (p125) Known for its trademark rubber-studded loafers.

Valentino (p125) Famous fashion brand founded in Rome in 1960 and still going strong.

Best Shoes

Calzoleria Petrocchi (p102) Handcrafting bespoke and ready-to-wear shoes since 1946.

Fausto Santini (p124) Rome's best-known shoe designer, known for beguilingly simple, architectural designs.

Giacomo Santini (p171) Outlet shop for end-of-season Fausto-designed shoes at a snip of the original price.

Marta Ray (p101) Women's ballerina flats in a rainbow of stylish colours.

Pietro da Cortona's frescoed ceiling at Gallerie Nazionali: Palazzo Barberini (p111)

Museums, Galleries & Historic Sites

With their ancient treasures and artistic riches, Rome's museums and historical sites are among Europe's most popular. That means crowds, and at peak times entering places like the Colosseum and Vatican Museums can be an ordeal. Here are the practicalities of ensuring a smooth visit to the city's top sights.

Avoiding Queues & Crowds

Queues are the norm at Rome's popular museums and sites, and in busy periods waits of up to two to three hours are not unheard of. To minimise waiting time, it pays to pre-book tickets and/or time your visit carefully. Pre-booking will help you skip the line at ticket offices, but you'll probably still have to queue for security checks.

Look out for night visits in summer, typically between April and October. These offer a unique chance to avoid the crowds and see the sights in a different light.

COLOSSEUM, ROMAN FORUM & PALATINO

Visit first thing in the morning or late in the afternoon. That way you'll avoid the midday heat, which can be draining in summer, and the worst of the crowds, which are at their heaviest between 11am and 2pm. These sites are free (and very busy) on the first Sunday of the month between October and March.

To book tickets, call 06 3996 7700 or go online at www.coopculture.it. You can buy standard admission tickets, which include entry to the Colosseum (p58), Roman Forum (p64) and Palatino (p60), or choose from a

NEED TO KNOW

Colosseum, Roman Forum & Palatino

Allow around two hours for the Colosseum (p58). You'll then need another two to three hours for the Roman Forum (p64) and Palatino (p60), which are covered on the same ticket. Pre-booking recommended.

Vatican Museums

Even moving quickly, reckon on around three hours for a whistle-stop tour, longer if you want to linger over the exhibits. Pre-booking tickets allows you to skip the ticket line, but you'll still have to queue for security checks.

St Peter's Basilica

The basilica is free to enter, but expect long, albeit fast-moving, queues. The main entrance is on St Peter's Square (p141) and is separate from the entrance to the Vatican Museums (p133). Dress rules are strictly applied.

Museo e Galleria Borghese

Visits are limited to two hours with admission at set times. You'll need to book your ticket and get an entry time.

Capitoline Museums

You could probably cover the highlights in around two hours, but give yourself longer for a more rewarding visit. Make sure to build in time for a break at the museums' panoramic cafe.

Pantheon

No tickets are necessary and there are rarely lines to get in. You can comfortably visit in around 30 minutes.

range of tours. Only the standard adult ticket can be printed at home; all other tickets must be picked up at the site. There's a booking fee of €2.

The new SUPER ticket (p72) gives skip-the-line admission and entry to several extra 'internal' sights at the Roman Forum and Palatino. It costs €6 more than the regular Colosseum ticket and is well worth considering.

VATICAN MUSEUMS & ST PETER'S BASILICA

Wednesday mornings are a good time to visit the Vatican Museums (p133) as everyone is at the pope's weekly audience. Mondays are very busy, as many of the city's other museums are shut. The museums are free (but busy) on the last Sunday of the month.

Book tickets through the museums' website, www.museivaticani.va. Once you've booked you'll receive an email voucher with a reservation code. Print this (or save it onto a smartphone or tablet) and present it at the museum entrance. Booking fee of €4.

St Peter's Basilica (p128) is free to visit, so it's not possible to pre-book or skip the line. Take heart, though: the queues might appear ominous at first, but they move quickly. The best times to visit are early morning (7am to 9am) or in the afternoon, after around 4pm. Avoid Wednesday mornings, and Saturdays when many day-trippers pour into town.

MUSEO E GALLERIA BORGHESE

Booking is compulsory for the Museo e Galleria Borghese (p204). Either call the museum direct or book online at www.tosc.it. Note you'll need to pick a day and time for your visit. Pick up tickets at the museum or print them at home. Booking fee of €2.

Discounts & Passes

Admission to state museums (which include the Colosseum and Castel Sant'Angelo) is free for under-18s and discounted for EU nationals aged 18 to 25. Similarly, city-run museums (most notably the Capitoline Museums) are free for kids under six and discounted for six to 25 year olds. In all cases, you'll need photo ID as proof of age.

The Pantheon, St Peter's Basilica and all the city's churches are free.

There are two main passes:

➡ Roma Pass (p21) Provides free admission to two museums or sites (or one with the 48-hour version), and reduced entry to extra sites. It does not cover the Vatican Museums. To get the best out of it, use the free entries on the more expensive sites.

➡ Omnia Card (p302) Is similar to the Roma Pass but also covers the Vatican Museums and several Vatican-managed sites as well as a hop-on, hop-off bus tour. To get your money's worth, you'll need to do everything the card offers and use public transport regularly.

Ancient Art

Capitoline Museums (p69) Rome's trademark wolf is the star of the museums' magnificent collection of classical sculpture.

Museo Nazionale Romano: Palazzo Massimo alle Terme (p152) Boasts some of Rome's finest ancient mosaics and frescoes.

Museo Nazionale Romano: Palazzo Altemps (p84) Frescoed halls set the stage for impressive Roman statuary.

Museo dell'Ara Pacis (p112) Modern architecture meets ancient sculpture in the form of Augustus' giant altar to peace.

Baroque Brilliance

Museo e Galleria Borghese (p204) Home to some of Rome's most spectacular baroque sculpture.

Gallerie Nazionali: Palazzo Barberini (p111) A majestic palace boasting unforgettable paintings and a blazing ceiling fresco.

St Peter's Basilica (p128) Baroque maestro Gian Lorenzo Bernini is the man behind the basilica's magnificent bronze *baldachino* (canopy over the altar).

Chiesa di San Luigi dei Francesi (p86) Three paintings by baroque bad boy Caravaggio adorn this historic church.

Under the Radar Sites & Museums

Galleria Doria Pamphilj (p90) Check out works by Caravaggio, Raphael, Titian, Velázquez and several Flemish masters.

Museo Nazionale Etrusco di Villa Giulia (p208) Beautiful museum showcasing Italy's finest collection of Etruscan treasures.

Villa dei Quintili (p221) A 2nd-century Roman villa set in bucolic greenery on Via Appia Antica.

Palazzo Farnese (p86) Rome's French Embassy boasts frescoes said to rival those of the Sistine Chapel.

Dramatic Settings

Castel Sant'Angelo (p141) Browse paintings, sculpture and medieval memorabilia at Rome's landmark castle.

Mercati di Traiano Museo dei Fori Imperiali (p72) Explore Trajan's towering 2nd-century complex overlooking the Imperial Forums.

Museo Capitoline Centrale Montemartini (p223) Ancient statues adorn furnaces and giant boilers at this decommissioned power station.

Catacombe di San Sebastiano (p219) This underground tunnel complex is one of several beneath Via Appia Antica.

Smaller Museums

Galleria Corsini (p176) Works by big-name artists hang in the halls of this overlooked Trastevere gallery.

Palazzo Spada (p86) Check out a celebrated optical illusion by baroque architect Francesco Borromini.

Villa Farnesina (p175) Fabulous frescoes by Raphael et al shine at this elegant 16th-century villa.

Museo di Roma (p85) Exhibits compete with palatial architecture and Piazza Navona views at this history museum.

Museum Cafes

Terrazza Caffarelli (p77) Stop by for refreshment and romantic views at the Capitoline Museums' fabulously sited 2nd-floor cafe.

Castel Sant'Angelo (p141) The castle's rooftop terrace provides a stunning setting for a quick cafe break.

Chiostro del Bramante (p85) Relax over a drink in the memorable confines of Bramante's Renaissance cloisters.

Modern Art

Museo Nazionale delle Arti del XXI Secolo (p207) Rome's premier contemporary-arts museum, housed in a Zaha Hadid–designed building.

La Galleria Nazionale (p207) Take in works by the giants of modern and contemporary art.

Museo d'Arte Contemporanea di Roma (p208) For experimental art in a slickly converted former brewery.

Mattatoio (p197) Rome's ex-abattoir has been revived as a contemporary-arts space.

Specialist Subjects

Keats-Shelley House (p113) One for Romantics, a small museum dedicated to Brit poet John Keats.

Museo Ebraico di Roma (p88) Housed in the city's synagogue, this museum tells of Rome's ancient Jewish community.

Cinecittà (p229) Rome's historic film studios have given rise to some of cinema's greatest hits.

Explore Rome

ROME'S TOP EXPERIENCES

Left St Peter's Basilica (p128)
IR STONE / SHUTTERSTOCK ©

Neighbourhoods at a Glance

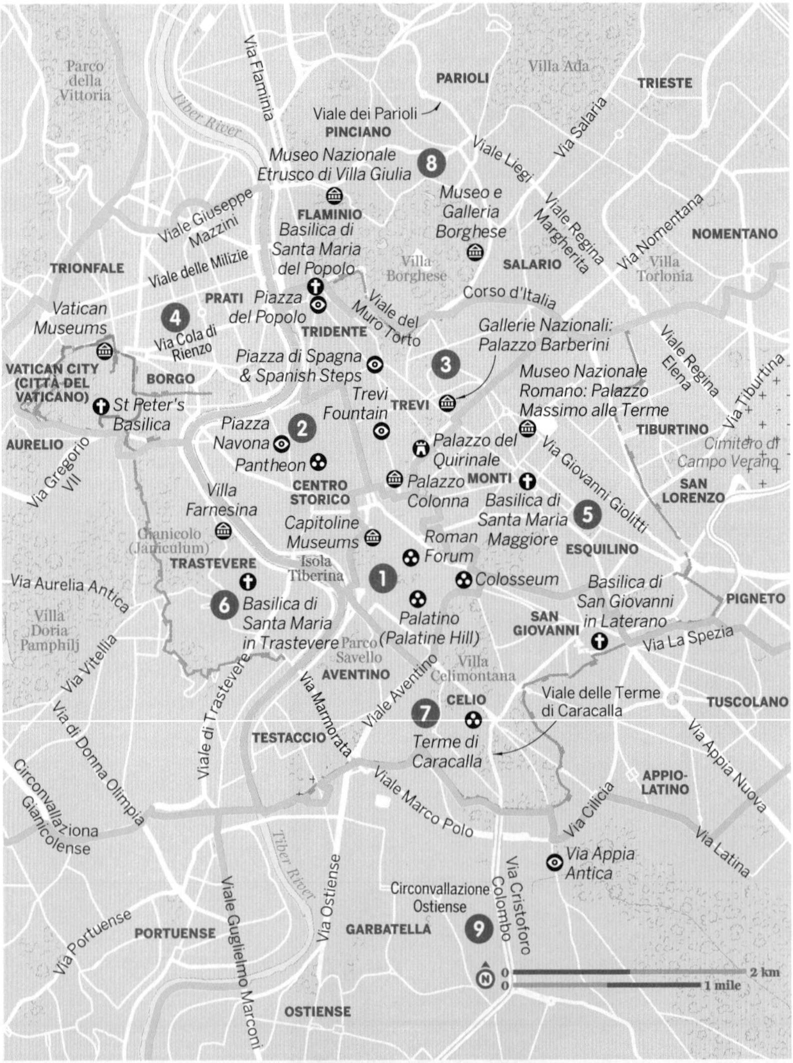

1 Ancient Rome p56

In a city of extraordinary beauty, Rome's ancient heart stands out. It's here you'll find the great icons of the city's past: the Colosseum; the Palatino; the forums; and the Campidoglio, the historic home of the Capitoline Museums. Touristy by day, it's quiet at night with few after-hours attractions.

2 Centro Storico p78

A tightly packed tangle of cobbled alleyways and baroque piazzas, the historic centre is the Rome many come to see. The Pantheon and Piazza Navona are the star turns, but its theatrical streets teem with monuments, museums, boutiques, bars, trattorias and art-laden churches.

3 Tridente, Trevi & the Quirinale p106

Counting the Trevi Fountain and Spanish Steps among its A-list sights, this part of Rome is debonair and touristy. Designer boutiques, swish hotels and historic cafes crowd the streets of Tridente, while the area around Piazza Barberini and the Trevi Fountain, within shouting distance of the president's palace on Quirinale hill, harbours multiple art galleries and eateries.

4 Vatican City, Borgo & Prati p126

The Vatican, the world's smallest sovereign state, sits over the river from Rome's historic centre. Radiating from the domed grandeur of St Peter's Basilica, it boasts some of Italy's most revered artworks, many in the Vatican Museums (home of the Sistine Chapel), as well as batteries of overpriced restaurants and souvenir shops. Nearby, the landmark Castel Sant'Angelo looms over the Borgo district and upscale Prati offers excellent accommodation, eating and shopping.

5 Monti, Esquilino & San Lorenzo p150

Centred on transport hub Stazione Termini, this large, cosmopolitan area can seem busy and overwhelming. But hidden among its traffic-noisy streets are some beautiful churches, Rome's best unsung art museum at Palazzo Massimo alle Terme, and any number of trendy bars and restaurants in the fashionable Monti, student-loved San Lorenzo and bohemian Pigneto districts.

6 Trastevere & Gianicolo p172

With its old-world cobbled lanes and boho vibe, ever-trendy Trastevere is one of Rome's most vivacious and Roman neighbourhoods. Endlessly photogenic and largely car-free, its labyrinth of backstreet lanes heaves after dark as crowds swarm to its fashionable restaurants, cafes and bars. Rising up behind, Gianicolo hill offers a breath of fresh air and superb views.

7 San Giovanni & Testaccio p188

Encompassing two of Rome's seven hills, this sweeping, multifaceted area offers everything from medieval churches and ancient ruins to colourful markets and popular trattorias. Its best-known drawcards are the Basilica di San Giovanni in Laterano and Terme di Caracalla. Down by the river, Testaccio is a trendy district known for its nose-to-tail Roman cuisine and weekend clubbing.

8 Villa Borghese & Northern Rome p202

This area encompasses Rome's most famous park (Villa Borghese) and its most expensive residential district (Parioli). Concert-goers head to the Auditorium Parco della Musica, while art lovers can choose between contemporary installations (MAXXI), Etruscan artefacts (Museo Nazionale Etrusco di Villa Giulia) or baroque treasures (Museo e Galleria Borghese).

9 Southern Rome p216

Boasting a wealth of diversions, this huge area extends to Rome's southern limits. Ancient ruins and subterranean catacombs await on Via Appia Antica, while post-industrial Ostiense offers edgy street art, superb dining and heaving nightlife. Then there's EUR, an Orwellian quarter of wide boulevards and linear buildings.

Ancient Rome

COLOSSEUM & PALATINO | THE FORUMS & AROUND | CAMPIDOGLIO | PIAZZA VENEZIA | FORUM BOARIUM & AROUND

Neighbourhood Top Five

❶ **Colosseum** (p58) Getting your first glimpse of Rome's iconic amphitheatre. An architectural masterpiece, this fearsome arena has been thrilling crowds since it first staged gladiatorial combat two millennia ago.

❷ **Palatino** (p60) Exploring the haunting ruins of the Palatine Hill, Rome's mythical birthplace and, in ancient times, its most exclusive neighbourhood.

❸ **Capitoline Museums** (p69) Going face to face with centuries of awe-inspiring art at the world's oldest public museums.

❹ **Roman Forum** (p64) Exploring the basilicas, temples and triumphal arches of what was once the nerve centre of the vast Roman Empire.

❺ **Vittoriano** (p75) Surveying the city spread out beneath you from atop this colossal marble extravaganza.

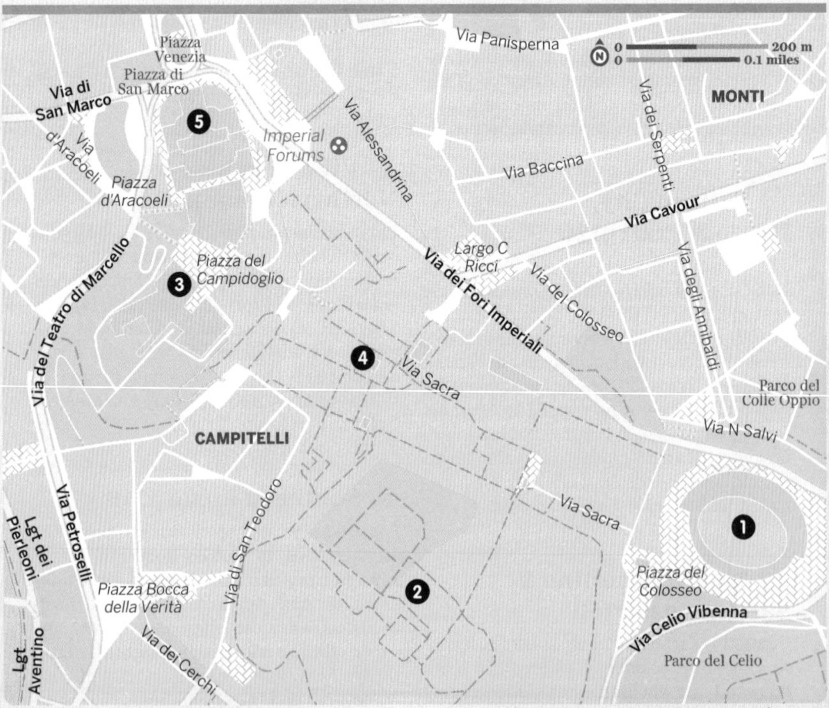

For more detail of this area see Map p324

Explore Ancient Rome

South of the city centre, this area contains the great ruins of the ancient city, all within easy walking distance of each other. They start to get crowded mid-morning and throng with tourists until mid- to late afternoon, although in peak season they can be busy all day.

The area has two focal points: the Colosseum (p58) to the southeast, and Campidoglio (Capitoline Hill; p74) to the northwest. In between lie the forums: the Roman Forum (p64) to the left of Via dei Fori Imperiali as you walk up from the Colosseum and the Imperial Forums (p74) to the right. Rising above the Roman Forum is the Palatino (p60), and behind that the grassy expanse of the Circo Massimo (p72). To the northwest of the Circo, you'll find the Bocca della Verità (p76) and a couple of early Roman temples in an area that used to be ancient Rome's cattle market (Forum Boarium).

To explore Ancient Rome, the obvious starting point is the Colosseum, which is easily accessible by metro. From there you could go directly up to the Roman Forum, but if you go first to the Palatino you'll get some wonderful views over the forums. Once you're done in the Roman Forum head up to Piazza del Campidoglio (p74) and the Capitoline Museums (p69). Nearby, the mammoth white Vittoriano (p75) is hard to miss.

Local Life

- **Exhibitions** While tourists clamber all over the Vittoriano, locals head inside to enjoy art at the Complesso del Vittoriano (p75). The gallery hosts temporary exhibitions, often by major modern artists.
- **Celebrations** Join Romans to celebrate the city's birthday, the Natale di Roma, on 21 April. The program varies each year but events are generally held around Via dei Fori Imperiali, Campidoglio (p74) and Circo Massimo (p72).
- **Via Crucis** Easter is a big deal in Rome. On Good Friday crowds gather at the Colosseum (p58) to witness the pope lead the traditional Via Crucis procession, an event that is televised and broadcast around the world.

Getting There & Away

- **Bus** Piazza Venezia in the northwest of the neighbourhood is an important hub. Many services stop on or near the square, including buses 40, 64, 87, 170, 916 and H.
- **Metro** Metro line B has stations at the Colosseum (Colosseo) and Circo Massimo. If taking the metro at Termini, follow signs for Line B 'direzione Laurentina'.

Lonely Planet's Top Tip

The big sights in this part of Rome are among the city's most visited. To avoid the worst of the crowds try to visit early morning or in the late afternoon, when it's cooler and the light is much better for taking photos. Also, be sure to wear comfy shoes as the ancient Roman cobblestones are murder on the feet and you'll be doing plenty of walking.

Best Places to Eat

- Terre e Domus (p77)
- 47 Circus Roof Garden (p77)
- Alimentari Pannella Carmela (p77)

For reviews, see p76.

Best Places to Drink

- Terrazza Caffarelli (p77)
- 0,75 (p77)
- Cavour 313 (p77)

For reviews, see p77.

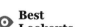

Best Lookouts

- Vittoriano (p75)
- Orti Farnesiani, Palatino (p63)
- Tabularium, Capitoline Museums (p70)
- Mercati di Traiano Museo dei Fori Imperiali (p72)

For reviews, see p72.

MARCO RUBINO / SHUTTERSTOCK ©

TOP EXPERIENCE
EXPERIENCE THE COLOSSEUM

An awesome, spine-tingling sight, the Colosseum is the most thrilling of Rome's ancient monuments. It was here that gladiators met in mortal combat and condemned prisoners fought off wild beasts in front of baying, bloodthirsty crowds. Two thousand years on and it's Italy's top tourist attraction, drawing more than seven million visitors a year.

The emperor Vespasian (r 69–79 CE) originally commissioned the amphitheatre in 72 CE in the grounds of Nero's vast Domus Aurea complex. He never lived to see it finished, though, and it was completed by his son and successor Titus (r 79–81) in 80 CE. To mark its inauguration, Titus held games that lasted 100 days and nights, during which some 5000 animals were slaughtered. Trajan (r 98–117) later topped this, holding a marathon 117-day killing spree involving 9000 gladiators and 10,000 animals.

The 50,000-seat arena was Rome's first, and greatest, permanent amphitheatre. For some five centuries it was used to stage lavish, crowd-pleasing spectacles to mark important anniversaries or military victories. Gladiatorial combat was eventually outlawed in the 5th century but wild animal shows continued until the mid-6th century.

Following the fall of the Roman Empire, the Colosseum was largely abandoned. It was used as a fortress by the powerful Frangipani family in the 12th century and later plundered of its precious building materials. Travertine and marble stripped from the Colosseum were used to decorate a number of Rome's notable buildings, including Palazzo Venezia, Palazzo Barberini and Palazzo Cancelleria.

TOP TIPS

- If queues are long, get your ticket at the Palatino at Via di San Gregorio 30.
- Alternatively, book tickets at www.coopculture.it (€2 booking fee); get the Roma Pass or SUPER ticket; join a tour.

PRACTICALITIES

- Colosseo
- Map p324, G6
- ☎06 3996 7700
- www.parcocolosseo.it
- Piazza del Colosseo
- adult/reduced incl Roman Forum & Palatino €12/7.50, SUPER ticket €18/13.50
- ⏲8.30am-1hr before sunset
- Ⓜ Colosseo

More recently, pollution and vibrations caused by traffic and the metro have taken a toll. To help counter this, it was given a major clean-up between 2014 and 2016, the first in its 2000-year history, as part of an ongoing €25 million restoration project sponsored by the luxury shoemaker Tod's.

The Exterior

The outer walls have three levels of arches, framed by decorative columns topped by capitals of the Ionic (at the bottom), Doric and Corinthian (at the top) orders. They were originally covered in travertine, and marble statues filled the niches on the 2nd and 3rd storeys. The upper level, punctuated with windows and slender Corinthian pilasters, had supports for 240 masts that held the awning over the arena, shielding the spectators from sun and rain. The 80 entrance arches, known as *vomitoria,* allowed the spectators to enter and be seated in a matter of minutes.

The Seating

The *cavea,* or spectator seating, was divided into three tiers: magistrates and senior officials sat in the lowest tier, wealthy citizens in the middle and the plebs in the highest tier. Women (except for Vestal Virgins) were relegated to the cheapest sections at the top. Tickets were numbered and spectators were assigned a precise seat in a specific sector – in 2015, restorers uncovered traces of red numerals on the arches, indicating how the sectors were numbered. The podium, a broad terrace in front of the tiers of seats, was reserved for the emperor, senators and VIPs.

The Arena

The stadium originally had a wooden floor covered in sand – *harena* in Latin, hence the word 'arena' – to prevent combatants from slipping and to soak up spilt blood. Trapdoors led down to the hypogeum, a subterranean complex beneath the arena floor.

Hypogeum

The hypogeum served as the stadium's backstage area. It was here stage sets were prepared and combatants would gather before showtime. Gladiators entered from the nearby Ludus Magnus (gladiator school) via an underground corridor, while a second tunnel, the Passaggio di Commodo (Passage of Commodus), allowed the emperor to arrive without having to pass through the crowds.

To hoist people, animals and scenery up to the arena, the hypogeum was equipped with a sophisticated network of 80 winch-operated lifts, all controlled by a single pulley system.

THE NAME

The arena was originally known as the Flavian Amphitheatre (Anfiteatro di Flavio) after Vespasian's family name, and although it was Rome's most famous arena, it wasn't the biggest – the Circo Massimo could hold up to 250,000 people. The name Colosseum, when introduced in the Middle Ages, wasn't a reference to its size but to the Colosso di Nerone, a giant statue of Nero that stood nearby.

Games staged at the Colosseum usually involved gladiators fighting wild animals or each other. Bouts rarely ended in death as the games' sponsor was required to pay compensation to a gladiator's owner if the gladiator died in action.

TICKETS & TOURS

When you buy a ticket online at www.coopculture.it, you'll have to commit to a specific entry time. Note also you'll need to book a guided tour to visit the underground area (hypogeum) and/or upper floors (Belvedere). These cost €9 (or €15 for both) plus the normal Colosseum ticket.

TOP EXPERIENCE
EXPLORE THE PALATINO

Sandwiched between the Roman Forum and the Circo Massimo, the Palatino (Palatine Hill) is an atmospheric area of towering pine trees, majestic ruins and memorable views. This is where Romulus supposedly founded the city in 753 BCE and Rome's emperors lived in palatial luxury.

Roman myth holds that Romulus founded Rome on the Palatino after he'd killed his twin Remus in a fit of anger. Archaeological evidence, however, puts the establishment of a village here to the early Iron Age (around 830 BCE).

As the most central of Rome's seven hills, and because it was close to the Roman Forum, the Palatino was ancient Rome's most exclusive neighbourhood. The emperor Augustus lived here all his life and successive emperors built increasingly opulent palaces. But after Rome's fall it fell into disrepair, and in the Middle Ages churches and castles were built over the ruins. Later, wealthy Renaissance families established gardens on the hill.

Most of the Palatino as it appears today is covered by the ruins of Emperor Domitian's vast complex, which served as the main imperial palace for 300 years. Divided into the Domus Flavia, Domus Augustana and a *stadio* (stadium), it was built in the 1st century .

Southern Path

On entering the Palatino from the main entrance on Via di San Gregorio, continue left until you come to a gate giving onto a path (open 9am to 3pm). This skirts the hill's southern flank, offering good views up to the ruins and

DON'T MISS

- Stadio
- Domus Augustana
- Casa di Livia and Casa di Augusto
- Orti Farnesiani

PRACTICALITIES

- Palatine Hill
- Map p324, D7
- ☎06 3996 7700
- www.parcocolosseo.it
- Via di San Gregorio 30, Piazza di Santa Maria Nova
- adult/reduced incl Colosseum & Roman Forum €12/7.50, SUPER ticket €18/13.50
- 8.30am-1hr before sunset; some SUPER ticket sites Mon, Wed, Fri & morning Sun only
- Ⓜ Colosseo

providing a clear chronology of the area's development – as you walk, you're essentially going back in time as the ruins become increasingly older.

Stadio

Back on the main site, the first recognisable construction you'll come across is the **stadio** (Map p324; Via di San Gregorio 30, Palatino; Ⓜ Colosseo). This sunken area, which was part of the imperial palace, was probably used by the emperors for private games and events.

A path to the side of it leads to the towering remains of a complex built by Septimius Severus, comprising the **Terme di Settimio Severo** baths (Map p324) and a palace, **Domus Severiana** (Map p324). Here you can enjoy views over the Circo Massimo and, if they're open, visit the **Arcate Severiane** (Severian Arches; Map p324; ⏲8.30am-6.45pm Tue & Fri summer, shorter hours Tue & Fri winter), a series of arches built to facilitate further development.

Domus Augustana & Domus Flavia

Next to the *stadio* are the ruins of the huge **Domus Augustana** (Emperor's Residence; Map p324), the emperor's private quarters in the imperial palace. This was built on two levels, with rooms leading off a *peristilio* (peristyle or porticoed courtyard) on each floor. You can't get down to the lower level, but from above you can see the basin of a big, square fountain and beyond it rooms that would originally have been paved in coloured marble.

Also here are the **Aula Isiaca** (Map p324; SUPER ticket adult/reduced €18/13.50; ⏲9am-6.30pm Mon, Wed & Fri, to 2pm Sun summer, 9am-3.30pm Mon, Wed & Fri, to 1pm Sun winter) and **Loggia Mattei**, two of several sites accessible with a SUPER ticket. The former is a frescoed room from a luxurious Republican-era house, while the latter is a Renaissance loggia decorated by Baldassarre Peruzzi.

To the north is the **Domus Flavia** (Map p324), the public part of the palace complex. This was centred on a grand columned peristyle – the grassy area you see with the base of an octagonal fountain – off which the main halls led. To the north was the emperor's audience chamber *(aula Regia);* to the west, a basilica where the emperor judged legal disputes; and to the south, a large banqueting hall, the *triclinium*.

Museo Palatino

The white building next to the Domus Augustana is the **Museo Palatino** (Map p324; Via di San Gregorio 30, Palatino; SUPER ticket adult/reduced €18/13.50; ⏲8.30am-1½hr before sunset; Ⓜ Colosseo), a small

SUPER SITES

Some of the internal sites on the Palatino can only be accessed with the SUPER ticket: the Casa di Augusto, Casa di Livia, Aula Isiaca and Loggia Mattei, all of which are open on Mondays, Wednesdays, Fridays and Sunday mornings; and the Museo Palatino and Criptoportico Neroniano, both open daily. Note also that access to the Casa di Augusto and Casa di Livia is by guided tour only. Numbers are limited so it's best to book an entry time when you buy your ticket.

The Palatino commands some stunning views. One of the best vantage points is the balcony of the Orti Farnesiani, which affords breathtaking panoramas over the Roman Forum. For a totally different perspective, there are terrific views up to the Arcate Severiane and Terme di Massenzio from the southern path around the base of the hill.

PALATINO (PALATINE HILL)

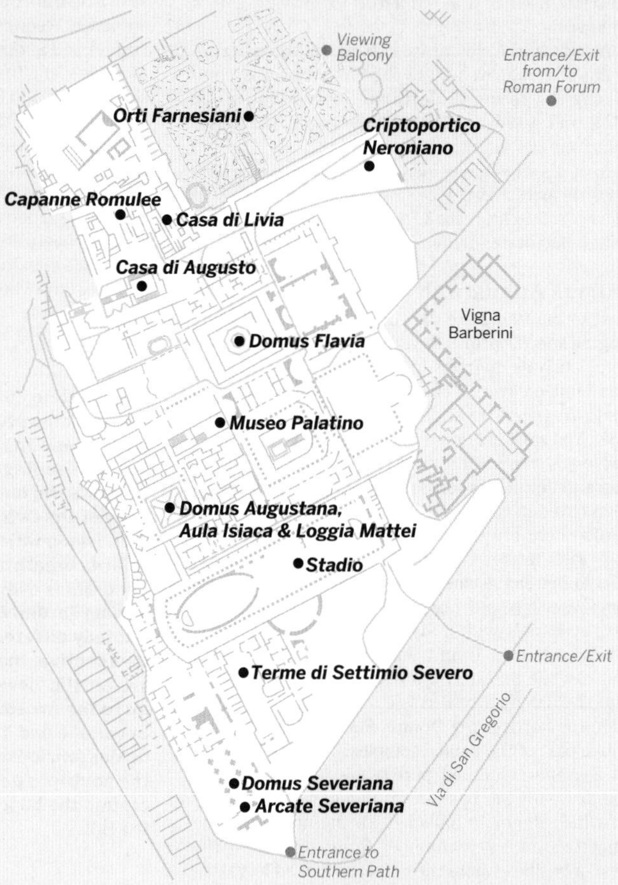
Viewing Balcony
Entrance/Exit from/to Roman Forum
Orti Farnesiani
Criptoportico Neroniano
Capanne Romulee
Casa di Livia
Casa di Augusto
Vigna Barberini
Domus Flavia
Museo Palatino
Domus Augustana, Aula Isiaca & Loggia Mattei
Stadio
Entrance/Exit
Terme di Settimio Severo
Via di San Gregorio
Domus Severiana
Arcate Severiana
Entrance to Southern Path

museum that charts the development of the Palatino through video presentations, models and archaeological finds. Highlights include busts of the imperial family and, in a room dedicated to Augustus, a marble pair of *Ali di Vittoria* (Victory Wings).

Casa di Livia & Casa di Augusto

Near the Domus Flavia, the **Casa di Livia** (Map p324; SUPER ticket adult/reduced €18/13.50; ⌚9am-6.30pm Mon, Wed & Fri, to 2pm Sun summer, 9am-3.30pm Mon, Wed & Fri, to 1pm Sun winter) is one of the Palatino's best-preserved buildings. Home to the emperor Augustus' wife Livia, it was built around an atrium leading onto what were once reception rooms, decorated with frescoes of mythological scenes, landscapes, fruits and flowers.

Nearby, the **Casa di Augusto** (Map p324; SUPER ticket adult/reduced €18/13.50; ⌚9am-6.30pm Mon, Wed & Fri, to 2pm Sun summer, 9am-3.30pm Mon, Wed & Fri, to 1pm Sun winter), Augustus' private residence, features some superb frescoes in vivid reds, yellows and blues. These are further enhanced by audio narrations and video projections explaining the layout of the house and its extensive decor.

Criptoportico Neroniano

Northeast of the Casa di Livia lies the **Criptoportico Neroniano** (Map p324; SUPER ticket adult/reduced €18/13.50; ⌚8.30am-1hr before sunset), a 130m tunnel where Caligula was thought to have been murdered, and which Nero later used to connect his Domus Aurea with the Palatino. Once decorated by elaborate stucco, it's now rather a dark, dank place despite the piped music and projections of ancient Roman decor.

Orti Farnesiani

The area west of the criptoportico was once Tiberius' palace, the Domus Tiberiana, but is now home to the 16th-century **Orti Farnesiani** (Map p324), one of Europe's earliest botanic gardens. A balcony at its northern end commands breathtaking views over the Roman Forum.

ROMULUS & REMUS

Rome's mythical founders were supposedly brought up on the Palatino by a shepherd, Faustulus, after a wolf saved them from death. Their shelter, the 8th-century-BCE **Capanne Romulee** (Romulean Huts), is situated near the Casa di Augusto. In 2007 the discovery of a mosaic-covered cave 15m beneath the Domus Augustana reignited interest in the legend. According to some scholars, this was the *Lupercale*, the cave where ancient Romans thought Romulus and Remus had been suckled by the wolf.

There are no great eating options in the immediate vicinity so consider bringing a picnic. A good spot to sit down is the Vigna Barberini (Barberini Vineyard), a grassy area off the path down to the Roman Forum. Note, however, you can't bring alcohol or glass containers onto the Palatino.

PALACE ROOTS

The Palatino's imperial connection has worked its way into the English language. The word 'palace' is a derivation of the hill's Latin name, *Palatium*.

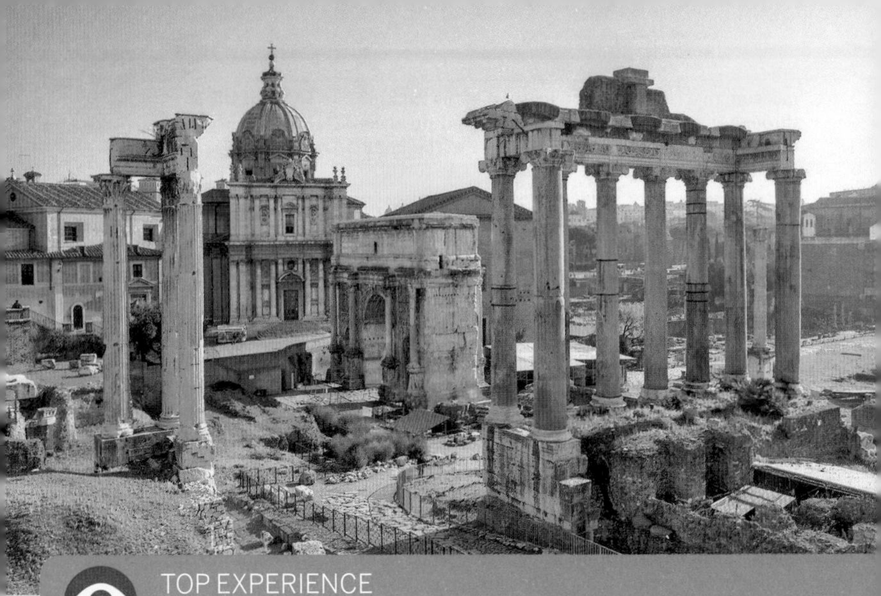

S.BORISOV / SHUTTERSTOCK ©

TOP EXPERIENCE

WONDER AT THE ROMAN FORUM

The Roman Forum was ancient Rome's showpiece centre, a grandiose district of temples, basilicas and vibrant public spaces. Nowadays, it's a collection of impressive, if sketchily labelled, ruins that can leave you drained and confused. But if you can get your imagination going, there's something wonderfully compelling about walking in the footsteps of Julius Caesar and other legendary figures of Roman history.

The site, which was originally a marshy burial ground, was first developed in the 7th century BCE, growing over time to become the social, political and commercial hub of the Roman empire.

Like many of ancient Rome's great urban developments, it fell into disrepair after the fall of the Roman Empire until eventually it was used as pasture land. In the Middle Ages it was known as the Campo Vaccino ('Cow Field') and extensively plundered for its stone and marble. The area was systematically excavated in the 18th and 19th centuries, and excavations continue to this day.

Via Sacra & Tempio di Giulio Cesare

Entering from Largo della Salara Vecchia – you can also enter directly from the Palatino or via an entrance near the Arco di Tito – you'll see the **Tempio di Antonino e Faustina** (Map p324) ahead to your left. Erected in 141 CE, this was transformed into a church in the 8th century, the **Chiesa di San Lorenzo in Miranda** (Map p324). To your right, the 179 BCE **Basilica Fulvia Aemilia** (Map p324) was a 100m-long public hall with a two-storey porticoed facade.

At the end of the path, you'll come to **Via Sacra** (Map p324), the Forum's main thoroughfare, and the

DON'T MISS

- Curia
- Arco di Settimio Severo
- Tempio di Saturno
- Chiesa di Santa Maria Antiqua
- Casa delle Vestali
- Basilica di Massenzio
- Arco di Tito

PRACTICALITIES

- Foro Romano
- Map p324, D5
- ☎06 3996 7700
- www.parcocolosseo.it
- Largo della Salara Vecchia, Piazza di Santa Maria Nova
- adult/reduced incl Colosseum & Palatino €12/7.50
- ⏲8.30am-1hr before sunset
- 🚌Via dei Fori Imperiali

Tempio di Giulio Cesare (Map p324) (also known as the Tempio del Divo Giulio). Built by Augustus in 29 BCE, this marks the spot where Julius Caesar's body was cremated after his assassination in 44 BCE. Caesar was the first Roman to be posthumously deified, a custom that was central to the Roman imperial cult.

Curia & Lapis Niger

Heading right up Via Sacra brings you to the **Curia** (Map p324), the seat of the Roman Senate. According to tradition, it was originally built by Tullo Ostilio, the third of Rome's seven kings, and later rebuilt by Silla around 80 BCE. Julius Caesar moved it to its current location, where it was subsequently modified by Augustus, Domitian and Diocletian, before being converted into a church in the Middle Ages. The brick barn-like construction you see today is a 1937 reconstruction of how it looked in the reign of Diocletian (r 284–305).

In front of the Curia, and hidden by scaffolding, the **Lapis Niger** (Map p324) is a large slab of black marble that covered an underground area said to contain the tomb of Romulus.

Arco di Settimio Severo & Rostri

At the end of Via Sacra, the 23m-high **Arco di Settimio Severo** (Arch of Septimius Severus; Map p324) is dedicated to the eponymous emperor and his two sons, Caracalla and Geta. The triumphal arch was built in 203 CE to commemorate Roman victories over the Parthians, and, if you can make them out, reliefs in the central panel depict the defeated Parthians being led away in chains.

Close by are the remains of the **Rostri** (Rostra; Map p324), an elaborate podium where Shakespeare had Mark Antony make his famous 'Friends, Romans, countrymen...' speech, and where local politicos would harangue the market crowds. Its name is a reference to several bronze beaks (*rostri*, or *rostra* in Latin) that were taken from ships captured at the battle of Antium in 338 BCE and used to decorate the giant platform.

Facing the Rostri, the **Colonna di Foca** (Column of Phocus; Map p324) rises above what was once the Forum's main square, **Piazza del Foro** (Map p324).

Tempio di Saturno & Around

The eight granite columns behind the Colonna di Foca are all that survive of the **Tempio di Saturno** (Temple of Saturn; Map p324), one of the Forum's landmark sights. Inaugurated in 497 BCE and subsequently rebuilt in the 1st century BCE, it was an important temple that doubled as the state treasury.

VESTAL VIRGINS

Despite privilege and public acclaim, life as a Vestal Virgin was no bed of roses. Every year, six physically perfect patrician girls aged between six and 10 were chosen by lottery to serve Vesta, goddess of hearth and household. Once selected, they faced a 30-year period of chaste servitude at the Tempio di Vesta. Their main duty was to ensure the temple's sacred fire never went out. If it did, the priestess responsible would be flogged. If a priestess were to lose her virginity, she risked being buried alive and her partner in crime being flogged to death.

The Forum's main drag, Via Sacra was the principal route of the Roman Triumph. This official victory parade, originally awarded by the Senate to victorious generals but later reserved for emperors, was a huge spectacle involving a procession from the *Porta Triumphalis* (Triumphal Gate) through the Forum to the Temple of Jupiter Capitolinus on the Capitoline Hill.

Roman Forum

A HISTORICAL TOUR

In ancient times, a forum was a market place, civic centre and religious complex all rolled into one, and the greatest of all was the Roman Forum (Foro Romano). Situated between the Palatino (Palatine Hill), ancient Rome's most exclusive neighbourhood, and the Campidoglio (Capitoline Hill), it was the city's busy, bustling centre. On any given day it teemed with activity. Senators debated affairs of state in the ❶ **Curia**, shoppers thronged the squares and traffic-free streets and crowds gathered under the ❷ **Colonna di Foca** to listen to politicians holding forth from the ❷ **Rostri**. Elsewhere, lawyers worked the courts in basilicas including the ❸ **Basilica di Massenzio**, while the Vestal Virgins quietly went about their business in the ❹ **Casa delle Vestali**.

Special occasions were also celebrated in the Forum: religious holidays were marked with ceremonies at temples such as ❺ **Tempio di Saturno** and ❻ **Tempio di Castore e Polluce**, and military victories were honoured with dramatic processions up Via Sacra and the building of monumental arches like ❼ **Arco di Settimio Severo** and ❽ **Arco di Tito**.

The ruins you see today are impressive but they can be confusing without a clear picture of what the Forum once looked like. This spread shows the Forum in its heyday, complete with temples, civic buildings and towering monuments to heroes of the Roman Empire.

TOP TIPS

➡ Get grandstand views of the Forum from the Palatino and Campidoglio.

➡ Visit first thing in the morning or late afternoon; crowds are worst between 11am and 2pm.

➡ In summer it gets hot in the Forum and there's little shade, so take a hat and plenty of water.

Colonna di Foca & Rostri
The free-standing, 13.5m-high Column of Phocus is the Forum's youngest monument, dating to AD 608. Behind it, the Rostri provided a suitably grandiose platform for pontificating public speakers.

Campidoglio (Capitoline Hill)

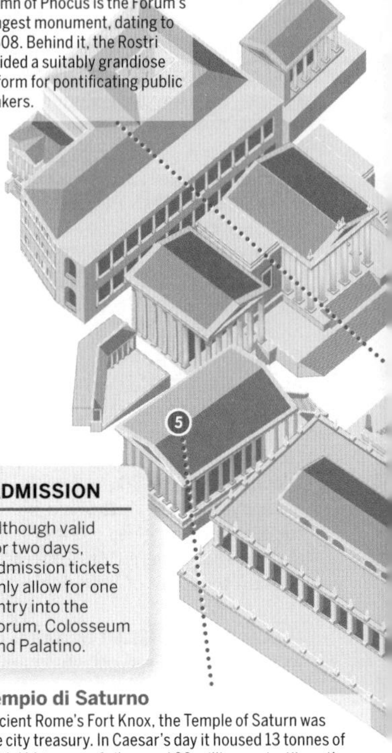

ADMISSION

Although valid for two days, admission tickets only allow for one entry into the Forum, Colosseum and Palatino.

Tempio di Saturno
Ancient Rome's Fort Knox, the Temple of Saturn was the city treasury. In Caesar's day it housed 13 tonnes of gold, 114 tonnes of silver and 30 million sestertii worth of silver coins.

IASCIC/SHUTTERSTOCK ©

VIACHESLAV LOPATIN/SHUTTERSTOCK ©

Tempio di Castore e Polluce
Only three columns of the Temple of Castor and Pollux remain. The temple was dedicated to the Heavenly Twins after they supposedly led the Romans to victory over the Latin League in 496 BC.

Arco di Settimio Severo

One of the Forum's signature monuments, this imposing triumphal arch commemorates the military victories of Septimius Severus. Relief panels depict his campaigns against the Parthians.

Curia

This big barn-like building was the official seat of the Roman Senate. Most of what you see is a reconstruction, but the interior marble floor dates to the 3rd-century reign of Diocletian.

Basilica di Massenzio

Marvel at the scale of this vast 4th-century basilica. In its original form the central hall was divided into enormous naves; now only part of the northern nave survives.

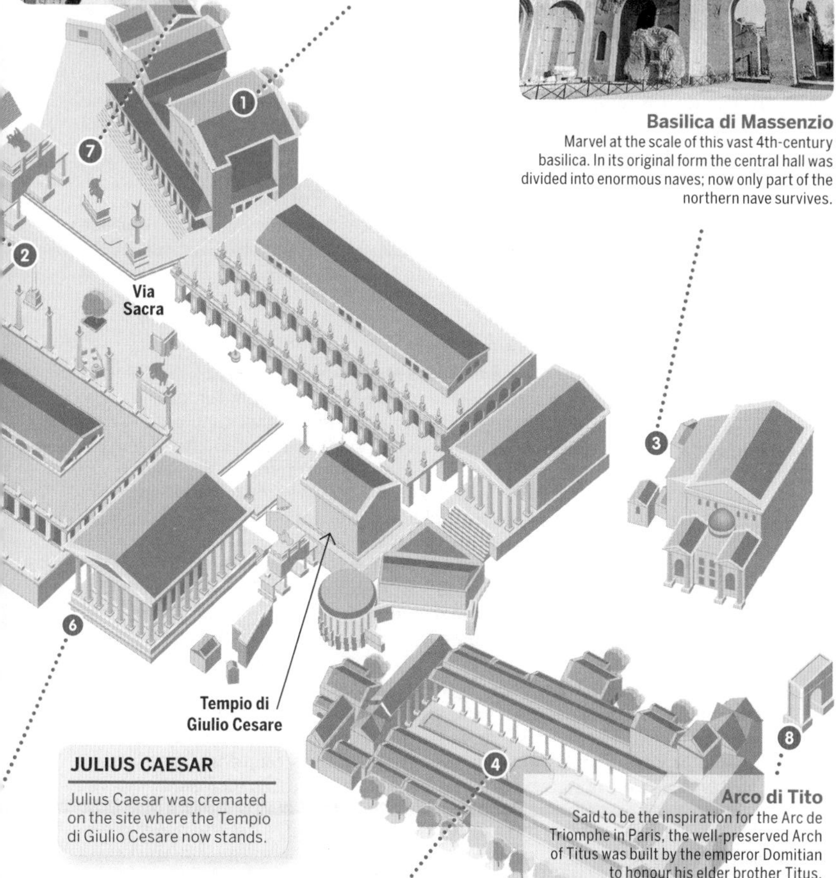

JULIUS CAESAR

Julius Caesar was cremated on the site where the Tempio di Giulio Cesare now stands.

Arco di Tito

Said to be the inspiration for the Arc de Triomphe in Paris, the well-preserved Arch of Titus was built by the emperor Domitian to honour his elder brother Titus.

Casa delle Vestali

White statues line the grassy atrium of what was once the luxurious 50-room home of the Vestal Virgins. The virgins played an important role in Roman religion, serving the goddess Vesta.

TAKE A BREAK

For a restorative coffee break, head up to the Campidoglio and the Terrazza Caffarelli (p77), the Capitoline Museums' panoramic rooftop cafe.

If you want something more substantial, search out Terre e Domus (p77), which serves excellent regional cuisine and fine local wines.

Behind it are: the ruins of the **Tempio della Concordia** (Temple of Concord; Map p324), a 1st-century reconstruction of an earlier 4th-century-BCE sanctuary; the 1st-century CE **Tempio di Vespasiano** (Temple of Vespasian and Titus; Map p324); and the 12-columned **Portico degli Dei Consenti** (Map p324) which belonged to one of ancient Rome's last pagan shrines, dating from the 4th century CE.

Basilica Giulia & Tempio di Castore e Polluce

On the southern side of Piazza del Foro, you'll see the stubby ruins of the **Basilica Giulia** (Map p324), which was begun by Caesar and finished by Augustus. At the end of the basilica, three columns remain from the 5th-century BCE **Tempio di Castore e Polluce** (Temple of Castor and Pollux; Map p324).

Chiesa di Santa Maria Antiqua

Nearby, the 6th-century **Chiesa di Santa Maria Antiqua** (Map p324; SUPER ticket adult/reduced €18/13.50; ⏲9am-6.30pm Tue, Thu & Sat, from 2pm Sun summer, 9am-3.30pm Tue, Thu & Sat, from 2pm Sun winter) is the oldest and most important Christian site on the forum. Its cavernous interior, reopened in 2016 after a lengthy restoration, is lined with exquisite 6th- to 9th-century frescoes. Particularly impressive is an image on the east wall showing Christ with the founding fathers of the Eastern and Western churches, and a hanging depiction of the Virgin Mary with child, one of the oldest icons in existence.

From the church you can access the **Rampa di Domiziano** (Domitian's Ramp; Map p324; SUPER ticket adult/reduced €18/13.50; ⏲9am-6.30pm Tue, Thu & Sat, from 2pm Sun summer, 9am-3.30pm Tue, Thu & Sat, from 2pm Sun winter), an underground passageway that allowed the emperors to enter the Forum from their palaces without being seen.

Casa delle Vestali & Basilica di Massenzio

Towards Via Sacra is the **Casa delle Vestali** (House of the Vestal Virgins; Map p324), home of the virgins who were charged with keeping the flame in the adjoining **Tempio di Vesta** (Map p324) permanently alight. At its centre is a grassy space lined with a string of statues, now mostly headless, depicting the Vestals.

Further on, past the circular **Tempio di Romolo** (Temple of Romulus; Map p324; SUPER ticket adult/reduced €18/13.50; ⏲9am-6.30pm Tue, Thu & Sat, from 2pm Sun summer, 9am-3.30pm Tue, Thu & Sat, from 2pm Sun winter), is the **Basilica di Massenzio** (Basilica di Costantino; Map p324; Piazza di Santa Maria Nova), the largest building on the Forum. Started by the Emperor Maxentius and finished by Constantine in 315 CE (it's also known as the Basilica di Costantino), it originally covered an area of approximately 100m by 65m, roughly three times what it now occupies.

Arco di Tito

Marking the Forum's southeastern entrance, the **Arco di Tito** (Arch of Titus; Map p324; Piazza di Santa Maria Nova) was built by the emperor Domitian in 81 CE to celebrate his brother Titus' military victories in Judea and the 70 CE sack of Jerusalem. In the past, Roman Jews would avoid passing under the arch, which is considered the historical symbol of the beginning of the Jewish Diaspora.

VIACHESLAV LOPATIN / SHUTTERSTOCK ©

TOP EXPERIENCE
WANDER THE CAPITOLINE MUSEUMS

Housed in two stately *palazzi* on Piazza del Campidoglio, the Capitoline Museums are the world's oldest public museums. Their origins date from 1471, when Pope Sixtus IV donated a number of bronze statues to the city, forming the nucleus of what is now one of Italy's finest collections of classical sculpture. There's also a formidable picture gallery with works by many big-name Italian artists.

The entrance to the museums is in **Palazzo dei Conservatori**, where you'll find the original core of the sculptural collection on the 1st floor, and the Pinacoteca (picture gallery) on the 2nd floor.

Before you head up to start on the sculpture collection proper, take a moment to admire the ancient masonry littered around the ground-floor courtyard, notably a mammoth head, hand and foot. These all come from a 12m-high statue of Constantine that originally stood in the Basilica di Massenzio in the Roman Forum.

Palazzo dei Conservatori

Of the sculpture on the 1st floor, the Etruscan *Lupa Capitolina* (Capitoline Wolf) is the most famous piece. Standing in the **Sala della Lupa**, the bronze wolf towers over her suckling wards, Romulus and Remus, who were added in 1471. Until recently, the she-wolf was thought to be a 5th-century BCE Etruscan work but carbon-dating has shown it probably dates from the 1200s.

Other highlights include the *Spinario,* a delicate 1st-century-BCE bronze of a boy removing a thorn from his foot in the **Sala dei Trionfi**, and two works by Gian Lorenzo Bernini:

TOP TIPS

- Note that ticket prices increase, typically to adult/reduced €15/13, when there's an exhibition on.
- Don't miss the views over the Roman Forum from the Tabularium.
- The ground-floor bookshop has a €15 museums guide.

PRACTICALITIES

- Musei Capitolini
- Map p324, B3
- 06 06 08
- www.museicapitolini.org
- Piazza del Campidoglio 1
- adult/reduced €11.50/9.50
- 9.30am-7.30pm, last admission 6.30pm
- Piazza Venezia

Medusa in the **Sala delle Oche** and a statue of Pope Urban VIII in the frescoed **Sala degli Orazi e Curiazi**.

Also on this floor, in the modern **Esedra di Marco Aurelio**, is the original of the equestrian statue of Marcus Aurelius that stands outside in Piazza del Campidoglio. Here you can also see foundations of the **Temple of Jupiter**, one of the ancient city's most important temples.

Pinacoteca

The 2nd floor of Palazzo dei Conservatori is given over to the Pinacoteca, the museum's picture gallery.

Each room harbours masterpieces but two stand out: the **Sala Pietro da Cortona**, which features Pietro da Cortona's famous depiction of the *Ratto delle Sabine* (Rape of the Sabine Women; 1630), and the **Sala di Santa Petronilla**, named after Guercino's huge canvas *Seppellimento di Santa Petronilla* (The Burial of St Petronilla; 1621–23). This airy hall also boasts two important works by Caravaggio: *La Buona Ventura* (The Fortune Teller; 1595), which shows a gypsy pretending to read a young man's hand but actually stealing his ring, and *San Giovanni Battista* (John the Baptist; 1602), an unusual nude depiction of the youthful saint with a ram.

Tabularium

A tunnel links Palazzo dei Conservatori to Palazzo Nuovo on the other side of the square via the Tabularium, ancient Rome's central archive, beneath **Palazzo Senatorio**. The tunnel is lined with panels and inscriptions from ancient tombs, but more inspiring are the views over the Roman Forum from the brick-lined Tabularium.

Palazzo Nuovo

Palazzo Nuovo is crammed to its elegant 17th-century rafters with classical Roman sculpture.

From the lobby, where the curly-bearded **Mars** glares ferociously at everyone who passes by, stairs lead up to the main galleries where you'll find some real showstoppers. Chief among them is the *Galata morente* (Dying Gaul) in the **Sala del Gladiatore**. One of the museum's greatest works, this sublime piece, actually a Roman copy of a 3rd-century-BCE Greek original, movingly captures the quiet, resigned anguish of a dying Gaul warrior.

Next door, the **Sala del Fauno** takes its name from the red marble statue of a faun.

Another superb figurative piece is the sensual yet demure portrayal of the *Venere Capitolina* (Capitoline Venus) in the **Gabinetto della Venere**, off the main corridor. Also worth a look are the busts of philosophers, poets and orators in the **Sala dei Filosofi**.

TREATY OF ROME

With frescoes depicting episodes from ancient Roman history and two papal statues – one of Urban VIII by Bernini and one of Innocent X by Algardi – the **Sala degli Orazi e Curiazi** provided the grand setting for one of modern Europe's key events. On 25 March 1957 the leaders of Italy, France, West Germany, Belgium, Holland and Luxembourg gathered here to sign the Treaty of Rome and establish the European Economic Community, the precursor of the European Union.

Stop by the Terrazza Caffarelli (p77) on the 2nd floor of Palazzo dei Conservatori for coffee and memorable views.

THE CONSERVATORI

Palazzo dei Conservatori takes its name from the *Conservatori* (elected magistrates) who used to hold their public hearings in the *palazzo* in the mid-15th century.

CAPITOLINE MUSEUMS

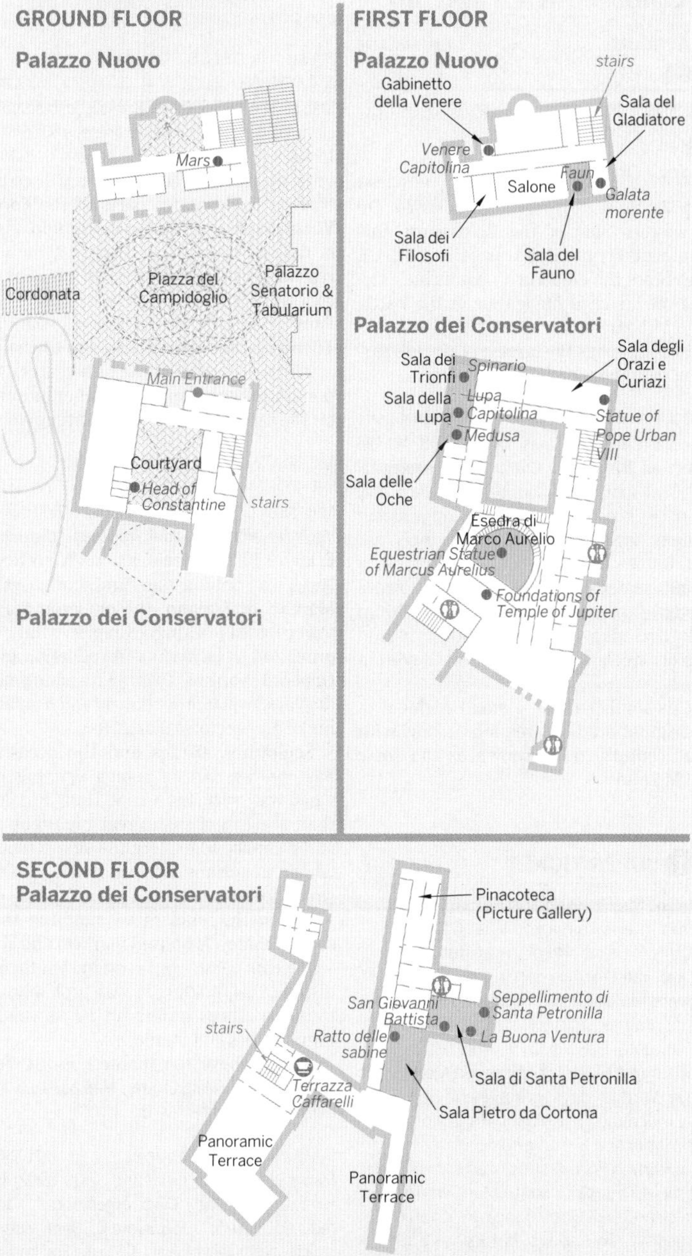
GROUND FLOOR
Palazzo Nuovo
Mars
Cordonata
Piazza del Campidoglio
Palazzo Senatorio & Tabularium
Main Entrance
Courtyard
Head of Constantine
stairs
Palazzo dei Conservatori
FIRST FLOOR
Palazzo Nuovo
stairs
Gabinetto della Venere
Sala del Gladiatore
Venere Capitolina
Faun
Salone
Galata morente
Sala dei Filosofi
Sala del Fauno
Palazzo dei Conservatori
Sala degli Orazi e Curiazi
Sala dei Trionfi
Spinario
Sala della Lupa
Lupa Capitolina
Statue of Pope Urban VIII
Medusa
Sala delle Oche
Esedra di Marco Aurelio
Equestrian Statue of Marcus Aurelius
Foundations of Temple of Jupiter
SECOND FLOOR
Palazzo dei Conservatori
Pinacoteca (Picture Gallery)
San Giovanni Battista
Seppellimento di Santa Petronilla
stairs
Ratto delle sabine
La Buona Ventura
Sala di Santa Petronilla
Terrazza Caffarelli
Sala Pietro da Cortona
Panoramic Terrace
Panoramic Terrace

SIGHTS

Colosseum & Palatino

COLOSSEUM AMPHITHEATRE
See p58.

PALATINO ARCHAEOLOGICAL SITE
See p60.

ARCO DI COSTANTINO MONUMENT
Map p324 (Via di San Gregorio; MColosseo) On the western side of the Colosseum, this monumental triple arch was built in 315 CE to celebrate the emperor Constantine's victory over his rival Maxentius at the Battle of the Milvian Bridge (312 CE). Rising to a height of 25m, it's the largest of Rome's surviving triumphal arches.

CIRCO MASSIMO HISTORIC SITE
Map p324 (Circus Maximus; 06 06 08; Via dei Cerchi; adult/reduced €5/4; archaeological area 10am-4pm Sat & Sun, by reservation only Tue-Fri; MCirco Massimo) Now a huge basin of dusty grass, Circo Massimo was ancient Rome's largest chariot racetrack, a 250,000-seater capable of holding up to a quarter of the city's population. The 600m track circled a wooden dividing island with ornate lap indicators and Egyptian obelisks.

At its southern end, a small segment of the original stadium remains along with a 12th-century tower known as the Torre della Moletta.

SUPER TICKET

To visit the Palatino and Roman Forum's internal sites you'll need to buy a SUPER ticket and plan carefully. The ticket, valid for two consecutive days, covers the Colosseum, Roman Forum and Palatino. On the Palatino, the Casa di Augusto, Casa di Livia, Aula Isiaca and Loggia Mattei are open on Mondays, Wednesdays, Fridays and Sunday mornings; the Museo Palatino and Criptoportico Neroniano open daily. The Roman Forum sites (Tempio di Romolo, Chiesa di Santa Maria in Antiqua, Rampa di Domiziano) are open on Tuesdays, Thursdays, Saturdays and Sunday afternoons.

The Forums & Around

ROMAN FORUM ARCHAEOLOGICAL SITE
See p64.

BASILICA DEI SS COSMA E DAMIANO BASILICA
Map p324 (06 699 08 08; www.cosmadamiano.com; Via dei Fori Imperiali 1; presepe €1; 10am-1pm & 3-6pm; Via dei Fori Imperiali) Backing onto the Roman Forum, this 6th-century basilica incorporates parts of the **Foro di Vespasiano** and **Tempio di Romolo**, visible at the end of the nave. However, the main reason to visit is to admire its fabulous 6th-century apse mosaic depicting Peter and Paul presenting saints Cosma, Damiano, Theodorus and Pope Felix IV to Christ.

Also worth a look is the 18th-century Neapolitan **presepe** (nativity scene) in a room off the salmon-orange 17th-century cloister.

MERCATI DI TRAIANO MUSEO DEI FORI IMPERIALI MUSEUM
Map p324 (06 06 08; www.mercatiditraiano.it; Via IV Novembre 94; adult/reduced incl exhibition €11.50/9.50; 9.30am-7.30pm; Via IV Novembre) This striking museum showcases the **Mercati di Traiano**, the emperor Trajan's towering 2nd-century complex, while also providing a fascinating introduction to the Imperial Forums (p74) with multimedia displays, explanatory panels and a smattering of archaeological artefacts.

Sculptures, friezes and the occasional bust are set out in rooms opening onto what was once the Great Hall. But more than the exhibits, the real highlight here is the chance to explore the vast structure, which historians believe housed the forums' administrative offices.

Originally, scholars thought the three-storey hemicycle housed markets and shops – hence its name – but more recent theories dispute this, holding it was probably used to house offices staffed by the forums' administrators and managers.

Rising above the markets is the **Torre delle Milizie** (Militia Tower; Map p324), a 13th-century red-brick tower.

CARCERE MAMERTINO HISTORIC SITE
Map p324 (Carcer Tullianum; 06 6992 4652; www.tullianum.org; Clivo Argentario 1; adult/reduced €10/5; 8.30am-6.30pm summer, shorter hours rest of year; Via dei Fori Imperiali) Hidden beneath the 16th-century **Chiesa di**

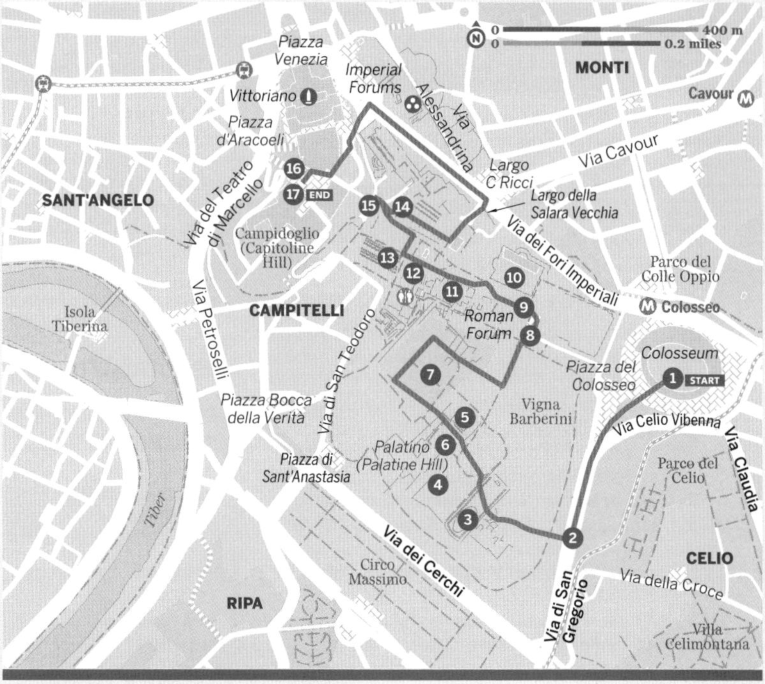

Walking Tour
Explore the Ruins

START COLOSSEUM
END CAPITOLINE MUSEUMS
LENGTH 1.5KM; FOUR HOURS

Start at the 1 **Colosseum** (p58), the great gladiatorial arena that more than any other monument encapsulates the drama of the ancient city. From there, follow Via di San Gregorio along to the 2 **Palatino** (p60), 1st-century Rome's most sought-after neighbourhood where the emperor lived alongside the cream of imperial society.

Beyond the 3 **stadio** (p61), you can still make out parts of the 4 **Domus Augustana** (p61), the emperor's private palace quarters, and the 5 **Domus Flavia** (p61), where he would hold official audiences. Pop into the nearby 6 **Museo Palatino** (p61), before heading up to the 7 **Orti Farnesiani** (p63). These 16th-century gardens weren't part of the ancient city but command stunning views over the Roman Forum. Next, work your way down to the Forum, entering near the 8 **Arco di Tito** (p68), one of the site's great triumphal arches. Beyond this, pick up 9 **Via Sacra** (p64), the Forum's main drag. Follow this down, passing the hulking 10 **Basilica di Massenzio** (p68), and after 100m or so you'll come to the 11 **Casa delle Vestali** (p68), where the legendary Vestal Virgins lived. Beyond the three columns of the 12 **Tempio di Castore e Polluce** (p68), you'll see an area littered with column bases and brick stumps. This is the 13 **Basilica Giulia** (p68), where lawyers and magistrates worked in the crowded law courts. Meanwhile, senators debated matters of state in the 14 **Curia** (p65), over on the other side of the Forum. Nearby, the 15 **Arco di Settimio Severo** (p65) commemorates the military victories of the emperor Septimius Severus.

From the Arco, double back to exit the Forum at Largo della Salara Vecchia. Work your way up to 16 **Piazza del Campidoglio** (p74) to round things off in style at the 17 **Capitoline Museums** (p69).

TOP EXPERIENCE
IMPERIAL FORUMS

The ruins over the road from the Roman Forum are known collectively as the Imperial Forums. Constructed between 42 BCE and 112 CE, they were mostly buried in 1933 when Mussolini bulldozed Via dei Fori Imperiali through the area, but excavations have since unearthed much of them. The standout sights are the **Mercati di Traiano** (p72) and the landmark **Colonna Traiana** (Trajan's Column).

Little recognisable remains of the **Foro di Traiano** (Trajan's Forum), except for some pillars from the **Basilica Ulpia** and the Colonna Traiana, whose minutely detailed reliefs depict Trajan's military victories over the Dacians.

To the southeast, three columns rise from the **Foro di Augusto** (Augustus' Forum). The 30m-high wall behind the forum was built to protect it from the fires that frequently swept down from the nearby Suburra slums.

The **Foro di Nerva** (Nerva's Forum) is now largely buried, although part of a temple to Minerva still stands. Originally, it would have connected the Foro di Augusto to the 1st-century **Foro di Vespasiano** (Vespasian's Forum), also known as the Foro della Pace or Tempio della Pace. Over the road, three columns are the most visible remains of the **Foro di Cesare** (Caesar's Forum).

TOP TIPS

➡ You get a good view of the ruins from Via dei Fori Imperiali.

➡ Look out for summer multimedia light shows (Viaggio nei Fori).

PRACTICALITIES

➡ Fori Imperiali

➡ Map p324, D2

➡ ☎06 06 08

➡ Piazza Santa Maria di Loreto

➡ adult/reduced €4/3, free 1st Sun of month Oct-Mar

➡ 🚌Via dei Fori Imperiali

San Giuseppe dei Falegnami, the Mamertine Prison was ancient Rome's maximum-security jail. St Peter did time here and, while imprisoned, supposedly created a miraculous stream of water to baptise his jailers.

On its bare stone walls, you can make out traces of medieval frescoes depicting Jesus, the Virgin Mary and saints Peter and Paul.

Visits take in a small street-level museum, a two-room affair with artefacts excavated on the site, while tablets provide graphic 3D illustration of how the complex developed over time.

From the museum, stairs lead down to the prison below, which is set on two levels: the 7th-century BCE *carcere* (prison) proper with its frescoed walls, and beneath that a dungeon known as the Tullianum. This chilling stone cell is where enemies of the state were thrown and left to die.

⊙ Campidoglio

Rising above the Roman Forum, the Campidoglio (Capitoline Hill) was one of the seven hills on which Rome was founded. At its summit were Rome's two most important temples: one dedicated to Jupiter Capitolinus (a descendant of Jupiter, the Roman equivalent of Zeus) and one to the goddess Juno Moneta (which housed Rome's mint). These days, politicians have replaced the gods and the hill is home to Rome's city hall (Palazzo Senatorio).

CAPITOLINE MUSEUMS — MUSEUM
See p69.

PIAZZA DEL CAMPIDOGLIO — PIAZZA
Map p324 (🚌Piazza Venezia) This hilltop piazza, designed by Michelangelo in 1538, is one of Rome's most beautiful squares. There are several approaches but the most dramatic is the graceful **Cordonata** (Map p324) staircase, which leads up from Piazza d'Aracoeli.

The piazza is flanked by **Palazzo Nuovo** and **Palazzo dei Conservatori**, together home to the Capitoline Museums, and **Palazzo Senatorio**, Rome's historic city hall. In the centre is a copy of an **equestrian statue** of Marcus Aurelius.

The original, which dates from the 2nd century CE, is in the Capitoline Museums.

~~1000~~

500
3000
~~1000~~
2000
1000
1500
140
200

9350

10/10

21,000
15,000
10,000
40,000
25,000
5,000

250
150
200
90
150
500
200
200

CHIESA DI SANTA MARIA IN ARACOELI CHURCH

Map p324 (☎06 6976 3837; Scala dell'Arce Capitolina; ⏰9am-6.30pm summer, 9.30am-5.30pm winter; 🚌Piazza Venezia) Atop the steep 124-step Aracoeli staircase, this 6th-century Romanesque church sits on the highest point of the Campidoglio. Its richly decorated interior boasts several treasures including a wooden gilt ceiling, an impressive Cosmatesque floor, and a series of 15th-century Pinturicchio frescoes illustrating the life of St Bernardino of Siena. Its chief claim to fame, though, is a wooden baby Jesus that's thought to have healing powers.

In fact, the Jesus doll – in the Cappella del S Bambino to the left of the main altar – is a copy. The original, which was supposedly made of wood from the garden of Gethsemane, was stolen in 1994 and has never been recovered.

The church sits on the site of the Roman temple to Juno Moneta and has long been associated with the nativity. According to legend, it was here that the Tiburtine Sybil told Augustus of the coming birth of Christ.

Piazza Venezia

VITTORIANO MONUMENT

Map p324 (Victor Emanuel Monument; Piazza Venezia; ⏰9.30am-5.30pm summer, to 4.30pm winter; 🚌Piazza Venezia) FREE Love it or loathe it, as many Romans do, you can't ignore the Vittoriano (aka the Altare della Patria, Altar of the Fatherland), the colossal mountain of white marble that towers over Piazza Venezia. Built at the turn of the 20th century to honour Italy's first king, Vittorio Emanuele II – who's immortalised in its vast equestrian statue – it provides the dramatic setting for the **Tomb of the Unknown Soldier** and, inside, the small **Museo Centrale del Risorgimento** (Map p324; ☎06 679 35 98; www.risorgimento.it; adult/reduced €5/2.50; ⏰9.30am-6.30pm), documenting Italian unification.

Also inside is the **Complesso del Vittoriano** (Map p324; ☎06 871 51 11; www.ilvittoriano.com; Via di San Pietro in Carcere; admission variable; ⏰9.30am-7.30pm Mon-Thu, to 10pm Fri & Sat, to 8.30pm Sun; 🚌Via dei Fori Imperiali), a gallery that regularly hosts major art exhibitions. But as impressive as any of the art on show are the glorious 360-degree

NAVIGATING THE ANCIENT SITES

As fascinating as Rome's ancient ruins are, they are not well labelled and it can be hard to know where to go and what to look at.

Entrances & Exits

The Roman Forum and Palatino form a single unified site. It's covered by one ticket (along with the Colosseum) and once you've entered it, you can walk freely between the two areas. There are three main entrances, all with associated ticket offices:

- Largo della Salara Vecchia for the Roman Forum.
- Via di San Gregorio 30 for the Palatino.
- Piazza di Santa Maria Nova (near the Arco di Tito) for both – go left for the Palatino or straight ahead for the Forum. Note the ticket office for this entrance is opposite the Colosseum on Piazza del Colosseo.

Exits are:

- at Largo della Salara Vecchia
- at Via di San Gregorio 30
- by the Basilica di Massenzio in the Forum.

Specialist Guides

Electa publishes a number of specialist guidebooks to Rome's archaeological sites, including the *Colosseum* (€5); the *Foro, Palatine and Colosseum* (€10); the *Archaeological Guide to Rome* (€12.90); *The Appian Way* (€8); and *The Baths of Caracalla* (€8). All are available, in English, at the **Colosseum Bookshop** (Map p324; www.parcocolosseo.it; Piazza del Colosseo, Colosseum; ⏰8.30am-1hr before sunset; Ⓜ Colosseo).

views from the top of the monument. See for yourself by taking the panoramic **Roma dal Cielo** (Map p324; adult/reduced €10/5; ⊙9.30am-7.30pm, last admission 6.45pm) lift up to the Terrazza delle Quadrighe.

ROMAN INSULA RUINS

Map p324 (☎06 06 08; Piazza d'Aracoeli; adult/reduced €4/3 plus cost of guide; ⊙guided tours by reservation only; 🚌Piazza Venezia) At the foot of the Campidoglio, next to the Aracoeli staircase, you'll see the ruins of a 2nd-century apartment block *(insula)*. The ground floor is thought to have served as a tavern, with four upper storeys given over to housing.

To visit you'll have to book a guided tour in advance (by phone), but you can get a pretty good idea of the cramped, squalid conditions many ancients lived in just by looking in from the street.

BASILICA DI SAN MARCO BASILICA

Map p324 (☎06 679 52 05; Piazza di San Marco 48; ⊙10am-1pm Tue-Sun & 4-6pm Tue-Fri, to 8pm Sat & Sun; 🚌Piazza Venezia) Now incorporated into Palazzo Venezia (p76), the early-4th-century Basilica di San Marco stands over the house where St Mark the Evangelist is said to have stayed while in Rome. Its main attraction is the golden 9th-century apse mosaic showing Christ flanked by several saints and Pope Gregory IV.

PALAZZO VENEZIA MUSEUM

Map p324 (☎06 6999 4388; www.museopalazzovenezia.beniculturali.it; Piazza Venezia 3; adult/reduced €10/5; ⊙8.30am-7.30pm Tue-Sun; 🚌Piazza Venezia) Built between 1455 and 1464, Palazzo Venezia was the first of Rome's great Renaissance palaces. For centuries it was the embassy of the Venetian Republic – hence its name – but it's most readily associated with Mussolini, who had his office here and famously made speeches from the balcony of the Sala del Mappamondo (Globe Room). Nowadays, it's home to the **Museo Nazionale del Palazzo Venezia** and its eclectic collection of Byzantine and early Renaissance paintings, ceramics, bronze figures, weaponry and armour.

Despite the museum's exhibits, the *palazzo* itself is the main draw. Particularly dramatic are the halls of the Appartamento Barbo, the original core of the palace built in the 15th century for the Venetian cardinal Pietro Barbo and now used to stage temporary exhibitions. Outside, a monumental two-tiered cloister, home to the museum's lapidarium, is another striking feature.

⊙ Forum Boarium & Around

BOCCA DELLA VERITÀ MONUMENT

Map p324 (Mouth of Truth; Piazza Bocca della Verità 18; voluntary donation; ⊙9.30am-5.50pm summer, to 4.50pm winter; 🚌Piazza Bocca della Verità) A bearded face carved into a giant marble disc, the *Bocca della Verità* is one of Rome's most popular curiosities. Legend has it that if you put your hand in the mouth and tell a lie, the Bocca will slam shut and bite it off.

The mouth, which was originally part of a fountain, or possibly an ancient manhole cover, now lives in the portico of the **Chiesa di Santa Maria in Cosmedin**, a handsome medieval church.

FORUM BOARIUM HISTORIC SITE

Map p324 (Piazza Bocca della Verità; 🚌Piazza Bocca della Verità) A busy thoroughfare, Piazza Bocca della Verità stands on what was once ancient Rome's cattle market, the Forum Boarium.

Little remains from that period except two tiny 2nd-century BCE temples: the circular **Tempio di Ercole Vincitore** (Tempio Rotondo, Round Temple; Map p324; ☎06 3996 7700; www.coopculture.it; guided tour €5.50, booking necessary; ⊙1st & 3rd Sun of the month), the oldest marble temple in Rome, and the **Tempio di Portunus** (Map p324; ☎06 3996 7700; www.coopculture.it; guided tour €5.50, booking necessary; ⊙1st & 3rd Sun of the month), dedicated to Portunus, god of rivers and ports. Both are visitable by guided tour.

EATING

This is a touristy part of town and most of the restaurants and trattorias around here are aimed squarely at the hungry hordes. But among the tourist traps you'll find a few gems hidden away, including a laid-back modern bistro overlooking the Imperial Forums and a romantic rooftop restaurant near the Bocca della Verità.

ALIMENTARI PANNELLA CARMELA
SANDWICHES €

Map p324 (Via dei Fienili 61; panini €3.50-4.80; 8.30am-2.30pm Mon-Sat & 5-8pm Mon-Fri; Via Petroselli) For a tasty lunchtime bite, ignore the area's touristy restaurants and search out this small, workaday food store. Hidden behind a curtain of creeping ivy, it's a local favourite supplying hungry workers with fresh, made-to-order *panini,* pizza slices and salads.

TERRE E DOMUS
LAZIO €€

Map p324 (06 6994 0273; Via Foro Traiano 82-4; meals €30-40; 9am-midnight Mon & Wed-Sat, from 10am Sun; Via dei Fori Imperiali) Staffed by young graduates from a local *scuola alberghiera* (catering college), this luminous modern restaurant is the best option in the touristy Forum area. With minimal decor and large windows overlooking the Colonna Traiana (p74), it's a relaxed spot to sit down to rustic local staples, all made with locally sourced ingredients, and a glass or two of regional wine.

Prices are quite high for the style of food, but that's largely down to the location.

47 CIRCUS ROOF GARDEN
RISTORANTE €€€

Map p324 (06 678 78 16; www.47circusroofgarden.com; Forty Seven Hotel, Via Petroselli 47; meals €65; 12.30-3.30pm & 7pm-10.30pm; Via Petroselli) With the Aventino hill rising in the background, the rooftop restaurant of the Forty Seven Hotel sets a romantic scene for contemporary Mediterranean cuisine. Seafood features heavily on the seasonal menu, appearing in creative antipasti, with pasta and in main courses.

DRINKING & NIGHTLIFE

There's little in the way of nightlife in this part of Rome and drinking is limited to a handful of cafes and bars. That said, if you like the sound of a cappuccino on the Capitoline Hill or cocktails on the Circo Massimo, you've come to the right place. Lovers of fine wine and craft beer will also find places to tickle their palate.

TERRAZZA CAFFARELLI
CAFE

Map p324 (Caffetteria dei Musei Capitolini; 06 6919 0564; Piazzale Caffarelli 4; 9.30am-7pm; Piazza Venezia) The Capitoline Museums' (p69) terrace cafe is a memorable place to relax over a sunset drink and swoon over magical views of the city's domes and rooftops.

It also does snacks and simple meals but it's the panoramas that you'll remember here. You don't need a museum ticket to reach the 2nd-floor cafe.

0,75
BAR

Map p324 (06 687 57 06; www.075roma.com; Via dei Cerchi 65; 11am-2am; ; Via dei Cerchi) This welcoming bar overlooking the Circo Massimo (p72) is good for a lingering evening drink, an *aperitivo* or casual meal (mains €6 to €17). It's a friendly place with a laid-back vibe, an international crowd, an attractive wood-beamed look and cool tunes.

CAVOUR 313
WINE BAR

Map p324 (06 678 54 96; www.cavour313.it; Via Cavour 313; 12.30-2.45pm daily & 6-11.30pm Mon-Thu, to midnight Fri & Sat, 7-11pm Sun, closed Aug; Cavour) Cavour 313 is a historic wine bar, a snug, wood-panelled retreat frequented by everyone from tourists to actors and politicians. It serves a selection of cold cuts and cheeses, as well as daily specials, but the headline act is the wine – with more than 1000 mainly Italian labels to choose from, you're sure to find something to tickle your palate.

SHOPPING

MERCATO CAMPAGNA AMICA AL CIRCO MASSIMO
MARKET

Map p324 (www.mercatocircomassimo.it; Via di San Teodoro 74; 8am-3pm Sat & Sun; Via dei Cerchi) One of Rome's best loved farmers markets, this weekly *mercato* provides a showcase for regional producers from Lazio and central Italy. Stalls sell all manner of edible fare, including potential take-home gifts: cheese, conserves, jars of honey, ready-made sauces, olive oils and wines.

Centro Storico

PANTHEON & AROUND | PIAZZA NAVONA & AROUND | CAMPO DE' FIORI & AROUND | JEWISH GHETTO & AROUND | ISOLA TIBERINA | PIAZZA COLONNA & AROUND

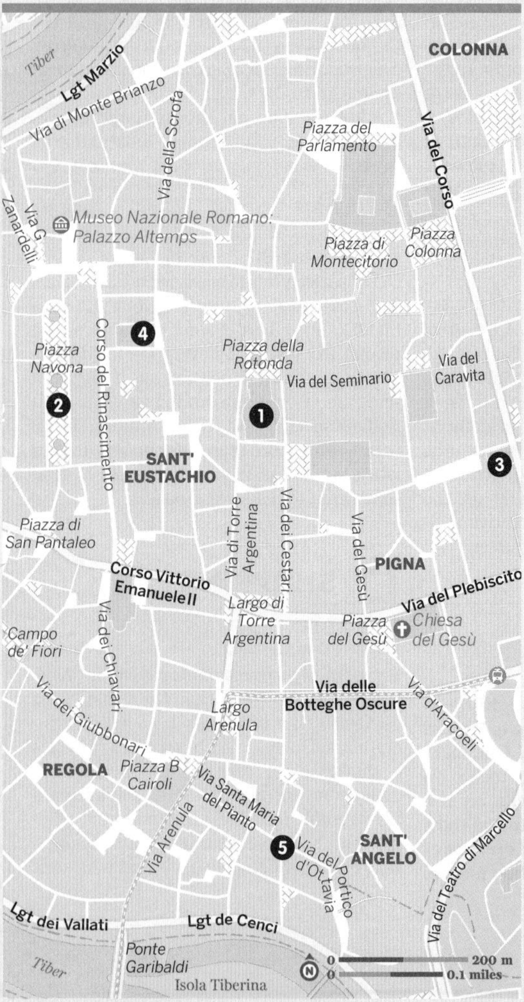

For more detail of this area see Maps p328 and p330

Neighbourhood Top Five

❶ **Pantheon** (p80) Stepping into this ancient temple and feeling the same sense of awe that the ancients must have felt 2000 years ago.

❷ **Piazza Navona** (p82) Marvelling at the beauty of this textbook baroque piazza with its flamboyant fountains and elegant domed *chiesa*.

❸ **Galleria Doria Pamphilj** (p90) Having the scion of the aristocratic Doria Pamphilj dynasty talk you through his family art collection at this fabulous private gallery.

❹ **Chiesa di San Luigi dei Francesi** (p86) Clocking three Caravaggio masterpieces at this historic church, one of Rome's many baroque treasures.

❺ **Historic Streets** (p83) Ditching your map and strolling the area's atmospheric lanes, taking in the colourful street life and hidden nooks.

Explore Centro Storico

Rome's *centro storico* (historic centre) is made for leisurely strolling, and although you could spend weeks exploring its every corner, you can cover most of the main sights in two or three days. Many people enter the area by bus, getting off at Largo di Torre Argentina (p83), from where it's a short walk up to the Pantheon (p80) and beyond that to Rome's political nerve centre Piazza Colonna (p89). Nearby, on Via del Corso, the Galleria Doria Pamphilj (p90) houses one of the capital's finest private art collections. To the west of the Pantheon, the narrow lanes around Piazza Navona (p82), itself one of Rome's great must-see sights, are a magnet for tourists and hip Romans with bohemian boutiques, cool bars and popular restaurants.

On the other side of Corso Vittorio Emanuele II, the main thoroughfare through the area, all roads lead to Campo de' Fiori (p86), home of a colourful daily market and hectic late-night drinking scene. From 'il Campo' you can shop your way down to the medieval Jewish Ghetto (p87), a wonderfully atmospheric neighbourhood of romantic corners, hidden piazzas and kosher trattorias.

Local Life

- **Snacking** Roman children are brought up on sliced pizza and the city is full of takeaways serving *pizza al taglio* (pizza by the slice). For some of the best head to Antico Forno Urbani (p96) in the Jewish Ghetto.
- **Shopping** Romans love wandering the *centro storico*, browsing its boutiques and artisans' studios. For a taster, head to streets like Via del Pellegrino near Campo de' Fiori (p86).
- **Exhibitions** Although an architectural masterpiece in its own right, locals tend to visit the Chiostro del Bramante (p85) for the art exhibitions it regularly stages.

Getting There & Away

- **Bus** The best way to access the *centro storico*. A whole fleet serves the area from Termini, including buses 40 and 64, which both stop at Largo di Torre Argentina and continue down Corso Vittorio Emanuele II.
- **Metro** There are no metro stations in the neighbourhood but it's within walking distance of Barberini, Spagna and Flaminio stations, all on line A.
- **Tram** Tram 8 runs from Piazza Venezia to Trastevere by way of Via Arenula.

Lonely Planet's Top Tip

The *centro storico* is an expensive part of town but there are ways of making your money go further. You can see masterpieces by the likes of Michelangelo, Raphael, Caravaggio and Bernini for nothing by visiting the area's churches, all of which are free to enter.

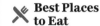

Best Places to Eat

- Pianostrada (p95)
- La Ciambella (p91)
- Forno Roscioli (p94)
- Antico Forno Urbani (p96)
- Retrobottega (p94)
- Salumeria Roscioli (p96)

For reviews, see p91.

Best Places to Drink

- Barnum Cafe (p100)
- Open Baladin (p100)
- Rimessa Roscioli (p99)
- Caffè Sant'Eustachio (p99)
- Roscioli Caffè (p100)

For reviews, see p99.

Best Art Churches

- Chiesa di San Luigi dei Francesi (p86)
- Chiesa del Gesù (p88)
- Chiesa di Sant'Ignazio di Loyola (p90)
- Basilica di Santa Maria Sopra Minerva (p83)

For reviews, see p83.

TOP EXPERIENCE

ADMIRE THE PANTHEON

A striking 2000-year-old temple, now a church, the Pantheon is Rome's best-preserved ancient monument and one of the most influential buildings in the Western world. Its greying, pockmarked exterior might look its age, but inside it's a different story, and it's a unique and exhilarating experience to pass through its vast bronze doors and gaze up at the largest unreinforced concrete dome ever built.

History

In its current form the Pantheon dates from around 125 CE. The original temple, built by Marcus Agrippa in 27 BCE, burnt down in 80 CE, and although it was rebuilt by Domitian, it was struck by lightning and destroyed for a second time in 110 CE. The emperor Hadrian had it reconstructed between 118 and 125 CE, and this is the version you see today.

Hadrian's temple was dedicated to the classical gods – hence the name Pantheon, a derivation of the Greek words *pan* (all) and *theos* (god) – but in 608 CE it was consecrated as a Christian church and it's now officially known as the Basilica di Santa Maria ad Martyres.

Thanks to this consecration, it was spared the worst of the medieval plundering that reduced Rome's ancient buildings to near dereliction. But it didn't escape entirely unscathed – its gilded-bronze roof tiles were removed and bronze from the portico was used by Bernini for his baldachin at St Peter's Basilica.

During the Renaissance, the building was much admired – Brunelleschi used it as inspiration for his cupola in Florence and Michelangelo studied it before designing the dome at St Peter's Basilica – and it became an important burial chamber. Today, you'll find the

TOP TIPS

- Mass is celebrated at 5pm on Saturdays and 10.30am on Sundays.
- The sloping marble floor has 22 almost-invisible holes to drain away the rain that gets in through the oculus.

PRACTICALITIES

- Map p328, F4
- www.pantheonroma.com
- Piazza della Rotonda
- admission free
- 8.30am-7.30pm Mon-Sat, 9am-6pm Sun
- Largo di Torre Argentina

tomb of the artist Raphael here alongside those of kings Vittorio Emanuele II and Umberto I.

Exterior

Originally, the Pantheon was on a raised podium, its entrance facing onto a rectangular porticoed piazza. Nowadays, the dark-grey pitted exterior faces onto busy, cafe-lined Piazza della Rotonda. And while its facade is somewhat the worse for wear, it's still an imposing sight. The monumental entrance **portico** consists of 16 Corinthian columns, each 11.8m high and each made from a single block of Egyptian granite, supporting a triangular **pediment**. Behind the columns, two 20-tonne bronze doors – 16th-century restorations of the originals – give onto the central rotunda.

Little remains of the ancient decor, although rivets and holes in the brickwork indicate where marble-veneer panels were once placed.

Interior

Although impressive from outside, it's only when you get inside that you can really appreciate the Pantheon's full size. With light streaming in through the **oculus** (the 8.7m-diameter hole in the centre of the dome), the cylindrical marble-clad interior seems vast, an effect that was deliberately designed to cut worshippers down to size before the gods.

Opposite the entrance is the church's main **altar**, over which hangs a 7th-century icon of the *Madonna col Bambino* (Madonna and Child). To the left (as you look in from the entrance) is the **tomb of Raphael**, marked by Lorenzetto's 1520 sculpture of the *Madonna del Sasso* (Madonna of the Rock). Neighbouring it are the **tombs of King Umberto I** and **Margherita of Savoy**. Over on the opposite side of the rotunda is the **tomb of King Vittorio Emanuele II**.

The Dome

The Pantheon's dome, considered the Romans' greatest architectural achievement, was the largest dome in the world until the 15th century when Brunelleschi beat it with his Florentine cupola. Its harmonious appearance is due to a precisely calibrated symmetry – its diameter is equal to the building's interior height of 43.4m. At its centre, the oculus, which symbolically connected the temple with the gods, plays a vital structural role by absorbing and redistributing the dome's huge tensile forces.

Radiating out from the oculus are five rows of 28 coffers (indented panels). These were originally ornamented but more importantly served to reduce the cupola's immense weight.

THE INSCRIPTION

For centuries the Latin inscription over the entrance led historians to believe that the current temple was Marcus Agrippa's original. Certainly, the wording suggests this, reading: 'M.AGRIPPA.L.F.COS. TERTIUM.FECIT' or 'Marcus Agrippa, son of Lucius, in his third consulate built this'. However, excavations in the 19th century revealed traces of an earlier temple and scholars realised that Hadrian had simply kept Agrippa's original inscription over his new temple.

The stripping of the Pantheon's bronze by the Barberini pope Urban VIII gave rise to the saying, still in use today: 'What the barbarians didn't do, the Barberini did.'

PENTECOST AT THE PANTHEON

Each Pentecost, tens of thousands of red petals are rained down on the Pantheon through the oculus. This centuries-old tradition represents the Holy Spirit descending to earth.

TOP EXPERIENCE

PEOPLE-WATCH AT PIAZZA NAVONA

With its showy fountains, graceful baroque *palazzi* and pavement cafes, Piazza Navona is central Rome's elegant showcase square. Long a hub of local life, it hosted Rome's main market for close on 300 years, and today attracts a colourful daily circus of street artists, hawkers, tourists and pigeons.

Stadio di Domiziano

Like many of the city's landmarks, the piazza sits atop an ancient monument, in this case the 1st-century-CE **Stadio di Domiziano** (Domitian's Stadium; ☎06 6880 5311; www.stadiodomiziano.com; Via di Tor Sanguigna 3; adult/reduced €8/6; ⏰10am-6.30pm Sun-Fri, to 7.30pm Sat). This 30,000-seat stadium, whose subterranean remains can be accessed from Via di Tor Sanguigna, used to host athletic meets – hence the name Navona, a corruption of the Greek word *agon*, meaning public games. Inevitably, though, it fell into disrepair and it wasn't until the 15th century that the crumbling arena was paved over and Rome's central market was transferred here from the Campidoglio.

TOP TIPS

- To catch the piazza at its most alluring, come first thing in the morning before the crowds arrive or after dark when the fountains are illuminated.
- In December the piazza stages a historic Christmas market that traditionally runs until 6 January.

PRACTICALITIES

- Map p328, E4
- 🚌Corso del Rinascimento

Fountains

The piazza's grand centrepiece is Gian Lorenzo Bernini's **Fontana dei Quattro Fiumi** (Fountain of the Four Rivers). Completed in 1651, this flamboyant fountain features a tapering Egyptian obelisk and muscular personifications of the Nile, Ganges, Danube and Plate rivers, representing the four continents of the then-known world. According to legend, the Nile figure is shielding his eyes to avoid looking at the Chiesa di Sant'Agnese in Agone designed by Bernini's bitter rival Borromini. In truth, Bernini had completed his fountain two years before Borromini started work on the church's facade and the gesture simply indicated that the source of the Nile was unknown at the time.

The **Fontana del Moro**, at the southern end of the square, was designed by Giacomo della Porta in 1576. Bernini added the Moor in the mid-17th century, but the surrounding Tritons are 19th-century copies.

At the northern end of the piazza, the 19th-century **Fontana del Nettuno** depicts Neptune fighting with a sea monster, surrounded by sea nymphs.

Chiesa di Sant'Agnese in Agone

With its theatrical facade and rich, domed interior, the **Chiesa di Sant'Agnese in Agone** (Map p328; ☎06 6819 2134; www.santagneseinagone.org; ⏰9am-1pm & 3-7pm Tue-Fri, 9am-1pm & 3-8pm Sat & Sun) is typical of Francesco Borromini's baroque style. The church, which regularly hosts classical music concerts, is said to stand on the spot where the martyr Agnes performed a miracle before being killed. Legend has it that after being stripped naked by her executioners her hair miraculously grew to cover her body and preserve her modesty.

Palazzo Pamphilj

Commissioned by Giovanni Battista Pamphilj to celebrate his election as Pope Innocent X, this elegant baroque **palazzo** (Map p328; http://roma.itamaraty.gov.br/it; ⏰by reservation only) was built between 1644 and 1650 by Borromini and Girolamo Rainaldi. Inside, there are some impressive frescoes by Pietro da Cortona but the building, which has been the Brazilian Embassy since 1920, can only be visited on a pre-booked guided tour.

SIGHTS

Bound by the River Tiber and Via del Corso, the *centro storico* is made for aimless wandering. Even without trying you'll come across some of Rome's great sights: the Pantheon, Piazza Navona and Campo de' Fiori, as well as a host of monuments, museums and churches. To the south, the lively Ghetto has been home to Rome's Jewish community since the 2nd century BCE.

Pantheon & Around

PANTHEON — CHURCH

See p80.

BASILICA DI SANTA MARIA SOPRA MINERVA — BASILICA

Map p328 (www.santamariasopraminerva.it; Piazza della Minerva 42; 6.55am-7pm Mon-Fri, 10am-12.30pm & 3.30-7pm Sat, 8.10am-12.30pm & 3.30-7pm Sun; Largo di Torre Argentina) Built on the site of three pagan temples, including one dedicated to the goddess Minerva, the Dominican Basilica di Santa Maria Sopra Minerva is Rome's only Gothic church. However, little remains of the original 13th-century structure and these days the main draw is a minor Michelangelo sculpture and the magisterial, art-rich interior.

Inside, to the right of the altar in the **Cappella Carafa** (also called the Cappella della Annunciazione), you'll find some superb 15th-century frescoes by Filipino Lippi and the majestic tomb of Pope Paul IV.

Left of the high altar is one of Michelangelo's lesser-known sculptures, *Cristo Risorto* (Christ Bearing the Cross; 1520), depicting Jesus carrying a cross while wearing some jarring bronze drapery. The latter wasn't part of the original composition and was added after the Council of Trent (1545–63) to preserve Christ's modesty.

Behind the statue to the left, you'll find the tomb of Fra' Angelico, the Dominican friar and painter, who is one of several luminaries buried in the church. The body of St Catherine of Siena, minus her head (which is in Siena), lies under the high altar, while the tombs of two Medici popes, Leo X and Clement VII, are in the apse.

ELEFANTINO — STATUE

Map p328 (Piazza della Minerva; Largo di Torre Argentina) Nicknamed the *pulcino della Minerva* ('Minerva's chick'), the Elefantino is a curious and much-loved statue of a puzzled-looking elephant carrying a 6th-century-BCE Egyptian obelisk. Commissioned by Pope Alexander VII and completed in 1667, the elephant, symbolising strength and wisdom, was sculpted by Ercole Ferrata to a design by Gian Lorenzo Bernini. The obelisk was taken from the nearby Basilica di Santa Maria Sopra Minerva.

LOCAL KNOWLEDGE

BIG FOOT

A giant marble foot, the **Piè di Marmo** (Map p328; Via di Santo Stefano del Cacco; Via del Corso) is one of the Roman's favourite monuments. It started life attached to a statue in a 1st-century temple dedicated to the Egyptian gods Isis and Serapis. Some 1600 years later it cropped up on the street that now bears its name, Via del Piè di Marmo. It was moved to its current position in 1878 to clear a path for King Vittorio Emanuele II's funeral procession to the Pantheon.

LARGO DI TORRE ARGENTINA — PIAZZA

Map p328 (Largo di Torre Argentina) A busy transport hub, Largo di Torre Argentina is set around the sunken **Area Sacra**, and the remains of four Republican-era temples, all built between the 2nd and 4th centuries BCE. These ruins, among the oldest in the city, are reckoned to be where Julius Caesar was murdered in 44 BCE and, while off limits to humans, are home to a thriving stray cat population and a volunteer-run **cat sanctuary** (Map p328; 06 6880 5611; www.gattidiroma.net; noon-6pm Mon-Fri, from 11am Sat & Sun).

On the piazza's western flank stands Teatro Argentina (p101), Rome's premier theatre.

MUSEO NAZIONALE ROMANO: CRYPTA BALBI — MUSEUM

Map p328 (06 678 01 67; www.museonazionaleromano.beniculturali.it; Via delle Botteghe Oscure 31; adult/reduced €10/5, incl Palazzo Altemps, Terme di Diocleziano & Palazzo Massimo alle Terme €12/6; 9am-7.45pm Tue-Sun; Via delle Botteghe Oscure) The least known of the Museo Nazionale Romano's four museums, the Crypta Balbi sits over the ruins of several medieval buildings, themselves set atop the Teatro di Balbo (13 BCE). Archaeological finds illustrate the urban development of the surrounding area, while the museum's underground excavations provide an interesting insight into Rome's multilayered past.

Piazza Navona & Around

PIAZZA NAVONA PIAZZA

See p82.

BASILICA DI SANT'AGOSTINO BASILICA

Map p328 (06 6880 1962; Piazza di Sant'Agostino 80; 7.45am-noon & 4-7.30pm; Corso del Rinascimento) The plain white facade of this early Renaissance church, built in the 15th century and renovated in the late 1700s, gives no indication of the impressive art inside. The most famous work is Caravaggio's *Madonna dei Pellegrini* (Madonna of the Pilgrims), in the first chapel on the left, but you'll also find a fresco by Raphael and a much-venerated sculpture by Jacopo Sansovino.

The *Madonna del Parto* (Madonna of Childbirth), Sansovino's 1521 statue of the Virgin Mary with baby Jesus, is a favourite with expectant mums who traditionally pray to it for a safe pregnancy. The Madonna also stars in Caravaggio's *Madonna dei Pellegrini,* which caused uproar when it was unveiled in 1604 due to its depiction of Mary's two devoted pilgrims as filthy, badly dressed beggars.

Painting almost a century before, Raphael provoked no such scandal with his fresco of Isaiah, visible on the third pillar on the left side of the nave.

CHIESA DI SANT'IVO ALLA SAPIENZA CHURCH

Map p328 (Corso del Rinascimento 40; 9am-noon Sun; Corso del Rinascimento) Hidden in the porticoed courtyard of Palazzo della Sapienza, this extraordinary church is a masterpiece of baroque architecture. Built by Francesco Borromini between 1642 and 1660, and based on an incredibly complex geometric plan, it combines alternating convex and concave walls with a circular interior capped by a twisted spire. Inside,

TOP EXPERIENCE

MUSEO NAZIONALE ROMANO: PALAZZO ALTEMPS

Just north of Piazza Navona, Palazzo Altemps is a beautiful late-15th-century *palazzo,* housing the best of the Museo Nazionale Romano's formidable collection of classical sculpture. Many pieces come from the celebrated Ludovisi collection, amassed by Cardinal Ludovico Ludovisi in the 17th century.

Prize exhibits include the beautiful 5th-century-BCE *Trono Ludovisi* (Ludovisi Throne), a carved marble block whose central relief shows a naked Venus (Aphrodite) being modestly plucked from the sea. In the neighbouring room, the *Ares Ludovisi,* a 2nd-century-BCE representation of a young, clean-shaven Mars, owes its right foot to a Gian Lorenzo Bernini restoration in 1622.

Another affecting work is the sculptural group *Galata suicida* (Gaul's Suicide), a melodramatic depiction of a Gaul knifing himself to death over a dead woman.

The building itself provides an elegant backdrop, with a grand central courtyard, a finely painted loggia and frescoed rooms. These include the **Sala delle Prospettive Dipinte**, which was adorned with landscapes and hunting scenes for Cardinal Altemps, the rich nephew of Pope Pius IV (r 1560–65) who bought the *palazzo* in the late 16th century.

TOP TIPS

- Entry is free on the first Sunday of the month between October and March.
- Check temporary exhibitions – online increases entry by €3.

PRACTICALITIES

- Map p328, E3
- 06 68 48 51
- www.museonazionaleromano.beniculturali.it
- Piazza Sant'Apollinare 46
- adult/reduced €10/5
- 9am-7.45pm Tue-Sun
- Corso del Rinascimento

its pure, light-filled interior features an altarpiece by Pietro da Cortona.

Palazzo della Sapienza, seat of Rome's university until 1935 and now home to the Italian state archive, is often used to stage temporary exhibitions.

MUSEO DI ROMA — MUSEUM

Map p328 (☎06 0608; www.museodiroma.it; Piazza di San Pantaleo 10 & Piazza Navona 2; adult/reduced €9.50/7.50, temporary exhibitions extra; ⊙10am-7pm Tue-Sun; 🚌Corso Vittorio Emanuele II) The baroque Palazzo Braschi houses the Museo di Roma's eclectic collection of paintings, photographs, etchings, clothes and furniture, charting the history of Rome from the Middle Ages to the early 20th century. But just as striking as the collection is the 17th-century *palazzo* itself, with its monumental baroque staircase, grand halls and views over Piazza Navona.

PASQUINO — STATUE

Map p328 (Piazza Pasquino; 🚌Corso Vittorio Emanuele II) This battered, armless figure is Rome's most famous 'talking statue'. During the 16th century, when there were no safe outlets for dissent, a Vatican tailor named Pasquino began sticking notes to the statue with satirical verses lampooning the church and aristocracy. Soon others joined in and, as the trend spread, talking statues popped up all over town.

The sculpture is now off limits to disgruntled Romans but there's a convenient board next to it where people still leave messages, traditionally known as *pasquinade.*

CHIESA DI SANTA MARIA DELLA PACE & CHIOSTRO DEL BRAMANTE — CHURCH

Map p328 (www.chiostrodelbramante.it; Via Arco della Pace 5; exhibitions adult/reduced €14/12; ⊙church 9.30am-6.30pm, cloister 10am-8pm Mon-Fri, to 9pm Sat & Sun; 🚌Corso del Rinascimento) Tucked away in the back streets behind Piazza Navona, this small baroque church boasts a columned semicircular facade by Pietro da Cortona and a celebrated Raphael fresco, *Sibille* (Sibyls; c 1515) – look up to the right as you enter.

The adjoining **Chiostro del Bramante** (Bramante Cloister), originally part of the same monastery complex, is a masterpiece of High Renaissance architectural styling that's now used to stage art exhibitions and cultural events.

The cloister, which you can visit freely by popping up to the 1st-floor cafe (p93), was the first work Bramante undertook in Rome after arriving from Milan in 1499. Its sober, geometric lines and perfectly proportioned spaces provide a marked counterpoint to the church's undulating facade, beautifully encapsulating the Renaissance aesthetic that Bramante did so much to promote.

VIA DEI CORONARI — STREET

Map p328 (🚌Corso del Rinascimento) This cobbled Renaissance street lined with antique shops, boutiques and costume jewellers is a lovely place for a stroll. It follows the course of the ancient Roman road that connected Piazza Colonna with the Tiber, but owes its name to the medieval *coronari* (rosary-bead sellers) who used to hang out here, hawking their wares to pilgrims as they passed en route to St Peter's Basilica.

VIA DEL GOVERNO VECCHIO — STREET

Map p328 (🚌Corso Vittorio Emanuele II) Striking off west from Piazza Pasquino, Via del Governo Vecchio is an atmospheric cobbled lane full of boutiques, lively restaurants and vintage clothes shops. The street, once part of the papal processional route between the Basilica di San Giovanni in Laterano and St Peter's, acquired its name (Old Government St) in 1755 when the pontifical government relocated from Palazzo Nardini at No 39 (now sadly dilapidated) to Palazzo Madama.

CHIESA NUOVA — CHURCH

Map p328 (Chiesa di Santa Maria in Vallicella; Piazza della Chiesa Nuova; ⊙7.30am-noon & 4.30-7.30pm; 🚌Corso Vittorio Emanuele II) Hardly new as its name would suggest, this imposing landmark church boasts a distinguished 17th-century facade and a vast baroque interior. Of particular note are the superb ceiling frescoes by Pietro da Cortona and a trio of paintings by Peter Paul Rubens.

Built in 1575 as part of a complex to house Filippo Neri's Oratorian order, it was originally a large plain church in accordance with Neri's wishes. But when Neri died in 1595 the artists moved in – Rubens painted over the high altar and Pietro da Cortona decorated the dome, tribune and nave. Neri was canonised in 1622 and is buried in a chapel to the left of the altar.

Next to the church is Borromini's **Oratorio dei Filippini**, and behind it the **Torre dell'Orologio** (Map p328; Piazza dell'Orologio), a clock tower built to decorate the adjacent convent.

TOP EXPERIENCE
CHIESA DI SAN LUIGI DEI FRANCESI

Church to Rome's French community since 1589, this opulent baroque *chiesa* is home to a celebrated trio of Caravaggio paintings: the *Vocazione di San Matteo* (The Calling of St Matthew), the *Martiro di San Matteo* (The Martyrdom of St Matthew) and *San Matteo e l'angelo* (St Matthew and the Angel), known collectively as the St Matthew cycle.

These three canvases, housed in the Cappella Contarelli, are among the earliest of Caravaggio's religious works, painted between 1600 and 1602, but they are inescapably his, featuring a down-to-earth realism and the stunning use of *chiaroscuro* (contrast of light and dark).

Caravaggio's refusal to adhere to the artistic conventions of the day and glorify his religious subjects often landed him in hot water, and his first version of *San Matteo e l'angelo,* which depicted St Matthew as a bald, bare-legged peasant, was originally rejected by his outraged patron, Cardinal Matteo Contarelli.

Before you leave the church, take a moment to enjoy Domenichino's faded 17th-century frescoes of St Cecilia in the second chapel on the right. St Cecilia is also depicted in the altarpiece by Guido Reni, a copy of a work by Raphael.

TOP TIPS

- The *chiesa* is a working church so is occasionally closed for religious functions.
- To ensure a good view of Caravaggio's works, take a €1 coin for the lighting meter.

PRACTICALITIES

- Map p328, E4
- Piazza di San Luigi dei Francesi 5
- 9.30am-12.45pm & 2.30-6.30pm Mon-Fri, 9.30am-12.15pm & 2.30-6.45pm Sat, 11.30am-12.45pm & 2.30-6.45pm Sun
- Corso del Rinascimento

Campo de' Fiori & Around

CAMPO DE' FIORI PIAZZA

Map p328 (Corso Vittorio Emanuele II) Colourful and always busy, *Il Campo* is a major focus of Roman life: by day it hosts one of the city's best-known markets; by night it heaves with tourists and young drinkers who spill out of its many bars and restaurants. For centuries the square was the site of public executions. It was here that philosopher Giordano Bruno was burned for heresy in 1600, now marked by a sinister statue of the hooded monk, created by Ettore Ferrari in 1889.

PALAZZO FARNESE HISTORIC BUILDING

Map p328 (www.inventerrome.com; Piazza Farnese; tours €9; guided tours 3pm, 4pm & 5pm Mon, Wed & Fri; Corso Vittorio Emanuele II) Home to the French embassy, this towering Renaissance *palazzo,* one of Rome's finest, was started in 1514 by Antonio da Sangallo the Younger, continued by Michelangelo and finished by Giacomo della Porta. Inside, it boasts frescoes by Annibale and Agostino Carracci that are said by some to rival Michelangelo's in the Sistine Chapel. The highlight, painted between 1597 and 1608, is the monumental ceiling fresco *Amori degli Dei* (The Loves of the Gods) in the Galleria dei Carracci.

Visits to the *palazzo* are by 45-minute guided tour (in English, French and Italian), for which you'll need to book at least a week in advance – see the website for details. Photo ID is required for entry and children under 10 are not admitted.

The twin fountains in the square outside are enormous granite baths taken from the Terme di Caracalla.

PALAZZO SPADA HISTORIC BUILDING

Map p330 (Palazzo Capodiferro; 06 683 24 09; www.galleriaspada.beniculturali.it; Piazza Capo Di Ferro 13; adult/reduced €5/2.50; 8.30am-7.30pm Wed-Mon; Corso Vittorio Emanuele II) With its stuccoed ornamental facade and handsome courtyard, this grand *palazzo* is a fine example of 16th-century mannerist architecture. Upstairs, a small four-room gallery houses the Spada family art collection with works by Andrea del Sarto, Guido Reni, Guercino and Titian, while downstairs Francesco Borromini's famous optical illusion, aka the *Prospettiva* (Perspective), continues to confound visitors.

The *Prospettiva* appears to be a 25m-long corridor lined with columns leading to a hedge and life-size statue but is, in fact, only 10m long. The sculpture, which was a later addition, is hip-height and the columns diminish in size not because of distance but because they actually get shorter. And look closer at that perfect-looking hedge – Borromini didn't trust the gardeners to clip a real hedge precisely enough so he made one of stone.

VIA GIULIA STREET

Map p328 (🚌Lungotevere dei Tebaldi) Designed by Bramante in 1508 as part of an urban development program ordered by Pope Julius II, Via Giulia is one of Rome's most charming streets, an elegant, largely car-free strip of churches, colourful Renaissance *palazzi* and discreet fashion boutiques.

BASILICA DI SAN GIOVANNI BATTISTA DEI FIORENTINI BASILICA

Map p328 (Piazza dell'Oro 2; ⏲7.30am-noon & 5-7pm Mon-Sat, 7.30am-1pm & 5-8pm Sun; 🚌Ponte Vittorio Emanuele II) The last resting place of Francesco Borromini and Carlo Maderno, this graceful 16th-century church was commissioned by Pope Leo X as a showcase for Florentine artistic talent. Jacopo Sansovino won a competition for its design, which was then executed by Antonio Sangallo the Younger and Giacomo della Porta. Carlo Maderno completed the elongated cupola in 1614, while the travertine facade was added by Alessandro Galilei in the mid-18th century.

PALAZZO DELLA CANCELLERIA HISTORIC BUILDING

Map p328 (Piazza della Cancelleria; exhibition adult/reduced €9/7; ⏲exhibition 9.30am-7.30pm; 🚌Corso Vittorio Emanuele II) One of Rome's most imposing Renaissance buildings, this huge *palazzo* was built for Cardinal Raffaele Riario between 1483 and 1513. It was later acquired by the Vatican and became the seat of the Papal Chancellery. It is still Vatican property and nowadays houses various Church offices, including the Roman Rota, the Holy See's highest ecclesiastical court.

The *palazzo* also provides the grand setting for a long-standing exhibition dedicated to machines designed by Leonardo da Vinci. If that doesn't appeal, it's still worth nipping through to the courtyard to take a peek at Bramante's glorious double loggia.

Incorporated into the *palazzo,* the 4th-century **Basilica di San Lorenzo in Damaso** (⏲7.30am-noon & 4.30-7.30pm Mon-Sat, 8.30am-1pm & 5-8pm Sun) is one of Rome's oldest churches.

CHIESA DI SANT'ANDREA DELLA VALLE CHURCH

Map p328 (☎06 686 13 39; Corso Vittorio Emanuele; ⏲7.30am-7.30pm; 🚌Corso Vittorio Emanuele II) A must for opera fans, this 17th-century church is where Giacomo Puccini set the first act of *Tosca*. Its most obvious feature is Carlo Maderno's soaring dome, the highest in Rome after St Peter's, but its cavernous baroque interior reveals a wonderful series of frescoes by Matteo Preti and Domenichino, and, in the dome, Lanfranco's heady depiction of heaven, *Gloria del Paradiso* (Glory of Paradise; 1625–28).

⊙ Jewish Ghetto & Around

The Jewish Ghetto, centred on lively Via del Portico d'Ottavia, is an atmospheric area studded with artisan's studios, small shops,

LOCAL KNOWLEDGE

HIDDEN COURTYARD

For one of Rome's most picture-perfect scenes, head to the **Arco degli Acetari** (Vinegar-Makers' Arch; Map p328; Via del Pellegrino 19; ⏲6.30am-11pm; 🚌Corso Vittorio Emanuele II), a dark archway just off Campo de' Fiori. The arch in itself isn't especially memorable, but go through it and you'll emerge onto a tiny medieval square enclosed by rusty orange houses and cascading plants. Cats and bicycles litter the cobbles, while overhead washing hangs off pretty flower-lined balconies.

TOP EXPERIENCE
CHIESA DEL GESÙ

An imposing example of Counter-Reformation architecture, this landmark *chiesa* is Rome's most important Jesuit church. Consecrated in 1584, it's fronted by a harmonious and much-copied facade by Giacomo della Porta. More than the masonry, though, the real draw here is the lavish interior and an astonishing **ceiling fresco**, the *Trionfo del Nome di Gesù* (Triumph of the Name of Jesus; 1679) by Giovanni Battista Gaulli. The artist, better known as Il Baciccia, also created much of the stucco decoration and the cupola frescoes.

Situated in the northern transept, the **Cappella di Sant'Ignazio** houses the tomb of Ignatius Loyola, the Spanish soldier who founded the Jesuits in 1540. Designed by baroque maestro Andrea Pozzo, the altar-tomb is a sumptious marble-and-bronze affair with lapis lazuli–encrusted columns, and, on top, a lapis lazuli globe representing the Trinity. On either side are sculptures whose titles neatly encapsulate the Jesuit ethos: to the left, *Fede che vince l'Idolatria* (Faith Defeats Idolatry); and on the right, *Religione che flagella l'Eresia* (Religion Lashing Heresy).

The Spanish saint lived in the church from 1544 until his death in 1556 and you can visit his private rooms to the right of the main church.

TOP TIPS

➡ Visit at 5.30pm to see the 'baroque machine' in action. This lowers the altar painting on St Ignatius' tomb to reveal a statue in a hidden niche.

➡ For more stunning art, visit the Sant'Ignazio rooms.

PRACTICALITIES

➡ Map p328, G6

➡ www.chiesadelgesu.org

➡ Piazza del Gesù

➡ ⏲6.45am-12.45pm & 4-7.30pm, St Ignatius rooms 4-6pm Mon-Sat, 10am-noon Sun

➡ 🚌Largo di Torre Argentina

kosher bakeries and popular trattorias. Crowning everything is the distinctive square dome of Rome's main synagogue.

As you stroll around look out for a series of brass cobblestones. These are memorial plaques commemorating the city's Holocaust victims: each one names a person and gives the date and destination of their deportation and death. They are placed outside the victims' homes.

Rome's Jewish community dates back to the 2nd century BCE, making it one of the oldest in Europe. The first Jews came as business envoys but many arrived as slaves following the Roman wars in Judaea and Titus' defeat of Jerusalem in 70 CE. Confinement to the Ghetto came in 1555 when Pope Paul IV ushered in a period of official intolerance that lasted, on and off, until the 20th century. Ironically, though, confinement meant that the Jewish cultural and religious identity survived intact.

FONTANA DELLE TARTARUGHE FOUNTAIN

Map p330 (Piazza Mattei; 🚋Via Arenula) This playful, much-loved fountain features four boys gently hoisting tortoises up into a bowl of water. Created by Giacomo della Porta and Taddeo Landini in the late 16th century, it's the subject of a popular local legend, according to which it was created in a single night.

MUSEO EBRAICO DI ROMA MUSEUM

Map p330 (Jewish Museum of Rome; ☎06 6840 0661; www.museoebraico.roma.it; Via Catalana; adult/reduced €11/8; ⏲10am-5.15pm Sun-Thu, to 3.15pm Fri summer, 9.30am-4.30pm Sun-Thu, 9am-2pm Fri winter; 🚌Lungotevere de' Cenci) The historical, cultural and artistic heritage of Rome's Jewish community is chronicled in this small but engrossing museum. Housed in the city's early-20th-century synagogue, Europe's second largest, it displays parchments, precious fabrics, marble carvings, and a collection of 17th- and 18th-century silverware. Documents and photos attest to life in the Ghetto and the hardships suffered by the city's Jewish people during WWII. Admission also includes a guided tour of the main synagogue, whose distinctive square dome towers over the neighbourhood.

To learn more about the Jewish Ghetto, the museum runs two daily tours of the neighbourhood, one in English and one in Italian (adult/reduced €8/5; about 45 minutes), bookable at the ticket office.

PORTICO D'OTTAVIA — RUINS

Map p330 (Via del Portica d'Ottavia 29; ⌚9am-7pm summer, to 6pm winter; 🚌Lungotevere de' Cenci) The Portico d'Ottavia is the oldest quadriporto (four-sided porch) in Rome. The columns, arches and fragmented pediment once formed part of a vast rectangular portico, supported by 300 columns and extending 132m by 119m. Much of what you see today is from a 3rd-century restoration of the portico Augustus built over the Portico di Metella (146 BCE) in 23 BCE. Named after the emperor's sister, Octavia, it housed Rome's fish market from the Middle Ages until the 19th century.

Behind the portico is the 8th-century Chiesa di Sant'Angelo.

TEATRO DI MARCELLO — HISTORIC BUILDING

Map p330 (Theatre of Marcellus; Via del Teatro di Marcello; ⌚9am-7pm summer, to 6pm winter; 🚌Via del Teatro di Marcello) Resembling a mini Colosseum, the Teatro di Marcello is the star turn of the dusty **Area Archeologica del Teatro di Marcello e del Portico di Ottavia**, a small site containing a smattering of ancient ruins. The 20,000-capacity theatre was planned by Julius Caesar and completed in 11 BCE by Augustus who named it after a favourite nephew, Marcellus. In the 16th century, a *palazzo*, which now contains several exclusive apartments, was built on top of the original structure.

BASILICA DI SAN NICOLA IN CARCERE — BASILICA

Map p330 (Via del Teatro di Marcello 46; excavations €3; ⌚basilica 7am-noon & 4-6pm, excavations 10am-6pm; 🚌Via del Teatro di Marcello) This innocuous-looking 11th-century basilica, hidden behind scaffolding when we last visited, harbours some fascinating underground ruins. Beneath the main church you can poke around the claustrophobic remains of three Republican-era temples and a series of cells that once served as currency exchange offices. The temples, which were used as a prison in medieval times – hence *carcere* (prison) in the church's name – were incorporated into the church's structure as witnessed by the marble columns in the basilica's side.

⊙ Isola Tiberina

ISOLA TIBERINA — ISLAND

Map p330 (Tiber Island; 🚌Lungotevere de' Cenci) One of the world's smallest inhabited islands, the boat-shaped Isola Tiberina has been associated with healing since the 3rd century BCE when the Romans built a temple here to the god of medicine Aesculapius. Still today people come to be cured, though they now head to the island's hospital, the **Ospedale Fatebenefratelli** (☎06 6 83 71; www.fatebenefratelli-isolatiberina.it; Piazza Fatebenefratelli).

The island is connected to the mainland by two bridges: the 62 BCE **Ponte Fabricio**, Rome's oldest standing bridge, which links with the Jewish Ghetto, and **Ponte Cestio**, which heads over to Trastevere.

Visible to the south are the remains of the Pons Aemilius. Also known as the **Ponte Rotto** (Broken Bridge; Map p330) or Broken Bridge, it was ancient Rome's first stone bridge, and was all but swept away in a 1598 flood.

CHIESA DI SAN BARTOLOMEO — CHURCH

Map p330 (☎06 687 79 73; www.sanbartolomeo.org; Piazza di San Bartolomeo all'Isola 22, Isola Tiberina; ⌚9.30am-1.30pm & 3.30-5.30pm Mon-Sat, 9.30am-1pm Sun; 🚌Lungotevere de' Cenci) Built on the ruins of the Roman temple to Aesculapius, the Graeco-Roman god of medicine, the Isola Tiberina's 10th-century church is an interesting hybrid of architectural styles. The facade and richly frescoed ceiling are baroque; the bell tower is 12th-century Romanesque; and the 28 columns that divide the interior date from ancient times.

⊙ Piazza Colonna & Around

PIAZZA COLONNA — PIAZZA

Map p328 (🚌Via del Corso) Together with the adjacent Piazza di Montecitorio, this stylish piazza is Rome's political nerve centre. On its northern flank, the 16th-century

Palazzo Chigi (Map p328; www.governo.it/visitare-i-palazzi-istituzionali/visitare-palazzo-chigi/palazzo-chigi-prenotazioni-e-calendario; Piazza Colonna 370; guided visits 9am-noon Sat, twice monthly Sep-Jul, bookings required) FREE has been the official residence of Italy's prime minister since 1961. In the centre, the 30m-high **Colonna di Marco Aurelio** (Map p328) was completed in 193 CE to honour Marcus Aurelius' military victories.

The column's vivid reliefs depict scenes from battles against the Germanic tribes (169–73) and, further up, the Sarmatians (174–76). In 1589 the emperor was replaced on the top of the column by a bronze statue of St Paul.

PALAZZO DI MONTECITORIO — HISTORIC BUILDING

Map p328 (800 012955; Piazza di Montecitorio; guided visits 10.30am-3.30pm 1st Sun of the month; Via del Corso) FREE Home to Italy's Chamber of Deputies, this baroque *palazzo* was built by Bernini in 1653, expanded by Carlo Fontana in the late 17th century, and given an art nouveau facelift in 1918. Visits take in the mansion's lavish reception rooms and the main chamber where the 630 deputies debate beneath a beautiful Liberty-style skyline.

The **obelisk** (Map p328) outside was brought from Heliopolis in Egypt by Augustus to celebrate his victory over Cleopatra and Mark Antony in 30 BCE.

PIAZZA DI PIETRA — PIAZZA

Map p328 (Via del Corso) This charming piazza, surrounded by popular bars and cafes, is overlooked by 11 huge Corinthian columns – all that's left of the 2nd-century **Tempio di Adriano** (Map p328). The temple formerly housed Rome's stock exchange and is now used to host conferences and business events.

CHIESA DI SANT'IGNAZIO DI LOYOLA — CHURCH

Map p328 (06 679 44 06; https://santignazio.gesuiti.it; Piazza di Sant'Ignazio; 7.30am-7pm Mon-Sat, from 9am Sun; Via del Corso) Flank-

TOP EXPERIENCE
GALLERIA DORIA PAMPHILJ

Hidden behind the grimy exterior of Palazzo Doria Pamphilj, this gallery boasts one of Rome's richest private art collections, with works by Raphael, Tintoretto, Titian, Caravaggio, Bernini and Velázquez, as well as several Flemish masters.

Masterpieces abound, but look out for Titian's *Salomè con la testa del Battista* (Salome with the Head of John the Baptist) and two early Caravaggios: *Riposo durante la fuga in Egitto* (Rest During the Flight into Egypt) and *Maddalene penitente* (Penitent Magdalen). Further highlights include Alessandro Algardi's bust of Donna Olimpia and the *Battaglia nel porto di Napoli* (Battle in the Bay of Naples), one of the few paintings in Rome by Pieter Bruegel the Elder.

The collection's undisputed star, though, is Velázquez' portrait of Pope Innocent X, who grumbled that the depiction was 'too real'. For a comparison, check out Bernini's sculptural interpretation of the same subject.

Palazzo Doria Pamphilj dates from the mid-15th century, but its present look was largely the work of its current owners, the Doria Pamphilj family, who acquired it in the 18th century. The Pamphilj's golden age, during which the family collection was started, came during the papacy of one of its own, Innocent X (r 1644–55).

TOP TIPS

- Get the free audio guide, narrated by Jonathan Pamphilj, which brings the gallery alive with family anecdotes and background information.
- The gallery's frescoed ceilings and ornate 18th-century decor are a sight in themselves.

PRACTICALITIES

- Map p328, H5
- 06 679 73 23
- www.doriapamphilj.it
- Via del Corso 305
- adult/reduced €12/8
- 9am-7pm, last entry 6pm
- Via del Corso

ing a delightful rococo piazza, this important Jesuit church boasts a Carlo Maderno facade and two celebrated trompe l'œil frescoes by Andrea Pozzo (1642–1709). One cleverly depicts a fake dome, while the other, on the nave ceiling, shows St Ignatius Loyola being welcomed into paradise by Christ and the Madonna.

For the best views of this dizzying work, stand on the small yellow spot on the nave floor and look up – alternatively, use the conveniently positioned mirror. Thanks to Pozzo's virtuoso use of perspective, a mass of figures, led by St Ignatius, appears to float heavenwards past a series of soaring columns and arches.

A second marble disc marks the best place to admire the dome, which is actually a flat canvas painted by Pozzo in 1685.

The church, which was built by the Jesuit architect Orazio Grassi in 1626, flanks **Piazza di Sant'Ignazio Loyola** (Map p328), an exquisite square laid out in 1727 to resemble a stage set. Note the exits into 'the wings' at the northern end and how the undulating surfaces create the illusion of a larger space.

EATING

Around Piazza Navona, Campo de' Fiori and the Pantheon you'll find all manner of places to eat, including some of the capital's best restaurants (both contemporary and old-school), several excellent gelaterie and a number of highly rated street-food joints. Needless to say, there are also hundreds of overpriced tourist traps. To the south, the atmospheric Ghetto is the place to head to for traditional Roman-Jewish cuisine.

Pantheon & Around

★LA CIAMBELLA ITALIAN €€

Map p328 (☎06 683 29 30; www.la-ciambella.it; Via dell'Arco della Ciambella 20; meals €35-45; ⏰noon-11pm Tue-Sun; 🚌Largo di Torre Argentina) Near the Pantheon but as yet largely undiscovered by the tourist hordes, this friendly restaurant beats much of the neighbourhood competition. Its handsome, light-filled interior is set over the ruins of the Terme di Agrippa, visible through transparent floor panels, setting an attractive stage for interesting, imaginative food.

ARMANDO AL PANTHEON ROMAN €€

Map p328 (☎06 6880 3034; www.armandoalpantheon.it; Salita dei Crescenzi 31; meals €40; ⏰12.30-3pm Mon-Sat & 7-11pm Mon-Fri; 🚌Largo di Torre Argentina) With its cosy wooden interior and unwavering dedication to old-school Roman cuisine, family-run Armando's is almost as well known as its neighbour, the Pantheon. It's been on the go for more than 50 years and remains as popular as ever, its cosy interior usually packed with locals and out-of-towners. Reservations essential.

GINGER BRASSERIE €€

Map p328 (☎06 6830 8559; www.gingersaporiesalute.com; Piazza Sant'Eustachio 54; meals €30-35; ⏰8am-midnight; 🚌Corso del Rinascimento) Boasting a casually contemporary white interior and al fresco seating on an unassuming piazza, this cool all-day brasserie is something of a jack of all trades. It serves everything from coffee and fresh fruit juices to burgers, gourmet *panini* and a full restaurant menu featuring the likes of *polpo e quinoa* (organic quinoa with steamed octopus) and *calamari* (squid) tacos.

OSTERIA DEL SOSTEGNO TRATTORIA €€

Map p328 (☎06 679 38 42; www.ilsostegno.it; Via delle Colonnelle 5; meals €35-40; ⏰12.30-3.30pm & 7.30-11pm, closed Sun dinner & Mon; 🚌Via del Corso) Follow the green neon arrow to the end of a narrow alley and you'll find this intimate trattoria. It's a long-standing favourite of business folk and politicians who sneak off here to dine on old-school staples such as *pasta e lenticchie* (pasta and lentils) and *abbacchio al forno* (roast lamb). Reservations recommended.

CASA COPPELLE RISTORANTE €€€

Map p328 (☎06 6889 1707; www.casacoppelle.com; Piazza delle Coppelle 49; meals from €65, lunch/dinner tasting menu €55/80; ⏰noon-3.30pm & 6.30-11.30pm; 🚌Corso del Rinascimento) Boasting an enviable setting near the Pantheon and a plush, theatrical look – think velvet drapes, black-lacquer tables and bookshelves – Casa Coppelle sets a romantic stage for high-end Italian-French cuisine. Gallic trademarks like foie gras and *vichyssoise* feature alongside updated Roman favourites such as *cacio e pepe*, here deconstructed as a cheese and pepper risotto with sauteed prawns. Book ahead.

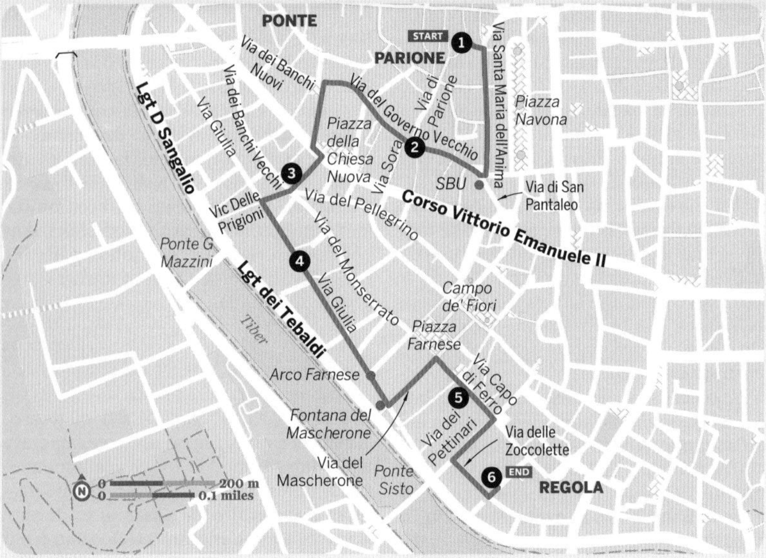

Local Life
A Day Out in the Centro Storico

Rome's historic centre casts a powerful spell. But it's not just visitors who fall for its romantic piazzas, suggestive lanes and streetside cafes. Away from the tourist spotlight, locals love to spend time here, shopping, unwinding over a drink, taking in an exhibition or simply hanging out with friends.

❶ An Exhibition at the Chiostro del Bramante

Tucked away in the backstreets near Piazza Navona, the Renaissance Chiostro del Bramante (p85) is a masterpiece of High Renaissance architectural styling that provides a stunning setting for modern-art exhibitions. Afterwards, pop upstairs for a coffee, light lunch or drink at the smart in-house cafe.

❷ Shopping around Via del Governo Vecchio

A charming street lined with indie boutiques, Via del Governo Vecchio (p85) strikes off Piazza Pasquino, home to a celebrated 'talking statue' (to which Romans used to stick notes lampooning the authorities). It can get touristy but locals love the vibe too and the area has some great shops, including hip jeans store SBU (p101).

❸ Street Food at Supplizio

A recent trend for street food has seen a number of quality fast-food joints spring up across town. At Supplizio (p95), Rome's favourite snack, the *supplì* (risotto balls), gets a gourmet makeover with predictably delicious results.

❹ Stroll Via Giulia

Lined with Renaissance *palazzi* and discreet fashion boutiques, Via Giulia (p87) is a picture-perfect strip to stroll. At its southern end, the **Fontana del Mascherone** (Map p330; Via Giulia; 🚌Lungotevere dei Tebaldi) depicts a seemingly gobsmacked 17th-century hippy spewing water from his mouth. Close by, the overhead **Arco Farnese** (Map p328; Via Giulia; 🚌Via Giulia) was part of an ambitious, unfinished project to link two Farnese palaces.

DIEGO FIORE / SHUTTERSTOCK ©

Via Giulia

5 An Optical Illusion at Palazzo Spada

Largely bypassed by the sightseeing hordes, Palazzo Spada (p86) is home to a celebrated optical illusion – the Prospettiva (Perspective) – created by the great baroque architect Francesco Borromini. What appears to be a 25m-long corridor lined with columns leading to a hedge and life-sized statue is, in fact, only 10m long, and the sculpture, a later addition, is only hip-height.

6 Wine Tasting at Rimessa Roscioli

A fantastic addition to Rome's drinking scene, Rimessa Roscioli (p99) is heaven-made for wine lovers. Exquisite wine-tasting dinners offer the chance to pair stellar wines with wonderful food (€33 to €65 for menus accompanied by three to seven wines).

Piazza Navona & Around

BAGUETTERIA DEL FICO SANDWICHES €

Map p328 (☎06 9604 5541; www.baguetteriadelfico.net; Via della Fossa 12; panini €6-9; ⏰11am-midnight; 🚌Corso del Risorgimento) This upmarket baguette bar is ideal for a midday bite or late snack. Choose your bread, then select from the rich selection of fillings – aged hams, pungent cheeses, marinated vegetables, salads and homemade sauces. Alternatively, go for a tasting platter, perhaps of smoked salmon or wafer-thin sliced tuna.

CAFFETTERIA CHIOSTRO DEL BRAMANTE CAFE €

Map p328 (☎06 6880 9036; www.chiostrodelbramante.it; Via Arco della Pace 5; meals €15-25; ⏰10am-8pm Mon-Fri, to 9pm Sat & Sun; 📶; 🚌Corso del Rinascimento) Few cafes are as beautifully located as this one on the 1st floor of Bramante's elegant Renaissance cloisters. With tables above the central courtyard and sofas in a vintage-styled room overlooking Raphael's frescoes in the Chiesa di Santa Maria della Pace, it serves everything from cakes and coffee to baguettes, risottos and avocado starters.

ALFREDO E ADA TRATTORIA €€

Map p328 (☎06 687 88 42; Via dei Banchi Nuovi 14; meals €25-30; ⏰noon-3pm & 7-10pm Tue-Sat; 🚌Corso Vittorio Emanuele II) For an authentic trattoria experience, search out this longstanding neighbourhood restaurant. It's distinctly no-frills with basic wooden tables, cheerful clutter and a simple menu but there's a warm, friendly atmosphere and the traditional Roman food is filling and flavoursome.

COROMANDEL RISTORANTE €€

Map p328 (☎06 6880 2461; www.coromandel.it; Via di Monte Giordano 60; breakfast €15, meals €35-40; ⏰8.30am-3pm Mon-Sat & 8-11pm Thu-Sat, 8.30am-4pm Sun; 🚌Corso del Rinascimento) A Roman *primo colazione* (breakfast) rarely consists of more than a coffee and a *cornetto* (croissant). Not here. Coromandel is renowned for its breakfasts and brunches – plates of rich French toast, waffles, pancakes and omelettes. Tea (or coffee) is served in dainty china cups, adding to its genteel tea-shop atmosphere. Reservations recommended.

EST ARTIGIANI DEL GUSTO ITALIAN €€

Map p328 (☎06 6880 3332; www.estartigianidelgusto.it; Vicolo della Cancelleria 11; meals €30-35; ⏲6.30am-10.15pm Mon-Sat; 🚌Corso Vittorio Emanuele II) A pearl among the tourist traps near Via del Governo Vecchio, this cosy bar-bistro is a good address to have up your sleeve. It's open all day, serving cooked breakfasts then seasonal Italian and Roman fare to a mixed crowd of tourists and office workers. It fills quickly, particularly at lunchtime, so booking is recommended.

VIVI BISTROT BISTRO €€

Map p328 (☎06 683 3779; www.vivibistrot.com; Palazzo Braschi, Piazza Navona 2; meals €25-35; ⏲10am-midnight Tue-Sun; 🖉; 🚌Corso del Rinascimento) Rustic decor goes hand in hand with baroque elegance at this handsome bistro on the ground floor of Palazzo Braschi. With its country wood tables, dried flowers and a menu that ranges from bruschetta starters to burgers, curries and vegan salads, it's a great spot to escape the hurly-burly outside.

LA CAMPANA ROMAN €€

Map p328 (☎06 687 52 73; www.ristorantelacampana.com; Vicolo della Campana 18; meals €35-40; ⏲12.30-3pm & 7.30-11pm Tue-Sun; 🚌Via di Monte Brianzo) Caravaggio, Goethe and Federico Fellini are among the luminaries who have dined at what is said to be Rome's oldest trattoria, dating from around 1518. Nowadays, locals and out-of-towners take to its soberly attired interior to dine on fresh fish and traditional Roman dishes in a warm, relaxed atmosphere. Bookings recommended.

LA FOCACCIA PIZZA €€

Map p328 (☎06 9761 7557; Via della Pace 11; pizzas €7-9.50, meals €30; ⏲noon-midnight; 🚌Corso del Rinascimento) This unassuming pizzeria-trattoria near the Chiostro del Bramante is an excellent choice for a simple meal in a warm, cheerful setting. In summer, the outside tables are the ones to go for, but come in winter and you'll find the surprisingly large interior full of happy diners. Kick off with a *supplì* (risotto ball) before launching into the main event: Neapolitan-style wood-fired pizza.

RETROBOTTEGA RISTORANTE €€€

Map p328 (☎06 6813 6310; www.retro-bottega.com; Via della Stelletta 4; à la carte meals €45, 4-/7-course menus €55/75; ⏲6.30-11.30pm Mon, from noon Tue-Sun; 🚌Corso del Rinascimento) Fine dining goes casual at trendy Retrobottega. Here you'll be sitting on a stool at a high communal table or chatting with the chef during plating of dishes at the counter. The food, in keeping with the experimental vibe and contemporary decor, is original and creative Italian.

CASA BLEVE RISTORANTE €€€

Map p328 (☎06 686 59 70; www.casableve.it; Via del Teatro Valle 48-49; meals €55-70; ⏲12.30-3pm & 7.30-11pm Mon-Sat; 🚌Largo di Torre Argentina) Ideal for a special-occasion dinner, this palatial restaurant dazzles with its column-lined dining hall and stained-glass roof. Its wine list, one of the best in town, accompanies a refined menu of classic Italian starters, seasonal pastas and sumptuous mains such as slow-cooked beef in Nebbiolo wine.

✕ Campo de' Fiori & Around

★FORNO ROSCIOLI BAKERY €

Map p328 (☎06 686 40 45; www.anticofornoroscioli.it; Via dei Chiavari 34; pizza slices from €2, snacks €2.50; ⏲7am-8pm Mon-Sat, 8.30am-7pm Sun; 🚋Via Arenula) This is one of Rome's top bakeries, much loved by lunching locals who crowd here for luscious sliced pizza, prize pastries and hunger-sating *supplì* (risotto balls). The pizza margherita is superb, if messy to eat, and there's also a counter serving hot pastas and vegetable side dishes.

TIRAMISÙ ZUM DESSERTS €

Map p328 (☎06 6830 7836; www.zumroma.it; Piazza del Teatro di Pompeo 20; tiramisu €4.50-6.50; ⏲11am-11pm Sun-Thu, to 1am Fri & Sat; 🚌Corso Vittorio Emanuele II) The ideal spot for a mid-afternoon pick-me-up, this fab dessert bar specialises in tiramisu, that magnificent marriage of mascarpone and liqueur-soaked biscuits. Choose between the classic version with its cocoa powdering or one of several tempting variations, flavoured with rum, forest fruits or Sicilian pistachio nuts.

I DOLCI DI NONNA VINCENZA PASTRIES €

Map p330 (☎06 9259 4322; www.dolcinonnavincenza.it; Via Arco del Monte 98a; pastries from €2.50; ⏲7.30am-8.30pm Mon-Sat, to 8am Sun; 🚋Via Arenula) Bringing the sweet flavours of Sicily to Rome, this pastry shop is a delight. Browse the traditional cakes and tempting *dolci* (sweet pastries) arrayed in the old wooden dressers, before adjourning to the adjacent bar to tear into creamy, flaky, puffy pastries and ricotta-stuffed *cannoli*.

SUPPLIZIO — FAST FOOD €

Map p328 (06 8987 1920; www.supplizioroma.it; Via dei Banchi Vecchi 143; supplì €3-7; noon-3.30pm & 5-10pm Mon-Sat; Corso Vittorio Emanuele II) Rome's favourite snack, the *supplì* (risotto ball), gets a gourmet makeover at this elegant street-food joint. Sit back on the vintage leather sofa and dig into a crispy classic model or push the boat out and try something different, perhaps a fishy version seasoned with butter and anchovies.

FORNO DI CAMPO DE' FIORI — BAKERY €

Map p328 (06 6880 6662; www.fornocampodefiori.com; Campo de' Fiori 22; pizza slices around €3; 7.30am-2.30pm & 4.45-8pm Mon-Sat, closed Sat afternoon Jul & Aug; Corso Vittorio Emanuele II) This buzzing bakery on Campo de' Fiori, divided into two adjacent shops, does a roaring trade in *panini* and delicious fresh-from-the-oven *pizza al taglio* (sliced pizza). Aficionados swear by the pizza *bianca* ('white' pizza with olive oil, rosemary and salt), which is great on its own or as a sandwich with artisanal mortadella.

MERCATO DI CAMPO DE' FIORI — MARKET €

Map p328 (Campo de' Fiori; 7am-2pm Mon-Sat; Corso Vittorio Emanuele II) The oldest and most picturesque – also the most expensive – of Rome's neighbourhood markets. Each weekday morning, shoppers mix with tourists and visitors amid the colourful stalls that take over the historic piazza. As well as seasonal fruit and veg, you can also pick up pasta, cheese, olive oil, balsamic vinegar, fruit juice and much more besides.

★PIANOSTRADA — RISTORANTE €€

Map p330 (06 8957 2296; www.facebook.com/pianostrada; Via delle Zoccolette 22; meals €40-45; 1-4pm & 7pm-midnight Tue-Fri, 10am-midnight Sat & Sun; Via Arenula) This uberhip bistro-restaurant, in a white space with vintage furnishings and a glorious summer courtyard, is a must. Reserve ahead, or settle for a stool at the bar and enjoy views of the kitchen at work. The cuisine is creative, seasonal and veg-packed, including gourmet open sandwiches and sensational focaccia, as well as full-blown mains.

EMMA PIZZERIA — PIZZA €€

Map p328 (06 6476 0475; www.emmapizzeria.com; Via del Monte della Farina 28-29; pizzas €8-18, meals €35; 12.30-3pm & 7-11.30pm; Via Arenula) Tucked in behind the Chiesa di San Carlo ai Catinari, Emma is a stylish set-up with outdoor seating and a spacious, art-clad interior. It specialises in cracking wood-fired pizzas, ranging from the

TOP GELATO STOPS

Gelateria del Teatro (Map p328; 06 4547 4880; www.gelateriadelteatro.it; Via dei Coronari 65; gelato from €3; 11am-8pm winter, 10am-10.30pm summer; Via Zanardelli) All the gelato served at this excellent gelateria is prepared on-site – look through the window and you'll see how. There are numerous flavours, all made from premium seasonal ingredients, ranging from evergreen favourites such as pistachio and hazelnut to inventive creations like rosemary, honey and lemon.

Fatamorgana (Map p328; 06 8881 8437; Via dei Chiavari 37; cones & tubs €2.50-5; noon-11pm; Corso Vittorio Emanuele II) Fatamorgana is a surefire bet for artisanal gelato made with top seasonal ingredients. There's a good choice of flavours ranging from the classic to more experimental creations such as *crema zenzero miele di castagno e limone* (ginger cream with chestnut honey and lemon).

Venchi (Map p328; 06 6992 5423; www.venchi.com; Via degli Orfani 87; gelato €3.20-5; 10am-11pm Sun-Thu, to midnight Fri & Sat; Via del Corso) Forget fancy flavours and experimental combinations, Venchi is all about the unadulterated enjoyment of chocolate. The wall shelves and counter displays feature myriad beautifully wrapped delicacies, from pralines to chilli chocolate bars, culminating in an assortment of decadent choc-based gelati. In peak times expect queues out of the door.

ever-present margherita to more inventive choices topped with guest ingredients such as Spanish *pata negra* ham and Cantabrian anchovies. Alternatively, go for a classic Roman pasta dish.

RENATO E LUISA ROMAN €€

Map p328 (☎06 686 96 60; www.renatoeluisa.it; Via dei Barbieri 25; meals €35-45; ⊙8pm-midnight Tue-Sun; 🚇Largo di Torre Argentina) A Roman favourite, this much-lauded backstreet trattoria is often packed. Chef Renato's menu features updated Roman classics that while modern and seasonal are also undeniably local, such as his signature *cacio e pepe e fiori di zucca* (pasta with *pecorino* cheese, black pepper and zucchini flowers). Bookings advised.

GRAPPOLO D'ORO TRATTORIA €€

Map p328 (☎06 689 70 80; www.hosteriagrappolodoro.it; Piazza della Cancelleria 80; meals €35; ⊙12.30-3pm & 6.30-11pm, closed Wed lunch; 🚇Corso Vittorio Emanuele II) This welcoming modern trattoria stands out among the many lacklustre options around Campo de' Fiori. The emphasis is on updated regional cuisine, so look out for dishes such as pasta with anchovies, pecorino and cherry tomatoes, and rich desserts like *zabaglione* spiked with fortified Marsala wine.

DITIRAMBO TRATTORIA €€

Map p328 (☎06 687 16 26; www.ristoranteditirambo.it; Piazza della Cancelleria 74; meals €35; ⊙12.40-3.15pm & 7-11pm, closed Mon lunch; 🌱; 🚇Corso Vittorio Emanuele II) Ditirambo wins diners over with its central location, informal trattoria vibe and seasonal, organic cuisine. Dishes cover many bases, ranging from traditional Roman pastas to thoughtful vegetarian offerings and regional creations such as baked Sardinian lamb served with chicory or potatoes. Book ahead.

★SALUMERIA ROSCIOLI RISTORANTE €€€

Map p330 (☎06 687 52 87; www.salumeriaroscioli.com; Via dei Giubbonari 21; meals €55; ⊙12.30-4pm & 7pm-midnight Mon-Sat; 🚇Via Arenula) The name Roscioli has long been a byword for foodie excellence in Rome, and this deli-restaurant is the place to experience it. Tables are set alongside the counter, laden with mouth-watering Italian and foreign delicacies, and in a small bottle-lined space behind. The food, including traditional Roman pastas, is top notch and there are some truly outstanding wines. Reservations essential.

IL PAGLIACCIO GASTRONOMY €€€

Map p328 (☎06 6880 9595; www.ristoranteilpagliaccio.com; Via dei Banchi Vecchi 129a; meals €85, lunch/8-/10-course tasting menus €75/150/170; ⊙7.30-10pm Tue, 12.30-2pm & 7.30-10pm Wed-Sat; 📶🌱; 🚇Corso Vittorio Emanuele II) Rome's only two-Michelin-starred restaurant, Il Pagliaccio is Italian fine dining at its best. Chef Anthony Genovese – who was born in France to Italian parents and honed his craft in Asia – draws vivid inspiration from his eclectic background, creating dishes such as lobster with passion fruit and *stracchino* (soft cheese), oyster and green-apple granita, and a memorable take on green curry.

Jewish Ghetto & Around

ANTICO FORNO URBANI BAKERY €

Map p330 (☎06 689 32 35; Piazza Costaguti 31; pizza slices from €1.50; ⊙7.40am-2.30pm & 5-7.45pm Mon-Fri, 8.30am-1.30pm Sat, 9.30am-1pm Sun; 🚇Via Arenula) This Ghetto kosher bakery makes some of the best *pizza al taglio* (sliced pizza) in town. It can get extremely busy but once you catch a whiff of the yeasty smell it's impossible to resist a quick stop. Everything's good, including its fabulous pizza *con patate* (pizza topped with thin slices of potato).

BEPPE E I SUOI FORMAGGI CHEESE €€

Map p330 (☎06 6819 2210; www.beppeeisuoiformaggi.it; Via Santa Maria del Pianto 9-11; meals €30-40; ⊙9-11pm Mon-Sat; 🚇Via Arenula) It's all in the name – Beppe and his cheeses. Serving cheese throughout the day, this small restaurant, attached to a well-stocked deli selling *formaggi* of all shapes and smells, is an aficionados' delight. Breakfast on ricotta and honey, lunch on *robiola*, and end the day with a luxurious fondue for two. Also does excellent charcuterie boards.

PIPERNO ROMAN €€€

Map p330 (☎06 6880 6629; www.ristorantepiperno.it; Via Monte de' Cenci 9; meals €45-55; ⊙12.45-2.30pm & 7.45-10.30pm, closed Sun dinner & Mon; 🚇Via Arenula) This historic Ghetto restaurant, complete with dated decor and a rather starchy atmosphere, is a top spot for traditional Jewish-Roman cooking.

LOCAL KNOWLEDGE

KOSHER ROME

If you want to eat kosher in Rome, head to Via del Portico d'Ottavia, the main strip through the Jewish Ghetto (p87). Lined with trattorias and restaurants specialising in Roman-Jewish cuisine, it's a lively hang-out, especially on hot summer nights when diners crowd the many pavement tables. For a taste of typical Ghetto cooking, try **Ba'Ghetto** (Map p330; ☎06 6889 2868; www.baghetto.com; Via del Portico d'Ottavia 57; meals €30-35; ⏰noon-11.30pm Mon-Thu & Sun, to 3pm Fri, 6-11.30pm Sat; 🚋Via Arenula), a long-standing neighbourhood restaurant that serves kosher food and local staples such as *carciofo alla guidia* (crisp fried artichoke). Further down the road, the unmarked **Cremeria Romana** (Map p330; ☎06 8898 3229; Via del Portico d'Ottavia 1b; gelato from €2.50; ⏰9am-9.30pm Mon-Thu & Sun, to 4pm Fri, 9pm-midnight Sat; 🚋Via Arenula) has a small selection of tasty kosher gelato.

Signature hits include deep-fried *filetti di baccalà* (cod fillets) and *animelle di agnello con carciofi* (lamb sweetbreads with artichokes). Bookings recommended.

Isola Tiberina

SORA LELLA ROMAN €€€

Map p330 (☎06 686 1601; www.trattoriasoralella.com; Via Ponte Quattro Capi 16; meals €45-50, tasting menus €48-60; ⏰12.30-2.45pm & 7.30-10.45pm Mon-Sat; 🌱; 🚌Lungotevere dei Cenci) This long-standing family-run restaurant enjoys a memorable setting in a tower on the Tiber's tiny island. Named after a much-loved actress – the current chef's *nonna* (grandma) – it serves a classic Roman menu spiced up with the occasional seafood dish. There are also homemade desserts and several tasting menus, including one for vegetarians – something of a rarity in meat-loving Rome.

Piazza Colonna & Around

DAL CAVALIER GINO TRATTORIA €€

Map p328 (Dal Gino al Parlamento; ☎06 687 34 34; Vicolo Rosini 4; meals €30-35; ⏰1-3.45pm & 8-11pm Mon-Sat; 🚌Via del Corso) Close to the Italian parliament, Gino's is a classic backstreet trattoria perennially packed with journalists, politicians, locals and tourists. Join the crowd for well-executed staples such as *tagliolini alla gricia* (flat spaghetti with lardons of cured pork) and *coniglio al vino bianco* (rabbit in a white-wine sauce), all served under gaudily painted murals. Reservations recommended. No credit cards.

MATRICIANELLA ROMAN €€

Map p328 (☎06 683 21 00; www.matricianella.it; Via del Leone 4; meals €40; ⏰12.30-3pm & 7.30-11pm Mon-Sat; 🚌Via del Corso) With its chintzy murals and fading prints, Matricianella is an archetypal neighbourhood trattoria, much loved for its traditional Roman cuisine. Its loyal locals keep coming back for evergreen crowd-pleasers such as artichoke *alla giudia* (fried, Jewish style) and *cotolette di abbacchio fritte e dorate* (breaded and fried lamb cutlets). Booking is highly recommended, particularly on Saturday nights.

OSTERIA DELL'INGEGNO ITALIAN €€

Map p328 (☎06 678 06 62; www.osteriadellingegno.com; Piazza di Pietra 45; meals €35-45; ⏰noon-midnight; 🚌Via del Corso) This fashionably casual restaurant wine-bar is an enticing spot with its colourful, art-filled interior and prime location on a charming central piazza. The daily menu hits all the right notes with a selection of seasonal pastas, inventive mains and homemade desserts, while the 200-strong wine list boasts some interesting Italian labels.

ENOTECA AL PARLAMENTO ACHILLI GASTRONOMY €€€

Map p328 (☎06 8676 1422; www.enotecalparlamento.com; Via dei Prefetti 15; meals from €90, tasting menu €160; ⏰12.30-2.30pm & 7.30-10.30pm Mon-Sat; 🚌Via del Corso) Housed in one of the capital's historic wine shops, chef Massimo Viglietti's Michelin-starred restaurant marries a classic, wood-panelled setting with audacious, experimental food and provocative deconstructions of Roman staples. The wine list is, unsurprisingly, excellent. Reservations recommended.

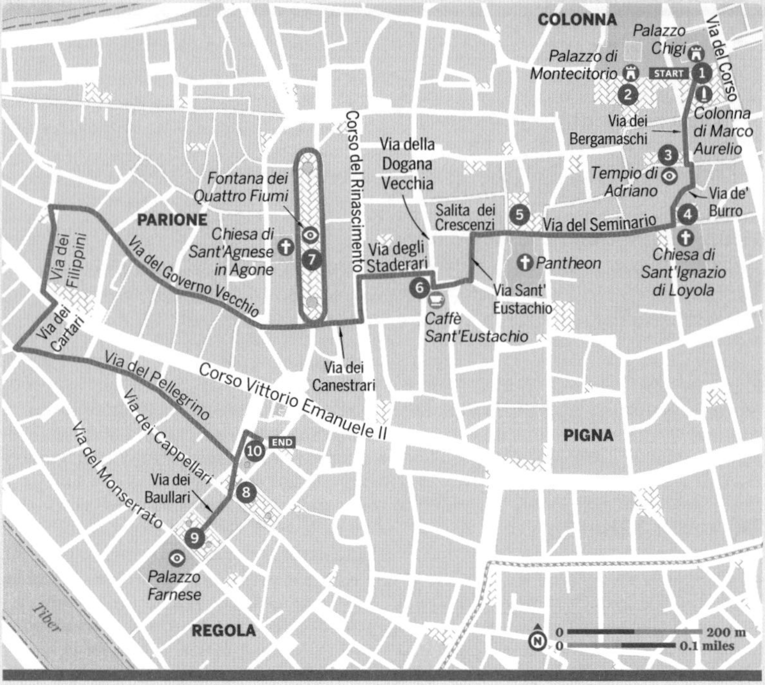

Neighbourhood Walk
Walking Tour: Centro Storico Piazzas

START PIAZZA COLONNA
END PIAZZA FARNESE
LENGTH 1.5KM; 2½ TO THREE HOURS

Start in 1 **Piazza Colonna** (p89), an elegant square dominated by the 30m-high Colonna di Marco Aurelio and flanked by Palazzo Chigi, the official residence of the Italian prime minister. Next door, and facing onto 2 **Piazza di Montecitorio**, is the impressive seat of Italy's Chamber of Deputies, Palazzo di Montecitorio. From Piazza Colonna follow Via dei Bergamaschi down to 3 **Piazza di Pietra** (p90), a refined rectangular space overlooked by the 2nd-century Tempio di Adriano. Continue down Via de' Burro to 4 **Piazza di Sant'Ignazio**, a small rococo piazza whose resident church boasts some magnificent trompe l'œil ceiling frescoes. From here, it's a short walk along Via del Seminario to 5 **Piazza della Rotonda**, where the Pantheon needs no introduction.

Leaving the Pantheon, head up Salita dei Crescenzi and go left along Via Sant'Eustachio to 6 **Piazza Sant' Eustachio**. On this small square, Caffè Sant'Eustachio is reckoned by many to serve the best coffee in town. Recharged, follow Via degli Staderari to Corso del Rinascimento, drop a quick left followed by a short right and you'll find yourself emerging onto 7 **Piazza Navona** (p82). Here you can compare the two giants of Roman baroque – Gian Lorenzo Bernini, creator of the Fontana dei Quattro Fiumi, and Francesco Borromini, author of the Chiesa di Sant'Agnese in Agone.

Exit the piazza and follow Via del Governo Vecchio. At the end, turn left down Via dei Filippini to Corso Vittorio Emanuele II, the busy thoroughfare that bisects the historic centre. Cross over and take Via dei Cartari to connect with Via del Pellegrino. Follow on to 8 **Campo de' Fiori** (p86), a colourful, chaotic market square, and beyond that, the more sober 9 **Piazza Farnese** overshadowed by the Renaissance Palazzo Farnese. To finish up, double back to **Grappolo d'Oro** (p96) where you can rest your feet over a relaxed trattoria meal.

DRINKING & NIGHTLIFE

With everything from cafes, wine bars, craft beer pubs and hidden speakeasies, there's plenty going on in the *centro storico.* Nightlife is centred on two main areas: the lanes around Piazza Navona and the rowdier area around Campo de' Fiori, where the crowd is younger and the drinking heavier. The area around the Pantheon is the place to go for coffee, with two of the city's most celebrated cafes competing for your custom.

Pantheon & Around

★CAFFÈ SANT'EUSTACHIO COFFEE

Map p328 (☎06 6880 2048; www.santeustachioilcaffe.it; Piazza Sant'Eustachio 82; ⏰7.30am-1am Sun-Thu, to 1.30am Fri, to 2am Sat; 🚌Corso del Rinascimento) Always busy, this workaday cafe near the Pantheon is reckoned by many to serve the best coffee in town.

To make it, the bartenders sneakily beat the first drops of an espresso with several teaspoons of sugar to create a frothy paste to which they add the rest of the coffee. The result is superbly smooth.

CLUB DERRIÈRE COCKTAIL BAR

Map p328 (☎393 5661077; www.facebook.com/clubderriereroma; Vicolo delle Coppelle 59; ⏰10pm-4am; 📶; 🚌Corso del Rinascimento) Found in the back room of an unassuming trattoria (Osteria delle Coppelle), Club Derrière is an enigmatic speakeasy where a suit of armour serves as unofficial bouncer.

Bartenders don ties and waistcoats and sling sleek cocktails (€12) often inspired by cultural figures, such as their Edgar Allan Poe: a heady mix of sherry, Knob Creek rye, chocolate and Angostura bitters.

LA CASA DEL CAFFÈ TAZZA D'ORO COFFEE

Map p328 (☎06 678 97 92; www.tazzadorocoffeeshop.com; Via degli Orfani 84-86; ⏰7am-8pm Mon-Sat, 10.30am-7.30pm Sun; 🚌Via del Corso) A busy cafe with burnished 1940s fittings, this is one of Rome's best coffee houses.

Its position near the Pantheon makes it touristy but its coffees are brilliant – the espresso hits the mark every time and there's a range of delicious *caffè* concoctions, including *granita di caffè,* a crushed-ice coffee served with whipped cream.

There's also a small shop and, outside, vending machines and a coffee bancomat for those out-of-hours caffeine emergencies.

Piazza Navona & Around

GIN CORNER COCKTAIL BAR

Map p328 (☎06 6880 2452; www.thegincorner.com; Hotel Adriano, Via Pallacorda 2; ⏰6pm-midnight; 🚌Via di Monte Brianzo) Forget fine wines and craft beers: this chic bar at Hotel Adriano is all about the undistilled enjoyment of gin.

Here the making of a simple G&T is raised to an art form as the skilled bar tenders select from more than 100 varieties of gin and premium tonics.

They also make excellent cocktails.

EX-CIRCUS BAR

Map p328 (☎06 9761 9258; www.facebook.com/circusromaofficial; Via della Vetrina 15; ⏰8am-10pm Mon-Thu, to 2am Fri & Sat, 9am-8pm Sun; 📶; 🚌Corso del Rinascimento) This is a great little bar tucked around the corner from Piazza Navona. Ex-Circus is a laid-back place with sofas, arty decor and free, fast wi-fi.

It's popular with young international folk who come here to work on their laptops and hang out over leisurely drinks.

The atmosphere hots up on weekend nights with regular gigs.

Campo de' Fiori & Around

★RIMESSA ROSCIOLI WINE BAR

Map p330 (☎06 6880 3914; www.winetastingrome.com; Via del Conservatorio 58; ⏰6.30-11.30pm Mon-Fri, noon-3pm & 6.30-11.30pm Sat & Sun; 📶; 🚌Lungotevere dei Tebaldi) An offshoot of the popular Roscioli empire, Rimessa is for wine lovers: labels from all over Italy and further afield crowd the shelves, while exquisite wine-tasting dinners (€33 to €65) unfold in both English and Italian.

Also available is a Tasting Bar option, where a sommelier crafts a tasting tailored to your budget and preferences.

★OPEN BALADIN CRAFT BEER

Map p330 (☎06 683 89 89; www.openbaladinroma.it; Via degli Specchi 6; ⊙noon-2am; 📶; 🚋Via Arenula) This modern pub near Campo de' Fiori has long been a leading light in Rome's craft-beer scene, and with more than 40 beers on tap and up to 100 bottled brews (many from Italian artisanal microbreweries) it's a top place for a pint. As well as great beer, expect a laid-back vibe and a young, international crowd.

★BARNUM CAFE CAFE

Map p328 (☎06 6476 0483; www.barnumcafe.com; Via del Pellegrino 87; ⊙9am-10pm Mon, 8.30am-2am Tue-Sat; 📶; 🚋Corso Vittorio Emanuele II) A laid-back *Friends*-style cafe, evergreen Barnum is the sort of place you could quickly get used to. With its shabby-chic furniture and white bare-brick walls, it's a relaxed spot for a breakfast cappuccino, a light lunch or a late-afternoon drink. Come evening, a coolly dressed-down crowd sips expertly mixed craft cocktails.

ROSCIOLI CAFFÈ CAFE

Map p330 (☎06 8916 5330; www.rosciolicaffe.com; Piazza Benedetto Cairoli 16; ⊙7am-11pm Mon-Sat, 8am-6pm Sun, closed mid-Aug; 🚋Via Arenula) In Rome, the Roscioli name is a guarantee of good things to come: the family runs one of Rome's most celebrated delis (p96) and a hugely popular bakery (p94), and this cafe doesn't disappoint either. The coffee is luxurious and the artfully crafted pastries, petits fours and *panini* taste as good as they look.

Behind the narrow, standing-room only bar is a back room where you can sit at a communal table and order from the daily food menu or sip evening cocktails.

ARGOT COCKTAIL BAR

Map p328 (☎06 4555 1966; Via dei Cappellari 93; ⊙10pm-4am Tue-Sun; 🚋Corso Vittorio Emanuele II) See out the night over craft cocktails in this intimate speakeasy. The vintage leather sofas, subdued lighting and friendly attitude create a cool underground vibe, abetted by a retro 1920s look and regular weekend gigs. There's a €10 membership fee for your first visit.

IL GOCCETTO WINE BAR

Map p328 (www.facebook.com/Ilgoccetto; Via dei Banchi Vecchi 14; ⊙noon-3pm Tue-Sat & 6pm-midnight Mon-Sat, closed mid-Aug; 🚋Corso Vittorio Emanuele II) This authentic, old-school *vino e olio* (wine and oil) shop has everything you could want in a wine bar: a woody, bottle-lined interior, a cheerful crowd of locals and first-timers, cheese and cured-meat platters, and a serious, 800-strong wine list.

JERRY THOMAS PROJECT COCKTAIL BAR

Map p328 (☎370 1146287, 06 9684 5937; www.thejerrythomasproject.it; Vicolo Cellini 30; ⊙10pm-4am Tue-Sat; 🚋Corso Vittorio Emanuele II) A speakeasy with a 1920s look and password to get in – check the website and call to book – this cult trendsetter has led the way in Rome's recent love affair with craft cocktails. Its master mixologists know their stuff and the retro decor gives it a real Prohibition-era feel. Note there's a €5 'membership' fee.

L'ANGOLO DIVINO WINE BAR

Map p328 (☎06 686 44 13; www.angolodivino.it; Via dei Balestrari 12; ⊙11am-3pm Tue-Sat & 5pm-1am daily; 🚋Corso Vittorio Emanuele II) This warm, timber-ceilinged wine bar is an oasis of calm in the backstreets around Campo de' Fiori. It offers a carefully curated wine list of mostly Italian labels, including natural and organic wines, platters of regional cheeses and cured meats, and a small daily menu of hot and cold dishes.

🍷 Piazza Colonna & Around

SALOTTO 42 BAR

Map p328 (☎06 678 58 04; www.salotto42.it; Piazza di Pietra 42; ⊙10.30am-2am; 🚋Via del Corso) The very picture of a glamorous lounge bar, Salotto 42 encapsulates Rome's *dolce vita* style. Set on a charming piazza facing ancient Roman columns, its bougainvillea-clad facade conceals an intimate, retro-cool interior of vintage 1950s armchairs, Murano lamps and heavyweight art books. This is the place to hang out with the beautiful people over an aperitif or cool cocktail.

☆ ENTERTAINMENT

ISOLA DEL CINEMA OUTDOOR CINEMA

Map p330 (www.isoladelcinema.com; Piazza San Bartolomeo all'Isola, Isola Tiberina; tickets adult/reduced €6/5; ⊙mid-Jun–Sep) From mid-June to September, the Isola Tiberina sets the stage for a season of outdoor cinema, featuring Italian and international films, some shown in their original language. There are also meetings with actors and directors, masterclasses and film-related events.

TEATRO ARGENTINA THEATRE

Map p328 (☎box office 06 684 000 311; www.teatrodiroma.net; Largo di Torre Argentina 52; tickets €12-40; 🚌Largo di Torre Argentina) Founded in 1732, Rome's top theatre is one of three managed by the Teatro di Roma, along with the Teatro India (p230) and Teatro di Villa Torlonia. Rossini's *Barber of Seville* premiered here in 1816, and these days it stages a wide-ranging program of classic and contemporary drama (mostly in Italian), plus dance and classical music.

SHOPPING

The area west of Piazza Navona is packed with small shops and indie boutiques selling everything from designer fashions to vintage clothes, handcrafted accessories and collectable antiques. Streets to target include Via del Governo Vecchio and, to the north, Via dei Coronari. Near Campo de' Fiori, you'll find more one-off boutiques on Via del Pellegrino and Via Monserrato, and several midrange clothing stores on Via dei Giubbonari.

Pantheon & Around

NAMASTÈY TEA

Map p328 (☎06 6813 5660; www.namastey.it; Via della Palombella 26; ⏰10.30am-7.30pm Mon-Sat, from 3pm Sun, closed Aug; 🚌Largo di Torre Argentina) After a visit to this charming shop, you'll be reminded of it every time you have a cup of tea. Set up like an apothecary with ceiling-high shelves and rows of jars, it stocks an encyclopaedic range of blends from across the globe, as well as everything you could ever need for your home tea ritual – teapots, cups, infusers and filters.

ALBERTA GLOVES FASHION & ACCESSORIES

Map p328 (☎06 679 73 18; Corso Vittorio Emanuele II 18; ⏰10am-7pm Mon-Sat; 🚌Largo di Torre Argentina) A throwback to a world without logos, this tiny family-run shop has a handmade glove for every conceivable occasion, from elbow-length silk evening gloves to tan-coloured driving mitts. Silk scarves and woolly hats too. Reckon on about €45 for a classic pair of leather gloves.

Piazza Navona & Around

★MARTA RAY SHOES

Map p328 (☎06 6880 2641; www.martaray.it; Via dei Coronari 121; ⏰10am-8pm; 🚌Via Zanardelli) Women's ballet flats and elegant, everyday bags in rainbow colours and super-soft leather, are the hallmarks of the Rome-born Marta Ray brand. At this store, one of three in town, you'll find a selection of trademark ballerinas as well as ankle boots and an attractive line in modern, beautifully designed handbags.

You'll find branch stores at Via della Reginella 4 in the Jewish Ghetto and Via del Moro 6 in Trastevere.

SBU CLOTHING

Map p328 (☎06 6880 2547; www.sbu.it; Via di San Pantaleo 68-69; ⏰10am-7.30pm Mon-Sat, noon-7pm Sun; 🚌Corso Vittorio Emanuele II) The flagship store of hip clothing label SBU, aka Strategic Business Unit, occupies a 19th-century workshop, complete with cast-iron columns and wooden racks. It's best known for its jeans, superbly cut from top-end Japanese denim, but you can also pick up casual shirts, jackets, hats, sweaters and T-shirts.

OFFICINA PROFUMO FARMACEUTICA DI SANTA MARIA NOVELLA COSMETICS

Map p328 (☎06 687 96 08; www.smnovella.com; Corso del Rinascimento 47; ⏰10am-7.30pm Mon-Sat; 🚌Corso del Rinascimento) This branch of one of Italy's oldest pharmacies stocks natural perfumes and cosmetics, herbal infusions, teas and potpourri, all shelved in wooden, glass-fronted cabinets under a flamboyant Murano chandelier. The original pharmacy was founded in Florence in 1612 by the Dominican monks of Santa Maria Novella, and many of its cosmetics are based on 17th-century herbal recipes.

LUNA & L'ALTRA FASHION & ACCESSORIES

Map p328 (☎06 6880 4995; www.facebook.com/Luna-laltra-159035367606825; Piazza Pasquino 76; ⏰3.30-7.30pm Mon, from 10.30am Tue-Sat; 🚌Corso Vittorio Emanuele II) This minimalist, all-white fashion boutique is one of a number of independent stores on and around Via del Governo Vecchio. In its austere, gallery-like interior, clothes by designers Comme des Garçons, Issey Miyake and Yohji Yamamoto are exhibited in reverential style.

ALDO FEFÈ ARTS & CRAFTS

Map p328 (☎06 6880 3585; Via della Stelletta 20b; ⊙8am-7.30pm Mon-Sat; 🚌Corso del Rinascimento) In his small, cluttered workshop, master craftsman Aldo Fefè patiently binds books and produces beautifully hand-painted notebooks, boxes, picture frames and albums (from €15). You can also buy Florentine wrapping paper and calligraphic pens.

CASALI ART

Map p328 (☎06 687 37 05; Via dei Coronari 115; ⊙10am-1pm & 3-7pm Mon-Fri, 10am-1pm Sat; 🚌Via Zanardelli) On Via dei Coronari, a street renowned for its antique shops, Casali deals in original and reproduction etchings and prints, many delicately hand coloured. The shop is small but the choice ranges from 16th-century botanical manuscripts to 18th-century maps of Rome and postcard prints.

PATRIZIA CORVAGLIA GIOIELLI JEWELLERY

Map p328 (☎06 4555 1441; www.patriziacorvaglia.it; Via dei Banchi Nuovi 45; ⊙11am-7.30pm Mon-Sat; 🚌Corso Vittorio Emanuele II) At her boutique in the former workshop of Renaissance goldsmith Benvenuti Cellini, Patrizia Corvaglia crafts her own line of jewellery. Her abstract, sometimes baroque, creations feature precious metals set with raw gemstones, often in geometric designs or patterns inspired by nature.

Campo de' Fiori & Around

★SALUMERIA ROSCIOLI FOOD & DRINKS

Map p330 (☎06 687 52 87; www.salumeriaroscioli.com; Via dei Giubbonari 21; ⊙8.30am-8.30pm Mon-Sat; 🚌Via Arenula) Rome's most celebrated deli showcases a smörgåsbord of prize products ranging from cured hams and cheeses to conserves, dried pastas, olive oils, aged balsamic vinegars and wines. Alongside celebrated Italian fare you'll also find top international foodstuffs such as French cheese, Iberian ham and Scottish salmon.

★IBIZ – ARTIGIANATO IN CUOIO FASHION & ACCESSORIES

Map p328 (☎06 6830 7297; www.ibizroma.it; Via dei Chiavari 39; ⊙10am-7.30pm Mon-Sat; 🚌Corso Vittorio Emanuele II) In her diminutive family workshop, Elisa Nepi and her team craft beautiful butter-soft leather wallets, bags, belts, keyrings and sandals in elegant designs and myriad colours. You can pick up a belt for about €35, while for a shoulder bag you should bank on around €145.

CHEZ DEDE CONCEPT STORE

Map p328 (☎06 8377 2934; www.chezdede.com; Via di Monserrato 35; ⊙3.30-7.30pm Mon, from 10.30am Tue-Sat; 🚌Lungotevere dei Tebaldi) This ultra-chic boutique offers a curated selection of hand-crafted accessories, fashions, homewares and books. Particularly sought after are its signature canvas and leather tote bags but you'll also find original artworks, hand-painted ceramics and limited edition perfumes, all displayed with effortless cool in the belle-époque-styled interior.

CALZOLERIA PETROCCHI SHOES

Map p328 (☎06 687 62 89; www.calzoleriapetrocchi.it; Vicolo Sugarelli 2; ⊙7am-1pm & 2-5.30pm Mon-Fri, 8am-1pm Sat, by appointment Sun; 🚌Corso Vittorio Emanuele II) This historic shoemaker has been hand-crafting leather shoes for well-heeled Romans and film icons such as Audrey Hepburn and Robert De Niro since 1946. Choose from the ready-to-wear collection or design a bespoke pair of your own: head artisan Marco Cecchi personally takes clients' measurements and customises shoes based on their selection of leather and style.

RACHELE CHILDREN'S CLOTHING

Map p328 (☎329 6481004; www.facebook.com/racheleart; Vicolo del Bollo 6; ⊙10.30am-2pm & 3.30-7.30pm Tue-Sat; 🚌Corso Vittorio Emanuele II) If your 12 year old (or younger child) needs a wardrobe update, look up Rachele in her delightful shop just off Via del Pellegrino. With everything from woolly hats and mitts to romper suits and jackets, all brightly coloured and all handmade, this sort of shop is a dying breed. Most items are around the €40 to €60 mark.

I COLORI DI DENTRO ART

Map p328 (☎06 683 24 94; www.mgluffarelli.com; Via dei Banchi Vecchi 29; ⊙11am-6.45pm Mon-Sat; 🚌Corso Vittorio Emanuele II) Take home some Mediterranean sunshine. Artist Maria Grazia Luffarelli's paintings are a riotous celebration of Italian colours, with sunny yellow landscapes, blooming flowers, Roman cityscapes and comfortable-looking cats. You can buy original watercolours or prints, as well as postcards, T-shirts, notebooks and calendars.

Jewish Ghetto & Around

IL MUSEO DEL LOUVRE — ART

Map p330 (☎328 162 60 75; Via della Reginella 8a; ⏲10.30am-7pm; tra Via Arenula) Giuseppe Casetti's collection of vintage black-and-white photos, art prints, leather-bound tomes, exhibition catalogues and posters is on show for all to browse at this, his fascinating gallery-bookshop. Everything is for sale but even if you're not buying it's a magical place to root through the wares, all relating to 20th-century design and culture.

Piazza Colonna & Around

★CONFETTERIA MORIONDO & GARIGLIO — CHOCOLATE

Map p328 (☎06 699 08 56; Via del Piè di Marmo 21-22; ⏲9am-7.30pm Mon-Sat; 🚌Via del Corso) Roman poet Trilussa was so smitten with this chocolate shop – established by the Torinese confectioners to the royal house of Savoy – that he was moved to mention it in verse. And we agree: it's a gem. Decorated like an elegant tearoom, it specialises in handmade chocolates and confections such as marrons glacés, many prepared according to original 19th-century recipes.

BARTOLUCCI — TOYS

Map p328 (☎06 6919 0894; www.bartolucci.com; Via dei Pastini 98; ⏲10am-10pm; 🚌Via del Corso) It's difficult to resist going into this magical toyshop where everything is carved out of wood. By the main entrance, a Pinocchio pedals his bike robotically, perhaps dreaming of the full-size motorbike parked nearby, while inside there are is all manner of ticking clocks, rocking horses, planes and more Pinocchios than you're likely to see in your whole life.

MONOCLE — FASHION & ACCESSORIES

Map p328 (☎06 683 36 68; www.monocle.it; Via di Campo Marzio 13; ⏲10.30am-7.30pm Mon-Sat, 11am-7pm Sun; 📶; 🚌Via del Corso) This luxury eyewear boutique has plenty of specs appeal: bold and unexpected designs from up-and-coming and indie designers such as Chrome Hearts, Katsura and Oliver Goldsmith are favoured over industrial brands. Monocle's own line of perfumes and colognes are also available in-store.

MATERIE — JEWELLERY

Map p328 (☎06 679 31 99; www.materieshop.com; Via del Gesù 73; ⏲10.30-7.30pm Mon-Sat; 🚌Via del Corso) Materie is a lovely showcase for unique handcrafted jewellery. Each year owner Viviana Violo travels to source new pieces from designers and artisans working in materials as diverse as silver, silicon, rubber, metal, plastic and stone. As well as jewellery, you'll also find a small choice of bags, scarves and accessories.

LE TARTARUGHE — FASHION & ACCESSORIES

Map p328 (☎06 679 22 40; www.letartarughe.eu; Via del Piè di Marmo 17; ⏲4-7.30pm Mon, from 10am Tue-Sat,; 🚌Via del Corso) Fashionable, versatile and elegant, Susanna Liso's seasonal designs adorn this relaxed, white-walled boutique. Her clothes, often blended from raw silks, cashmere and fine merino wool, provide vibrant modern updates on classic styles. You'll also find a fine line in novelty accessories.

JOHN HARPER / GETTY IMAGES ©

1. Piazza del Campidoglio (p74) **2.** Piazza Navona (p82) **3.** Piazza del Popolo (p112) **4.** Spanish Steps and Barcaccia fountain, Piazza di Spagna (p108)

NICOLA FORENZA / GETTY IMAGES ©

Showtime on Centro Storico's Piazzas

From the baroque splendour of Piazza Navona to the clamour of Campo de' Fiori and the majesty of St Peter's Square, Rome's piazzas encapsulate much of the city's beauty, history and drama.

Piazza Navona

In the heart of the historic centre, **Piazza Navona** (p82) is the picture-perfect Roman square. Graceful baroque *palazzi* (mansions), flamboyant fountains, packed pavement cafes and costumed street artists set the scene for the daily invasion of camera-toting tourists.

St Peter's Square

The awe-inspiring approach to St Peter's Basilica, this monumental **piazza** (p141) is a masterpiece of 17th-century urban design. The work of Bernini, it's centred on a towering Egyptian obelisk and flanked by two grasping colonnaded arms.

Piazza del Popolo

Neoclassical **Piazza del Popolo** (p112) is a vast, sweeping spectacle. In centuries past, executions were held here; nowadays crowds gather for political rallies, outdoor concerts or just to hang out.

Piazza del Campidoglio

The centrepiece of the Campidoglio (Capitoline Hill), this Michelangelo-designed **piazza** (p74) is thought by many to be the city's most beautiful. Surrounded on three sides by *palazzi,* it's home to the Capitoline Museums.

Campo de' Fiori

Home to one of Rome's historic markets and a boozy bar scene, **Campo de' Fiori** (p86) buzzes with activity day and night.

Piazza di Spagna

In Rome's swank shopping district, **Piazza di Spagna** (p108) has long attracted foreigners who come to walk down the iconic Spanish Steps (p108) to the Barcaccia fountain below.

Tridente, Trevi & the Quirinale

PIAZZA DEL POPOLO & AROUND | PIAZZA DI SPAGNA & AROUND | PIAZZA DI TREVI, QUIRINALE HILL & AROUND | PIAZZA BARBERINI & AROUND | PIAZZA DI TREVI, QUIRINALE & AROUND

Neighbourhood Top Five

❶ **Spanish Steps** (p108) Indulging in some people-watching and selfie-snapping while climbing this icon.

❷ **Basilica di Santa Maria del Popolo** (p109) Marvelling at Caravaggio's command of light and shade in his two masterworks adorning the basilica's Cerasi Chapel.

❸ **Villa Medici** (p113) Joining a guided tour of this Renaissance villa with its formal gardens, frescoed garden studio and wonderful views.

❹ **Palazzo Barberini** (p111) Admiring paintings by Raphael, Caravaggio, El Greco and their contemporaries, as well as a magnificent baroque ceiling fresco in a palace built for a pope.

❺ **Shopping** (p123) Browsing (or buying!) high and boutique fashion, artisanal perfume, silverware crafted by third-generation goldsmiths, and dozens of other desirable items on and around Via dei Condotti.

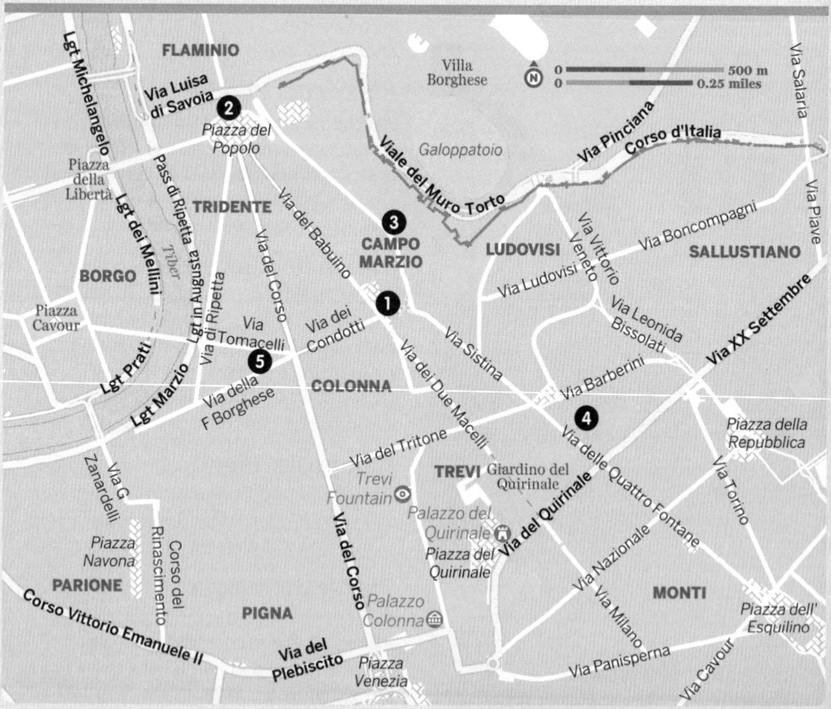

For more detail of this area see Map p332

Explore Tridente, Trevi & the Quirinale

Tridente is Rome's most glamorous district, full of designer boutiques, fashionable bars and swish hotels. It's worth devoting a full day to exploring it, as there are a number of sights to visit too. Start with a coffee standing at the bar in historic Antico Caffè Greco (p122), and then intersperse time at the Spanish Steps (p108), Piazza del Popolo (p112) and one or two of the lesser sights – Museo dell'Ara Pacis (p112), Casa di Goethe (p113), Keats-Shelley House (p113) – with some shopping and a leisurely lunch. Dinner options abound, too. The area is easily explored on foot – it's only a short walk from the Centro Storico or Piazza Venezia and is easily accessible from the Spagna and Flaminio metro stations.

Exploring the Quirinale and Trevi areas will take another day – maybe more. There are plenty of art galleries, churches, ancient sites and palaces to visit – we suggest prioritising the Trevi Fountain (p110), Palazzo Barberini (p111) and Chiesa di San Carlino alle Quattro Fontane (p114) and then slotting in other sights if time allows. Stay for dinner as there are plenty of tempting options to be found among the tourist-trap restaurants surrounding the Trevi Fountain. Busy during the day, these areas are sleepy after dark.

Local Life

- **Ambling** Wander along ivy-draped Via Margutta (p112), once home to film-maker Federico Fellini and now studded with art galleries and antique shops.
- **Boutique bargains** Ignore the ultra-expensive big-name boutiques on Via dei Condotti and instead shop on artisanal Via dell'Oca near the Piazza del Popolo.
- **Brunch** Join locals hovering over the tempting buffet spreads at Il Margutta (p116), Bistrot del Quirino (p119) and (on weekends only) Babette (p117).

Getting There & Away

- **Metro** The Trevi and Quirinale areas are closest to the Barberini metro stop, while Spagna and Flaminio stations are perfectly placed for Tridente. All three stops are on line A.
- **Bus** Numerous buses run down to Piazza Barberini; many stop at the southern end of Via del Corso and on Via del Tritone, ideal for a foray into Tridente.

Lonely Planet's Top Tip

Plan your itinerary in advance to accommodate differing opening hours: Gallerie Colonna is only open Saturday morning; book in advance to tour the Palazzo del Quirinale; Villa Medici and Palazzo Barberini are closed on Monday; and many local churches close over lunch so are best visited in the morning or late afternoon.

Best Places to Eat

- Colline Emiliane (p120)
- Hostaria Romana (p119)
- Il Margutta (p116)
- Fatamorgana Corso (p116)
- Il Chianti (p119)

For reviews, see p116.

Best Places to Drink

- Zuma Bar (p120)
- Stravinskij Bar (p120)
- Il Palazzetto (p122)
- Antico Caffè Greco (p122)
- Caffè Ciampini (p122)

For reviews, see p120.

Best Churches

- Basilica di Santa Maria del Popolo (p109)
- Chiesa di Sant'Andrea al Quirinale (p114)
- Chiesa di San Carlino alle Quattro Fontane (p114)
- Chiesa di Santa Maria della Vittoria (p116)

For reviews, see p112.

TOP EXPERIENCE

TAKE SNAPS AT THE SPANISH STEPS

Forming a picture-perfect backdrop to Piazza di Spagna, this statement sweep of stairs is one of the city's major icons and public meeting points. Though officially named the *Scalinata della Trinità dei Monti,* the stairs are popularly called the Spanish Steps.

Piazza di Spagna was named after the Spanish Embassy to the Holy See, but the staircase – 135 gleaming steps designed by the Italian Francesco de Sanctis – was built in 1725 with a legacy from the French. The dazzling stairs, which reopened in September 2016 after a €1.5 million clean-up funded by Italian jewellers' Bulgari, are crowned by the hilltop Chiesa della Trinità dei Monti (p113). To their south, the Keats-Shelley House (p113) is the last home of Romantic poet John Keats who died there in 1821.

At the foot of the steps, the fountain of a sinking boat, the 1627 **Barcaccia** (pictured above; Map p332), is believed to be by Pietro Bernini, father of the more famous Gian Lorenzo Bernini. It's fed from an aqueduct, the ancient Roman Aqua Virgo (also known as the Acqua Vergine), as are the fountains in Piazza del Popolo and the Trevi Fountain. Here there's not much pressure, so it's sunken as a clever piece of engineering. Bees and suns decorate the structure, symbols of the commissioning Barberini family.

To the southeast of the piazza, adjacent Piazza Mignanelli is dominated by the **Colonna dell'Immacolata**, built in 1857 to celebrate Pope Pius IX's declaration of the Immaculate Conception. On 8 December each year, the pope comes here to offer a bouquet of flowers to celebrate the Feast of the Conception.

TOP TIPS

- It's forbidden to sit, eat and drink on the staircase or wheel suitcases and prams up the steps. Doing so risks a fine of up to €400.
- A prime photo op is during the springtime festival Mostra delle Azalee, held late March/early April, when hundreds of vases of bright pink azaleas in bloom adorn the steps.

PRACTICALITIES

- Map p332, D4
- (M) Spagna

TOP EXPERIENCE

GAZE AT BASILICA DI SANTA MARIA DEL POPOLO

A magnificent repository of art, this is one of Rome's earliest and richest Renaissance churches, parts of which were designed by Bramante and Bernini. The lavish chapels, decorated by Caravaggio, Bernini, Caracci, Pinturicchio and others, were commissioned by local noble families.

History

The first chapel was built here in 1099 to exorcise the ghost of Nero, who was secretly buried in the tomb of the Domitii family on this spot. Its name reflected the fact that it was funded by the *popolo Romano* (people of Rome). The church's most important renovation came at the end of the 15th century when Bramante redid the choir, Raphael designed the Chigi Chapel and Pinturicchio added a series of frescoes. Also in the Bramante-designed apse are Rome's first stained-glass windows, crafted by Frenchman Guillaume de Marcillat in the early 16th century. The church's most famous works, by Caravaggio, were added in 1601, and Bernini further reworked the church in the 17th century.

Cerasi Chapel

The church's dazzling highlight is the Cappella Cerasi, to the left of the main altar, with its two facing works by Caravaggio: the *Conversion of St Paul* (1600-01; aka *The Conversion of Saul*) and the *Crucifixion of St Peter* (1601). The former is the second version, as the first was rejected by the patron. The latter is frighteningly realistic: the artist has used perspective to emphasise the weight of the cross, and St Peter's facial expression as he is upturned is heart-rendingly human. The central altarpiece painting is the *Assumption* (c 1660) by Annibale Carracci.

Chigi Chapel

Raphael designed this chapel on the left-hand side of the church (second from the entrance). It was dedicated to his patron, the enormously wealthy banker Agostino Chigi. Sadly, Raphael never lived to see it completed. Bernini finished the job for him more than 100 years later, contributing statues of Daniel and Habakkuk to the altarpiece, which was built by Sebastiano del Piombo. Only the floor mosaics were retained from Raphael's original design, including that of a kneeling skeleton, placed there to remind the living of the inevitable.

Della Rovere Chapel

The frescoes in the lunettes on this chapel on the right-hand side of the church depict the stories of St Jerome, to whom the chapel is dedicated. They and the *Adoration of the Christ Child* here were painted by Pinturicchio in the late 15th century, and glow with jewel-bright colours.

TOP TIPS

Come armed with a stash of €1 coins to illuminate the Caravaggio masterpieces – pop a coin in the slot and enjoy a couple of minutes admiring the paintings. You'll also need coins to listen to the information display in front of the Della Rovere Chapel.

PRACTICALITIES

- Map p332, A1
- 392 3612243
- www.smariadelpopolo.com
- Piazza del Popolo 12
- 7am-noon & 4-7pm Mon-Sat, 8am-1.30pm & 4.30-7.30pm Sun
- Flaminio

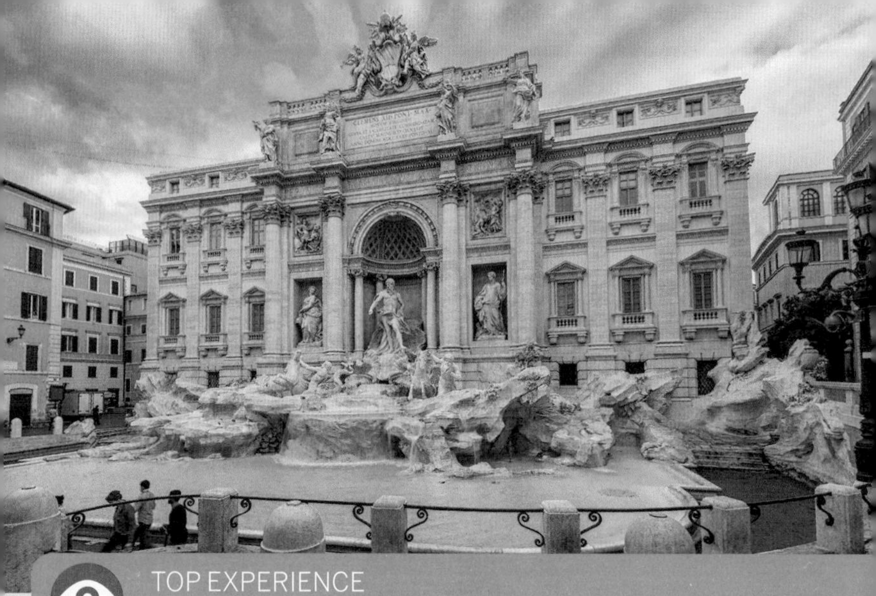

CATARINA BELOVA / SHUTTERSTOCK ©

TOP EXPERIENCE

TOSS A COIN INTO THE TREVI FOUNTAIN

Rome's most famous fountain, the iconic Fontana di Trevi, is a baroque extravaganza – a foaming white-marble and emerald-water masterpiece filling an entire piazza. The flamboyant ensemble, 20m wide and 26m high, was designed by Nicola Salvi in 1732 and depicts the chariot of the sea-god Oceanus being led by Tritons accompanied by seahorses that represent the moods of the sea.

The fountain's water comes from the Aqua Virgo, a 2000-year-old aqueduct that brings water from the Salone springs around 19km away. The *tre vie* (three roads) that converge at the fountain give it its name.

To the eastern side of the fountain is a large round stone urn. The story goes that during the fountain's construction, Salvi was harassed by a barber, who had a nearby shop and was critical of the work in progress. Thus the sculptor added the urn in order to block the irritating critic.

The famous tradition (inaugurated in the 1954 film *Three Coins in the Fountain*) is to toss a coin into the fountain, thus ensuring your return to Rome. An estimated €3000 is thrown into the Trevi each day. This money is collected daily and goes to the Catholic charity Caritas, with its yield increasing significantly since the crackdown on people extracting the money for themselves.

Most famously, Trevi Fountain is where movie star Anita Ekberg cavorted in Federico Fellini's classic *La Dolce Vita* (1960); apparently she wore waders under her iconic black dress but still shivered during the winter shoot.

More recently in 2016, fashion house Fendi staged a show at the fountain following its €2.18 million sponsorship of the fountain's restoration.

TOP TIPS

- Coin-tossing etiquette: throw with your right hand, over your left shoulder with your back to the fountain.
- Paddling or bathing is strictly forbidden, as is eating and drinking on the steps. Both crimes risk an on-the-spot fine of up to €500.
- Visit in the evening when the fountain's beautifully lit.

PRACTICALITIES

- Fontana di Trevi
- Map p332, D6
- Piazza di Trevi
- Ⓜ Barberini

TOP EXPERIENCE
SEE THE MASTERS AT PALAZZO BARBERINI

Home to an eclectic and magnificent collection of art that includes masterpieces by Raphael, Caravaggio, Giovanni Bellini and Filippo Lippi, this museum is housed in a baroque palace. The architecturally notable features include the monumental staircases and an extraordinary reception room frescoed by Pietro da Cortona.

The Palace
The palace was commissioned by Florentine-born Maffeo Barberini (1568–1644), who was elected pope in 1623 and took the name of Urban VIII. It was designed by three of the most important architects of the 1600s: Carlo Maderno, Gian Lorenzo Bernini and Francesco Borromini. Its distinctive elements include two staircases: a square-shafted staircase designed by Bernini and an extraordinary oval helicoidal one by Borromini. Barberini family members lived in the palazzo until 1955.

Ground Floor
Start in Rooms 1 to 6, which showcase ancient icons and early Renaissance paintings from Tuscany, Umbria and the Marche. The standout work, in Room 3, is Filippo Lippi's luminous *Annunciazione* (Annunciation; 1440–45), portraying the Virgin learning of her divine motherhood; a *hortus conclusus* (uncontaminated garden) in the background symbolises her virginity. Over the corridor, Rooms 7 to 9 hold works from Lombardy, Emilia Romagna and the Veneto as well as the *Sala delle Colonne* (Hall of the Columns) decorated by Pietro da Cortona.

1st Floor
The 1st floor showcases art from the 15th and 16th centuries. Room 10 contains works by Piero di Cosimo and Andrea del Sarto, while Room 12 is home to one of the museum's most famous works, Raphael's *La Fornarina* (The Baker's Girl), painted c 1520 and believed to be a portrait of his mistress Margherita Luti, the daughter of a baker in Trastevere. Also on this floor are major works by El Greco, Perugino, Bronzino and Guido Reni – the latter's *Portrait of Beatrice Cenci* (1599) takes as its subject a young girl convicted of patricide and beheaded in 1599. Public sentiment was on Beatrice's side – her father was known to have abused her – but she was executed regardless. Caravaggio – whose *San Francesco d'Assisi in meditazione* (St Francis in Meditation; 1606), *Narciso* (Narcissus; 1597–98) and *Giuditta e Oloferne (Judith Beheading Holophernes;* c 1598–99) are also on this floor – was said to have been a witness to Beatrice's execution.

Salone Pietro da Cortona
One of the gallery's major draws is this huge reception room, home to Pietro da Cortona's frescoed ceiling *The Triumph of Divine Providence and the Fulfilment of its Purposes under Pope Urban VIII.* Painted by the Umbrian-born artist and his pupils between 1632 and 1639, it celebrates the spiritual and political power of the Barberini family.

TOP TIPS
- Your ticket also allows entrance to the Galleria Corsini (p176) in Trastevere, another masterpiece-rich art museum, and is valid for 10 days from purchase.

PRACTICALITIES
- Galleria Nazionale d'Arte Antica
- Map p332, F5
- ☎06 481 45 91
- www.barberinicorsini.org
- Via delle Quattro Fontane 13
- adult/reduced €12/6
- 8.30am-6pm Tue-Sun
- Ⓜ Barberini

SIGHTS

There are some big-hitting sights in this part of town: the Spanish Steps, the Trevi Fountain, the Basilica di Santa Maria del Popolo and the Palazzo Barberini, to name only a few. And when the crowds at these get too much – and crowds are a given, especially at the Spanish Steps and Trevi Fountain – there are a handful of lesser-known, more intimate villas, churches and monuments where you can find peace surrounded by magnificent art and architecture.

Piazza del Popolo & Around

BASILICA DI SANTA MARIA DEL POPOLO — BASILICA

See p109.

VIA MARGUTTA — STREET

Map p332 (MSpagna) Small antique shops, commercial art galleries and artisanal boutiques are arrayed along Via Margutta, one of Rome's prettiest pedestrian cobbled lanes. Strung with ivy-laced *palazzi,* the street is named after a 16th-century family of barbers but has long been associated with art and artists: Picasso worked at a gallery at No 54 and the Italian Futurists had their first meeting here in 1917.

MUSEO DELL'ARA PACIS — MUSEUM

Map p332 (☎06 06 08; www.arapacis.it; Lungotevere in Augusta; adult/reduced €10.50/8.50; ⏲9.30am-6.30pm; MFlaminio) The first modern construction in Rome's historic centre since WWII, Richard Meier's glass-and-marble pavilion houses the remnants of the *Ara Pacis Augustae* (Altar of Peace), Augustus' great monument to peace. One of the most important works of ancient Roman sculpture, the vast marble altar –

TOP EXPERIENCE
PIAZZA DEL POPOLO

Laid out in 1538 as a grand entrance for what was then Rome's main northern gateway, this huge piazza connects the city with Via Flaminia and the north. The piazza has been remodelled multiple times, most significantly in 1823 by Giuseppe Valadier, who created the huge busker-filled ellipse we see today. It was the site of public executions until 1826.

The 36m-high **obelisk** (Map p332) in its centre was brought by Augustus from Heliopolis, in ancient Egypt, and originally stood in Circo Massimo. To the east lies a viewpoint of the **Pincio Hill Gardens** (Map p348). This is not one of Rome's original seven hills, as it lay outside the original city boundary; it was included within the city from the 3rd century.

Guarding the piazza's southern end are Carlo Rainaldi's twin 17th-century baroque churches, **Chiesa di Santa Maria dei Miracoli** (Map p332; ☎06 361 02 50; Via del Corso 528; ⏲7.30am-12.30pm & 4.30-7.30pm) and **Basilica di Santa Maria in Montesanto** (Chiesa degli Artisti; Map p332; www.chiesadegliartisti.it; Via del Babuino 198; ⏲10am-noon & 5-8pm Mon-Fri, 10am-noon Sat, 11am-1.30pm Sun). Over on the northern flank is the magnificent art-rich **Basilica di Santa Maria del Popolo** (p109) and the **Porta del Popolo** (Map p332; People's Gate), created by Bernini to celebrate Queen Christina of Sweden's defection to Catholicism and subsequent arrival in Rome.

TOP TIPS

- The stiff climb up to the Pincio Hill Gardens rewards with lovely views over to St Peter's and Gianicolo Hill.
- Visit at the end of the day when sunset casts a golden glow over the square – best savoured over an *aperitivo* on one of the piazza's cafe terraces.

PRACTICALITIES

- Map p332, A1
- MFlaminio

measuring 11.6m by 10.6m by 3.6m – was completed in 13 BCE and was put on show in this purpose-built pavilion in 2006. The entrance ticket is overpriced considering how little there is to see.

CASA DI GOETHE MUSEUM

Map p332 (☎06 3265 0412; www.casadigoethe.it; 1st fl, Via del Corso 18; adult/reduced €5/3; ⏰10am-6pm Tue-Sun; Ⓜ Flaminio) Once a gathering place for German intellectuals, the Via del Corso apartment is where writer Johann Wolfgang von Goethe enjoyed a happy Italian sojourn (despite complaining of the noisy neighbours) from 1786 to 1788. Today it's now a lovingly maintained small museum. Exhibits include fascinating Piranesi engravings of 18th-century Rome, as well as Goethe's sketches and letters, plus some lovely sketches of him by his friend Tischbein. With advance permission, ardent fans can use the library full of first editions.

⊙ Piazza di Spagna & Around

PIAZZA DI SPAGNA & THE SPANISH STEPS PIAZZA

See p108.

CHIESA DELLA TRINITÀ DEI MONTI CHURCH

Map p332 (☎06 679 41 79; http://trinitadeimonti.net/it/chiesa/; Piazza Trinità dei Monti 3; ⏰10.15am-8pm Tue-Thu, noon-9pm Fri, 9.15am-8pm Sat, 9am-8pm Sun; Ⓜ Spagna) Sitting in majesty above the Spanish Steps (p108), this landmark church was commissioned by King Louis XII of France and consecrated in 1585. Apart from the great views over Rome offered from its front staircase, it is notable for impressive frescoes by Daniele da Volterra. His *Deposizione* (Deposition), in the second chapel on the left, is regarded as a masterpiece of mannerist painting.

VILLA MEDICI PALACE

Map p332 (☎06 676 13 11; www.villamedici.it; Viale Trinità dei Monti 1; guided tour adult/reduced €12/6; ⏰10am-7pm Tue-Sun; Ⓜ Spagna) Built for Cardinal Ricci da Montepulciano in 1540, this sumptuous Renaissance palace was purchased by Ferdinando de' Medici in 1576 and remained in Medici hands until 1801, when Napoleon acquired it for the French Academy. Guided tours (1½ hours) in multiple languages take in the sculpture-filled gardens and orchard, a garden studio exquisitely frescoed by Jacopo Zucchi in 1577 and the cardinal's private apartments. Note the pieces of ancient Roman sculpture from the Ara Pacis embedded in the villa's walls.

KEATS-SHELLEY HOUSE MUSEUM

Map p332 (☎06 678 42 35; www.keats-shelley-house.org; Piazza di Spagna 26; adult/reduced €5/4; ⏰10am-1pm & 2-6pm Mon-Sat; Ⓜ Spagna) Poet John Keats died of tuberculosis aged only 25 in this house in 1821. Keats had come to Rome in 1820 hoping to improve his health in the Italian climate, and rented two rooms on the 3rd floor of this building next to the Spanish Steps with painter companion Joseph Severn (1793–1879). The bookshelf-lined rooms, practically unchanged since 1909 when the museum was dedicated, evoke the impoverished lives of Keats and Severn, and house displays about the Romantic poets.

VIA DEI CONDOTTI AREA

Map p332 (Ⓜ Spagna) High-rolling shoppers and window-dreamers take note: this is Rome's smartest shopping strip. At the eastern end, near Piazza di Spagna, Antica Caffè Greco (p122) was a favourite meeting point of 18th- and 19th-century writers. Other top shopping streets in the area include Via Frattina, Via della Croce, Via delle Carrozze and Via del Babuino.

⊙ Piazza di Trevi, Quirinale Hill & Around

TREVI FOUNTAIN FOUNTAIN

See p110.

PIAZZA DEL QUIRINALE PIAZZA

Map p332 (🚌Via Nazionale, Ⓜ Repubblica) A wonderful spot to enjoy a glowing Roman sunset, this piazza, which is dominated by the imposing presidential palace of Palazzo del Quirinale (p114), marks the summit of Quirinal Hill. The central obelisk was moved here from the **Mausoleo di Augusto** (Map p332; www.mausoleodiaugusto.it; Piazza Augusto Imperatore; 🚌Piazza Augusto Imperatore) in 1786 and is flanked by 5.5m statues of Castor and Pollux reining in a couple of rearing horses. Catch the weekly changing of the guards on Sunday at 6pm in summer, and 4pm the rest of the year.

TOP EXPERIENCE
PALAZZO DEL QUIRINALE

This huge palace sitting atop one of the seven hills of Rome, the Quirinale Hill, was formerly the papal summer residence. After hosting the popes for nearly three centuries, its keys were begrudgingly handed over to Italy's new king in 1870. Since 1948 it has been home of the Presidente della Repubblica, Italy's head of state.

Pope Gregory XIII (r 1572–85) originally chose the site, and over the next century and a half it was worked on by the top architects of the day, including Francesco Borromini, Gian Lorenzo Bernini, Domenico Fontana and Carlo Maderno.

There are shorter guided tours on offer – these visit the reception rooms, while a longer tour also includes the gardens and the carriages; all are in Italian. Catch the weekly changing of the guards outside the palace on Sunday at 6pm in summer, and 4pm the rest of the year.

On the other side of the piazza, the palace's former stables, the **Scuderie al Quirinale** (Map p332; ☎06 8110 02 56; www.scuderiequirinale.it; Via XXIV Maggio 16; adult/reduced €15/13; ⏲10am-8pm Sun-Thu, to 9.30pm Fri & Sat), is now a magnificent space that hosts art exhibitions; recent shows have included exhibits by Matisse and Frida Kahlo.

TOP TIPS

- Visits are by guided tour only. Book at least five days ahead by phone or online at www.coopculture.it.
- Tours (only in Italian) use the tradesmen's entrance on Via del Quirinale; arrive 15 minutes before your allotted time and bring your passport or ID card.

PRACTICALITIES

- Map p332, E7
- www.quirinale.it
- Piazza del Quirinale
- ⏲9.30am-4pm Tue, Wed & Fri-Sun, closed Aug
- 🚌Via Nazionale, Ⓜ Repubblica

CHIESA DI SANT'ANDREA AL QUIRINALE — CHURCH

Map p332 (☎06 481 93 99; https://santandrea.gesuiti.it; Via del Quirinale 29; ⏲9am-noon & 3-6pm Tue-Sun; Ⓜ Repubblica) It's said that in his old age Bernini liked to come and enjoy the peace of this late-17th-century church, regarded by many as one of his greatest. Faced with severe space limitations, he managed to produce a sense of grandeur by designing an elliptical floor plan with a series of chapels opening onto the central area. Look for the cherubim looking down on worshippers from the lantern and altar.

CHIESA DI SAN CARLINO ALLE QUATTRO FONTANE — CHURCH

Map p332 (☎06 488 32 61; Via del Quirinale 23; cloister €1; ⏲10am-1pm Mon-Sat, from noon Sun; Ⓜ Repubblica) A masterpiece of Roman baroque, this tiny building was the first church designed by Francesco Borromini. His clever design – which includes a play of convex and concave surfaces and a dome illuminated by hidden windows – cleverly transforms the small space into a place of light and beauty. Completed in 1641, it stands at the intersection known as the Quattro Fontane, named after the late-16th-century fountains on its four corners, representing Fidelity, Strength and the rivers Arno and Tiber.

LE DOMUS ROMANE DI PALAZZO VALENTINI — ARCHAEOLOGICAL SITE

Map p332 (☎06 2276 1280; www.palazzovalentini.it; Via Foro Traiano 85; adult/reduced €12/8; ⏲9.30am-6.30pm Wed-Mon; 👪; Ⓜ Barberini) Underneath a grand mansion that's been the seat of the Province of Rome since 1873 lie the archaeological remains of several lavish ancient Roman houses; the excavated fragments have been turned into a fascinating multimedia 'experience'. Tours are held every 30 minutes, but rotate between Italian, English, French, German and Spanish. Book ahead online or by phone (advance booking fee €1.50), especially during holiday periods.

BASILICA DEI SANTI APOSTOLI CHURCH

Map p332 (Piazza dei Santissimi Apostoli; ⌚7am-noon & 4-7pm; Ⓜ Repubblica) This much-altered 6th-century church is dedicated to the apostles James and Philip, whose relics are in the crypt. Its most obvious attraction is the portico, which has Renaissance arches, and the two-tier facade topped by 13 towering figures. Inside, the flashy baroque interior was completed in 1714 by Carlo and Francesco Fontana. Highlights include the ceiling frescoes by Baciccia and Antonio Canova's grandiose tomb of Pope Clement XIV.

Piazza Barberini & Around

PIAZZA BARBERINI PIAZZA

Map p332 (Ⓜ Barberini) More a traffic thoroughfare than a place to linger, this noisy square is named after the Barberini family, one of Rome's great dynastic clans. It's home to two Bernini-designed fountains, the **Fontana del Tritone** (Fountain of the Triton) in the centre and the **Fontana delle Api** (Fountain of the Bees) in square's northeastern corner.

CONVENTO DEI CAPPUCCINI MUSEUM

Map p332 (☎06 8880 3695; www.cappucciniviaveneto.it; Via Vittorio Veneto 27; adult/reduced €8.50/5; ⌚9am-6.30pm; Ⓜ Barberini) This church and convent complex safeguards what is possibly Rome's strangest sight: crypt chapels where everything from the picture frames to the light fittings is made of human bones. Between 1732 and 1775 resident Capuchin monks used the bones of 3700 of their departed brothers to create this macabre *memento mori* (reminder of death) – a 30m-long passageway ensnaring six crypts, each named after the type of bone used to decorate (skulls, shin bones, pelvises etc).

There's an arch crafted from hundreds of skulls, vertebrae used as fleurs-de-lis, and light fixtures made of femurs. The accompanying multimedia museum tells the story of the Capuchin order of monks and is home to a work attributed to Caravaggio: *St Francis in Meditation* (c 1603). Don't miss the adjoining **Chiesa dei Cappuccini** (1626), accessible via the outside staircase. Hiring an audio tour (in Italian, English or Spanish) costs €5.

TOP EXPERIENCE PALAZZO COLONNA

Home to the patrician Colonna family, this is the largest private palace in Rome and now functions as both a residence and house museum. On Saturdays, it offers excellent guided tours introducing visitors to the family's art collection, reception salons and formal garden. During the tours, guides convey anecdotes about family members including Marcantonio II, a hero of the 1571 Battle of Lepanto.

The purpose-built gallery, constructed in the 17th century, has six rooms crowned by fantastical ceiling frescoes dedicated to Marcantonio. It is also home to major paintings including Carracci's *Mangiafagioli* (The Bean Eater; 1580–90) and Bronzino's *Venus, Cupid and a Satyr* (1554). The gallery's **Great Hall** was used as a set in the 1953 film *Roman Holiday*, directed by William Wyler. Look for the cannonball that became lodged in the gallery's marble stairs during the 1849 siege of Rome.

Combination tickets allow visitors to take in both the garden and the 'Princess Isabelle Apartment', a wing of the palace named after Beirut-born Isabelle Colonna, née Sursock, who married into the family.

TOP TIPS

- The gallery is only open Saturday morning.
- Guided tours in English, included in the ticket price, depart every Saturday at noon.

PRACTICALITIES

- Map p332, D8
- ☎06 678 43 50
- www.galleriacolonna.it
- Via della Pilotta 17
- adult/reduced €12/10
- ⌚9am-1.15pm Sat, closed Aug
- Ⓜ Colosseo

CHIESA DI SANTA MARIA DELLA VITTORIA CHURCH

Map p344 (☎06 4274 0571; www.chiesasantamariavittoriaroma.it; Via XX Settembre 17; ⏰7am-noon & 3.30-7.15pm; Ⓜ Repubblica) Designed by Carlo Maderno, this modest church is an unlikely setting for an extraordinary work of art – Bernini's extravagant and sexually charged *Santa Teresa trafitta dall'amore di Dio* (Ecstasy of St Teresa). This daring sculpture depicts Teresa, engulfed in the folds of a flowing cloak, floating in ecstasy on a cloud while a teasing angel pierces her repeatedly with a golden arrow. It's in the fourth chapel on the north side.

GAGOSIAN GALLERY GALLERY

Map p332 (☎06 420 86 498; www.gagosian.com; Via Francesco Crispi 16; ⏰10.30am-7pm Tue-Sat; Ⓜ Barberini) FREE The Rome branch of Larry Gagosian's contemporary art empire has hosted the big names of contemporary art since it opened in 2007: Cy Twombly, Damien Hirst and Lawrence Weiner, to name only a few. The gallery is housed in an artfully converted 1920s bank, and was designed by Roman architect Firouz Galdo and Englishman Caruso St John.

EATING

Classy eateries are sandwiched between fashion boutiques in this designer district, with kitchens covering the whole gamut of Roman cooking styles. In the Quirinale and Trevi Fountain area, take care selecting where to eat: avoid tourist restaurants with English menus, waiters touting for business on the street outside or (worst of all) plastic plates of food showcased on a table on the street out the front. But gems still sparkle among the stones, with some notable restaurants around the presidential palace and parliament – Italian politicians are a discerning bunch when it comes to dining out.

Piazza del Popolo & Around

FATAMORGANA CORSO GELATO €

Map p332 (☎06 3265 22 38; www.gelateriafatamorgana.com; Via Laurina 10; cups & cones €2.50-5; ⏰noon-11pm; Ⓜ Flaminio) The wonderful all-natural, gluten-free gelato served at Fatamorgana is arguably Rome's best artisanal ice cream. Innovative and classic ambrosial flavours abound, all made from the finest seasonal ingredients. There are several branches around town.

GELATERIA DEI GRACCHI GELATO €

Map p332 (☎06 322 47 27; www.gelateriadeigracchi.it; Via di Ripetta 261; cones & tubs €2.50-5.50; ⏰noon-10pm Tue-Sun; Ⓜ Flaminio) This outpost of the venerable Gelataria dei Gracchi, by the Vatican, is known for its superb ice cream made from the best ingredients. Flavours are classic. Located between Piazza del Popolo and the Spanish Steps, it stays open until midnight in summer from Thursday to Sunday.

★**IL MARGUTTA** VEGETARIAN €€

Map p332 (☎06 3265 0577; www.ilmargutta.bio; Via Margutta 118; lunch buffet weekdays/weekends €15/25, meals €35; ⏰8.30am-11.30pm; 🌶; Ⓜ Spagna) This chic art-gallery-bar-restaurant is packed at lunchtime with Romans feasting on its good-value, all-you-can-eat buffet deal. Everything on its menu is organic, and the evening menu is particularly creative – vegetables and pulses combined and presented with care and flair. Among the various tasting menus is a vegan option.

LA BUCA DI RIPETTA ITALIAN €€

Map p332 (☎06 321 93 91; www.labucadiripetta.com/roma; Via di Ripetta 36; meals €45; ⏰noon-3.30pm & 7-11pm; Ⓜ Flaminio) Popular with locals, who know a good thing when they taste it, this trattoria serves traditional dishes with a refreshingly refined execution – there's nothing stodgy or overly rich on the menu here. Together, the food, attractive surrounds and friendly service make for an extremely satisfying dining experience.

AL GRAN SASSO TRATTORIA €€

Map p332 (☎06 321 48 83; www.algransasso.com; Via di Ripetta 32; meals €35; ⏰noon-3.30pm & 7-11pm Sun-Fri Sep-Jul; ❄📶; Ⓜ Flaminio) A top lunchtime spot, this is a classic, dyed-in-the-wool trattoria specialising in old-school country cooking. It's a relaxed place offering a welcoming vibe and tasty, value-for-money meat and fish dishes. The fried dishes are excellent, as are the daily specials, chalked up on the board outside. Cash only.

LOCAL KNOWLEDGE

FLEE THE CROWDS: HIDDEN CURIOSITIES

When the camera-wielding Trevi Fountain crowd gets too much, nip up the church steps and into **Chiesa di Santi Vincenzo e Anastasio** (Map p332; www.santivincenzo eanastasio.it; Vicolo dei Modelli 72; ⏲9am-1pm & 4-8pm; Ⓜ Barberini). Originally known as the 'papal church' due to its proximity to the papal residence on Quirinal Hill, this 17th-century church overlooking Rome's most spectacular fountain safeguards the hearts and internal organs of dozens of popes – preserved in amphorae in a tiny gated chapel to the right of the apse. This practice began under Pope Sixtus V (r 1585–90) and continued until the 20th century when Pope Pius X (r 1903–1914) decided it was not for him.

To admire another hidden treasure *senza* crowds, meander west from Trevi Fountain, along pedestrian Via delle Muratte, and duck a block south to **Galleria Sciarra** (Map p332; Via Marco Minghetti 9-10; Ⓜ Barberini), a stunning interior courtyard with an art nouveau glass roof and vibrant frescoes depicting the late-19th-century aristocratic Roman woman in all her feminine guises: as wife, mother, musician and so on. Hidden away inside 16th-century Palazzo Sciarra Colonna di Carbognano, the frescoes and unusual glass roof date from 1890 when the courtyard was remodelled and spruced up by the wealthy Sciarra family. Spot the single man in the frescoes: late Romantic writer Gabriele d'Annunzio.

EDY RISTORANTE TRATTORIA €€

Map p332 (☎06 3600 1738; www.ristoranteedy.it; Vicolo del Babuino 4; meals €42; ⏲noon-3pm & 6.30-11pm Mon-Sat; Ⓜ Spagna) The high-ceilinged interior of this classy neighbourhood restaurant is peppered with paintings, and is very atmospheric. Despite the tourist-central location, it caters to mainly Italian clientele; the food is excellent. In nice weather there are a few tables outside on the cobbled street.

BABETTE ITALIAN €€€

Map p332 (☎06 3211559; www.babetteristorante.it; Via Margutta 1d-3; meals €55; ⏲9am-midnight Tue-Sun; 🖉; Ⓜ Spagna) This charming bistro is run by two sisters who formerly produced a fashion magazine, hence the chic interior. The kitchen turns out Italian dishes with a contemporary twist: risotto may be presented in crisp pan-fried blocks, soups can be laced with coconut milk and fresh herbs are used to excellent effect. Be sure to order the homemade bread basket.

Romans flock here at weekends for Babette's good-value lunch buffet (€28; 1pm to 3pm), which includes water, bread, dessert and coffee. Breakfast (dishes €3 to €15) is popular, too.

DAL BOLOGNESE ITALIAN €€€

Map p332 (☎06 322 27 99; www.dalbolognese.it; Piazza del Popolo 1; meals €80; ⏲12.45-3pm & 8.15-11pm Tue-Sun, closed Aug; Ⓜ Flaminio) Moneyed Romans mingle with models and celebs at this historically chic restaurant. Dine inside, surrounded by wood panelling and exotic flowers, or outside, people-watching with views over Piazza del Popolo (p112). As the name suggests, Emilia-Romagna dishes are the name of the game; everything is good, but try the tortellini in soup, *tagliatelle* with *ragú*, or the damn fine fillet steak.

OSTERIA MARGUTTA OSTERIA €€€

Map p332 (☎06 323 10 25; www.osteriamargutta.it; Via Margutta 82; meals €55; ⏲12.30-3pm & 7.30-11pm Tue-Sat, 12.30-3pm Sun; Ⓜ Spagna) This vintage *osteria* (tavern), around since 1965, oozes theatre: a rich interior mixes blue glass with rich reds and fringed lampshades, while the flower- and ivy-strewn street terrace is one of summertime's prettiest. Plaques on the chairs testify to the famous thespians who've dined on its classic regional dishes here. Top wine list and occasional live jazz too.

✕ Piazza di Spagna & Around

POMPI DESSERTS €

Map p332 (☎06 6994 17 52; www.barpompi.it; Via della Croce 82; tiramisu €4; ⏲11am-9.30pm Mon-Thu, to 10.30pm Fri-Sun; Ⓜ Spagna) Now a chain operation, Rome's most famous vendor of tiramisu (which literally means 'pick me up') sells takeaway cartons of the deliciously rich yet light-as-air dessert. As well as classic, flavours include strawberry, pistachio and banana-chocolate. Eat on the spot (standing) or buy frozen portions that will keep for a few hours until you're ready to tuck in at home.

VENCHI GELATO €

Map p332 (☎06 6979 7790; www.venchi.com; Via della Croce 25-26; cones from €3.50; ⏲10.30am-11pm Sun-Thu, to midnight Fri & Sat; Ⓜ Spagna) A wall in this gorgeous boutique features a cascade of shiny dark chocolate – 350kg in all, mixed with a spot of olive oil. Shop here for chocolates and gelato, crafted with pride by the Turin chocolate house since 1878. The chocolate gelato, served in a dipped cone and topped with whipped cream and/or hazelnuts if you choose, is predictably divine.

PASTIFICIO GUERRA FAST FOOD €

Map p332 (☎06 679 31 02; Via della Croce 8; pastas €4; ⏲1-9.30pm; Ⓜ Spagna) A brilliant budget find, this old-fashioned pasta shop (1918) serves up two choices of pasta from its kitchen hatch. It's fast food, Italian style – freshly cooked (if you time it right) pasta, with a glass of water included. Grab a space to stand and eat between shelves packed with packets of dry pasta or take it away.

VYTA ENOTECA REGIONALE DEL LAZIO ITALIAN €€

Map p332 (☎06 8771 60 18; www.vytaenoteca lazio.it/en; Via Frattina 94; cicchetti from €3, platters €15, restaurant meals €55; ⏲9am-11pm Sun-Thu, to midnight Fri & Sat; Ⓜ Spagna) Showcasing food and wine of the Lazio region, this mega-stylish address owes its design to fashionable Roman architect Daniela Colli and its contemporary menu to chef Dino De Bellis. The burnished copper bar is a perfect perch for enjoying *panini*, *cicheti* (snacks) and *taglieri* (cheese and meat plates) – it also offers a tempting *aperitivo* spread. Upstairs, a glam restaurant awaits.

FIASCHETTERIA BELTRAMME TRATTORIA €€

Map p332 (☎06 6979 7200; Via della Croce 39; meals €45; ⏲11.15-3pm & 7.30-11.30pm; Ⓜ Spagna) This 19th-century *fiaschetteria* (meaning 'wine seller') is a stuck-in-time place with a short menu and a long list of local devotees. At lunch, regulars dig into huge serves of traditional Roman pastas (carbonara, *cacio e pepe*) and simple mains from recipes unchanged since the 1930s. At night, most tables are claimed by tourists and the vibe isn't quite as *autentico*.

In the evening, you may end up dining at a communal table.

BABINGTON'S TEA ROOMS CAFE €€

Map p332 (☎06 678 60 27; www.babingtons.com; Piazza di Spagna 23; tea menus €17-33; ⏲10am-9.15pm; Ⓜ Spagna) Founded in 1893 by two English women, these tea rooms were an instant hit with the hordes of English tourists in Rome desperate for a decent cup of tea. Little has changed in the ensuing century and Babington's properly made pots of tea (China, India, Ceylon and herbal), cream teas and dainty finger sandwiches remain its unique selling point.

The high-tea menus are pricey, but it's perfectly acceptable to order one along with an extra cup of tea and share between two people.

IMÀGO ITALIAN €€€

Map p332 (☎06 6993 4726; www.imagorestaurant.com; Piazza della Trinità dei Monti 6, Roma Hassler; tasting menus €130-170; ⏲7-10.30pm Feb-Dec; ✎; Ⓜ Spagna) Even in a city of great views, the panoramas from the Michelin-starred romantic rooftop restaurant at Roma Hassler (p245) are special, extending over a sea of roofs to the great dome of St Peter's Basilica; request the corner table. Complementing the views are the bold, modern Italian creations.

NINO TUSCAN €€€

Map p332 (☎06 679 56 76; www.ristorantenino.it; Via Borgognona 11; meals €60; ⏲12.30-3pm & 7.30-11pm Mon-Sat; Ⓜ Spagna) With a look that has endured since this restaurant opened in 1934 (wrought-iron chandeliers, polished dark wood and white tablecloths), Nino is enduringly popular with well-heeled locals. Waiters can be brusque if you're not on the A-list, but the food is quality Tuscan fare, including memorable bean soup and steaks.

Piazza di Trevi, Quirinale Hill & Around

★PICCOLO ARANCIO TRATTORIA €€

Map p332 (☎06 678 61 39; www.piccoloarancio.it; Vicolo Scanderbeg 112; meals €38; ⏲noon-3pm & 7pm-midnight Tue-Sun; Ⓜ Barberini) In a 'hood riddled with tourist traps, this backstreet eatery – tucked inside a little house next to grandiose Palazzo Scanderberg – stands out. The kitchen mixes Roman classics with more contemporary options and, unusually, includes a hefty number of seafood choices – the *linguini alla pescatora* (handmade pasta with shellfish and baby tomatoes) is sensational. Bookings essential.

Tables spill onto the quaint cobbled street in summer. Service can be abrupt but the food is so good that we tend to overlook this.

IL CHIANTI TUSCAN €€

Map p332 (☎06 679 24 70; www.vineriailchianti.com; Via del Lavatore 81-82a; pizzas €8-12, taglieri €14, meals €50; ⏲noon-11.30pm; ⓂBarberini) The name says it all: this pretty ivy-clad place specialises in Tuscan-style wine and food. Cosy up inside its bottle-lined interior or grab a table on the lovely street terrace and dig into Tuscan favourites including crostini (toasts with toppings), *taglieri* (platters of cheese and cured meats), hearty soups, handmade pasta and Florence's iconic T-bone steak. Selected pizzas are available, too.

BISTROT DEL QUIRINO ITALIAN €€

Map p332 (☎06 9887 8090; www.bistrotquirino.com; Via delle Vergini 7; weekday/weekend brunch €10/15, à la carte €30; ⏲noon-3.30pm & 4pm-2am; 🚌Via del Corso) For unbeatable value near Trevi Fountain (p110), reserve a table at this arty bistro adjoining **Teatro Quirino** (☎box office 06 679 45 85; www.teatroquirino.it; tickets €13-34). Theatre posters add bags of colour to the spacious interior, where a banquet of a 'brunch' buffet – salads, antipasti, and hot and cold dishes – is laid out for in-the-know Romans to feast on.

From 4pm, the bistro morphs into a cafe – until 6.30pm when the *aperitivo* session kicks in.

NANÀ VINI E CUCINA TRATTORIA €€

Map p332 (☎06 6919 0750; www.nanaviniecucina.it; Via della Panettaria 37; meals €45; ⏲12.30-3pm & 7-11pm Tue-Sun; ⓂBarberini) Nanà's menu harks from Italy's south, with loads of fish and seafood choices; try the *polpo rosticciato con crema di patate* (roasted octopus with potato cream) or the *scialatielli ai frutti di mare* (homemade pasta with clams, mussels and cherry tomato). Sit inside and watch the chefs work in the open kitchen, or claim a table in the piazzetta.

LE TAMERICI SEAFOOD €€€

Map p332 (☎06 6920 0700; www.letamerici.com; Vicolo Scavolino 79; meals €60; ⏲12.30-3pm Mon-Fri, 7-11pm Mon-Sat, closed Aug; ⓂBarberini) Exceptional seafood and top-notch wine are a winning epicurean combo at this elegant escape from the Trevi Fountain hubbub. Hidden down an alleyway, it impresses with its wine list, range of *digestivi* and light-as-air homemade pasta dishes – served in two intimate rooms with bleached-wood beamed ceilings. Consider ordering one of the tasting menus (€60 to €90) with matching wines (€20).

AL MORO ITALIAN €€€

Map p332 (☎06 678 34 96; www.ristorantealmororoma.com; Vicolo delle Bollette 13; meals €65; ⏲12.30-3.30pm & 7.30-11.30pm Mon-Sat; ⓂBarberini) A pair of potted olive trees marks the entrance to this one-time Fellini haunt, a step back in time with its picture-gallery dining rooms, Liberty wall lamps, cantankerous buttoned-up waiters and old-money regulars. You'll dine on a daily menu including classics such as *trippa alla romana* (tripe with tomato and pecorino) and *scaloppina di vitella con i carciofi* (veal escalopes with artichokes).

Piazza Barberini & Around

CRISPY HEALTH FOOD €

Map p332 (☎06 4201 4040; Via Francesco Crispi 80; dishes €9.50-12; ⏲10.30am-7.30pm Mon-Fri; 📶🥗; ⓂBarberini) Homemade soups, quiches, wraps, salads, cookies and cakes jam-packed with natural goodness make for a super-powered lunch at this organic market and bistro, run by talented baker Flaminia and partner Matthew. Don't miss the creative fruit and veg juices (€6.50). Eat in, at bar stools around high tables between shelves of herbal teas, grains and pulses, or take away.

★HOSTARIA ROMANA TRATTORIA €€

Map p332 (☎06 474 52 84; www.hostariaromana.it; Via del Boccaccio 1; meals €45; ⏲12.30-3pm & 7.15-11pm Mon-Sat; ⓂBarberini) Beloved of locals and tourists alike, this bustling place in Trevi is everything an Italian trattoria should be. Order an antipasto or pasta (excellent) and then move onto a main – traditional Roman dishes including *saltimbocca* (pan-fried, prosciutto-wrapped veal escalopes) and tripe are on offer, as are lots of grilled meats.

★COLLINE EMILIANE ITALIAN €€

Map p332 (☎06 481 75 38; www.collineemiliane.com; Via degli Avignonesi 22; meals €45; ⊙12.45-2.45pm & 7.30-10.45pm Tue-Sat, 12.45-2.45pm Sun; MBarberini) Serving sensational regional cuisine from Emilia-Romagna, this restaurant has been operated by the Latini family since 1931; the current owners are Paola (dessert queen) and Anna (watch her making pasta each morning in the glassed-off lab). Our three recommendations when eating here: start with the *antipasti della casa* (€26 for two persons), progress to pasta and don't skimp on dessert.

The kitchen flies the flag for Emilia-Romagna, the well-fed Italian province that has blessed the world with Parmesan cheese, balsamic vinegar, bolognese sauce and Parma ham. Seasonal delights include white truffles in winter and fresh porcini mushrooms in spring, but the menu is delectable whatever the season. Service can be uneven; we find it most friendly at lunch.

DRINKING & NIGHTLIFE

Rome's shopping district is subdued after dark: hobnobbing with Roman fashionistas over cocktails in glamorous rooftop bars and sipping cappuccino on the terraces of historic cafes lacing Piazza del Popolo and the streets around the Spanish Steps is about as racy as it gets in this distinguished part of the city.

Piazza del Popolo & Around

★STRAVINSKIJ BAR BAR

Map p332 (☎06 3288 88 74; www.roccofortehotels.com/hotels-and-resorts/hotel-de-russie; Via del Babuino 9, Hotel de Russie; ⊙9am-1am; MFlaminio) Can't afford to stay at the celeb-magnet Hotel de Russie (p246)? Then splash out on a drink at its swish bar. There are sofas inside, but the sunny courtyard is the fashionable choice, with sun-shaded tables overlooked by terraced gardens.

CAFFÈ RIPETTA CAFE

Map p332 (☎06 321 05 24; 39 Via della Frezza; ⊙8.30am-11pm; MFlaminio) Buzzing with a buoyant, young, staunchly Roman crowd, this sassy corner cafe is a relaxed and easy spot for lapping up a bit of local *dolce vita* over a love-heart-topped cappuccino – inside at the all-white bar or on the street-smart pavement terrace, which is heated in winter. Serves pizza (€8.50 to €11) and *panini* (€4.50 to €12) too.

LOCARNO BAR BAR

Map p332 (www.hotellocarno.com; Via della Penna 22, Hotel Locarno; ⊙7pm-1am; MFlaminio) Fashionistas and style gurus congregate at this rakish lounge bar for their 7pm *aperitivo* (pre-dinner drinks). Part of the art deco Hotel Locarno (p246) near Piazza del Popolo, it's an inspiring spot for a sundowner, with romantic corners, a shaded outdoor terrace, heavy cast-iron tables and a decadent Agatha Christie–era feel.

ROSATI CAFE

Map p332 (☎06 322 58 59; www.barrosati.com; Piazza del Popolo 5; ⊙7.30am-11.30pm; MFlaminio) Overlooking the vast disc of Piazza del Popolo, this historic 1922 cafe was once the hang-out of the left-wing chattering classes. Authors Italo Calvino and Alberto Moravia drank here while their right-wing counterparts went to the Canova across the square. Today tourists are the main clientele, but the views are as good as ever.

Piazza di Spagna & Around

★ZUMA BAR COCKTAIL BAR

Map p332 (☎06 9926 6622; www.zumarestaurant.com; Via della Fontanella di Borghese 48, Palazzo Fendi; ⊙6pm-1am Sun-Thu, to 2am Fri & Sat; 📶; MSpagna) Dress up for a drink on the rooftop terrace of Palazzo Fendi of fashion-house fame – few cocktail bars in Rome are as sleek, hip or achingly sophisticated as this. City rooftop views are predictably fabulous; cocktails mix exciting flavours like shiso with juniper berries, elderflower and prosecco.

Should you be feeling peckish, the Zuma restaurant is on-site with its superb Japanese kitchen serving up izakaya-style cuisine designed to be shared by the entire table. Bookings recommended.

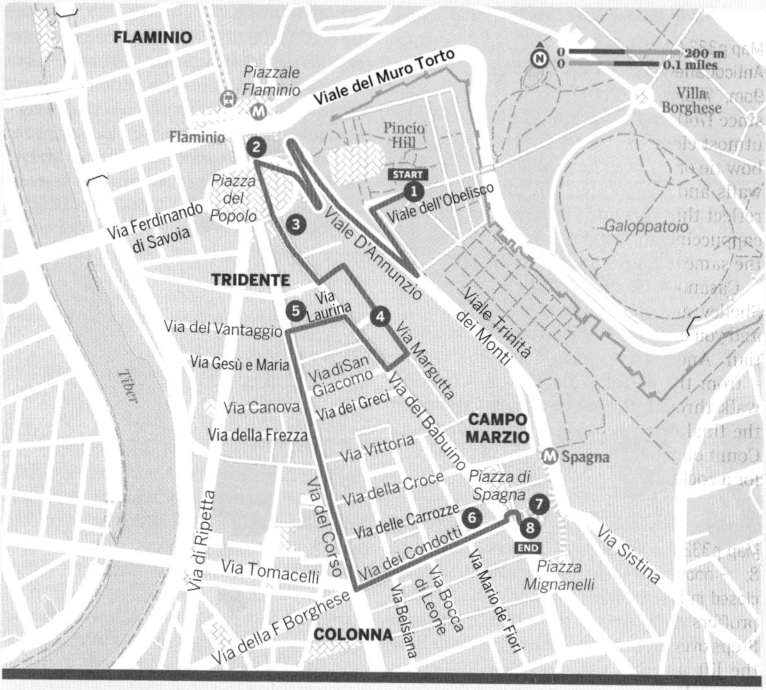

Neighbourhood Walk
Literary Footsteps

START PINCIO HILL GARDENS
END KEATS-SHELLEY HOUSE
LENGTH 1KM; 2½ HOURS

This walk explores the literary haunts, both real and fictional, that speckle the streets around the Spanish Steps.

Begin your walk in **1 Pincio Hill Gardens** (p112), where Henry James' Daisy Miller walked with Frederick Winterborne. Then make your way downhill to Piazza del Popolo and visit the church of **2 Santa Maria del Popolo** (p109), the subject of Thom Gunn's 1958 poem *In Santa Maria del Popolo* (The Conversion of St Paul).

From here it's a few steps to **3 Hotel de Russie** (p246), favoured by the artistic avant-garde in the early 20th century. French writer and film-maker Jean Cocteau stayed here with Picasso in 1917; Cocteau wrote a letter home in which he described plucking oranges from outside his window.

Running parallel to Via del Babuino is **4 Via Margutta** (p112). Famous for its artistic and cinematic connections, this picturesque street was where Truman Capote wrote his short story *Lola*. Fellini, Picasso, Stravinsky and Puccini all lived here, and Gregory Peck's character in the 1953 film *Roman Holiday* had his apartment here (exteriors were shot at No 51).

Next make your way to Via del Corso, to see the **5 Casa di Goethe** (p113) where Goethe stayed from 1786 to 1788. Head down Via del Corso then turn left up into Via dei Condotti, where William Thackeray stayed in 1854, stopping at **6 Antico Caffè Greco** (p122), a former haunt of Casanova, Goethe, Keats, Byron and Shelley. Leaving here, you're almost at the **7 Spanish Steps** (p108), which Dickens described in his *Pictures from Italy*. Byron stayed on Piazza di Spagna, at No 66, in 1817. Just south of the steps is the apartments where Keats died of tuberculosis, aged just 25. The **8 Keats-Shelley House** (p113) is now a small museum devoted to the romantic poets.

★ANTICO CAFFÈ GRECO CAFE

Map p332 (06 679 17 00; www.facebook.com/AnticoCaffeGreco; Via dei Condotti 86; 9am-9pm; Spagna) Rome's oldest cafe, open since 1760, is still working the look with the utmost elegance: waiters in black tails and bow tie or frilly white pinnies, scarlet flock walls and age-spotted gilt mirrors. Prices reflect this amazing heritage: pay €9 for a cappuccino sitting down or join locals for the same (€2.50) standing at the bar.

Casanova, Goethe, Wagner, Keats, Byron, Shelley and Baudelaire were all regulars, and you can even flop down on Hans Christian Andersen's ginger-coloured canapé – from the entrance on Via dei Condotti, walk through the series of eight rooms to the final drawing room with grand piano. Count on paying €12 for a cup of tea or €21 for a cocktail.

★IL PALAZZETTO COCKTAIL BAR

Map p332 (06 6993 4560; Vicolo del Bottino 8; noon-6pm winter, 4pm-midnight summer, closed in bad weather; Spagna) No terrace proffers such a fine view of the Spanish Steps over an expertly shaken cocktail. Ride the lift up from the discreet entrance on narrow Vicolo del Bottino or look for stairs leading to the bar from the top of the steps. Given everything is al fresco, the bar is only open in warm, dry weather.

CAFFÈ CIAMPINI CAFE

Map p332 (06 678 56 78; Viale Trinità dei Monti; 8am-11pm Mar-Oct; Spagna) Hidden away a short walk from the top of the Spanish Steps towards the Pincio Hill Gardens (p112), this cafe has a vintage garden-party vibe, with green wooden latticework and orange trees framing its white-clothed tables. There are lovely views over the backstreets behind Spagna, and the gelato – particularly the *tartufo al cioccolato* (chocolate truffle) – is renowned. Serves food too.

BAR FRATTINA CAFE

Map p332 (06 679 26 93; www.barfrattina.com; Via Frattina 142; 7am-11pm; Spagna) Yes, the Spanish Steps offer a primo people-watching opportunity. But so too does the streetside terrace of this nearby cafe, which has been hugely popular with local workers and residents ever since opening back in the 1950s. Come for coffee or a drink, not to eat.

CANOVA TADOLINI CAFE

Map p332 (06 3211 0702; www.canovatadolini.com; Via del Babuino 150a/b; 8am-10.30pm; Spagna) In 1818 sculptor Antonio Canova signed a contract for this studio that agreed it would be forever preserved for sculpture. The place is still stuffed with statues and it's a unique experience to sit among the great maquettes and sip a cappuccino, beer or wine over snacks, cake, a *panino* or a full meal. Pay first at the till then head left to the bar.

Piazza di Trevi, Quirinale Hill & Around

FARO – LUMINARI DEL CAFFÈ CAFE

Map p348 (06 4281 5714; www.farorome.com; Via Piave 55; 7am-6pm Mon-Fri, 8am-5pm Sat & Sun; Calabria) Coffee connoisseurs can't miss Faro, where the Florentine Marzocco espresso machine concocts a life-changing *caffè* with 100% Arabica beans, hand-picked to ensure they're ripe and at their most flavourful. The passionate staff will discourage you from adding sugar to your cappuccino (it's perfect as it is) and will patiently help you select the brew that's best for you.

Piazza Barberini & Around

UP SUNSET BAR COCKTAIL BAR

Map p332 (06 8791 6652; www.upsunsetbar.com; Via del Tritone 61; 10am-11pm; Barberini) Perched on the top two floors of luxury department store La Rinascente, this flirty bar promises plenty of champagne, dishes by Michelin-starred chef Riccardo Di Giacinto, and a swish front-row seat to Rome's stunning skyline. Or come in the morning for a cappuccino and *cornetto* (croissant) breakfast with the city sprawled at your feet.

☆ ENTERTAINMENT

GREGORY'S JAZZ CLUB JAZZ

Map p332 (06 679 63 86, 327 8263770; www.gregorysjazz.com; Via Gregoriana 54d; obligatory drink €15-20; 7.30pm-2am Tue-Sun; Barberini) If Gregory's were a tone of voice, it'd be husky: unwind over a whisky in the downstairs bar, then unwind some more on squashy sofas upstairs to slinky live jazz

LUXURY SPAS

Kami Spa (Map p332; ☎06 4201 0039; www.kamispa.com; Via degli Avignonesi 11-12; massage €120-280; ⏰10am-10pm; Ⓜ Barberini) A luxurious spa not far from the Trevi Fountain (p108), this is a soothing place to recover from bouts of frantic sightseeing. Think hot stone massages, Balinese palm massages, massages with Moroccan rose petal oil, turmeric and sandalwood body wraps, and green-tea body cocoons.

Hotel De Russie Spa (☎06 3288 8820; www.roccofortehotels.com/it; Via del Babuino 9, Hotel De Russie; ⏰6.30am-10pm; Ⓜ Flaminio) This glamorous and gorgeous day spa in one of Rome's top hotels (p246) boasts a salt-water hydropool, steam room, Finnish sauna and well-equipped gym. A wide array of treatments is available (for him and her), including shiatsu and deep-tissue massages; count on at least €110 for a 50-minute massage.

and swing, with quality local performers who also like to hang out here.

SHOPPING

Tridente is queen of Rome shopping. Main street Via del Corso and the streets surrounding it are lined cheek by jowl with beautiful boutiques selling everything from savvy street wear and haute-couture fashion to handmade paper stationery, artisanal jewellery, perfume, homewares and food. Specialist streets include quaint Via Margutta for antiques; Via dei Condotti for designer fashion; and Via della Pugna for small, independent boutiques.

Piazza del Popolo & Around

★CHIARA BASCHIERI — CLOTHING

Map p332 (☎333 6364851; www.chiarabaschieri.it; Via Margutta, cnr Vicolo Orto di Napoli; ⏰11am-7pm Tue-Sat; Ⓜ Spagna) One of Rome's most impressive independent designers, Chiara Baschieri produces classic, meticulously tailored clothing featuring exquisite fabrics. Her style has echoes of 1960s Givenchy – if Audrey Hepburn had ever stopped by, Chiara would no doubt have gained another fan.

★BOMBA — CLOTHING

Map p332 (☎06 361 28 81; www.cristinabomba.com; Via dell'Oca 39; ⏰11am-7.30pm Tue-Sat, from 3.30pm Mon; Ⓜ Flaminia) Opened by designer Cristina Bomba over four decades ago, this gorgeous boutique is now operated by her fashion-designing children Caterina (womenswear) and Michele (menswear). Using the highest-quality fabrics, their creations are tailored in the next-door atelier (peek through the front window); woollens are produced at a factory just outside the city. Pricey but oh so worth it.

ARTISANAL CORNUCOPIA — DESIGN

Map p332 (☎342 8714597; www.artisanalcornucopia.com; Via dell'Oca 38a; ⏰10.30am-7.30pm Tue-Sat, from 3.30pm Mon, from 4.30pm Sun; Ⓜ Flaminio) One of several stylish independent boutiques on Via dell'Oca, this chic concept store showcases exclusive handmade pieces by Italian designers: the delicate gold necklaces and other jewellery crafted by Giulia Barela are a highlight, but there are loads of bags, shoes, candles, homewares and other objects to covet.

BORSALINO — HATS

Map p332 (☎06 323 33 53; www.borsalino.com; Piazza del Popolo 20; Ⓜ Flaminia) Humphrey Bogart, Ingrid Bergman, Marcello Mastroianni and Jean Paul Belmondo all wore them, and now you can too. Borsalino has been producing quality men's and women's hats since 1857 and still does so – the must-buy numbers are the classic straw and felt models but there are many other styles to choose from.

PATRIZIA FABRI — HATS

Map p332 (☎320 7964125; www.facebook.com/patriziafabrihats; Via dell'Oca 34; ⏰10.30am-1pm & 2-7.30pm Tue-Sat, from 3pm Mon; Ⓜ Flaminio) When in Rome, buy a beautiful hat handcrafted by Rome-based milliner Patrizia Fabri at her tiny boutique near Piazza del Popolo. Be it a stylish turban, beanie, traditional hand-pressed sunhat, straw cap or

LEAVES OF STONE

In a conservative city essentially known for its extraordinary ancient art and architecture, contemporary art installations in public spaces are a rare breed. Enter *Foglie di Pietra* (Leaves of Stone; 2016), a sensational sculpture outside the Fendi flagship store on posh shopping strip Largo Carlo Goldoni in Tridente. Donated to the city of Rome by the homegrown Fendi fashion house and unveiled in spring 2017, the sculpture by Italian artist Giuseppe Penone comprises two life-sized bronze trees supporting an 11-tonne marble block with their interlocked branches. The trees tower 18m and 9m high into the sky and represent a definite breath of contemporary fresh air in Rome's art scene.

felt panama, this designer does not disappoint. Hats are made at her workshop, an original 1930s atelier near the Vatican.

LA BOTTEGA DEL MARMORARO ART

Map p332 (☎06 320 76 60; Via Margutta 53b; ⏱8am-7.30pm Mon-Sat; Ⓜ Flaminio) Watch *marmoraro* (marble artist) Sandro Fiorentini chip away in this atelier filled with his decorative marble plaques engraved with various inscriptions: *la dolce vita, la vita e bella* (life is beautiful) etc. Plaques start at €10 and Sandro will engrave any inscription you like (from €15).

FABRIANO ARTS & CRAFTS

Map p332 (☎06 3260 0361; www.fabrianoboutique.com; Via del Babuino 173; ⏱10am-8pm; Ⓜ Flaminio) Fabriano makes distinctive stationery including deeply desirable leather-bound diaries, decorative notebooks and products embossed with street maps of Rome. It's perfect for picking up a gift, with other items including leather key rings and quirky paper jewellery by local designers.

Piazza di Spagna & Around

★GENTE FASHION & ACCESSORIES

Map p332 (☎06 320 76 71; www.genteroma.com; Via del Babuino 77; ⏱10.30am-7.30pm Mon-Fri, to 8pm Sat, 11.30am-7.30pm Sun; Ⓜ Spagna) This multi-label boutique was the first in Rome to bring all the big-name luxury designers – Italian, French and otherwise – under one roof and its vast emporium-styled space remains an essential stop for every serious fashionista. Labels include Dolce & Gabbana, Prada, Alexander McQueen, Sergio Rossi and Missoni.

Its men's store is across the road, at Via Babuino 185. A second women's store on Via Frattina focuses on **accessories** (Map p332; ☎06 678 91 32; Via Frattina 92; 🚌 Via del Corso).

★FAUSTO SANTINI SHOES

Map p332 (☎06 678 41 14; www.faustosantini.com; Via Frattina 120; ⏱10am-7.30pm Mon-Sat, 11am-7pm Sun; Ⓜ Spagna) Rome's best-known shoe designer, Fausto Santini is famous for his beguilingly simple, architectural shoe designs, with beautiful boots and shoes made from butter-soft leather. Colours are beautiful and the quality is impeccable.

FEDERICO BUCCELLATI JEWELLERY

Map p332 (☎06 679 03 29; www.facebook.com/federico-buccellati-orafo-311172238241; Via dei Condotti 31; ⏱10am-1.30pm & 3-7pm Tue-Fri, 10am-1.30pm & 2-6pm Sat, 3-7pm Mon; Ⓜ Spagna) Run today by the third generation of one of Italy's most prestigious silver- and goldsmiths, this historical shop opened in 1926. Everything is handcrafted and often delicately engraved with decorative flowers, leaves and nature-inspired motifs. Don't miss the Silver Salon on the 1st floor showcasing some original silverware and jewellery pieces by grandfather Mario.

FENDI FASHION & ACCESSORIES

Map p332 (☎06 3345 0890; www.fendi.com; Largo Carlo Goldoni 420, Palazzo Fendi; ⏱10am-7.30pm Mon-Sat, from 10.30am Sun; Ⓜ Spagna) With travertine walls, stunning contemporary art and sweeping red-marble staircase, the flagship store of Rome's iconic fashion house inside 18th-century Palazzo Fendi is dazzling. Born in Rome in 1925 as a leather and fur workshop on Via del Plebiscit, this luxurious temple to Roman fashion is as much concept store as *maison* selling ready-to-wear clothing for men and women.

ANGLO AMERICAN BOOKSHOP BOOKS

Map p332 (06 679 52 22; www.aab.it; Via della Vite 102; 10.30am-7.30pm Tue-Sat, from 3.30pm Mon; Spagna) Particularly good for university reference books, the Anglo American Bookshop is well stocked and well known. It has an excellent range of literature, travel guides, children's books and maps, and if it hasn't got the book you want, staff will order it in.

VALENTINO CLOTHING

Map p332 (06 9451 57 10; www.valentino.com; Piazza di Spagna 38; 10am-7.30pm Mon-Sat, to 7pm Sun; Spagna) Rome's most famous couturier, Valentino Garavani, opened his first store on Via dei Condotti in 1960. The brand now sells its creations from this nearby boutique.

CATELLO D'AURIA FASHION & ACCESSORIES

Map p332 (06 679 33 64; www.catellodauria.it; Via dei Due Macelli 55; 9.30am-7.30pm; Spagna) Making leather gloves since 1894, this traditional Roman business retains its walls of original glove drawers, which are filled with examples made from leather and lined with silk, merino wool and cashmere. It also sells socks and woollen hats.

MANDARINA DUCK FASHION & ACCESSORIES

Map p332 (06 678 64 14; www.mandarinaduck.com; Via dei Due Macelli; 10am-7.30pm Mon-Sat, from 10.30am Sun; Spagna) Now a global brand, this Italian company produces handbags, wallets and suitcases with a distinctive contemporary design. Prices are extremely reasonable considering the quality.

BALENCIAGA FASHION & ACCESSORIES

Map p332 (06 8750 2260; www.balenciaga.com; Via Borgognona 7e; 10am-7pm; Spagna) Design lovers will adore this boutique of French fashion label Balenciaga, which is set inside a 19th-century *palazzo* with vintage furniture and a fabulous 'aristocratic residence' vibe. The decor features old marquetry and theatrical overhead lighting by the Italian architect and lighting designer Gae Aulenti (1927–2012). Oh, and the clothes are pretty good, too.

LAURA BIAGIOTTI FASHION & ACCESSORIES

Map p332 (06 679 12 05; www.laurabiagiotti.it; Via Belsiana 57; 10.30am-1pm & 3.30-7.30pm Tue-Sat, 10am-7.30pm Sun, from 3pm Mon; Spagna) A stiletto strut from the Spanish Steps, the boutique of this well-established Roman fashion designer unfolds over three floors. Inside, ethnic-inspired printed fabrics and cashmere and silk pieces woo fashionistas on the lookout for the latest bold design by one of Italy's best-known high-street designers.

TOD'S SHOES

Map p332 (06 6821 0066; www.tods.com; Via della Fontanella di Borghese 56a; 10.30am-7.30pm Mon-Sat, 10am-2pm & 3-7.30pm Sun; Via del Corso) The trademark of this luxury Italian brand is its rubber-studded loafers – perfect weekend footwear for kicking back at your country estate. There's a second store nearby, at Via Condotti 53a. Tod's is known more recently as the generous benefactor behind the much-needed clean-up of the northern and southern facades of the Colosseum.

C.U.C.I.N.A. HOMEWARES

Map p332 (06 679 12 75; www.cucinastore.com; Via Mario de' Fiori 65; 10am-7.30pm Tue-Fri, from 10.30am Sat, from 3.30pm Mon; Spagna) Make your own *cucina* (kitchen) look the part with the designer goods from this famous kitchenware shop, which stocks everything from classic *caffettiere* (Italian coffee makers) to cutlery and myriad devices you'll decide you simply must have.

Piazza di Trevi, Quirinale & Around

GALLERIA ALBERTO SORDI SHOPPING CENTRE

Map p332 (06 6919 0769; www.galleriaalbertosordi.it; Galleria di Piazza Colonna, Piazza Colonna; 8.30am-9pm Mon-Fri, to 10pm Sat, 9.30am-9pm Sun; Via del Corso) This elegant stained-glass arcade appeared in Alberto Sordi's 1973 classic film, *Polvere di stelle* (Stardust), and has since been renamed in his honour. It's a good place to find high-street stores such as Zara and Feltrinelli.

Vatican City, Borgo & Prati

VATICAN CITY | BORGO & AROUND | PRATI

Neighbourhood Top Five

❶ **Sistine Chapel** (p136) Gazing heavenwards at Michelangelo's most celebrated masterpieces: his cinematic Genesis frescoes on the ceiling, and his terrifying vision of the *Last Judgment* on the western wall.

❷ **St Peter's Basilica** (p128) Being blown away by the super-sized opulence of this, the most important church in the Catholic world.

❸ **St Peter's Square** (p141) Trying to line up the columns on the Vatican's central square – it is possible.

❹ **Castel Sant'Angelo** (p141) Revelling in the wonderful rooftop views from this landmark castle on the Tiber.

❺ **Stanze di Raffaello** (p133) Marvelling at the vibrant colours of these fabulously frescoed chambers in the Vatican Museums. They're home to Raphael's greatest painting, *La Scuola di Atene*.

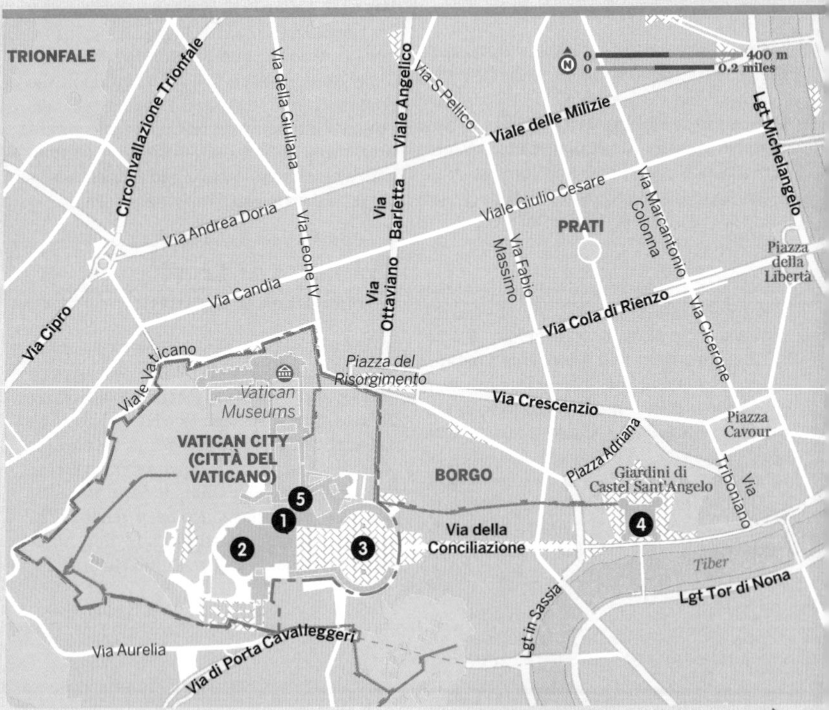

For more detail of this area see Map p336 ➡

Explore Vatican City, Borgo & Prati

The Vatican stands atop the low-lying Vatican hill west of the Tiber. Much of its 44 hectares are covered by the Vatican Gardens and the Palazzo Apostolico, the sprawling palace that houses the pope's official residence and the Vatican Museums.

You'll need at least a morning to do justice to the Vatican Museums (p133). The highlight is the Michelangelo-frescoed Sistine Chapel (p133), but there's enough art on display to keep you busy for years. If you're with a tour guide, or you can sneakily tail onto a group, you can pass directly from the Chapel through to St Peter's Basilica (p128); otherwise you'll have to walk around and approach from St Peter's Square (p141). Once finished in the basilica, you'll be ready for a break. There are a couple of good eating options in the Vatican itself, but the nearby Prati district is full of trattorias, takeaways and restaurants.

Between the Vatican and the river lies the Borgo. Little remains of the original medieval district, which was largely destroyed in 1936 to make way for Via della Conciliazione, the monumental road that runs from St Peter's Square to Castel Sant'Angelo (p141).

Local Life

➡ **Fast food** Quick eats are the order of the day and there are many excellent takeaways in Prati. Grab a *pizza al taglio* at Panificio Bonci (p142), *panini* at Fa-Bìo (p142) or go sweet at Gelateria dei Gracchi (p142).

➡ **Shopping** Prati is good shopping territory. Via Cola di Rienzo is the area's central strip, lined with department stores and midrange clothes shops.

➡ **Catch a gig** Join the locals for sweet melodies at Alexanderplatz (p146), Rome's most famous jazz joint. Another top venue is Fonclea (p146), which offers an eclectic program of nightly gigs.

Getting There & Away

➡ **Bus** From Termini, bus 40 is the quickest one to the Vatican – it'll drop you off near Castel Sant'Angelo. You can also take the 64, which runs a similar route but stops more often. Bus 81 runs to Piazza del Risorgimento, passing through San Giovanni and the *centro storico* (historic centre).

➡ **Metro** Take metro line A to Ottaviano-San Pietro. From the station, signs direct you to St Peter's or the Vatican Museums.

➡ **Tram** No 19 serves Piazza del Risorgimento by way of San Lorenzo, Viale Regina Margherita and Villa Borghese.

Lonely Planet's Top Tip

Beware the touts around Ottaviano metro station selling skip-the-line tours of the Vatican Museums. They're on commission to round up clients, and the tours they're pushing could cost more than the museums' official tours. The Vatican Museums' website lists an array of tour packages taking in the museums and sites across Vatican territories.

Best Places to Eat

➡ Bonci Pizzarium (p143)
➡ Enoteca La Torre (p145)
➡ L'Arcangelo (p145)
➡ Fa-Bìo (p142)
➡ Gelateria dei Gracchi (p142)

For reviews, see p142.

Best Places to Drink

➡ Sciascia Caffè (p146)
➡ L'Osteria di Birra del Borgo Roma (p146)
➡ Passaguai (p146)
➡ Be.re (p146)

For reviews, see p145.

Best Over & Underground

➡ St Peter's Basilica Dome (p131)
➡ Terrace of Castel Sant'Angelo (p141)
➡ Tomb of St Peter (p132)
➡ Vatican Grottoes (p132)
➡ Necropoli Via Triumphalis (p141)

For reviews, see p141.

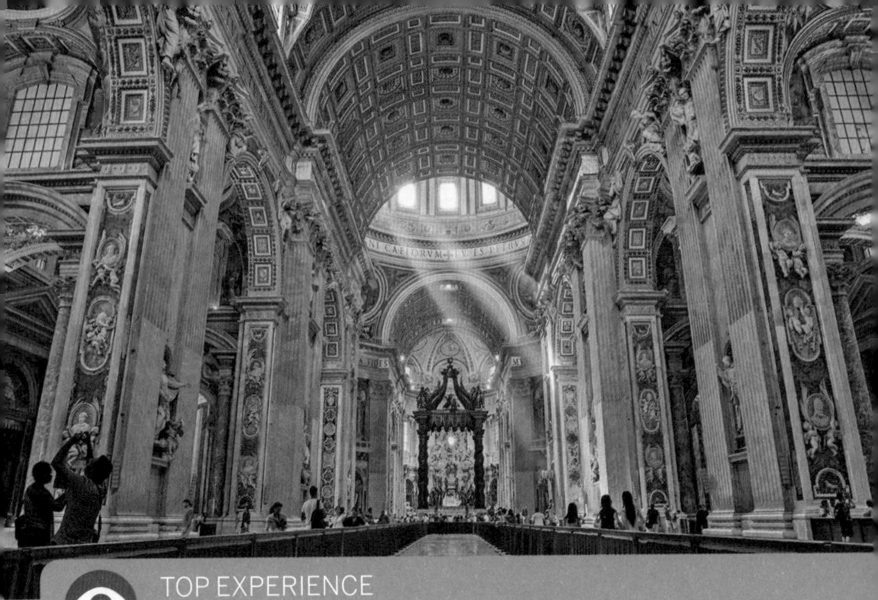

IHSAN GERCELMAN / SHUTTERSTOCK ©

TOP EXPERIENCE
GAZE IN AWE AT ST PETER'S BASILICA

In a city of outstanding churches, none can hold a candle to St Peter's, Italy's largest, richest and most spectacular basilica. A monument to centuries of artistic genius, it boasts many spectacular works of art, including three of Italy's most celebrated masterpieces: Michelangelo's *Pietà*, his soaring dome, and Bernini's 29m-high bronze baldachin (canopy) over the papal altar.

History

The original St Peter's – which lies beneath the current basilica – was commissioned by the Emperor Constantine and built around 349 on the site where St Peter is said to have been buried between 64 and 67 CE. But like many medieval churches, it eventually fell into disrepair and it wasn't until the mid-15th century that efforts were made to restore it, first by Pope Nicholas V and then, rather more successfully, by Julius II.

In 1506 construction began on Bramante's design for a new basilica based on a Greek-cross plan, with four equal arms and a huge central dome. But on Bramante's death in 1514, building ground to a halt as architects, including Raphael and Antonio da Sangallo, tried to modify his original plans. Little progress was made and it wasn't until Michelangelo took over in 1547 at the age of 72 that the situation changed. Michelangelo simplified Bramante's plans and drew up designs for what was to become his greatest architectural achievement, the dome. He never lived to see it built, though, and it was left to Giacomo della Porta and Domenico Fontana to finish it in 1590.

TOP TIPS

- Dress appropriately if you want to get in – no shorts, miniskirts or bare shoulders.
- Queues are inevitable at the security checks, but they move quickly.
- Lines are generally shorter during lunch hours and in the late afternoon.

PRACTICALITIES

- Basilica di San Pietro
- Map p336, C5
- ☎06 6988 3731
- www.vatican.va
- St Peter's Sq
- admission free
- 7am-7pm Apr-Sep, to 6pm Oct-Mar
- Piazza del Risorgimento, M Ottaviano-San Pietro

With the dome in place, Carlo Maderno inherited the project in 1605. He designed the monumental facade and lengthened the nave towards the piazza.

The basilica was finally consecrated in 1626.

The Facade

Built between 1608 and 1612, Maderno's immense facade is 48m high and 115m wide. Eight 27m-high columns support the upper attic on which 13 statues stand representing Christ the Redeemer, St John the Baptist and the 11 apostles. The central balcony is known as the **Loggia della Benedizione**, and it's from here that the pope delivers his *Urbi et Orbi* blessing at Christmas and Easter.

Running across the entablature is an inscription, 'IN HONOREM PRINCIPIS APOST PAVLVS V BVRGHESIVS ROMANVS PONT MAX AN MDCXII PONT VII', which translates as 'In honour of the Prince of Apostles, Paul V Borghese, Roman, Pontiff, in the year 1612, the seventh of his pontificate'.

In the grand atrium, the **Porta Santa** (Holy Door) is opened only in Jubilee years.

Interior – The Nave

Dominating the centre of the basilica is Bernini's 29m-high **baldachin**. Supported by four spiral columns and made with bronze taken from the Pantheon, it stands over the **papal altar**, also known as the Altar of the Confession. In front, Carlo Maderno's **Confessione** stands over the site where St Peter was originally buried.

Above the baldachin, Michelangelo's **dome** soars to a height of 119m. Based on Brunelleschi's design for the Duomo in Florence, it's supported by four massive stone **piers**, each named after the saint whose statue adorns its Bernini-designed niche. The saints are all associated with the basilica's four major relics: the lance **St Longinus** supposedly used to pierce Christ's side; the cloth with which **St Veronica** was said to have wiped Jesus' face; a fragment of the Cross collected by **St Helena**; and the head of **St Andrew**.

At the base of the **Pier of St Longinus** is Arnolfo di Cambio's much-loved 13th-century bronze **statue of St Peter**, whose right foot has been worn down by centuries of caresses.

Behind the altar, the tribune is home to Bernini's extraordinary **Cattedra di San Pietro**. A vast gilded bronze throne held aloft by four 5m-high saints, it's centred on a wooden seat that was once thought to have been St Peter's but in fact dates from the 9th century. Above, light shines through a yellow window framed by a gilded mass of golden angels and adorned with a dove to represent the Holy Spirit.

TOURS

Free, two-hour English-language tours of the basilica are run by seminarians from the Pontifical North American College (www.pnac.org). These generally start at 2.15pm Monday, Wednesday and Friday, leaving from the Ufficio Pellegrini e Turisti (p305). No tickets are necessary, but check the website to verify tour dates.

For a bite to eat, avoid the tourist traps around the basilica and head to nearby Prati. For a salad or tasty *panino* stop off at hit organic takeaway Fa-Bìo (p142), while for something more substantial, join the fashionable neighbourhood diners at Il Sorpasso (p144).

MASS

For all its artistic treasures, St Peter's is still a working church and mass is held daily in the basilica's chapels. For a timetable, in Italian, see www.vatican.va/various/basiliche/san_pietro/it/vita_liturgica/orari.htm.

ST PETER'S BASILICA

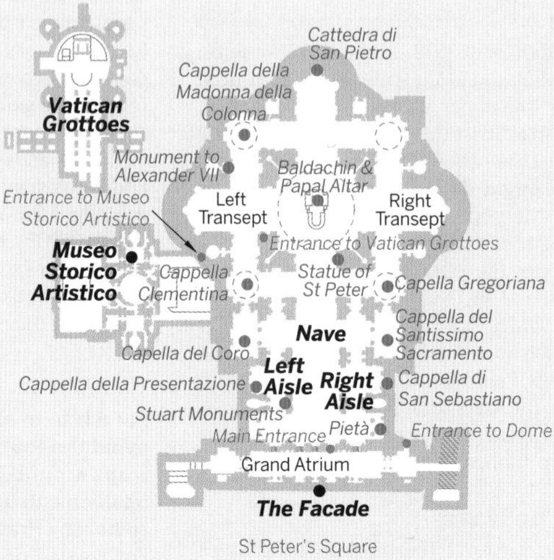

To the right of the throne, Bernini's **monument to Urban VIII** depicts the pope flanked by the figures of Charity and Justice.

Interior – Left Aisle

In the roped-off left transept, the **Cappella della Madonna della Colonna** takes its name from the Madonna that stares out from Giacomo della Porta's marble altar. To its right, above the **tomb of St Leo the Great**, is a fine relief by Alessandro Algardi. Under the next arch is Bernini's last work in the basilica, the **monument to Alexander VII**.

Halfway down the left aisle, the **Cappella Clementina** is named after Clement VIII, who had Giacomo della Porta decorate it for the Jubilee of 1600. Beneath the altar is the **tomb of St Gregory the Great** and, to the left, a **monument to Pope Pius VII** by Thorvaldsen.

The next arch shelters Alessandro Algardi's 16th-century **monument to Leo XI**. Beyond it, the richly decorated **Cappella del Coro** was created by Giovanni Battista Ricci to designs by Giacomo della Porta. The **monument to Innocent VIII** by Antonio Pollaiuolo in the next aisle arch is a recreation of a monument from the old basilica.

Continuing on, the **Cappella della Presentazione** contains two of St Peter's most modern works: a black relief **monument to John XXIII** by Emilio Greco, and a **monument to Benedict XV** by Pietro Canonica.

Under the next arch are the so-called **Stuart monuments**. On the right is the monument to Clementina Sobieska, wife of James Stuart, by Filippo Barigioni, and on the left is Canova's vaguely erotic monument to the last three members of the Stuart clan, the pretenders to the English throne who died in exile in Rome.

Michelangelo's *La Pietà*

Interior – Right Aisle

At the head of the right aisle is Michelangelo's hauntingly beautiful **La Pietà**. Sculpted when he was only 25 (in 1499), it's the only work the artist ever signed – his signature is etched into the sash across the Madonna's breast.

Nearby, a **red floor disc** marks the spot where Charlemagne and later Holy Roman emperors were crowned by the pope.

On a pillar just beyond the *Pietà,* Carlo Fontana's gilt and bronze **monument to Queen Christina of Sweden** commemorates the far-from-holy Swedish monarch who converted to Catholicism in 1655.

Moving on, you'll come to the **Cappella di San Sebastiano**, home of Pope John Paul II's tomb, and the **Cappella del Santissimo Sacramento**, a sumptuously decorated baroque chapel with works by Borromini, Bernini and Pietro da Cortona.

Beyond the chapel, the grandiose **monument to Gregory XIII** sits near the roped-off **Cappella Gregoriana**, a chapel built by Gregory XIII from designs by Michelangelo.

Much of the right transept is closed off, but you can still make out the **monument to Clement XIII**, one of Canova's most famous works.

Dome

Entry to the **dome** (with/without lift €10/8; ⌚8am-6pm Apr-Sep, to 5pm Oct-Mar) is to the far right of the basilica's main portico, where you also buy your ticket. A small lift can take you halfway up, but it's still a

FACE IN THE BALDACHIN

The frieze on Bernini's baldachin contains a hidden narrative that begins at the pillar to the left (looking with your back to the entrance). As you walk clockwise around the baldachin note the woman's face carved into the frieze of each pillar. On the first three pillars her face seems to express the increasing agony of childbirth; on the last one, it's replaced by that of a smiling baby. The woman was a niece of Pope Urban VIII, who gave birth as Bernini worked on the baldachin.

Contrary to popular belief, St Peter's Basilica is not the world's largest church – the Basilica of Our Lady of Peace in Yamoussoukro on the Ivory Coast is bigger. Still, its measurements are pretty staggering – it's 187m long and covers more than 15,000 sq metres. Bronze floor plates in the nave indicate the respective sizes of the 14 next-largest churches.

CHRISTINA, QUEEN OF SWEDEN

Famously portrayed by Greta Garbo in the 1933 film *Queen Christina*, the Swedish monarch is one of only three women buried in St Peter's Basilica – the other two are Queen Charlotte of Cyprus, a minor 15th-century royal, and Agnesina Colonna, a 16th-century Italian aristocrat. Christina earned her place by abdicating the Swedish throne and converting to Catholicism in 1655. She spent much of her later life in Rome, where she enjoyed fame as a brilliant patron of the arts, even as salacious rumours of affairs with courtiers and acquaintances abounded.

long climb to the top (320 steps to be exact). Press on and you're rewarded with stunning rooftop views from a perch 120m above St Peter's Square. It's well worth the effort, but bear in mind that it's a long climb and not recommended for anyone who suffers from claustrophobia or vertigo.

Museo Storico Artistico

Accessed from the left nave, the **Museo Storico Artistico** (Tesoro, Treasury; ☎06 6988 1840; €5 incl audioguide; ⏲9am-6.10pm Apr-Sep, to 5.10pm Oct-Mar, last entrance 30min before closing) sparkles with sacred relics. Highlights include a tabernacle by Donatello; the *Colonna Santa*, a 4th-century Byzantine column from the earlier church; and the 6th-century *Crux Vaticana* (Vatican Cross), a jewel-encrusted crucifix presented by the emperor Justinian II to the original basilica.

Vatican Grottoes

Extending beneath the basilica, the **Vatican Grottoes** (⏲8am-5pm Apr-Sep, to 4pm Oct-Mar) FREE contain the tombs and sarcophagi of numerous popes, as well as several columns from the original 4th-century basilica. The entrance is in the Pier of St Andrew.

Tomb of St Peter

Excavations beneath the basilica have uncovered part of the original church and a necropolis with what archaeologists believe is the **Tomb of St Peter** (☎06 6988 5318; www.scavi.va; €13).

In 1942 the bones of an elderly, strongly built man were found in a box hidden behind a wall covered by pilgrims' graffiti. And while the Vatican has never definitively claimed that the bones belong to St Peter, in 1968 Pope Paul VI said they had been identified in a way that the Vatican considered 'convincing'. Then, in 2013, Pope Francis publicly displayed the relics for the first time.

The excavations can only be visited by guided tour. For further details, and to book a tour (this must be done well in advance), check out the website of the **Ufficio Scavi** (Excavations Office; Fabbrica di San Pietro; ☎06 6988 5318; www.scavi.va; €13; ⏲9am-6pm Mon-Fri, to 5pm Sat).

KIEVVICTOR / SHUTTERSTOCK ©

TOP EXPERIENCE
VISIT THE VATICAN MUSEUMS

Visiting the Vatican Museums is a thrilling and unforgettable experience. With some 7km of exhibitions and more masterpieces than many small countries can call their own, this vast museum complex boasts one of the world's greatest art collections. Highlights include a spectacular collection of classical statuary in the Museo Pio-Clementino, a suite of rooms frescoed by Raphael, and the Michelangelo-decorated Sistine Chapel.

Founded by Pope Julius II in the early 16th century, the museums are housed in the lavishly decorated halls and galleries of the Palazzo Apostolico Vaticano. This immense 5.5-hectare complex consists of two palaces – the original Vatican palace (nearer to St Peter's) and the 15th-century Palazzetto di Belvedere – joined by two long galleries. On the inside are three courtyards: the Cortile della Pigna, the Cortile della Biblioteca and, to the south, the Cortile del Belvedere. You'll never cover it all in one day, so it pays to be selective.

Pinacoteca

Often overlooked by visitors, the papal picture gallery displays paintings dating from the 11th to 19th centuries, with works by Giotto, Fra' Angelico, Filippo Lippi, Perugino, Titian, Guido Reni, Guercino, Pietro da Cortona, Caravaggio and Leonardo da Vinci.

Look out for a trio of paintings by Raphael in Room VIII – the *Madonna di Foligno* (Madonna of Folignano), the *Incoronazione della Vergine* (Crowning of the Virgin), and *La Trasfigurazione* (Transfiguration), which was completed

TOP TIPS

- Last Sunday of the month museums are free (and busy).
- Exhibits are simply labelled – consider an audioguide (€8) or *Guide to the Vatican Museums and City* (€13).
- Check website for excellent tours.

PRACTICALITIES

- Musei Vaticani
- Map p336, C3
- ☎06 6988 4676
- www.museivaticani.va
- Viale Vaticano
- adult/reduced €17/8
- 🕘9am-6pm Mon-Sat, to 2pm last Sun of month, last entry 2hr before close
- 🚌Piazza del Risorgimento, Ⓜ Ottaviano-San Pietro

QUEUE-JUMPING

To avoid horrendous queues, book tickets (€4 fee) online (http://biglietteriamusei.vatican.va/musei/tickets/do; print the voucher and swap it for a ticket at the appointed time at the entrance) or at Ufficio Pellegrini e Turisti (p305). Alternatively, sign up for a tour. Also, time your visit: Tuesdays and Thursdays are quietest; Wednesday mornings are good too; afternoon is better than morning; and avoid Mondays when other museums close, and rainy days.

VISITORS WITH DISABILITIES

Free guided tours are available for blind visitors (a multisensory tour) and deaf visitors (in Italian sign language) and must be reserved in advance. Wheelchairs are available to borrow from the Special Permits desk in the entrance hall (you must have an ID for deposit). People with disabilities, and in some cases a companion, may skip the ticket queue. For further details, see the Services for Visitors section of the museums' website.

by his students after his death in 1520. Other highlights include Filippo Lippi's *L'Incoronazione della Vergine con Angeli, Santo e donatore* (Coronation of the Virgin with Angels, Saints and Donors); Leonardo da Vinci's haunting and unfinished *San Gerolamo* (St Jerome); and Caravaggio's *Deposizione* (Deposition from the Cross).

Museo Chiaramonti & Braccio Nuovo

This museum is effectively the long corridor that runs down the lower east side of the Palazzetto di Belvedere. Its walls are lined with thousands of statues and busts representing everything from immortal gods to playful cherubs and ugly Roman patricians.

Near the end of the hall, off to the right, is the Braccio Nuovo (New Wing), which contains a celebrated statue of the Nile as a reclining god covered by 16 babies.

Museo Pio-Clementino

This stunning museum (pictured on p133) contains some of the Vatican's finest classical statuary, including the peerless *Apollo Belvedere* and the 1st-century BCE *Laocoön,* both in the **Cortile Ottagono** (Octagonal Courtyard).

Before you go into the courtyard, take a moment to admire the 1st-century *Apoxyomenos,* one of the earliest known sculptures to depict a figure with a raised arm.

To the left as you enter the courtyard, the *Apollo Belvedere* is a 2nd-century Roman copy of a 4th-century-BCE Greek bronze. A beautifully proportioned representation of the sun god Apollo, it's considered one of the great masterpieces of classical sculpture. Nearby, the *Laocoön* depicts the mythical death of the Trojan priest who warned his fellow citizens not to take the wooden horse left by the Greeks.

Back inside, the **Sala degli Animali** is filled with sculpted creatures and magnificent 4th-century mosaics. Continuing on, you come to the **Sala delle Muse** (Room of the Muses), centred on the *Torso Belvedere,* another of the museum's must-sees. A fragment of a muscular 1st-century-BCE Greek sculpture, this was found in Campo de' Fiori and used by Michelangelo as a model for his *ignudi* (male nudes) in the Sistine Chapel.

The next room, the **Sala Rotonda** (Round Room), contains a number of colossal statues, including a gilded-bronze *Ercole* (Hercules) and an exquisite floor mosaic. The enormous basin in the centre of the room was found at Nero's Domus Aurea and is made out of a single piece of red porphyry stone.

Museo Gregoriano Egizio

Founded by Pope Gregory XVI in 1839, this Egyptian museum displays pieces taken from Egypt in ancient Roman times. There are fascinating exhibits, including a fragmented statue of the pharaoh Ramses II on his throne, vividly painted sarcophagi dating from around 1000 BCE, and a macabre mummy.

Museo Gregoriano Etrusco

At the top of the 18th-century Simonetti staircase, this fascinating museum contains artefacts unearthed in the Etruscan tombs of northern Lazio, as well as a superb collection of vases and Roman antiquities. Of particular interest is the *Marte di Todi* (Mars of Todi), a black bronze of a warrior dating from the late 5th century BCE, located in Room III.

Galleria dei Candelabri & Galleria degli Arazzi

Originally an open loggia, the **Galleria dei Candelabri** is packed with classical sculpture and several elegantly carved candelabras that give the gallery its name. The corridor continues through to the **Galleria degli Arazzi** (Tapestry Gallery) and its huge hanging tapestries. The best, on the left, were woven in Brussels in the 16th century.

Galleria delle Carte Geografiche & Sala Sobieski

One of the unsung heroes of the Vatican Museums, the 120m-long Map Gallery is hung with 40 huge topographical maps. These were created between 1580 and 1583 for Pope Gregory XIII based on drafts by Ignazio Danti, one of the leading cartographers of his day. Beyond the gallery, the **Sala Sobieski** is named after an enormous 19th-century painting depicting the victory of the Polish King John III Sobieski over the Turks in 1683.

Stanze di Raffaello

These four frescoed chambers, currently undergoing partial restoration, were part of Pope Julius II's private apartments. Raphael himself painted the **Stanza della Segnatura** (1508–11) and the **Stanza d'Eliodoro** (1512–14), while the **Stanza dell'Incendio di Borgo** (1514–17) and **Sala di Costantino** (1517–24) were decorated by students following his designs.

The first room you come to is the **Sala di Costantino**, originally a ceremonial reception room, which is dominated by the *Battaglia di Costantino contro Maxentius* (Battle of the Milvian Bridge) showing the victory of Constantine, Rome's first Christian emperor, over his rival Maxentius.

Leading off the *sala,* but often closed to the public, the **Cappella Niccolina**, Pope Nicholas V's private chapel, boasts superb frescoes by Fra' Angelico.

The **Stanza d'Eliodoro**, which was used for the pope's private audiences, takes its name from the *Cacciata d'Eliodoro* (Expulsion of Heliodorus from the Temple), reflecting Pope Julius II's policy of forcing foreign powers off Church lands. To its right, the *Messa di Bolsena* (Mass of Bolsena) shows Julius paying homage to the relic of a 13th-century miracle at the lakeside town of Bolsena. Next is the *Incontro di Leone Magno con Attila* (Encounter of Leo the Great with Attila), and, on the fourth wall, the *Liberazione di San Pietro* (Liberation of St Peter), a brilliant work illustrating Raphael's masterful ability to depict light.

The **Stanza della Segnatura**, Julius' study and library, was the first room that Raphael painted, and it's here that you'll find his great masterpiece, *La Scuola di Atene* (The School of Athens), featuring philosophers and scholars gathered around Plato and Aristotle. The seated figure in front of the steps is believed to be Michelangelo, while the figure of Plato is said to be a portrait of Leonardo da Vinci, and Euclide (the bald man bending over) is Bramante. Raphael also included a self-portrait in the lower right corner – he's the second figure from the right in the black hat. Opposite is *La Disputa del Sacramento* (Disputation on the Sacrament), also by Raphael.

The most famous work in the **Stanza dell'Incendio di Borgo**, the former seat of the Holy See's highest court and later a dining room, is the *Incendio di Borgo* (Fire in the Borgo). This depicts Leo IV extinguishing a fire by making the sign of the cross. The ceiling was painted by Raphael's master, Perugino.

From the Raphael Rooms, stairs lead to the **Appartamento Borgia** and the Vatican's collection of modern religious art.

Sistine Chapel

The jewel in the Vatican crown, the **Sistine Chapel** (Cappella Sistina) is home to two of the world's most famous works of art – Michelangelo's ceiling frescoes and his *Giudizio Universale* (Last Judgment).

continued on p138

Museum Tour
Vatican Museums

LENGTH THREE HOURS

Follow this tour to see the museums' hits, culminating in the Sistine Chapel.

Once you've passed through the entrance complex, head up the modern spiral ramp (or escalator) to ❶ **Cortile delle Corazze**, the starting point for all routes through the museums. While here take a moment to nip out to the terrace for views over St Peter's dome and the Vatican Gardens. Re-enter and follow through to ❷ **Cortile della Pigna**, named after the huge Augustan-era bronze pine cone in the monumental niche. Cross the courtyard and enter the long corridor that is ❸ **Museo Chiaramonti**. Don't stop here, but continue left, up the stairs, to the Museo Pio-Clementino, home of the Vatican's finest classical statuary. Follow the flow of people through to the ❹ **Cortile Ottagono** (Octagonal Courtyard), where you'll find the mythical masterpieces, the *Laocoön* and *Apollo Belvedere*. Continue through a series of rooms – ❺ **Sala degli Animali** (Animal Room); ❻ **Sala delle Muse** (Room of the Muses), home of the famous *Torso Belvedere;* and ❼ **Sala Rotonda** (Round Room), centred on a vast red basin. From neighbouring ❽ **Sala Croce Greca** (Greek Cross Room), the Simonetti staircase leads up to ❾ **Galleria dei Candelabri** (Gallery of the Candelabra), the first of three galleries along a lengthy corridor. It gets very crowded up here as you're funnelled through ❿ **Galleria degli Arazzi** (Tapestry Gallery) and onto ⓫ **Galleria delle Carte Geografiche** (Map Gallery), a 120m-long hall hung with huge topographical maps. At the end of the corridor, carry on through ⓬ **Sala Sobieski** to ⓭ **Sala di Costantino**, the first of the four Stanze di Raffaello (Raphael Rooms) – the others are ⓮ **Stanza d'Eliodoro**, ⓯ **Stanza della Segnatura**, featuring Raphael's superlative *La Scuola di Atene*, and ⓰ **Stanza dell'Incendio di Borgo**. (Note: sometimes guards have you tour the rooms in a different order.) Anywhere else these magnificent frescoed chambers would be the star attraction, but here they serve as the warm-up for the grand finale, the ⓱ **Sistine Chapel**.

VATICAN MUSEUMS

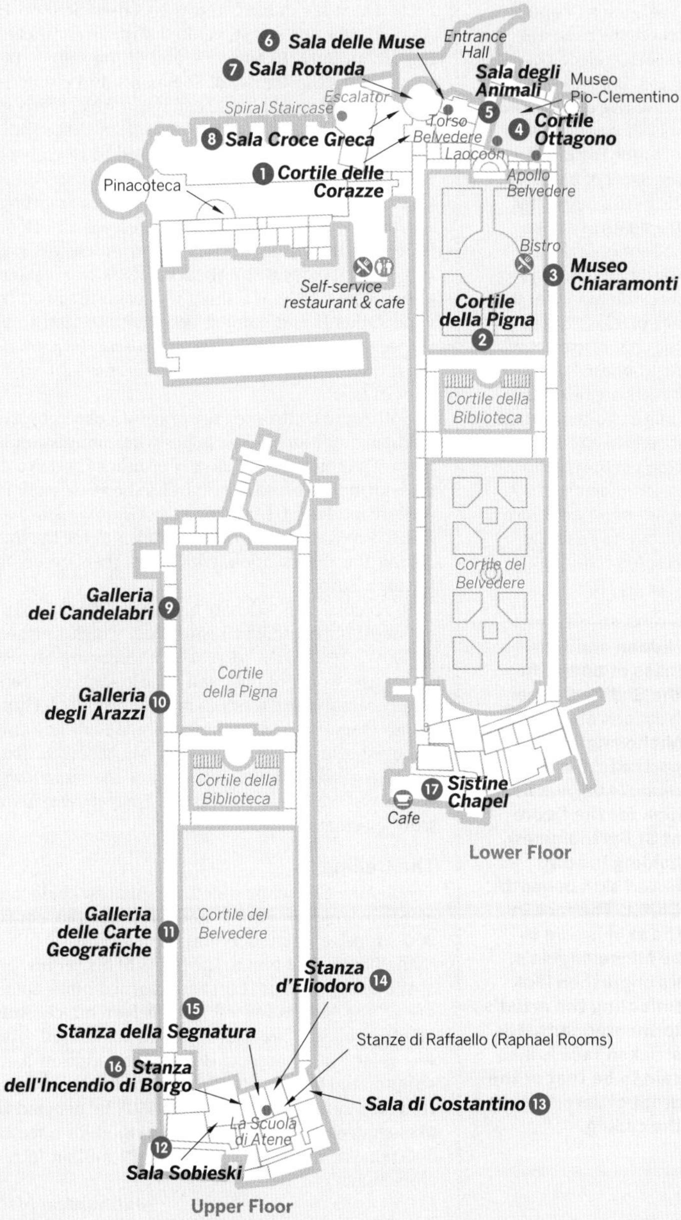

6 Sala delle Muse
Entrance Hall
7 Sala Rotonda
Sala degli Animali
Museo Pio-Clementino
Escalator
Spiral Staircase
5
Torso Belvedere
4 Cortile Ottagono
8 Sala Croce Greca
Laocoön
1 Cortile delle Corazze
Apollo Belvedere
Pinacoteca
Bistro
Self-service restaurant & cafe
3 Museo Chiaramonti
Cortile della Pigna
2
Cortile della Biblioteca
Cortile del Belvedere
17 Sistine Chapel
Cafe
Lower Floor
Galleria dei Candelabri 9
Galleria degli Arazzi 10
Cortile della Pigna
Cortile della Biblioteca
Galleria delle Carte Geografiche 11
Cortile del Belvedere
Stanza d'Eliodoro 14
15
Stanza della Segnatura
Stanze di Raffaello (Raphael Rooms)
16 Stanza dell'Incendio di Borgo
Sala di Costantino 13
La Scuola di Atene
12
Sala Sobieski
Upper Floor

CONCLAVE

The Sistine Chapel is where the conclave meets to elect a new pope. Dating from 1274, give or take a few modifications, the rules of the voting procedure are explicit: between 15 and 20 days after the death of a pope, the entire College of Cardinals (comprising all cardinals under the age of 80) is locked in the chapel to elect a new pontiff. Four secret ballots are held a day until a two-thirds majority has been secured. News of the election is communicated by emitting white smoke through a specially erected chimney.

Hidden amid the mass of bodies in the Sistine Chapel frescoes are two Michelangelo self-portraits. On the *Giudizio Universale* look for the figure of St Bartholomew, holding his own flayed skin beneath Christ. The face in the skin is said to be Michelangelo's, its anguished look reflecting the artist's tormented faith. His stricken face is also said to be that of the prophet Jeremiah on the ceiling.

History

The chapel was originally built for Pope Sixtus IV, after whom it's named, and was consecrated on 15 August 1483. It's a vast, vaulted structure, measuring 40.2m long, 13.4m wide and 20.7m high – the same size as the Temple of Solomon – and even pre-Michelangelo would have been impressive. Frescoes by the leading artists of the day adorned the walls and the vaulted ceiling was coloured to resemble a blue sky with golden stars. Underneath everything was a patterned floor in inlaid polychrome marble.

However, apart from the wall frescoes and floor, little remains of the original decor, which was sacrificed to make way for Michelangelo's two masterpieces. The first, the ceiling, was commissioned by Pope Julius II and painted between 1508 and 1512; the second, the spectacular *Giudizio Universale* (Last Judgment), was completed almost 30 years later in 1541.

Both were controversial works influenced by the political ambitions of the popes who commissioned them. The ceiling came as part of Julius II's drive to transform Rome into the Church's showcase capital, while Pope Paul III intended the *Giudizio Universale* to serve as a warning to Catholics to toe the line during the Reformation, which was then sweeping through Europe.

In recent decades debate has centred on the chapel's multi-million-dollar restoration, which finished in 1999 after nearly 20 years. In removing almost 450 years' worth of dust and candle soot, restorers finally revealed the frescoes in their original technicolour glory. But some critics claimed that they also removed a layer of varnish that Michelangelo had added to darken them and enhance their shadows. Whatever the truth, the Sistine Chapel remains a truly spectacular sight.

The Ceiling

The Sistine Chapel provided the greatest challenge of Michelangelo's career and painting the entire 800-sq-metre vaulted ceiling at a height of more than 20m pushed him to the limits of his genius.

When Pope Julius II first approached him – some say at the suggestion of his chief architect, Bramante, who was keen for Michelangelo to fail – he was reluctant to accept. He regarded himself as a sculptor and had no experience of painting frescoes. However, Julius persisted and in 1508 he persuaded Michelangelo to accept the commission for a fee of 3000 ducats (more or less €1.5 to €2 million in today's money).

continued on p140

SISTINE CHAPEL CEILING

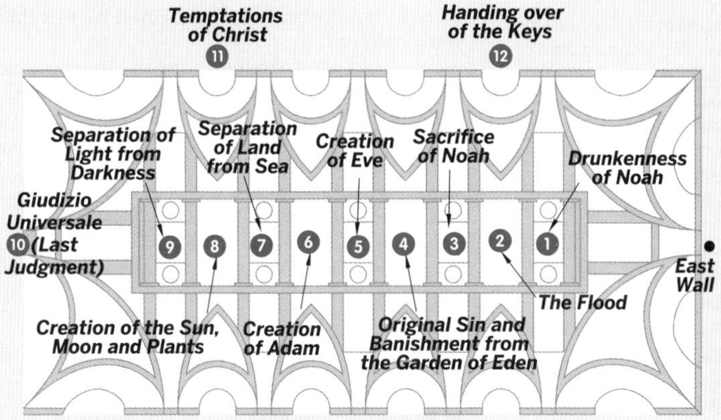

Museum Tour
Sistine Chapel

LENGTH 30 MINUTES

On entering the chapel, head over to the main entrance in the far (east) wall for the best views of the ceiling.

Michelangelo's design, which took him four years to complete, covers the entire 800-sq-metre surface. With painted architectural features and a colourful cast of biblical figures, it centres on nine panels depicting stories from the Book of Genesis.

As you look up from the east wall, the first panel is the 1 **Drunkenness of Noah**, followed by 2 **The Flood**, and the 3 **Sacrifice of Noah**. Next, 4 **Original Sin and Banishment from the Garden of Eden** famously depicts Adam and Eve being sent packing after accepting the forbidden fruit from Satan, represented by a snake with the body of a woman coiled around a tree. The 5 **Creation of Eve** is then followed by the 6 **Creation of Adam**. This, one of the most famous images in Western art, shows a bearded God pointing his finger at Adam, thus bringing him to life. Completing the sequence are the 7 **Separation of Land from Sea**; the 8 **Creation of the Sun, Moon and Plants**; and the 9 **Separation of Light from Darkness**, featuring a fearsome God reaching out to touch the sun. Set around the central panels are 20 athletic male nudes, the so-called *ignudi*.

Straight ahead of you on the west wall is Michelangelo's mesmeric 10 **Giudizio Universale** (Last Judgment), showing Christ – in the centre near the top – passing sentence over the souls of the dead as they are torn from their graves to face him. The saved get to stay up in heaven (in the upper right) while the damned are sent down to face the demons in hell (in the bottom right).

The chapel's side walls also feature stunning Renaissance frescoes, representing the lives of Moses (to the left) and Christ (to the right). Look out for Botticelli's 11 **Temptations of Christ** and Perugino's great masterpiece, the 12 **Handing over of the Keys**.

BLUE SKY ABOVE

One of the striking features of the *Giudizio Universale* is the amount of ultramarine blue in the painting – in contrast with the ceiling frescoes, which don't have any. In the 16th century, blue paint was made from the hugely expensive stone lapis lazuli, and artists were reluctant to use it unless someone else was paying. In the case of the *Giudizio Universale,* the pope picked up the tab for all Michelangelo's materials; on the ceiling, however, the artist had to cover his own expenses and so used less costly colours.

There's a fine bistro in the Cortile della Pigna (dishes €6 to €22) and a complex of self-service cafeterias (meals €12.50), as well as a cafe (snacks €5) with an outdoor patio near the Pinacoteca.

NIGHT OPENINGS

From mid-April to October, the museums open late every Friday evening (7pm to 11pm). To visit at this special time you'll need to book online.

Originally, Pope Julius wanted Michelangelo to paint the 12 apostles and a series of decorative architectural elements. But the artist rejected this and came up with a more complex design based on stories from the book of Genesis. And it's this that you see today.

The focus of the ceiling frescoes are the nine central panels, but set around them are 20 athletic male nudes, known as *ignudi.* These models caused a scandal when they were first revealed and still today art historians are divided over their meaning – some claim they are angels, others that they represent Michelangelo's neo-Platonic vision of ideal man.

Also depicted are five sibyls and seven prophets. These pagan and Christian figures are thought to symbolise mankind's continuous wait for redemption.

Wall Frescoes

If you can tear your eyes from the Michelangelos, the Sistine Chapel also boasts some superb wall frescoes. These formed part of the original chapel decoration and were painted between 1481 and 1482 by a crack team of Renaissance artists, including Botticelli, Ghirlandaio, Pinturicchio, Perugino and Luca Signorelli. They represent events in the lives of Moses (to the left, looking at the *Giudizio Universale*) and Christ (to the right). Most famous of all is Perugino's masterpiece showing Christ handing the keys of heaven to a kneeling St Peter.

Giudizio Universale (Last Judgment)

Michelangelo's second stint in the Sistine Chapel, from 1535 to 1541, resulted in the *Giudizio Universale* (Last Judgment), his depiction of Christ's second coming on the 200-sq-metre western wall.

The project, which was commissioned by Pope Clement VII and encouraged by his successor Paul III, was controversial from the start. Critics were outraged when Michelangelo destroyed two Perugino frescoes while preparing the wall – it had to be replastered so that it tilted inwards to protect it from dust – and when it was unveiled in 1541, five years after Michelangelo had started painting, its swirling mass of 391 predominantly naked bodies also provoked outrage. So fierce were feelings that the Church's top brass, meeting at the 1564 Council of Trent, ordered the nudity to be covered up. The task fell to Daniele da Volterra, one of Michelangelo's students, who added fig leaves and loincloths to 41 nudes, earning himself the nickname *il braghettone* (the breeches maker).

For his part Michelangelo rejected the criticism. He even got his own back on one of his loudest critics, Biagio de Cesena, the papal master of ceremonies, by depicting him as Minos, judge of the underworld, with donkey ears and a snake wrapped around him.

SIGHTS

Boasting priceless treasures at every turn, the Vatican is home to some of Rome's most popular attractions. The Vatican Museums and St Peter's Basilica are the star turns, but Castel Sant'Angelo, one of the city's most recognisable landmarks, is also well worth a visit.

Vatican City

VATICAN MUSEUMS — MUSEUM

See p133.

ST PETER'S BASILICA — BASILICA

See p128.

ST PETER'S SQUARE — PIAZZA

Map p336 (Piazza San Pietro; Piazza del Risorgimento, Ottaviano-San Pietro) Overlooked by St Peter's Basilica (p128), the Vatican's central square was laid out between 1656 and 1667 to a design by Gian Lorenzo Bernini. Seen from above, it resembles a giant keyhole with two semicircular colonnades, each consisting of four rows of Doric columns, encircling a giant ellipse that straightens out to funnel believers into the basilica. The effect was deliberate – Bernini described the colonnades as representing 'the motherly arms of the church'.

The scale of the piazza is dazzling: at its largest it measures 320m by 240m. There are 284 columns and, atop the colonnades, 140 saints. The 25m **obelisk** in the centre was brought to Rome by Caligula from Heliopolis in Egypt and later used by Nero as a turning post for the chariot races in his circus.

Leading off the piazza, the monumental approach road, **Via della Conciliazione**, was commissioned by Mussolini and built between 1936 and 1950.

★VATICAN GARDENS — GARDENS

Map p336 (www.museivaticani.va; adult/reduced incl Vatican Museums €33/24, by open-air bus €37/23; by reservation only; Piazza del Risorgimento, Ottaviano-San Pietro) Up to a third of the Vatican is covered by the perfectly manicured Vatican Gardens, which contain fortifications, grottoes, monuments, fountains, and the state's tiny heliport and train station. Visits are by guided tour only – either on foot (two hours) or by open-air bus (45 minutes) – for which you'll need to book at least a week in advance. After the tour you're free to visit the Vatican Museums on your own; admission is included in the ticket price.

NECROPOLI VIA TRIUMPHALIS — ARCHAEOLOGICAL SITE

Map p336 (www.museivaticani.va; adult/reduced incl Vatican Museums €27/20, incl Vatican Museums & Gardens €38/29; by reservation only; Ottaviano-San Pietro) Not to be confused with the Tomb of St Peter, this ancient Roman cemetery extends beneath the Vatican hill. Guided tours, which must be prebooked, take in the tombs and burial chambers that extended along the ancient road known as Via Triumphalis.

Borgo & Around

★CASTEL SANT'ANGELO — MUSEUM, CASTLE

Map p336 (06 681 9111; www.castelsantangelo.beniculturali.it; Lungotevere Castello 50; adult/

PAPAL AUDIENCES & MASS AT ST PETER'S SQUARE

Papal audiences are held at 10am on Wednesdays, usually in St Peter's Square but sometimes in the nearby Aula delle Udienze Pontificie Paolo VI (Paul VI Audience Hall). To attend you'll need to book free tickets in advance.

You'll also need tickets if you want to attend a papal mass. These often run out quickly, so apply early, especially for Easter and Christmas services.

➡ For further details, see the Vatican website (www.vatican.va/various/prefettura/index_en.html).

➡ You can also get tickets in advance via the Pontifical North American College (www.pnac.org).

➡ The Swiss Guard sometimes gives away tickets on the morning of the audience (from their station left of the basilica entrance or from their office at Porta Sant'Anna) – but don't count on it.

No tickets are required for the pope's Sunday blessing at noon in St Peter's Square.

reduced €14/7, free 1st Sunday of the month Oct-Mar; ⌚9am-7.30pm, ticket office to 6.30pm; 🚌Piazza Pia) With its chunky round keep, this castle is an instantly recognisable landmark. Built as a mausoleum for the emperor Hadrian, it was converted into a papal fortress in the 6th century and named after an angelic vision that Pope Gregory the Great had in 590. Nowadays, it is a moody and dramatic keep that houses the **Museo Nazionale di Castel Sant'Angelo** and its grand collection of paintings, sculpture, military memorabilia and medieval firearms.

Many of these weapons were used by soldiers fighting to protect the castle, which, thanks to a 13th-century **secret passageway to the Vatican** (*Passetto di Borgo*), provided sanctuary to many popes in times of danger. Most famously, Pope Clemente VI holed up here during the 1527 sack of Rome.

The castle's upper floors are filled with elegant Renaissance interiors, including the lavish **Sala Paolina** with frescoes depicting episodes from the life of Alexander the Great. Two storeys up, the **terrace**, immortalised by Puccini in his opera *Tosca*, offers unforgettable views over Rome and has a busy little cafe (snacks €2.50 to €5).

Fascinating Secret Castle (Il Castello Segreto) tours (€5; twice daily in English) take in the hidden *Passetto di Borgo*, the prisons and the beautifully painted, steam-heated papal baths of Leo X and Clemente VII.

Ticket prices may increase during temporary exhibitions.

PONTE SANT'ANGELO — BRIDGE

Map p336 (🚌Piazza Pia) The emperor Hadrian built the Ponte Sant'Angelo in 136 to provide an approach to his mausoleum, but it was Bernini who brought it to life, designing the angel sculptures in 1668. The three central arches of the bridge are part of the original structure; the end arches were restored and enlarged in 1892–94 during the construction of the Lungotevere embankments.

EATING

Beware, hungry travellers: there are an unholy number of overpriced tourist traps around the Vatican and St Peter's. A much better bet is nearby Prati, which has everything from gourmet takeaways and artisanal gelaterie to old-school trattorias and hybrid restaurant-cafes. Many of these cater to the legions of lawyers and media execs who work in the area..

Prati

★GELATERIA DEI GRACCHI — GELATO

Map p336 (☎06 321 66 68; www.gelateriadeigracchi.it; Via dei Gracchi 272; gelato from €2.50; ⌚noon-12.30am; 🚌Piazza Cola Di Rienzo) This is the original location of the small chain of gelato shops that has taken Rome by storm. The proprietors here only use fresh fruit in season – no fruit concentrate, no peach gelato in January etc. The flavours vary by day and season, but you're always assured of a top treat. Try one of the chocolate-covered gelato bars.

★PANIFICIO BONCI — BAKERY €

Map p336 (☎06 3973 4457; www.bonci.it; Via Trionfale 36; snacks €2-6; ⌚8.30am-3pm & 5-8.30pm Mon-Thu, 8.30am-8.30pm Fri & Sat; 🌶; 🚌Largo Trionfale) From Gabriele Bonci of the vaunted Bonci Pizzarium, this mellow bakery and deli offers a wide range of splendid takeaway fare, starting with the signature thin and crispy pizza slices. There are sandwiches, wholegrain breads and superb pastries. Seating (there's none) will be your main challenge. Enjoy *panini* stuffed with slow-roasted porchetta (pork) and tangy gorgonzola.

★FA-BÌO — SANDWICHES €

Map p336 (☎06 3974 6510; Via Germanico 71; meals €5-7; ⌚10.30am-5.30pm Mon-Fri, to 4pm Sat; 🚌Piazza del Risorgimento, MOttaviano-San Pietro) 🍃 Sandwiches, wraps, salads and fresh juices are all prepared with speed, skill and fresh organic ingredients at this busy takeaway. Locals, Vatican tour guides and in-the-know visitors come here to grab a quick lunchtime bite. If you can't find room in the small interior, there are stools along the pavement.

FATAMORGANA — GELATO €

Map p336 (☎06 3751 9093; www.gelateriafatamorgana.it; Via Leone IV 52; gelato €2.50-5; ⌚noon-11pm summer, to 9pm winter; MOttaviano-San Pietro) The Prati branch of Rome's trendy gelateria chain. As well as all the classic flavours, there are some wonderfully esoteric creations, including a delicious *basilico, miele e noci* (basil, honey and hazelnuts), carrot cake, and pineapple and ginger.

FORNO FELIZIANI — ITALIAN €

Map p336 (☎06 3973 7362; Via Candia 61; meals €8, slice of pizza €1.50; ⏲7.30am-8.30pm Mon-Sat; 📶🍴; ⓂCipro) Ditch the tourist traps around the Vatican Museums in favour of this *tavola calda,* Italy's version of fast food. Instead of ordering from a menu, you choose from dishes that are ready and waiting: waitstaff usher homey pastas, roasted vegetables, pizza by the slice and handmade pastries from the glassed-in kitchen to the counter – the perfect fuel for before or after sightseeing.

PANINO DIVINO — DELI €

Map p336 (☎06 3973 7803; www.paninodivino.it; Via dei Gracchi 11a; snacks from €4; ⏲10am-9pm Mon-Sat; 📶🍴👪; ⓂOttaviano) After a long trek through the Vatican Museums, this nearby sandwich shop hits the spot. Polish off *panini* stuffed with everything from slow-roasted porchetta, to tangy gorgonzola, marinated veggies, spicy tomato jam and much more. Dine on pavement stools around old wine barrels.

MO'S GELATERIE — GELATO €

Map p336 (☎06 687 43 57; Via Cola di Rienzo 174; gelato €2.50-6; ⏲8am-7.30pm; 🚌Piazza del Risorgimento) Chocoholics should make a beeline for Mo's, a small gelateria nestled between shops. The choice of flavours is limited, but the artisanal gelato really hits the mark. The dark chocolate is wonderful, and the banana has a lot of appeal. Insiders go nuts for the pistachio.

CACIO E PEPE — LAZIO €

Map p348 (☎06 321 72 68; www.trattoriacacioepepeprati.com; Via Avezzana 11; meals €20-25; ⏲12.30-3pm Mon-Sat & 7.30-11.30pm Mon-Fri; 🚌Piazza delle Cinque Giornate, 🚋Piazza delle Cinque Giornate) A local institution, this humble eatery is about as hardcore as it gets with its blackboard menu of Roman staples, spartan interior and no-frills service. Grab a table at one of the many pavement tables and dig into the namesake *cacio e pepe* (pasta with pecorino cheese and black pepper) followed by ever-welcome *polpette* (meat balls in a tomato sauce).

LOCAL KNOWLEDGE

SLICED PIZZA TO DIE FOR

Bonci Pizzarium (Map p336; ☎06 3974 5416; www.bonci.it; Via della Meloria 43; pizza slices €5; ⏲11am-10pm Mon-Sat, from noon Sun; ⓂCipro), the takeaway of Gabriele Bonci, Rome's acclaimed pizza emperor, serves Rome's best sliced pizza, bar none. Scissor-cut squares of soft, springy base are topped with original combinations of seasonal ingredients and served for immediate consumption. Often jammed, there are only a couple of benches and stools for the tourist hordes; head across to the plaza at the metro station for a seat. Also worth trying are the freshly fried *supplì* (risotto balls).

FRANCHI — DELI €

Map p336 (☎06 686 55 64; www.franchi.it; Via Cola di Rienzo 198; snacks from €1.50; ⏲7.30am-9pm Mon-Sat; 🚌Via Cola di Rienzo) One of Rome's historic delis, Franchi is great for a swift bite. Cheerful assistants work with practised dexterity slicing hams, cutting cheese, weighing olives and preparing *panini.* Make a picnic or enjoy in air-con comfort standing or at one of the few tables. There is also fried *suppli* and various daily pastas. The prepared foods are often gone by 3pm.

DOLCE MANIERA — BAKERY €

Map p336 (☎06 370 05 70; Via Barletta 27; snacks €0.50-2; ⏲24hr; ⓂOttaviano-San Pietro) For that late-night snack, nowhere beats this decades-old 24-hour basement bakery. When the munchies strike, head here to load up on cheap-as-chips *cornetti,* slabs of pizza, *panini,* pastries, cakes and biscuits. Just follow the olfactory siren song of sweet smells.

MONDO ARANCINA — FAST FOOD €

Map p336 (☎06 9761 9213; www.mondoarancina.it; Via Marcantonio Colonna 38; arancini from €3; ⏲10am-midnight; ⓂLepanto) All sunny yellow ceramics, hungry lunch crowds and tantalising deep-fried snacks, this bustling small takeaway brings a little corner of Sicily to Rome. Classic fist-sized *arancini* – fried rice balls stuffed with fillers ranging from the classic *ragù* to more exotic fare such as *zucca* (pumpkin) and gorgonzola – are the draw.

GELARMONY GELATO €

Map p336 (06 320 23 95; www.gelarmony.it; Via Marcantonio Colonna 34; gelato €2.50-4; 6.30am-midnight winter, to 2am summer; Lepanto) The real appeal at this popular Sicilian gelateria is the busy coffee bar. There's an ample selection of not bad fruit and cream *gelati* but for a typically Sicilian flavour go for pistachio or cassata. Alternatively, try a brioche *con panna* (with cream).

OLD BRIDGE GELATO €

Map p336 (328 411 94 78; http://gelateriaoldbridge.com; Viale dei Bastioni di Michelangelo 5; gelato €2-6; 10am-2am Mon-Sat, 2.30pm-2am Sun; Piazza del Risorgimento) Exhausted museum-goers besiege this tiny gelateria. It's been in business for more than 25 years and still does a roaring trade in creamy gelato, served in standard flavours and large portions. As an alternative, it also has yoghurts and refreshing sorbets. The cream used is organic.

HOSTARIA-PIZZERIA GIACOMELLI PIZZA €

Map p336 (06 372 59 10; Via Emilio Faà di Bruno 25; pizzas €5.50-13; 12.30-2.30pm & 7.30-11pm Tue-Sun; Ottaviano-San Pietro) This fine old-school neighbourhood pizzeria has been slinging out thin, crispy Roman pizzas for as long as most locals can remember. Little has changed over the years: the spartan tiled decor is dated, service is gruff, and the menu is much as it always has been, with bruschetta, fried starters, classic pizzas and frozen desserts. There are pavement tables.

IL SORPASSO ITALIAN €€

Map p336 (06 8902 4554; www.sorpasso.info; Via Properzio 31-33; meals €20-35; 7.30am-1am Mon-Fri, 9am-1am Sat; ; Piazza del Risorgimento) A bar-restaurant hybrid sporting a vintage cool look – vaulted stone ceilings, exposed brick, rustic wooden tables and summertime outdoor seating – Il Sorpasso is a Prati hotspot. Open throughout the day, it caters to a fashionable crowd, serving everything from salads and pasta specials to *trapizzini* (pyramids of stuffed pizza), cured meats and cocktails.

STILELIBERO ITALIAN €€

Map p336 (06 321 96 57; Via Fabio Massimo 68; meals €30-40; noon-3pm & 7pm-1am Tue-Sun; ; Lepanto) This eclectic restaurant and bar seamlessly marries fashion, food and cocktails. Italian dishes are playfully revisited, such as *amatriciana*-stuffed *tortello,* while bags and accessories from local designers adorn the walls, doubling as decor. Downstairs, a sleek cocktail bar with a piano serves up drinks and live music till late.

VELAVEVODETTO AI QUIRITI LAZIO €€

Map p336 (06 3600 0009; www.ristorantevelavevodetto.it; Piazza dei Quiriti 4/5; meals €30-40; 12.30-3pm & 7.45-11pm; Lepanto) This welcoming restaurant wins you over with its unpretentious Roman food and honest prices. The menu reads like a directory of local staples; standout choices include *fettuccine con asparagi, guanciale e pecorino* (pasta ribbons with asparagus, *guanciale* and *pecorino* cheese) and *polpette di bollito* (meatballs). Pavement tables overlook the fountain on the Piazza dei Quiriti.

OSTERIA DELL'ANGELO TRATTORIA €€

Map p336 (06 372 94 70; Via Bettolo 24; fixed-price menu €25-35; 12.30-2.30pm Mon-Fri, 8-11pm Mon-Sat; Ottaviano-San Pietro) With rugby paraphernalia on the walls and basic wooden tables, this hectic eatery offers an authentic neighbourhood trattoria experience. The fixed-price menu features a mixed antipasti, a robust Roman-style pasta and a choice of hearty mains. To finish off, spiced biscuits are served with sweet dessert wine. Reservations recommended and no credit cards. Order a bottle of house wine (€10).

DEL FRATE ITALIAN €€

Map p336 (06 323 64 37; www.enotecadelfrate.it; Via degli Scipioni 122; meals €40-45; 12.30-3pm Tue-Sat, 6-11.45pm Mon-Sat; Ottaviano-San Pietro) Locals love this upmarket *enoteca* (wine bar) with its simple wooden tables and high-ceilinged brick-arched rooms. Dishes are designed to complement the extensive wine list, so there's a formidable selection of cheeses (from Sicilian ricotta to Piedmontese *robiola*) and small bites suitable for vino, alongside a refined menu of starters, salads, fresh pastas and main courses (dinner served from 8pm).

DAL TOSCANO TUSCAN €€

Map p336 (06 3972 5717; www.ristorantedaltoscano.it; Via Germanico 58-60; meals €35-50; 12.30-3pm & 8-11.15pm Tue-Sun; Ottaviano-San Pietro) Immerse yourself in the tastes of

Tuscany at this old-fashioned *ristorante*. Meat is a highlight, with cured hams and salamis served as starters followed by grilled steaks. Menu highlights include a colossal chargrilled *bistecca alla Fiorentina* (Florentine-style steak) and *ribollito,* a thick Tuscan soup, served as a first course. Reservations recommended. Enjoy a table outside on the quiet street.

HOSTARIA DINO E TONI LAZIO €€

Map p336 (☎06 3973 3284; www.facebook.com/h.dinoetony; Via Leone IV 60; meals €25-30; ⏲12.30-3pm & 7-11pm Mon-Sat, closed Aug; ⓂOttaviano-San Pietro) A bustling old-school trattoria, Dino e Toni offers simple, no-frills Roman cooking. Kick off with its house antipasto and a minor meal of fried *supplì,* olives and pizza, before plunging into its signature pasta dish, *rigatoni all'amatriciana* (pasta tubes with bacon-like *guanciale,* chilli and tomato sauce). It has tables with checked tablecloths outside along the busy street.

AMALFI PIZZA €€

Map p336 (☎06 3973 3165; http://amalfiristoranti.com; Via dei Gracchi 12; pizzas €6.50-11, meals €30-35; ⏲11am-12.30am; 🚌Piazza del Risorgimento, ⓂOttaviano-San Pietro) On a quiet side street just off the main route from Ottaviano-San Pietro metro station to St Peter's, this brassy pizzeria-cum-restaurant draws a mainly touristy crowd who enjoy the many outdoor tables. It offers decent Neapolitan-inspired food – buffalo mozzarella starters, soft, doughy pizzas, seafood pastas, salads and grilled meats.

L'ARCANGELO LAZIO €€€

Map p336 (☎06 321 09 92; www.larcangelo.com; Via Giuseppe Gioachino Belli 59; meals €45-80, lunch set menu €30; ⏲1-2.30pm Mon-Fri, 8-11pm Mon-Sat; 🚌Piazza Cavour) Styled as an informal bistro with wood panelling, leather banquettes and casual table settings, L'Arcangelo enjoys a stellar local reputation.

Dishes are modern and creative yet still undeniably Roman in their use of traditional ingredients such as sweetbreads and *baccalà* (cod). A further plus is the well-curated wine list. Whimsical touches include toy cars on tables.

DRINKING & NIGHTLIFE

Once the Vatican tourists have left and Prati's army of office workers have gone home for the day, this is a quiet part of town. There are a few bars and cafes dotted around the place, but the local drinking scene is pretty low-key, and nightlife is limited to a few live-music venues and theatres.

MICHELIN-STARRED DINING

For fine-dining in the shadow of the Vatican, follow the Michelin star to these two acclaimed restaurants:

Tordomatto (Map p336; ☎06 6935 2895; www.tordomattoroma.com; Via Pietro Giannone 24; meals €65-125; ⏲1-2.30pm Fri-Sun, 7.30-10.45pm Thu-Tue; 🚌Trionfale/Telesio) The dining room is elegant simplicity itself at this Michelin-starred restaurant, which puts the food ahead of fuss. With a corner spot on genteel streets, Tordomatto promises a relaxed evening of fine cuisine. See the Michelin-starred chefs in action by booking the kitchen table well in advance. Look for Roman classics, exquisitely imagined and prepared.

Enoteca La Torre (Map p348; ☎06 4566 8304; www.enotecalatorreroma.com; Villa Laetitia, Lungotevere delle Armi 22; fixed-price lunch menu €60, tasting menus €105-130; ⏲12.30-2.30pm Tue-Sat, 7.30-10.30pm Mon-Sat; 🚌Lungotevere delle Armi) The romantic art nouveau Villa Laetitia (p247) provides an aristocratic setting for this refined Michelin-starred restaurant. It's a solid member in good standing in Rome's fine-dining scene, and people book weeks in advance. Expect sophisticated contemporary cuisine with seasonal dishes beautifully presented. The wine list is stellar and the service sublime. Many come just to gape at the noted interior dining-room windows.

CRAFT BEER BARS

L'Osteria di Birra del Borgo Roma (Map p336; ☎06 8376 2316; http://osteria.birradelborgo.it; Via Silla 26; ⏲noon-2am; Ⓜ Ottaviano-San Pietro) Italy is no longer just about wine: for years a generation of brewers has been developing great craft beers. Try some of the best at this chic, contemporary bar with a soaring ceiling and stylish vats of brewing beer. It has a short menu of Italian standards at night and fine antipasto choices all day.

Be.Re. (Map p336; ☎06 9442 1854; www.be-re.eu; Piazza del Risorgimento, cnr Via Vespasiano; ⏲11am-2am; 🚌Piazza del Risorgimento) With its exposed-brick decor, high vaulted ceilings and narrow pavement tables, this is a good spot for Italian craft beers. And should hunger strike, there's a branch of hit takeaway Trapizzino right next door that offers table service at Be.re. Lactose-intolerant coffee drinkers will enjoy the attached Pergamino as it includes concoctions made with soy milk.

★SCIASCIA CAFFÈ — CAFE

Map p336 (☎06 321 15 80; http://sciasciacaffe1919.it; Via Fabio Massimo 80/a; ⏲7am-9pm; Ⓜ Ottaviano-San Pietro) There are several contenders for the best coffee in town, but in our opinion nothing tops the *caffè eccellente* served at this polished old-school cafe.

A velvety smooth espresso served in a delicate cup lined with melted chocolate, it's nothing short of magnificent, and has been since 1919.

PASSAGUAI — WINE BAR

Map p336 (☎06 8745 1358; www.passaguai.it; Via Leto 1; ⏲10am-2am Mon-Fri, 6pm-2am Sat & Sun; 📶; 🚌Piazza del Risorgimento) A basement bar with tables in a cosy stone-clad interior and on a quiet side street, Passaguai feels pleasingly under the radar.

It's a great spot for a post-sightseeing cocktail or glass of wine – there's an excellent choice of both – accompanied by cheese and cold cuts, or even a full meal from the small menu.

MAKASAR BISTROT — WINE BAR

Map p336 (☎06 687 46 02; www.makasar.it; Via Plauto 33; ⏲noon-midnight Mon-Thu, to 2am Fri & Sat, 5pm-midnight Sun; 📶; 🚌Piazza del Risorgimento) Recharge your batteries with a quiet drink at this bookish *bistrot*.

Pick your tipple from the 250-variety tea menu or opt for an Italian wine and sit back in the softly lit earthenware-hued interior. For something to eat, there's a small menu of salads, bruschette, baguettes and hot dishes.

☆ ENTERTAINMENT

ALEXANDERPLATZ — JAZZ

Map p336 (☎06 8377 5604; www.alexanderplatzjazzclub.com; Via Ostia 9; tickets €15-20; ⏲8.30pm-1.30am; Ⓜ Ottaviano-San Pietro) Intimate, underground and hard to find – look for the discreet black door near the corner – Rome's most celebrated jazz club draws top Italian and international performers and a respectful cosmopolitan crowd. Book a table for the best stage views or to dine here, although note that it's the music that's the star act. Performances begin at 10pm.

FONCLEA — LIVE MUSIC

Map p336 (☎06 689 63 02; www.fonclea.it; Via Crescenzio 82a; cover after 8pm €10; ⏲6pm-2am Sep-May, concerts 9.30pm; 📶; 🚌Piazza del Risorgimento) Fonclea is a great little pub venue, with nightly gigs by bands playing everything from jazz and soul to pop, rock and doo-wop. Get in the mood with a drink during happy hour (6pm to 8.30pm daily). There are several cocktail bars nearby with outdoor tables.

AUDITORIUM CONCILIAZIONE — LIVE PERFORMANCE

Map p336 (☎06 683 22 56; www.auditoriumconciliazione.it; Via della Conciliazione 4; ⏲box office 9am-8pm Mon-Sat, to 5pm Sun; 🚌Piazza Pia) On the main approach road to St Peter's Basilica, this large auditorium plays host to a wide range of events – classical and contemporary concerts, cabarets, dance spectacles, theatre productions, film screenings, exhibitions and conferences.

SHOPPING

Unless you're in the market for rosary beads and religious souvenirs, the Vatican has little in the way of shopping. Prati is a different story, and its shop-lined streets offer plenty of scope for browsing. The main drag, Via Cola di Rienzo, specialises in department stores and midrange clothes outlets while the backstreets harbour some wonderful boutiques and artisanal studios.

★PACIOTTI SALUMERIA — FOOD & DRINKS

Map p336 (06 3973 3646; www.paciottisalumeria.it; Via Marcantonio Bragadin 51/53; 7.30am-8.30pm Mon-Wed, Fri & Sat, 12.30-8.30pm Thu; M Cipro) This family-run deli is a fantasyland of Italian edibles. Whole prosciutto hams hang in profusion. Cheeses, olive oil, dried pasta, balsamic vinegar, wine and truffle pâtés crowd the shelves, and can be bubbled-wrapped and vacuum-sealed for travel. Patriarch Antonio Paciotti and his three affable sons merrily advise customers in both Italian and English.

★IL SELLAIO — FASHION & ACCESSORIES

Map p336 (06 3211719; www.serafinipelletteria.it; Via Caio Mario 14; 9.30am-7.30pm Mon-Fri, 9.30am-1pm & 3.30-7.30pm Sat; M Ottaviano-San Pietro) During the 1960s Ferruccio Serafini was one of Rome's most sought-after artisans, making handmade leather shoes and bags for the likes of Liz Taylor and Marlon Brando. Nowadays, his daughter Francesca runs the family shop where you can pick up beautiful hand-stitched bags, belts and accessories. Have designs made to order or get your leather handbags and luggage reconditioned.

ANTICA MANIFATTURA CAPPELLI — HATS

Map p336 (06 3972 5679; www.antica-cappelleria.it; Via degli Scipioni 46; 9am-7pm Mon-Sat; M Ottaviano-San Pietro) A throwback to a more elegant age, the prim, hat-size atelier-boutique of milliner Patrizia Fabri offers a wide range of beautifully crafted hats. Choose from the off-the-peg line of straw Panamas, vintage cloches, felt berets and tweed deerstalkers, or have one made to measure. Prices range from about €70 to €300. Ordered hats can be delivered within the day.

MOSAIC COURSES

If the sight of so much art in the Vatican has inspired you, head to the **Art Studio Lab** (Map p336; 348 6099758, 344 0971721; box@savellireligious.com; Savelli Arte e Tradizione, Via Paolo VI 27-29; 9.30am-4pm, shop to 6pm; Lungotevere in Sassia), a mosaic school in the Savelli Arte e Tradizione shop near St Peter's Square. Its expert mosaicists offer a range of individually tailored sessions and courses, including a basic three-hour workshop during which you'll learn how to cut marble and enamels and make your own frames, mirrors or tiles. Reckon on €90/80 per adult/child, including lunch, for a group of one to three people.

LA TRADIZIONE — FOOD & DRINKS

Map p336 (06 3972 0349; www.latradizione.it; Via Cipro 8; 8am-2pm & 4.30-8.30pm Mon-Sat; M Cipro) With a window bedecked with fresh black truffles, you know you've found a source for Italian foods of the highest order. This traditional shop (note the name) has excellent cheeses, meats, prepared foods, chocolates and much more.

ENOTECA COSTANTINI — WINE

Map p336 (06 320 35 75; https://enotecacostantinipiero.it; Piazza Cavour 16; 9am-1pm Tue-Sat, 4.30-8pm Mon-Sat; Piazza Cavour) If you're after a hard-to-find grappa or a special wine, this excellent *enoteca* is the place. Piero Costantini's superbly stocked shop is a point of reference for aficionados, with its 800-sq-metre basement cellar and a colossal collection of Italian and international wines, champagnes and more than 1000 spirits. Note the beautiful wrought-iron grapevines on the facade.

1. Bocca della Verità at Chiesa di Santa Maria in Cosmedin (p76)
2. Michelangelo's *Moses* at Basilica di San Pietro in Vincoli (p154)
3. Basilica di Santa Maria in Trastevere (p174) **4.** St Peter's Basilica (p128)

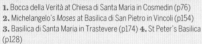

MMAC72 / GETTY IMAGES ©

Rome's Churches

Rome is a visual feast, and whatever your faith, it's impossible not to be awestruck by its riches. Nowhere will you be able to visit such a splendid array and wealth of ecclesiastic architecture, from the stark simplicity of Basilica di Santa Sabina (p194) and the tiny perfection of Tempietto di Bramante (p177) to the awe-inspiring grandeur of St Peter's Basilica (p128) – the world's greatest church – and the Sistine Chapel (p136). Rome's other inspirational pilgrimage sites include huge edifices such as the basilicas of San Lorenzo Fuori le Mura (p157), Santa Maria Maggiore (p153) and San Giovanni in Laterano (p190), and the Chiesa di Santa Croce in Gerusalemme (p155).

Ancient Architecture

Whether they're baroque, medieval or Renaissance, many churches also feature a form of recycling that's uniquely Roman, integrating leftover architectural elements from imperial Rome. For example, you'll see ancient columns in the Basilica di Santa Maria in Trastevere (p174), and the famous ancient mask, the Bocca della Verità (p76), in the beautiful medieval Chiesa di Santa Maria in Cosmedin. Taking the idea to the limit, the mesmerising Pantheon (p80) is an entire Roman temple converted into a church.

Divine Art

Rome's churches, which dot almost every street corner, also serve as free art galleries, bedecked in gold, inlay-work, mosaics and carvings. The wealth of the Roman Catholic Church has benefited from centuries of virtuoso artists, architects and artisans who descended here to create their finest and most heavenly works in the glorification of God. Without paying a cent, anyone can wander in off the street to see this glut of masterpieces, including works by Michelangelo in Basilica di San Pietro in Vincoli (p154) and St Peter's Basilica, Caravaggio in Santa Maria del Popolo (p109) and San Luigi dei Francesi (p86), and Bernini in Santa Maria della Vittoria (p116).

Monti, Esquilino & San Lorenzo

MONTI | ESQUILINO | PIAZZA DELLA REPUBBLICA & AROUND | SAN LORENZO & BEYOND

Neighbourhood Top Five

❶ **Palazzo Massimo alle Terme** (p152) Evoking the ancient past when viewing exquisite jewel-coloured frescoes from the villas of imperial Rome at one of the city's finest museums.

❷ **Monti** (p154) Pottering around Rome's romantic, bohemian-chic neighbourhood, lingering at wine bars, sipping coffee on pavement terraces and browsing artisan boutiques en route.

❸ **Pigneto** (p167) Joining young locals partying in the many bars scattered across this iconic working-class district, which was immortalised by film director Pier Paolo Pasolini.

❹ **Basilica di Santa Maria Maggiore** (p153) Marvelling at the Byzantine and baroque splendours of one of Rome's four patriarchal basilicas.

❺ **Domus Aurea** (p155) Exploring the subterranean remains of Nero's massive golden palace, now lying beneath Oppian Hill.

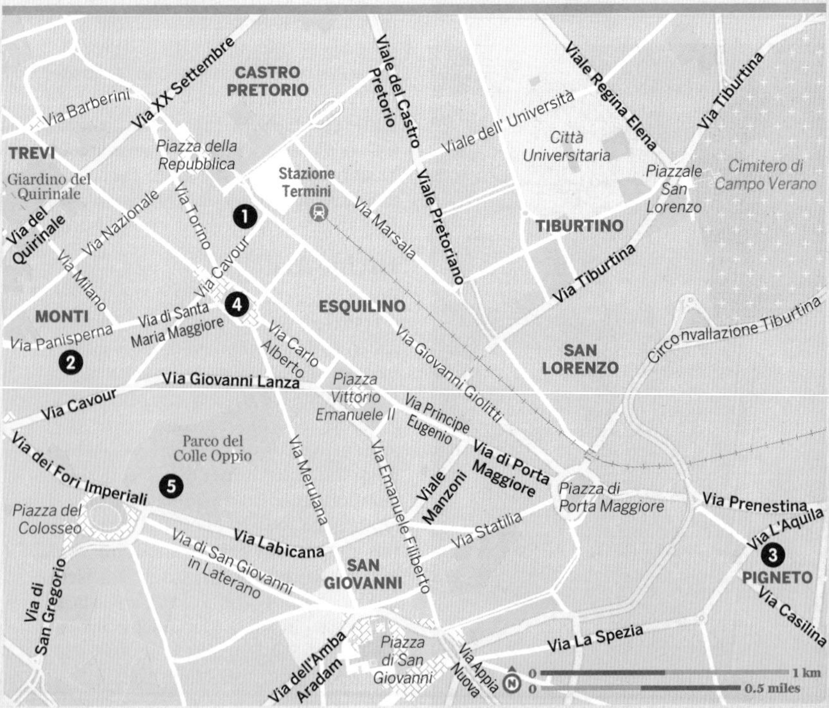

For more detail of this area see Maps p343 and p344

Explore Monti, Esquilino & San Lorenzo

Allow a full day to explore Esquilino, named after one of Rome's seven hills and incorporating the down-at-heel streets around Stazione Termini and Piazza Vittorio Emanuele II. The magnificent Basilica di Santa Maria Maggiore (p153) is located here, as is the Museo Nazionale Romano: Palazzo Massimo alle Terme (p152) with its stunning classical art. Head elsewhere in the evening, though, as Esquilino can be a bit dodgy after dark.

Heading downhill, Monti was ancient Rome's notorious Suburra slum – a red-light district and the childhood home of Julius Caesar. Now gentrified, its cafes, bistros, boutiques and *enoteche* (wine bars) lend it bags of charm. Dedicate at least a day to it and be sure to dine here at least once.

East of Termini, the lively student quarter of San Lorenzo won't appeal to everyone and by day it feels decidedly hungover. Consider heading to the Basilica di San Lorenzo, Fuori le Mura (p157) in the late afternoon, followed by some bar hopping. The student nightlife scene kicks in after dark.

Pigneto (p167), a quick tram ride from Termini, is known for its bars. Eating is disappointing here, though.

Local Life

➡ **Coffee hang-outs** Every neighbourhood has its own iconic cafe: La Bottega del Caffè (p164) in Monti; Dagnino (p167) in Esquilino; Bar Celestino (p168) and Gente di San Lorenzo (p168) in San Lorenzo; and Necci dal 1924 (p167) in Pigneto.

➡ **Aperitivo** After-work drinking destinations proliferate: in Monti, Ai Tre Scalini (p164) or Barzilai Bistro (p164); in Esquilino, Gatsby Café (p165); in San Lorenzo Artisan (p167) and Officina Beat (p167) are good for craft beer devotees.

Getting There & Away

➡ **Metro** The Cavour metro stop (line B) is most convenient for Monti, while the Termini (lines A and B), Castro Pretorio (line B) and Vittorio Emanuele (line A) stations are useful for Esquilino.

➡ **Bus** Termini is the city's main bus hub, connected to places all over the city. Access Monti from buses stopping on Via Nazionale or Via Cavour. San Lorenzo is served by buses 71 and 492; Pigneto is served by buses 81, 810 and 105, and night bus n12.

➡ **Tram** An easy way to access San Lorenzo (trams 3 or 19) or Pigneto (trams 5, 14 or 19).

Lonely Planet's Top Tip

After visiting the Basilica di Santa Maria Maggiore, pop in to admire the Byzantine mosaics at the nearby **Basilica di Santa Prassede** (p154), a diminutive and serenely beautiful church rarely visited by tourists.

Best Places to Eat

➡ Alle Carrette (p159)
➡ La Barrique (p160)
➡ Panella (p161)
➡ Said (p163)
➡ Pasticceria Regoli (p162)
➡ Trattoria Da Danilo (p162)

For reviews, see p159.

Best Places to Drink

➡ Ai Tre Scalini (p164)
➡ Blackmarket Hall (p164)
➡ Gatsby Café (p165)
➡ La Bottega del Caffè (p164)
➡ Artisan (p167)
➡ Necci dal 1924 (p167)

For reviews, see p164.

Best Churches

➡ Basilica di Santa Maria Maggiore (p153)
➡ Basilica di San Pietro in Vincoli (p154)
➡ Basilica di San Lorenzo Fuori le Mura (p157)
➡ Basilica di Santa Prassede (p154)

For reviews, see p154.

ANNA PAKUTINA / SHUTTERSTOCK ©

TOP EXPERIENCE

FIRE YOUR IMAGINATION AT MUSEO NAZIONALE: PALAZZO MASSIMO ALLE TERME

One of Rome's finest museums, this oft-empty branch of the Museo Nazionale is packed with spectacular classical art. Start your visit on the 2nd floor, in order to see its wonders when you're fresh – the frescoes and mosaics here offer a scintillating evocation of what the interiors of grand ancient Roman villas looked like.

The 2nd-floor showstopper is in Room 2, where frescoes from Villa Livia, one of the homes of Augustus' wife Livia Drusilla, are displayed. These decorated a summer triclinium, a large living and dining area built half underground to provide protection from the heat, and depict a lush garden filled with flowering plants and fruit trees under a deep-blue, bird-filled sky.

Frescoes and intricate mosaic floors from Villa Farnesia are displayed in Rooms 3 to 5. There are friezes of garland-carrying caryatids (sculpted female figures serving as an architectural support); frescoed still lifes; and bedrooms decorated with images of the goddesses Artemis and Aphrodite. A multimedia presentation gives an excellent idea of what the villa, which was rediscovered in Trastevere in 1879, would have looked like.

The ground and 1st floors are devoted to sculpture. On the 1st floor, don't miss a mid-3rd century BCE marble statue known as the *Anzio Maiden*, which depicts a young girl participating in a Dionysian Ritual (Room 6). On the ground floor, the highlights are two 2nd-century-BCE Greek bronzes, *The Boxer* and *The Prince* (Room 7); and the 4th-century-BCE marble *Dying Niobid* statue in Room 6.

In the basement, the coin collection is far more absorbing than you might expect, tracing the history of the Roman Empire via coinage. There's also jewellery dating back several millennia that looks as good as new.

TOP TIPS

- Rent an audio guide at the main ticket desk for €5.
- Buy a combination ticket which also covers the Terme di Diocleziano, Palazzo Altemps and Crypta Balbi.

PRACTICALITIES

- Map p344, E3
- 06 3996 7700
- www.coopculture.it
- Largo di Villa Peretti 1
- adult/reduced €10/5
- 9am-7.45pm Tue-Sun
- M Termini

FELIX LIPOV / SHUTTERSTOCK ©

TOP EXPERIENCE

WANDER THE BASILICA DI SANTA MARIA MAGGIORE

Crowning the Esquiline Hill, this monumental building is one of Rome's four patriarchal basilicas. It was constructed on the spot where snow is said to have fallen in the summer of 358 CE and each 5 August the snowstorm is recreated at the festival of La Madonna della Neve, a light show in Piazza Santa Maria Maggiore.

Before entering the basilica look up to admire the magnificent 13th-century mosaics inside the loggia. The 18.8m-high column outside came from the Basilica of Massenzio in the Roman Forum and the basilica's 75m campanile, the highest in Rome, is 14th-century Romanesque.

The vast interior retains its 5th-century structure as well as 5th-century mosaics in the triumphal arch and nave. In the apse, the central image shows the Virgin Mary's coronation and dates from the 13th century. The nave floor is a handsome example of 12th-century Cosmati paving.

The baldachin (canopy) over the high altar is adorned with cherubs and the altar is a porphyry sarcophagus that's said to contain the relics of martyrs including St Matthew. A plaque in the floor marks the spot where Gian Lorenzo Bernini and his father Pietro are buried. Steps lead down to the *confessio* where a statue of Pope Pius IX kneels before a reliquary said to contain a fragment of Jesus' manger.

One of a number of side chapels, the graceful **Cappella Sforza** was one of Michelangelo's final architectural commissions.

The upper loggia, accessible only by 30-minute guided tours, was designed by Ferdinand Fuga in the late 18th century. On the tour you can admire the iridescent mosaics it screens, as well as a 'hidden' helical staircase by Gian Lorenzo Bernini.

TOP TIPS

- When you arrive, book yourself a guided tour of the loggia straight away; tours run every hour or so in English, Italian or Spanish.
- Visit early in the morning to have the basilica all to yourself.

PRACTICALITIES

- Map p344, E5
- 06 6988 6800
- Piazza Santa Maria Maggiore
- basilica free, adult/reduced museum €3/2, loggia €5
- 7am-6.45pm, loggia guided tours 9.30am-5.45pm
- M Termini or Cavour

SIGHTS

Grand 19th-century buildings line the streets of Esquilino, the area around Rome's central train station, Termini. It might not be Rome's prettiest 'hood, and some parts feel downright dodgy, but it's studded with some stupendous churches, museums and archaeological sites, including Santa Maria Maggiore (p153) and San Pietro in Vincoli (p154; home to Michelangelo's *Moses*), Nero's Domus Aurea (p155) and two masterpiece-packed outposts of the Museo Nazionale Romano (p152 and p156). To the southeast, San Lorenzo is home to the Basilica di San Lorenzo Fuori le Mura (p157), one of Rome's four patriarchal basilicas.

Monti

BASILICA DI SAN PIETRO IN VINCOLI — BASILICA

Map p344 (06 9784 4950; Piazza di San Pietro in Vincoli 4a; 8am-12.20pm & 3-6.50pm summer, to 5.50pm winter; Cavour) Pilgrims and art lovers flock to this 5th-century basilica for two reasons: to marvel at Michelangelo's colossal *Moses* sculpture (1505) and to see the chains that are said to have bound St Peter when he was imprisoned in the Carcere Mamertino ('in Vincoli' means 'in Chains'). Also of note is a lovely 7th-century mosaic icon of St Sebastian. Access to the church is via a steep flight of steps leading up from Via Cavour and passing under a low arch.

The church was built specially to house the shackles of St Peter, which had been sent to Constantinople after the saint's death, but were later returned as relics. They arrived in two pieces and legend has it that when they were reunited they miraculously joined together. They are now displayed under the altar.

To the right of the altar, Michelangelo's *Moses* forms the centrepiece of his unfinished tomb for Pope Julius II. The prophet strikes a muscular pose with well-defined biceps, a magnificent waist-length beard and two small horns sticking out of his head. These were inspired by a mistranslation of a biblical passage: where the original said that rays of light issued from Moses' face, the translator wrote 'horns'. Michelangelo was aware of the mistake, but gave Moses horns anyway. Flanking Moses are statues of Leah and Rachel, probably completed by Michelangelo's students. A statue of Julius lolls somewhat saucily in the centre, above Moses.

The tomb, despite its imposing scale, was never finished – Michelangelo originally envisaged 40 statues, but got sidetracked by the Sistine Chapel – and Pope Julius II was buried in St Peter's Basilica.

Esquilino

BASILICA DI SANTA MARIA MAGGIORE — BASILICA

See p153.

BASILICA DI SANTA PRASSEDE — CHURCH

Map p344 (Via Santa Prassede 9a; 7am-noon & 4-6.30pm; Cavour) Famous for its brilliant Byzantine mosaics, which have been preserved in their original state, this small 9th-century church is dedicated to St Praxedes, an early Christian heroine who hid Christians fleeing persecution and buried those she couldn't save in a well. The position of the well is now marked by a marble disc on the floor of the nave.

The mosaics entirely cover the walls and vault. They were produced by artists whom Pope Paschal I had brought in specially from Byzantium and bear all the hallmarks of their eastern creators, with bold gold backgrounds and a marked Christian symbolism. The apse mosaics depict Christ flanked by Sts Peter, Pudentiana and Zeno on the right, and Paul, Praxedes and Paschal on the left. All the figures have golden halos except for Paschal, whose head is shadowed by a blue nimbus to indicate that he was still alive at the time.

Further treasures await in the heavily mosaiced **Cappella di San Zenone**, including a piece of the column to which Christ is said to have been tied when he was flogged, brought back from Jerusalem – it's in the glass case on the right.

CHIESA DI SAN MARTINO AI MONTI — CHURCH

Map p344 (Viale del Monte Oppio 28; 9am-noon & 4.30-7pm; Cavour) This was already a place of worship in the 3rd century, when Christians would meet in what was then the home of a Roman named Equitius. In the 4th century, after Christianity was legalised, a church was constructed on the site, and later rebuilt in the 6th and 9th centuries. It was then completely transformed by Filippo Gagliardi in the 1650s.

The church is of particular interest for Gagliardi's frescoes showing the Basilica di San Giovanni in Laterano before it was rebuilt in the mid-17th century and St Peter's Basilica before it assumed its present 16th-century look. Remnants of the more distant past include the ancient Corinthian columns dividing the nave and aisles.

DOMUS AUREA ARCHAEOLOGICAL SITE

Map p344 (Golden House; ☎06 3996 7700; www.coopculture.it; Viale della Domus Aurea, Parco del Colle Oppio; adult/under 6yr €14/free; ⏲9.15am-4.15pm Sat & Sun; Ⓜ Colosseo) Nero had his Domus Aurea constructed after the fire of 64 CE (which he is rumoured to have started to clear the area). Named after the gold that lined its facade and interiors, it was a huge complex covering almost one third of the city. Making some use of video and virtual reality, multi-language guided tours of its ruins shed light on how it would have appeared in its prime. Advance online reservations (€2) are obligatory. Enter from Via Labicana.

The Domus was full of architectural invention, and was a more splendid palace than had ever been seen before. However, Nero's successors attempted to raze all trace of his megalomania. Vespasian drained Nero's ornamental lake and, in a symbolic gesture, built the Colosseum in its place. Domitian built a palace on the Palatino, while Trajan sacked and destroyed the 1st floor and then entombed the lower level in earth and used it for the foundations of his public baths complex, which was abandoned by the 6th century. This burial of the palace preserved it; the section that has been excavated lies beneath Oppian Hill.

In winter, wear warm clothes to visit as the palace now lies underground and is damp. Remarkably, the humidity has helped preserve the frescoes in the chambers, though these may only be seen in a couple of cleaned areas – the rest have been destroyed or are yet to be restored. Tours last 75 minutes and are guided by archaeologists.

During the Renaissance, artists (including Raphael and Pinturicchio) lowered themselves into the ruins, climbing across the top of Trajan's rubble in order to study the frescoed grottoes. In fact, Raphael reproduced some of their motifs in his work on the Vatican.

LOCAL KNOWLEDGE

VILLA ALDOBRANDINI

If you're in need of a breather around Via Nazionale or are in search of somewhere for a picnic, follow Via Mazzarino off the main road and walk up the steps, past 2nd-century ruins, to this graceful, sculpture-dotted garden (Map p344; Via Mazzarino; ⏲dawn-dusk; 🚍Via Nazionale) with gravel paths and benches beneath fragrant orange trees, palms and camellias.

PALAZZO MERULANA MUSEUM

Map p339 (☎06 3996 7800; www.palazzomerulana.it; Via Merulana 121; adult/reduced €5/4; ⏲Mon & Wed-Fri 2-7pm, Sat & Sun from 10am; Ⓜ Manzoni) Housed within the splendidly restored Palazzo Merulana, this impressive museum exhibits artworks sourced from the Elena and Claudio Cerasi Foundation (p207; the Cerasis own the construction firm responsible for major projects such as the MAXXI). The majority of the pieces on display come from Roman and Italian artists active in the first half of the 20th century, including de Chirico, Pirandello and Capagrossi. Additional perks include a spacious outdoor terrace, stylish coffee bar and excellent gift shop. Audio guides cost €5.

MUSEO STORICO DELLA LIBERAZIONE MUSEUM

Map p343 (Museum of Liberation of Rome; ☎06 700 38 66; www.museoliberazione.it; Via Tasso 145; entry by donation; ⏲9am-1.15pm & 2.15-7.15pm; Ⓜ Manzoni) The apartment block at Via Tasso 145 was the headquarters of the German SS during the Nazi occupation of Rome (1943–44), and now a small and sombre museum recounts the story the reign of terror in the city. Members of the local Resistance were interrogated, tortured and imprisoned here and you can still see graffiti scrawled on the walls by condemned prisoners. Exhibits include photos, documents and artefacts charting the events of the occupation. English-language audio guides are provided.

To enter, ring the bell for apartment 2.

THE CULT OF ANNA PERENNA

One of Rome's lesser-visited major museums, the Museo Nazionale Romano: Terme di Diocleziano is home to an enthralling exhibition on the role that magic played in ancient Rome. The exhibit focuses on artefacts found during the excavation of the Fontana di Anna Perenna (Fountain of Anna Perenna), a cult centre where this ancient nymph was worshipped from the 5th century BCE to the 5th century CE.

Discovered in 1999 during works to construct an underground car park in Parioli, the fountain is considered to be one of the most important discoveries relating to magic ever made. During the excavation archaeologists unearthed magical artefacts including 523 coins, 75 votive lamps, amulets, containers for spells, a large copper pot used to concoct potions, and a huge variety of curses inscribed on tablets – these were directed towards individuals, thieves and even chariot teams.

A video presentation in Italian and English recreates the wild festival celebrating Anna Perenna's cult, which was held on 15 March each year and was recounted in Ovid's epic poem, the *Fasti*.

CHIESA DI SANTA CROCE IN GERUSALEMME CHURCH

Map p343 (☎06 7061 30 53; www.santacroceroma.it; Piazza di Santa Croce in Gerusalemme 12; ⏰7am-12.45pm & 3.30-7.30pm Mon-Sat, from 7.30am Sun; ⓂSan Giovanni) One of Rome's seven pilgrimage churches, the Church of the Holy Cross in Jerusalem was founded in 320 by St Helena, mother of the emperor Constantine, in the grounds of her Roman palace.

It takes its name from the Christian relics here – including a piece of the cross on which Jesus was crucified and a nail from the crucifixion – that St Helena supposedly brought to Rome from Jerusalem. These are housed in a modern chapel to the left of the altar.

MUSEO NAZIONALE DEGLI STRUMENTI MUSEUM

Map p343 (National Museum of Musical Instruments; ☎06 702 41 53; http://museostrumentimusicali.beniculturali.it; Piazza di Santa Croce in Gerusalemm 9A; adult/reduced €5/2.50; ⏰9am-6.30pm Tue-Sun; 🚊Piazza di Porta Maggiore) This little-known museum behind the church of Santa Croce stands on the site of the former home of St Helena.

It's undeservedly but refreshingly deserted, with a collection of over 3000 exquisite musical instruments that includes gorgeously painted, handle-operated 18th-century Neapolitan street pianos, and one of the oldest known pianos (1722).

⊙ Piazza della Repubblica & Around

MUSEO NAZIONALE ROMANO: PALAZZO MASSIMO ALLE TERME MUSEUM

See p152.

MUSEO NAZIONALE ROMANO: TERME DI DIOCLEZIANO MUSEUM

Map p344 (☎06 3996 7700; www.coopculture.it; Viale Enrico de Nicola 78; adult/reduced €10/5; ⏰9am-6.30pm Tue-Sun; ⓂTermini) Able to accommodate some 3000 people, the Terme di Diocleziano was ancient Rome's largest bath complex. Now an epigraphic museum, its exhibits provide a fascinating insight into ancient Roman life, with the highlight being the upstairs exhibition relating to cults. There's also a temporary exhibition area in the massive baths hall and a 16th-century cloister that was built as part of the charterhouse of Santa Maria degli Angeli e dei Martiri. The cloister's design was based on drawings by Michelangelo.

The cloister is home to classical sarcophagi, carved funerary altars and huge sculpted animal heads thought to have come from the Foro di Traiano.

As you wander around the museum, you'll see glimpses of the original complex, which was completed in the early 4th century as a state-of-the-art combination of baths, libraries, concert halls and gardens – the Aula Ottagona and Basilica di Santa Maria degli Angeli buildings were also once part of this enormous endeavour. It fell into disrepair after the aqueduct that fed the baths was destroyed by invaders in about 536 CE.

Note that the museum is one of four that collectively make up the Museo Nazionale Romano. A combined ticket (€12/6), which is valid for three days, includes admission to the other three sites: Palazzo Massimo alle Terme (p152), Palazzo Altemps (p84) and the Crypta Balbi (p813).

BASILICA DI SANTA MARIA DEGLI ANGELI E DEI MARTIRI — BASILICA

Map p344 (06 4880812; www.santamariadegliangeliroma.it; Piazza della Repubblica; 7.30am-6.30pm Mon-Sat, to 8pm Sun; M Repubblica) This hulking basilica occupies what was once the central hall of Diocletian's baths complex. It was originally designed by Michelangelo, but only the great vaulted ceiling remains from his plans. There's often an organ recital here on Saturdays at 6pm.

PIAZZA DELLA REPUBBLICA — PIAZZA

Map p344 (M Repubblica) Flanked by grand 19th-century neoclassical colonnades, this landmark piazza near Termini was laid out as part of Rome's post-unification makeover. It follows the lines of the semicircular exedra (benched portico) of Diocletian's baths complex and was originally known as Piazza Esedra. The elegant **Fontana delle Naiadi** (Fountain of the Water Nymphs; Map p344) is located in the centre of the piazza.

PALAZZO DELLE ESPOSIZIONI — CULTURAL CENTRE

Map p344 (06 3996 7500; www.palazzoesposizioni.it; Via Nazionale 194; 10am-8pm Tue-Thu & Sun, to 10.30pm Fri & Sat; Via Nazionale) This neoclassical palace was built in 1882 as an exhibition centre, though it has since served as headquarters for the Italian Communist Party, a mess hall for Allied servicemen, a polling station and even a public loo. Nowadays it's a splendid cultural hub, with cathedral-scale exhibition spaces hosting blockbuster art exhibitions and sleekly designed art labs, as well as an upmarket restaurant (p163) serving dinner and a bargain-priced weekday lunch or weekend brunch buffet beneath a dazzling all-glass roof.

San Lorenzo & Beyond

BASILICA DI SAN LORENZO FUORI LE MURA — BASILICA

Map p343 (Piazzale San Lorenzo; 8am-noon & 4-6.30pm; Piazzale del Verano) One of Rome's four patriarchal basilicas, San Lorenzo Fuori le Mura (St Lawrence Outside the Walls) has an unusually restrained interior. It was the only major Roman church to suffer bomb damage in WWII, and is a hotchpotch of rebuilds and restorations as a result. Despite this, it is worth visiting for its magnificent Cosmati floor and front portico, which features a fresco of St Lawrence, one of Rome's martyrs, being roasted alive on a spit.

St Lawrence was martyred in 258 CE, and Constantine had the original basilica constructed in the 4th century over his burial place, which was rebuilt 200 years later. Subsequently, a nearby 5th-century church dedicated to the Virgin Mary was incorporated into the building, resulting in the church you see today. The nave, portico and much of the decoration date from the 13th century.

The remains of St Lawrence and St Stephen are in the church crypt beneath the high altar. A pretty barrel-vaulted cloister contains inscriptions and sarcophagi, and leads to the Catacombe di Santa Ciriaca, where St Lawrence was initially buried.

CIMITERO DI CAMPO VERANO — CEMETERY

Map p343 (www.cimitericapitolini.it; Piazzale del Verano 1; 7.30am-6pm Apr-Sep, to 5pm Oct-Dec, to 1pm Jan-Mar; Piazzale del Verano, Piazzale del Verano) The city's largest cemetery dates from the Napoleonic occupation of Rome (1804–14), when an edict ordered that the city's dead must be buried outside the city walls. Between the 1830s and the 1980s virtually all Catholics who died in Rome (with the exception of popes, cardinals and royalty) were buried here. On All Souls' Day (2 November), thousands of Romans flock here to leave flowers on the tombs of loved ones.

FONDAZIONE PASTIFICIO CERERE — GALLERY

Map p343 (06 4542 2960; www.pastificiocerere.com; Via degli Ausoni 7; 3-7pm Mon-Fri, 4-8pm Sat; Reti) A former pasta factory that hung up its spaghetti racks in 1960

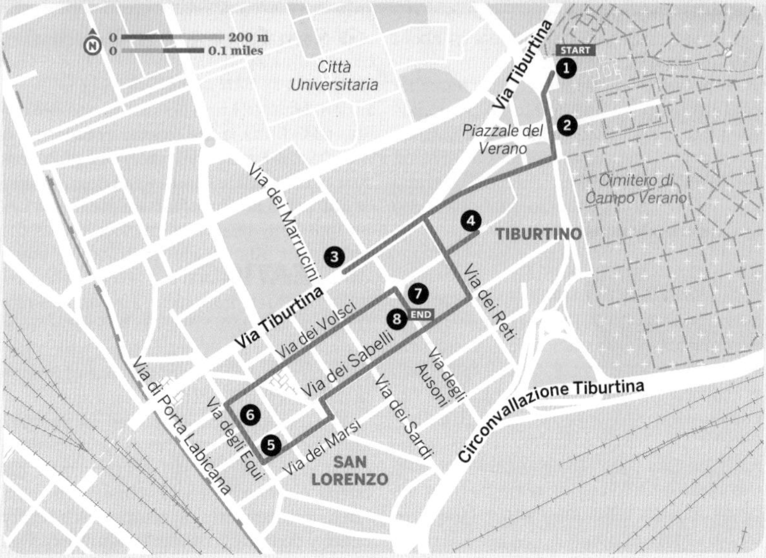

Local Life
Hanging Out in San Lorenzo

The presence of the huge Sapienza University of Rome, founded way back in 1303, gives this area immediately southeast of Termini Station a lively feel, with bars, clubs and budget eateries solidly geared towards students. It's also popular with left-wing bohemian types, who patronise the art galleries, cultural centres and performance venues found on almost every graffiti-clad street.

❶ Basilica di San Lorenzo Fuori le Mura

Standing on the site of St Lawrence's burial place, this basilica (p157) is a popular venue for local weddings and baptisms. It suffered bomb damage in WWII but retains a stunning Cosmati floor and 13th-century frescoed portico.

❷ Explore the Cimitero di Campo Verano

Next door to the basilica, the Cimitero di Campo Verano (p157) is a strangely moving place. Avenues of grandiose tombs criss-cross the cemetery, Rome's largest, which dates from the Napoleonic occupation of Rome (1804–14).

❸ Chocolate Stop

Now that you've got your sightseeing out of the way, it's time to delve into the drinking and art scenes that San Lorenzo is known for. Start at stylish Said (p163), a hybrid boutique cafe-bar and restaurant set in a cleverly reimagined 1920s factory. Order a hot chocolate, chocolate martini or other chocolatey temptation.

❹ Esc Atelier

Pop in to visit the left-leaning artists and local residents who operate this hybrid arts space and neighbourhood centre (p169). You're bound to find someone keen to brief you on the local visual art, literary and political scenes.

❺ Craft Beer

The friendly bar staff at hipster hotspot Artisan (p167) are always happy to recommend particular craft beers from its large range, which is sourced from across the globe.

❻ Eat with the Beats

The book-lined walls and vintage furnishings at Officina Beat (p167) provide a

Cimitero di Campo Verano (p155)

suitably boho setting for a drink (craft beers and cocktails are the tipples of choice) or a simple meal.

❼ Nuovo Cinema Palazzo

Now fully fuelled, head to this palace of alternative culture (p169) to experience one of the creative happenings that it hosts – everything from film screenings to theatre performances and jazz concerts to breakdance classes. The piazza out the front is popular with street artists.

❽ Last Drinks

Bring your day's exploration to a close at Bar Celestino (p168), which opened for business way back in 1904. If you can fight your way through the crowd and claim a seat inside, kudos to you. If not, join the grungy regulars drinking on the pavement and street.

after 55 years of business, this is now a contemporary art hub, with regular shows in the building's galleries and courtyards. The Pastificio came to prominence in the 1980s as home of the Nuova Scuola Romana (New Roman School), a group of six artists who still still show here, alongside a new generation that includes Maurizio Savini, famous for his pink chewing gum sculptures.

EATING

Monti is one of Rome's most vibrant eating and drinking neighbourhoods. The cafes, wine bars and trattorias here are casual, and there are plenty of ethnic and fast-food options. Less-endearing Esquilino has a few popular local pizzerias, trattorias and bakeries – most are in the budget price range. Mooching east into the vibrant student area of San Lorenzo, there are pizzerias, burger joints and the occasional traditional trattoria. Again, most are in the budget price range.

Monti

★ALLE CARRETTE PIZZA €

Map p344 (☎06 679 27 70; www.facebook.com/allecarrette; Via della Madonna dei Monti 95; pizza €5.50-9; ⏰11.30am-4pm & 7pm-midnight; Ⓜ Cavour) Authentic pizza, super-thin and swiftly cooked in a wood-fired oven, is what this traditional Roman pizzeria on one of Monti's prettiest streets has done well for decades. Romans pile in here at weekends for good reason – it's cheap, friendly and delicious. All of the classic toppings are available, as well as gourmet choices such as anchovy and zucchini flower (yum!).

Consider beginning your local feast with some fried *supplì* (risotto balls) or *baccalà* (salted cod). And note that if you order the Pizza Amnesty (tomato, mozzarella, ricotta and aubergine), €1 is donated to Amnesty International. The rear laneway seating is popular in summer.

ZIA ROSETTA SANDWICHES €

Map p344 (☎06 3105 2516; www.ziarosetta.com; Via Urbana 54; salads €6-8, panini mini €2-3.50, regular €4.50-7; ⏰11am-4pm Mon-Thu, to 10pm Fri-Sun; Ⓜ Cavour) Grab a pew at a marble-topped table and brace your taste buds for a torturous choice between 25 or so gourmet *panini* and another dozen specials – all creatively stuffed with unexpected combinations, and with catchy names like Amber Queen, Strawberry Hill and Lady Godiva.

If you really can't decide, pick a trio of mini *panini*. Freshly squeezed juices (€3.50), too. Glam and gluten-free.

AROMATICUS HEALTH FOOD €

Map p344 (☎06 488 13 55; www.aromaticus.it; Via Urbana 134; dishes €7-12; ⏰11.30am-9.30pm Tue-Sun; 📶✍; Ⓜ Cavour) Few addresses exude such a healthy vibe. Set within a shop selling aromatic plants and edible flowers, this inventive little cafe is the perfect place to satisfy cravings for fresh and unadorned food. Its daily changing menu features creative salads, soups, and dishes suitable for vegans and those who are gluten-free. To drink, order a juice or detox smoothie.

Order at the bar, set your own table and collect your food when it's ready.

GREZZO PASTRIES €

Map p344 (☎06 48 34 43; www.grezzoitalia.it; Via Urbana 130; desserts €5.50-7; ⏰11am-11pm Mon-Thu & Sun, to midnight Fri & Sat; ✍; Ⓜ Cavour) The chocolate smell that greets visitors to this chic boutique is quite intoxicating, bodying well for those who are in the mood for a sweet treat. Choose from exquisite tiramisu miniatures, tarts and tortes, cheesecakes, ice creams and one-bite pralines – everything is raw, organic and gluten-free. Take away or squat on stools around low tables. Good hot chocolate, too.

GREEN & GO HEALTH FOOD €

Map p344 (www.facebook.com/GreenandGo Roma; Via del Boschetta 20; lunch dishes €9; ⏰11am-4pm Mon-Fri, noon-3pm Sat; Ⓜ Cavour) When the urge for hardcore greens strikes, duck into this pocket-size organic salad bar for homemade soups, gazpacho, made-to-order salads and vegan desserts. Freshly pressed juices and smoothies too, all to enjoy around a couple of bar-stool tables or to take away.

FORNO DA MILVIO PIZZA €

Map p344 (☎06 4893 0145; Via dei Serpenti 7; pizza slice from €3.50; ⏰6.30am-late; Ⓜ Cavour) This small *pizza al taglio* (pizza by the slice) place cooks up a tasty range of light and crispy pizza, served by weight (€15 per kilo), alongside fried *supplì* (risotto balls), zucchini flowers, *baccalà* (salted cod) and other Roman 'fast-food' staples. Sit on a bar stool and listen to the radio blaring, or take away. Also makes *panini*.

FATAMORGANA MONTI GELATO €

Map p344 (www.gelateriafatamorgana.com; Piazza Zingari 5; gelato €2.50-5; ⏰1.30-9.30pm Mon, to 10.30pm Tue-Thu, to 11pm Fri-Sun; Ⓜ Cavour) One of Rome's finest artisanal gelaterie, Fatamorgana whips up delicious, gluten-free gelato in a range of fantastic flavours – citrus and ricotta, peanut or seed-studded pumpkin, among others. Sit and enjoy on the pretty cobbled square in front, or contemplate the large photo behind the counter (from the classic film *La Banda degli Onesti* starring Totò, shot just around the corner).

CIURI CIURI PASTRIES €

Map p344 (☎06 4544 4548; www.ciuri-ciuri.it; Via Leonina 18; snacks around €4; ⏰8.30am-midnight Sun-Thu, to 2am Fri & Sat; Ⓜ Cavour) What's not to love about a Sicilian ice cream and pastry shop? Pop in for delectable homemade sweets such as *cannoli* freshly filled with ricotta, *cassata* (sponge cake, cream, marzipan, chocolate and candied fruit) and *pasticini di mandorla* (almond pastries). It's not all sweet, though; there

MERCATO CENTRALE

A gourmet oasis for hungry travellers at Stazione Termini (p293), this **food hall** (Map p344; www.mercatocentrale.it/roma; Stazione Termini, Via Giolitti 36; snacks/meals from €3/10; ⏰8am-midnight; 📶; Ⓜ Termini) with its vaulted 1930s ceiling hosts stalls selling good-quality fast food and fresh produce. Consider purchasing a *panino* filled with artisanal cheese from Beppe Giovali; a slice of focaccia or pizza from Gabriele Bonci; or a Chianina burger from Enrico Lagorio. A *birreria* (beer house) sells craft beer.

Grab something quick from one of the ground-floor stalls and eat it at one of the tables in the walkways, or head upstairs to 1st-floor **Il Ristorante di Oliver Glowig** (meals €45; open noon to 3pm and 7pm to 11pm), which offers a menu signed off by the Rome-based Michelin-starred chef.

are also excellent freshly made *arancini* (deep-fried rice balls) and other snacks. Eat in or out.

★LA BARRIQUE ITALIAN €€

Map p344 (☎06 4782 5953; www.facebook.com/la.barrique.94; Via del Boschetto 41b; meals €40; ⏱1-2.30pm & 7.30-11pm Mon-Fri, 7.30-11.30pm Sat; Ⓜ Cavour) This traditional *enoteca* is a classy yet casual place to linger over a meal. There's a large wine list, mostly sourced from small producers, with lots of natural wines to choose from. A small menu of creative pastas and mains provide a great accompaniment – this is one of the best places to eat in Monti. Bookings recommended.

LA TAVERNA DEI FORI IMPERIALI TRATTORIA €€

Map p344 (☎06 679 86 43; www.latavernadeiforiimperiali.com; Via della Madonna dei Monti 9; meals €40; ⏱12.30-3pm & 7.30-10.30pm Mon-Wed; ❄; Ⓜ Cavour) It's easy to dismiss a restaurant as being 'too touristy', but this can be unjust. Yes, this family-operated trattoria is popular with foreign tourists. And yes, Roman patrons are few and far between. But its staff are friendly and multilingual, its food is consistently tasty and its pleasant surrounds evoke old Rome. We reckon that makes it a good choice.

TEMAKINHO SUSHI €€

Map p344 (☎06 4201 6656; www.temakinho.com; Via dei Serpenti 16; dishes €8-15; ⏱12.30-3.30pm & 7pm-midnight; 📶; Ⓜ Cavour) In a city where most food is still resolutely (though deliciously) Italian, this branch of a chain of Brazilian-Japanese hybrid restaurants makes for a refreshing change. As well as sushi and ceviche, it serves delicious, strong *caipirinha* cocktails, which combine Brazilian *cachaça,* sugar, lime and fresh fruit; there are also 'sakehinhas' made with sake. It's very popular so book ahead.

DA VALENTINO TRATTORIA €€

Map p344 (☎06 488 06 43; Via del Boschetto 37; meals €35; ⏱12.30-2.45pm & 8-11pm Mon-Sat; Ⓜ Repubblica) A 1930s sign on the front of this neighbourhood trattoria says 'Birra Peroni' and the evocative interior feels little changed from this time. Locals tend to order bruschetta, grilled meats and *scamorza,* an Italian cheese that's grilled and melted atop myriad different ingredients: tomato and rocket, artichokes, *lardo di colonnata* (pork fat) slices from Tuscany and porcini mushrooms. Book ahead.

URBANA 47 ITALIAN €€

Map p344 (☎06 4788 4006; www.urbana47.it; Via Urbana 47; pizzas $8-14, meals €42; ⏱8am-midnight; 📶✎; Ⓜ Cavour) 🌿 This place promises more than it delivers. We love the fact that it operates the 'zero kilometre' rule (as much as possible), meaning that most things you eat here will be sourced from Lazio, but the food itself can be disappointing. Nevertheless, its stylish decor and healthy-eating emphasis attracts a young, chic Roman crowd.

✕ Esquilino

★PANELLA BAKERY €

Map p344 (☎06 487 24 35; www.panellaroma.com; Via Merulana 54; meals €7-15; ⏱7am-11pm Mon-Thu & Sun, to midnight Fri & Sat; Ⓜ Vittorio Emanuele) Freshly baked pastries, fruit tartlets, *pizza al taglio* (pizza by the slice) and focaccia fill display cases in this famous bakery, and there's also a *tavola calda* ('hot table') where an array of hot dishes is on offer. Order at the counter and eat at bar stools between shelves of gourmet groceries, or sit on the terrace for waiter service.

PALAZZO DEL FREDDO DI GIOVANNI FASSI GELATO €

Map p343 (☎06 446 47 40; www.palazzodelfreddo.it; Via Principe Eugenio 65; ice cream from €1.60; ⏱noon-10pm Mon-Thu, to midnight Fri & Sat, 10am-11pm Sun; Ⓜ Vittorio Emanuele) Established in 1880, this vast temple to gelato is now operated by the founder's great-grandson, Andrea Fassi. Choose from myriad flavours of gelato, or opt for an iced dessert instead – the *tronchetto* (ice-cream cake), cassata, *Sanpietrino* (a semifreddo of zabaglione, coffee, nuts and chocolate) and *tramezzini* (ice-cream wafer 'sandwiches' filled with *Sanpietro*) deserve special mention.

VECCHIA ROMA PIZZA €

Map p344 (☎06 446 71 43; www.trattoriavecchiaroma.it; Via Ferruccio 12c; pizzas €6-9, pastas €9.50-12; ⏱noon-3pm & 7-11pm; 📶; Ⓜ Vittorio Emanuele) It's not at all unusual to see groups of locals queuing outside the door to this century-old basement favourite – the rock-bottom prices, convivial atmosphere and tasty food ensure that it is usually full to the gills. The pizzas are good, but the standout dishes are the *flambé* pastas – opt for the *spaghetti alla parmigiana* or the *bucatini all'amatriciana*. Cash only.

PASTICCERIA REGOLI BAKERY €

Map p344 (☎06 487 28 12; www.pasticceriaregoli.com; Via dello Statuto 60; cakes €6; ⏰cafe 6.30am-6.45pm Wed-Mon, shop to 8.20pm; Ⓜ Vittorio Emanuele) At weekends a queue marks the entrance to this elegant chandelier-lit *pasticceria*, much-loved since 1916. Its *crostate* (latticed jam tarts) are iconic, as are its berry-topped *crostatine fragoline di bosco*. Take a number from the machine next to the register, order when it's called and then pay.

A *maritozzi con panna* (sweet bread bun filled to bursting with whipped cream) is the downright wicked speciality to order in the next-door cafe, which also serves good coffee.

FORNO ROSCIOLI PIETRO BAKERY €

Map p344 (☎06 446 71 46; www.facebook.com/fornorosciolipietro; Via Buonarroti 46-48; pizza slices €3.50; ⏰7am-8pm Mon-Sat; Ⓜ Vittorio Emanuele) This slightly off-the-beaten-track branch of one of Rome's best bakeries serves delicious *pizza al taglio* (pizza by the slice), pasta dishes and other goodies that make it ideal for a swift lunch or stocking up for a picnic.

It's on a road leading off Piazza Vittorio Emanuele II.

TRATTORIA DA DANILO TRATTORIA €€

Map p344 (☎06 7720 0111; www.trattoriadadanilo.com; Via Petrarca 13; meals €40; ⏰1-3.30pm & 7.30-11pm Tue-Sat, 7.45-11pm Mon; Ⓜ Vittorio Emanuele, Manzoni) Da Danilo offers well-cooked Roman specialities served in rustic, atmospheric surrounds.

It's renowned for its *pasta cacio e pepe* (pasta with *caciocavallo* cheese and pepper), which is served theatrically from a huge hulled cheese. The carbonara is also excellent.

When booking (essential), specify a seat in the upstairs dining room and not the basement. Service can be rude.

TRATTORIA MONTI TRATTORIA €€

Map p344 (☎06 446 65 73; Via di San Vito 13a; meals €45; ⏰1-2.45pm & 8-10.45pm Tue-Sat, 1-2.45pm Sun; Ⓜ Vittorio Emanuele) The Camerucci family runs this elegant brick-arched trattoria proffering refined traditional dishes from the Marches region. There are wonderful *fritti* (fried things), delicate hand-made pastas and a range of *secondi*, including game and *porchetta* (suckling pig); sadly, the chef is over-fond of salt. Service is multilingual and excellent. Book ahead.

MEID IN NEPOLS NEAPOLITAN €€

Map p344 (☎06 4470 4131; www.meidinnepols.com; Via Varese 54; pizza €4.50-12.50, meals €40; ⏰12.15-3pm & 7.15-11pm Mon-Sat, 7-11pm Sun; Ⓜ Termini) For a steaming bowl of *impepata di cozze* (pepper-spiced mussels) or *frittura Napoletana* (fry-up of battered anchovies and salmon) near Stazione Termini, try this casual Neapolitan eatery. Or follow the lead of the many regulars who head here to enjoy pizza and craft beer. Chocolate lovers should order the house-special *pizza sciù sciù*, a calzone filled with warm gooey Nutella.

Note that pizzas aren't available at lunch on Saturday.

LA GALLINA BIANCA PIZZA €

Map p344 (☎06 474 37 77; www.lagallinabiancaroma.it; Via A Rosmini 5-12; pizzas €7-12; ⏰noon-3pm & 6pm-midnight; Ⓜ Termini) The 'White Hen' is a friendly pizzeria restaurant amid the minefield of substandard eateries around Termini. Large and airy, it serves thick-crust Neapolitan pizzas made from slow-risen dough, bruschetta and a good range of antipasti.

Piazza della Repubblica & Around

AMODEI BANCO E BOTTEGA ITALIAN €

Map p344 (☎06 482 31 38; www.facebook.com/amodeiroma; Via Principe Amedeo 7; meals €18; ⏰10am-11.30pm; 📶; Ⓜ Termini) Dodge the tourist traps scattered around Termini Station and opt for lunch or dinner at this cheery deli.

Thoughtfully composed meat and cheese boards, Italian comfort food (meatballs and lasagne) and crostoni with porchetta are the heart of the menu.

It also doubles as a gourmet food shop, brimming with edible souvenirs such as biscotti, wine, cheese and pâtés.

ANTONELLO COLONNA OPEN

GASTRONOMY €€€

Map p344 (☎06 4782 2641; www.antonellocolonna.it; Via Milano 9a; lunch/brunch €16/30, à la carte meals €80-100; ⏲12.30-3.30pm & 7-11pm Tue-Sat, 12.30-3.30pm Sun; ❄; Ⓜ Repubblica) Spectacularly set at the back of the Palazzo delle Esposizioni (p157), Antonello Colonna's restaurant lounges dramatically under a dazzling all-glass roof. Cuisine is new Roman – innovative takes on traditional dishes, cooked with wit and flair. On sunny days, dine al fresco on the rooftop terrace. The all-you-can-eat weekday lunch buffet and weekend brunch are cheap but unremarkable.

San Lorenzo & Beyond

★SAID

DESSERTS €

Map p343 (☎06 446 92 04; www.said.it; Via Tiburtina 135; praline assortment €8, desserts €8-10; ⏲10am-12.30am Tue-Thu, to 1.30am Fri, noon-1.30am Sat, noon-midnight Sun; 📶; 🚊Reti) Housed in a 1920s chocolate factory, this hybrid cafe-bar, restaurant and boutique is San Lorenzo's most fashionable address. Its top-quality chocolate can be indulged in here or purchased to take home. Enjoying a coffee, dessert or meal in the urban-chic interior will give you lots of opportunities to people-watch as the place literally heaves at night, particularly on weekends.

For a wickedly decadent treat, order a chocolate cocktail (€10) or hot chocolate (€4 to €6).

VITAMINAS 24

VEGETARIAN €

Map p343 (☎331 2045535; www.facebook.com/vitaminas24; Via Ascoli Piceno 40-42; meals €15; ⏲noon-midnight; 📶🥄; Ⓜ Pigneto, 🚊Prenestina/Officine Atac) 🌿 Produce from Rome's agricultural surrounds goes into the delicious 100% organic smoothies, soups, dips, wraps, salads, burgers and other vegetarian and vegan cuisine cooked up at this bistro. The Brazilian heritage of creative owner Giuliana injects an appealing tropical vibe, and her veggie-packed *vellutate* ('velvet' soups) are a local legend.

MOZZICO

INTERNATIONAL €

Map p343 (☎06 9453 2800; www.facebook.com/mozzico; Via dei Volsci 80; panini €11-12, meals €30; ⏲6.30pm-midnight; 🚌Via Tiburtina) Cool jazz wafts out into the street when the door to this simple bistro and *birreria* (beer house) opens. The shabby chic interior has an open kitchen as its focal point, and it's kept busy making *stuzzichini* (bite-size snacks), bruschetta, *panini*, burgers and pastas, all of which are washed down with craft beers and cocktails.

PIZZERIA FORMULA 1

PIZZA €

Map p343 (☎06 445 38 66; www.facebook.com/pizzeriaformula1roma; Via degli Equi 13; pizzas €5-7; ⏲6.30pm-12.30am Mon-Sat; 🚊Reti) This basic San Lorenzo pizzeria is as adrenaline-fuelled as its name: waiters zoom around under whirring fans, delivering tomato-loaded bruschetta, fried zucchini flowers, *supplì* (risotto balls) and piping-hot thin-crust pizza to crowds of feasting students and wallet-savvy locals. Cash only.

PIGNETO QUARANTUNO

RISTORANTE €€

Map p343 (☎06 7039 9483; www.pignetoquarantuno.it; Via del Pigneto 41-45; meals €32; ⏲6pm-midnight; 🚊Prenestina/Officine Atac) Traditional dishes including pasta carbonara and Roman-style tripe mingle with more creative *primi* and *secondi* on the menu at this small and stylish Pigneto bistro. Its wine list is both affordable and interesting, with options by the glass and bottle.

It's also open for Sunday lunch between mid-September and mid-June.

TRAM TRAM

TRATTORIA €€

Map p343 (☎06 49 04 16; www.tramtram.it; Via dei Reti 44; meals €35; ⏲noon-3pm & 7-11pm Tue-Sun; 🚊Reti) Taking its name from the trams that rattle by outside, this old-style trattoria is known as a Slow Food hub.

A family-run affair, its kitchen mixes classical Roman dishes with seafood from Puglia in Italy's sultry south. Taste sensation *tiella riso, patate e cozze* (baked rice dish with rice, potatoes and mussels) is not to be missed. Book ahead.

EX PASTIFICIO

INTERNATIONAL €€€

Map p343 (☎06 3397 46 28; info@expastifico.it; Via Tiburtina 196; meals €50; ⏲6pm-1am Mon-Sat; 📶; 🚊Reti) Specialising in barbecued meats and featuring Australian Black Angus, Japanese Wagyu and Tuscan T-bone steak, this hybrid restaurant and cocktail bar next to the Fondazione Pastificio Cerere (p157) is quite unlike other eateries in San Lorenzo.

Its chic surrounds, low lighting and jazz-dominated soundtrack would be equally at home in New York, London or Sydney.

DRINKING & NIGHTLIFE

Few districts buzz after dark quite like Monti, a neighbourhood littered with stylish cafes, old-world *enoteche* (wine bars) and a slew of contemporary bars. Many of these serve decent food, too. For edgy clubs, live music and craft beer, wander off the beaten track into the grungy student 'hood of San Lorenzo or further east into boho Pigneto, a gritty district known for its alternative nightlife.

Monti

★BLACKMARKET HALL — COCKTAIL BAR

Map p344 (☎339 7351926; www.facebook.com/blackmarkethall; Via de Ciancaleoni 31; ⌚6pm-3am; Ⓜ Cavour) One of Monti's best bars, this multi-roomed speakeasy in a former monastery has an eclectic vintage-style decor and plenty of cosy corners where you can enjoy a leisurely, convivial drink.

It serves food up till midnight (burgers €12 to €15) and hosts live music – often jazz – on weekends. There's a second venue nearby on Via Panisperna 101.

★AI TRE SCALINI — WINE BAR

Map p344 (☎06 4890 7495; www.facebook.com/aitrescalini; Via Panisperna 251; ⌚12.30pm-1am; Ⓜ Cavour) A firm favourite since 1895, the 'Three Steps' is always packed, with predominantly young patrons spilling out of its bar area and into the street.

It's a perfect spot to enjoy an afternoon drink or a simple meal of cheese, salami and dishes such as *polpette al sugo* (meatballs with sauce), washed down with superb choices of wine or beer.

★LA BOTTEGA DEL CAFFÈ — CAFE

Map p344 (☎06 474 15 78; Piazza Madonna dei Monti 5; ⌚8am-2am; 📶; Ⓜ Cavour) On one of Rome's prettiest squares in Monti, La Bottega del Caffè – named after a comedy by Carlo Goldoni – is the hotspot in Monti for lingering over excellent coffee, drinks, snacks and lunch or dinner. Heaters in winter ensure balmy al fresco action year-round.

BARZILAI BISTRO — BAR

Map p344 (☎06 487 49 79; Via Panisperna 44; ⌚5.30pm-midnight; Ⓜ Cavour) Opposite Monti's much-loved Ai Tre Scalini, this bohemian bar-bistro accommodates the people who can't squeeze in over the road but are seeking a similarly casual place to enjoy a drink and something to eat.

Sit at one of the tables under the huge chandelier or stand at the bar; when it's full, they're happy to serve drinks through the window.

LA CASETTA A MONTI — CAFE

Map p344 (☎06 482 77 56; www.facebook.com/lacasettadeimonti; Via della Madonna dei Monti 62; ⌚8.30am-8.30pm Mon-Thu, to 10pm Fri & Sat, to 9pm Sun; 📶; Ⓜ Cavour) Doll's house in size, seating only 16 in a cramped space, this cafe in the cobbled heart of Monti serves decent coffee, *panini*, pastries and a fruit and yoghurt bowl.

It's set in a low-lying house ('casetta' means cottage) with big windows and foliage-draped facade.

AL VINO AL VINO — WINE BAR

Map p344 (☎06 48 58 03; Via dei Serpenti 19; ⌚10.30am-2.30pm & 6pm-12.30am Mon-Thu, to 1.30am Fri & Sat, from 11.30am Sun; Ⓜ Cavour) Mixing lovely ceramic-topped bistro tables with bottle-lined walls and the odd contemporary painting, this rustic *enoteca* is an attractive spot in which to linger over a fine collection of wine, including several *passiti* (sweet wines).

The other speciality is *distillati* – grappa, whisky and so on.

LIBRERIA CAFFÈ BOHEMIEN — BAR

Map p344 (☎339 7224622; www.caffebohemien.it; Via degli Zingari 36; ⌚5pm-1am Sun, Mon, Wed & Thu, to 2am Fri & Sat; Ⓜ Cavour) This hybrid wine bar, tearoom and bookshop lives up to its name, resembling something you might stumble on in Left Bank Paris.

It's small, with mismatched vintage furniture and an eclectic crowd enjoying wine by the glass, aperitifs, tea and coffee.

ICE CLUB BAR

Map p344 (☎06 9784 5581; www.facebook.com/iceclubroma; Via della Madonna dei Monti 18; ⊙5pm-1am Mon-Thu, 2pm-2am Fri & Sat, to 1am Sun; Ⓜ Cavour) Novelty value is what the Ice Club is all about. Pay €15 (you get a free vodka cocktail served in a glass made of ice), don a (completely unflattering) hospital-blue thermal cloak and mittens, and enter the bar, in which everything is made of ice (temperature: -5°C/23°F).

Most people won't chill here for too long. Extended hours in summer.

FAFIUCHÉ WINE BAR

Map p344 (☎06 699 09 68; www.facebook.com/fafiuchemonti; Via della Madonna dei Monti 28; ⊙5.30pm-1am Mon-Sat; Ⓜ Cavour) Fafiuché roughly translates as 'playful' or 'unusual' in Piedmontese dialect, and this narrow, bottle-lined bar more than lives up to that.

Come to *liberate la gola* (literally 'clear your throat', but something more akin to 'free your taste buds') with fine wine, artisanal beers and dishes from all over Italy. It's a popular spot for wine and *merende* (afternoon snacks).

Esquilino

GATSBY CAFÉ BAR

Map p344 (☎06 6933 9626; www.facebook.com/gatsbycafe; Piazza Vittorio Emanuele II 106; ⊙8am-midnight Sun-Wed, to 1am Thu, to 2am Fri & Sat; Ⓜ Vittorio Emanuele) There's good reason why the friendly bartenders here all wear flat caps, feather-trimmed trilbys and other traditional gents' hats: this fabulous 1950s-styled space with vintage furniture and flashes of geometric wallpaper was originally a milliner's shop called Galleria Venturini.

Delicious *spritz,* craft cocktails, gourmet *panini* and *taglieri* (salami and cheese platters) make it a top *aperitivo* spot.

Don't miss the intimate lounge on the 2nd floor, where live jazz gigs are sometimes staged, and the vintage hat collection displayed behind glass on the 1st floor.

YELLOW BAR BAR

Map p344 (☎06 4470 2868; www.the-yellow.com; Via Palestro 40; ⊙24hr; 📶; Ⓜ Castro Pretorio) Cleverly designed to look like a vintage joint, the Yellow Hostel's around-the-clock bar is constantly packed with young international travellers.

DJs spin tunes, bands play live sets on weekends and patrons play beer pong and put the karaoke set to good use (fortunately, not all at the same time).

There are also burgers, tacos and quesadillas on offer (€4 to €8.50).

ZEST BAR BAR

Map p344 (Radisson Blu es. Hotel; ☎06 4448 4384; Via Filippo Turati 171; ⊙10.30am-midnight; 📶; Ⓜ Vittorio Emanuele) In need of a cocktail in the Termini district? Pop up to the 7th-floor bar at the slinkily designed **Radisson Blu Es.** (Map p344; ☎06 44 48 41; www.radissonblu.com/eshotel-rome; Via Filippo Turati 171; r €225-250; ❄@≋; Ⓜ Vittorio Emanuele II) hotel.

Chairs are by Jasper Morrison, views are through plate glass, and there's a sexy outdoor rooftop pool to gaze at, open May to September.

TRIMANI WINE BAR

Map p344 (☎06 446 96 30; www.trimani.com; Via Cernaia 37b; ⊙11.30am-3pm & 5.30pm-12.30am Mon-Sat; Ⓜ Termini) Part of the Trimani family's wine empire (their vast *enoteca* around the corner on Via Goito stocks 4000-odd Italian and international labels), this is an unpretentious and welcoming place with knowledgeable, multilingual staff.

Its wine list includes loads of Italian regional wines by the glass and bottle, and its food menu includes pasta, antipasti and cheese platters (dishes €9 to €19).

RACE CLUB SPEAKEASY COCKTAIL BAR

Map p339 (☎06 9604 4048; www.theraceclubspeakeasyroma.com; Via Labicana 52; ⊙10pm-3am; 📶; Ⓜ Colosseo) Like any good speakeasy, this bar lies underground, and visitors are expected to formally request entrance via a doorbell; they also need to pay €5 for a membership card.

Decor is an off-kilter mix of mirrors, black-and-white snapshots, and glimmery Christmas lights.

Cash only and table reservations recommended.

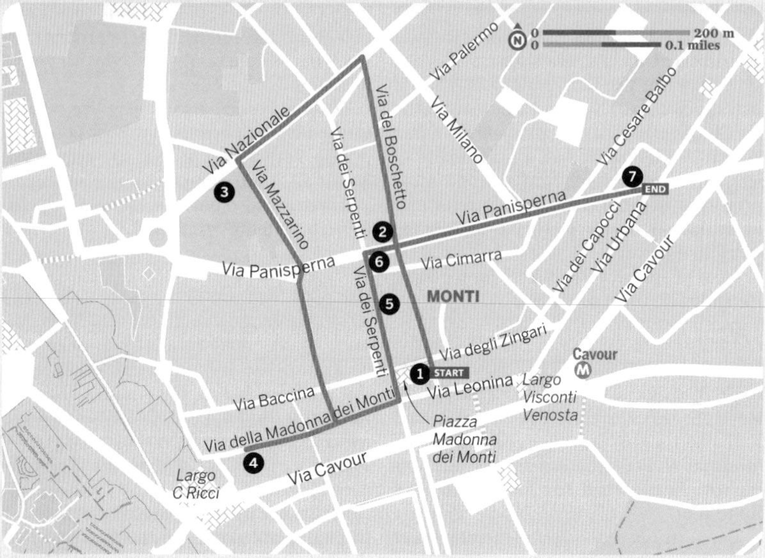

Local Life
Bars & Boutiques in Monti

The first residential *rione* (district) established beyond the walls of the Imperial city, Monti was once a working-class area infamous for its brothels, seedy wine shops and general air of debauchery. These days, the brothels have been replaced by artisanal boutiques, the wine shops have morphed into bohemian bars and the ambience is local, arty and pretension-free.

❶ Morning Coffee

Set on the eastern edge of pocket-sized Piazza della Madonna dei Monti with its pretty Fontana dei Catecumeni, a fountain named for adults initiated to the Catholic Church, La Bottega del Caffè (p164) serves the best coffee in Monti, and also has the most alluring terrace. Colonise a table and watch local life unfold in front of you.

❷ Via del Boschetto

Sauntering along this street proves that Monti's much-hyped reputation as an alternative fashion hub is fully justified. Clothing boutiques such as Tina Sondergaard (p170) have led the way, joined by vintage outlets, jewellery stores and other tempting businesses.

❸ Villa Aldobrandini

During the high season Monti can be a maelstrom of crowds, so it's a relief to know that there is a tranquil bolthole available just off traffic-choked Via Nazionale. This sculpture-dotted garden (p155) in front of a 16th-century villa has a scattering of benches beneath perfumed orange trees, where it's easy to catch one's breath.

❹ Pizza Refuel

Every neighbourhood needs a welcoming pizzeria, and Monti has one of the best in town. Alle Carrette (p159) serves up thin-crust, piping-hot pizza to a constant stream of locals and tourists, and is just as popular at lunch as it is later in the evening. Sit inside in winter and in the rear laneway during the warmer months.

❺ Via dei Serpenti

Another excellent shopping street, Via dei Serpenti has a view of the Colosseum from its southern end and a garland of tempting boutiques stretching north on each side of the road, including one of the city's best vintage clothing shops, Pifebo (p170).

Via del Boschetto

❻ Ai Tre Scalini

A popular local hang-out since 1895, the Three Steps (p164) is perennially packed with young Romans – many local – who catch up with friends over beers, glasses of wines and generous cheese and *salumi* platters. Those who can't cram in often adjourn to Barzilai Bistro (p164), opposite.

❼ Into the Wee Hours

Monti has more than its fair share of bars, all with their own character. Multi-roomed speakeasy Blackmarket Hall (p164) is popular with locals who want to enjoy a quiet drink and conversation rather than hang out in one of the noisy local wine bars. The volume picks up at weekends, though, when live music acts perform.

Piazza della Repubblica & Around

DAGNINO CAFE

Map p344 (☎06 481 86 60; Via Vittorio Emanuele Orlando 75; ⏰7am-11pm; Ⓜ Repubblica) Secreted in the Esedra Arcade near Piazza della Repubblica, this cafe has retained its original 1960s decor, including murals – you'll feel like you're entering a time warp when enjoying a coffee and one of the Sicilian-style treats (*cannoli*, *cassatas* etc) displayed in the long display case. The gelato here is also good.

CAFFÈ E PASTICCERIA U. GIULIANI CAFE

Map p344 (Via Solferino 8; ⏰7am-midnight; Ⓜ Termini) Our recommendation of this 1897 cafe comes with a couple of caveats: we don't recommend paying for table service or eating anything other than the Sicilian-style sweet pastries that the place is known for. If you pay at the register for a coffee (good) and pastry (even better) and enjoy them standing at the bar, you should be happy.

San Lorenzo & Beyond

★NECCI DAL 1924 CAFE

(☎06 9760 1552; www.necci1924.com; Via Fanfulla da Lodi 68; ⏰8am-1am Sun-Thu, to 2am Fri & Sat; 📶👪; 🚊Prenestina/Officine Atac) An all-round hybrid in Pigneto, iconic Necci opened as a gelateria in 1924 and later became a favourite drinking destination of film director Pier Paolo Pasolini. These days it caters to a buoyant hipster crowd, offering a laid-back vibe, retro interior and all-day food. Huge kudos for the fabulous summertime terrace, which is very family friendly.

ARTISAN CRAFT BEER

Map p343 (☎327 9105709; www.facebook.com/art.isan.90; Via degli Arunci 9; ⏰6pm-1am Sun & Mon, to 2am Tue-Thu, to 3am Fri & Sat; 🚊Reti) A mecca for those who enjoy drinking craft beer, this hipster bar stocks artisanal tipples from around the globe and serves simple but tasty global food, too.

OFFICINA BEAT COCKTAIL BAR

Map p343 (☎06 9521 87 79; https://officinebeat.it; Via degli Equi 29; ⏰6pm-1am Sun-Thu, to 2am Fri & Sat; 📶; 🚊Reti) We like Officina's style.

A friendly drinking den with tiled floor, vintage furniture and book-lined walls, it focuses on quality craft beers and expertly made cocktails, but also offers good food. Reason alone to head to San Lorenzo.

CARGO BAR

Map p343 (☎349 7404620; www.facebook.com/cargoalpigneto; Via del Pigneto 20; ⏲5pm-2am; 📶; 🚋Prenestina/Officine Atac) This long-standing favourite is known for its cocktails and antipasti platters. If you get here early you may be able to lay claim to a seat on the zebra-skin couch.

BAR CELESTINO BAR

Map p343 (☎06 4547 2483; www.facebook.com/bar-celestino; Via degli Ausoni 62-64; ⏲7.30am-2am Mon-Sat; 🚋Reti) Few places evoke the San Lorenzo student vibe quite like this grungy drinking den near Piazza dei Sanniti. A diehard icon of this working-class neighbourhood, Celestino first opened in 1904 and is still going strong thanks to its simple, unpretentious atmosphere. Grab a seat or standing spot on the pavement or head inside. Find party updates on its Facebook page.

CO.SO COCKTAIL BAR

(☎06 4543 5428; www.facebook.com/COSOROMA/?rf=326992017442044; Via Braccio da Montone 80; ⏲6.30pm-3am Mon-Sat; 🚋Via Prenestina/Officine Atac) Tiny Co.So (meaning 'Cocktails & Social') was founded by Massimo D'Addezio (a former master mixologist at Hotel de Russie) and is hipster to the hilt. Think Carbonara Sour cocktails (with pork-fat-infused vodka), bubblewrap coasters, and popcorn and M&M bar snacks.

GUERRA AL PIGNETO BAR

Map p343 (☎333 2986996; Via del Pigneto 18; ⏲11am-3pm & 7pm-12.30am Tue-Sun; 🚋Prenestina/Officine Atac) Forget the other bars that line Pigneto's main pedestrianised drag. If you want authenticity, this traditional shop is the place, with its cheap beer and wine, and menu of antipasti and *porchetta* (pork roasted in herbs). Outside seating only.

IL TIASO BAR

Map p343 (☎349 5891498; www.facebook.com/ilTiasoalPigneto; Via Ascoli Piceno 25; ⏲6pm-2am; 📶; 🚋Prenestina/Officine Atac) Think living room with zebra-print chairs, walls of indie art, Lou Reed biographies wedged between wine bottles, and owner Gabriele playing his favourite New York Dolls album to neo-beatnik chicks, corduroy-clad professors and the odd neighbourhood dog. Expect well-priced wine, an intimate chilled vibe, regular live music and a lovely pavement terrace.

LOCANDA ATLANTIDE CLUB

Map p343 (☎06 9604 5875; www.facebook.com/locanda.atlantide; Via dei Lucani 22b; cover varies; ⏲9pm-late Oct-Jun; 🚋Scalo San Lorenzo) Come and tickle Rome's grungy underbelly. Descend through a door in a graffiti-covered wall into this cavernous basement dive, packed to the rafters with studenty, alternative crowds and featuring everything from prog-folk to techno and psychedelic trance. It's good (or is it?) to know that punk is not dead.

IL SORÌ WINE BAR

Map p343 (☎393 4318681; www.ilsori.it; Via dei Volsci 51; ⏲6pm-2am Mon-Sat; 🚋Reti) The ambience here is laid-back and the surrounds atmospheric – we just wish that the quality of the food was better (supermarket-quality cheese straight from the refrigerator does not make for a satisfying cheese board). Stop in for a glass of wine from the chalkboard menu; if you would like some help navigating Italian varietals staff will be happy to help.

BIRRA PIÙ BAR

Map p343 (☎06 7061 3106; www.facebook.com/birra.piu; Via del Pigneto 105; ⏲5pm-1am Mon-Thu, to 2am Fri & Sat, 6pm-1am Sun; 🚋Prenestina/Officine Atac) A small, relaxed bar, Birra Plus attracts a laid-back crowd who drape themselves over blonde-wood bar stools and tables. There's plenty of craft beer on offer: on tap or in bottles.

YEAH! PIGNETO BAR

(☎06 6480 1456; www.yeahpigneto.com; Via Giovanni de Agostini 43; ⏲8am-midnight Mon-Thu, to 2am Fri & Sat; 🚋Prenestina/Officine Atac) Keen on '80s pop and rock? You'll hear lots of it on the sound system at this cafe-bar, which has walls covered in collages and classic album covers, and a large collection of music on vinyl.

GENTE DI SAN LORENZO BAR

Map p343 (☎06 445 44 25; www.facebook.com/pages/category/Restaurant/Gente-di-San-Lorenzo-230221323683500; Via degli Aurunci 42; ⏲6.30am-10pm Mon-Wed, to 2am Thu-Sat; 📶;

Via dei Reti) San Lorenzo's signature neighbourhood bar is a chilled place to hang with students over a drink, snack or meal. The interior is modern and welcoming enough, but the real action happens on the pavement terrace where there are prime people-watching views of Piazza dell'Immacolata and its throngs of students lazing beneath orange trees on balmy nights.

ENTERTAINMENT

NUOVO CINEMA PALAZZO — ARTS CENTRE

Map p343 (www.nuovocinemapalazzo.it; Piazza dei Sanniti 9a; hours vary; Via Tiburtina) Students, artists and activists are breathing new life into San Lorenzo's former Palace Cinema with a bevy of exciting creative happenings: think film screenings, theatre performances, DJs, concerts, live music, breakdance classes and other arty events. In warm weather, the action spills outside onto the street terrace. Check the Facebook page for event details.

TEATRO DELL'OPERA DI ROMA — OPERA

Map p344 (06 48 16 01; www.operaroma.it; Piazza Beniamino Gigli 1; box office 10am-6pm Mon-Sat, 9am-1.30pm Sun; Repubblica) Rome's premier opera house boasts a dramatic red-and-gold interior, a Fascist 1920s exterior and an impressive history: it premiered both Puccini's *Tosca* and Mascagni's *Cavalleria rusticana*. Opera and ballet performances are staged between November and June.

CHARITY CAFÉ — LIVE MUSIC

Map p344 (06 4782 5881; www.charitycafe.it; Via Panisperna 68; 6pm-2am Tue-Sun; Cavour) Think narrow space, spindly tables, dim lighting and a laid-back vibe: this is a place to snuggle down and listen to some slinky live jazz or blues. Civilised, relaxed, untouristy and very Monti. Gigs usually take place from 10pm; *aperitivo* is between 6pm and 9pm. Check the website to see who's performing. It's closed on Sundays in summer.

WISHLIST — LIVE MUSIC

Map p343 (349 7494659; www.facebook.com/wishlistclub; Via dei Volsci 126b; 9.30pm-2am Thu, to 4am Fri & Sat, 9pm-2am Sun; Via dei Reti) A black door marks the entrance to this music club housed in a low-lying building on one of San Lorenzo's grungiest streets. Check the Twitter feed for gig details.

ESC ATELIER — LIVE MUSIC

Map p343 (www.escatelier.net; Via dei Volsci 159; 3-11pm Tue-Sat; Reti) This alternative arts centre, tucked down a grungy San Lorenzo street, hosts cultural events including festivals, live gigs and club nights: expect electronica DJ sets, discussions, exhibitions, political events and more. Check its Facebook page for events.

TEATRO AMBRA JOVINELLI — THEATRE

Map p343 (06 8308 2884; www.ambrajovinelli.org; Via G Pepe 43; Vittorio Emanuele) A home away from home for many famous Italian actors, the Ambra Jovinelli is a historic venue for alternative comedians and satirists. Nowadays, its program runs the gamut, ranging from stand-up comedy and musicals to drama and contemporary work.

ISTITUZIONE UNIVERSITARIA DEI CONCERTI — LIVE MUSIC

Map p343 (IUC; 06 361 00 51; www.concertiiuc.it; Piazzale Aldo Moro 5; Verano) The IUC organises a season of concerts in the Aula Magna of La Sapienza University, including many visiting international artists and orchestras. Performances cover a wide range of musical genres, including baroque, classical, contemporary and jazz.

SPACE CINEMA MODERNO — CINEMA

Map p344 (06 892 111; www.thespacecinema.it; Piazza della Repubblica 45; Repubblica) Film premieres are often held at this multiplex, which screens blockbusters from Hollywood (both in English and Italian) and major-release Italian films.

SHOPPING

While not a prime shopping area, it's worth heading to this part of town to browse Monti's artisanal clothing and jewellery boutiques, as well as its growing number of vintage shops.

Monti

★PERLEI — JEWELLERY

Map p344 (06 4891 3862; www.perlei.com; Via del Boschetto 35; 10am-8pm Mon-Sat, 11am-2pm & 3-7pm Sun; Cavour) Pieces of

MARKETS

Nuovo Mercato Esquilino (Map p343; Via Filippo Turati 160; ⊙5am-3pm Mon, Wed & Thu, to 5pm Tue, Fri & Sat; Ⓜ Vittorio Emanuele) Throw yourself into the real Rome at this buzzing covered food market where budget-conscious Romans and students shop for fresh fruit, veg, exotic herbs, spices and more.

Mercato Monti Urban Market (Map p344; www.mercatomonti.com; Via Leonina 46; ⊙10am-8pm Sat & Sun Sep-Jun; Ⓜ Cavour) Vintage clothes, accessories and one-off pieces by local designers: this market in the hip 'hood of Monti is well worth a rummage if you're here on a weekend.

avant-garde body jewellery catch the eye in the window of this tiny artisanal jeweller situated on Monti's best shopping street. Inside, handmade pieces by Tammar Edelman and Elinor Avni will appeal to those with a modernist aesthetic – their graceful arcs, sinuous strands and architectural arrangements are elegant and eye-catching.

★TINA SONDERGAARD — FASHION & ACCESSORIES

Map p344 (☎06 8365 57 61; www.facebook.com/tina.sondergaard.rome; Via del Boschetto 1d; ⊙10.30am-7.30pm Mon-Sat, closed Aug; Ⓜ Cavour) Sublimely cut and whimsically retro-esque, Tina Sondergaard's handmade creations for women are a hit with the local fashion cognoscenti. Styles change by the week rather than the season, femininity is the leitmotif, and you can have adjustments made (included in the price). Everything is remarkably well priced considering the quality of the fabrics and workmanship.

CENTOVENTISETTE — CLOTHING

Map p344 (Via del Boschetto 127; ⊙10.30am-7.30pm Mon-Sat; Ⓜ Cavour) Monti's streets are home to a number of clothing ateliers, and this is one of the best of them. The pieces sold here have an elegant simplicity and are extremely well priced, too.

FLAMINGO VINTAGE — CLOTHING

Map p344 (☎06 4890 67 33; Via del Boschetto 123; ⊙11am-7.30pm Mon-Sat, from 3pm Sun; Ⓜ Cavour) Owner Carlotta has a great eye, and manages to source vintage finds from the 1940s and every subsequent decade to sell in this cute boutique.

LE NOU — CLOTHING

Map p344 (☎06 3105 6339; www.facebook.com/Le-NoU-210998585605889; Via del Boschetto 111; ⊙11am-8pm Tue-Sat; 📶; Ⓜ Cavour) This clothing store in Monti is run by the startlingly talented Eugenia Barbati, who graduated from fashion school and promptly opened up her own place. Her hipster designs can be bought off the rack, or you can pick the fabric and garment style of your choice and she'll whip you up a bespoke piece in no time.

PIFEBO — VINTAGE

Map p344 (☎06 8901 5204; www.pifebo.com; Via dei Serpenti 141; ⊙11am-3pm & 4-8pm Mon-Sat, noon-8pm Sun; 📶; Ⓜ Cavour) Seek out a secondhand steal at Pifebo, the city's top vintage boutique. Shelves and racks brim with sunglasses, boots, clothing, bags and an impressive sports jersey collection, all hailing from the '70s, '80s and '90s. The shop also specialises in rehabbing and restoring leather items, handily returning them to their original splendour.

PODERE VECCIANO — FOOD

Map p344 (☎06 4891 3812; www.poderevecciano.com; Via dei Serpenti 33; ⊙10am-8pm Tue-Sun; Ⓜ Cavour) Selling produce from its Tuscan farm, this shop is a great place to pick up presents to take home. Choose from different varieties of pesto, honey and marmalade, selected wines, olive-oil-based cosmetics and beautiful olive-wood chopping boards. There's even an olive tree growing in the middle of the shop.

ABITO — FASHION & ACCESSORIES

Map p344 (☎06 488 10 17; www.facebook.com/ABITO61; Via Panisperna 60; ⊙10.30am-2pm & 3-8pm Mon-Sat, from noon Sun; Ⓜ Cavour) Wilma Silvestre, founder of local label Le Gallinelle, designs elegant clothes with a difference. You can browse her chic, laid-back styles and buy off the rack at her Monti boutique. Silvestre's Le Gallinelle boutique is located on the opposite side of the road.

Esquilino

ROMA LIUTERIA DI MATHIAS MENANTEAU MUSICAL INSTRUMENTS

Map p344 (339 3517677; www.romaliuteria.it; Via di Santa Maria Maggiore 150; 10am-1pm & 3-7pm Mon-Sat; MCavour, Termini) A vintage ceramic-tiled wood burner casts a golden glow on this old-fashioned artisanal workshop where French luthier Mathias Menanteau crafts and restores cellos and violins by hand.

GIACOMO SANTINI SHOES

Map p344 (06 488 09 34; Via Cavour 106; 10am-1pm & 3.30-7.30pm Mon-Fri, 10am-1.30pm & 3-7.30pm Sat; MCavour) This Fausto Santini outlet, named after the Roman accessory designer's father Giacomo, sells last season's and discounted Fausto Santini boots, shoes and bags. Expect to pay a snip of the regular retail price for a pair of his exquisite designs in soft leather. Sizes can be limited. Look for the 'Calzaturo' sign above the boutique.

Piazza della Repubblica & Around

FELTRINELLI INTERNATIONAL BOOKS

Map p344 (06 482 78 78; www.lafeltrinelli.it; Via VE Orlando 84-86; 9am-8pm Mon-Sat, 10.30am-1.30pm & 4-8pm Sun; MRepubblica) The international branch of Italy's ubiquitous bookseller has a splendid collection of books in English, Italian, Spanish, French, German and Portuguese. You'll find everything from recent bestsellers to dictionaries, travel guides, DVDs and maps.

San Lorenzo & Beyond

TRANSMISSION MUSIC

Map p343 (06 4470 4370; www.transmissionroma.com; Via Salentini 27; 10am-2pm & 3-8pm Mon-Sat; Via Tiburtina) One of a growing number of shops serving Rome's record collectors, this San Lorenzo store has a devoted clientele. Its eclectic collection of vinyl LPs, CDs, 7-inch singles, DVDs and Blu-rays covers the musical gamut, ranging from classical music and 1950s oldies to jazz, reggae, punk, new wave and modern dance.

SPORTS & ACTIVITIES

DIVULGAZIONE LINGUA ITALIANA LANGUAGE

Map p344 (06 446 25 93; www.dilit.it; Via Marghera 22; 8.30am-7pm Mon-Fri) School offering language and cultural courses. Check the website for course dates and prices.

Trastevere & Gianicolo

EAST OF VIALE DI TRASTEVERE | WEST OF VIALE DI TRASTEVERE | GIANICOLO & AROUND

Neighbourhood Top Five

❶ **Basilica di Santa Maria in Trastevere** (p174) Admiring the exquisite interior and exterior mosaics in this beautiful church, followed by people-watching on the square out the front.

❷ **Trattoria dining** (p178) Feasting on the perfect Roman carbonara, *pasta cacio e pepe* or seasonal artichoke at traditional trattorias hidden away on tiny cobbled piazzas.

❸ **Villa Farnesina** (p175) Savouring the breathtaking interior decor by Raphael inside Trastevere's elegant Renaissance villa.

❹ **Trastevere nightlife** (p181) Sampling inventive cocktails, trying a flight of fine wines or hobnobbing with hipsters in a secret speakeasy.

❺ **Gianicolo** (p182) Hiking to the top of Rome's highest hill for a magnificent, soul-soaring panorama of the city.

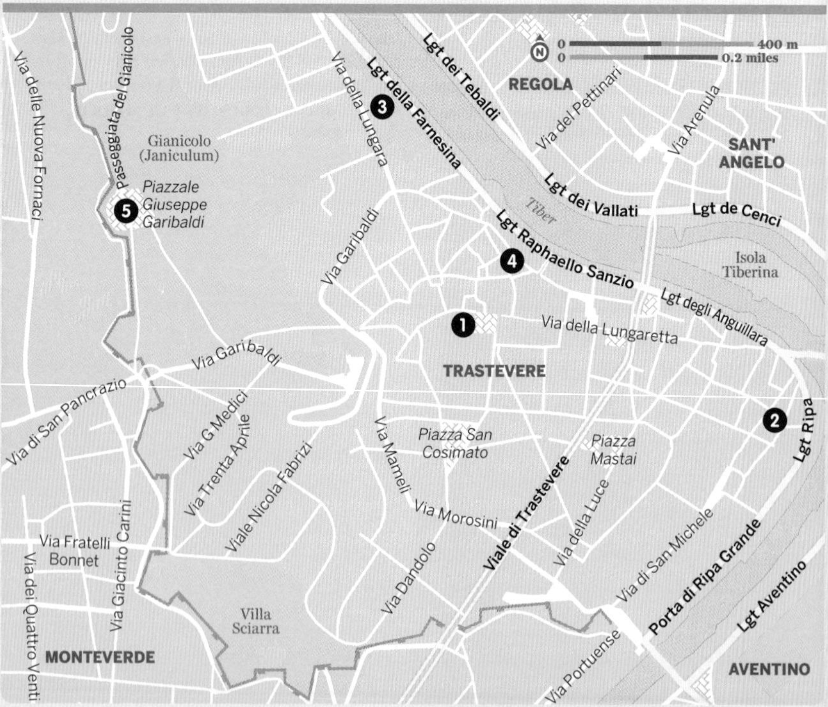

For more detail of this area see Map p340

Explore Trastevere & Gianicolo

Cradled in a left-bank curve of the River Tiber, medieval Trastevere is made for walking – or rather aimless, contented wandering punctuated by photo stops, coffee breaks, and some of Rome's finest home cooking in vintage trattorias. Allow at least a day to explore: key sights include glittering Basilica di Santa Maria in Trastevere (p174); Villa Farnesina (p175), a breathtaking mansion with decor by Raphael and others; and Galleria Corsini (p176), with its dazzling yet often overlooked art collection. End your sightseeing with a green moment in Trastevere's botanic gardens or, should you be up for the stiff hike, atop Gianicolo (p182) – don't miss Tempietto di Bramante (p177) on your way up.

Come dusk, bars unveil banquets of nibbles and finger foods for that sacrosanct *aperitivo*. Many are clustered in the small lanes around Piazza Trilussa; Via Benedetta is the street for international-style pubs (much loved by American foreign-exchange students).

Local Life

- **Cafe culture** No cafe terrace is as no-frills or busy as veteran favourite Bar San Calisto (p181), notorious for serving the cheapest beer in Rome.
- **Home cooking** Join locals queuing at Antica Caciara Trasteverina (p185) for ingredients to make an authentic Roman carbonara.
- **Summer nights** Trendy pop-up bars pepper Trastevere's riverside between Ponte Mazzini and Ponte Cestio in summer, making the river *the* cool place to be.
- **Meeting point** Locals always meet up at 'the steps', the wide flight of steps leading up to the fountain on **Piazza Trilussa** (Map p340; Piazza Trilussa); in summer the steps are packed with people sitting here, drink in hand.

Getting There & Away

- **Tram** From Largo di Torre Argentina tram 8 runs along the main drag of Viale di Trastevere, ending up at Villa Doria Pamphilj. Tram 3 also stops at the southern end of Viale Trastevere, connecting with Testaccio (Via Marmorata), Colosseo, San Giovanni and Villa Borghese.
- **Bus** From Termini, bus H runs to Viale di Trastevere, while the 780 runs from Piazza Venezia. For Gianicolo, if you don't fancy the steep steps from Via G Mameli, take bus 870 from Piazza della Rovere or bus 115 from Viale di Trastevere.

Lonely Planet's Top Tip

With its century-old biscuit shops and bakeries, family-run trattorias, open-air food market and superb food purveyors replete with carefully sourced, zero-kilometre farm produce, Trastevere is a naturally gourmet destination. To get the most out of it, consider a guided food tour with locals in the know: **Casa Mia** (p36), **GT Food & Travel** (p346) or **The Tour Guy** (p297).

Best Places to Eat

- Trattoria Da Cesare al Casaletto (p181)
- La Tavernaccia (p178)
- Da Enzo (p178)
- Fior di Luna (p179)
- Supplì (p179)

For reviews, see p177.

Best Places to Drink

- Niji Roma (p183)
- Bar San Calisto (p181)
- Terra Satis (p181)
- Keyhole (p183)
- Il Baretto (p184)

For reviews, see p180.

Best Artworks

- Basilica di Santa Maria in Trastevere (p174)
- Basilica di Santa Cecilia in Trastevere (p176)
- Villa Farnesina (p175)
- Galleria Corsini (p176)

For reviews, see p176.

TOP EXPERIENCE

LINGER AT BASILICA DI SANTA MARIA IN TRASTEVERE

This glittering church is said to be the oldest church in Rome dedicated to the Virgin Mary. It was first constructed in the early 3rd century over the spot where, according to legend, a fountain of oil miraculously sprang from the ground. Its current Romanesque form is the result of a 12th-century revamp.

The church facade is decorated with a beautiful medieval mosaic depicting Mary feeding Jesus surrounded by 10 women bearing lamps. Two are veiled and hold extinguished lamps, symbolising widowhood, while the lit lamps of the others represent their virginity. The portico was added by Carlo Fontana in 1702, with its balustrade decorated with statues of four popes.

Inside, it's the golden 12th-century mosaics that stand out. In the apse, look out for the dazzling depiction of Christ and his mother flanked by various saints and, on the far left, Pope Innocent II holding a model of the church. Beneath this is a series of six mosaics (pictured above) by Pietro Cavallini (c 1291) illustrating the life of the Virgin.

Note the 24 Roman columns, some plundered from the Terme di Caracalla; the fragments of Roman carved marbles forming an informal mosaic on the porch; the wooden ceiling designed in 1617 by Domenichino; and, on the right of the altar, a spiralling Cosmati candlestick, on the exact spot where the oil fountain is said to have sprung. The Cappella Avila is also worth a look for its stunning 17th-century dome. The spiralling Cosmatesque floor was relaid in the 1870s, a recreation of the 13th-century original.

TOP TIPS

- Allow plenty of time to linger on the piazza in front of the church afterwards – it's Trastevere's focal square and a prime people-watching spot.
- Visit early in the morning or at the end of the day when the softer light shows off the beautiful Romanesque facade fresh from a painstaking restoration.

PRACTICALITIES

- Map p330
- 06 581 48 02
- Piazza Santa Maria in Trastevere
- 7.30am-9pm Sep-Jul, 8am-noon & 4-9pm Aug
- Viale di Trastevere, Belli

TOP EXPERIENCE

DELIGHT AT THE VILLA FARNESINA

This 16th-century villa is serenely and symmetrically proportioned on the outside and fantastically frescoed from top to bottom on the inside.

Villa Farnesina was built for Agostino Chigi, the immensely wealthy papal banker. At his banquets he'd encourage his guests to throw their solid gold plates out of the window once they'd finished (servants would stand beneath the windows to catch them in nets). The house was bought by Cardinal Alessando Farnese in 1577.

The architect was Baldassare Peruzzi, formerly Bramante's assistant; he also painted several of the frescoes. On the ground floor is the **Loggia of Galatea**, attributed to Raphael and depicting a sea nymph, with the vault frescoed by Peruzzi, and mythological scenes by Sebastiano del Piombio. Next door, the **Loggia of Cupid and Psyche** was also frescoed by Raphael and seethes with naked figures and muscular cupids.

On the 1st floor, Peruzzi's frescoes in the **Salone delle Prospettive** are a superb illusionary perspective of a panorama of 16th-century Rome, while Chigi's bedchamber is filled with cavorting cherubs, gods and goddesses.

TOP TIPS

- With the exception of the 2nd Sunday of the month, the villa is only open before 2pm – plan accordingly.
- Show your Vatican Museums ticket (within seven days) to get a reduced admission rate.
- On most Saturdays, there's an English-language guided tour (€4), departing at 10am.

PRACTICALITIES

- Map p328
- 06 6802 7268
- www.villafarnesina.it
- Via della Lungara 230
- adult/reduced €6/5
- 9am-2pm Mon-Sat, to 5pm 2nd Sun of the month
- Lungotevere della Farnesina

SIGHTS

Trastevere tucks away a peppering of exquisite churches and Renaissance *palazzi* and villas stuffed with largely unsung artworks. Yet some of its most memorable sights are picturesque glimpses down narrow, ochre-and-orange-shaded lanes strung with the morning's washing. North of Trastevere rise the hilly slopes of Gianicolo. Today a tranquil and leafy area that combines Rome's finest views, embassies, monuments, piazzas, Rome's botanical gardens and some beautiful architecture, it's difficult to imagine that in 1849 the Gianicolo was the scene of fierce and bloody fighting against French troops sent to restore papal rule. Escape here for fresh air and fabulous city views.

East of Viale di Trastevere

★BASILICA DI SANTA CECILIA IN TRASTEVERE — BASILICA

Map p338 (06 4549 2739; www.benedettinesantacecilia.it; Piazza di Santa Cecilia 22; fresco & crypt each €2.50; basilica & crypt 10am-12.30pm & 4-6pm Mon-Sat, 11.30am-12.30pm & 4.30-6.30pm Sun, fresco 10am-12.30pm Mon-Sat, 11.30am-12.30pm Sun; Viale de Trastevere, Belli) The last resting place of the patron saint of music features Pietro Cavallini's stunning 13th-century fresco in the nuns' choir of the hushed convent adjoining the church. Inside the church itself, Stefano Maderno's mysterious sculpture depicts St Cecilia's miraculously preserved body, unearthed in the Catacombs of San Callisto in 1599. You can also visit the excavations of Roman houses, one of which was possibly Cecilia's. The church is fronted by a gentle fountain surrounded by roses.

CHIESA DI SAN FRANCESCO D'ASSISI A RIPA GRANDE — CHURCH

Map p340 (06 581 9020; www.sanfrancescoaripa.it/san-francesco; Piazza di San Francesco d'Assisi 88; 7am-1pm & 2-7.30pm; Viale di Trastevere, Trastevere/Mastai) St Francis is said to have stayed here in 1219, and in his cell you can still see the rock that he purportedly used as a pillow and his crucifix. Rebuilt several times, the church's current incarnation dates from the 1680s. It contains one of Bernini's most daring works, the *Beata Ludovica Albertoni* (Blessed Ludovica Albertoni; 1674), a work of highly charged sexual ambiguity. Note how the marble has been transformed into flowing robes.

West of Viale di Trastevere

BASILICA DI SANTA MARIA IN TRASTEVERE — BASILICA

See p174.

VILLA FARNESINA — HISTORIC BUILDING

See p175.

★GALLERIA CORSINI — GALLERY

Map p340 (Palazzo Corsini; 06 6880 2323; www.barberinicorsini.org; Via della Lungara 10; adult/reduced incl Palazzo Barberini €12/6; 8.30am-7pm Wed-Mon; Lungotevere della Farnesina) Once home to Queen Christina

STUMBLING STONES

Watch your footing when meandering Trastevere's impossibly quaint, old-world lanes and alleys. Among the uneven, well-worn square-shaped cobblestones (dangerously slippery in rain), you will occasionally stumble across a *pietri d'inciampo* (literally 'stumbling stone' in Italian) glinting in the sunlight. Each one of these polished brass stones, shaped square like a Roman cobble and engraved with the name of a local Jewish resident, marks the exact spot where the Holocaust victim was rounded up by Nazi soldiers during WWII and deported to Auschwitz or other death camps. Most stumbling blocks are embedded in pavements in front of private homes and invariably count more than one – a stone for each member of entire Jewish families.

The stumbling stones are part of a Europe-wide memorial project initiated by German artist Gunter Demning. Some 200 pave the historic streets of Rome to date, predominantly in Trastevere, such as those at **Viale Trastevere 114** (Map p340; Trastevere/Bernardino Da Feltre), and the old Jewish Ghetto directly across the river.

of Sweden, whose bedroom reputedly witnessed a steady stream of male and female lovers, the 16th-century Palazzo Corsini was designed by Ferdinando Fuga in grand Versailles style, and houses part of Italy's national art collection. Highlights include Caravaggio's *San Giovanni Battista* (St John the Baptist), Guido Reni's *Salome con la Testa di San Giovanni Battista* (Salome with the Head of John the Baptist), and Fra' Angelico's Corsini Triptych, plus works by Rubens, Poussin and Van Dyck.

TRIUMPHS & LAMENTS PUBLIC ART

Map p340 (Lungotevere della Farnesina; 🚌Lungotevere dei Tebaldi) This vast and fading frieze adorns the River Tiber walls between Ponte Sisto and Ponte Mazzini. The creation of South African artist William Kentridge, it stretches for 550m and comprises more than 80 figures, some up to 12m high, illustrating episodes from Rome's history. Look for depictions of Roman emperor Marcus Aurelius, Mussolini, and actor Marcello Mastroianni who's shown kissing Anita Ekberg in a re-creation of the famous Trevi Fountain scene from *La Dolce Vita*.

Gianicolo & Around

TEMPIETTO DI BRAMANTE & CHIESA DI SAN PIETRO IN MONTORIO CHURCH

Map p340 (☎06 581 3940; www.sanpietroinmontorio.it; Piazza San Pietro in Montorio 2; ⏰chiesa 8.30am-noon & 3-4pm Mon-Fri, tempietto 10am-6pm Tue-Sun; 🚌Via Garibaldi) Considered the first great building of the High Renaissance, Bramante's sublime tempietto (Little Temple; 1508) is a perfect surprise, squeezed into the courtyard of the Chiesa di San Pietro in Montorio, on the spot where St Peter is said to have been crucified. It's small but perfectly formed; its classically inspired design and ideal proportions epitomise the Renaissance zeitgeist.

VIEWPOINT VIEWPOINT

(Passeggiata del Gianicolo; 🚌Ospedale pediatrico Bambin Gesù) Many of the vaunted viewpoints along Gianicolo (aka Janiculum) are obscured by trees, but this lesser known overlook at the north end has sweeping views across Rome. There's a small cafe, a few benches, the usual weeds and a bittersweet little toy stand selling gifts for patients in the nearby children's hospital, Ospedale pediatrico Bambin Gesù.

ORTO BOTANICO GARDENS

Map p340 (Botanical Garden; ☎06 4991 7107; Largo Cristina di Svezia 24; adult/reduced €8/4; ⏰9am-6.30pm Mon-Sat summer, to 5.30pm winter; 🚌Lungotevere della Farnesina, Piazza Trilussa) Formerly the private grounds of Palazzo Corsini, Rome's 12-hectare botanical gardens are a little-known, slightly neglected gem and a great place to unwind in a tree-shaded expanse covering the steep slopes of the Gianicolo. Plants have been cultivated here since the 13th century and the current gardens were established in 1883, when the grounds of Palazzo Corsini were given to the University of Rome. They now contain up to 8000 species, including some of Europe's rarest plants.

FONTANA DELL'ACQUA PAOLA FOUNTAIN

Map p340 (Via Garibaldi; 🚌Via Garibaldi) Featured in the opening scene of Paolo Sorrentino's Oscar-winning *La grande bellezza* (The Great Beauty; 2013), this monumental white fountain with its thundering water was built in 1612 to celebrate the restoration of a 2nd-century aqueduct that supplied (and still supplies) water from Lago di Bracciano, 35km north of Rome. Four of the fountain's six columns are made from pink stone and came from the facade of the old St Peter's Basilica, while much of the marble was pillaged from the Roman Forum.

VILLA DORIA PAMPHILJ PARK

Map p340 (⏰sunrise-sunset; 🚌Via di San Pancrazio) Lorded over by the 17th-century Villa Doria Pamphilj is Rome's largest landscaped park – many a Roman's favourite place to escape the city noise and bustle. Once a private estate, it was laid out around 1650 for Prince Camillo Pamphilj, nephew of Pope Innocent X. It's a huge expanse of rolling parkland, shaded by Rome's distinctive umbrella pines. At its centre is the prince's summer residence, Casino del Belrespiro (used for official functions today), with its manicured gardens and citrus trees.

EATING

Traditionally working class and poor but nowadays chic and pricey, picturesque Trastevere is packed with restaurants, trattorias, cafes and pizzerias. The better places dot the maze of side streets, and it pays to be selective, as many of the restaurants are bog-standard tourist

traps. But it's not just tourists here – Romans like to eat in Trastevere too, especially in the leafy outer reaches.

East of Viale di Trastevere

C'È PASTA... E PASTA! ITALIAN €

Map p350 (06 5832 0125; Via Ettore Rolli 29; meals €15-25; 8.30am-3pm Sun-Fri, 5-9.30pm Sun-Thu, meals served from noon; Stazione Trastevere) Fresh pasta sold here is ready for you to prepare and eat at home; ready to eat and wrapped for takeaway; or ready to eat at one of the simple tables here, inside or out. Everything is superb (and kosher), especially the artichoke ravioli and the traditional Roman-style lasagne. Browse the cases filled with edible joy and assemble a great-value meal.

PIZZERIA AI MARMI PIZZA €

Map p340 (Panattoni; 06 580 09 19; http://facebook.com/aimarmi; Viale di Trastevere 53; meals €10-20; 6.30pm-2am Thu-Tue; Viale di Trastevere, Trastevere/Mastai) Also called *l'obitorio* (the morgue) because of its vintage marble-slab tabletops, this is Trastevere's most popular pizzeria. Think super-thin pizzas, a clattering buzz, testy waiters, a huge street terrace and some fantastic fried starters – the *supplì* (risotto balls), *baccalà* (salted cod) and zucchini flowers are all heavenly. Skip the pastas. They're serious here: the menu notes the few toppings that are frozen.

SEU PIZZA ILLUMINATI PIZZA €

Map p350 (06 588 33 84; http://seu-pizza-illuminati.business.site; Via Angelo Bargoni 10-18; meals €20-25; 7pm-midnight Wed-Mon; P ; Ippolito Nievo) 'In pizza we trust' is the cheeky motto of this Trastevere pizzeria helmed by Pier Daniele Seu. Inspired combos range from burrata, tuna tartare, pistachio and lime zest to *guanciale* (cured pig's cheek), pecorino cream, red onion and coffee. A selection of classics like the margherita keep purists happy. Expect an unapologetically thick Neapolitan crust.

★LA TAVERNACCIA TRATTORIA €€

Map p350 (06 581 27 92; www.latavernacciaroma.com; Via Giovanni da Castel Bolognese 63; meals €30-45; 12.45-3pm & 7.30-11pm Thu-Tue; Stazione Trastevere) This family-run trattoria bustles every minute it's open. Book in advance to get one of Rome's most sought-after tables. The setting is simplicity itself, and the food is sensational. Roman classics get stellar treatment here. First courses include various preserved meats and hams that melt away. Besides pastas there are many roasts. Staff are cheery and helpful.

★DA ENZO TRATTORIA €€

Map p340 (06 581 22 60; www.daenzoal29.com; Via dei Vascellari 29; meals €30-35; 12.30-3pm & 7.30-11pm Mon-Sat; Lungotevere Ripa, Belli) Vintage ochre walls, yellow-checked tablecloths and a traditional menu featuring all the Roman classics: what makes this tiny and staunchly traditional trattoria exceptional is its careful sourcing of local, quality products, many from nearby farms in Lazio. The seasonal, deep-fried Jewish artichokes and the *pasta cacio e pepe* (cheese and black-pepper pasta) are among the best in Rome.

SPIRITO DIVINO ITALIAN €€

Map p340 (06 589 66 89; www.ristorantespiritodivino.com; Via dei Genovesi 31; meals €35-45; 7pm-midnight Mon-Sat; Belli) Chef and Slow Food aficionado Eliana Catalani buys ingredients directly from local producers. The restaurant's trademark dish is *maiale alla mazio,* an ancient pork and red-wine stew said to have been a favourite of Caesar. Between courses diners can visit the wine cellar, which dates from 80 BCE. Note the ancient columns on the side facade with old Hebrew inscriptions.

TRATTORIA DA TEO TRATTORIA €€

Map p340 (06 581 83 55; www.facebook.com/Trattoria.da.teo; Piazza dei Ponziani 7; meals €35-45; 12.30-3pm & 7.30-11.30pm Mon-Sat; Viale di Trastevere, Belli) One of Rome's classic trattorias, Da Teo buzzes with locals digging into steaming platefuls of Roman standards, such as carbonara, *pasta cacio e pepe* and the most fabulous seasonal artichokes – both Jewish (deep-fried) and Roman-style (stuffed with parsley and garlic, and boiled). In keeping with hardcore trattoria tradition, Teo's homemade gnocchi is only served on Thursday. Reservations essential.

LA GENSOLA SICILIAN €€€

Map p340 (06 581 63 12; www.osterialagensola.it; Piazza della Gensola 15; meals €45-55; 12.30-3pm & 7.30-11.30pm, closed Sun summer; Viale di Trastevere, Belli) Enjoy delicious traditional cuisine with an emphasis on seafood at this upmarket trattoria. Begin with a half-dozen oysters or wafer-thin slices of raw tuna, amberjack or seabass carpaccio, followed perhaps by a heap of *spaghellini* with fingernail-sized clams or seared anchovies with chicory. Meat lovers can tuck into Roman classics like *coda alla vaccinara* (oxtail stew) or *trippa* (tripe).

West of Viale di Trastevere

★FIOR DI LUNA GELATO €

Map p340 (06 6456 1314; http://fiordiluna.com; Via della Lungaretta 96; gelato from €2.50; 1-8pm Sun & Mon, 1-11pm Tue-Sat; Belli, Viale di Trastevere) For many Romans this busy little hub makes the best handmade gelato and sorbet in the world. It's produced in small batches using natural, seasonal ingredients. Seasonal favourites include pear and banana, blueberry yoghurt, strawberry and pistachio (the nuts are ground by hand). Get a kick with a cup of *cafe bio* (organic coffee, €1). Note the 'no franchising' sign.

SUPPLÌ ITALIAN €

Map p340 (06 589 71 10; www.suppliroma.it; Via di San Francesco a Ripa 137; pizza & fritti €2.50-6; 9am-10pm Mon-Sat; Viale di Trastevere) This blink-and-you-miss-it Trastevere *tavola calda* (hot table) has Roman street food down to an art. Locals queue for its namesake *supplì:* fried risotto balls spiked with *ragù* (meat and tomato sauce) and mozzarella. The family-run eatery also gets top marks for pizza by the slice. Daily specials include gnocchi (Thursday) and fried fish and calamari (Tuesday and Friday).

GISELDA ITALIAN €

Map p340 (06 4566 5090; http://giseldafornoroma.com; Viale di Trastevere 52; meals from €9; 7am-11pm;) The coffee bar at this bright and airy cafe buzzes all day. Grab a table amid the industrial chic and tuck into one of the €6 lunch specials. It's all Italian standards made with care, passion and the best ingredients. The bakery sells pizza slices topped with buttery mortadella that will make you weep. Also good are the pastries and the desserts.

ANTICA NORCINERIA IACOZZILLI DELI €

Map p340 (06 581 27 34; Via Natale del Grande 15; sandwich €4.50; 9am-1pm & 4.30-8.30pm Mon-Sat; ; Trastevere/Mastai) Three generations of the Iacozzilli family work in this old-school deli that dates from 1924. It's hailed for its *porchetta:* seasoned with salt and rosemary, this slow-roasted pork is juicy in the middle and exquisitely crispy on top. Ask for a *porchetta panino,* find a wall outside to lean on and relish the savoury goodness.

> **LOCAL KNOWLEDGE**
>
> **GRATTACHECCA**
>
> It's summertime, the living is easy, and Romans like nothing better in the sultry evening heat than to amble down to the river and partake of some *grattachecca* (crushed ice covered in fruit and syrup). It's the ideal way to cool down, and there are kiosks along the riverbank satisfying this very Roman need; try **Sora Mirella Caffè** (Map p340; Lungotevere degli Anguillara; treats €3-6; 11am-3am May-Sep; Lungotevere degli Anguillara), next to Ponte Cestio. Down by the water, shaved ice in hand, meander north along the river to **Ponte Sisto** and watch the marauding seagulls.

LA RENELLA BAKERY €

Map p340 (06 581 72 65; http://larenella.com; Via del Moro 15; pizza slices from €2.50; 7am-midnight Sun-Thu, to 3am Fri & Sat; Piazza Trilussa) Watch pizza masters at work at this historic Trastevere bakery. Savour the wood-fired ovens, bar-stool seating and heavenly aromas of pizza, bread (get the *casareccia*, crusty Roman-style bread) and biscuits. Piled-high toppings (and fillings) vary seasonally, to the joy of everyone from punks with big dogs to old ladies with little dogs. It's been in the biz since 1870.

LE LEVAIN BAKERY €

Map p340 (06 6456 2880; www.lelevainroma.it; Via Luigi Santini 22-23; snacks from €3; 8am-6.30pm winter, to 8.30pm summer; ; Via Mameli, Trastevere/Mastai) Many locals come here for their daily dose of rich and creamy butter, albeit it in the guise of authentic croissants, *pains au chocolat* and other irresistible French pastries. Traditional French sweet treats – colourful cream-filled macarons, flaky millefeuilles and miniature *tartes aux pommes* (apple tarts) – are equally authentic. Enjoy your indulgence on a stool inside or on the nearby piazza.

PROSCIUTTERIA – CANTINA DEI PAPI TUSCAN €

Map p340 (06 6456 2839; Via della Scala 71; snacks from €5; 11am-11.30pm; Via della Scala) For a taste of Tuscany in Rome, consider a stop at this cheery Florentine *prosciutteria* (salami shop). Made-to-measure *taglieri* (wooden chopping boards) come loaded with cold cuts, cheeses, fruit and pickles and are best devoured over a glass of Brunello di Montalcino or Chianti Classico. Dozens of hams and salami dangle above the smattering of stools.

MERCATO DI PIAZZA SAN COSIMATO MARKET

Map p340 (Piazza San Cosimato; 7am-2pm Mon-Sat; Viale di Trastevere, Trastevere/Mastai) Trastevere's open-air neighbourhood market is a top spot to stock up on globe and violet artichokes, *broccolo romanesco* (Roman broccoli), dandelion greens and other seasonal foodstuffs, as has been the case for at least a century. Bring your own bag or basket. Get a snack and enjoy it in the small park while squealing children play.

OSTERIA DA ZI UMBERTO LAZIO €

Map p340 (06 581 66 46; Piazza di San Giovanni della Malva 14; meals €20-25; 12.30-3pm & 7.30-11.30pm Tue-Sun; Piazza Trilussa) If you know a joke in Italian, tell it to break through the theatrically gruff Roman exteriors of the staff at this classic local joint. Tourists often outnumber locals, but this basic trattoria still exudes authenticity. Roman standards like *pasta cacio e pepe* (pasta with cheese and pepper) are excellent and much recommended. In summer, tables occupy the small square.

RUMI BOTTEGA ORGANICA MARKET €

Map p340 (06 581 49 88; www.rumibottegaorganica.it; Via di San Francesco a Ripa 133; meals from €10; 10am-9pm Mon-Sat; Viale di Trastevere, Trastevere/Mastai) There is a real charm to this tiny down-to-earth *bottega organica* (organic market) in Trastevere where a knowing crowd lingers over sassy farro- and pulse-packed salads, and sandwiches made from organic, naturally leavened bread. Craft beer and organic wine are natural companions, and the picnic-handy deli offers healthy treats to take away.

DAR POETA PIZZA €€

Map p340 (06 588 05 16; www.darpoeta.com; Vicolo del Bologna 45; meals €25-35; noon-midnight; Piazza Trilussa) Visitors flock to Dar Poeta for filling wood-fired pizzas and a buzzing atmosphere. As well as the usual selection of pizzas, served with crusts that are somewhere between wafer-thin Roman and Neapolitan deep pan, it's also famous for its trademark ricotta and Nutella calzone. Tables inside and out on the quiet street have red-checked tablecloths.

ZIA RESTAURANT FUSION €€€

Map p340 (06 2348 8093; www.ziarestaurant.com; Via Goffredo Mameli 45; meals €30-55; 7.30-10pm Mon-Wed, 12.30-2pm & 7.30-10pm Thu-Sat; Trastevere/Min P Istruzione) Having cut his teeth in the kitchens of a few of the culinary world's most reputable names (think Georges Blanc and Gordon Ramsay), up-and-coming chef Antonio Ziantoni has forged out on his own with solo venture Zia. The menu exquisitely mates Italian and French cuisine; pasta stuffed with blue cheese in an onion and clove broth and foie gras macarons shine.

GLASS HOSTARIA ITALIAN €€€

Map p340 (06 5833 5903; www.glass-restaurant.it; Vicolo del Cinque 58; menus €90-150, meals €90-140; 7.30-11pm Tue-Sun; Piazza Trilussa) Michelin-starred Glass creates innovative cuisine in a contemporary, sophisticated space with a mezzanine. Law graduate-turned-chef Cristina Bowerman creates inventive, delicate dishes that combine seasonal ingredients with traditional elements to delight and surprise the palate – best experienced with a tasting menu. There's a vegetarian menu, too. It has one of Rome's most interesting wine lists. Let the staff recommend something special.

DRINKING & NIGHTLIFE

Trastevere is one of the city's most popular areas to wander, drink and decide what to do afterwards. Foreign visitors often love it, as do those who love foreign visitors, but it's also a local haunt. The streets in summer are packed, with the drinking action spilling outside onto pretty pavement terraces –

WORTH A DETOUR

MONTEVERDE DINING

For a wonderful tourist-free meal, venture to the leafy Monteverde neighbourhood southwest of Trastevere.

Trattoria Da Cesare al Casaletto (06 53 60 15; www.trattoriadacesare.it; Via del Casaletto 45; meals €25-50; 12.45-3pm & 8-11pm Thu-Tue; Casaletto) Rome's best trattoria? Many think so and you will too after an amazing meal of Roman standards where virtually every dish is prepared just *so*. The restaurant is simplicity itself: dozens of tables in a plain setting – that in summer move outside under a vine-covered arbour on a vast terrace. The food is rightfully the star. The service is efficient and relaxed.

Litro (Map p340; 06 4544 7639; www.facebook.com/litrovineria; Via Fratelli Bonnet 5; meals €30-35; 12.30-3.30pm & 6pm-midnight Mon-Fri, 12.30pm-1am Sat; ; Via Fratelli Bonnet) Crunchy bread comes in a paper bag and the 1950s clocks on the wall – all three dozen of them – say a different time at this understated vintage-styled bistro-bar in wonderfully off-the-beaten-tourist-track Monteverde. The creative Roman kitchen is predominantly organic, with ingredients sourced from small local producers, and the choice of natural and organic wines is among the best in Rome.

it can be a bit overcrowded and won't be to everyone's taste (especially locals clamouring for stricter regulations on nightlife). But beyond the places touting beer pong and cheap shots are venues that capture Rome's sense of style.

East of Viale di Trastevere

★TERRA SATIS — CAFE, WINE BAR

Map p340 (06 9893 6909; Piazza dei Ponziani 1a; 7am-1am Mon-Thu, to 2am Fri & Sat; ; Viale di Trastevere, Belli) This hip neighbourhood cafe and wine bar in Trastevere has it all: newspapers, great coffee and charming bar staff, not to mention vintage furniture, comfy banquette seating and really good snacks. On warm days the laid-back action spills out onto its bijou, vine-covered terrace on cobbled Piazza di Ponziani. Good wine and beer selection.

HÝBRIS — CAFE

Map p340 (06 9437 6374; www.hybrisartgallery.com; Via della Lungaretta 164; 10am-2am; ; Viale di Trastevere, Belli) This boho cafe-bar on pedestrian- and shop-strewn Via della Lungaretta is an arty spot for early-evening drinks and bites between marble busts and artworks. Vintage typewriters, a piano and armchairs add a generous dose of trendy old-world ambience, and the marble balustrade bar gets top marks for design. Occasional live jazz and blues, DJ sets and art exhibitions too.

West of Viale di Trastevere

★RIVENDITA LIBRI, CIOCCOLATA E VINO — COCKTAIL BAR

Map p340 (06 5830 1868; www.facebook.com/cioccolateriatrastevere; Vicolo del Cinque 11a; 6.30pm-2am Mon-Fri, 2pm-2am Sat & Sun; Piazza Trilussa) Think of this as Ground Zero of Rome's recent crack-down on debauched drinking. The drinks of a million hen parties – French Kiss, Orgasm and One Night Stand – highlight the cocktail list. The bar is packed every night from around 10pm with a squealing, drinking-pounding crowd.

★BAR SAN CALISTO — CAFE

Map p340 (Piazza San Calisto 3-5; 6am-2am Mon-Sat; Viale di Trastevere, Viale di Trastevere) Head to 'Sanca' for its basic, stuck-in-time atmosphere, cheap prices and large terrace. It attracts everyone from intellectuals to people-watching idlers and foreign students. It's famous for its chocolate – come for hot chocolate with cream in winter, and chocolate gelato in summer.

KEYHOLE — COCKTAIL BAR

Map p340 (Via dell'Arco di San Calisto 17; midnight-5am; Viale di Trastevere, Belli) This hip, underground speakeasy ticks all

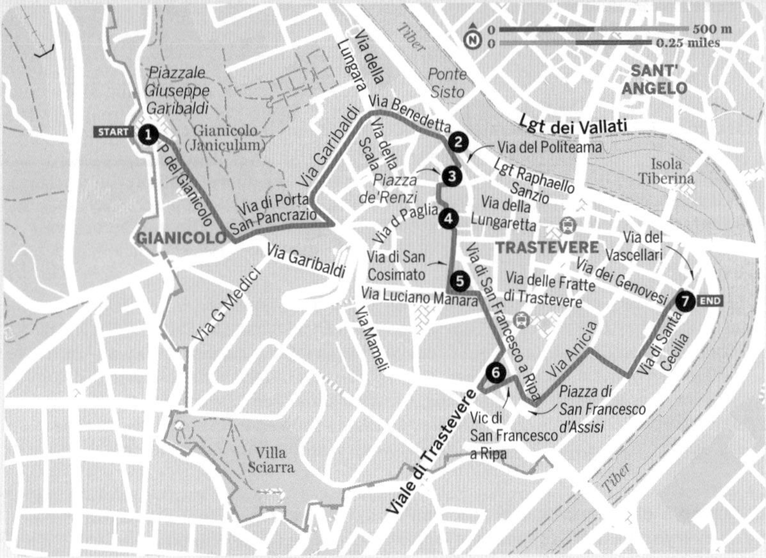

Local Life
A Night Out in Trastevere & Gianicolo

With its enchanting lanes, vibrant piazzas and carnival atmosphere, Trastevere is one of the city's favourite after-dark hang-outs. Foreigners love it, but it's also a local haunt and Romans come here in droves, particularly on balmy summer nights when street sellers set up camp on the picturesque alleyways and bar crowds spill out onto the streets.

❶ Views on the Gianicolo

The early evening is a good time to enjoy sweeping panoramic views from the **Gianicolo** (Janiculum; Map p340; 🚌115, 870). This leafy hill, Rome's highest, was the scene of vicious fighting during Italian unification but is now a tranquil, romantic spot. Lap up the vibe at Bar Stuzzichini or another drink vendor on Piazzale Giuseppe Garibaldi.

❷ Aperitivo at Freni e Frizioni

Once back down in the fray, head to **Freni e Frizioni** (Map p340; ☎06 4549 7499; www.freniefrizioni.com; Via del Politeama 4-6; ⏲6.30pm-2am; 🚌Piazza Trilussa) for an *aperitivo*. This perennially cool bar pulls in a spritz-loving young crowd that swells onto the small piazza outside to sip cocktails (from €10) and fill up at the bar buffet (7pm to 10pm).

❸ Dinner at Da Augusto

Bag a rickety table outside **Da Augusto** (Map p340; ☎06 580 37 98; Piazza de' Renzi 15; meals €25-35; ⏲12.30-3pm & 8-11pm; 🚌Via della Scala, 🚊Belli) and tuck into fabulous family-style cooking on one of Trastevere's most atmospheric piazza terraces. All the Roman classics are dished up here. Be prepared to queue and expect basic bathrooms.

❹ Hanging out on Piazza di Santa Maria in Trastevere

Trastevere's main square, **Piazza di Santa Maria in Trastevere** (Map p340; 🚌Viale di Trastevere, 🚊Belli), is prime people-watching territory. By day it's full of cheery locals and guidebook-toting tourists, but by night foreign students, marauding Romans and high-jinks-minded visitors take over.

❺ A Sweet Pause at Otaleg

Let the precious flavours of Marco Radicioni tickle your taste buds at **Otaleg** (Map p340; ☎338 6515450; www.otaleg.com; Via di San Cosimato 14a; gelato from €2; ⏲noon-midnight; 🖉; 🚊Trastevere/Mastai) (gelato spelled

Piazza di Santa Maria in Trastevere

backwards). Try the pistachio, lemon and dark chocolate or seasonal surprises like prickly pear and acacia honey. Savour your little (melting) scoop of joy while strolling the cobblestones.

6 Blues at Big Mama

To wallow in the Eternal City blues, there's only one place to go – **Big Mama** (Map p340; ☎06 581 25 51; www.bigmama.it; Vicolo di San Francesco a Ripa 18; ⏱9pm-1.30am, shows 10.30pm, closed summer; 🚌Viale di Trastevere, 🚊Trastevere/Mastai), a cramped Trastevere basement. There are weekly residencies from well-known Italian musicians, and frequent blues, jazz, funk, soul and R&B concerts by international artists.

7 Cocktails at Niji Roma

Finish your night late at **Niji Roma** (Map p340; ☎06 581 95 20; www.facebook.com/niji.cafe.roma; Via dei Vascellari 35; ⏱7pm-3am; 🚊Belli), a chic and arty bar with a surreal vibe – almost like a film set designed to embody exactly these qualities. Cocktails are exquisitely poured and presented, and almost too pretty to drink. The mellow atmosphere is the perfect end to a fine night.

the boxes: no identifiable name or signage outside; a black door smothered in keyhole plates; and Prohibition-era decor including Chesterfield sofas, dim lighting and a craft cocktail menu. Not sure what to order? The mixologists will create your own bespoke cocktail (around €10). No password is required to get into Keyhole, but you need to fill in a form to become a member (€5). No phones.

PIMM'S GOOD BAR

Map p340 (☎06 9727 7979; www.pimmsgood.it; Via di Santa Dorotea 8; ⏱10am-2am; 📶; 🚌Piazza Trilussa) 'Anyone for Pimm's?' is the catchphrase of both the namesake fruity English liqueur and this eternally popular bar. It has a part red-brick ceiling and does indeed serve Pimm's – the classic way or in a variety of cocktails. The lively bartenders are serious mixologists and well-crafted cocktails are their thing. Look for the buzzing street-corner pavement terrace.

MA CHE SIETE VENUTI A FÀ PUB

Map p340 (☎06 6456 2046; www.football-pub.com; Via Benedetta 25; ⏱11am-2am; 🚌Piazza Trilussa) Named after a football chant, which translates politely as 'What did you come here for?', this pint-size Trastevere pub is a beer-buff's paradise, packing in around 15 international craft beers on tap and even more by the bottle. Although it could easily be a cliché, the vibe here is real, and every surface is covered in beer labels.

CAFFÈ LUNGARA 1940 CAFE

Map p340 (☎06 687 56 26; http://lungara1940.com; Via della Lungara 14; ⏱6.30am-10pm Mon-Fri, 7am-10pm Sat, to 3pm Sun; 📶; 🚌Piazza Triussa) Run with much pride, passion and creativity by the Nardecchia family for almost 80 years, Caffè Lungara is an address Romans love, from students to arts-loving elderly couples. Pop in before or after visiting the neighbouring botanical gardens, Galleria Corsini or Villa Farnesina for a cappuccino, Aperol *spritz* sundowner or full meal in a sharp, bright, white interior.

MECCANISMO BAR

Map p340 (☎06 581 61 11; www.meccanismoroma.com; Piazza Trilussa 34; ⏱7.30am-2am Mon-Sat, to midnight Sun; 📶; 🚌Piazza Trilussa) This welcoming all-rounder is a prime spot in which to lounge in comfort (grab an

MUSIC ON THE GIANICOLO

Started in 2017, the **Gianicolo in Musica** (☎331 7098854; www.ilgianicolo.it; Piazza Giuseppe Garibaldi; most events free; ⊙Jul-Sep; 🚌Piazza Giuseppe Garibaldi) festival atop Gianicolo Hill was an immediate success. It's hoped it will become a long-running annual event. Based around the festival bar, Bar Dei Mille, top acts perform jazz, blues, funk, tango, swing and more on an outdoor stage with all of Rome as a backdrop.

armchair if you can) over breakfast, lunch, afternoon tea, or a dusk-time *aperitivo* or craft beer with nibbles until 9pm. Burgers, salads and some vegetarian dishes appease hunger pangs and there's pavement seating from which to people-watch on Piazza Trilussa. Monday is live-music night.

Gianicolo & Around

IL BARETTO BAR

Map p340 (☎06 589 60 55; Via Garibaldi 27; ⊙7am-2am; 🚌Via Garibaldi) Venture up a steep flight of steps from Trastevere – go on, it's worth it. Because here you'll discover this good-looking cocktail bar where the bass lines are meaty, the bar staff hip, and the interior a mix of vintage and pop art. Better yet, stop here on your way *down* from Gianicolo and have something cold on the tree-shaded terrace.

ENTERTAINMENT

LETTERE CAFFÈ LIVE MUSIC

Map p340 (☎340 0044154; www.letterecaffe.org; Via di San Francesco a Ripa 100/101; ⊙6pm-2am, closed mid-Aug–mid-Sep; 🚌Viale di Trastevere, 🚋Trastevere/Mastai) Like books? Poetry? Blues and jazz? Then you'll love this place: a clutter of bar stools and books, where there are regular live gigs, poetry slams, comedy and gay nights, plus DJ sets playing electronic, indie and new wave. *Aperitivo,* with a tempting vegetarian buffet, is served between 7pm and 9pm. Enjoy one of the cheap cocktail specials under the whirling fans.

NUOVO SACHER CINEMA

Map p340 (☎06 581 81 16; www.sacherfilm.eu; Largo Ascianghi 1; 🚌Viale di Trastevere, 🚋Trastevere/Mastai) Owned by cult Roman film director Nanni Moretti, this small cinema with classic red-velvet seats is the place to catch the latest European art-house offerings. There are regular screenings of Italian and international films, most in their original language (with Italian subtitles).

SHOPPING

The main medieval throughway, Via della Lungaretta, makes a good starting point with its pleasurable line-up of shops and small family-run boutiques. Otherwise, shopping in Trastevere is a matter of losing yourself in its labyrinth of alleys and seeing what you can find. Expect artisanal workshops, gourmet groceries, century-old bakeries and cake shops, fashionable boutiques and open-air markets.

East of Viale di Trastevere

★**BISCOTTIFICIO INNOCENTI** FOOD

Map p340 (☎06 580 39 26; www.facebook.com/biscottificioInnocenti; Via della Luce 21; ⊙8am-8pm Mon-Sat, 9.30am-2pm Sun; 🚌Viale di Trastevere, 🚋Belli) For homemade biscuits, bite-sized meringues and fruit tarts large and small, there is no finer address in Rome than this vintage *biscottificio* with ceramic-tiled interior, fly-net door curtain and a set of old-fashioned scales on the counter to weigh biscuits (€17 to €25 per kilo). The shop has been run with much love and passion for several decades by the ever-dedicated Stefania.

MERCATO DI PORTA PORTESE MARKET

Map p340 (Piazza Porta Portese; ⊙6am-2pm Sun; 🚌Viale di Trastevere, 🚋Trastevere/Min P Istruzione) Head to this mammoth flea market to see Rome bargain-hunting. Thousands of stalls sell everything from rare books and fell-off-a-lorry bikes to Peruvian shawls and off-brand phones. It's crazily busy and a lot of fun. Keep your valuables safe and wear your haggling hat for the inevitable discovery of a treasure amid the dreck.

West of Viale di Trastevere

★ANTICA CACIARA TRASTEVERINA FOOD & DRINKS

Map p340 (06 581 28 15; www.facebook.com/anticacaciaratrasteverina; Via di San Francesco a Ripa 140; 7.30am-8pm Mon-Sat; Viale di Trastevere, Trastevere/Mastai) The fresh ricotta is a prized possession at this century-old deli, and it's usually gone by lunchtime. If you're too late, take solace in the luscious *ricotta infornata* (oven-baked ricotta), wheels of famous, black-waxed *pecorino romano*, and garlands of *guanciale* (pig's jowl) ready for the perfect carbonara. The lovely, caring staff answer questions and plastic-wrap cheese and hams for transport home.

LES VIGNERONS WINE

Map p340 (06 6477 1439; www.lesvignerons.it; Via Mameli 61; 4-9pm Mon, 11am-9pm Tue-Thu, to 9.30pm Fri & Sat; Viale di Trastevere, Trastevere/Min P Istruzione) If you're looking for interesting vintages, search out this lovely Trastevere wine shop. It boasts one of the capital's best collections of natural wines, mainly from small Italian and French producers, as well as a comprehensive selection of spirits and international craft beers. Staff offer great advice.

ALMOST CORNER BOOKSHOP BOOKS

Map p340 (06 583 69 42; www.facebook.com/almostcornerbookshop; Via del Moro 45; 11am-7pm Mon-Fri, to 8pm Sat-Sun; Piazza Trilussa) A crammed haven full of reads – every millimetre of wall space contains English-language fiction and nonfiction (including children's) and travel guides.

ACID DROP FASHION & ACCESSORIES

Map p340 (06 9603 5643; www.acidrop.com; Via del Moro 14; 11am-8.30pm Tue-Thu, to 10pm Fri & Sat, noon-8.30pm Sun; Piazza Trilussa) Mother-daughter duo Ileana and Eleonora Ottini prove creativity is inherited at their quirky boutique. Unconventional statement pieces include punchy silk-screened T-shirts, steampunk-inspired accessories, hand-painted bags, and jewellery inspired by everything from *The Little Prince* and Frida Kahlo to the phases of the moon. All is made from scratch.

ARTIGIANINO TRASTEVERE FASHION & ACCESSORIES

Map p340 (06 8917 1689; www.artigianino.com; Vicolo del Cinque 49; 11am-1pm & 4-9pm Mon-Fri, to 11pm Sat, 3.30-9pm Sun; Piazza Trilussa) For buttery leather bags, purses and accessories at a reasonable price, those in the know head to this Trastevere boutique. Browse slouchy bag styles in bold colours, classic wallets and briefcases in neutral hues. Belts, key chains, passport holders and men's accessories round out the collection.

1

Rome Street Life

As in many sunny countries, much of life in Rome is played out on the street. In the morning, you can watch the city slowly wake up. Shop shutters are cranked open, rubbish collectors do the rounds, restaurants set out their tables: Rome is readying itself for its close-up.

Day to Night

During the next phase, the fruit and veg markets in every *rione* (neighbourhood) will swell with people, with a predominance of matriarchs wielding grocery trolleys and showing a reckless disregard for queuing.

Throughout the day, people come and go on Rome's piazzas and public spaces. In Campo de' Fiori (p86), there's a busy food market during the day, then the character of the piazza changes towards the evening when its bars become busy, taking over corners of the square.

Pedestrianised Via del Pigneto, to Rome's northeast, follows a similar trajectory: market in the morning, bars and cafes creating a party atmosphere in the evening. In the historic centre, locals and tourists flock to the Spanish Steps and Piazza di Spagna (p108), but these empty as night falls.

Day or evening, the stadium-size Piazza Navona (p82) ebbs and flows with people-watching entertainment, with hawkers, caricaturists and occasional street performers.

La Passeggiata

In the early evening, the *passeggiata* (early evening stroll) is an important part of Roman life, as it is elsewhere in Italy. Locals will usually dress up before

JJFARQ / SHUTTERSTOCK ©

DIEGO FIORE / SHUTTERSTOCK ©

1. Via del Corso (p29)
2. Campo de' Fiori (p86)
3. Via dei Condotti (p113)

LUIS SANTOS / SHUTTERSTOCK ©

heading out. Like many other parts of everyday life, such as coffee-drinking, Italians have elevated a seemingly simple practice into something special.

Romans will usually head to the area that's most convenient for them. Trastevere (p172) tends to be a broader mix of tourists and young people. Villa Borghese (p2057) and the Pincio Hill Gardens (p1102) attract more families and are more tranquil. Via del Corso (p29) is popular among younger window-shoppers, while Rome's smartest shopping strip, Via dei Condotti (p113), attracts a mix of ages. In summer, there's the Lungo il Tevere festival (p27) on Isola Tiberina, and stalls along the riverside create a new area for early-evening wanders.

Instead of paying €6 or so to sit and drink at a bar, many people out on the stroll opt to stop for a more affordable gelato, which they can eat on their way. In summer, you'll see lots of people enjoying *grattachecca* – flavoured, crushed ice – along the banks of the Tiber.

The *bella figura* ('beautiful figure', better explained as 'keeping up appearances') is important here, and the *passeggiata* is as much about checking everyone else out as it is about enjoying the atmosphere. The *passeggiata* reaches its height in summer, around 5pm or 6pm when the heat of the day subsides. There's not much else to do, so why not head out into the street?

San Giovanni & Testaccio

SAN GIOVANNI & THE CELIO | AVENTINO & AROUND | TESTACCIO | AVENTINO & AROUND

Neighbourhood Top Five

❶ **Basilica di San Giovanni in Laterano** (p190) Facing up to the monumental splendour of what was once Rome's most important church. You'll feel very small as you explore the echoing baroque interior of the city's oldest Christian basilica.

❷ **Terme di Caracalla** (p191) Being overawed by the colossal remnants of this vast baths complex.

❸ **Villa del Priorato di Malta** (p194) Looking through the unmarked keyhole to take in a magical view of the dome crowning St Peter's Basilica.

❹ **Basilica di San Clemente** (p192) Going underground at this medieval basilica. Before you descend, check the church's 12th-century apse mosaic.

❺ **Traditional trattorias** (p195) Enjoying a leisurely meal at one of Testaccio's trattorias is a quintessential Roman experience.

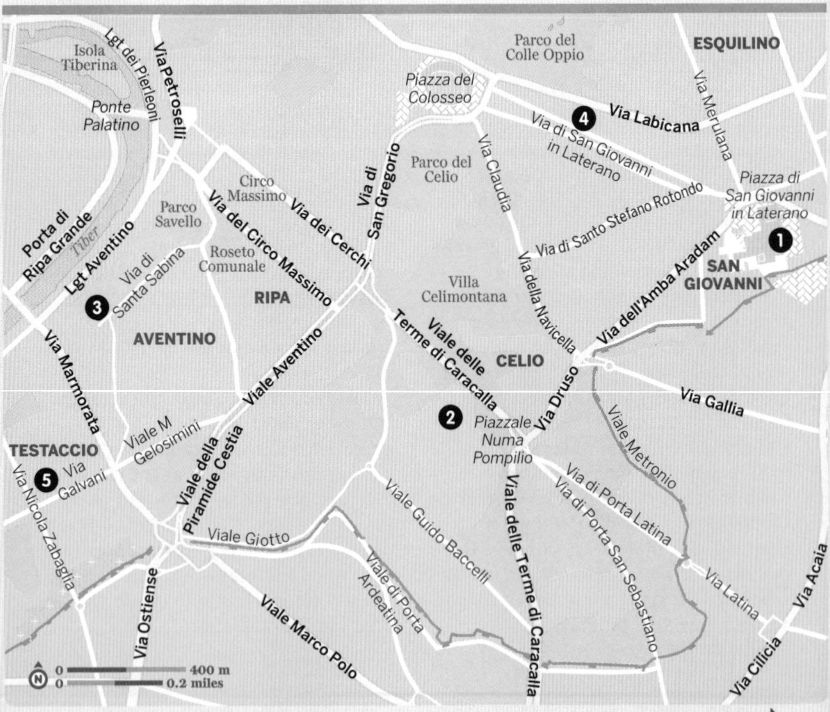

For more detail of this area see Maps p338 and p339 ➡

Explore San Giovanni & Testaccio

Extending south of the city centre, this is a large area that rewards a measured approach. It can easily be divided into two separate patches: San Giovanni and the Celio; and Aventino and Testaccio. A day in each is more than enough to cover the main sights.

Start off at the landmark Basilica di San Giovanni in Laterano (p190), the focal point of the largely residential San Giovanni neighbourhood. Once you've explored the basilica and surrounding piazza, head down Via di San Giovanni in Laterano towards the Colosseum. Near the bottom, the Basilica di San Clemente (p192) is a fascinating church with some eerie underground ruins. From there, you can walk across to the Celio, the green hill that rises south of the Colosseum. There's not a lot to see but the graceful Villa Celimontana (p193) park is a great place to escape the crowds. Further south, the towering ruins of the Terme di Caracalla (p191) are a thrilling sight.

To the west, on the banks of the Tiber, the once working-class area of Testaccio is a foodie hotspot with some excellent trattorias and a popular nightlife strip. Rising above it, the Aventino hill boasts a number of serene medieval churches and one of Rome's great curiosities – a famous keyhole view of St Peter's dome.

Local Life

➡ **Romance** Local Lotharios out to impress their loved ones take them to enjoy sunset views from Parco Savello (p194) on the Aventino.

➡ **Offal** Testaccio is the spiritual home of Roman 'blood-and-guts' cooking. It's not for everyone, but savvy locals head to long-standing trattorias such as Da Felice (p199) to eat it.

➡ **Market life** Testaccio's market (p196) has long been a focus of neighbourhood life: traders and local shoppers cheerfully shout at each other and lunchers flock to its popular street-food stalls.

Getting There & Away

➡ **Bus** Useful bus routes include 85 and 87, both of which stop in San Giovanni, and 714, which serves San Giovanni and the Terme di Caracalla.

➡ **Metro** San Giovanni is accessible by metro lines A and C. For Testaccio take line B to Piramide. The Aventino is walkable from Testaccio, and Circo Massimo station (line B).

➡ **Tram** No 3 runs from San Giovanni along Viale Aventino, through Testaccio and on to Trastevere.

Lonely Planet's Top Tip

If you like music and ballet, check www.operaroma.it for details of summer performances at the **Terme di Caracalla** (p201). If contemporary art in a gritty urban setting is more your thing, look out for exhibitions and installations at Testaccio's **Mattatoio** (p197), a gallery space in Rome's former abattoir.

Best Places to Eat

➡ Flavio al Velavevodetto (p196)

➡ Sbanco (p195)

➡ Aroma (p197)

➡ Trapizzino (p198)

➡ Marco Martini Restaurant (p197)

For reviews, see p195.➡

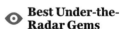

Best Places to Drink

➡ Wine Concept (p199)

➡ Blind Pig (p199)

➡ Barnaba (p197)

➡ Rec 23 (p200)

➡ L'Oasi della Birra (p200)

For reviews, see p199.➡

Best Under-the-Radar Gems

➡ Villa del Priorato di Malta (p194)

➡ Cimitero Acattolico per gli Stranieri (p194)

➡ Chiesa di Santo Stefano Rotondo (p193)

➡ Basilica dei SS Quattro Coronati (p192)

For reviews, see p192.➡

TOP EXPERIENCE

EXPLORE THE BREATHTAKING BASILICA DI SAN GIOVANNI IN LATERANO

This monumental church, the oldest of the city's four papal basilicas, is Rome's official cathedral and the pope's seat as the Bishop of Rome. Dating from the 4th century, it's revered as the *mater et caput* (mother and head) of all Catholic churches and was the pope's main place of worship for almost a thousand years.

The first Christian basilica built in the city, it was originally commissioned by the Emperor Constantine and consecrated by Pope Sylvester I in 324 CE. From then until 1309, when the papacy moved to Avignon, it was the principal pontifical church, and the adjacent Palazzo Laterano was the pope's official residence. Both buildings fell into disrepair during the pope's French interlude and when Pope Gregory XI returned to Rome in 1377 he chose to move to the fortified Vatican.

Little now remains of the original church, which was revamped several times over the centuries. Its current form is largely the result of a baroque makeover by Francesco Borromini in the mid-17th century.

The Facade

Crowned by 15 7m-high statues – Christ, with St John the Baptist, John the Evangelist and the 12 apostles – Alessandro Galilei's immense late-baroque facade was added in 1735. In the portico behind the colossal columns, look out for the **central bronze doors** which were moved here from the Curia in the Roman Forum, and, on the far right, the **Holy Door**, which is only opened in Jubilee years.

TOP TIPS

- Look down as well as up – the basilica's inlaid mosaic floor is a wonderful work of art in its own right.
- In the cloister, look out for a slab of porphyry on which it's said Roman soldiers threw lots to win the robe of the crucified Christ.

PRACTICALITIES

- Map p339, D2
- ☎06 6988 6493
- Piazza di San Giovanni in Laterano 4
- basilica free, cloister €5 incl Museo del Tesoro
- ⏱7am-6.30pm, cloister 9am-6pm
- Ⓜ San Giovanni

The Interior

The echoing, marble-clad interior is a breathtaking sight. Designed by Francesco Borromini for the 1650 Jubilee, it features a golden gilt **ceiling**, a 15th-century **mosaic floor**, and a wide **central nave** lined with 18th-century sculptures of the apostles, each 4.6m high and set in its own dramatic niche.

At the head of the nave, an elaborate Gothic **baldachin** (canopy) towers over the papal altar. Dating from the 14th century, it's said to contain the relics of the heads of saints Peter and Paul. In front of it, at the base of the altar, the Renaissance tomb of Pope Martin V lies in the **confessio** along with a wooden statue of St John the Baptist.

The massive **apse** is decorated with sparkling mosaics, some of which survive from the original 4th-century basilica. Most, however, were added in the 1800s. To the right, a modest gift shop leads onto the **Museo del Tesoro** and its small collection of religious artefacts and vestments.

At the other end of the basilica, you'll find an incomplete **Giotto fresco** on the first pillar in the right-hand nave. While admiring this, listen carefully – on the next column is a monument to Pope Sylvester II (r 999–1003) that's said to creak when the death of a pope is imminent.

The Cloister

Entered from left of the altar, the basilica's 13th-century cloister is a charming oasis of peace. Set around a central garden, its ambulatories are lined with graceful twisted columns and marble fragments from the original church, including the remains of a 5th-century papal throne and inscriptions of two papal bulls.

RAFAEL DIAS KATAYAMA / SHUTTERSTOCK ©

TOP EXPERIENCE

TOUR THE TERME DI CARACALLA

One of Rome's most awe-inspiring sights, the towering ruins of this vast baths complex hint at the monumental scale of the ancient city. The *thermae*, inaugurated by the emperor Caracalla in 216 CE, covered 10 hectares and comprised baths, gyms, libraries, shops and gardens. Up to 8000 people passed through daily, while below ground hundreds of slaves sweated in a 9.5km tunnel network, tending to the complex plumbing systems.

The baths were used until 537, when invading Visigoths cut off Rome's water supply. Over successive centuries the site was plundered for building materials and frequently excavated. Most notably, digs in the 16th century unearthed a number of important sculptures, many of which later found their way into the Farnese family's art collection. More recently, archaeologists have discovered an underground **Mithraeum** (temple) dedicated to the Persian god Mithras. Unfortunately, this is rarely open to visitors.

Most of what you see today are the remains of the central bathhouse. This was a huge rectangular edifice flanked by two **palestre** (gyms) and centred on a **frigidarium** (cold room), where bathers would cool off after spells in the warmer **tepidarium** and dome-capped **caldaria** (hot room). In summer, music and ballet performances are staged here.

TOP TIPS

- To see the baths as they looked in their heyday, hire a virtual-reality headset (€7), which recreates the various environments within the complex.
- Admission is free on the first Sunday of the month between October and March.

PRACTICALITIES

- Map p339, A4
- 06 3996 7700
- www.coopculture.it
- Viale delle Terme di Caracalla 52
- adult/reduced €8/4
- 9am-1hr before sunset Tue-Sun, 9am-2pm Mon
- Viale delle Terme di Caracalla

SIGHTS

Rome is a city of churches and this district boasts some of the capital's finest, from San Giovanni's namesake basilica to a series of austere medieval gems on the Celio and Aventino. There are also underground treasures, towering ancient ruins and a couple of beautiful parks: Villa Celimontana and Parco Savello, famous for its orange trees and inspiring views.

San Giovanni & the Celio

BASILICA DI SAN GIOVANNI IN LATERANO — BASILICA

See p190.

TERME DI CARACALLA — RUINS

See p191.

SANTUARIO DELLA SCALA SANTA & SANCTA SANCTORUM — CHRISTIAN SITE

Map p339 (www.scala-santa.it; Piazza di San Giovanni in Laterano 14; Scala free, Sancta €3.50; Scala 6am-2pm & 3-7pm summer, to 6.30pm winter, Sancta Sanctorum 9.30am-12.45pm & 3-4.45pm Mon-Sat; MSan Giovanni) The Scala Santa, said to be the staircase Jesus walked up in Pontius Pilate's palace in Jerusalem, was brought to Rome by St Helena in the 4th century. Pilgrims consider it sacred and climb it on their knees, saying a prayer on each of the 28 steps. At the top, behind an iron grating, is the richly decorated Sancta Sanctorum (Holy of Holies), formerly the pope's private chapel.

Behind the sanctuary building you will see a showy brick facade adorned with a gold apse mosaic. This is the **Triclinium Leoninum**, an 18th-century reconstruction of a wall from the original Palazzo Laterano.

PALAZZO LATERANO — HISTORIC BUILDING

Map p339 (Piazza di San Giovanni in Laterano; MSan Giovanni) Palazzo Laterano was the official papal residence until the pope moved to the Vatican in 1377. Adjacent to the Basilica di San Giovanni in Laterano (p190), it's still technically Vatican property and today houses offices of the Vicariate of Rome. Much altered over the centuries, it owes its current form to a 16th-century facelift by Domenico Fontana. It's not open to the public.

OBELISK — MONUMENT

Map p339 (Piazza di San Giovanni in Laterano) Overlooking Palazzo Laterano, this is said to be the world's largest standing Egyptian obelisk. Topping off at almost 46m, it's also the oldest of Rome's 13 ancient obelisks, dating from the 15th century BCE. It originally stood in a temple in Thebes but was shipped to Rome by Constantine II and, after various relocations, placed in its current position in 1588.

BASILICA DEI SS QUATTRO CORONATI — BASILICA

Map p339 (335 495248; Via dei Santi Quattro 20; cloisters €2, Oratorio di San Silvestro €1; basilica 6.30am-12.45pm & 3.30-8pm, cloisters 9.45am-11.45am & 3.45-5.45pm Mon-Sat; Via di San Giovanni in Laterano) This brooding fortified church harbours some lovely 13th-century frescoes and a delightful hidden cloister, accessible from the left-hand aisle. The frescoes, in the **Oratorio di San Silvestro**, depict the story of Constantine and Pope Sylvester I and the so-called Donation of Constantine (p258), a notorious forged document with which the emperor supposedly ceded control of Rome and the Western Roman Empire to the papacy.

To access the Oratorio, ring the bell in the second courtyard.

The basilica, which dates from the 6th century, took on its present form in the 12th century after the original was destroyed by Normans in 1084. Its name – the Basilica of the Four Crowned Martyrs – is a reference to four Christian sculptors who were supposedly killed by Diocletian for refusing to make a statue of a pagan god.

Its frescoed **Aula Gotica** (Gothic Hall), on the 1st floor of the Torre Maggiore, is a rare example of Gothic architecture in Rome. To visit you'll need to sign up for one of the bimonthly guided tours (€10 per person) – see www.aulagoticasantiquattrocoronati.it for details.

★BASILICA DI SAN CLEMENTE — BASILICA

Map p339 (06 774 00 21; www.basilicasanclemente.com; Piazza di San Clemente; basilica free, excavations adult/reduced €10/5; 9am-12.30pm & 3-6pm Mon-Sat, 12.15-6pm Sun; Via Labicana) Nowhere better illustrates the various stages of Rome's turbulent past than this fascinating multilayered church. The ground-level 12th-century basilica sits atop a 4th-century church, which, in turn, stands over a 2nd-century pagan temple and a 1st-century Roman house. Beneath everything are foundations dating from the Roman Republic.

The street-level *basilica superiore* features a marvellous 12th-century apse mosaic depicting the *Trionfo della Croce* (Triumph of the Cross) and some wonderful 15th-century frescoes by Masolino in the **Cappella di Santa Caterina** showing a crucifixion scene and episodes from the life of St Catherine.

Steps lead down to the 4th-century *basilica inferiore,* mostly destroyed by Norman invaders in 1084, but with some faded 11th-century frescoes illustrating the life of St Clement, a 1st-century bishop who became the fourth pope in 88 CE. Follow the steps down another level and you'll come to a 1st-century Roman house and a dark 2nd-century temple to Mithras, with an altar showing the god slaying a bull. Beneath it all, you can hear the eerie sound of a subterranean river flowing through a Republic-era drain.

SUBTERRANEAN CULT

The cult of Mithraism was hugely popular in ancient military circles. According to its mythology, the Sun ordered Mithras, a young, handsome god, to slay a wild bull. As the animal died, it gave life, its blood causing wheat and other plants to grow.

Mithraic temples, known as Mithraeums, were almost always in underground locations or caves, reflecting the cult's belief that caverns represented the cosmos. In these Mithraeums, devotees underwent complex initiation rites, and ate bread and water to symbolise the body and blood of the bull. Sound familiar? The early Christians thought so too, and were fervently opposed to the cult.

CHIESA DI SANTO STEFANO ROTONDO — CHURCH

Map p339 (www.santo-stefano-rotondo.it; Via di Santo Stefano Rotondo 7; ⏲10am-1pm & 2-5pm Tue-Sun winter, 10am-1pm & 3.30-6.30pm Tue-Sun summer; 🚌Via Claudia) Set in its own secluded grounds, this haunting church boasts a porticoed facade and a round, columned interior. But what really gets the heart racing is the graphic wall decor – a cycle of 16th-century frescoes depicting the tortures suffered by many early Christian martyrs.

Describing them in 1846, Charles Dickens wrote: 'Such a panorama of horror and butchery no man could imagine in his sleep, though he were to eat a whole pig, raw, for supper.'

The church, one of Rome's oldest, dates from the late 5th century, although it was subsequently altered in the 12th and 15th centuries.

VILLA CELIMONTANA — PARK

Map p339 (Via della Navicella 12; ⏲7am-sunset; 🚌Via della Navicella) With its grassy banks and colourful flower beds, this leafy park is a wonderful place to escape the crowds and enjoy a summer picnic. At its centre is a 16th-century villa housing the Italian Geographical Society, while to the south stands a 12m-plus Egyptian obelisk.

BASILICA DEI SS GIOVANNI E PAOLO AL CELIO — BASILICA

Map p339 (☎06 700 57 45; Piazza dei Santi Giovanni e Paolo; ⏲8.30am-noon & 3.30-6pm; 🚌Via Claudia) A popular wedding location, this handsome medieval church dates to the 4th century when it was built over the houses of two Roman martyrs. It has since been much altered, though you can still explore the ancient houses that lie beneath it, the so-called Case Romane.

CASE ROMANE — CHRISTIAN SITE

Map p339 (☎06 7045 4544; www.caseromane.it; Clivo di Scauro; adult/reduced €8/6; ⏲10am-1pm & 3-6pm Thu-Mon; 🚌Via Claudia) According to tradition, two Roman soldiers, John and Paul (not to be confused with the Apostles), lived in these houses before they were beheaded by the emperor Julian. There's no direct evidence for this, although research has revealed that the houses were used for Christian worship. There are more than 20 rooms, many of them richly decorated.

CHIESA DI SAN GREGORIO AL CELIO — CHURCH

Map p339 (☎church 06 700 09 87, oratory 06 7049 4966; www.sangregorioalcelio.com; Piazza di San Gregorio 1; ⏲9am-1pm & 3.30-7pm; Ⓜ Colosseo, Circo Massimo) Ring for admission to this landmark church standing on the spot where Pope Gregory the Great supposedly dispatched St Augustine to convert the British. Originally the pope's family home, in 575 he converted it into a monastery. It was rebuilt in the 17th century and given a baroque makeover a century later.

Inside, the **Cappella Salviati**, a 16th-century chapel by Carlo Maderno, contains a fresco of a *Madonna with Child* that is said to have spoken to St Gregory.

Aventino & Around

BASILICA DI SANTA SABINA — BASILICA

Map p338 (06 57 94 01; Piazza Pietro d'Illiria 1; 6.30am-12.45pm & 3-8pm; Lungotevere Aventino) This solemn basilica, one of Rome's most beautiful early Christian churches, was founded by Peter of Illyria around 422 CE. It was enlarged in the 9th century and again in 1216, just before it was given to the newly founded Dominican order – note the tombstone of Muñoz de Zamora, one of the order's founding fathers, in the nave floor. The interior was further modified by Domenico Fontana in 1587. A 20th-century restoration subsequently returned it to its original look.

One of the few elements to have survived since the 5th century are the basilica's cypress-wood doors. These feature 18 carved panels depicting biblical events, including one of the oldest Crucifixion scenes in existence. It's quite hard to make out in the top left, but it depicts Jesus and the two thieves, although, strangely, not their crosses.

Inside, 24 custom-made columns support an arcade decorated with a faded red-and-green frieze. Light streams in from high nave windows that were added in the 9th century, along with the carved choir, pulpit and bishop's throne.

Behind the church is a garden and a meditative 13th-century cloister.

PARCO SAVELLO — PARK

Map p338 (Via di Santa Sabina; 7am-9pm summer, to 6pm winter; Via del Circo Massimo) Known to Romans as the *Giardino degli Aranci* (Orange Garden), this walled park is a romantic haven. Head down the central avenue, passing towering umbrella pines and lawns planted with blooming orange trees, to bask in heavenly sunset views of St Peter's dome and the city's rooftops.

VILLA DEL PRIORATO DI MALTA — HISTORIC BUILDING

Map p338 (Villa Magistrale; Piazza dei Cavalieri di Malta; Lungotevere Aventino) Fronting an ornate cypress-shaded piazza, the Roman headquarters of the Sovereign Order of Malta, aka the *Cavalieri di Malta* (Knights of Malta), boasts one of Rome's most celebrated views. It's not immediately apparent, but look through the keyhole in the villa's green door and you'll see the dome of St Peter's Basilica perfectly aligned at the end of a hedge-lined avenue.

ROSETO COMUNALE — GARDENS

Map p338 (Municipal Rose Garden; 06 574 68 10; rosetoromacapitale@comune.roma.it; Via di Valle Murcia 6; 8.30am-7.30pm mid-Apr–mid-Jun; Circo Massimo) FREE Stretched out on the slopes of the Aventine Hill, this idyllic garden boasts more than 1100 of the rarest roses, coaxed into life each spring by a team of horticultural experts. The ancient Circo Massimo (p72) plays backdrop, and is just as striking as the grounds themselves.

Testaccio

★CIMITERO ACATTOLICO PER GLI STRANIERI — CEMETERY

Map p338 (06 574 19 00; www.cemeteryrome.it; Via Caio Cestio 6; voluntary donation €3; 9am-5pm Mon-Sat, to 1pm Sun; Piramide) Despite the roads that surround it, Rome's 'non-Catholic' cemetery is a verdant oasis of peace. An air of Grand Tour romance hangs over the site where up to 4000 people are buried, including poets Keats and Shelley, and Italian political thinker Antonio Gramsci.

Among the gravestones and cypress trees, look out for the *Angelo del Dolore* (Angel of Grief), a much-replicated 1894 sculpture that US artist William Wetmore Story created for his wife's grave.

PIRAMIDE DI CAIO CESTIO — TOMB

Map p338 (06 3996 7700; www.coopculture.it; tour €5.50, booking required; guided tour 11am 2nd, 3rd & 4th Sat & Sun of month, closed Aug; Piramide) Sticking out like, well, an Egyptian pyramid, this distinctive landmark looms over a busy traffic junction near Piramide metro station. A 36m-high marble-and-brick tomb, it was built for Gaius Cestius, a 1st-century-BCE magistrate, and some 200 years later was incorporated into the Aurelian walls near Porta San Paolo.

The surrounding area is today known as Piramide.

Note that the hour-long guided tours are in Italian.

EATING

Testaccio is one of Rome's foodie hotspots. It's home to some wonderful old-school trattorias, mostly specialising in traditional Roman cuisine, as well as several popular takeaways and market food stalls. Elsewhere, you'll find some surprisingly good eateries among the tourist traps southeast of the Colosseum, and several interesting new places in San Giovanni.

San Giovanni & the Celio

★SBANCO PIZZA €

Map p350 (06 78 93 18; https://sbanco.eatbu.com; Via Siria 1; pizzas €7-13; 7.30pm-midnight Mon-Sat, from 1pm Sun; Piazza Zama) With its informal warehouse vibe and buzzing atmosphere, Sbanco is one of the capital's best modern pizzerias. Since opening in 2016, it's made a name for itself with its sumptuous fried starters and inventive, wood-fired pizzas, including a *cacio e pepe* (*pecorino* and black pepper) pizza. To top things off, you can quaff on delicious craft beer.

CAFÈ CAFÈ BISTRO €

Map p339 (06 7045 1303; www.cafecafebistrot.it; Via dei Santi Quattro 44; meals €15-20; 9.30am-8.30pm Wed-Mon, to 4pm Tue; Via di San Giovanni in Laterano) Cosy, relaxed and welcoming, this cafe-bistro is a far cry from the many impersonal eateries around the Colosseum. With its rustic wooden tables, butternut walls and wine bottles, it's a charming spot for a breakfast pancake, lunch salad or afternoon tea and cake. It will also do you a sandwich and water to take away for €5, ideal for a picnic.

LI RIONI PIZZA €

Map p339 (06 7045 0605; www.lirioni.it; Via dei Santi Quattro 24; meals €15-20; 7pm-midnight Wed-Mon; Via di San Giovanni in Laterano) Always busy, this boisterous joint serves the best pizza in the Colosseum neighbourhood. Locals and tourists squeeze into the noisy interior – set up as a Roman street scene – and tuck into crispy fried starters and bubbling wood-charred pizzas in the thin-crust Roman style.

CHARLOTTE PASTICCERIA DESSERTS €

Map p350 (06 2539 9727; www.charlotteroma.it; Via Vercelli 12-14; pastries from €2.50, desserts €5; 10am-8.30pm Tue-Sun; Re di Roma) Named for the owner's beloved spaniel, French-inspired patisserie Charlotte bakes, caramelises and stacks edible wonders. Valrhona chocolate cake swirled on a biscuit base with raspberry filling, vanilla mousse with a cherry centre dipped in white chocolate, and *robiola* cheesecake topped with a tumble of berries are ultra-photogenic and make the case that room should always be saved for dessert.

BARRED GASTRONOMY €€

Map p350 (06 9727 3382; www.barred.it; Via Cesena 30; meals €35; 5pm-midnight Mon-Sat; Re di Roma) Helmed by brothers and sommelier-chef duo Tiziano and Mirko Palucci, Barred impresses with its casual vibe and inventive food. A tapas menu and daring starters such as lemon brioche with marinated sardines and caper gelato are on offer, while a gin-based cocktail menu and plenty of Italian craft beers and wines keep guests and the atmosphere buzzing.

IL BOCCONCINO LAZIO €€

Map p339 (06 7707 9175; www.ilbocconcino.com; Via Ostilia 23; meals €30-35; 12.30-3.30pm & 7.30-11.30pm Thu-Tue; Via Labicana) One of the better options in the touristy pocket near the Colosseum, this easy-going trattoria stands out for its authentic regional cooking. Daily specials are chalked up on blackboards or there's a regular menu of classic Roman pastas, grilled meats and imaginative desserts.

DIVIN OSTILIA ITALIAN €€

Map p339 (06 7049 6526; Via Ostilia 4; meals €30-35; noon-11.30pm, wine bar to 1am; Via Labicana) A popular choice near the Colosseum, Divin Ostilia is a model wine bar with a high brick ceiling and wooden shelves lined with bottles. It's a small place and its cosy interior can get pretty toasty at mealtimes as diners squeeze in to feast on cheese and cured meats, classic pastas and grilled steaks.

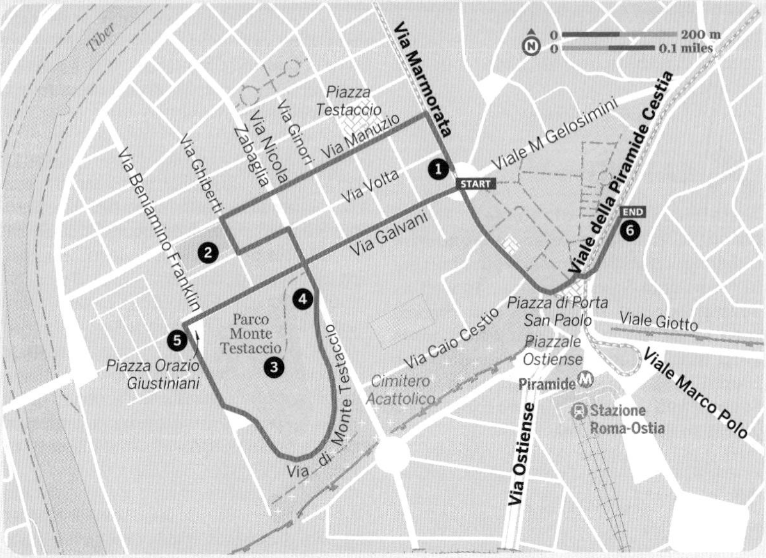

Local Life
A Taste of Testaccio

With its working-class roots and renown as the birthplace of traditional Roman cuisine, Testaccio offers a glimpse of another, less-touristy Rome. It's not completely off the beaten path but it retains a distinct neighbourhood character and its historic market and popular trattorias are much loved locally. Food apart, there's also contemporary art and a grassy hill made of ancient rubbish.

❶ Breakfast at Barberini

Start your day with a bar breakfast at **Pasticceria Barberini** (☎06 5725 0431; www.pasticceriabarberini.it; Via Marmorata 41; cappuccino & cornetto €2; ⏱6am-9pm; 📶✍; Ⓜ Piramide). To do it Roman-style, stand at the counter and have a *caffè* (or cappuccino) and *cornetto* (croissant filled with jam or rich chocolate cream).

❷ A Trip to the Market

Testaccio's neighbourhood market, the **Nuovo Mercato di Testaccio** (entrances Via Beniamino Franklin, Via Volta, Via Manuzio, Via Ghiberti; ⏱7am-3.30pm Mon-Sat; 🚌Via Marmorata), is as much about people-watching as shopping. Throughout the morning, stall-holders cheerfully bellow at each other as shoppers browse the piles of colourful produce and displays of shoes, hats and clothes. Come lunchtime and the market's popular food stalls burst into life, serving crowds of local workers and visitors.

❸ Monte Testaccio

Get to the heart of the local landscape at **Monte Testaccio** (☎06 06 08; Via Nicolo Zabaglia 24, cnr Via Galvani; adult/reduced €4/3, plus cost of tour; ⏱group visits only, reservation necessary; 🚌Via Marmorata). This 54m-high grass-capped mound is essentially a huge pile of amphorae fragments (*testae* in Latin), dating from the time when Testaccio was ancient Rome's river port. The amphorae were used to transport wine and oil; once emptied they were smashed and their fragments carefully stacked.

❹ Carbonara at Flavio al Velavevodetto

Testaccio is the ideal place to experience a trattoria meal and nowhere serves better *cucina romana* (Roman cuisine) than **Flavio al Velavevodetto** (☎06 574 41 94; www.ristorantevelavevodetto.it; Via di Monte Testaccio 97-99; meals €30-35; ⏱12.30-3pm & 7.45-11pm; 🚌Via Galvani). To keep it local, try *carciofo alla*

FABIANODP / SHUTTERSTOCK ©

Fresh produce on display at Nuovo Mercato di Testaccio

giudia (deep-fried artichoke) followed by superlative *rigatoni alla carbonara* (pasta tubes wrapped in a silky egg sauce spiked with morsels of cured pig's cheek).

5 Modern Art at the Mattatoio

Spend the afternoon admiring art at the **Mattatoio** (06 3996 7500; www.mattatoioroma.it; Piazza Orazio Giustiniani 4; adult/reduced €6/5; 2-8pm Tue-Sun; Via Marmorata), one of Rome's top contemporary arts venues. The 19th-century complex, itself a fine example of industrial architecture, has long been a local landmark and until 1975 was the city's main abattoir. Nowadays, it plays host to exhibitions and performances.

6 Wine at Barnaba

Round the day off with some wine-tasting at **Barnaba** (06 2348 4415; www.facebook.com/barnabawinebarecucina; Via della Piramide Cestia 45-51; meal €38; 12.30pm-12.30am; ; Piramide), a popular addition to the neighbourhood's lively drinking scene. A fashionable wine bar, it has a strong selection of natural and independent Italian labels as well as champagnes and more than 20 wines by the glass.

CAFFÈ PROPAGANDA BISTRO €€

Map p339 (06 9453 4256; www.caffepropaganda.it; Via Claudia 15; meals €35-40; 8.30am-2am Tue-Sun; Via Claudia) This modish Parisian-inspired bistro is a good-looking place with a striking zinc bar, 5m-high ceilings, and bric-a-brac on the white-tiled walls. Divided into a bar and restaurant, it serves refined, artfully plated Italian food, as well as more humble bar food in the evening. There's also a thoughtful wine list and excellent cocktails.

AROMA GASTRONOMY €€€

Map p339 (06 9761 5109; www.aromarestaurant.it; Via Labicana 125; meals €120-180; 12.30-3pm & 7.30-11.30pm; Via Labicana) One for a special occasion, the rooftop restaurant of the luxury Palazzo Manfredi hotel offers once-in-a-lifetime views of the Colosseum and Michelin-starred food that rises to the occasion. Overseeing the kitchen is chef Giuseppe Di Iorio, whose seasonal menus reflect his passion for inventive, forward-thinking Mediterranean cuisine.

Aventino & Around

TORCÈ GELATO €

Map p338 (06 574 68 76; www.claudiotorce.it; Viale Aventino 59; gelato €2.70-6; 11am-midnight Wed-Sun, to 9pm Mon & Tue; Viale Aventino) This is the Aventine outpost of Rome's gelato king, Claudio Torcè. His creamy creations are seasonal, healthy – his recipes use fructose in place of white sugar – and often quite bonkers. Anyone for mortadella or gorgonzola gelato?

MARCO MARTINI RESTAURANT GASTRONOMY €€€

Map p338 (06 4559 7350; http://marcomartinichef.com; Viale Aventino 121; meals from €65, tasting menus from €100; 12.30-2.30pm & 7-10pm, closed Sat lunch & Sun; ; Viale Aventino, Viale Aventino) A lush garden pavilion at the Corner Townhouse provides the lovely setting for this casual fine-dining restaurant. The man with his name on the menu is one of Rome's youngest Michelin-starred chefs, whose inventive dishes often riff on Italian culinary traditions. Order à la carte or opt for one of several tasting menus, including one for vegetarians.

LOCAL KNOWLEDGE

ALL ABOUT OFFAL

The hallmark of an authentic Roman menu is the presence of offal. The Roman love of nose-to-tail eating arose in Testaccio around the city abattoir, and many of its neighbourhood trattorias serve traditional offal-based dishes. So whether you want to avoid them or give them a go, look out for *pajata* (veal intestines), *trippa* (tripe), *coratella* (heart, lung and liver), *animelle* (sweetbreads), along with coda alla vaccinara (oxtail), *testarella* (head), *lingua* (tongue) and *zampe* (trotters).

Testaccio

★TRAPIZZINO FAST FOOD €

Map p338 (06 4341 9624; www.trapizzino.it; Via Branca 88; trapizzini from €3.50; noon-1am Tue-Sun; Via Marmorata) The original of what is now a growing countrywide chain, this is the birthplace of the *trapizzino,* a kind of hybrid sandwich made by stuffing a cone of doughy focaccia with fillers like *polpette al sugo* (meatballs in tomato sauce) or *pollo alla cacciatore* (stewed chicken). They're messy to eat but quite delicious.

PARAPONZIPÒ SANDWICHES €

Map p338 (06 4542 8690; www.paraponzipo.it; Piazza di Porta San Paolo 9; sandwiches €5-6; 10.30am-10pm Thu-Sat, to 5pm Tue, Wed & Sun, to 4pm Mon; ; MPiramide) Paraponzipò proves that the best thing since sliced bread is superb Italian salumi and cheese packed between said bread. An impressive selection of cold cuts such as mortadella, porchetta and bresaola stands alongside piled-high fish and vegetarian options – everything from sun-dried tomatoes and *pecorino* to truffle cream. Seating is sparse – grab your *panino* to take away.

MORDI E VAI STREET FOOD €

Map p338 (339 1343344; www.mordievai.it; Box 15, Nuovo Mercato di Testaccio; panini €4-5; 8am-3pm Mon-Sat; Via Galvani) Come at lunchtime and you'll have to elbow your way through the crowds at Sergio Esposito's critically acclaimed market stall. What they're coming for is traditional Roman street food and the stall's signature *panino con l'allesso di scottona* (bread roll filled with tender slow-cooked beef).

PIZZERIA DA REMO PIZZA €

Map p338 (06 574 62 70; Piazza Santa Maria Liberatrice 44; meals €15; 7pm-1am Mon-Sat; Via Marmorata) For an authentic Roman experience, join the noisy crowds here at one of the city's best-known and most popular pizzerias. It's a spartan-looking place, but the crispy wafer-thin pizzas, served charred and spilling over the plate's edges, are the business, and there's a cheerful, boisterous vibe. Expect to queue after 8.30pm.

100% BIO VEGETARIAN €

Map p338 (06 574 77 78; www.centopercento.bio; Piazza di Porta San Paolo 6a; buffet per kg €2.60, pannini €4.50; 7.30am-9pm Mon-Sat, 8am-4pm Sun; ; MPiramide) Veggies star at this cosy bistro a quick jaunt from the Piramide di Caio Cestio (p194). All dishes are vegan or vegetarian and rich in legumes, grains and greens; come for the lunch buffet, which boasts more than 30 homemade dishes. Ingredients are 100% certified organic, and your cappuccino can be brewed with soy, rice or almond milk.

An abundant *aperitivo* buffet is also available in the evening.

CUPS STREET FOOD €

Map p338 (Box 44, Nuovo Mercato di Testaccio; dishes €5-8; 8am-3.30pm Mon-Sat; Via Galvini) This gourmet market stall, part of celebrity chef Cristina Bowerman's ever-growing Roman empire, takes its name from the carton cups used to serve soups and freshly prepared staples such as meatballs in tomato sauce. If that doesn't appeal, slide along to Romeo, another Bowerman outfit, next door, for sliced pizza and cured meat platters.

FOODIE FRESH MARKET VEGETARIAN €

Map p338 (06 8953 7350; Piazza Testaccio 35; dishes €4.50-6; 8am-8pm Mon-Sat; ; Via Marmorata) A fruit-and-veg shop doubling as a salad and juice bar, this friendly outfit is a vegetarian oasis in the homeland of Rome's carnivorous cuisine. As well as freshly squeezed juices and fruit shakes, it serves ready-made quiches and salads, to eat in or take away, and a choice of veggie burgers and wraps.

DA FELICE ROMAN €€

Map p338 (☎06 574 68 00; www.feliceatestaccio.it; Via Mastro Giorgio 29; meals €30-40; ⏰12.30-3pm & 7-11.30pm; 🚌Via Marmorata) This historic trattoria, much frequented by locals and tourists alike, is renowned for its unswerving dedication to Roman soul food. In contrast to the light-touch modern decor, the menu is pure old school with hallowed city staples such as *tonnarelli a cacio e pepe* (thick spaghetti with *pecorino* cheese and ground black pepper). Reservations essential.

LA VILLETTA ROMAN €€

Map p338 (☎06 575 05 97; www.lavillettadal1940.com; Viale della Piramide Cestia 53; meals €30; ⏰12.30-2.45pm & 7.30-11.30pm; 📶✍; Ⓜ Piramide) This mellow Testaccio trattoria has won over locals since 1940 with its excellent *cucina romana* (Roman cuisine) and generous meat and cheese boards. Despite (or perhaps because of) its down-to-earth charm, La Villetta is a favourite of countless Italian celebrities, including legendary footballer Francesco Totti, who dined here after his final game for AS Roma.

LA TORRICELLA RISTORANTE €€

Map p338 (☎06 574 63 11; www.la-torricella.com; Via Torricelli 2-12; meals €30-35; ⏰12.30-3pm & 7.30pm-midnight; 🚌Lungotevere Testaccio) A long-standing local favourite, La Torricella is a copybook neighbourhood restaurant with formal white-starched tablecloths and a menu to cover all bases. The Roman classics are all there, as well as pizzas and steaks, but it's the seafood that draws the regulars, dishes like fried *moscardini* (octopus) and sea bream with roast potatoes.

TAVERNA VOLPETTI ITALIAN €€

Map p338 (☎06 5744 306; www.tavernavolpetti.it; Via Volta 8; meals €25-35; ⏰noon-11pm Tue-Sat, to 3pm Sun & Mon; 🚌Via Marmorata) Just round the corner from the famous Volpetti deli (p201), this casual restaurant serves a cosmopolitan menu of beloved Roman pastas and creative modern mains. However, its forte is its selection of cured meats and cheeses, served on platters showcasing fine Parma prosciutto, Alpine *formaggio* and prize Iberian hams.

CHECCHINO DAL 1887 ROMAN €€€

Map p338 (☎06 574 38 16; www.checchino-dal-1887.com; Via di Monte Testaccio 30; meals €40, tasting menus €40-65; ⏰12.30-3pm & 8pm-11.45pm, closed Sun dinner & Mon; 🚌Via Galvani) A pig's whisker from the city's former slaughterhouse, this old-school restaurant is a long-standing champion of the *quinto quarto* (fifth quarter – or insides of the animal). Signature dishes include *coda all vaccinara* (oxtail stew) and *rigatoni alla pajata* (pasta with a sauce of tomato and veal intestines).

DRINKING & NIGHTLIFE

With kicking clubs, suave wine bars and cafes full of old-timers, this area has most tastes covered. There are two main nightlife districts: Testaccio, which is home to a string of bars and clubs catering to cocktail lovers, craft-beer fans and weekend partygoers; and the area around Via di San Giovanni in Laterano, which hosts a more mellow scene centred on wine bars and a couple of popular gay-friendly nightspots.

San Giovanni & the Celio

WINE CONCEPT WINE BAR

Map p339 (☎06 7720 6673; www.wineconcept.it; Via Capo d'Africa 21; ⏰noon-3pm & 6pm-midnight Mon-Thu, noon-3pm & 6pm-1am Fri, 6pm-1am Sat; 🚌Via Labicana) Wine buffs looking to excite their palate should search out this *enoteca* (wine bar). Run by expert sommeliers, it has an extensive list of Italian regional labels and European vintages, as well as a daily food menu. Wines are available to drink by the glass or to buy by the bottle.

BLIND PIG COCKTAIL BAR

(☎06 8775 07 14; Via La Spezia 72; ⏰6.30pm-2am; Ⓜ Lodi) Cocktail bars have been a thing in Rome for some time but the trend shows no sign of waning and new places continue to open. This good-looking relative newcomer hits all the right notes with its dim lighting, green-and-black decor and professionally mixed cocktails. And that's without even mentioning its delicious focaccia.

ANTICAFÉ ROMA CAFE

Map p350 (☎06 7049 4442; Via Veio 4B; ⏰9am-9pm Mon-Fri, from 10am Sat & Sun; 📶; Ⓜ San Giovanni) If you've time to kill, this relaxed cafe

LOCAL KNOWLEDGE

GAY LIFE

The bottom end of Via di San Giovanni in Laterano, the sloping street that runs from the Basilica di San Giovanni to near the Colosseum, is a favourite haunt of Rome's LGBTIQ+ community. In the evenings, bars like **Coming Out** (Map p339; ☎06 700 98 71; www.comingout.it; Via di San Giovanni in Laterano 8; ⌚7am-5.30am; 🚇Via Labicana) and **My Bar** (Map p339; ☎06 700 44 25; Via di San Giovanni in Laterano 12; ⌚9am-2am; 🚇Via Labicana) burst into life, attracting large crowds of mostly gay men.

is the answer. Anticafé doesn't charge for its drinks, rather you pay for the time you spend there – €4 for the first hour, then €4 for successive hours. With that you're free to hang out and do pretty much whatever – use the wi-fi, play board games, read on the sofa, drink... You can BYO alcohol or there's a bar with free drinks (coffees and fruit juices) and snacks.

Aventino & Around

CASA MANFREDI CAFE

Map p338 (☎06 9760 5892; Viale Aventino 91-93; ⌚7am-9pm Mon-Fri, from 8am Sat, 8am-8pm Sun; 🚇Viale Aventino, 🚌Viale Aventino) A good-looking cafe-*pasticceria* in the wealthy Aventine neighbourhood. Join its well-dressed habitués for a quick coffee in the gleaming glass-and-chandelier interior, a light al fresco lunch or chic evening *aperitivo*. It also does a tasty line in picture-perfect pastries and artisanal gelato.

Testaccio

REC 23 BAR

Map p338 (☎06 8746 2147; www.rec23.com; Piazza dell'Emporio 2; ⌚6.30pm-2am daily, plus 12.30-3.30pm Sat & Sun; 🚇Via Marmorata) All exposed brick and mismatched furniture, this large, New York–inspired venue caters to all moods, serving *aperitivo* (drink plus buffet €10), restaurant meals and a weekend brunch (€18). Arrive thirsty to take on a 'Testaccio mule', one of its original cocktails, or keep it simple with an Italian prosecco, Scottish whisky or Latin American rum.

L'OASI DELLA BIRRA BAR

Map p338 (☎06 574 61 22; Piazza Testaccio 41; ⌚4.30pm-1am Mon-Sat, from 6pm Sun; 🚇Via Marmorata) Housed in the Palombi Enoteca bottle shop, L'Oasi della Birra is exactly that – an oasis of beer. With hundreds of labels, from German heavyweights to British bitters and Belgian brews, plus wines, cheeses and cold cuts, it's ideally set up for an evening's quaffing, either in the cramped cellar or on the piazza-side terrace. Good *aperitivo* buffet too (€10).

TRAM DEPOT BAR

Map p338 (www.facebook.com/tramdepotroma; Via Marmorata 13; ⌚7.30am-2am Mon-Fri, from 9am Sat & Sun May-Oct; Ⓜ Piramide) When temperatures climb in the capital, this charming little bar springs to life, serving up coffee and cocktails (€5) until long after sunset. Its outdoor seating, vintage porch swings, twinkly tea lights and a verdant stretch of grass flanked by trees conjure up a garden-party vibe smack in the centre of the city.

LINARI CAFE

Map p338 (☎06 578 23 58; Via Nicola Zabaglia 9; ⌚6.30am-9.30pm; 🚇Via Marmorata) A part of the neighbourhood furniture, this long-standing cafe-*pasticceria* has the busy clatter of a good bar, with excellent pastries, splendid coffee and plenty of raucous banter. There are a few tables positioned outside – ideal for a cheap lunch (pastas and mains €5.50) but you'll have to outfox the neighbourhood locals to get one.

L'ALIBI CLUB

Map p338 (☎320 3541185; Via di Monte Testaccio 44; ⌚11pm-4am Thu, 11.30pm-5am Fri & Sat; 🚇Via Galvani) Gay-friendly L'Alibi is one of Rome's best-known clubs, hosting regular parties and serving up a mash of house, hip-hop, Latino, pop and dance music to a young, mixed crowd.

It can get pretty steamy inside, particularly on packed weekend nights, but you can grab a mouthful of air outside on the spacious summer terrace.

ENTERTAINMENT

TERME DI CARACALLA OPERA

Map p339 (www.operaroma.it; Viale delle Terme di Caracalla 52; tickets from €30; Jun & Jul; Viale delle Terme di Caracalla) The hulking ruins of this vast 3rd-century baths complex (p191) set the memorable stage for the Teatro dell'Opera's summer season of music and ballet.

It features shows by big-name Italian and international performers.

CONTESTACCIO LIVE MUSIC

Map p338 (www.facebook.com/contestaccio; Via di Monte Testaccio 65b; 6pm-5am Wed-Sat; Via Galvani) A fixture on Rome's music scene, ConteStaccio is one of the city's top venues on the Testaccio clubbing strip.

It's known for its free gigs, which feature both emerging groups as well as established performers, spanning a range of styles – indie, pop, rock, acoustic, reggae and new wave.

VILLAGGIO GLOBALE LIVE MUSIC

Map p338 (www.facebook.com/pages/Villaggio-Globale/161652650554595; Lungotevere Testaccio 1; gigs 10pm-late; Via Marmorata) For a taste of the underground, head to this historic *centro sociale* (an ex-squat turned into a cultural centre) that occupys the city's graffiti-sprayed former slaughterhouse.

It stages gigs – everything from techno to ska, as well as DJ sets, workshops and cultural events.

SHOPPING

Foodie shoppers are well catered for in Testaccio, home to a covered daily market and one of Rome's most celebrated and best-stocked delis. In San Giovanni, bargain-hunters can look for new and secondhand clothes, while vinyl junkies can get their fix at one of the capital's longest-standing record shops.

VOLPETTI FOOD & DRINKS

Map p338 (06 574 23 52; www.volpetti.com; Via Marmorata 47; 8.30am-2pm & 4.30-8.15pm Mon-Fri, 8.30am-8.30pm Sat; Via Marmorata) This super-stocked deli, one of the best in town, is a treasure trove of gourmet delicacies. Helpful staff will guide you through its extensive selection of Italian cheese, homemade pasta, olive oil, vinegar, cured meat, wine and grappa. It also serves excellent, though pricey, sliced pizza.

PIFEBO VINTAGE

Map p339 (06 9818 5845; https://pifebo.com; Via dei Valeri 10; noon-8pm Mon-Sat; Via dell'Ambra Aradam) One of Rome's best-stocked secondhand and vintage clothes stores. There's a definite rocker theme to the stock, which includes endless racks of leather jackets, denims, cut-off shorts and cowboy boots. Dig further through the red-painted rooms and you'll discover plenty more to pimp up your wardrobe.

SOUL FOOD MUSIC

Map p339 (06 7045 2025; www.haterecords.com; Via di San Giovanni in Laterano 192; 10.30am-1.30pm & 3.30-7.30pm Tue-Sat; Via di San Giovanni in Laterano) Run by Hate Records, Soul Food is a laid-back record store with an encyclopaedic collection of vinyl that runs the musical gamut from '60s garage and rockabilly to punk, indie, new wave, folk and soul. You'll also find retro T-shirts, posters, fanzines and even vintage toys.

ETEL SHOES

Map p338 (06 575 84 15; www.facebook.com/ETeLRomaTestaccio; Piazza Testaccio 44; 10am-7.30pm Mon-Sat; Via Marmorata) A hot find for footwear fiends, Etel stocks a carefully curated collection of fashionable women's shoes by mainly Italian labels. Designs range from richly coloured ankle boots to elegant high-heeled sandals and wooden-soled suede lace-ups.

Villa Borghese & Northern Rome

VILLA BORGHESE & AROUND | FLAMINIO | SALARIO | NOMENTANO | PARIOLI

Neighbourhood Top Five

❶ **Museo e Galleria Borghese** (p204) Getting to grips with artistic genius at this lavish gallery. Bernini's sculptures are the star turn, but you'll also find masterpieces by Canova, Caravaggio, Titian and Raphael.

❷ **Villa Borghese** (p207) Escaping the crowds as you explore the leafy lanes and bosky glades of Rome's most famous park.

❸ **Museo Nazionale Etrusco di Villa Giulia** (p208) Applauding Italy's most comprehensive collection of Etruscan treasures at this splendid museum.

❹ **La Galleria Nazionale** (p207) Going face to face with the giants of modern art in the halls of a stately belle époque palace.

❺ **Auditorium Parco della Musica** (p213) Catching a world-class concert and admiring Renzo Piano's trend-setting architecture at this eye-catching cultural centre.

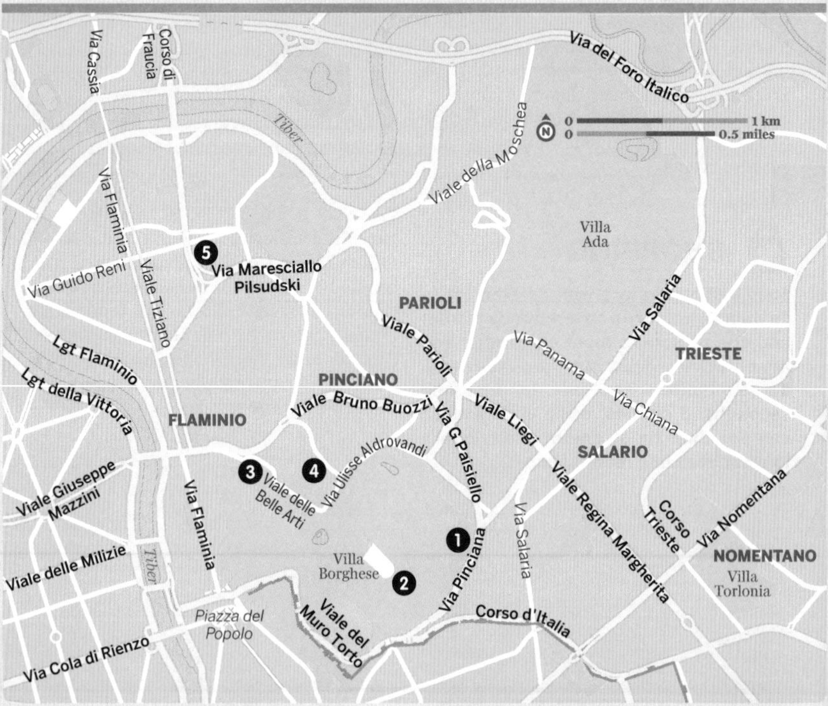

For more detail of this area see Map p348 ➡

Explore Villa Borghese & Northern Rome

Although less packed with traditional sights than elsewhere, this large swath of northern Rome is rich in interest. The obvious starting point is Villa Borghese (p207), an attractive park counting the city's zoo, its largest modern-art gallery and a stunning Etruscan museum among its myriad attractions. But its great scene-stealing highlight is the Museo e Galleria Borghese (p204), one of Rome's top art museums.

From Piazzale Flaminio, a tram heads up Via Flaminia to two of Rome's most important modern buildings: Renzo Piano's concert centre, the Auditorium Parco della Musica (p213), and Zaha Hadid's contemporary-art gallery, MAXXI (p207). Continue up the road and you come to Ponte Milvio (p208), a handsome footbridge. Over the river, Piazzale di Ponte Milvio is a favourite hang-out, its cafes and busy eateries much frequented by the area's well-to-do residents. To the west, crowds flock to the Stadio Olimpico (p213) for football, rugby and the occasional rock concert.

To the east of Villa Borghese, Via Salaria, the old Roman *sale* (salt) road, runs through a smart residential and business district. To the north, Villa Ada park expands northwards while, to the south, Via Nomentana traverses hectares of housing as it heads out of town. On Via Nomentana, Villa Torlonia (p209) is a captivating park, and the Basilica di Sant'Agnese Fuori le Mura (p209) claims Rome's oldest Christian mosaics.

Local Life

- **Concerts and events** Rome's culture vultures keep a close eye on what's going on at the Auditorium Parco della Musica (p213). Also check for events at the MAXXI (p207) and MACRO (p208) art galleries.
- **Parks** Tourists tend to stop at Villa Borghese (p207), but locals often head to Villa Torlonia (p209) or Villa Ada (p209).
- **Football** Sunday is match day. And for Rome's ardent fans that means a pilgrimage to the Stadio Olimpico (p213) to cheer their team on (Roma or Lazio).

Getting There & Away

- **Bus** Buses 53 and 160 go to Villa Borghese from Via Vittorio Veneto near Barberini metro station. There are also regular buses along Via Nomentana and Via Salaria.
- **Metro** Villa Borghese is accessible from Flaminio and Spagna stations (both line A).
- **Tram** No 2 serves Via Flaminia and Viale Tiziano from Piazzale Flaminio; no 3 connects Villa Borghese with San Lorenzo, Testaccio and Trastevere; and no 19 runs from Piazza del Risorgimento to Villa Borghese.

Lonely Planet's Top Tip

Monday is not a good day to explore Villa Borghese. Sure, you can walk in the park, but all of the museums and galleries are shut – they open Tuesday to Sunday. Remember to book tickets for the **Museo e Galleria Borghese** (p204). It's easy to do, either online (plus a €2 booking fee) or by phoning the museum directly. You won't get in without a reservation.

Best Places to Eat

- Metamorfosi (p212)
- All'Oro (p211)
- Osteria Flaminio (p211)
- Pro Loco Pinciano (p212)
- Neve di Latte (p211)

For reviews, see p210.

Best Places to Drink

- Momart (p212)
- Lanificio 159 (p213)
- Enoteca Mostó (p212)
- Chioschetto di Ponte Milvio (p212)

For reviews, see p212.

Best Museums & Galleries

- Museo e Galleria Borghese (p204)
- Museo Nazionale Etrusco di Villa Giulia (p208)
- La Galleria Nazionale (p207)
- MAXXI (p207)
- MACRO (p208)

For reviews, see p207.

TOP EXPERIENCE

DON'T MISS THE MUSEO E GALLERIA BORGHESE

If you only have the time or inclination for one art gallery in Rome, make it this one. Housing what's often referred to as the 'queen of all private art collections', it boasts some of the city's finest art treasures, including a series of sensational sculptures by Gian Lorenzo Bernini and important paintings by the likes of Caravaggio, Titian, Raphael and Rubens.

The Villa

The museum's collection was formed by Cardinal Scipione Borghese (1577–1633), the most knowledgeable and ruthless art collector of his day. It was originally housed in the cardinal's residence near St Peter's, but in the 1620s he had it transferred to his new villa just outside Porta Pinciana. And it's in the villa's central building, the Casino Borghese, that you'll see it today.

Over the centuries the villa has undergone several overhauls, most notably in the late 1700s when Prince Marcantonio Borghese added much of the lavish neoclassical decor. But while the villa remained intact, the collection did not. Much of the antique statuary was carted off to the Louvre in the early 19th century, and other pieces were gradually sold off. In 1902 the Italian State bought the casino, but it wasn't until 1997 that the collection was finally put on public display.

The villa is divided into two parts: the ground-floor museum, with its superb sculptures, intricate Roman floor mosaics and hypnotic trompe l'œil frescoes; and the upstairs picture gallery.

DON'T MISS

- *Ratto di Proserpina*
- *Venere vincitrice*
- *Ragazzo col Canestro di Frutta*
- *La Deposizione di Cristo*
- *Amor Sacro e Amor Profano*

PRACTICALITIES

- Map p348, F6
- 06 3 28 10
- http://galleriaborghese.beniculturali.it
- Piazzale del Museo Borghese 5
- adult/child €15/8.50
- 9am-7pm Tue-Sun
- Via Pinciana

Ground Floor

Stairs lead up to a portico flanking the grand entrance hall, decorated with 4th-century floor mosaics of fighting gladiators and a 2nd-century *Satiro Combattente* (Fighting Satyr). High on the wall is a gravity-defying bas-relief of a horse and rider falling into the void *(Marco Curzio a Cavallo)* by Pietro Bernini (Gian Lorenzo's father).

The statuesque scene-stealer in **Sala I** is Antonio Canova's daring depiction of Napoleon's sister, Paolina Bonaparte Borghese, reclining topless as *Venere vincitrice* (1805–08). Its suggestive pose and technical virtuosity (look at the cushion!) is typical of Canova's elegant, mildly erotic neoclassical style.

Further on, in **Sala III**, Gian Lorenzo Bernini's *Apollo e Dafne* (1622–25), one of a series depicting pagan myths, captures the exact moment Daphne's hands start morphing into leaves. **Sala IV** is home to Bernini's masterpiece *Ratto di Proserpina* (1621–22). This flamboyant sculpture brilliantly reveals the artist's virtuosity – just look at Pluto's hand pressing into the seemingly soft flesh of Persephone's thigh.

Caravaggio dominates **Sala VIII**. There's a dissipated-looking self-portrait *Bacchino malato* (Young Sick Bacchus; 1592–95), the strangely beautiful *La Madonna dei Palafrenieri* (Madonna with Serpent; 1605–06), and *San Giovanni Battista* (St John the Baptist; 1609–10), probably Caravaggio's last work. There's also the much-loved *Ragazzo col Canestro di Frutta* (Boy with a Basket of Fruit; 1593–95), and the dramatic *Davide con la Testa di Golia* (David with the Head of Goliath; 1609–10) – Goliath's severed head is also said to be a self-portrait.

Pinacoteca

Upstairs, the picture gallery offers a wonderful snapshot of Renaissance art.

Don't miss Raphael's extraordinary *La Deposizione di Cristo* (The Deposition; 1507) in **Sala IX**, and his *Dama con Liocorno* (Lady with a Unicorn; 1506). In the same room is Fra Bartolomeo's superb *Adorazione del Bambino* (Adoration of the Christ Child; 1495) and Perugino's *Madonna con Bambino* (Madonna and Child; first quarter of the 16th century).

Next door in **Sala X**, Correggio's *Danäe* (1530–31) shares the room with a willowy Venus, as portrayed by Cranach in his *Venere e Amore che Reca Il Favo do Miele* (Venus and Cupid with Honeycomb; 1531). And don't miss the gorgeous ceiling!

Moving on, **Sala XIV** boasts two self-portraits by Bernini. **Sala XVIII** is home to Rubens' *Susanna e I Vecchioni* (Susanna and the Elders; 1605–07).

To finish off, Titian's early masterpiece *Amor Sacro e Amor Profano* (Sacred and Profane Love; 1514), in **Sala XX**, is one of the collection's most prized works.

BOOKING TICKETS

To limit numbers, visitors are admitted at two-hourly intervals – you'll need to pre-book your ticket well in advance and get an entry time. To book, either phone the museum directly or buy tickets online at www.tosc.it. If you have a Roma Pass (p21), you can only book by phone. Pick your ticket up from the basement ticket office 30 minutes before your entry time. Take ID.

Cardinal Scipione Caffarelli Borghese (1577–1633) was one of the most influential figures in Rome's baroque art world. Nephew of Pope Paul V, he sponsored the greatest artists of the day, including Caravaggio, Bernini, Domenichino, Rubens and Guido Reni. Yet while he promoted the artists, he didn't always see eye to eye with them and was quite prepared to play dirty to get his hands on their works: he had Cavaliere d'Arpino jailed in order to confiscate his canvases and Domenichino arrested to force him to surrender *La Caccia di Diana* (The Hunt of Diana).

MUSEO E GALLERIA BORGHESE

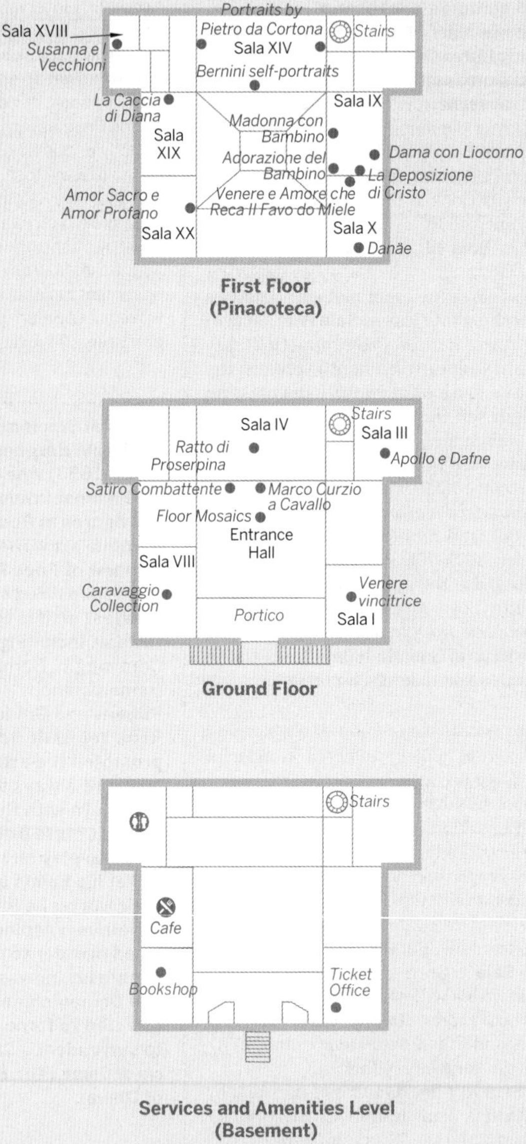

Sala XVIII
Susanna e I Vecchioni
Portraits by Pietro da Cortona
Sala XIV
Stairs
Bernini self-portraits
La Caccia di Diana
Sala XIX
Madonna con Bambino
Sala IX
Dama con Liocorno
Adorazione del Bambino
La Deposizione di Cristo
Amor Sacro e Amor Profano
Venere e Amore che Reca Il Favo do Miele
Sala XX
Sala X
Danäe
First Floor (Pinacoteca)
Sala IV
Stairs
Sala III
Ratto di Proserpina
Apollo e Dafne
Satiro Combattente
Marco Curzio a Cavallo
Floor Mosaics
Entrance Hall
Sala VIII
Caravaggio Collection
Venere vincitrice
Portico
Sala I
Ground Floor
Stairs
Cafe
Bookshop
Ticket Office
Services and Amenities Level (Basement)

SIGHTS

Ballooning northwards from the city centre, Villa Borghese is the obvious focus of this extensive area. Rome's central park provides a welcome respite from the city's hectic streets and harbours a number of outstanding museums. Elsewhere, you'll find several high-profile sights, including Rome's flagship cultural centre and two contemporary-art museums.

Villa Borghese & Around

MUSEO E GALLERIA BORGHESE — MUSEUM

See p204.

MUSEO NAZIONALE ETRUSCO DI VILLA GIULIA — MUSEUM

See p208.

★VILLA BORGHESE — PARK

Map p348 (entrances at Piazzale San Paolo del Brasile, Piazzale Flaminio, Via Pinciana, Via Raimondo, Largo Pablo Picasso; sunrise-sunset; Via Pinciana) Locals, lovers, tourists, joggers – no one can resist the lure of Rome's most celebrated park. Originally the 17th-century estate of Cardinal Scipione Borghese, it covers about 80 hectares of wooded glades, gardens and grassy banks. Among its attractions are several excellent museums, the landscaped **Giardino del Lago**, **Piazza di Siena**, a dusty arena used for Rome's top equestrian event in May, and a panoramic terrace on the Pincio Hill (p112).

Film buffs should head to the area around the Piazzale San Paolo del Brasile entrance, where the **Casa del Cinema** (Map p348; 06 06 08; www.casadelcinema.it) hosts regular film-related events, and the **Cinema dei Piccoli** (Map p348; 06 855 34 85; www.cinemadeipiccoli.it; tickets Mon-Fri €5, Sat & Sun €6) is one of the world's smallest cinemas.

Bike hire is available at various points, including the **Bici Pincio** (cnr Viale dell'Orologio & Viale Medici) kiosk in the southern part of the park for €5/15 per hour/day, as are four-seater electric bikes (€20 per hour). Or try **Villa Borghese Bike Rental** (Largo Pablo Picasso).

★LA GALLERIA NAZIONALE — GALLERY

Map p348 (Galleria Nazionale d'Arte Moderna e Contemporanea; 06 3229 8221; http://lagallerianazionale.com; Viale delle Belle Arti 131, accessible entrance Via Antonio Gramsci 71; adult/reduced €10/5; 8.30am-7.30pm Tue-Sun; Piazza Thorvaldsen) Housed in a vast belle époque palace, this oft-overlooked modern-art gallery, known locally as GNAM, is an unsung gem. Its superlative collection runs the gamut from neoclassical sculpture to abstract expressionism, with works by many of the most important exponents of 19th- and 20th-century art.

There are canvases by the *macchiaioli* (Italian Impressionists) and futurists Boccioni and Balla, as well as sculptures by Canova and major works by Modigliani, de Chirico and Guttuso. International artists represented include Van Gogh, Cézanne, Monet, Klimt, Kandinsky, Mondrian and Man Ray.

Flaminio

MUSEO NAZIONALE DELLE ARTI DEL XXI SECOLO — GALLERY

Map p348 (MAXXI; 06 320 19 54; www.maxxi.art; Via Guido Reni 4a; adult/reduced €12/9; 11am-7pm Tue-Fri & Sun, to 10pm Sat; Viale Tiziano) The Zaha Hadid–designed building that Rome's leading contemporary-art gallery occupies is as much a highlight as the art it contains. Formerly a barracks, the curved concrete structure is striking inside and out, with a multilayered geometric facade and a cavernous light-filled interior full of snaking walkways and suspended staircases.

The gallery has an outstanding permanent collection of 20th- and 21st-century works, of which a selection are on free display in Gallery 1, but even more interesting are its international exhibitions.

AUDITORIUM PARCO DELLA MUSICA — CULTURAL CENTRE

Map p348 (06 8024 1281; www.auditorium.com; Viale Pietro de Coubertin; 11am-8pm Mon-Sat, 10am-8pm Sun summer, to 6pm winter; Viale Tiziano) Designed by starchitect Renzo Piano and inaugurated in 2002, Rome's flagship cultural centre is an audacious work of architecture consisting of three silver pod-like concert halls set round a 3000-seat amphitheatre. There's a pleasant cafe in the central square and the grounds include a children's park. There's also a fabulous book and music store.

TOP EXPERIENCE
MUSEO NAZIONALE ETRUSCO DI VILLA GIULIA

Pope Julius III's 16th-century villa provides the charming setting for Italy's finest collection of Etruscan and pre-Roman treasures. Exhibits, many of which came from tombs in the surrounding Lazio region, range from bronze figurines and black **bucchero** tableware to temple decorations, terracotta vases and dazzling jewellery.

Must-sees include a polychrome terracotta statue of Apollo from the Etruscan town of Veio, just north of Rome, and the so-called **Lamine di Pyrgi** (Pyrgi Tablets): three gold sheets discovered during excavations of Pyrgi, Cerveteri's ancient sea port. Dating from the end of the 6th century BCE, they are inscribed with texts written in both Etruscan and Phoenician. But the museum's most famous piece is the 6th-century BCE **Sarcofago degli Sposi** (Sarcophagus of the Betrothed). This astonishing work, originally unearthed in a tomb in Cerveteri, depicts a husband and wife reclining on a stone banqueting couch. And although called a sarcophagus, it was actually designed as an elaborate urn for the couple's ashes.

Further finds relating to the Umbri and Latin peoples are housed in the nearby **Villa Poniatowski** (Map p348; incl in Museo Nazionale Etrusco di Villa Giulia ticket; ⌚10am-1pm Thu, 3-6pm Sat).

TOP TIPS

- Plan for time to stroll the villa's beautiful grounds.
- For a change of period, go to **La Galleria Nazionale** (p207) for modern art.

PRACTICALITIES

- Map p348, D5
- ☎06 322 65 71
- www.villagiulia.beniculturali.it
- Piazzale di Villa Giulia
- adult/reduced €8/4
- ⌚9am-8pm Tue-Sun
- 🚊Via delle Belle Arti

Excavations during its construction revealed remains of an ancient Roman villa, some of which are now on show in the Auditorium's small **Museo Archeologico** (⌚10am-8pm summer, 11am-6pm Mon-Sat, 10am-6pm Sun winter) FREE.

PONTE MILVIO BRIDGE

Map p348 (🚊Lungotevere Maresciallo Diaz) A cobbled footbridge, Ponte Milvio is best known as the site of the ancient Battle of the Milvian Bridge. It was first built in 109 BCE to carry Via Flaminia over the Tiber and survived intact until 1849, when Garibaldi's troops partially destroyed it to stop advancing French soldiers. Pope Pius IX had it rebuilt a year later.

FORO ITALICO ARCHITECTURE

Map p348 (Viale del Foro Italico; 🚊Lungotevere Maresciallo Cadorna) At the foot of the heavily wooded **Monte Mario**, the Foro Italico is a grandiose Fascist-era sports complex, centred on the Stadio Olimpico (p213), Rome's 70,000-seat football stadium. Most people pass through en route to a football or rugby match, but if you're interested in Fascist architecture, it's worth a look.

EXPLORA – MUSEO DEI BAMBINI DI ROMA MUSEUM

Map p348 (☎06 361 37 76; www.mdbr.it; Via Flaminia 80-86; €8, children 1-3yr €5, under 1yr free; ⌚entrance 10am, noon, 3pm & 5pm Tue-Sun, no 10am entrance in Aug; 👪; Ⓜ Flaminio) Rome's only dedicated kids' museum, Explora is aimed at the under-12s. It's divided into thematic sections, and with everything from a play pool and fire engine to a train driver's cabin, it's a hands-on, feet-on, full-on experience that your nippers will love. Outside there's also a free play park open to all.

Booking is recommended for the timed entrance and required on weekends.

Salario

MUSEO D'ARTE CONTEMPORANEA DI ROMA ARTS CENTRE

Map p348 (MACRO; ☎06 69 62 71; www.museomacro.org; Via Nizza 138, cnr Via Cagliari; ⌚10am-8pm Tue-Fri & Sun, to 10pm Sat; 🚊Via Nizza) FREE Along with MAXXI (p207), this is Rome's most important contemporary-art centre. Vying with the exhibits and performances for your attention is the museum's sleek black-and-red interior design. The work of French architect Odile Decq, this retains much of the building's original structure (a converted Peroni brewery), while also incorporating a sophisticated steel-and-glass finish.

CATACOMBE DI PRISCILLA CHRISTIAN SITE

Map p348 (☎06 8620 6272; www.catacombepriscilla.com; Via Salaria 430; guided visit adult/reduced €8/5; ⏱9am-noon & 2-5pm Tue-Sun; 🚌Via Salaria) Dug between the 2nd and 5th centuries, this vast network of moody tunnels was known as the Queen of Catacombs. It was an important early Christian burial site and numerous martyrs and popes are buried in the 40,000 tombs and chambers that line the 13km of tunnels.

Tours (35 minutes; alternating in English and Italian throughout the day) take in a decorated 3rd-century-CE Greek chapel and a rough fresco of the Virgin Mary with the baby Jesus on her lap. Dating from around 230 CE, this is thought to be the oldest existing image of the Madonna.

VILLA ADA PARK

Map p348 (entrances at Via Salaria, Via di Ponte Salario, Via di Monte Antenne, Via Panama; ⏱7am-sunset; 🚌Via Salaria) Once the private estate of King Vittorio Emanuele III, Villa Ada is a big rambling park, about 160 hectares, with shady paths, lakes, lawns and woods. It's popular with locals and explodes into life in summer when outdoor concerts are staged during the Roma Incontro il Mondo festival.

⊙ Nomentano

★BASILICA DI SANT'AGNESE FUORI LE MURA & MAUSOLEO DI SANTA COSTANZA BASILICA

(www.santagnese.com; entrances at Via Nomentana 349 & Via di Sant'Agnese 3; basilica & mausoleo free, catacombs guided visit adult/reduced €8/5; ⏱basilica 8am-noon & 4-7.30pm, mausoleo 9am-noon & 3-6pm, catacombs 9am-noon Mon-Sat & 3-5pm daily; 🚌Via Nomentana) Although a bit of a hike, it's well worth searching out this intriguing medieval church complex. Set over the catacombs where St Agnes was buried, it comprises the Basilica di Sant'Agnese Fuori le Mura, home to a stunning Byzantine mosaic of the saint, and the Mausoleo di Santa Costanza, a circular 4th-century mausoleum decorated by some of Christendom's oldest mosaics.

The original basilica, remains of which can be seen in a field adjacent to the current complex, was built in the 4th century for Costanza, daughter of the emperor Costantino. It was subsequently abandoned in the 7th century and replaced by the current basilica, which has itself been much modified over the centuries. Its star attraction, and one of the few original features, is its golden apse mosaic. This is one of the best examples of Byzantine art in Rome and has survived intact. It shows St Agnes, flanked by Popes Honorius and Symmachus, standing over the signs of her martyrdom – a sword and a flame. According to tradition, the 13-year-old Agnes was sentenced to be burnt at the stake, but when the flames failed to kill her she was beheaded on Piazza Navona and buried beneath this church.

Up from the main basilica is the Mausoleo di Santa Costanza. This squat circular building has a dome supported by 12 pairs of granite columns and a vaulted ambulatory decorated with beautiful 4th-century mosaics. Bring a €0.50 piece to turn on its lights.

VILLA TORLONIA PARK

Map p348 (Via Nomentana 70; ⏱7am-7pm winter, to 8.30pm summer; 🚌Via Nomentana) Full of towering pine trees, atmospheric palms and scattered villas, this splendid but often ungroomed 19th-century park once belonged to Prince Giovanni Torlonia (1756–1829),

QUARTIERE COPPEDÈ

The compact **Quartiere Coppedè** (Map p348; 🚊Viale Regina Margherita), centring around the magnificent Piazza Mincio, is one of Rome's most extraordinary neighbourhoods. Conceived and built by the little-known Florentine architect, Gino Coppedè, between 1913 and 1926, it's a fairy-tale series of palazzos with Tuscan turrets, Liberty sculptures, Moorish arches, Gothic gargoyles, frescoed facades and palm-fringed gardens.

At the heart of the piazza, the whimsical froggy **Fontana delle Rane** (Fountain of the Frogs) is a modern take on the better known Fontana delle Tartarughe in the Jewish Ghetto.

a powerful banker and landowner. His large neoclassical villa, Casino Nobile, later became the Mussolini family home (1925–43) and, in the latter part of WWII, Allied headquarters (1944–47). These days it's part of the Musei di Villa Torlonia museum. By appointment you can tour Mussolini's bunker under the park.

VILLA TORLONIA BUNKER HISTORIC SITE

Map p348 (www.bunkertorlonia.it; Villa Torlonia, Via Nomentana 70; adult/child €10/free; by reservation; Via Nomentana) Beneath the greenery of Villa Torlonia lie reminders of a dark chapter in Rome's history. Between 1940 and 1943, Mussolini had two air-raid shelters and an underground bunker built beneath what was, at the time, his family estate. Guided 1½-hour tours take you down into these bare underground chambers, complete with anti-gas doors and air-filtration systems. The bunker, whose 4m-thick walls lie 6m below the Casino Nobile, was still being worked on when the Duce was arrested on 25 July 1943.

MUSEI DI VILLA TORLONIA MUSEUM

Map p348 (06 06 08; www.museivillatorlonia.it; Villa Torlonia, Via Nomentana 70; adult/reduced Casino Nobile €7.50/6.50, Casina delle Civette €6/5, combined €9.50/7.50; 9am-7pm Tue-Sun; Via Nomentana) Housed in three villas – Casino Nobile, Casina delle Civette and Casino dei Principi – this museum boasts an eclectic collection of sculpture, paintings, furnishings and decorative stained glass.

The main ticket office is just inside the Via Nomentana entrance to Villa Torlonia.

With its oversized neoclassical facade – added by architect Giovan Battista Caretti to embellish an earlier overhaul by Giuseppe Valadier – **Casino Nobile** (adult/reduced €7.50/6.50, combined with Casina delle Civette €9.50/7.50) makes quite an impression. In the lavishly decorated interior you can admire the Torlonia family's fine collection of classically inspired sculpture and early-20th-century paintings from the *Scuola Romana* (Roman School of Art).

To the northeast, the much smaller **Casina delle Civette** (adult/reduced €6/5, combined with Casino Nobile €9.50/7.50) is a bizarre mix of Swiss cottage, Gothic castle and twee farmhouse decorated in art nouveau style. Built between 1840 and 1930, it's now a museum dedicated to stained glass.

Casino dei Principi (adult/reduced incl Casino Nobile €7.50/6.50) houses the archive of the *Scuola Romana* and opens only to stage temporary exhibitions.

PORTA PIA GATE

Map p348 (Piazzale Porta Pia; Via XX Settembre) Michelangelo's last architectural work, this crenellated structure was commissioned by Pope Pius IV to replace Porta Nomentana, one of the original gates in the Aurelian Walls, and was built between 1561 and 1564.

Bitter street fighting took place here in 1870 as Italian troops breached the adjacent walls on 20 September to wrest the city from the pope and claim it for the nascent kingdom of Italy.

EATING

Eating options range from takeaways and neighbourhood trattorias to smart cafes, gourmet gelaterie and critically acclaimed restaurants. Head to the wealthy Parioli district for Michelin-starred cuisine and fine dining, while Piazzale di Ponte Milvio boasts a number of popular, casual eateries. Villa Borghese itself is something of a foodie wasteland, but you'll find a few choice options in the area east of the park.

Villa Borghese & Around

SERENELLA PIZZA €

Map p348 (06 6478 1660; www.facebook.com/pizzeriaserenellaroma; Via Salaria 70; pizza slices from €2; 8am-10pm; Via Salaria) For the best sliced pizza near Villa Borghese park, search out this humble takeaway. Pizzas come capped with a selection of imaginative toppings and a light, fluffy base, the result of a 72-hour preparation and the use of natural yeast. For a cheap, easy-to-eat snack, the *pizza bianca* (plain white pizza) is excellent.

DOLCE SWEETS €

Map p348 (06 841 62 79; www.officinadolce.it; Via Savoia 52; sweets from €1.50; 8.30am-8pm Mon-Sat, 9.30am-2pm Sun; Fiume) Dolce, a charming cake and pie shop, offers exquisitely crafted sweets, from muffins to sea-

LOCAL KNOWLEDGE

GELATO GEMS

This neck of Rome harbours some outstanding gelaterie. They're not the easiest to find, though, and unless you know where to look you're unlikely to stumble upon them. A case in point is **Neve di Latte** (Map p348; ☎06 320 84 85; www.facebook.com/NevedilatteRomaFlaminio; Via Poletti 6; gelato €2.50-5; ⏰noon-11pm Sun-Thu, to midnight Fri & Sat summer, noon-10pm winter; 🚋Viale Tiziano), an innocuous-looking place near MAXXI that serves some of the best classical gelato in town. **Gelateria dei Gracchi** (Map p348; ☎06 8535 3508; www.gelateriadeigracchi.it; Viale Regina Margherita 212; small gelato €2.50; ⏰noon-midnight Sun-Thu, to 12.30am Fri & Sat) and, over the river, **Al Settimo Gelo** (Map p348; ☎06 3725 567; www.alsettimogelo.it; Via Vodice 21a; gelato €2-5; ⏰10am-11.30pm Tue-Sat, 11am-2pm & 4-11.30pm Sun summer, 10am-8.30pm Tue-Sat, 11am-2pm & 3.30-8.30pm Sun winter; 🚌Piazza Giuseppe Mazzini) are other much-lauded gelaterie, known for their creative flavours and use of natural ingredients.

sonal fruit-inspired cakes. A tiny clutch of vintage tables allows for leisurely tasting and tea drinking.

CAFFÈ DELLE ARTI RISTORANTE €€

Map p348 (☎06 3265 1236; www.caffedelleartiroma.com; Via Gramsci 73; meals €40-45; ⏰8am-5pm Mon, 8am-midnight Tue-Sun; 🚋Piazza Thorvaldsen) The cafe-restaurant of La Galleria Nazionale (p207) sits in neoclassical splendour in a tranquil corner of Villa Borghese. An elegant venue, it's at its best on warm sunny days when you can sit on the terrace and enjoy the romantic setting over a lunch salad, cocktail or dinner of classic Italian cuisine.

Flaminio

ANTICA PIZZERIA DA MICHELE PIZZA €

Map p348 (☎06 3260 0432; www.damicheleroma.it; Via Flaminia 82; pizza €9; ⏰noon-5pm & 7pm-midnight; 📶🍴; Ⓜ Flaminio) The Rome location of the famed Neapolitan pizzeria imports the same rules that work so well at its original eatery in the south: no reservations, thick-crusted pies hanging off your plate, a strict duo of pizzas (marinara or margherita) and a scattering of generously stuffed calzones as the only options on the menu.

Da Michele is located inside Explora (p208) children's museum.

OSTERIA FLAMINIO RISTORANTE €€

Map p348 (☎06 323 69 00; www.osteriaflaminio.com; Via Flaminia 297; lunch buffet €9-12, meals €30-35; ⏰12.30-3.30pm & 7.30pm-midnight Mon-Fri, 7.30pm-midnight Sat, noon-3.30pm Sun; 🚋Via Flaminia) This friendly eatery makes for a fine lunch stop after a visit to the MAXXI (p207) art museum. The vibe is casual and its interior is a handsome mix of dark-wood floors, large windows and muted greys and whites. Foodwise, it serves a popular lunch buffet (vegetarian on Mondays, fish on Fridays) and a menu of modern Italian and international fare.

★ALL'ORO RISTORANTE €€€

Map p348 (☎06 9799 6907; www.ristorantealloro.it; Via Giuseppe Pisanelli 23-25; tasting menus €88-150; ⏰7-11pm daily, 1-2.45pm Sat & Sun; Ⓜ Flaminio) This Michelin-starred restaurant, in the five-star H'All Tailor Suite hotel, is one of Rome's top fine-dining tickets. At the helm is chef Riccardo Di Giacinto, whose artfully presented food is modern and innovative while still being recognisably Italian. Complementing the cuisine, the decor strikes a contemporary club look with dark-wood ceilings, brass lamps and a fireplace.

Salario

PASTICCERIA GRUÈ PASTRIES €

Map p348 (☎06 841 22 20; www.gruepasticceria.it; Viale Regina Margherita 95; pastries from €1.50; ⏰7am-9pm Sun-Fri; 🚋Viale Regina Margherita) One of many eateries on Viale Regina Margherita, this sleek *pasticceria*-cafe is a local hotspot – suits and sharply dressed office workers lunch here on delicate *panini* and daily pastas, while evening sees the aperitif crowd move in. But its real calling cards are the exquisitely designed pastries and chocolates that stare out from beneath the counter.

LOCAL KNOWLEDGE

KIOSK BARS

A recurring feature of Rome's streetscape are its green kiosks. Many of these are occupied by vendors selling newspapers, magazines and public transport tickets. Some, however, harbour long-standing and much-loved bars. On the river, the **Chioschetto di Ponte Milvio** (Map p348; ☎347 6957141; www.facebook.com/ilchioschettodipontemilvio; Piazzale di Ponte Milvio; ⏲6pm-2am summer, 5pm-2am Thu-Sat, 8am-10.30pm Sun winter; 🚌Ponte Milvio) is a classic case in point: a neighbourhood meeting point that buzzes on warm summer nights. Another prime example is **Lemoncocco** (Map p348; ☎335 1618376; Piazza Buenos Aires; ⏲10am-2am; 🚌Viale Regina Margherita), a local institution famous for its trademark lemon-and-coconut drink.

PRO LOCO PINCIANO LAZIO €€

Map p348 (☎06 841 41 36; www.prolocopinciano.it; Via Bergamo 18; meals €20-35; ⏲12.30-3pm & 7.30-11.30pm, closed lunch Tue; 🚌Via Salaria) Like a number of Rome's newer, popular eateries, Pro Loco Pinciano is something of a culinary all-rounder. It serves regional cured meats and cheeses from a well-furnished deli counter, delicious wood-fired pizzas, and a seasonal menu of salads, pastas and mains. All this in a good-looking interior of exposed-brick walls and trendy mismatched furniture.

Nomentano

PIZZERIA ITALIA DAL 1987 PIZZA €

Map p348 (☎06 4424 9771; Corso d'Italia 103; slice from €2; ⏲9am-9pm Mon-Sat; 🚌Porta Pia) With rustic, delicious, no-nonsense pizza by the slice (changing daily), this hole-in-the-wall shop is always packed at lunch with local workers noshing.

Parioli

★**METAMORFOSI** RISTORANTE €€€

Map p348 (☎06 807 68 39; www.metamorfosiroma.it; Via Giovanni Antonelli 30; tasting menus €100-130; ⏲12.30-2.30pm & 8-10.30pm, closed Sat lunch & Sun; 🚌Via Giovanni Antonelli) This Michelin-starred Parioli restaurant provides one of Rome's best dining experiences, offering international fusion cuisine and a contemporary look that marries linear clean-cut lines with warm earthy tones. Chef Roy Caceres' cooking is eclectic, often featuring playful updates of traditional Roman dishes, such as his signature Uovo 65° carbonara antipasto, a deconstruction of Rome's classic pasta dish.

MOLTO RISTORANTE €€€

Map p348 (☎06 808 29 00; www.moltoitaliano.it; Viale dei Parioli 122; meals €50-60; ⏲12.30-3pm & 7.30-11pm, to 11.30pm Fri & Sat; 🚌Viale Parioli) Fashionable and quietly chic, Molto is a Parioli favourite. The discreet entrance gives onto an elegant, modern interior and open-air terrace, while the menu offers everything from cured meat and cheese starters to traditional Roman pastas and succulent roast meats. Saturday features a burger menu, and there's brunch on Sunday (€40).

DRINKING & NIGHTLIFE

Many of the galleries and museums in this area have good in-house cafes. Otherwise, the drinking scene is centred on Piazzale di Ponte Milvio, a popular hang-out for north Rome's young well-to-do crowd. Partygoers should head out to the suburbs where there are a couple of top venues, both hosting live gigs and thumping club nights.

ENOTECA MOSTÓ WINE BAR

Map p348 (☎392 2579616; www.facebook.com/enotecamosto; Viale Pinturicchio 32; ⏲6.30pm-2am Tue-Sun; 🚌Pinturicchio) Modern and busy, Enoteca Mostó is a popular local watering hole and eatery. Cram into the small space for top-shelf wines, knowledgeable staff and small tapas-style plates.

MOMART CAFE

(☎06 8639 1656; www.momartcafe.it; Viale XXI Aprile 19; ⏲noon-2am Mon-Thu, to 3am Fri, 11.30am-3am Sat, to 2am Sun; 🚌Viale XXI Aprile) A modish restaurant-cafe in the university district near Via Nomentana, Momart serves one of Rome's most bountiful spreads of *apericena* (an informal evening meal involving *aperitivi* and tapas-style food). A mixed crowd of students and local professionals flocks here to fill up on the ample buffet (€12) and kick back over cocktails on the pavement terrace.

LANIFICIO 159 CLUB

(☎06 4178 0081; www.lanificio.com; Via Pietralata 159a; ⊙club nights 11pm-4.30am Fri & Sat Sep-May; 🚌Via Pietralata) Occupying an ex-wool factory in Rome's northeastern suburbs, this cool underground venue hosts live gigs and hot clubbing action, led by top Roman crews and international DJs. The club is part of a larger complex that stages more reserved events such as Sunday markets, exhibitions and *aperitivi.*

BRANCALEONE CLUB

(☎339 5074012; www.facebook.com/BrancaleoneRoma; Via Levanna 11; ⊙typically 10pm-late; 🚌Via Nomentana) Starting life as an anti-establishment *centro sociale,* Brancaleone serves up popular club nights with top DJs and live gigs. Rap, hip-hop, drum and bass, reggae and techno feature heavily, and there's a regular calendar of events and one-off evenings. The club is in the outlying Montesacro district.

ENTERTAINMENT

★AUDITORIUM PARCO DELLA MUSICA CONCERT VENUE

Map p348 (☎06 8024 1281; www.auditorium.com; Viale Pietro de Coubertin; 🚋Viale Tiziano) The hub of Rome's thriving cultural scene, the Auditorium is the capital's premier concert venue. Its three concert halls offer superb acoustics and, together with a 3000-seat open-air arena, stage everything from classical music concerts to jazz gigs, public lectures and film screenings.

The Auditorium is also home to Rome's Orchestra dell'Accademia Nazionale di Santa Cecilia (www.santacecilia.it).

STADIO OLIMPICO STADIUM

Map p348 (☎06 3685 7563; Viale dei Gladiatori 2, Foro Italico; 🚌Lungotevere Maresciallo Cadorna) A trip to Rome's impressive Stadio Olimpico offers an unforgettable insight into Rome's sporting heart. Throughout the football season (late August to May) there's a game on most Sundays featuring one of the city's two Serie A teams (Roma or Lazio), and during the Six Nations rugby tournament (February to March) it hosts Italy's home games.

SILVANO TOTI GLOBE THEATRE THEATRE

Map p348 (☎06 06 08; www.globetheatreroma.com; Largo Aqua Felix, Villa Borghese; tickets €10-30; 🚌Piazzale Brasile) Like London's Globe Theatre but with better weather, Villa Borghese's open-air Elizabethan theatre serves up Shakespeare (performances mostly in Italian) from late June through to early October.

TEATRO OLIMPICO THEATRE

Map p348 (☎06 326 59 91; www.teatroolimpico.it; Piazza Gentile da Fabriano 17; 🚌Piazza Mancini, 🚋Piazza Mancini) The Teatro Olimpico hosts a varied program of opera, dance, solo shows, musicals and comedies, as well as classical-music concerts by the Accademia Filarmonica Romana.

SHOPPING

BIALETTI HOMEWARES

Map p348 (☎06 8778 4222; www.bialettistore.it; Via Salaria 52; ⊙10am-8pm Mon-Sat, 10am-1.30pm & 4-8pm Sun; 🚌Via Salaria) In 1933 Alfonso Bialetti revolutionised domestic coffee-making by creating his classic *moka caffettiera.* His design has by now become a household staple, as ubiquitous in Italian kitchens as kettles in British homes. Here at this gleaming shop you'll find a full range, as well as all manner of cool kitchenware.

ENOTECA BULZONI WINE

Map p348 (☎06 807 04 94; www.enotecabulzoni.it; Viale dei Parioli 36; ⊙8.30am-2pm & 4.30-8.30pm Mon-Sat; 🚌Viale Parioli) This historic *enoteca* has been supplying Parioli's wine buffs since 1929. It has a formidable collection of Italian regional wines, as well as European and New World labels, and a carefully curated selection of champagne, liqueur, craft beer, olive oil and gourmet delicacies.

1

Roman Catacombs

Ancient Roman law forbade burying the dead within the city walls, for reasons of hygiene. Rome's persecuted Jewish and Christian communities didn't have their own cemeteries, so in the 2nd century CE they built an extensive network of subterranean burial grounds outside the city.

Construction

The tombs were dug by specialised gravediggers, who tunnelled out the galleries. Bodies were wrapped in simple shrouds and then either placed individually in carved-out niches, called *loculi*, or in larger family tombs. Many tombs were marked with elaborate decorations, from frescoes to stucco work, which remain remarkably well preserved. A great many tombs discovered here bear touching inscriptions, such as: 'Apuleia Crysopolis, who lived for 7 years, 2 months; (her) parents made (this) for their dearest daughter'.

Symbolism

An almost secretive language of symbols evolved to represent elements of the Christian faith. Since many early Christians could not read and write, these symbols served as both a secret code and a means to communicate among the illiterate. The most common of the symbols included the fish, the Greek word for which is *ichthys*, standing for Iesous Christos Theou Yios Soter (Jesus Christ, son of God, Saviour). The anchor, which also appears regularly, symbolises the belief in Christ as a safe haven, a comforting thought in times of persecution. It's thought, too, that this was again an example of Greek wordplay:

1. Catacombe di Priscilla (p209)
2. Catacombe di Santa Domitilla (p220)
3. Fresco, Catacombe di San Callisto (p220)

ankura resembling *en kuriol*, which means 'in the Lord'. A dove with an olive branch in the beak is a reference to the biblical dove, meaning salvation.

Abandonment

The catacombs began to be abandoned as early as 313, when Constantine issued the Edict of Milan for religious tolerance and Christians were thus able to bury their dead in churchyards.

In about 800, after frequent incursions by invaders, the bodies of the martyrs and first popes were transferred to the basilicas inside the city walls for safekeeping. The catacombs were abandoned and by the Middle Ages many had been forgotten.

Since the 19th century, more than 30 catacombs have been uncovered in the area. The warren of tunnels are fascinating to explore, and sections of four sets of catacombs are accessible via guided tour. Unless you're passionate about catacombs, visiting one set will be sufficient.

TOP 5 CATACOMB READS

- ➡ *The Roman Catacombs*, by James Spencer Northcote (1859)
- ➡ *Tombs and Catacombs of the Appian Way: History of Cremation*, by Olinto L Spadoni (1892)
- ➡ *Valeria, the Martyr of the Catacombs*, by WH Withrow (1892)
- ➡ *Christian Rome: Past and Present: Early Christian Rome Catacombs and Basilicas*, by Philippe Pergola (2002)
- ➡ *The Churches and Catacombs of Early Christian Rome: A Comprehensive Guide*, by Matilda Webb (2001)

Southern Rome

VIA APPIA ANTICA | OSTIENSE & SAN PAOLO | GARBATELLA | VIA APPIA ANTICA & AROUND | OSTIENSE & SAN PAOLO

Neighbourhood Top Five

❶ **Via Appia Antica** (p218) Tracing the route of a thousand ancient Roman footsteps by bike, on foot or both along this urban 'countryside' trail, sprinkled with ancient Roman ruins.

❷ **Catacombe di San Sebastiano** (p219) Exploring the ancient Christian burial catacombs in the depths of subterranean Rome.

❸ **Street art** (p225) Checking out the vibrant, edgy gallery of open-air art in ex-industrial and alternative Ostiense.

❹ **Museo Capitoline Centrale Montemartini** (p223) Wandering around the ingenious location for the overflow from the Capitoline Museums – a former power station.

❺ **Basilica de San Paolo Fuori le Mura** (p223) Feeling dwarfed by the majesty of the second-largest church in Rome after St Peter's.

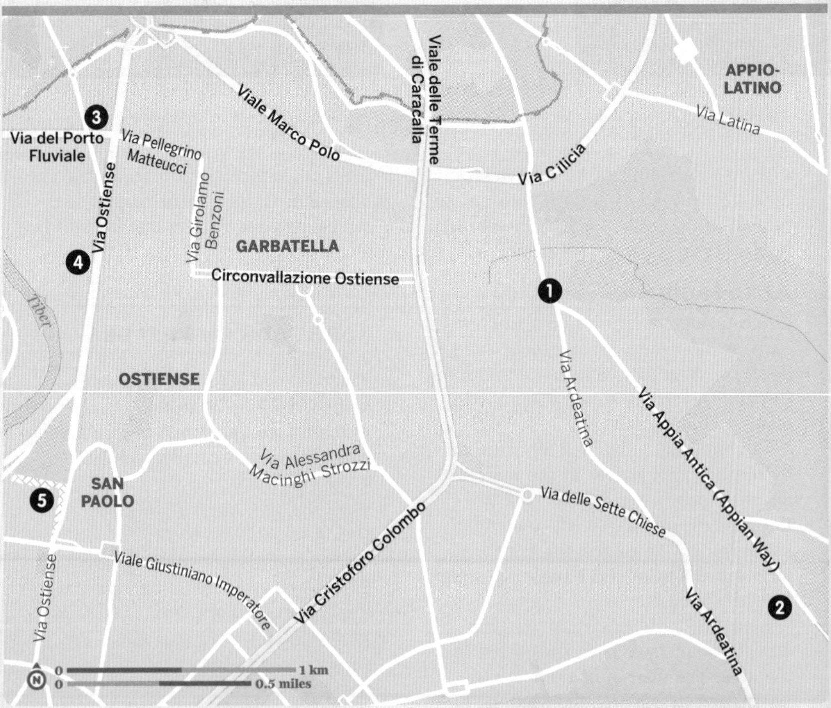

For more detail of this area see Map p350

Explore Southern Rome

Southern Rome is a sprawling neighbourhood that comprises four distinct areas of interest to tourists: the Via Appia Antica (p218), famous for its Roman ruins, catacombs and bucolic country air; post-industrial Ostiense with its rainbow of street art (p225) and cutting-edge nightlife; picturesque Garbatella (p223); and EUR (p226), Mussolini's futuristic building development spearheaded today by Italian fashion house Fendi, which has its global headquarters here. It's all quite spread out, but public transport connections are decent.

Allow at least a day for the Appian Way, best kept for when you have the urge to 'get out of town'. Fields surround the rickety, stone-paved road – one of the world's oldest roads and a much-prized Roman address. The main sights can be done on foot, but to really cover some old paving stones on the road, originally 212km long and requiring a journey of five days when the Romans built it in 312 BCE, rent a bicycle.

To the west, Via Ostiense presents a very different picture. Explore by day if you are here to track down street art, admire superb classical statuary in a defunct power station at the Museo Capitoline Centrale Montemartini (p223), or visit the gargantuan Basilica di San Paolo Fuori le Mura (p223), one step removed from Ostiense's gritty soul. Otherwise, come after dark when tagged, disused factories and warehouses buzz with some of the best clubs in town.

Local Life

➡ **Clubbing** Some of the coolest clubs on Roman earth – Vinile (p228), Neo Club (p228), Circolo Degli Illuminati (p228), Goa (p228) – are clustered on and around Via Libetta, at the southern end of Via Ostiense.

➡ **Weekend brunch** Roman families pile into Porto Fluviale (p227) for Sunday brunch, while cent-saving students jam Vinile (p228) to the rafters.

➡ **Cycling** Escape from the frenetic city centre along the evocative Via Appia Antica (p218).

➡ **Food, glorious food** There is no finer spot to shop for, and taste, the very best of Italian food products than at Eataly (p224).

Getting There & Away

➡ **Metro** Metro line B runs to Piramide, Garbatella, Basilica San Paolo, EUR Palasport and EUR Fermi.

➡ **Bus** There are bus connections to Porta San Sebastiano (77, 118 and 218), Via Ostiense (23 and 769) and Via Appia Antica (118 and 660).

Lonely Planet's Top Tip

Originally paved with huge *basoli* (polygonal cobbles of basalt rock) and wide enough for two carriages to pass, the Appian Way is today something of a hair-raising racetrack for loony Roman drivers out for a Sunday spin – visit on a weekday when the road is quieter.

Best Places to Eat

➡ Trattoria Pennestri (p227)
➡ Doppiozeroo (p224)
➡ Al Ristoro degli Angeli (p227)
➡ Verde Pistacchio (p225)
➡ Pizzeria Ostiense (p225)

For reviews, see p224.➡

Best Places to Drink

➡ Circolo Degli Illuminati (p228)
➡ Goa (p228)
➡ Vinile (p228)
➡ Neo Club (p228)

For reviews, see p228.➡

Best Roman Ruins

➡ Villa dei Quintili (p221)
➡ Circo di Massenzio (p218)
➡ Villa di Massenzio (p218)
➡ Mausoleo di Cecilia Metella (p218)

For reviews, see p223.➡

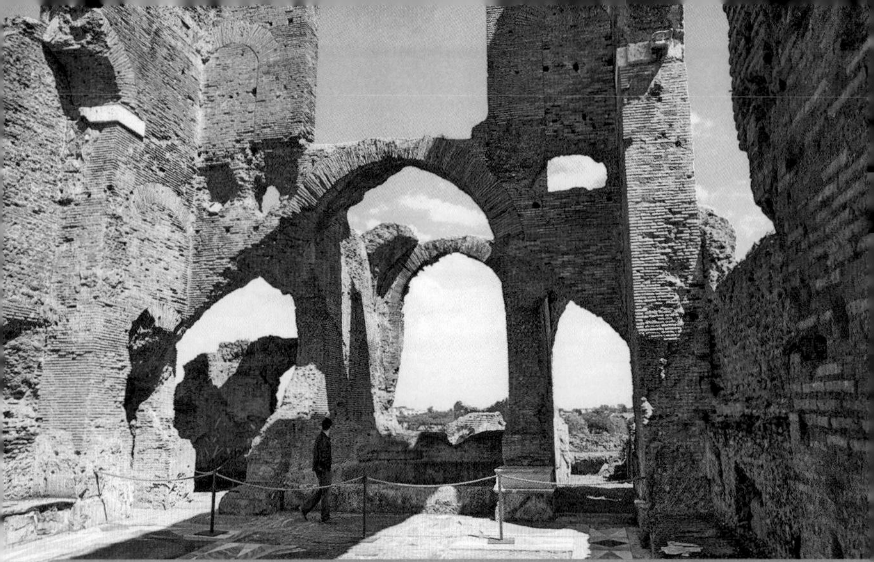

FRANCISCO JAVIER DIAZ / SHUTTERSTOCK ©

TOP EXPERIENCE
STROLL THE VIA APPIA ANTICA

The Appian Way was known to the Romans as Regina Viarum (Queen of Roads). Named after Appius Claudius Caecus, who laid the first 90km section in 312 BCE, it was extended in 190 BCE to reach Brindisi on the Adriatic coast. Today it's one of Rome's most exclusive addresses, a beautiful cobbled thoroughfare flanked by fields, Roman ruins and towering pines.

Northern Section

Porta San Sebastiano & Museo delle Mura

Marking the start of Via Appia Antica, the 5th-century **Porta San Sebastiano** (Map p350; 06 06 08; www.museodellemuraroma.it; Via di Porta San Sebastiano 18; museum 9am-2pm Tue-Sun; Porta San Sebastiano) FREE is the largest of the gates in the Aurelian Wall. During WWII the Fascist Party secretary Ettore Muti lived here; today it houses the modest **Museo delle Mure**, which offers the chance to walk along the top of the walls for around 50m as well as displaying the history of the city's fortifications.

Mausoleo di Cecilia Metella

Resembling a huge can of tomatoes, this **mausoleum** (06 3996 7700; www.coopculture.it; Via Appia Antica 161; adult/reduced €5/2.50, incl Villa dei Quintili & Complesso di Santa Maria Nova €10; 9am-1pm & 2-5pm Mon-Fri, 9am-2pm Sat) from the 1st century BCE encloses a now roofless burial chamber. In the 14th century it was converted into a fort by the politically connected Caetani family (they were related to Pope Boniface VIII) and used to collect tolls from passing traffic.

Villa di Massenzio

Maxentius' huge 4th-century palace complex features the **Circo di Massenzio** (06 06 08; Via Appia Antica 153; 10am-4pm Tue-Sun; Via Appia Antica) FREE, Rome's best-preserved

TOP TIPS

- The further south you go, the quieter and more evocative the Appian Way becomes.
- Visits to the catacombs are by guided tour only. Wear sensible shoes and dress warmly.

PRACTICALITIES

- Appian Way
- Map p350, E3
- www.parcoappiaantica.it
- main site 24hr, individual sites hours vary
- Via Appia Antica

ancient racetrack – you can still make out the starting stalls used for chariot races. The 10,000-seat arena was built by Maxentius around 309, but he died before ever seeing a race here. Above the arena are the ruins of Maxentius' imperial residence. Near the racetrack, the **Mausoleo di Romolo** (Tombo di Romolo) FREE was built by Maxentius for his 17-year-old son Romulus.

Overlooking the vast site, the namesake **Villa di Massenzio** (www.villadimassenzio.it) FREE itself is closed for long-term archaeological investigations.

Basilica & Catacombe di San Sebastiano

One of the two main Appian Way catacombs, this complex contains frescoes, stucco work, epigraphs and several immaculately preserved mausoleums. The catacombs extend for more than 12km and once harboured more than 65,000 tombs.

The 4th-century **basilica** (Map p350; ☎06 780 88 47; www.sansebastianofuorilemura.org; Via Appia Antica 136; ⏰8.30am-6.30pm) that was built here by the emperor Constantine was mostly destroyed by Saracen raids in the 9th century; the church you see today dates mainly from the 17th century. It is dedicated to St Sebastian, who was martyred and buried here in the late 3rd century. In 826 his body was transferred to St Peter's for safekeeping, but he was re-interred here in the 12th century. In the **Capella delle Reliquie** you'll find one of the arrows used to kill him and the column to which he was tied. On the other side of the church is a marble slab with Jesus' footprints.

A warren of tunnels that lie beneath the church and beyond, the **Catacombe di San Sebastiano** (☎06 785 03 50; www.catacombe.org; adult/reduced €8/5; ⏰10am-5pm Mon-Sat Jan-Nov) were the first catacombs to be so called, the name deriving from the Greek *kata* (near) and *kymbas* (cavity), because they were located near a cave. During the persecution of Christians by the emperor Vespasian from 258 CE, some believe that the catacombs were used as a safe haven for the remains of St Peter and St Paul.

Within the catacombs there are three beautifully preserved and decorated **mausoleums**. Each of the monumental facades features a door, above which are inscribed symbols and the names of the owners.

Mausoleo delle Fosse Ardeatine

This **memorial** (Map p350; ☎06 513 67 42; www.mausoleofosseardeatine.it; Via Ardeatina 174; ⏰8.15am-3.30pm Mon-Fri, to 4.30pm Sat & Sun; 🚌Fosse Ardeatine) FREE is about 500m southeast of the Catacombe di Santa Domitilla and is a 10-minute walk west of the main Appian Way sights. It's dedicated to the 335 Romans shot by the Germans on 24 March 1944 as a reprisal for a partisan attack. There is a memorial, a tomb, sculptures, the cave where the shootings occurred and a museum.

TOURIST INFORMATION

Service Center Appia Antica (Map p350; ☎06 513 53 16; www.parcoappiaantica.it; Via Appia Antica 58-60; ⏰9.30am-1pm & 2pm-dusk Mon-Fri, 9.30am-sunset Sat & Sun; 🚌Via Appia Antica) A good source of information on the Appian Way and the Appia Antica Regional Park, this office at the northern start of the road sells useful maps (€1.50) and organises guided tours by bike, on foot or by electric golf cart. It also **rents** (per hr/day bike €3/15, per hr/day e-bike €6/30) bicycles and e-bikes for adults and children and has toddler bike seats.

The Appia Antica, peaceful today, resounds with history: it's where Spartacus and 6000 of his slave rebels were crucified in 71 BCE, and around it lie 300km of underground tunnels carved out of soft tufa rock, used as burial chambers by the early Christians. Corpses were wrapped in simple white sheets and usually placed in rectangular niches carved into the walls.

ACCESSING VIA APPIA ANTICA

There are several ways to access the Appian Way.

➡ **Northern Start** Take metro line B to Circo Massimo then bus 118 to Via Appia Antica where you can start your walk south. This is mainly an uphill walk.

➡ **Midway** Take metro line A to the Colli-Albani metro stop, then bus 660 to the end of the line at Appia Antica Caffè. From here you can walk north along the Appian Way, passing the core sights and enjoying glimpses of Rome ahead as you walk gently downhill. Also, you can rent a bike at the cafe and head south to explore the much-less-visited section of the Appian Way.

➡ **Villa dei Quintili** An ambitious walk that covers almost everything of note on the Appian Way. From the metro line A station Arco di Travertino, take bus 663 or 664 to Via Appia Nuova and the Villa dei Quintili stop. Use the east entrance to the vast villa site, then exit out the main entrance and head north on a beautiful and lonely stretch of the Via Appia Antica. After a total of about 7km, you reach the northern start point.

Note that Rome transit maps show bus 789 crossing Via Appia Antica at the Villa dei Quintili. Don't take this bus as there's no Appian Way stop; rather, the closest stop is 1km away along an extremely hazardous road completely unsuitable for walkers.

Catacombe di Santa Domitilla

About 500m west of the Catacombe di San Callisto and well away from the main swath of Via Appia Antica sights, these **catacombs** (Map p350; ☎06 511 03 42; www.domitilla.info; Via delle Sette Chiese 282; adult/reduced €8/5; ⏲9am-noon & 2-5pm Wed-Mon mid-Jan–mid-Dec) feature the evocative underground **Chiesa di SS Nereus e Achilleus**, a 4th-century church dedicated to two Roman soldiers martyred by Diocletian.

On a tour, you'll see the church, some exquisite Christian wall art and just a fraction of the tunnels, which extend roughly 17km. The site is below what was the private burial ground of Flavia Domitilla, niece of the emperor Domitian and a member of the wealthy Flavian family.

Catacombe di San Callisto

The most-visited **catacombs** (☎06 513 01 51; www.catacombe.roma.it; Via Appia Antica 110-126; adult/reduced €8/5; ⏲9am-noon & 2-5pm Thu-Tue Mar-Jan) in Rome, these extend for more than 20km in a tangle of tunnels. Visits are only by tour, and you'll visit just a fraction of what lies below ground. Still, you will see a selection of tombs that includes 16 popes, scores of martyrs and thousands upon thousands of Christians.

There are staircases cut into the soft strata, and in addition to the lighted tunnels that you traverse, you'll see scores of tunnels curving off into the dark distances – if you weren't with a group, it would be very creepy. Guides offer up a wealth of information about early Christian life and point out the various tombs and decorations used for the more notable people buried here.

Tours last about 45 minutes and are offered in several languages, including English. They depart regularly. The site is on a pleasant access road that is a good alternative to a car-filled stretch of the Via Appia Antica.

Chiesa del Domine Quo Vadis

This otherwise small and unremarkable **church** (☎06 512 04 41; Via Appia Antica 51; ⏲8am-7.30pm summer, to 6.30pm winter) at the northern end of the Via Appia Antica marks the place where St Peter, fleeing Rome, met a vision of Jesus. When Peter asked, *'Domine, quo vadis?'* (Lord, where are you going?), Jesus replied, *'Venio Roman iterum crucifigi'* (I am coming to Rome to be crucified again). Reluctantly following his lead, Peter returned to the city, where he was arrested and executed.

Southern Section

Capo di Bove

This sight combines the remains of a **villa** (☎06 7839 2729; www.parcoarcheologicoappiaantica.it/luoghi/complesso-di-capo-di-bove; Via Appia Antica 222; ⏰9am-5pm winter, to 6.30pm summe) FREE, the highlights of which are the elaborate mosaics. At the rear of the sight, an office sells a good guide to the Appian Way. Nearby, there is a building with extensive displays showing the Appian Way over the past two centuries. As the modern world encroaches, efforts to preserve the road and its sights are detailed in fascinating displays and huge aerial photos.

Tombs & Monuments

Following the Via Appia Antica on the quiet section running south from the Capo di Bove, you will often encounter various Roman tombs and monuments along the side of the road. They range in size and condition. Most take some aspect of their design from the Greeks and some include small altars for offerings. The guide sold at the Capo di Bove has details on many of these stone constructions.

Villa dei Quintili

Sprawling across wide open meadows, this 2nd-century **villa** (pictured on p218; ☎06 3996 7700; www.coopculture.it; main entrance: Via Appia Antica 251, east entrance: Via Appia Nuova 1092; adult/reduced incl Mausoleo di Cecilia Metella valid for 2 days €5/2.50; ⏰9am-1hr before sunset Tue-Sun; 🚌Via Appia Nuova) is one of Rome's least-visited major sights. It was the lavish home of two consuls, the Quintili brothers, but its luxurious excess was their downfall: the emperor Commodus had them both killed and seized the villa for himself. The emperor expanded the complex and the remaining ruins retain their opulence. Don't miss the baths complex with a pool, *caldarium* (hot bath room) and *frigidarium* (cold bath room) and the small museum, which offers useful context.

Casal Rotondo

Over eight very historic kilometres from the start of the Appian Way, this **ruin** FREE was once a tomb dating to the 1st century BCE. In the eons since it has been a watchtower, farmhouse, stable and more. It's a moody mess today and for many it marks the end of their Appian Way trek by foot or bike.

GRAB A BITE

Take a coffee or beer break in the tree-shaded garden of Appia Antica Caffè (p228); it sells light snacks and prepares picnics too. Enjoy a garden lunch beneath orange trees at Il Giardino di Giulia e Fratelli (p224), almost opposite the Mausoleo di Cecilia Metella.

On the scenic stretch of the Via Appia Antica south of the Capo di Bove, you'll encounter many original stretches of the Appian Way. The large, weathered grey paving stones have remained in place for over 2000 years and show the passage of the centuries. Large parallel ruts suggest they were made by the wheels of countless chariots. Note that cyclists will find these sections very rough going. Use the parallel dirt horse tracks instead.

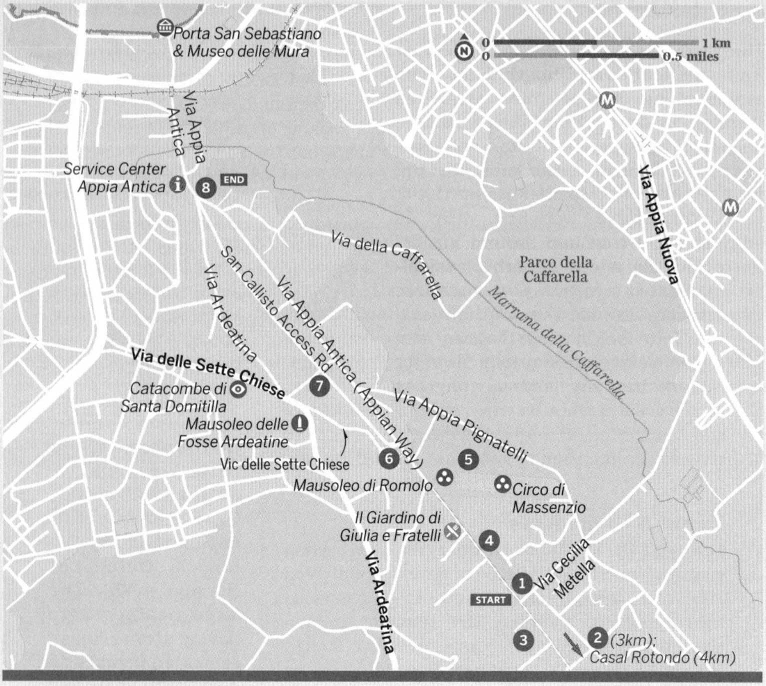

Walking Tour Via Appia Antica

LENGTH FOUR HOURS (SIX HOURS WITH OPTIONAL BIKE RIDE)

This walk covers the core of the Via Appia Antica and lets you enjoy glimpses of Rome luring you on as you walk north. It's also generally gently downhill. Start at the handy hub, 1 **Appia Antica Caffè**, accessed by taking metro line A to the Colli-Albani stop, then bus 660 to the end of the line.

Here you have the option of renting a bike and detouring south along a less-visited stretch of the Via Appia Antica before returning and beginning the walk north. On this southern section, you'll see dozens of ancient tombs lining the road, long stretches of original 2000-year-old cobblestones and the sensational 2 **Villa dei Quintili**.

Whether or not you do the bike detour, make your first walking stop the 3 **Capo di Bove**, a Roman villa with beautiful mosaics. Buy the excellent Appian Way guidebook and map in the office here.

Walk north, stopping at these unmissable sights: the 4 **Mausoleo di Cecilia Metella**, a cylindrical burial chamber with precious relics, and the 5 **Villa di Massenzio**, a vast site that includes the largest surviving Roman circus **Circo di Massenzio**.

Next up is the baroque, 6 **Basilica di San Sebastiano**, which has a Bernini bust and Christ's footprints. Down below are the labyrinthine **Catacombe di San Sebastiano** and its early Christian and pagan Roman burial sites.

Immediately north, you'll see a turn-off on the Via Appia Antica for the 7 **Catacombe di San Callisto**. This 1.5km access road is an excellent alternative to the parallel Via Appia Antica: it's quiet, shady and smooth with verdant views. The catacombs of San Sebastiano and San Callisto offer compelling but similar experiences; we recommend visiting one rather than both.

Continue north on the San Callisto access road, at the bottom you'll be at the cute little 8 **Chiesa del Domine Quo Vadis**. From here you can catch bus 118 or 218 back towards the heart of Rome.

SIGHTS

The key sights are split between four distinct neighbourhoods. The awe-inspiring Appian Way stretches through fields south of Rome and is peppered with ancient Roman ruins and subterranean catacombs. To the west, south from Stazione Roma-Ostia, is post-industrial Ostiense with its edgy street art on and around Via del Porto Fluviale and a superb classical-art museum in a former power station. Immediately east, at the southern end of Via Ostiense, are Garbatella and EUR. The latter, essentially Rome's business district with several congress and conference centres, is only really of interest to architecture enthusiasts.

Via Appia Antica

VIA APPIA ANTICA — HISTORIC SITE

See p218.

Ostiense & San Paolo

BASILICA DI SAN PAOLO FUORI LE MURA — BASILICA

Map p350 (Basilica of St Paul Outside the Walls; ☎06 6988 0803; www.basilicasanpaolo.org; Piazzale San Paolo 1; cloisters adult/reduced €4/3; ⏲7am-6.30pm; Ⓜ Basilica San Paolo) The largest church in Rome after St Peter's (and the world's third-largest), this vast basilica stands on the site where St Paul was buried after being decapitated in 67 CE. Built by Constantine in the 4th century, it was largely destroyed by fire in 1823 and much of what you see is a 19th-century reconstruction. The echoey results have a modern feel and draw large groups of pilgrims who are dwarfed by the huge interior.

However, many treasures survived, including the 5th-century **triumphal arch**, with its heavily restored mosaics, and the Gothic marble **tabernacle** over the high altar. This was designed around 1285 by Arnolfo di Cambio together with another artist, possibly Pietro Cavallini. To the right of the altar, the elaborate Romanesque Paschal candlestick was fashioned by Nicolò di Angelo and Pietro Vassalletto in the 12th century and features a grim cast of animal-headed creatures. The **cloisters** would be a wonderful lavender-scented refuge if they let you sit down (there are no benches or seats).

St Paul's tomb is in the nearby **confessio**, somewhat lost in the unfortunately weed-choked grounds.

Looking upwards, doom-mongers should check out the papal portraits beneath the nave windows. Every pope since St Peter is represented here, and legend has it that when there is no longer room for the next portrait, the world will fall. Note that there are only six blank spots left after Francis.

Also well worth a look is the polychromatic 13th-century Cosmati mosaic work that decorates the columns of the **cloisters** of the adjacent Benedictine abbey.

MUSEO CAPITOLINE CENTRALE MONTEMARTINI — MUSEUM

Map p350 (Museums at Centrale Montemartini; ☎06 06 08; www.centralemontemartini.org; off Via Ostiense 106; adult/reduced €7.50/6.50, incl Capitoline Museums €12.50/10.50, ticket valid 7 days; ⏲9am-7pm Tue-Sun; 🚌Via Ostiense) Housed in a former power station, this bold outpost of the Capitoline Museums (Musei Capitolini) juxtaposes classical sculpture against diesel engines and giant furnaces. The collection's highlights are in the Sala Caldaia, where ancient statuary strike poses around the giant furnace. Beautiful pieces include the *Fanciulla Seduta* (Seated Girl) and *Musa Polimnia* (Muse Polyhymnia), and there are also some exquisite Roman mosaics, depicting favourite subjects such as hunting scenes and foodstuffs.

Garbatella

QUARTIERE GARBATELLA — AREA

Map p350 (Ⓜ Garbatella) A favourite location for films and TV, Quartiere Garbatella was originally conceived as a workers' residential quarter, but in the 1920s the Fascists hijacked the project and used the area to house people who'd been displaced by construction work in the city. Many people were moved into *alberghi suburbani* (suburban hotels), big housing blocks designed by Innocenzo Sabbatini, the leading light of the Roman School of architecture; the most famous, **Albergo Rosso** (Map p350; Piazza Michele da Carbonara; Ⓜ Garbatella), is typical of the rather brutish style. Nearby is the other trademark building, Teatro Palladium (p229).

EATING

The gentrifying southern areas of Ostiense and Garbatella feature some excellent neighbourhood restaurants, including a lovely vegetarian choice near Basilica di San Paolo Fuori le Mura and every type of cuisine under the Italian sun in Ostiense's Eataly complex. Via Appia Antica's rural setting includes some traditional trattorias with flowery summertime gardens, or stock up on picnic supplies in central Rome before hitting the ancient southern trail.

Via Appia Antica

IL GIARDINO DI GIULIA E FRATELLI — ITALIAN €

Map p350 (☎347 5092772; Via Appia Antica 176; meals €10-30; ⏲noon-3pm & 7-11.30pm Tue-Sat; 👪; 🚌Via Appia Antica) Just north of the tomb of Cecilia Metella, this garden restaurant is a bucolic delight. Book one of the well-spaced tables beneath the orange trees and feast on standard Italian fare or *panini* (sandwiches) amid flowery green views. On Sundays, locals in their finery gather for family lunches. There's even a playground.

QUI NUN SE MORE MAI — LAZIO €€

Map p350 (☎06 780 39 22; www.facebook.com/qvinunsemoremai; Via Appia Antica 198; meals €35-45; ⏲noon-3pm & 7.30-11.45pm Tue-Sat, 12.30-3pm Sun; 🚌Via Appia Antica) This small, charismatic restaurant in an old stone house has an open fire for grilling, plus a small terrace. The menu offers Roman classics such as pasta *amatriciana* (pig's cheek with onions and tomato), carbonara, *alla gricia* (cured pork and *pecorino* cheese) and *cacio e pepe* (cheese and pepper) – just the thing to set you up for the road ahead.

TRATTORIA PRISCILLA — TRATTORIA €€

Map p350 (☎06 513 63 79; www.trattoriapriscilla.it; Via Appia Antica 68; meals €25-30; ⏲noon-3pm daily, 7-11.30pm Mon-Sat; 🚌Via Appia Antica) Set in a 16th-century former stable, this family-run trattoria has been feeding hungry travellers along the Appian Way for more than a hundred years, serving up traditional *cucina Romana* – gutsy platefuls of spaghetti laced in carbonara, *amatriciana* and *cacio e pepe*. The tiramisu wins plaudits. The dining room is all simplicity.

RISTORANTE CECILIA METELLA — ITALIAN €€

Map p350 (☎06 512 67 69; www.ceciliametella.it; Via Appia Antica 125; menu €40, meals €35-45; ⏲12.30-3pm & 7.30-10pm Tue-Sun; 🚌Via Appia Antica) Near the catacombs of San Callisto, Cecilia Metella has romantic outside seating, set on a low hill under a vine canopy and with glimpses of the jewel-green countryside. The interior has a 1960s wedding-function vibe, but the food is reasonable – the grilled meats are recommended. Set menus include one with seafood.

L'ARCHEOLOGIA RISTORANTE — ITALIAN €€€

Map p350 (☎06 788 04 94; www.larcheologia.it; Via Appia Antica 139; meals €50; ⏲12.30-3pm & 8-11pm; 📶; 🚌Via Appia Antica) At home in a rambling old horse exchange on the Appian Way, this 19th-century inn exudes vintage charm. Dining is elegant, with white-tablecloth-covered tables beneath age-old beams or in front of the fireplace. In summer, dining is al fresco and fragrant due to the blooms of a magnificent 300-year-old wisteria. Cuisine is traditional Roman and the wine list exemplary. Reservations recommended.

Ostiense & San Paolo

★DOPPIOZEROO — ITALIAN €

Map p350 (☎06 5730 1961; www.doppiozeroo.com; Via Ostiense 68; meals €12-35; ⏲7am-2am; 🚌Via Ostiense, Ⓜ Piramide) This easy-going bar was once a bakery, hence the name ('double zero' is a type of flour). But today the sleek, modern interior attracts hungry, trendy Romans who pile in here for its cheap, canteen-style lunches, pizza slices, famously lavish *aperitivi* (pre-dinner drinks and snacks; 6pm to 9pm) and abundant weekend brunch (12.30pm to 3.30pm). It's all wine bar after 9pm. There are pavement tables.

EATALY — ITALIAN €

Map p350 (☎06 9027 9201; www.eataly.net; Piazzale XII Ottobre 1492; meals €10-50; ⏲shops 9am-midnight, restaurants typically noon-3.30pm & 7-11pm; 📶; Ⓜ Piramide, 🚆Ostiense) Be prepared for some serious taste-bud titillation in this flash food emporium of gargantuan proportions built in the former terminal for airport buses. Four shop floors showcase every conceivable Italian food product (dried and fresh), while multiple themed food stalls and restaurants offer plenty of opportunity to taste or feast on Italian cuisine.

STREET ART IN THE SUBURBS

Street art in Rome is edgy, exciting, progressive and a fabulous excuse to delve into the city's gritty southern suburbs when you need a break from Ancient Rome's tourist crowds and top-billing sights. Tourist kiosks have maps marked up with key street-art works, and 15 street-art itineraries can be found under 'Itineraries' at the official tourism website, www.turismoroma.it.

With over 30 works, ex-industrial and alternative Ostiense is one of the best parts of Rome in which to lap up the outdoor gallery of colourful wall murals. Note, however, that these works are ephemeral and many past masterpieces have faded away or been destroyed by development.

Highlights include the fading murals at **Caserma dell'Aeronautica** (Map p350; Via del Porto Fluviale; MPiramide), a former military warehouse where Bolognese artist **Blu** (www.blublu.org) painted a rainbow of sinister faces across the entire building in 2014. He transformed the 48 arched windows into eyes, apparently to represent the evils of homelessness on a building that has been a long-term squat. Walk around the side of the building to admire a fantastical mural of a boat topped by cranes and robots.

The signature stencil art of well-known Italian street artists **Sten & Lex** (http://stenlex.com) is well-represented in Ostiense with a B&W wall mural of an anonymous student at Via delle Conce 14 (neighbouring a menacing bald gangster spray-painted by French artist **MTO**, guarding the entrance to the now-closed Rising Love nightclub next door at No 12) and the giant **Peassagio Urbano XVIII** (2016) emblazoning the pedestrian entrance to Stazione Roma-Ostiense next to Eataly on Piazzale XII Ottobre. Nearby, on Via dei Magazzini Generali, a line-up of larger-than-life portraits by Sten & Lex provide an admiring audience for the iconic *Wall of Fame* by Rome's very own **JBRock** (www.jbrock.it).

Two alternative galleries give Rome's street-art scene instant street cred and bags of buzz. East of the Appian Way, in the offbeat district of Quadraro, **MURo** (Museo di Urban Art di Roma; www.muromuseum.blogspot.it; Via dei Lentuli, Quadraro; walking/bicycle tour €10/20; MPorta Furba Quadraro) runs highly recommended guided tours – on foot or by bicycle – of the wealth of murals, many by big-name international artists, decorating its streets. In 2017 the ruins of 19th-century soap factory Mira Lanza (1899) in Ostiense opened its doors as a gallery, the **Ex Mira Lanza Museum** (Map p350; 351 0317563; www.999contemporary.com/exmiralanza; Via Amedeo Avogadro; 24hr; MStazione Trastevere) FREE. This public-art project invited French globe-painter **Seth** (www.seth.fr) to spruce up the site with a series of large-scale art installations and murals. Free guided tours with museum curator Stefan Antonelli can be reserved in advance. See the website for detailed access information to the site.

Graze on Italian street food at Scottadito, gorge yourself on chocolate at La Cioccolateria Venchi and indulge in the wood-fired flavours of Tuscany at Il Bosco Umbro. Sample Italian craft beers on tap in La Birreria (Beer Hall) or different coffee beans in the cafe. There are also cooking classes, demonstrations and wine tastings too.

VERDE PISTACCHIO VEGETARIAN, VEGAN €

Map p350 (06 4547 5965; www.facebook.com/verdepistacchioroma; Via Ostiense 181; meals €12-25; 11am-4pm & 6pm-midnight Mon-Thu, 11am-4pm & 6pm-2am Fri, 5.30pm-2am Sat & Sun; ; Via Ostiense, MGarbatella) Camilla, Raffaele and Francesco are the friends behind Green Pistachio, a stylish bistro-cafe with a minimalist, vintage interior and pavement tables among a little strip of good eateries and cafes. The kitchen cooks up fantastic vegetarian and vegan cuisine, and the lunchtime deal is a steal. Lunch here before or after visiting Rome's second-largest church just over the road.

PIZZERIA OSTIENSE PIZZA €

Map p350 (06 5730 5081; www.pizzeriaostiense.it; Via Ostiense 56; meals from €10; 6.30pm-1am, closed Tue winter; Via Ostiense, MPiramide) Run by folks formerly of the much-lauded classic Roman pizzeria Remo in Testaccio, Pizzeria Ostiense offers

SOUTHERN ROME EATING

WORTH A DETOUR

ROMAN UNIVERSAL EXHIBITION (EUR) DISTRICT

One of the few planned developments in Rome's history, **EUR** (MEUR Palasport) was built for an international exhibition in 1942. There are a few museums here, but the area's interest lies in its spread of rationalist architecture, beautifully expressed in a number of distinctive *palazzi*, including the iconic **Palazzo della Civiltà Italiana** (Palace of Italian Civilisation; 06 3345 0970; www.fendi.com; Quadrato della Concordia; depends on exhibition; MEUR Magliana) FREE. Other monumentalist architecture includes the **Chiesa Santi Pietro e Paolo** (www.santipietroepaoloroma.it; Piazzale dei Santi Pietro e Paolo; 6.30am-noon & 4-7pm Mon-Sat, 7.30am-1pm & 4-8pm Sun; MEUR Palasport), the **Palazzo dello Sport** (Palalottomatica; 06 54 09 01; www.palazzodellosportroma.it; Piazzale dello Sport 1; MEUR Palasport) and **Palazzo dei Congressi** (Piazza JF Kennedy 1; MEUR Fermi).

Massimiliano and Doriana Fuksas' cutting-edge 2016 **Roma Convention Centre** (06 5451 3710; www.romaconventiongroup.it; Viale Asia, entrance cnr Via Cristoforo Colombo; MEUR Fermi) – the largest new building to open in Rome in half a century – is the most dramatic piece of contemporary architecture. The striking building comprises a transparent, glass-and-steel box called 'Le Theca' (The Shrine), inside of which hangs organically shaped *Nuvola* (Cloud).

Rome's grand new aquarium **Sea Life Roma** (045 644 97 77; www.visitsealife.com; Piazza Umberto Elia Terracini) has been under construction for a good chunk of the 21st century and will contain more than 5000 sea creatures, 30 tanks with almost 3.8 million litres of water and a 360-degree glass tunnel for viewing sharks and stingrays.

EUR's best option for a meal, a snack or a cocktail is the large, bustling **Caffè Palombini** (06 591 17 00; www.palombini.com; Piazzale Konrad Adenauer 12; meals €10-20; 7am-10pm Sun-Thu, 7am-1am Fri & Sat). For a sweet treat, grab a cone or dish of impossibly creamy gelato at the legendary **Giolitti** (06 592 45 07; https://giolittieur.it; Viale Oceania 90; gelato from €2; 7am-midnight;).

Also in EUR is Rome's largest public swimming pool, **Piscina delle Rose** (06 5422 0333; www.piscinadellerose.it; Viale America 20; adult/reduced €16/10, 90min pass Mon-Fri €10, under 10yr free; 9am-9pm Mon-Fri, to 7pm Sat & Sun summer; MEUR Palasport). It gets crowded, so arrive early to grab a deck chair.

Finally, pedestrians take note: cars are king and queen in the EUR. You won't find many walkers about.

similarly fab paper-thin, crispy bases with delicious fresh toppings and scrumptious *fritti* (fried zucchini flowers) in unfussy surroundings. There's an upbeat vibe.

ANDREOTTI PASTRIES €

Map p350 (06 575 07 73; www.andreottiroma.it; Via Ostiense 54; treats from €1.50; 7.30am-10pm; ; Via Ostiense, MPiramide) Try not to drool on the cases full of luscious pastry and gelato displays crafted at this 1934 *pasticceria* (pastry shop). Treats range from buttery *crostate* (tarts) to piles of golden *sfogliatelle romane* (ricotta-filled pastries). Hanging out with a coffee on the sunny pavement terrace is a warm-weather delight. Andreotti cooks up simple meals; pasta dishes ring in at around €6.

Film director and Ostiense local Ferzan Ozpetek (*Loose Cannons/Mine Vaganti;* 2010) is such a fan of the pastries that he's been known to cast them in his films.

ANGELINA ITALIAN €

Map p350 (06 4368 8415; www.ristoranteangelina.com; Via Porto Fluviale 5; meals €15-30; 8am-2am; MPiramide) This relaxed bar-lounge-bistro-cafe manages to be almost all things to all people. It has a country-house feel and serves comfort food from a bit after dawn until well past midnight. There are baked goods in the morning, followed by Italian dishes hot and cold. At any time you can enjoy a range of beers, wines and cocktails. Who said Ostiense was gritty?

GELATERIA ROMANA GELATO €

Map p350 (06 5730 2253; www.gelateriaromana.com; Via Ostiense 48; 3-scoop cone €2.70; noon-midnight Mon-Fri, to 1am Sat; MPiramide) This brightly lit outpost of the huge pan-European gelato chain lacks the intimacy of smaller, artisanal ice-cream shops. But enticing flavours include panna cotta with toasted pine nuts and caramel, Sicilian blood-red orange, Black Forest and ricotta with caramelised fig.

★TRATTORIA PENNESTRI LAZIO €€

Map p350 (☎06 574 24 18; www.facebook.com/TrattoriaPennestri; Via Giovanni da Empoli 5; meals €25-35; ⏲noon-3pm Fri-Sun, 7-11pm Tue-Sun; ; MPiramide) Headed by a Danish-Italian chef Tommaso Pennestri, this mellow trattoria pays its respects to staunch Roman classics (think carbonara and tripe) but is at its best when dishing out bright, bold comfort food, such as gnocchi tumbled with prawns and *stracciatella* cheese or suckling pig glazed in juniper with apple chutney. Save room for the heavenly chocolate and rosemary mousse.

PORTO FLUVIALE ITALIAN €€

Map p350 (☎06 574 31 99; www.portofluviale.com; Via del Porto Fluviale 22; meals €25-30; ⏲10.30am-2am Sun-Thu, to 3am Fri & Sat; ; MPiramide) A hip, buzzing corner restaurant-bar laden with industrial-chic, Porto Fluviale attracts a mixed crowd – lots of families included – with its spacious lounge-style interior and good-value kitchen, which turns out everything from pasta, pizza and *cicchetti* (tapas-style appetisers) to burgers and meal-sized salads (some available in half-portions). Choose a table or a leather sofa and let the hours roll past.

Between meals, relax over a coffee, an *aperitivo* or an evening drink to a jazz soundtrack.

TRATTORIA ZAMPAGNA TRATTORIA €€

Map p350 (☎06 574 23 06; www.trattoria-romana.it/da/zampagna; Via Ostiense 179; meals €30-35; ⏲noon-3pm & 5.30-11pm Mon-Sat; Via Ostiense, MGarbatella) One of a line-up of cute little restaurants with terraces overlooking the hulk of Basilica de San Paolo Fuori le Mura, this humble trattoria offers up wholesome home-cooking as it's done for the past 80-odd years. Tuck into gnocchi – as Roman tradition demands – on Thursday, *baccalà* (salted cod) on Friday, and tripe on Saturday. The homemade tiramisu is exceptional. There's also a garden with tables at the back.

ESTROBAR ITALIAN €€

Map p350 (☎06 5728 9141; www.estrobar.com; Via Pellegrino Matteucci 20; menu €29, meals €35-50; ⏲9am-midnight; MPiramide, Via Ostiense) Designer denizens head to this hybrid restaurant-bar-gallery inside Testaccio's hip Hotel Abitart (p250) to deconstruct the likes of Claudio di Carlo over a bottle of Brut or fruit- or veggie-based cocktail. Fuelling the cultured conversations are chef Francesco Bonanni's Italo-fusion flavours and a wine list spanning 200 Italian drops. DJ sets and live music too.

SEACOOK SEAFOOD €€€

Map p350 (☎06 5730 1512; www.seacook.it; Via del Porto Fluviale 7d-e; meals €45-60; ⏲noon-3.30pm & 6.30-11.45pm; ; MPiramide) For stylish seafood dining in a chic aquatic ambience, look no further than this glorious white Nordic corner restaurant in Ostiense, with bar-stool seating, potted plants and bamboo lampshades. *Cuochi e Pescatori* (Cooks and Fishermen) is the strapline, and the fish is fresh from southern Italy's Salento. There are many daily specials depending on what's fresh.

Garbatella

NERO VANIGLIA PASTRIES €

Map p350 (☎06 578 03 06; info@nerovaniglia.it; Circonvallazione Ostiense 201; pastries €2.50; ⏲6am-8pm Tue-Sat, 7am-8pm Sun; ; MGarbatella) This cosy patisserie in the Garbatella neighbourhood coaxes sugar and butter into sweet treats such as *cornetti* (croissants) brimming with custard, *bignè* (cream puffs), and a slew of miniaturised desserts like tiramisu and panna cotta. A glassed-in kitchen gives guests a glimpse of the bakers at work.

AL RISTORO DEGLI ANGELI LAZIO €€

Map p350 (☎06 5143 6020; www.ristorodegliangeli.it; Via Luigi Orlando 2; meals €30-45; ⏲12.30-3pm Sat, 7-11.30pm Mon-Sat; MGarbatella) Right under the arches in a landmark Garbatella building, this refined trattoria packs in locals in the know, who come for sterling renditions of Roman classics. You won't go wrong with any pasta dish, but there's also fresh seafood as well as finely prepared seasonal vegetables. Book a table outside under an arch.

DRINKING & NIGHTLIFE

The ex-industrial area of Ostiense is the zone to head for after dark. Fertile clubbing land, this is where party-loving Romans dance the night away in grungy warehouses, motorbike repair workshops and vintage, graffiti-tagged factories. Serious clubbers can expect electro, nu-house, nu-funk and all sorts of other eclectica spun by some top DJs. Head to Via Giuseppe Libetta for a range of choices.

Via Appia Antica & Around

APPIA ANTICA CAFFÈ — CAFE

(☎06 8987 9575; www.appiaanticacaffe.it; Via Appia Antica 175; ⏱9am-sunset Tue-Sun, to 2pm Mon; 🚌Via di Cecilia Metella) Heading south along the Appian Way, you come to this tiny streetside cafe with pavement tables shaded by a gnarled old olive tree, a hunger-appeasing selection of *panini,* pastries and light snacks, and a fantastic garden out the back. The cafe also rents out bicycles and can provide you with a picnic lunch to take away.

Ostiense & San Paolo

★AZIENDA CUCINERIA & CIRCOLO DEGLI ILLUMINATI — LOUNGE

Map p350 (☎327 7615286; www.circolodegli illuminati.it; Via Giuseppe Libetta 3; ⏱kitchen 8pm-midnight Tue-Sat, club 10.30pm-late Thu-Sat; MGarbatella) Enjoy showy cocktails and stylish bites at this lounge. It has a courtyard garden with potted plants and olive trees, which is a gorgeous space to kick-start the evening beneath the stars. Late in the night from Thursday to Saturday, it opens up into a club, Circolo Degli Illuminati. Tech house, hip-hop, chill music and top DJs rev up clubbers.

★GOA — CLUB

Map p350 (☎06 574 82 77; www.goaclub.com; Via Giuseppe Libetta 13; ⏱11.30pm-5am Thu-Sat; MGarbatella) At home in a former motorbike-repair shop down a bamboo-lined dead-end alley, Goa is Rome's serious super-club with exotic India-inspired decor and international DJs mixing house and techno. Expect a fashion-forward crowd, podium dancers, thumping dance floor, sofas to lounge on and heavies on the door.

VINILE — CLUB

Map p350 (☎06 5728 8666; www.vinileroma.it; Via Giuseppe Libetta 19; ⏱8pm-2am Tue & Wed, to 3am Thu, to 4am Fri & Sat, 12.30-3.30pm & 8pm-2am Sun; MGarbatella) On weekends a mixed bag of Romans hit the dance floor at Vinyl, a buzzing bar and club cooking up food, music and party happenings on the Via Giuseppe Libetta strip. Inside its cavernous interior – with part-vegetal, part-frescoed ceiling – the night starts with an *aperitivo* banquet available from 8pm; DJ sets start at 11.30pm. On Sunday mornings students pile in for the unbeatable-value brunch.

GAZOMETRO 38 — COCKTAIL BAR

Map p350 (☎06 5730 2106; www.gazometro38.com; Via del Gazometro 38; ⏱12.30-3pm & 6.30-11.30pm Tue-Fri, 6.30pm-midnight Sat & Sun; 🚌Via Ostiense, MPiramide) It's not so much about the food as the eye-catching industrial design at this contemporary lounge-bar/restaurant in ever-more-hip Ostiense. Hobnob over an Elderflower Mule or Raspberry Basil Smash cocktail and a plate of *fritti* or *supplì* (rice balls) in the lounge area with sofa seating or at a table in the alley-entrance, plastered with B&W industrial-scene murals.

NEO CLUB — CLUB

Map p350 (☎338 9492526; www.piovra.it; Via degli Argonauti 18; ⏱11pm-late Fri & Sat; MGarbatella) This small, dark two-level club has an underground feel, and it's one of the funkiest choices in the zone, featuring a danc-etastic mish-mash of breakbeat, techno and old-school house.

PLANET ROMA — CLUB

Map p350 (☎06 574 78 26; www.planetroma.com; Via del Commercio 36; ⏱hours vary; MPiramide) Planet Roma is one of Rome's largest nightclubs, getting its freak on to an eclectic array of sounds in its four rooms, from live jazz gigs to house to retro to Latino nights. 'Glam', a mixed gay and lesbian night, rocks out to house and pop on Saturday.

WORTH A DETOUR

ROME'S CINEMA CITY

Cinecittà (☎06 7229 3269; http://cinecittasimostra.it; Via Tuscolana 1055; adult/reduced incl guided tour €15/13; ⏰9.30am-6.30pm Wed-Mon, last admission 4.30pm; Ⓜ Cinecittà) is Italy's foremost film studio, founded in 1937 by Mussolini and used for many iconic Italian and international films. It's possible to take a tour of the studios (Cinecittà Si Mostra, or Cinecittà Shows Off), where you get to visit several impressive sets, including 1500s Florence and ancient Rome, and there are interesting exhibitions, one dedicated to the work of Federico Fellini, and another exploring the studio's history. Of the thousands of films shot here, almost 50 have won Oscars.

Originally intended by Mussolini to turn out propaganda pictures, the studios were used during WWII variously as a refugee camp and hospital, but postwar they went from strength to strength. In the 1950s many major Hollywood films were made here, including *Cleopatra*, and Rome earned the nickname Hollywood on the Tiber. This was also to become Fellini's stomping ground – he even had a bedroom here – and *La Dolce Vita* was filmed in Theatre 5, within which the director recreated Via Veneto. Later, spaghetti westerns dominated the schedule. Recently it was used for the HBO series *Rome* and Paolo Sorrentino's *The Young Pope*.

At certain times guided tours of the sets are offered in English; check the website for further details.

Note, movie-themed amusement park **Cinecittà World** is located 25km southwest of Rome.

RASHŌMON BAR & CLUB — CLUB

Map p350 (☎391 7307386; www.rashomonclub.com; Via degli Argonauti 16; ⏰10pm-4am Tue-Sat Oct-May; Ⓜ Garbatella) Rashōmon is sweaty, not posey, and the place to head when you want to dance until dawn. Shake it to a music-lover's feast of underground sound, especially house, funk, techno and electronica.

Garbatella

ENOTECA IL MELOGRANO — WINE BAR

Map p350 (☎06 511 56 09; www.enograno.it; Via Guglielmo Massaia 9; ⏰11am-3pm & 7.30pm-midnight Mon-Fri; Ⓜ Garbatella) This small, snug *enoteca* (wine bar) in Garbatella is run by two knowledgeable brothers who suggest the best wines from their 300-strong list without making you feel like a *stupido*. There's a cheap set-dinner menu or you can choose dishes such as *bruschette* (grilled bread topped with tomatoes), *crostini* (toasts with toppings) and *carpaccio* (sliced cured meat) à la carte. Desserts are homemade and best accompanied by a fragrant dessert wine.

ENTERTAINMENT

CAFFÈ LETTERARIO — LIVE MUSIC

Map p350 (☎06 5730 2842; www.caffeletterarioroma.it; Via Ostiense 95; ⏰10am-2am Tue-Fri, 4pm-2am Sat & Sun; 🚌Via Ostiense, Ⓜ Piramide) Caffè Letterario is an intellectual hang-out housed in the funky, somewhat underground, post-industrial space of a former garage. It combines designer looks, a bookshop, gallery, co-working space, performance area and lounge bar. There are regular gigs, usually starting from around 10pm, ranging from soul and jazz to blues and Indian dance.

TEATRO PALLADIUM — THEATRE

Map p350 (☎box office 06 5733 2768; http://teatropalladium.uniroma3.it; Piazza Bartolomeo Romano; tickets adult/reduced €18/12; Ⓜ Garbatella) Once at risk of being turned into a bingo hall, the historic Teatro Palladium (1926), with a beautifully renovated 1920s interior, stages a rich repertoire of theatre, classical-music concerts, cinema and art exhibitions.

PALALOTTOMATICA — LIVE MUSIC

(☎06540901; www.palazzodellosportroma.it; Piazzale dello Sport 1; Ⓜ EUR Palasport) Originally built for the 1960 Olympics, this multipurpose venue hosts top rock stars and Italian swooners as well as staging musicals, theatrical performances and big-bash spectacles.

LA CASA DEL JAZZ JAZZ

Map p350 (☎06 8024 1281; www.casajazz.it; Viale di Porta Ardeatina 55; ⏲hours vary; 🚌Viale di Porta Ardeatina) In the middle of a park in the southern suburbs, the Jazz House resides in a three-storey 1920s villa that once belonged to the boss of the *banda del Magliana,* a powerful local Mafia outfit. When he was caught, Rome Council converted it into a jazz complex with a 150-seat auditorium, rehearsal rooms, cafe and restaurant. It books some big names.

Admission to shows varies; some events are free.

TEATRO INDIA THEATRE

Map p350 (☎06 8775 2210; www.teatrodiroma.net; Lungotevere Vittorio Gassman 1; 🚊Stazione Trastevere) Inaugurated in 1999 in the post-industrial landscape of Rome's southern suburbs, the India is the younger sister of Teatro Argentina. It's a stark, modern space in a converted industrial building, a fitting setting for its cutting-edge program, with a calendar of international and Italian works.

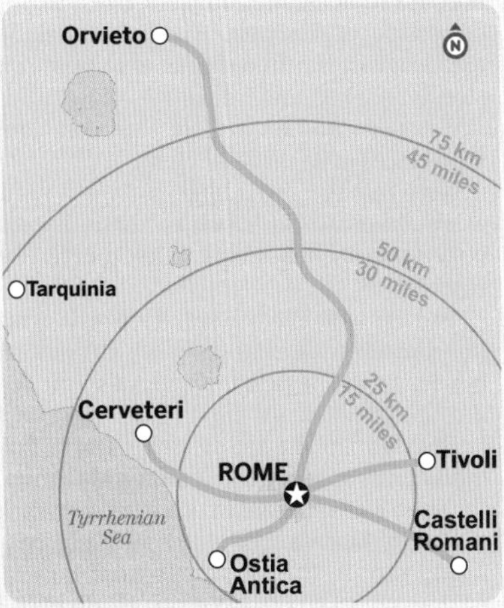

Day Trips from Rome

Ostia Antica p232

Wander through complete streets, gape at ancient toilets and clamber over an amphitheatre at the ancient port of Ostia Antica, Rome's very own Pompeii.

Tivoli p233

This hilltop town is home to two Unesco World Heritage sites: Villa Adriana, the emperor Hadrian's colossal country estate, and Villa d'Este, famous for its landscaped gardens and lavish fountains.

Castelli Romani p234

South of Rome, the pretty Coli Albani (Alban Hills) and its 13 towns have long provided a green escape for overheated Romans.

Cerveteri p236

The evocative tombs and archaeological treasures of this once important Etruscan city provide a window into a mysterious ancient world.

Orvieto p238

Home to one of Italy's most awe-inspiring Gothic cathedrals, this hilltop Umbrian town makes for a rewarding day trip.

Ostia Antica

Explore

An easy train ride from Rome, Ostia Antica is one of Italy's most thrilling archaeological sites.

Founded in the 4th century BCE, Ostia started life as a fortified military camp guarding the mouth of the Tiber – hence the name, a derivation of the Latin word *ostium* (mouth). It quickly grew, and by the 2nd century CE it had become a thriving port with a population of around 50,000.

Decline set in after the fall of the Roman Empire, and by the 9th century it had largely been abandoned, its citizens driven off by barbarian raids and outbreaks of malaria. Over subsequent centuries, it was plundered of marble and building materials and its ruins were gradually buried in river silt, thus ensuring their survival.

The Best...

➡ **Sight** Terme di Nettuno

Top Tip

Bring a picnic or time your visit so that you can eat at a restaurant as the on-site canteen gets extremely busy.

Getting There & Away

➡ **Train** From Rome, take the Roma–Lido train from Stazione Porta San Paolo (next to Piramide metro) to Ostia Antica (every 15 minutes). The 25-minute trip is covered by a standard Rome public transport ticket.

➡ **Car** Take Via del Mare, which runs parallel to Via Ostiense, and follow signs for the *scavi* (excavations).

Need to Know

➡ **Location** 25km southwest of Rome

SIGHTS

★AREA ARCHEOLOGICA DI OSTIA ANTICA — ARCHAEOLOGICAL SITE

(☎06 5635 8099; www.ostiaantica.beniculturali.it/; Viale dei Romagnoli 717; adult/reduced €10/5; ⏲8.30am-7.15pm Tue-Sun summer, last admission 6.15pm, shorter hours winter) One of Lazio's prize sights, the ruins of ancient Rome's seaport are wonderfully complete, like a smaller version of Pompeii. Highlights include the Terme di Nettuno (Baths of Neptune), a steeply stacked amphitheatre, some exquisite mosaics and an ancient cafe, complete with traces of its original menu.

Note that the site is huge and you'll need a few hours to do it justice. Also, it gets busy at weekends but is much quieter on weekdays.

To help with navigation, it's worth arming yourself with a site map, which you can buy for €2 at the ticket office. Audio guides are also available for €5.

Just beyond the ticket office, **Porta Romana** gives onto the **Decumanus Maximus**, the site's central drag, which runs over 1km to **Porta Marina**, the city's original sea-facing gate. At the time of research, however, it was blocked off about two-thirds of the way down, by the Tempio dei Fabri Navales.

On the Decumanus, the **Terme di Nettuno** is a must-see. This baths complex, one of 20 that originally stood in town, dates from the 2nd century and boasts some superb mosaics, including one of Neptune riding a seahorse chariot. In the centre of the complex are the remains of an arcaded **palestra** (gym).

Near the Terme is the **Teatro**, an amphitheatre originally built at the end of the 1st century BCE by Agrippa and later enlarged to hold 4000 people.

The grassy area behind the amphitheatre is the **Piazzale delle Corporazioni** (Forum of the Corporations), home to the offices of Ostia's merchant guilds. The mosaics that line the perimeter – ships, dolphins, a lighthouse, elephants – are thought to have represented the businesses housed on the square: ships and dolphins indicated shipping agencies, while elephants probably signalled businesses involved in the ivory trade.

Further down the Decumanus, the **Forum**, Ostia's main square, is overlooked by what remains of the **Capitolium**, a temple built by Hadrian and dedicated to Jupiter, Juno and Minerva.

Nearby is another highlight: the **Thermopolium**, an ancient cafe, complete with bar, fragments of its original frescoed menu, and a small courtyard where customers would have relaxed around a fountain. To the north of this are two of the so-called **case decorate**. These frescoed houses are off limits to unaccompanied visitors but can be entered on a free guided tour at 10.30am each Sunday – see the website for booking details.

Over on the other side of the Decumanus are the remains of the 2nd-century **Terme del Foro**, originally the city's largest and most important baths complex. Here, in the *forica* (public toilet), you can see 20 well-preserved latrines set sociably in a long stone bench.

For more modern facilities, you'll find a cafeteria, toilets and a gift shop to the north of the Decumanus (head up Via dei Molini). Also here is a small **museum** displaying statues and sarcophagi excavated on the site.

EATING

RISTORANTE MONUMENTO ITALIAN €€

(☎06 565 00 21; www.ristorantemonumento.it; Piazza Umberto I 8; meals €30-35; ⏰12.30-3.30pm & 8-11pm Tue-Sun) In Ostia's tiny medieval centre, this historic restaurant started life in the 19th century, catering to the labourers working on reclaiming the local marshlands. Nowadays, it does a brisk business feeding sightseers from the nearby ruins. Particularly good are seafood dishes such as *spaghetti alle vongole* (with clams).

Bookings recommended, particularly at weekends.

Tivoli

Explore

A summer retreat for ancient Romans and the Renaissance rich, the hilltop town of Tivoli is home to two Unesco World Heritage Sites: Villa Adriana, the sprawling estate of Emperor Hadrian, and the 16th-century Villa d'Este, a Renaissance retreat famous for its landscaped gardens and lavish fountains.

The Best...

- **Sight** The *canopo* at Villa Adriana

Top Tip

To cover Tivoli's two main sites in a day, visit Villa d'Este first, then have lunch in the centre, before heading down to Villa Adriana. To get to Villa Adriana from the centre, take local CAT bus 4 or 4X (€1.30, 10 minutes, half-hourly) from Piazza Garibaldi.

Getting There & Away

- **Bus** Tivoli, 30km east of Rome, is accessible by **Cotral bus** (€1.30, 50 minutes, at least twice hourly) from Rome's Ponte Mammolo metro station.
- **Car** Take Via Tiburtina or the quicker Rome–L'Aquila autostrada (A24).
- **Train** Trains run from Rome's Stazione Tiburtina to Tivoli (€2.60, one to 1¼ hours, at least hourly).

Need to Know

- **Area Code** ☎0774
- **Location** 30km east of Rome
- **Tourist Information Point** (☎0774 31 35 36; Piazzale delle Nazioni Unite; ⏰9.30am-5.30pm)

SIGHTS

★VILLA ADRIANA ARCHAEOLOGICAL SITE

(☎0774 38 27 33; www.villaadriana.beniculturali.it; Largo Marguerite Yourcenar 1; adult/reduced €10/5; ⏰8.30am-1hr before sunset) The ruins of Hadrian's vast country estate, 5km outside of Tivoli proper, are quite magnificent, easily on a par with anything you'll see in Rome. Built between 118 and 138 CE, the villa was one of the largest in the ancient world, encompassing more than 120 hectares, about 40 of which are now open to the public. You'll need about three hours to explore it fully.

From the entrance, a road leads 400m or so up to a pavilion where you can see a plastic model of the original villa, much of which was designed by Hadrian himself. The emperor was a great traveller and enthusiastic architect, and he based many of his ideas on buildings he'd seen around the world. The **pecile**, the large pool area near the walls, is a reproduction of a building in Athens. Similarly, the **canopo** is a copy of a sanctuary in the Egyptian town of Canopus, with a narrow 120m-long pool flanked by sculptural figures. At its head, the **Serapaeum** is a semi-circular *nymphaeum* (shrine to the water nymph) that was once used to host summer banquets. Flanking the water is the **antiquarium** where temporary exhibitions (adult/reduced €5/2.50) are now held.

Northeast of the *pecile*, the **Teatro Marittimo** is one of the site's signature buildings. A circular mini-villa set in an artificial pool, this was Hadrian's personal refuge that could only be accessed by swing bridges.

To the southeast, **Piazza d'Oro** makes for a memorable picture, particularly in spring, when its grassy centre is cloaked in wild yellow flowers.

There are also several bath complexes, temples and barracks. Parking (€3) is available at the site.

VILLA D'ESTE HISTORIC BUILDING

(☎0774 33 29 20; www.villadestetivoli.info; Piazza Trento 5; adult/reduced €10/5; ⏲8.30am-7.45pm Tue-Sun, from 2pm Mon, gardens close sunset, ticket office closes 6.45pm) In the hilltop centre, the steeply terraced grounds of Villa d'Este are a superlative example of a Renaissance garden, complete with monumental fountains, tree-lined avenues and landscaped grottoes. The villa, originally a Benedictine convent, was converted into a luxury retreat by Lucrezia Borgia's son, Cardinal Ippolito d'Este, in the late 16th century and later provided inspiration for composer Franz Liszt, who wrote *The Fountains of the Villa d'Este* after spending time here between 1865 and 1886.

Before heading out to the gardens, take time to admire the villa's rich mannerist frescoes. Outside, the manicured park features water-spouting gargoyles and shady lanes flanked by lofty cypress trees and extravagant fountains, all powered by gravity alone. Look out for the Bernini-designed **Fountain of the Organ**, which uses water pressure to play music through a concealed organ, and the 130m-long **Avenue of the Hundred Fountains**.

EATING

VAPOFORNO PLEBISCITO BAKERY €

(☎0774 31 13 23; Piazza del Plebiscito 6; meals €10-15; ⏲7am-3pm & 4.30-8pm Mon-Fri, 7am-3pm & 5-11pm Sat) Overlooking Tivoli's historic market square, this attractive bakery is a fine place for a casual meal. You can nip in for a quick slice of pizza or grab a table in the back and linger over a sit-down meal, perhaps a freshly made salad or a hearty plate of stew.

SLEEPING

★RESIDENZE GREGORIANE BOUTIQUE HOTEL €€€

(☎0774 43 69 03, 347 7136854; www.residenzegregoriane.it; Via Domenico Giuliani 92; ste €230-250; ❄📶🚭) Steeped in history, the Residenze Gregoriane offers a night to remember. Its four suites, all decorated in classic antique style, occupy the 16th-century Palazzo Mancini-Torlonia. Frescoes adorn the historic building, many by the same artists who worked on Villa d'Este, and there's a magnificent internal courtyard adorned with ceramic tiles and seashell mosaics.

Castelli Romani

Explore

A pretty pocket of verdant hills and volcanic lakes 20km southeast of Rome, the Colli Albani (Alban Hills) and their 13 towns are collectively known as the Castelli Romani. Since ancient times they've provided a green refuge from the city and still today Romans flock to the area on hot summer weekends. Highlights include the famous wine town of Frascati, hilltop Castel Gandolfo, and the scenic Lago Albano.

The Best...

- **Sight** Lago Albano
- **Place to Eat** Cacciani
- **Place to Drink** Frascati

Top Tip

In Frascati, search out a *cantina* (cellar-cum-trattoria) and settle down for a simple feast of *porchetta* (herb-roasted pork) and fresh local wine.

Getting There & Away

- **Train** During the week hourly trains run from Rome's Stazione Termini to Frascati (€2.10, 30 minutes) and Castel Gandolfo (€2.10, 45 minutes); on Sundays, services are very two hours. For Castel Gandolfo, take the Albano Laziale train.

➡ **Car** Exit Rome on Via Tuscolana (SS215) for Frascati or Via Appia Nuova (SS7) for Castel Gandolfo and Lago Albano.

Getting Around

To travel between the Castelli towns, you'll need to take the bus. From Frascati's Piazza Marconi, Cotral (p296) buses connect with Grottaferrata (€1.10, 10 minutes) and Castel Gandolfo (€1.30, 30 minutes).

If driving, Grottaferrata is signposted from Frascati and is an easy 4km away on the SR218. For Castel Gandolfo, continue past Grottaferrata for another 5km or so.

Need to Know

➡ **Location** 20km southeast of Rome

SIGHTS

Frascati

CATTEDRALE DI SAN PIETRO CHURCH
(☎06 942 02 38; Piazza San Pietro; ⏲7am-1pm & 3-7pm) Frascati is a long way from Scotland but it's here, in the town's 16th-century cathedral, that the heart of Charles Edward Stuart, aka Bonnie Prince Charlie, is buried – the rest of his body is at St Peter's Basilica in Rome. The church's main feature is its bombastic two-tone baroque facade, the creation of architect Girolamo Fontana.

SCUDERIE ALDOBRANDINI MUSEUM
(☎06 941 71 95; www.scuderiealdobrandini.it; Piazza Marconi 6; adult/reduced €3/1.50, plus exhibition €5.50/3; ⏲10am-6pm Tue-Fri, to 7pm Sat & Sun) The former stables of Villa Aldobrandini, restored by architect Massimiliano Fuksas, house Frascati's single museum of note, the **Museo Tuscolano**. Dedicated to local history, its collection includes ancient Roman artefacts and models of the Ville Tuscolane, a series of patrician villas built in the surrounding countryside between the 16th and 17th centuries.

VILLA ALDOBRANDINI GARDENS GARDENS
(☎06 942 25 60; Via Cardinal Massai 18; ⏲8.30am-5.30pm Mon-Fri) FREE Looming over Frascati's main square, Villa Aldobrandini is a haughty 16th-century villa designed by Giacomo della Porta and built by Carlo Maderno. It's closed to the public, but you can visit its baroque gardens, complete with a celebrated water theatre and panoramic terrace.

Castel Gandolfo

GIARDINI DI VILLA BARBERINI GARDENS
(Villa Barberini Gardens; ☎06 6988 3145; www.museivaticani.va; Via Rosselli; tours adult/reduced €20/15, Sat morning walk €12/5; ⏲9.30am-2.30pm) For centuries a closed world, the papal gardens at Castel Gandolfo can now be visited, albeit accompanied and in groups. The regular one-hour tour involves a mini-train ride through the extensive gardens, taking in Roman ruins, flower displays, woods, fruit-and-veg patches and the papal helipad.

To explore on foot, there are scheduled Saturday morning visits when you're free to walk around accompanied by Vatican staff – see the website for details of this and other visitor packages.

PALAZZO APOSTOLICO PALACE
(☎06 6988 3145; www.museivaticani.va; Piazza della Libertà; adult/reduced €11/5; ⏲8.30am-2pm Mon-Fri, to 5.30pm Sat, 10am-3pm Sun) Dominating Castel Gandolfo's skyline, the 17th-century Palazzo Apostolico was the pope's traditional summer residence. However, since 2016 it has been open to the public and you can now visit the papal apartments and explore the palace's marble halls. Look out for portraits of around 50 popes as well as costumes, robes and assorted Vatican paraphernalia, including the BMW that Pope John Paul II used when he stayed at the palace.

Lago Albano

★**LAGO ALBANO** LAKE
The larger and more developed of the Castelli's two volcanic lakes – the other is Lago di Nemi – Lago Albano is set in a steeply banked wooded crater. It's a popular hangout, particularly in spring and summer, when Romans flock here to top up their tans and eat in the many lakeside restaurants and trattorias.

The lake is accessible from Castel Gandolfo, or from a branch road off Via Appia Nuova (SS7).

EATING

Frascati

CANTINA SIMONETTI OSTERIA €

(☎347 6300269; Piazza San Rocco 4; meals €25; ⌚8pm-midnight Tue-Sun summer, 1-4pm Sat & Sun & 8pm-midnight Wed-Sun winter) For an authentic *vino e cucina* (wine and food) experience, search out this traditional *cantina* and sit down to a mountainous meal of *porchetta*, cold cuts, cheese and Roman pastas, all accompanied by jugs of local white wine. In keeping with the food, the decor is rough-and-ready rustic with strings of hanging garlic and plain wooden tables.

OSTERIA SAN ROCCO PIACENTE OSTERIA €€

(☎06 9428 2786; Via Cadorna 1; meals €25-30; ⌚noon-4pm Sat & Sun & 7pm-12.30am daily) To try a typical *osteria*, head to this popular spot. Just make sure you arrive hungry if you want to get beyond the rich starters of *porchetta* and fried zucchini flowers. Make it and you can continue with evergreen staples such as homemade ravioli and richly seasoned meatballs.

★CACCIANI RISTORANTE €€€

(☎06 942 03 78; www.cacciani.it; Via Armando Diaz 13; meals €50; ⌚12.30-2.30pm & 8-10.30pm, closed Sun dinner & Mon) One of Frascati's most renowned restaurants, Cacciani offers fine food and twinkling terrace views. The menu lists much-loved regional classics like *tonnarello a cacio e pepe* (egg spaghetti with pecorino cheese and black pepper) alongside more modern compositions prepared with seasonal ingredients from small local producers. Aficionados will also appreciate the weighty wine list.

Castel Gandolfo

ANTICO RISTORANTE PAGNANELLI RISTORANTE €€€

(☎06 936 00 04; www.pagnanelli.it; Via Gramsci 4; meals €60; ⌚noon-3.30pm & 6.30-11.45pm) A local landmark for more than a century, this colourful wisteria-clad restaurant oozes romance, particularly on warm summer nights when the views over Lago Albano melt the heart. The seasonally driven Italian food rises to the occasion too, especially when paired with outstanding wine from the terrific list – bottles are racked in an amazing cellar carved into tufa rock.

Cerveteri

Explore

A quiet provincial town 35km northwest of Rome, Cerveteri is home to one of Italy's great Etruscan treasures – the Necropoli di Banditaccia. This ancient burial complex, now a Unesco World Heritage Site, is all that remains of the formidable Etruscan city that once stood here.

Founded in the 9th century BCE, the city the Etruscans knew as Kysry, and Latin-speakers called Caere, was a powerful member of the Etruscan League. For a period between the 7th and 5th centuries, it was one of the Mediterranean's most important commercial centres. It eventually came into conflict with Rome and in 358 BCE was annexed into the Roman Republic.

The Best...

➡ **Sight** Necropoli di Banditaccia

Top Tip

Don't miss Cerveteri's Etruscan museum, which provides context for the tombs and brings the ancient era to life.

Getting There & Away

➡ **Bus** Cerveteri is easily accessible from Rome by Cotral (p296) bus (€2.80, one to 1¼ hours, twice hourly Monday to Saturday, hourly Sunday) from Cornelia metro station (line A).

➡ **Car** Take either Via Aurelia (SS1) or the Civitavecchia autostrada (A12) and exit at Cerveteri–Ladispoli.

Need to Know

➡ **Area Code** 06

➡ **Location** 35km northwest of Rome

➡ **Tourist Information Point** (☎06 9955 2637; Piazza Aldo Moro; ⌚9.30am-12.30pm & 5.30-7.30pm Tue-Sat, 10am-1pm Sun summer, 9.30am-12.30pm Tue-Sat, 10am-1pm Sun winter)

WORTH A DETOUR

TARQUINIA

Some 90km northwest of Rome, Tarquinia is the pick of Lazio's Etruscan towns. The highlight is the magnificent Unesco-listed necropolis and its extraordinary frescoed tombs, but there's also a fantastic Etruscan museum (the best outside of Rome) and an atmospheric medieval centre. Legend holds that Tarquinia was founded towards the end of the Bronze Age in the 12th century BCE. It was later home to the Tarquin kings of Rome, reaching its peak in the 4th century BCE, before a century of struggle ended with surrender to Rome in 204 BCE.

The **Museo Archeologico Nazionale Tarquiniense** (☎0766 85 60 36; www.polomusealelazio.beniculturali.it/index.php?it/145/antichit; Via Cavour 1; adult/reduced €6/2, incl necropolis €10/4; ⏰8.30am-7.30pm Tue-Sun), beautifully housed in the 15th-century Palazzo Vitelleschi, is a treasure trove of locally found Etruscan artefacts.

To see one of Italy's most important Etruscan sites, head to the **Necropoli di Tarquinia** (Necropoli dei Monterozzi; ☎0766 85 63 08; www.polomusealelazio.beniculturali.it/index.php?it/145/antichit; Via Ripagretta; adult/reduced €6/2, incl museum €10/4; ⏰8.30am-7.30pm Tue-Sun summer, to 1hr before sunset winter), a remarkable 7th-century BCE necropolis. At first sight, it doesn't look like much – a green field littered with corrugated huts – but once you start ducking into the tombs and seeing the vivid frescoes, you'll realise what all the fuss is about. Some 6000 tombs have been excavated in this area since digs began in 1489, of which 140 are painted and 22 are currently open to the public. For the best frescoes search out the **Tomba della Leonessa**, the **Tomba della Caccia e della Pesca**, which boasts some wonderful hunting and fishing scenes, the **Tomba dei Leopardi**, and the **Tomba della Fustigazione**.

To get to the necropolis, which is about 1.5km from the centre, take bus D (€1) from near the tourist office. Alternatively, it's 20 minutes on foot – head up Corso Vittorio Emanuele, turn right into Via Porta Tarquinia and continue along Via Ripagretta.

The best way to reach Tarquinia from Rome is by train from Termini (€5.60, 1½ hours, hourly). From Tarquinia station, catch the hourly BC bus to the hilltop historic centre (€1). By car, take the A12 autostrada for Civitavecchia and then Via Aurelia (SS1).

SIGHTS

★NECROPOLI DI BANDITACCIA — ARCHAEOLOGICAL SITE

(☎06 994 00 01; www.polomusealelazio.beniculturali.it/index.php?it/145/antichit; Via della Necropoli 43/45; adult/reduced €6/2, incl museum €10/4; ⏰8.30am-1hr before sunset Tue-Sun) This haunting, 12-hectare Etruscan necropolis is a veritable city of the dead, with streets, squares and terraces of *tumuli* (circular tombs cut into the earth and capped by turf). Some tombs, including the 6th-century-BCE **Tomba dei Rilievi**, retain traces of painted reliefs; many illustrate endearingly domestic household items, as well as figures from the underworld.

Another interesting tomb is the 7th-century BCE **Tumulo Mengarelli**, whose plain interior shows how the tombs were originally structured.

MUSEO NAZIONALE CERITE — MUSEUM

(☎06 994 13 54; www.polomusealelazio.beniculturali.it/index.php?en/145/antiquity; Piazza Santa Maria 1; adult/reduced €6/2, incl necropolis €10/4; ⏰8.30am-7.30pm Tue-Sun) Housed in a medieval fortress on what was once Caere's acropolis, this interesting little museum houses archaeological artefacts unearthed at the nearby Necropoli di Banditaccia.

Exhibits include terracotta vases, bucchero tableware and jewellery. The highlight is the *Euphronios Krater*, a 1st-century BCE vase that returned to Cerveteri in 2015 after an extended period in New York and Rome.

EATING

DA BIBBO — OSTERIA €€

(☎388 6598858; Via Agillina 41; meals €30-35; ⏰noon-3pm & 7-11pm) A popular choice in Cerveteri's historic centre, this coolly casual *osteria* looks the part with its low brick arches, exposed stone walls and decorative wine cases. Food-wise, it serves an imaginative menu of modern, well-executed *mare* (sea) and *terra* (land) dishes prepared with prime Italian ingredients.

Orvieto

Explore

Set atop a gigantic plug of rock above fields streaked with vines, olive groves and cypress trees, Orvieto is one of Umbria's star attractions. Its austere medieval centre is a classic of its kind with weaving lanes, brown stone houses and cobbled piazzas, and its location between Rome and Florence ensures a constant stream of visitors. But what sets the town apart from its medieval neighbours is its breathtaking cathedral. This extraordinary vision, one of Italy's greatest Gothic churches, is stunning inside and out, with a sensational facade and frescoes that are said by some to rival Michelangelo's in the Sistine Chapel.

The Best...

- **Sight** Duomo di Orvieto
- **Place to Eat** I Sette Consoli
- **Place to Drink** Bottega Vera

Top Tip

Stay overnight to experience the medieval atmosphere of the town once all the day trippers have ebbed away.

Getting There & Away

- **Bus** Buses depart from the station near Piazza Cahen, often also stopping at the train station. Destinations include Todi (€6.30, two hours, one daily Monday to Saturday during school term time) and Terni (€6.90, 2¼ hours, one daily Monday to Saturday).
- **Car** Orvieto is on the Rome–Florence A1 autostrada, while the SS71 heads north to Lago Trasimeno. Your best bet for parking is the **Parcheggio Campo della Fiera** (per hr/day €1.50/12) which has a free lift up to the historic centre.
- **Train** Orvieto's **train station** (www.trenitalia.com; Via Antonio Gramsci, Orvieto Scalo) is located 4km west of the *centro storico* (historic centre) in Orvieto Scalo. Direct trains run to/from Rome (€8.25 to €17.50, one to 1½ hours, hourly) and Florence (€14.90 to €16.70, two to 2½ hours, eight daily). Services to Perugia (€8.05 to €14.25, 1½ to two hours, hourly) involve a change at Orte or Terontola-Cortona.

Getting Around

- **Funicular** A century-old **funicular** (€1.30; every 10min 7.15am-8.30pm Mon-Sat, every 15min 8am-8.30pm Sun) creaks up the wooded hill from Orvieto's train station (west of the centre) to Piazza Cahen. The fare includes a bus ride from Piazza Cahen to Piazza Duomo. Outside of funicular hours, bus 1 runs up to the old town from the train station (€1.30).
- **Bus** Local bus A (€1.30) connects Piazza Cahen with Piazza Duomo.

Need to Know

- **Area Code** 0763
- **Location** 120km northwest of Rome
- **Tourist Office** (0763 34 17 72; Piazza Duomo 24; 8.15am-1.50pm & 4-7pm Mon-Fri, 10am-6pm Sat & Sun)

SIGHTS

★**DUOMO** CATHEDRAL

(0763 34 24 77; www.opsm.it; Piazza Duomo 26; €4, incl Museo dell'Opera del Duomo di Orvieto €5; 9.30am-7pm Mon-Sat, 1-5.30pm Sun summer, shorter hours winter) Nothing can prepare you for the visual feast that is Orvieto's soul-stirring Gothic cathedral. Dating from 1290, it sports a black-and-white banded exterior fronted by what is perhaps the most astonishing facade to grace any Italian church: a mesmerising display of rainbow frescoes, jewel-like mosaics, bas-reliefs and delicate braids of flowers and vines.

The building took 30 years to plan and three centuries to complete. It was started by Fra Bevignate and later additions were made by Sienese master Lorenzo Maitani, Andrea Pisano (of Florence Cathedral fame) and his son Nino, Andrea Orcagna and Michele Sanmicheli.

Of the art on show inside, it's Luca Signorelli's *Giudizio Universale* that's the star turn. The artist began work on this vast fresco in 1499 and over the course of the next four years covered every inch of the Cappella di San Brizio with a swirling, and at times grotesque, depiction of the *Last Judgment*. Michelangelo is said to have taken inspiration from it. Indeed, to some, Michelangelo's masterpiece runs a close second to Signorelli's creation.

On the other side of the transept, the **Cappella del Corporale** houses a 13th-century altar cloth stained with blood that is believed to have miraculously poured from the communion bread of a priest who doubted the transubstantiation.

MUSEO DELL'OPERA DEL DUOMO DI ORVIETO MUSEUM

(☎0763 34 24 77; www.opsm.it; Piazza Duomo 26; €4, incl Duomo €5; ⏲9.30am-7pm daily summer, to 5pm Tue-Sun winter) Housed in a complex of papal palaces, the Palazzi Papali, this museum showcases a fine collection of religious relics from the Duomo and paintings by artists such as Arnolfo di Cambio and the three Pisanos (Andrea, Nino and Giovanni). A separate exhibition in Palazzo Soliano is dedicated to sculptor and medallist Emilio Greco (1913–95).

MUSEO CLAUDIO FAINA E CIVICO MUSEUM

(☎0763 34 15 11; www.museofaina.it; Piazza Duomo 29; adult/reduced €4.50/3; ⏲9.30am-6pm summer, 10am-5pm winter, closed Mon Nov-Feb) Stage your own archaeological dig at this fantastic museum opposite the Duomo. It houses one of Italy's foremost collections of Etruscan finds, comprising plenty of stone sarcophagi, terracotta pieces and some amazing bronzeware. Also of note are a series of decorative Greek amphorae.

ORVIETO UNDERGROUND HISTORIC SITE

(☎0763 340688; www.orvietounderground.it; Piazza Duomo 23; adult/reduced €7/5; ⏲visits 11am, 12.15pm, 4pm & 5.15pm) The coolest place in Orvieto (literally), this series of 440 caves (out of 1200 in the system) has been used for millennia by locals for various purposes – WWII bomb shelters, refrigerators, wine cellars, wells and, during many a pesky Roman or barbarian siege, as dovecotes to trap the usual one-course dinner: pigeon (still seen on local menus as *palombo*).

EATING & DRINKING

AL POZZO ETRUSCO UMBRIAN €€

(☎0763 34 10 50; www.alpozzoetruscodagiovanni.it; Piazza dei Ranieri 1a; meals €30-35; ⏲12.30-2.30pm & 7.30-9.30pm Wed-Mon; 📶) Named after an ancient Etruscan well that graces its basement, this is a firm local favourite. Your host, Giovanni, will guide you through his seasonal menu of updated Umbrian delights, best enjoyed al fresco on the charming candlelit terrace. Pastas are seasoned with herbed meats and flavoursome vegetables, paving the way for original mains such as beef cheeks stewed in red beer.

★I SETTE CONSOLI ITALIAN €€€

(☎0763 34 39 11; www.isetteconsoli.it; Piazza Sant'Angelo 1a; meals €40-45, tasting menu €45; ⏲12.30-3pm & 7.30-10pm, closed Wed & Sun dinner) This refined restaurant walks the culinary high wire in Orvieto, serving inventive, artfully presented dishes, from joyful starters such as *panzanella* (a bread-based salad typical of central Italy) with vegetables and anchovies to pasta so light it almost floats off the fork. In good weather, try to get a table in the back garden. Dress for dinner and reserve ahead.

BOTTEGA VERA WINE BAR

(☎349 4300167; www.casaveraorvieto.it/it/bottega.html; Via del Duomo 36; ⏲8.30am-8.30pm Mon-Fri & Sun, to 10pm Sat; 📶) This gourmet deli and wine shop has been pouring the good stuff since 1938, when it was started by grandmother of current host Cesare, who will expertly guide you through his daily selections of wine by the glass (from €3).

SLEEPING

★B&B RIPA MEDICI B&B €

(☎0763 34 13 43, 328 7469620; www.ripamedici.com; Vicolo Ripa Medici 14; s €50, d €75-90; P❄📶) Hugging the walls on the edge of Orvieto's old town, this gracious B&B takes the concept of a 'room with a view' to another level, gazing longingly out across undulating countryside. But the dreamy views are just one of its attractions. The immaculate guest room and two apartments ooze charm and are lovingly furnished with antique pieces, timber beams and English farmhouse decor.

★MISIA RESORT BOUTIQUE HOTEL €€

(☎0763 34 23 36; www.misiaresort.it; Località Rocca Ripesena 51; s/d/ste €80/130/160; P❄📶👪) You won't regret going the extra mile to this boutique hotel in Rocca Ripesena, a panoramic hilltop hamlet 6km west of Orvieto. Its light, spacious rooms and suites, in the main hotel building and spread across the stone village, feature soft, earthy tones and stylish vintage touches – a chesterfield sofa here, a distressed wood beam there.

Sleeping

Rome is expensive and busy; book ahead to secure the best deal. Accommodation ranges from five-star hotels to hostels, B&Bs, pensioni and private rooms; there's also a growing number of boutique suite and apartment hotels.

Pensions & Hotels

The bulk of Rome's accommodation consists of *pensioni* (pensions) and *alberghi* (hotels).

A *pensione* is a small, family-run hotel, often in a converted apartment. Rooms are usually fairly simple, though most come with a private bathroom.

Most hotels in Rome's historic centre tend to be three-star and up. As a rule, a three-star room will come with a hairdryer, minibar (or fridge), safe, air-con and wi-fi. Roman hotel rooms tend to be small, especially in the *centro storico* (historic centre) and Trastevere. In these areas, many hotels are housed in centuries-old *palazzi* (mansions).

B&Bs & Guesthouses

Alongside traditional B&Bs, Rome has many boutique-style guesthouses offering chic, upmarket accommodation at midrange to top-end prices.

Breakfast in a Roman B&B usually consists of bread rolls, croissants, yoghurt, ham and cheese. Some B&Bs offer breakfast (usually coffee and a pastry) in a nearby cafe.

Hostels

Rome's hostels cater to everyone from backpackers to budget-minded families. Many offer hotel-style rooms alongside traditional dorms. The city's new breed of hostels are chic, designer pads with trendy bar-restaurants, bike rental, the occasional rooftop garden and a fantastic array of tours and activities.

Apartment Rentals

An excellent option for families, groups of friends and self-caterers, short-term apartment stays can often work out considerably less expensive than an extended hotel sojourn. Many booking services require a minimum stay. You'll often need to pay a cleaning levy when you leave.

Seasons & Rates

Rome doesn't have a low season as such, but rates are at their lowest from November to March (excluding Christmas and New Year) and from mid-July through August. Expect to pay top whack in spring (April to June) and autumn (September and October) and over the main holiday periods (Christmas, New Year and Easter).

Most midrange and top-end hotels accept credit cards. Budget places might, but it's always best to check in advance.

Useful Websites

- **Lonely Planet** (www.lonelyplanet.com/italy/rome) Author-reviewed accommodation options.
- **Cross Pollinate** (☎06 9936 9799; www.cross-pollinate.com) Personally vetted rooms and apartments by the team behind Rome's Beehive (p247) hostel.
- **Bed & Breakfast Italia** (☎06 8837 3407; www.bbitalia.it) Italian B&B network listing many Rome options.
- **Rome Accommodation.net** (www.rome-accommodation.net) Apartment and vacation-home rentals.

Lonely Planet's Top Choices

Argentina Residenza Style Hotel (p244) Sleek boutique choice in a central location.

RomeHello (p247) Stay at this fab hostel and you'll be supporting local charities.

Residenza Maritti (p243) Inspiring Forum views cap this hidden gem.

Arco del Lauro (p248) Exemplary B&B in a quiet pocket of Trastevere.

Best by Budget

€

RomeHello (p247) Fabulous street-art-adorned hostel operated as a social enterprise.

Generator Hostel (p247) Urban-chic (non-)hostelling in Esquilino.

Althea Inn Roof Terrace (p249) Designer comfort at budget prices.

Beehive (p247) Sustainable, friendly and stylish hostel near Termini.

€€

Residenza Maritti (p243) Hidden treasure with captivating views over the Forums.

Palm Gallery Hotel (p250) Delightful hotel in elegant residential neighbourhood.

Arco del Lauro (p248) B&B bolthole with ultra-friendly hosts.

€€€

Villa Spalletti Trivelli (p248) Stately style in a city-centre mansion.

Eitch Borromini (p244) Elegant rooms and two roof terraces overlooking Piazza Navona.

Argentina Residenza Style Hotel (p244) Charming boutique choice occupying a former monastery.

Best Boutique Hotels

Villa Laetitia (p247) Revel in tasteful decor at this Fendi-designed riverside villa.

Inn at the Roman Forum (p243) Modern styling and Roman ruins meet at this elegant bolthole.

Villa Spalletti Trivelli (p248) Glorious mansion with 16th-century furnishings, garden and Jacuzzi-clad roof terrace.

Best With Rooftop Terraces

Villa Della Fonte (p249) Seventeenth-century townhouse with a trio of rooftop gardens strewn with sun loungers.

Lungarno Collection: Portrait Roma (p245) A 360-degree city panorama unfolds on the terrace of this designer choice.

First Roma (p245) The rooftop restaurant and bar here are among the city's best.

9 Hotel Cesàri (p243) Enjoy views of *centro storico* rooftops from this hotel's top-floor bar.

Best B&Bs

Arco del Lauro (p248) Modern rooms, perfectly placed on the quiet side of Trastevere.

Villa Della Fonte (p249) Scale this 17th-century townhouse to its rooftop gardens and understand what *la dolce vita* is really all about.

Althea Inn Roof Terrace (p249) A hidden gem near Testaccio.

NEED TO KNOW

Price Ranges

Price ranges refer to a high-season double room with private bathroom, including breakfast unless stated otherwise.

€	less than €110
€€	€110–200
€€€	more than €200

Accommodation Tax

Everyone overnighting in Rome pays a room-occupancy tax on top of their bill:

- €3 per person per night in one- and two-star hotels
- €3.50 in B&Bs and room rentals
- €4/6/7 in three-/four-/five-star hotels

The tax applies for a maximum of 10 consecutive nights. Prices in reviews don't include tax.

Reservations

- Always try to book ahead, especially in high season (Easter to September, and over the Christmas–New Year period) and during major religious festivals.
- Ask for a *camera matrimoniale* for a room with a double bed; a *camera doppia* has twin beds.

Checking In & Out

- When you check in, you'll need to present your passport or ID card.
- Checkout is usually between 10am and noon. In hostels it's around 9am.
- Most guesthouses and B&Bs require you to arrange a time to check in.

Where to Stay

NEIGHBOURHOOD	FOR	AGAINST
Ancient Rome	Close to major sights such as Colosseum, Roman Forum and Capitoline Museums; quiet at night.	Not cheap and has few budget options; restaurants are touristy.
Centro Storico	Atmospheric area with everything on your doorstep – Pantheon, Piazza Navona, restaurants, bars, shops.	Most expensive part of town; few budget options; can be noisy.
Tridente, Trevi & the Quirinale	Good for Spanish Steps, Trevi Fountain and designer shopping; excellent midrange and top-end options; good transport links.	Upmarket area with prices to match; subdued after dark.
Vatican City, Borgo & Prati	Near St Peter's Basilica and Vatican Museums; decent range of accommodation; some excellent shops and restaurants; on the metro.	Expensive near St Peter's; not much nightlife; sells out quickly for religious holidays.
Monti, Esquilino & San Lorenzo	Many hostels and budget hotels around Stazione Termini; top eating options in Monti and thriving nightlife in studenty San Lorenzo; good transport links.	Some dodgy streets in Termini area, which is not Rome's most characterful.
Trastevere & Gianicolo	Gorgeous, atmospheric area; party vibe with hundreds of bars, cafes and restaurants; some interesting sights.	Can be noisy, particularly on summer nights – try to stay in the 'quiet' side, east of Viale di Trastevere.
San Giovanni & Testaccio	Authentic atmosphere with good eating and drinking options; Aventino is a quiet, romantic area; Testaccio is a top food and nightlife district.	Few options available; not many big sights.
Villa Borghese & Northern Rome	Largely residential area good for the Auditorium and some top museums; generally quiet after dark.	Out of the centre; few budget choices.

Ancient Rome

★**RESIDENZA MARITTI** GUESTHOUSE €€
Map p324 (06 678 82 33; www.residenzamaritti.com; Via Tor de' Conti 17; s €100, d €130-180, tr €150-200, q €170-210; ; Cavour) Boasting stunning views over the nearby forums and Vittoriano, this hidden gem has 13 rooms spread across three floors. Some are bright and modern, others are more cosy with antiques, original tiled floors and family furniture. There's a fully equipped kitchen and a buffet breakfast is served in the bistro next door.

CAESAR HOUSE GUESTHOUSE €€
Map p324 (06 679 26 74; www.caesarhouse.com; Via Cavour 310; s €80-120, d €100-164, ste €250-308; ; Cavour) Quiet and friendly, yet in the thick of it on Via Cavour, this 2nd-floor hideaway has six bright rooms in a renovated apartment. From the small white reception area, a hallway leads to the attractive high-ceilinged rooms, each decorated with tiled floors, soothing colours and a mix of modern and classical furniture.

★**INN AT THE ROMAN FORUM** BOUTIQUE HOTEL €€€
Map p324 (06 6919 0970; www.theinnattheromanforum.com; Via degli Ibernesi 30; d €228-422; Cavour) Hidden on a quiet backstreet near the Imperial Forums, this chic boutique hotel offers five-star service and a refined contemporary look. Rooms are individually styled, marrying modern design with timber beams and Murano chandeliers, while up top there's a terrace for aperitifs and romantic views. Check out the hotel's own ancient ruins – a 1st-century BC tunnel complex.

NERVA BOUTIQUE HOTEL BOUTIQUE HOTEL €€€
Map p324 (06 678 18 35; www.hotelnerva.com; Via Tor de' Conti 3; d €175-300; ; Cavour) This friendly hotel is tucked away behind the Imperial Forums. Its snug rooms display a contemporary look in shades of cream, grey and black, with padded leather bedsteads, parquet floors, pop art and the occasional coffee-table tome.

Centro Storico

★**NAVONA ESSENCE** BOUTIQUE HOTEL €€
Map p328 (06 8760 5186; www.navonaessencehotel.it; Via dei Cappellari 24; d €70-200; ; Corso Vittorio Emanuele II) Bed down in the heart of the action at this snug boutique hotel. Situated on a narrow backstreet near Campo de' Fiori, it's something of a squeeze but its location is handy for pretty much everywhere and its rooms are attractive, sporting a pared-down modern look and designer bathrooms.

9 HOTEL CESÀRI HISTORIC HOTEL €€
Map p328 (06 674 97 01; www.9-hotel-cesari-rome.it; Via di Pietra 89a; s €130-170, d €145-280; ; Via del Corso) This friendly three-star has been welcoming guests since 1787 and both Stendhal and Giuseppe Mazzini are said to have slept here. Modern-day visitors can expect traditionally attired rooms, a stunning rooftop terrace and a wonderful central location. The panoramic terrace bar, which is also open to nonguests, opens daily in summer from 6pm to midnight but closes on Sundays and Mondays in winter.

HOTEL NAVONA HOTEL €€
Map p328 (06 6821 1392; www.hotelnavona.com; 2nd fl, Via dei Sediari 8; s €110-170, d €125-260, q €195-400; ; Corso del Rinascimento) This well-placed hotel offers a range of handsome rooms in a 15th-century *palazzo* near Piazza Navona. The fresh, crisp decor marries white walls with blond-wood floors, large padded bedsteads and the occasional ceiling fresco to striking effect. Family rooms, including a deluxe suite as large as a mid-size apartment, are also available. Breakfast costs €10 extra.

HOTEL BARRETT PENSION €€
Map p328 (06 686 8481; www.pensionebarrett.com; Largo di Torre Argentina 47; s €115-135, d €135-150, tr €165-175; ; Largo di Torre Argentina) This exuberant *pensione* is quite unique. Boasting a convenient central location, its decor is flagrantly over the top with statues, busts and vibrant stucco set against a forest of leafy pot plants. Rooms, which are on the small side, come with thoughtful extras like foot spas, coffee machines and fully stocked fridges.

HOTEL MIMOSA
PENSION €€

Map p328 (☑06 6880 1753; www.hotelmimosa.
net; 2nd fl, Via di Santa Chiara 61; s €95-135,
d €125-145, tr €135-175, q €145-185; ❄@🛋;
🖳Largo di Torre Argentina) This long-standing
pensione makes an excellent central base,
offering a warm welcome and a top location near the Pantheon. Rooms are spacious
and comfortable with jazzy patterned wallpaper, laminated floors and cooling low-key
colours.

DIMORA DEGLI DEI
GUESTHOUSE €€

Mapp328(☑0668193267;www.pantheondimora
deglidei.com; Via del Seminario 87; r €140-300;
❄🛋; 🖳Largo di Torre Argentina) Location and
discreet style are the selling points of this
elegant guesthouse near the Pantheon. On
the 1st floor of a centuries-old *palazzo,* it
has six tasteful high-ceilinged rooms featuring honey-coloured parquet floors, the
occasional wood beam and minimal decor. Breakfast (included) is served in your
room or you can opt for a €10 buffet in a
nearby cafe.

⭐ARGENTINA RESIDENZA
STYLE HOTEL
BOUTIQUE HOTEL €€€

Map p328 (☑06 6821 9623; www.argentina
residenzastylehotel.com; Via di Torre Argentina
47, 1st fl; r €180-280; ❄🛋; 🖳Largo di Torre Argentina) A prime central location, stellar service and sleek contemporary design await
at this elegant boutique hotel. Housed in a
former monastery, its 12 individually styled
rooms sport a minimalist white look while
effortlessly incorporating features from the
original building: wood-beamed ceilings,
frescoes, stone door frames. Extras include
a popular daily aperitif served in the timber
beamed breakfast hall.

⭐HOTEL CAMPO
DE' FIORI
BOUTIQUE HOTEL €€€

Map p328 (☑06 6880 6865; www.hotelcampo
defiori.com; Via del Biscione 6; r €280-430, apt
€230-350; ❄@🛋; 🖳Corso Vittorio Emanuele
II) This rakish four-star has got the lot –
enticing boudoir decor, an enviable location off Campo de' Fiori, super-helpful staff
and a fabulous panoramic roof terrace. The
interior feels delightfully decadent with
its boldly coloured walls, low wooden ceilings, gilt mirrors and heavy crimson dam-
ask. Also available are 13 apartments, each
sleeping two to five people.

⭐EITCH BORROMINI
HOTEL €€€

Map p328 (☑06 686 14 25; www.eitchborromini.
com; Via di Santa Maria dell'Anima 30; r €300-
600; ❄🛋; 🖳Corso del Rinascimento) A sense
of history pervades this ravishing hotel,
housed in a 17th-century *palazzo* designed
by Borromini and overlooking Piazza Navona. Rooms are bright and quietly elegant
with understated period furniture, wood-
beamed ceilings and even the occasional
fresco, and there are dreamy views from
two panoramic roof terraces.

ARGENTINA RESIDENZA
GUESTHOUSE €€€

Map p328 (☑06 6819 3267; www.argentina
residenza.com; Via di Torre Argentina 47, 3rd fl;
d €140-320; ❄🛋; 🖳Largo di Torre Argentina)
A classy boutique guesthouse, Argentina
Residenza provides a stylish bolthole in the
heart of the historic centre. Its six rooms cut
a contemporary dash with their white and
pearl-grey palettes, parquet floors, design
touches and sparkling bathrooms. Service
is excellent and the ample buffet breakfast
makes a great start to the day.

🛏 Tridente, Trevi & the Quirinale

LA CONTRORA
HOSTEL €

Map p332 (☑06 9893 7366; rome@lacontrora.
com; Via Umbria 7; d/tr €110/120; ❄@🛋;
Ⓜ Barberini, Ⓜ Repubblica) Quality budget accommodation is thin on the ground in the
upmarket area north of Piazza Repubblica,
but this great little hostel is a top choice. It
has a friendly, laid-back vibe, helpful staff
and rooms with private bathrooms; email
and ask about the possibility of a dorm bed
(€40). Minimum two-night stay.

⭐CASA FABBRINI:
CAMPO MARZIO
B&B €€

Map p332 (☑06 324 37 06; https://campo
marzio.casafabbrini.it; Vicolo delle Orsoline 13; r
from €155; 🛋; Ⓜ Spagna) There are only four
B&B rooms on offer in this 16th-century
townhouse secreted in a pedestrianised
lane near the Spanish Steps, ensuring an
intimate stay. Owner Simone Fabbrini has
furnished these with a mix of antiques and
contemporary pieces, and the result is quite
delightful. Common areas include a mezzanine lounge and a kitchen where breakfast
is served.

HOTEL MODIGLIANI · HOTEL €€

Map p332 (☑06 4281 5226; www.hotelmodigliani.
com; Via della Purificazione 42; s/d €175/200;
❄ 🛜; MBarberini) Run by Italian writer
Marco and musician Giulia, this three-
star hotel is all about attention to detail.
Twenty-three modern rooms sport a soothing, taupe-and-white palette; all have good
bathrooms and some have balconies with
superb views. The garden apartments sleep
up to six and are great choices for families.
Pretty courtyard patio garden, too.

HOTEL FORTE · HISTORIC HOTEL €€

Map p332 (☑06 320 76 25; www.hotelforte.
com; Via Margutta 61; s & d €200, tr €210; ❄🛜;
MSpagna) Elegant 18th-century Palazzo
Alberto is on one of Rome's prettiest ivy-
draped streets, and this three-star hotel
within it is a reliable midrange choice for
those seeking an old-style Roman ambience (it opened in 1923) and a convenient
location. Its 20 well-maintained rooms are
comfortable, with satellite TV. Good buffet
breakfast.

HOTEL MOZART · HOTEL €€

Map p332 (☑06 3600 1915; www.hotelmozart.
com; Via dei Greci 23b; s €150, d €170-200, tr
€200-230; P❄@🛜; MSpagna) The Mozart
ticks all the boxes: its location is central;
the 56 classic rooms (some with balcony)
are comfortable and well-equipped with
satellite TV and kettles; the breakfast buffet
is generous; and its far-better-than-average
facilities include a sun-flooded rooftop garden and lounge with fireplace.

It also manages the Vivaldi Luxury
Suites and several apartments nearby. Look
out for special offers on the website.

BDB LUXURY ROOMS · GUESTHOUSE €€

Map p332 (☑06 6821 0020; www.bdbluxury
rooms.com; Via Margutta 38; r from €75; ❄🛜;
MFlaminio) For your own designer pied-à-
terre on one of Rome's prettiest and most
peaceful pedestrian streets, reserve yourself
one of the seven well-equipped rooms on
the upper floors (no lift) of this 17th-century
palazzo on Via Margutta. The ground-floor
reception is, in fact, a contemporary art gallery and bold wall art is a prominent feature of the decor. Breakfast costs €10.

⭐PALAZZO SCANDERBEG · BOUTIQUE HOTEL €€€

Map p332 (☑06 8952 9001; www.palazzoscan
derbeg.com; Piazza Scanderbeg 117; r/ste from
€360/1000; ❄🛜; MBarberini) Suite hotels
are a dime a dozen in central Rome, but few
are as attractive and comfortable as this
boutique offering in a 15th-century palazzo
near the Trevi Fountain. All of the guest
rooms are spacious and elegantly appointed; suites have kitchens. Enjoy breakfast in
the chic breakfast room or have the butler
bring it to your room.

FENDI PRIVATE SUITES · DESIGN HOTEL €€€

Map p332 (☑06 9779 8080; www.fendiprivate
suites.com; Via della Fontanella di Borghese 48,
Palazzo Fendi; ste €950; P❄@🛜; 🖥Via del
Corso) Comfortably at home on the 3rd
floor of Palazzo Fendi (the Roman fashion
house's flagship store is below), this exclusive boutique hotel is pure class. Original
artworks, photographs of the city snapped
by Fendi creative director Karl Lagerfield,
Fendi Casa furniture and haute-couture
fabrics in soothing greys and blues adorn
the seven spacious suites. Dress the part.

LUNGARNO COLLECTION: PORTRAIT ROMA · BOUTIQUE HOTEL €€€

Map p332 (☑06 6938 0742; www.portraitsuites.
com; Via Bocca di Leone 23; ste €670-2800;
P❄🛜; MFlaminio) As exclusive as Roman
accommodation comes, this residence
boasts exquisite suites in a townhouse
near the Spanish Steps. Interiors evoke the
1950s style and panache of Italian design
king Salvatore Ferragamo, and rooms have
comforts and gadgets galore; all have a
kitchenette and one has its own sauna and
mini-gym. The 360-degree city panorama
from the roof terrace is exhilarating.

ROMA HASSLER · HOTEL €€€

Map p332 (☑06 69 93 40; www.hotelhassler
roma.com; Piazza della Trinità dei Monti 6; r €600-
900, ste from €2000; ❄@🛜; MSpagna) Sur-
mounting the Spanish Steps, the historic
Hassler is a byword for old-school luxury.
A long line of VIPs have stayed here, enjoying the ravishing views and sumptuous
hospitality. Its Michelin-starred restaurant
Imàgo (p118) has one of the finest city vis-
tas. Under the same management is nearby
boutique hotel Il Palazzetto (Map p332; ☑06
6993 4560; www.ilpalazzettoroma.com; Vicolo
del Bottino 8; d €330-360; ❄@🛜; MSpagna),
with views over the Spanish Steps.

FIRST ROMA · DESIGN HOTEL €€€

Map p332 (☑06 4561 7070; www.thefirsthotel.
com; Via del Vantaggio 14; r/ste from €470/650;

Flaminio) Noble 19th-century *palazzo* turned 'luxury art hotel' is the essence of this boutique, five-star choice. Room decor features walls of art and shelves of books; amenities include Nespresso machines and Acqua Di Parma toiletries. The rooftop garden (with restaurant and cocktail bar) is one of Rome's best.

HOTEL LOCARNO HOTEL €€€

Map p332 (06 361 08 41; www.hotellocarno.com; Via della Penna 22; d €320-440, ste €470-830; Flaminio) With its stained-glass doors and rattling cage-lift, this 1925 hotel is an art nouveau classic – the kind of place Agatha Christie's famous detective Hercule Poirot might stay if he were in town. Rooms have period furniture, marble bathrooms and vintage charm. The roof garden, wisteria-draped courtyard, restaurant and fin-de-siècle cocktail bar (p120) with wintertime fireplace are major draws.

GIUTURNA BOUTIQUE HOTEL BOUTIQUE HOTEL €€€

Map p332 (06 6228 9629; www.giuturnaboutiquehotel.com; Largo del Tritone 153; d/tr €240/260; Barberini) A hop, skip and coin's throw from Trevi Fountain, this stylish boutique hotel is a peaceful and elegant retreat from the madding crowds. Rooms mix parquet flooring and original architectural features including polished 18th-century beams and wooden floors with contemporary furniture. Reception doubles as a drawing room and lounge, with complimentary coffee. A continental breakfast costs €8.

HOTEL DE RUSSIE HOTEL €€€

Map p332 (06 32 88 81; www.roccofortehotels.com/it; Via del Babuino 9; d from €600; Flaminio) The historic Hotel de Russie is almost on Piazza del Popolo and has exquisite terraced gardens. The decor is softly luxurious in many shades of grey, and the rooms offer state-of-the-art entertainment systems, massive mosaic-tiled bathrooms and all the luxuries. There's a lovely courtyard bar (p120) and a fab, five-star spa (p123).

MARGUTTA 54 HOTEL €€€

Map p332 (06 3229 5295; www.romeluxurysuites.com/margutta/default-en.html; Via Margutta 54; d €340-380; Spagna) Book one of the four sleek suites in this building of former artists' studios and you'll be given your own key to the street entrance, letting you emulate the locals. Overlooking a courtyard off picturesque Via Margutta, the suites are spacious, with living areas and luxe bathrooms.

Vatican City, Borgo & Prati

COLORS HOTEL HOTEL €

Map p336 (06 687 40 30; www.colorshotel.com; Via Boezio 31; s €70-95, d €80-130, q €120-160; Via Cola di Rienzo) This welcoming hotel in an elegant four-storey building impresses with its fresh, artful design and clean, colourful rooms. These come in various shapes and sizes, including cheaper ones with shared toilets (sinks and showers in the room). A buffet breakfast is included in some web rates. There's a small rooftop terrace.

CASA DI ACCOGLIENZA PAOLO VI MONASTERY €

Map p336 (06 390 91 41; www.casapaolosesto.it; Viale Vaticano 92; s/d/tr/q €40/70/90/100; Viale Vaticano) Stay at this tranquil, palm-shaded convent and you're ideally placed to be first in the line at the Vatican Museums. The resident nuns keep everything ship-shape and the 30 small, sunny rooms are clean as a pin, if institutional in feel. No breakfast, but there's a fridge and microwave for guests to use plus a small rooftop terrace.

HOTEL SAN PIETRINO HOTEL €

Map p336 (06 370 01 32; www.sanpietrino.it; Via Bettolo 43; s €40-70, d €55-80, tr €75-100, q €95-130; Ottaviano-San Pietro) Within easy walking distance of St Peter's Basilica, this family-run *pensione* is an excellent budget choice. Its 11 compact rooms, squeezed into a 3rd-floor apartment (with elevator), are characterful and prettily decorated with terracotta-tiled floors and the occasional statue. It's a good location near cafes.

★**LE STANZE DI ORAZIO** BOUTIQUE HOTEL €€

Map p336 (06 3265 2474; www.lestanzediorazio.com; Via Orazio 3; r €80-200; Via Cola di Rienzo, Lepanto) This five-room boutique hotel makes for an attractive home away from home in the heart of the elegant Prati district, a single metro stop from the Vatican. The rooms have refined decor from a modern colour palette. There are top-end luxuries and well-appointed bathrooms. The breakfast area is small and stylish.

QUOD LIBET B&B €€

Map p336 (347 1222642; www.quodlibetroma.com; 4th fl, Via Barletta 29; r €140-240; ; Ottaviano-San Pietro) A family-run guest-house offers four big colourful rooms and a convenient location near Ottaviano-San Pietro metro station. Rooms are spacious with hand-painted bright watercolours and homey furnishings, and it also has a kitchen for guest use plus an elevator. Enjoy breakfast on the large garden terrace. Hosts Gianluca and Connie extend a warm welcome.

VATICAN STYLE BOUTIQUE HOTEL €€

Map p336 (06 687 63 36; www.vaticanstyle.com; 6th fl, Via del Mascherino 46; d €130-194; ; Piazza del Risorgimento) A short hop from St Peter's, this stylish bolthole has 12 rooms spread over two floors of a large residential building. There's a hushed air about the place with its white, light-filled rooms, modern decor and occasional rooftop view. Cheaper rates are available without breakfast.

FABIO MASSIMO DESIGN HOTEL DESIGN HOTEL €€

Map p336 (06 321 30 44; www.hotelfabiomassimo.com; Viale Giulio Cesare 71; r €115-230; ; Ottaviano-San Pietro) Easily walkable from Ottaviano-San Pietro metro station, this design hotel is convenient as well as modestly stylish. From the 4th-floor reception and breakfast area, corridors lead off to nine rooms, each carpeted and coloured in slate greys and whites with touches of deep red, flower motifs and hanging lamps. It has an elevator and a tiny bar.

★**VILLA LAETITIA** BOUTIQUE HOTEL €€€

Map p348 (06 322 67 76; www.villalaetitia.com; Lungotevere delle Armi 22; r €140-400; ; Lungotevere delle Armi) Gorgeous Villa Laetitia is in a riverside art nouveau villa. Its 20 rooms and mini-apartments, spread over the main building and a separate Garden House, were all individually designed by Anna Venturini Fendi of the famous fashion house. Interiors marry modern design touches with family furniture, vintage pieces and rare finds, such as a framed Picasso scarf in the Garden Room.

Also in the hotel is the Enoteca La Torre (p145), one of Rome's Michelin-starred fine-dining restaurants.

Monti, Esquilino & San Lorenzo

★**ROMEHELLO** HOSTEL €

Map p344 (06 9686 0070; https://theromehello.com; Via Torino 45; dm/r from €15/45; ; Repubblica) Funnelling all of its profits into worthy social enterprises, this street-art-adorned hostel is the best in the city. Opened in 2018, it offers 200 beds, a communal kitchen, courtyard, lounge and laundry. Dorms max out at 10 beds (most have four) and have good mattresses and en-suite bathrooms; each bed has a locker, reading light, USB plug and powerpoint.

★**BEEHIVE** HOSTEL €

Map p344 (06 4470 4553; www.the-beehive.com; Via Marghera 8; dm from €25, s €70, without bathroom €50, d €100, without bathroom €80; reception 7am-11pm; ; Termini) More boutique chic than backpacker grungy, this small and stylish hostel has a glorious summer garden and a friendly traveller vibe. Dynamic American owners Linda and Steve exude energy and organise yoga sessions, storytelling evenings and tri-weekly vegetarian and organic dinners around a shared table (€10). Private rooms come with or without bathrooms and air-con; dorms are mixed or female-only.

GENERATOR HOSTEL HOSTEL €

Map p344 (06 49 23 30; https://generatorhostels.com; Via Principe Amedeo 251; dm/d from €15/40; ; Vittorio Emanuele) Rome is blessed with a number of designer hostels, and this is one of the best. Though small, private rooms are bright and have good bathrooms. Comfortable dorms sleep between three and six. Facilities include a bar and a cafe where breakfast (€5) is served. Sadly, the hostel is located in one of central Rome's least-attractive pockets.

MEININGER ROMA HOSTEL HOSTEL €

Map p344 (06 9480 1352; www.meininger-hotels.com; Via San Martino della Bataglia 16; dm/s/tw/tr/f from €17/49/50/63/68; ; Castro Pretorio) This family-friendly German-owned place is a very different proposition to its party-focused competitors.

Rooms have single beds, and dorms – most of which have four beds – have a mix of single beds and bunks; all have excellent bathrooms. Facilities include a communal kitchen, bar and breakfast room where a generous buffet (€7.90) is served.

YELLOW HOSTEL HOSTEL €

Map p344 (06 446 35 54; www.the-yellow.com; Via Palestro 51; dm/d €45/130; Castro Pretorio) This sharp, 374-bed party hostel offers mixed and female-only dorms (some with en suites), private en-suite rooms, two communal lounges and a clean, well-equipped kitchen. Each dorm bed has a reading light, powerpoint and luggage cage (BYO padlock). The hostel is rapidly colonising the entire street – aka the 'Yellow Square' – with its restaurant, bar, gelateria and bike shop.

★66 IMPERIAL INN B&B €€

Map p344 (06 4890 7682, 333 3520294; www.66imperialinn.com; Via del Viminale 66, 4th fl; d €150, tr & q €210; Via Nazionale) A particularly charming B&B, this place on an upstairs floor of an attractive building near Rome's opera house offers five rooms, each named after a colour (or animal in the case of B&W-striped Zebra). All have cable TV, a kettle and a good-sized marble bathroom. Guests love the complimentary water and bottle of wine. Book ahead.

RESIDENZA CELLINI B&B €€

Map p344 (06 4782 5204; www.residenzacellini.it; Via Modena 5; r from €190; Repubblica) Six comfortable and attractive rooms with bathrooms so clean they gleam are on offer at this elegant 3rd-floor B&B on a quiet side road near busy Via Nazionale. All are equipped with tea and coffee set-up (Twinings, no less), cable TV and double-glazed windows. Off-season, rates plummet.

HOTEL DUCA D'ALBA HOTEL €€

Map p344 (06 48 44 71; www.hotelducadalba.com; Via Leonina 14; r €164-200; Cavour) This appealing four-star hotel in the heart of the Monti action has 27 small but charming rooms. Some rooms have traditional decor and others have been given a slick makeover; all of those facing the street have double-glazed windows. The best rooms have gorgeous little balconies overlooking the Monti rooftops. Economy rooms don't include breakfast.

TOP FLOOR COLOSSEO GUESTHOUSE €€

Map p339 (393 0327195; www.topfloorcolosseo.com; Via Labicana 72, 5th fl; r €95-130; Colosseo) Bright rooms, a friendly welcome and a convenient location near the Colosseum await on the Top Floor. It's all reasonably basic, but rooms are both clean and comfortable – some even offer a fleeting view of the Colosseum if you stick your head out of the window. Breakfast is served in your room; on-site parking costs €30.

★VILLA SPALLETTI TRIVELLI BOUTIQUE HOTEL €€€

Map p344 (06 4890 7934; www.villaspalletti.it; Via Piacenza 4; d/ste from €540/830; Repubblica) Furnished with 16th-century tapestries, antique books and original period furnishings, this mansion was built by Gabriella Rasponi, niece of Carolina Bonaparte (Napoleon's sister), and its magnificent salons evoke this illustrious past quite wonderfully. The 14 romantic rooms and suites are elegantly decorated, with excellent bathrooms and amenities. Guests are offered personalised service, a lavish buffet breakfast and complimentary daily *aperitivo.*

THE LIBERTY BOUTIQUE HOTEL €€€

Map p344 (06 495 92 61; www.hoteltheliberty.com; Via Palestro 64; r/f €250/380; Castro Pretorio) This boutique hotel occupies a handsome heritage villa designed in the Liberty style – Italy's version of art nouveau. Decor, service and facilities are all excellent, but the location in Rome's scruffy hostel precinct is unfortunate. That said, this place is cheaper than most boutique picks, and has draws including a garden, on-site parking and TVs with Netflix. Low-season prices drop dramatically.

Trastevere & Gianicolo

★ARCO DEL LAURO GUESTHOUSE €€

Map p340 (06 9784 0350; www.arcodellauro.it; Via Arco de' Tolomei 27; r €120-175; Viale di Trastevere, Viale di Trastevere) Perfectly placed on a peaceful cobbled lane on the 'quiet side' of Trastevere, this ground-floor guesthouse sports six gleaming white rooms with parquet floors, a modern low-key look and well-equipped bathrooms. Guests share a fridge, a complimentary fruit bowl and cakes. Breakfast (€5) is served in a nearby cafe. Daniele and Lorenzo, who run the place, could not be friendlier or more helpful.

★RELAIS LE CLARISSE HOTEL €€

Map p340 (☎06 5833 4437; www.leclarissetrastevere.com; Via Cardinale Merry del Val 20; r €120-200; ❄ 📶; 🚌Viale di Trastevere, 🚋Trastevere/Mastai) Set around a pretty internal courtyard with a gnarled old olive tree, orange trees and a scattering of tables, this is a peaceful 18-room oasis in Trastevere's bustling core. In contrast to the urban mayhem outside, the hotel is all farmhouse charm. Rooms are decorated in rustic style with wrought-iron bedsteads and wood-beamed ceilings. Suites open on to the garden.

★VILLA DELLA FONTE B&B €€

Map p340 (☎06 580 37 97; www.villafonte.com; Via della Fonte d'Olio 8; s €150-170, d €160-200; ❄ 📶; 🚌Via della Scala) A lovely terracotta-hued, ivy-shrouded gem in a 17th-century townhouse, Villa della Fonte is precisely what Rome's *la dolce vita* is about. Five rooms with basic decor, some with original red brick and wood-beam ceilings, are comfortable. The crowning glory is the trio of rooftop gardens, strewn with sun lounges, potted pomegranate trees and fragrant citrus plants.

B&B SUITES TRASTEVERE B&B €€

Map p350 (☎347 0744086; http://bbsuites.com/trastevere; Viale di Trastevere 248; r €70-140; ❄ 📶; 🚌Viale di Trastevere, 🚋Trastevere/Pascarella) Find this guesthouse on the 3rd floor of a honey-hued *palazzo*. Owner and ultimate good host Marco is an utter angel. You won't forget you're in Rome staying here – each of the rooms and suites is dramatically frescoed with local sights, such as the Colosseum and Trevi Fountain. Breakfast is served in the kitchen, which is open to guests throughout the day.

RESIDENZA ARCO DEI TOLOMEI GUESTHOUSE €€

Map p340 (☎06 5832 0819; www.bbarcodeitolomei.com; Via Arco de' Tolomei 27; s/d from €165/190; ❄ @ 📶; 🚌Viale di Trastevere, 🚋Belli) Polished antiques and rich fabrics decorate this old-world guesthouse, on the 2nd floor of an old building in backstreet Trastevere. There are six rooms, each named after a Roman road – Appia, Aurelia and so on. Breakfast is around a shared wooden table beneath wood beams and faux glass chandeliers.

★DONNA CAMILLA SAVELLI HOTEL HOTEL €€€

Map p340 (☎06 58 88 61; www.hoteldonnacamillasavelli.com; Via Garibaldi 27; r €200-300; ❄ @ 📶; 🚌Via Garibaldi) It's seldom you can stay in a 16th-century convent designed by baroque genius Borromini. This four-star hotel is exquisitely appointed – muted colours complement the serene concave and convex curves of the architecture – and service is excellent. The best rooms overlook the cloister garden or have views of Rome. Enjoy the roof garden and view with a drink from the bar.

BUONANOTTE GARIBALDI B&B €€€

Map p340 (☎06 5833 0733; www.buonanottegaribaldi.com; Via Garibaldi 83; r €210-280; ⌚reception 9am-7pm; ❄ @ 📶; 🚌Via Garibaldi) With only three rooms in a divinely pretty villa set around a courtyard in Gianicolo, this upmarket B&B is a haven. The rooms – themed Rome (inspired by the magnificent sunsets over Rome as seen from Gianicolo), Chocolate and Tinto – are beautifully decorated. There are works of art and sculpture all over the place; this is artist Luisa Longo's house.

HOTEL SANTA MARIA HOTEL €€€

Map p340 (☎06 589 46 26; www.hotelsantamariatrastevere.it; Vicolo del Piede 2; s/d from €200/220, q from €250; ❄ @ 📶; 🚌Viale della Scala) Squirrelled away behind a wall in the heart of Trastevere is this old convent, today a 20-room hotel arranged around a courtyard peppered with orange trees. An alley of lemon trees and ivy leads up to the modern, low-lying building. Functional rooms evoke the sun with terracotta floors and Provençal colour schemes. Quads with bunk beds cater to families. Free bicycles provided.

🛏 San Giovanni & Testaccio

★ALTHEA INN ROOF TERRACE B&B €

Map p338 (☎339 4353717, 06 9893 2666; www.altheainnroofterrace.com; Via dei Conciatori 9; d €100-120; ❄ 📶; Ⓜ Piramide) In a workaday apartment block near the Aurelian Walls, this friendly B&B offers superb value for money and easy access to Testaccio's bars, clubs and restaurants. Its spacious, light-filled rooms sport a modish look with white walls and tasteful modern furniture, and some also come with their own al fresco terrace.

HOTEL LANCELOT HOTEL €€

Map p339 (☎06 7045 0615; www.lancelothotel.com; Via Capo d'Africa 47; s €80-128, d €100-196, f €230-278; P ❄ 📶; 🚌Via di San Giovanni in Laterano) A great location near the Colosseum, striking views and super-helpful English-speaking staff – the family-run Lancelot scores across the board. The lobby and communal areas gleam with marble and crystal while the airy rooms exhibit a more restrained classic style. The best, on the 6th floor, also come with their own terrace.

Parking is available on request for €10 per day.

HOTEL VALERI HOTEL €€

Map p339 (☎06 7759 1793; www.hotelvaleri.com; Largo dell'Ambra Aradam 3; d €90-135, tr €150-160; ❄ 📶; 🚌Via dell'Ambra Aradam) Situated between San Giovanni and the Celio, this discreet three-star feels well off the beaten track, yet is only a 15-minute walk from the Colosseum. It's a small operation with 10 snug rooms and a low-key modern look. Francesco, the manager, is a wealth of local information and is happy to suggest itineraries and book tickets.

★HOTEL SANT'ANSELMO BOUTIQUE HOTEL €€€

Map p338 (☎06 57 00 57; www.aventinohotels.com; Piazza Sant'Anselmo 2; s €129-254, d €179-334; ❄ 📶; 🚌Via Marmorata) A ravishing hideaway in the romantic Aventino district. Housed in an elegant villa, its individually decorated rooms are not the biggest but they are stylish, juxtaposing parquet floors, Liberty-style furniture and ornate decorative flourishes with modern touches and contemporary colours. They also come with smartphones which guests are free to use during their stay.

Villa Borghese & Northern Rome

★PALM GALLERY HOTEL HOTEL €€

Map p348 (☎06 6478 1859; www.palmgalleryhotel.com; Via delle Alpi 15d; s/d/f from €140/180/250; ❄ 📶 🏊; 🚌Via Nomentana, 🚌Viale Regina Margherita) Housed in a 1905 Liberty-style villa, this gorgeous hotel sports an eclectic look that effortlessly blends African and Middle Eastern art with original art deco furniture, exposed brickwork and hand-painted tiles. Rooms are individually decorated, with the best offering views over the wisteria and thick greenery in the surrounding streets. In an adjacent building, a small swimming pool provides a welcome respite from the summer heat.

MY GUEST ROMA B&B B&B €€

(☎06 8632 4590; www.myguestroma.it; Viale XXI Aprile 12; s/d/tr/q €75/120/135/170; ❄ 📶; 🚌Viale XXI Aprile, MBologna) Run by the super-friendly Stefano, My Guest Roma has various guest rooms, including a quad with bunk bed, spread over two floors of a big 1930s *palazzo*. It's slightly out of the centre but only three metro stops from Termini, and with its colourful rooms, Ikea-style furnishings and relaxed air, it's a real home away from home. Kosher and gluten-free breakfasts are available.

Southern Rome

HOTEL ABITART HOTEL €€

Map p350 (☎06 454 31 91; www.abitarthotel.com; Via Pellegrino Matteucci 10-20; r €120-170; 🚌Via Ostiense, MPiramide) Changing contemporary-art exhibitions by local Roman artists decorate this stylish 66-room hotel in gentrifying Ostiense. Standard rooms are a riot of bright colours, and themed suites evoke different art periods (cubism, 1970s, pop art) and genres (poetry, photography). Pluses include the hotel restaurant-bar Estrobar (p227) with its attractive summertime terrace, and garage parking (€25 per night) right next door.

Catacombe di San Callisto (p220)

SUN_SHINE/SHUTTERSTOCK ©

Understand Rome

History

Rome's history spans three millennia, from the classical myths of vengeful gods to the follies of Roman emperors, from Renaissance excess and papal plotting to swaggering 20th-century fascism. Everywhere you go in this remarkable city, you're surrounded by the past. Martial ruins, Renaissance *palazzi* (mansions) and flamboyant baroque basilicas all have tales to tell – of family feuding, historic upheavals, artistic rivalries, intrigues and dark passions.

Ancient Rome, the Myth

As much a mythical construct as a historical reality, ancient Rome's image has been carefully nurtured throughout history. Intellectuals, artists and architects have sought inspiration from this skilfully constructed legend, while political and religious rulers have invoked it to legitimise their authority and serve their political ends.

Imperial Spin Doctors

In 2014 excavations under the Lapis Niger in the Roman Forum unearthed a wall dating to between the end of the 9th century BCE and the early 8th century BCE. This would suggest that Rome was founded a century or so before its traditional birth date of 753 BCE.

Rome's original myth-makers were the first emperors. Eager to reinforce the city's status as *caput mundi* (capital of the world), they turned to writers such as Virgil, Ovid and Livy to create an official Roman history. These authors, while adept at weaving epic narratives, were less interested in the rigours of historical research and frequently presented myth as reality. In the *Aeneid,* Virgil brazenly draws on Greek legends and stories to tell the tale of Aeneas, a Trojan prince who arrives in Italy and establishes Rome's founding dynasty. Similarly, Livy, a writer celebrated for his monumental history of the Roman Republic, makes liberal use of mythology to fill the gaps in his historical narrative.

Ancient Rome's rulers were sophisticated masters of spin, and under their tutelage, art, architecture and public ceremony were employed to perpetuate the image of Rome as an invincible and divinely sanctioned power. Monuments such as the Ara Pacis, the Colonna di Traiano and the Arco di Costantino celebrated imperial glories, while gladiatorial games highlighted the Romans' physical superiority. The Colosseum, the Roman Forum and the Pantheon were not only sophisticated feats of engineering, they were also symbols of Rome's eternal might.

TIMELINE

753 BCE

According to legend, Romulus kills his twin brother Remus and founds Rome. Archaeological evidence exists of an 8th-century settlement on the Palatino.

509 BCE

On the death of the king Tarquinius Superbus, the Roman Republic is founded, paving the way for Rome's rise to European domination.

146 BCE

Carthage is razed to the ground at the end of the Third Punic War, and mainland Greece is conquered by rampant legionaries. Rome becomes undisputed master of the Mediterranean.

The Past as Inspiration

During the Renaissance, a period in which ancient Rome was hailed as the high point of Western civilisation, the city's great monuments inspired a whole generation of artists and architects. Bramante, Michelangelo and Raphael modelled their work on classical precedents as they helped rebuild Rome as the capital of the Catholic Church.

But more than anyone, it was Italy's 20th-century fascist dictator Benito Mussolini who invoked the glories of ancient Rome. Il Duce spared no effort in his attempts to identify his fascist regime with imperial Rome – he made Rome's traditional birthday, 21 April, an official fascist holiday, he printed stamps with images of ancient Roman emperors, and he commissioned archaeological digs to unearth further proof of Roman might. His idealisation of the Roman Empire underpinned much of his colonialist ideology.

Nowadays, the myth of Rome is used less as a rallying cry and more as an advertising tool – and with some success. However cynical and world-weary you are, it's difficult to deny the thrill of seeing the Colosseum for the first time or visiting the Palatino, the hill where Romulus is said to have founded the city in 753 BCE.

Ancient Rome on Screen

Spartacus (1960; Stanley Kubrick)

Quo Vadis (1951; Mervyn LeRoy)

Gladiator (2000; Ridley Scott)

I, Claudius (1976; BBC)

Rome (2005–07; HBO, BBC)

ROMULUS & REMUS, ROME'S LEGENDARY TWINS

The most famous of Rome's many legends is the story of Romulus and Remus and the foundation of the city on 21 April 753 BCE.

According to myth, Romulus and Remus were the children of the vestal virgin Rhea Silva and the god of war, Mars. While still babies they were set adrift on the Tiber to escape a death penalty imposed by their great-uncle Amulius, who at the time was battling their grandfather Numitor for control of Alba Longa. However, they were discovered near the Palatino by a she-wolf, who suckled them until a shepherd, Faustulus, found and raised them.

Years later the twins decided to found a city on the site where they'd originally been saved. They didn't know where this was, so they consulted the omens. Remus, on the Aventino, saw six vultures; his brother over on the Palatino saw 12. The meaning was clear and Romulus began building, much to the outrage of his brother. The two argued and Romulus killed Remus.

Romulus continued building and soon had a city. To populate it, he created a refuge on the Campidoglio, Aventino, Celio and Quirinale hills, to which a ragtag population of criminals, ex-slaves and outlaws soon decamped. However, the city still needed women. Romulus therefore invited everyone in the surrounding country to celebrate the Festival of Consus (21 August). As the spectators watched the festival games, Romulus and his men pounced and abducted all the women, an act that was to go down in history as the Rape of the Sabine Women.

73–71 BCE

Spartacus leads a slave revolt against dictator Cornelius Sulla. Defeat is inevitable; punishment is brutal. Spartacus and 6000 followers are crucified along Via Appia Antica.

49 BCE

'Alea iacta est' (The die is cast). Julius Caesar leads his army across the River Rubicon and marches on Rome. In the ensuing civil war, Caesar defeats rival Pompey.

44 BCE

On the Ides of March (15 March), soon after Julius Caesar is proclaimed dictator for life, he is stabbed to death in the Teatro di Pompeo (on modern-day Largo di Torre Argentina).

14 CE

Augustus dies after 41 years as Rome's first emperor. His reign is successful, unlike those of his mad successors, Tiberius and Caligula, who go down in history for their cruelty.

Legacy of an Empire

Rising out of the bloodstained remains of the Roman Republic, the Roman Empire was the Western world's first great superpower. At its zenith under the emperor Trajan (r 98–117 CE), it extended from Britannia in the north to North Africa in the south, from Hispania (Spain) in the west to Palestina (Palestine) and Syria in the east. Rome itself had more

A WHO'S WHO OF ROMAN EMPERORS

Of the 250 or so emperors of the Roman Empire, only a few were truly heroic. Here we highlight 10 of the best, worst and completely insane.

➡ **Augustus (27 BCE–14 CE)** Rome's first emperor. Ushers in a period of peace and security; the arts flourish and many monuments are built, including the Ara Pacis and the original Pantheon.

➡ **Caligula (37–41)** The third emperor, after Augustus and Tiberius. Remains popular until illness leads to the depraved behaviour for which he becomes infamous. Is murdered by his bodyguards on the Palatino.

➡ **Claudius (41–54)** Expands the Roman Empire and conquers Britain. Is eventually poisoned, probably at the instigation of Agrippina, his wife and Nero's mother.

➡ **Nero (54–68)** Initially rules well but later slips into madness – he has his mother murdered, persecutes the Christians and attempts to turn half the city into a palace, the Domus Aurea. He is eventually forced into suicide.

➡ **Vespasian (69–79)** First of the Flavian dynasty, he imposes peace and cleans up the imperial finances. His greatest legacy is the Colosseum.

➡ **Trajan (98–117)** Conquers the east and rules over the empire at its zenith. He revamps Rome's city centre, adding a forum, marketplace and column, all of which still stand.

➡ **Hadrian (117–38)** Puts an end to imperial expansion and constructs walls to mark the empire's borders. He rebuilds the Pantheon and has one of the ancient world's greatest villas built at Tivoli.

➡ **Aurelian (270–75)** Does much to control the rebellion that sweeps the empire at the end of the 3rd century. Starts construction of the city walls that still today bear his name.

➡ **Diocletian (284–305)** Splits the empire into eastern and western halves in 285. Launches a savage persecution of the Christians as he struggles to control the empire's eastern reaches.

➡ **Constantine I (306–37)** Although based in Byzantium (later renamed Constantinople in his honour), he legalises Christianity and embarks on a church-building spree in Rome.

64

Rome is ravaged by a huge fire that burns for five and a half days. Some blame Nero, although he was in Anzio when the conflagration broke out.

67

Sts Peter and Paul become martyrs as Nero massacres Rome's Christians. The persecution is a thinly disguised ploy to win back popularity after the great fire of 64 CE.

80

The 50,000-seat Flavian Amphitheatre, better known as the Colosseum, is inaugurated by the emperor Titus. Five thousand animals are slaughtered in the 100-day opening games.

285

To control anarchy within the Roman Empire, Diocletian splits it into two. The eastern half is later incorporated into the Byzantine Empire; the western half falls to the barbarians.

The Roman Empire

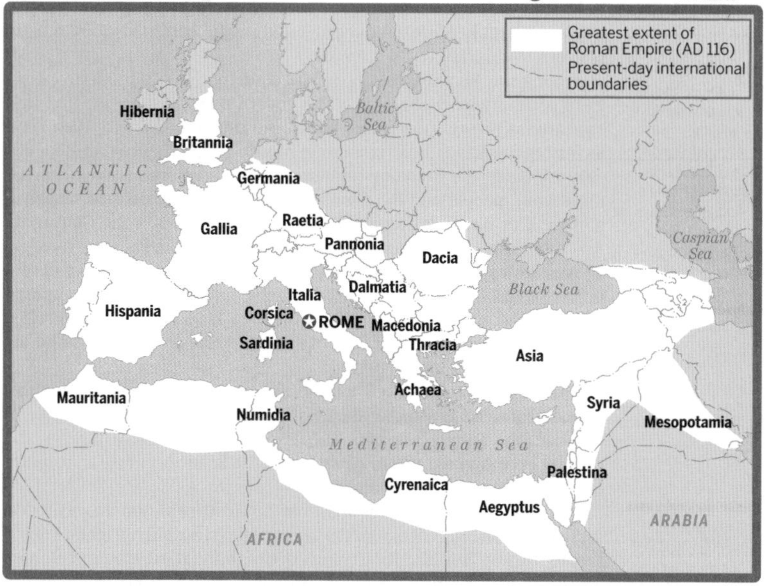

than 1.5 million inhabitants and the city sparkled with the trappings of imperial splendour: marble temples, public baths, theatres, circuses and libraries. Decline eventually set in during the 3rd century, and by the latter half of the 5th century the city was in barbarian hands.

Europe Divided

The empire's most immediate legacy was the division of Europe into east and west. In 285 CE the emperor Diocletian, prompted by widespread disquiet across the empire, split the Roman Empire into eastern and western halves – the west centred on Rome, the east on Byzantium (later called Constantinople) – in a move that was to have far-reaching consequences. In the west, the fall of the Western Roman Empire in 476 CE paved the way for the emergence of the Holy Roman Empire and the Papal States, while in the east, Roman (later Byzantine) rule continued until 1453 when the empire was conquered by Ottoman armies.

You'll see the letters SPQR everywhere in Rome. They were adopted during the Roman Republic and stand for Senatus Populusque Romanus (the Senate and People of Rome).

313

A year after his victory at the Battle of Milvian Bridge, the emperor Constantine issues the Edict of Milan, officially establishing religious tolerance and legally ending Christian persecution.

476

The fall of Romulus Augustulus marks the end of the Western Empire. This had been on the cards for years: in 410 the Goths sacked Rome; in 455 the Vandals followed suit.

754

Pope Stephen II and Pepin, king of the Franks, cut a deal resulting in the creation of the Papal States. The papacy is to rule Rome until Italian unification.

800

Pope Leo III crowns Pepin's son, Charlemagne, Holy Roman Emperor during Christmas mass at St Peter's Basilica. A red disk in the basilica marks the spot where it happened.

Democracy & the Rule of Law

Via Appia Antica is named after Appius Claudius Caecus, the Roman censor who initiated its construction in 312 BCE. He also built Rome's first aqueduct, the Aqua Appia, which brought water in from the Sabine Hills.

In broader cultural terms, Roman innovations in language, law, government, art, architecture, engineering and public administration remain relevant to this day.

Among the Romans' most striking contributions to modern society were certain aspects of democratic government. Democracy had first appeared in 5th-century-BCE Athens, and the Romans, with their genius for organisation, took it to another level. Under the Roman Republic (509–47 BCE), the Roman population was divided into two categories: the Roman people and the Senate. Both held clearly defined responsibilities. The people, through three assembly bodies – the Centuriate Assembly, the Tribal Assembly and the Council of the People – voted on all new laws and elected two annual tribunes who had the power of veto in the Senate. The Senate, for its part, elected and advised two annual consuls who acted as political and military leaders. It also controlled the Republic's purse strings and, in times of grave peril, could nominate a dictator for a six-month period.

This system worked well for the duration of the republic, and remained more or less intact during the empire – at least on paper. In practice, the Senate assumed the assemblies' legislative powers and the emperor claimed power of veto over the Senate, a move that pretty much gave him complete command.

Gladiatorial combat was part of the public games *(ludi)* put on at the Colosseum. Gladiators were prisoners of war, condemned criminals or volunteers who would fight in bouts of 10 to 15 minutes. Surprisingly, these rarely ended in death.

The observance of law was an important feature of Roman society. As far back as the 5th century BCE, the republic had a bill of rights, known as the Twelve Tables. This remained the foundation stone of Rome's legal system until the emperor Justinian (r 527–65) produced his mammoth *Corpus Iurus Civilis* (Body of Civil Law) in 529. This not only codified all existing laws, but also included a systematic treatise on legal philosophy. In particular, it introduced a distinction between *ius civilis* (civil law – laws particular to a state), *ius gentium* (law of nations – laws established and shared by states) and *ius naturale* (natural law – laws concerning male–female relationships and matrimony).

Latin

More than the laws themselves, Rome's greatest legacy to the legal profession was the Latin language. Latin was the lingua franca of the Roman Empire and was later adopted by the Catholic Church, a major reason for its survival. It is still one of the Vatican's official languages, and until the second Vatican Council (1962–65), it was the only language in which Catholic Mass could be said. As the basis for modern Romance languages such as Italian, French and Spanish, it provides the linguistic roots of many modern words.

1084

Rome is sacked by a Norman army after Pope Gregory VII invites them in to help him against the besieging forces of the Holy Roman Emperor Henry IV.

1300

Pope Boniface VIII proclaims Rome's first ever Jubilee, offering a full pardon to anyone who makes the pilgrimage to the city. Up to 200,000 people are said to have come.

1309

Fighting between French-backed pretenders to the papacy and Roman nobility ends in Pope Clement V transferring to Avignon. Only in 1377 does Pope Gregory XI return to Rome.

1347

Cola di Rienzo, a local notary, declares himself dictator of Rome. Surprisingly, he's welcomed by the people; less surprisingly, he's later driven out of town by the hostile aristocracy.

Christianity & Papal Power

For much of its history Rome has been ruled by the pope, and still today the Vatican wields immense influence over the city.

Before the arrival of Christianity, the Romans were remarkably tolerant of foreign religions. They themselves worshipped a cosmopolitan pantheon of gods, ranging from household spirits and former emperors to deities appropriated from Greek mythology (Jupiter, Juno, Neptune, Minerva etc). Religious cults were also popular – the Egyptian gods Isis and Serapis enjoyed a mass following, as did Mithras, a heroic saviour-god of vaguely Persian origin, who was worshipped by male-only devotees in underground temples.

Longest-Serving Popes

St Peter (r 30–67)

Pius XI (r 1846–78)

John Paul II (r 1978–2005)

Leo XIII (r 1878–1903)

Pius VI (r 1775–99)

Emergence of Christianity

Christianity entered Rome's religious cocktail in the 1st century CE, sweeping in from Judaea, a Roman province in what is now Israel and the West Bank. Its early days were marred by persecution, most notably under Nero (r 54–68), but Christianity slowly caught on, thanks to its popular message of heavenly reward and the evangelising efforts of Sts Peter and Paul. However, it was the conversion of the emperor Constantine (r 306–37) that really set Christianity on the path to European domination. In 313 Constantine issued the Edict of Milan, officially legalising Christianity, and later, in 378, Theodosius (r 379–95) made it Rome's state religion. By this time, the Church had developed a sophisticated organisational structure based on five major sees: Rome, Constantinople, Alexandria, Antioch and Jerusalem. At the outset, each bishopric carried equal weight, but in subsequent years Rome emerged as the senior party. The reasons for this were partly political (Rome was the wealthy capital of the Roman Empire) and partly religious (early Christian doctrine held that St Peter, founder of the Roman Church, had been sanctioned by Christ to lead the universal Church).

The patron saints of Rome, Peter and Paul, were both executed during Nero's persecution of the Christians between 64 and 68. Paul, who as a Roman citizen was entitled to a quick death, was beheaded, while Peter was crucified head down on Nero's Circus on the Vatican Hill.

Papal Control

But while Rome had control of Christianity, the Church had yet to conquer Rome. This it did in the dark days that followed the fall of the Roman Empire. And although no one person can take credit for this, Pope Gregory the Great (r 590–604) did more than most to lay the groundwork. A leader of considerable foresight, he won many friends by supplying free bread to Rome's starving citizens and restoring the city's water supply after it had been cut by barbarian invaders. He also stood up to the menacing Lombards, who presented a very real threat to the city.

1378–1417

Squabbling between factions in the Catholic Church leads to the Great Schism. The pope rules in Rome while the alternative anti-pope sits in Avignon.

1506

Pope Julius II employs 150 Swiss mercenaries to protect him. The Swiss Guard, all practising Catholics from Switzerland, are still responsible for the pope's personal safety.

1508

Michelangelo starts painting the Sistine Chapel, while down the hall Raphael decorates Pope Julius II's private apartments, now known as the Stanze di Raffaello (Raphael Rooms).

1527

Pope Clement VII takes refuge in Castel Sant'Angelo as Rome is sacked by troops loyal to Charles V, king of Spain and Holy Roman Emperor.

DONATION OF CONSTANTINE

The most famous forgery in medieval history, the Donation of Constantine is a document with which Emperor Constantine purportedly grants Pope Sylvester I (r 314–35) and his successors control of Rome and the Western Roman Empire, as well as primacy over the holy sees of Antioch, Alexandria, Constantinople, Jerusalem and all the world's churches.

No one is exactly sure when the document was written, but the consensus is that it dates to the mid- or late 8th century. Certainly this fits with the widespread theory that the author was a Roman cleric, possibly working with the knowledge of Pope Stephen II (r 752–57).

For centuries the donation was accepted as genuine and used by popes to justify their territorial claims. But in 1440 the Italian philosopher Lorenzo Valla proved that it was a forgery. By analysing the Latin used in the document he was able to show that it was inconsistent with the Latin used in the 4th century.

It was this threat that pushed the papacy into an alliance with the Frankish kings, an alliance that resulted in the creation of the two great powers of medieval Europe: the Papal States and the Holy Roman Empire. In Rome, the battle between these two superpowers translated into endless feuding between the city's baronial families and frequent attempts by the French to claim the papacy for their own. This political and military fighting eventually culminated in the papacy transferring to the French city of Avignon between 1309 and 1377, and the Great Schism (1378–1417), a period in which the Catholic world was headed by two popes, one in Rome and one in Avignon.

As both religious and temporal leaders, Rome's popes wielded influence well beyond their military capacity. For much of the medieval period, the Church held a virtual monopoly on Europe's reading material (mostly religious scripts written in Latin) and was the authority on virtually every aspect of human knowledge. All innovations in science, philosophy and literature had to be cleared by the Church's hawkish scholars, who were constantly on the lookout for heresy.

The pope's personal fiefdom, the Papal States were established in the 8th century after the Frankish King Pepin drove the Lombards out of northern Italy and donated large tracts of territory to Pope Stephen II. At the height of their reach, the States encompassed Rome and much of central Italy.

Modern Influence

Almost a thousand years on and the Church is still a major influence on modern Italian life. Its rigid stance on social and ethical issues such as birth control, abortion, same-sex marriage and euthanasia informs much public debate, often with highly divisive results.

The relationship between the Church and Italy's modern political establishment has been a fact of life since the founding of the Italian

1540

Pope Paul III officially recognises the Society of Jesus, aka the Jesuits. The order is founded by Ignatius de Loyola, who spends his last days in the Chiesa del Gesù.

1555

As fear pervades Counter-Reformation Rome, Pope Paul IV confines the city's Jews to the area known as the Jewish Ghetto. Official intolerance continues on and off until the 20th century.

1626

After more than 150 years of construction, St Peter's Basilica is consecrated. The hulking basilica remains the largest church in the world until well into the 20th century.

1632

Galileo Galilei is summoned to appear before the Inquisition. He is forced to renounce his belief that the earth revolves around the sun and is exiled to Florence.

Republic in 1946. For much of the First Republic (1946–94), the Vatican was closely associated with the Christian Democrat party (Democrazia Cristiana; DC), Italy's most powerful party and an ardent opponent of communism. At the same time, the Church, keen to weed communism out of the political landscape, played its part by threatening to excommunicate anyone who voted for Italy's Communist Party (Partito Comunista Italiano; PCI).

Today, no one political party has a monopoly on Church favour, and politicians across the spectrum tread warily around Catholic sensibilities. But this reverence isn't limited to the purely political sphere; it also informs much press reporting and even law enforcement. In September 2008 Rome's public prosecutor threatened to prosecute a comedian for comments made against the pope, invoking the 1929 Lateran Treaty under which it is a criminal offence to 'offend the honour' of the pope and the Italian president. The charge, which ignited a heated debate on censorship and the right to free speech, was eventually dropped by the Italian justice minister.

Historical Reads

SPQR: A History of Ancient Rome (Mary Beard; 2015)

Rome: The Biography of a City (Christopher Hibbert; 1985)

Absolute Monarchs (John Julius Norwich; 2011)

Italian Hours (Henry James; 1909)

New Beginnings, Protest & Persecution

Bridging the gap between the Middle Ages and the modern era, the Renaissance (*Rinascimento* in Italian) was a far-reaching intellectual, artistic and cultural movement. It emerged in 14th-century Florence but quickly spread to Rome, where it gave rise to one of the greatest makeovers the city had ever seen. Not everyone was impressed, though, and in the early 16th century the Protestant Reformation burst into life. This, in turn, provoked a furious response by the Catholic Church, the Counter-Reformation.

Humanism & Rebuilding

The intellectual cornerstone of the Renaissance was humanism, a philosophy that focused on the central role of humanity within the universe; this was a major break from the medieval world view, which had placed God at the centre of everything. It was not anti-religious, though. Many humanist scholars were priests and most of Rome's great works of Renaissance art were commissioned by the Church. In fact, it was one of the most celebrated humanist scholars of the 15th century, Pope Nicholas V (r 1447–55), who is generally considered the harbinger of the Roman Renaissance.

When Nicholas became pope in 1447, Rome was not in good shape. Centuries of medieval feuding had reduced the city to a semi-deserted battleground, and its bedraggled population lived in constant fear of plague, famine and flooding (the Tiber regularly broke its banks). In

The Borgias, led by family patriarch Rodrigo, aka Pope Alexander VI (r 1492–1503), were one of Renaissance Rome's most notorious families. Machiavelli supposedly modelled *Il Principe* (The Prince) on Rodrigo's son, Cesare, while his daughter, Lucrezia, earned notoriety as a femme fatale with a penchant for poisoning her enemies.

1656–67

Gian Lorenzo Bernini lays out St Peter's Square for Pope Alexander VII. Bernini, along with his great rival Francesco Borromini, are the leading exponents of Roman baroque architecture.

1798

Napoleon marches into Rome, forcing Pope Pius VI to flee. A republic is announced, but it doesn't last long and in 1801 Pius VI's successor, Pius VII, returns to Rome.

1870

Nine years after Italian unification, Rome's city walls are breached at Porta Pia and Pope Pius IX is forced to cede the city to Italy. Rome becomes the Italian capital.

1885

To celebrate Italian unification and honour Italy's first king, Vittorio Emanuele II, construction work begins on Il Vittoriano, the mountainous monument dominating Piazza Venezia.

political terms, the papacy was recovering from the trauma of the Great Schism and attempting to face down Muslim encroachment in the east.

It was against this background that Nicholas decided to rebuild Rome as a showcase for Church power. To finance his plans, he declared 1450 a Jubilee year, a tried and tested way of raising funds by attracting hundreds of thousands of pilgrims to the city (in a Jubilee year anyone who comes to Rome and confesses receives a full papal pardon).

Over the course of the next 80 years or so, Rome underwent a complete overhaul. Pope Sixtus IV (r 1471–84) had the Sistine Chapel built and, in 1471, gave the people of Rome a selection of bronzes that became the first exhibits of the Capitoline Museums. Julius II (r 1503–13) laid Via del Corso and Via Giulia, and ordered Bramante to rebuild St Peter's Basilica. Michelangelo frescoed the Sistine Chapel and designed the dome of St Peter's, while Raphael inspired a whole generation of painters with his masterful grasp of perspective.

The Roman Inquisition was set up in the 16th century to counter the threat of Protestantism. It was responsible for prosecuting people accused of heresy, blasphemy, immorality and witchcraft, and although it did order executions, it often imposed lighter punishments such as fines and the recital of prayers.

The Sack of Rome & Protestant Protest

Rome's Renaissance rebuild wasn't all plain sailing. By the early 16th century, the long-standing conflict between the Holy Roman Empire, led by the Spanish Charles V, and the Italian city states remained the main source of trouble. This simmering tension came to a head in 1527 when Rome was invaded by Charles' marauding army and ransacked while Pope Clement VII (r 1523–34) hid in Castel Sant'Angelo. The sack of Rome, regarded by most historians as the nail in the coffin of the Roman Renaissance, was a hugely traumatic event. It left the papacy reeling and gave rise to the view that the Church had been greatly weakened by its own moral shortcomings. That the Church was corrupt was well known, and it was with considerable public support that Martin Luther pinned his *95 Theses* to a church door in Wittenberg in 1517, thus sparking the Protestant Reformation.

The Counter-Reformation

The Counter-Reformation, the Catholic response to the Protestant Reformation, was marked by a second wave of artistic and architectural activity as the Church once again turned to bricks and mortar to restore its authority. But in contrast to the Renaissance, the Counter-Reformation was also a period of persecution and official intolerance. With the full blessing of Pope Paul III, Ignatius Loyola founded the Jesuits in 1540, and two years later the Holy Office was set up as the Church's final appeals court for trials prosecuted by the Inquisition. In 1559 the Church published the *Index Librorum Prohibitorum* (Index of Prohibited Books) and began to persecute intellectuals and freethinkers.

1922

Some 40,000 fascists march on Rome. King Vittorio Emanuele III, worried about the possibility of civil war, invites the 39-year-old Mussolini to form a government.

1929

Keen to appease the Church, Mussolini signs the Lateran Treaty, creating the state of the Vatican City. To celebrate, Via della Conciliazione is bulldozed through the medieval Borgo.

1944

On 24 March, 335 Romans are shot by Nazi troops in an unused quarry on Via Ardeatina. The massacre is a reprisal for a partisan bomb attack in Via Rasella.

1946

The Italian republic is born after a vote to abolish the monarchy. Two years later, on 1 January 1948, the Italian constitution becomes law.

Galileo Galilei (1564–1642) was forced to renounce his assertion of the Copernican astronomical system, which held that the earth moved around the sun. He was summoned by the Inquisition to Rome in 1632 and exiled to Florence for the rest of his life. Giordano Bruno (1548–1600), a freethinking Dominican monk, fared worse. Arrested in Venice in 1592, he was burned at the stake eight years later in Campo de' Fiori.

Despite, or perhaps because of, the Church's policy of zero tolerance, the Counter-Reformation was largely successful in re-establishing papal prestige. And in this sense it can be seen as the natural finale to the Renaissance that Nicholas V had kicked off in 1450. From being a rural backwater with a population of around 20,000 in the mid-15th century, Rome had grown to become one of Europe's great 17th-century cities.

Political Reads

Good Italy: Bad Italy (Bill Emmott; 2012)

The Dark Heart of Italy (Tobias Jones; 2003)

Modern Italy: A Political History (Denis Mack Smith; 1959)

The Sack of Rome (Alexander Stille; 2006)

Power & Corruption

The exercise of power has long gone hand in hand with corruption. And no one enjoyed greater power than Rome's ancient emperors and Renaissance popes.

Imperial Follies & Papal Foibles

Of all ancient Rome's cruel, despotic leaders, few are as notorious as Caligula. A byword for depravity, he was initially hailed as a saviour when he inherited the empire from his hated great-uncle Tiberius in 37 CE. But this optimism was soon to prove ill-founded, and after a bout of serious illness, Caligula began showing disturbing signs of mental instability. He forced his senators to worship him and infamously tried to make his horse a senator. By 41 CE everyone had had enough of him, and on 24 January the leader of his own Praetorian Guard stabbed him to death.

Debauchery on such a scale was rare in the Renaissance papacy, but corruption was no stranger to the corridors of ecclesiastical power. It was not uncommon for popes to father illegitimate children and nepotism was rife. The Borgia pope Alexander VI (r 1492–1503) had two illegitimate children with the first of his two high-profile mistresses. The second, Giulia Farnese, was the sister of the cardinal who was later to become Pope Paul III (r 1534–59), himself no stranger to earthly pleasures. When not persecuting heretics during the Counter-Reformation, the Farnese pontiff managed to father four children.

Tangentopoli

The early 1990s was a traumatic time for Italy's political establishment, which was virtually brought to its knees during the so-called *Tangentopoli* (Kickback City) scandal. Against a backdrop of steady

1957

Leaders of Italy, France, West Germany, Belgium, Holland and Luxembourg meet in the Capitoline Museums to sign the Treaty of Rome and establish the European Economic Community.

1960

Rome stages the Olympic Games while Federico Fellini films *La Dolce Vita* at Cinecittà studios. Three years later, Elizabeth Taylor falls for Richard Burton while filming *Cleopatra* there.

1968

Widespread student unrest results in mass protests across Italy. In Rome, students clash with police at La Sapienza's architecture faculty, an event remembered as the Battle of Valle Giulia.

1978

Former PM Aldo Moro is kidnapped and shot by a cell of the extreme left-wing Brigate Rosse (Red Brigades) during Italy's *anni di piombo* (years of lead).

economic growth, the controversy broke in Milan in 1992 when a routine corruption case – accepting bribes in exchange for contracts – blew up into a nationwide crusade against corruption.

Led by magistrate Antonio di Pietro, the Mani Pulite (Clean Hands) investigations exposed a political and business system riddled with corruption. Politicians, public officials and business people were investigated, and for once no one was spared, not even the powerful Bettino Craxi (prime minister between 1983 and 1989), who rather than face trial fled Rome in 1993. He was subsequently convicted in absentia on corruption charges and died in self-imposed exile in Tunisia.

The Rubygate affair centred on Silvio Berlusconi's trial for paying for sex with an underage dancer nicknamed Ruby the Heartstealer. He was found guilty, but his conviction was later overturned on appeal. In 2018, he was indicted for bribing witnesses in the case.

Contemporary Controversy

Controversy and lurid gossip were a recurring feature of Silvio Berlusconi's three terms as prime minister (1994, 2000–06 and 2008–11). Berlusconi himself faced a series of trials on charges ranging from abuse of power to paying for sex with an underage prostitute. To date, he has only been convicted once, for tax fraud in 2012, but that could change depending on the outcome of an ongoing trial in which he's accused of bribing witnesses in an earlier case.

Rome's City Hall has also been embroiled in scandal. In 2014, the so-called Mafia Capitale case broke as allegations surfaced that the city's municipal council had been colluding with a criminal gang to skim public funds. An investigation, the largest anti-corruption operation since the Mani Pulite campaign of the 1990s, culminated in convictions for 41 people, including former mayor Gianni Alemanno who was sentenced to six years in jail for corruption and illegal financing.

The First Tourists

Pilgrims have been pouring into Rome for centuries but it was the classically minded travellers of the 18th and 19th centuries who established the city's reputation as a holiday hotspot.

Religious Pilgrimages

As seat of the Catholic Church, Rome was already one of the main pilgrim destinations in the Middle Ages when, in 1300, Pope Boniface VIII proclaimed the first ever Holy Year (Jubilee). Promising full forgiveness for anyone who made the pilgrimage to St Peter's Basilica and the Basilica di San Giovanni in Laterano, his appeal to the faithful proved a resounding success. Hundreds of thousands answered his call, and the Church basked in popular glory.

1992–93	2000	2001	2005
A nationwide anti-corruption crusade, Mani Pulite (Clean Hands), shakes the political and business establishment. Many high-profile figures are arrested and former PM Bettino Craxi flees the country.	Pilgrims pour into Rome from all over the world to celebrate the Catholic Church's Jubilee year. A high point is a mass attended by two million people at Tor Vergata university.	Colourful media tycoon Silvio Berlusconi becomes prime minister for the second time. His first term in 1994 was a short-lived affair; his second lasts the full five-year course.	Pope John Paul II dies after 27 years on the papal throne. He is replaced by his long-standing ally Josef Ratzinger, who takes the name Benedict XVI.

Some 700 years later and the Holy Year tradition is still going strong. Up to 24 million visitors descended on the city for Pope John Paul II's Jubilee, while it's estimated around 21 million pilgrims passed through the holy doors of St Peter's Basilica during Pope Francis' 2016 Holy Year.

Romantic poet John Keats lived the last months of his short life in a house by the Spanish Steps. He died aged 25 in February 1821 and, along with fellow poet Percy Bysshe Shelley, was buried in Rome's Cimitero Acattolico per gli Stranieri.

The Grand Tour

While Rome has long been a pilgrimage site, its history as a modern tourist destination can be traced back to the late 1700s and the fashion for the Grand Tour. The 18th-century version of a gap year, the Tour was considered an educational rite of passage for wealthy young men from northern Europe, and Britain in particular.

The overland journey through France and into Italy followed the medieval pilgrim route, entering Italy via the St Bernard Pass and descending the west coast before cutting in to Florence and then down to Rome. After a sojourn in the capital, tourists would venture down to Naples, where the newly discovered ruins of Pompeii and Herculaneum were causing much excitement, before heading up to Venice.

Rome, enjoying a rare period of peace, was perfectly set up for this English invasion. The city was basking in the aftermath of the 17th-century baroque building boom, and a craze for all things classical was sweeping Europe. Rome's papal authorities were also crying out for money after their excesses had left the city coffers bare, reducing much of the population to abject poverty.

Thousands came, including Goethe, who stopped off to write his travelogue *Italian Journey* (1817), as well as Byron, Shelley and Keats, who all fuelled their romantic sensibilities in the city's vibrant streets. So many English people stayed around Piazza di Spagna that locals christened the area *er ghetto de l'inglesi* (the English ghetto).

Artistically, rococo was the rage of the moment. The Spanish Steps, built between 1723 and 1726, proved a major hit with tourists, as did the exuberant Trevi Fountain.

In his 1818 work *Childe Harold's Pilgrimage*, the English poet Lord Byron quotes the words of the 8th-century monk Bede: 'While stands the Coliseum, Rome shall stand; When falls the Coliseum, Rome shall fall! And when Rome falls – the World.'

The Ghosts of Fascism

Rome's fascist history is a highly charged subject. Historians on both sides of the political spectrum have accused each other of recasting the past to suit their views: left-wing historians have criticised their right-wing counterparts for glossing over the more unpleasant aspects of Mussolini's regime, while right-wingers have attacked their left-wing colleagues for whitewashing the facts to perpetuate an overly simplistic anti-fascist narrative. In 2018, mayor Virginia Raggi announced that the city will rename streets still named after fascists.

2008

Gianni Alemanno, a former member of the neo-fascist MSI (Movimento Sociale Italiano), sweeps to victory in Rome's mayoral elections. The news makes headlines across the world.

2012

On 31 October the Pope leads a vespers prayer service in the Sistine Chapel to celebrate the 500th anniversary of Michelangelo's celebrated ceiling frescoes.

2013

The anti-establishment Movimento 5 Stelle (Five Star Movement), led by charismatic rabble rouser, blogger and former comedian Beppe Grillo, takes a quarter of the vote in Italy's general election.

2013

Pope Benedict XVI becomes the first pope to resign since Gregory XII in 1415. He is replaced by the Argentinian cardinal Jorge Mario Bergoglio who is elected Pope Francis.

Mussolini

Benito Mussolini was born in 1883 in Forlì, a small town in Emilia-Romagna, a region of northern Italy. As a young man he was a member of the Italian Socialist Party, but service in WWI and Italy's subsequent descent into chaos led to a change of heart, and in 1919 he founded the Italian Fascist Party. Calling for rights for war veterans, law and order, and a strong nation, the party won support from disillusioned soldiers, many of whom joined the squads of Blackshirts that Mussolini used to intimidate his political enemies.

In 1921 Mussolini was elected to the Chamber of Deputies. His parliamentary support was limited but on 28 October 1922 he marched on Rome with 40,000 black-shirted followers. Fearful of civil war between the fascists and socialists, King Vittorio Emanuele III responded by inviting Mussolini to form a government. His first government was a coalition of fascists, nationalists and liberals, but victory in the 1924 elections left him better placed to consolidate his power, and by the end of 1925 he had seized complete control of Italy. In order to silence the Church he signed the Lateran Treaty in 1929, which made Catholicism the state religion and recognised the sovereignty of the Vatican State.

Nowhere more vividly displays the fascist obsession with sport and the male ideal than the Foro Italico sports complex. The entrance is marked by an obelisk inscribed with the words Mussolini Dux, while inside 59 giant marble nudes strike muscular poses at the Stadio dei Marmi (Stadium of the Marbles).

On the home front, Mussolini embarked on a huge building program in Rome: Via dei Fori Imperiali and Via della Conciliazione were laid out; parks were opened on the Oppio Hill and at Villa Celimontana; the Imperial Forums and the temples at Largo di Torre Argentina were excavated; and the monumental Foro Italico sports complex and EUR were built.

Abroad, Mussolini invaded Abyssinia (now Ethiopia) in 1935 and sided with Hitler in 1936. In 1940, standing on the balcony of Rome's Palazzo Venezia, he announced Italy's entry into WWII to a vast, cheering crowd. The good humour didn't last, as Rome suffered, first at the hands of its own fascist regime then, after Mussolini was ousted in 1943, at the hands of the Nazis. Rome was liberated from German occupation on 4 June 1944.

Postwar Period

Defeat in WWII didn't kill off Italian fascism, and in 1946 hardline Mussolini supporters founded the Movimento Sociale Italiano (MSI; Italian Social Movement). For close on 50 years this overtly fascist party participated in mainstream Italian politics, while at the other end of the spectrum the Partito Comunista Italiano (PCI; Italian Communist Party) grew into Western Europe's largest communist party. The MSI was finally dissolved in 1994, when Gianfranco Fini rebranded it as the post-fascist Alleanza Nazionale (AN; National Alliance). AN remained

2014

Ex-mayor Gianni Alemanno and up to 100 politicians and public officials are placed under police investigation as the so-called *Mafia Capitale* scandal rocks Rome.

2015

Rome's presidential palace, Palazzo del Quirinale, gets a new resident as Sergio Mattarella replaces 89-year-old Giorgio Napolitano as Italy's Presidente della Repubblica.

2016

Onlookers applaud the Colosseum's polished new look after completion of an extensive three-year clean-up, the first in its 2000-year history. The makeover comes as part of a €25 million restoration project.

2016

Virginia Raggi, a 37-year-old lawyer from the anti-establishment Five Star Movement, becomes Rome's first woman, and youngest, mayor. Her term is beset by scandal and popular disapproval.

an important political player until it was incorporated into Silvio Berlusconi's former Popolo della Libertà (PdL; People of Freedom) party in 2009. More than a decade on, the far-right is once again a major political force under its two high-profile leaders: Matteo Salvini, head of the Lega (League) party, and Giorgia Meloni of the rival Fratelli d'Italia (Brothers of Italy) party.

Outside the political mainstream, fascism (along with communism) was a driving force of the domestic terrorism that rocked Rome and Italy during the *anni di piombo* (years of lead), between the late 1960s and early '80s. Terrorist groups emerged on both sides of the ideological spectrum, giving rise to a spate of politically inspired violence. In one of the era's most notorious episodes, the communist Brigate Rosse (Red Brigades) kidnapped and killed former prime minister Aldo Moro in 1978, leaving his bullet-riddled body in the boot of a car on Via Michelangelo Caetani near the Jewish Ghetto.

2017

As Brexit shockwaves continue to rock Europe, 27 EU leaders gather on the Capitoline Hill to celebrate the EU's 60th anniversary. The 1957 Treaty of Rome paved the way for the birth of the union.

2018

Giuseppe Conte is sworn in as PM, heading a populist coalition formed by the Five Star Movement and hard-right League party.

2020

Rome shuts up shop as Italy becomes the first European country to impose a nationwide anti-COVID lockdown. Citizens keep spirits high by singing on their apartment balconies.

2021

'Super' Mario Draghi, former chief of the European Central Bank, becomes PM after Conte's coalition collapses. Top of his agenda: defeating COVID and promoting economic recovery.

The Arts

Rome's turbulent history and magical cityscape have long provided inspiration for painters, sculptors, film-makers, writers and musicians. The great classical works of Roman antiquity fuelled the imagination of Renaissance artists; Counter-Reformation persecution led to baroque art and popular street satire and the trauma of Mussolini and WWII found expression in neo-realist cinema. More recently, urban art has flourished and film-making has returned to the streets of Rome.

Painting & Sculpture

Home to some of the Western world's most recognisable art, Rome is a visual feast. Its churches alone contain more masterpieces than many small countries, and the city's galleries are laden with works by world-famous artists.

The best-surviving examples of Etruscan frescoes are found in Tarquinia, where up to 6000 tombs have been discovered. Particularly impressive are the illustrations in the Tomba delle Leonesse (*Tomb of the Lionesses*).

Etruscan Groundwork

Laying the groundwork for much later Roman art, the Etruscans placed great importance on their funerary rites, and they developed sepulchral decoration into a highly sophisticated art form. Elaborate stone sarcophagi were often embellished with a reclining figure or a couple, typically depicted with a haunting, enigmatic smile. A stunning example is the *Sarcofago degli Sposi* (Sarcophagus of the Betrothed) in the Museo Nazionale Etrusco di Villa Giulia. Underground funerary vaults were further enlivened with bright, exuberant frescoes.

The Etruscans were also noted for their bronze work and filigree jewellery. Bronze ore was abundant and was used to craft everything from chariots to candelabras, bowls and polished mirrors. Etruscan jewellery was unrivalled throughout the Mediterranean, and goldsmiths produced elaborate pieces using sophisticated filigree and granulation techniques.

For Italy's best collection of Etruscan art, head to the Museo Nazionale Etrusco di Villa Giulia (p208); to see Etruscan treasures in situ, head up to Cerveteri and Tarquinia.

One of Rome's great medieval artists was Pietro Cavallini (c 1240–1330). Little is known about this Roman-born painter, but his most famous work is the *Giudizio universale* (Last Judgment) fresco in the Chiesa di Santa Cecilia in Trastevere.

Roman Developments

In art, as in architecture, the ancient Romans borrowed heavily from the Etruscans and Greeks. In terms of decorative art, the Roman use of mosaics and wall paintings was derived from Etruscan funerary decoration. By the 1st century BCE, floor mosaics were a popular form of home decor. Typical themes included landscapes, still lifes, geometric patterns and depictions of gods. Later, as production and artistic techniques improved, mosaics were displayed on walls and in public buildings. In the Museo Nazionale Romano: Palazzo Massimo alle Terme (p152), you'll find some spectacular wall mosaics from Nero's villa in Anzio, as well as a series of superb 1st-century-BCE frescoes from Villa Livia, one of the homes of Livia Drusilla, Augustus' wife.

Sculpture

Sculpture was an important element of Roman art, and was largely influenced by Greek styles. In fact, early Roman sculptures were often made by Greek artists. They were largely concerned with the male physique and generally depicted visions of male beauty in mythical settings – the *Apollo Belvedere* and *Laocoön* in the Vatican Museums' Museo Pio-Clementino are classic examples.

However, over time Roman sculpture began to focus on accurate representation, mainly in the form of sculptural portraits. Browse the collections of the Capitoline Museums (p69) or the Museo Nazionale Romano: Palazzo Massimo alle Terme (p152) and you'll be struck by how lifelike so many of the marble faces are.

In terms of function, Roman art was highly propagandistic. From the time of Augustus (r 27 BCE to 14 CE), art was increasingly used to serve the state, and artists came to be regarded as little more than state functionaries. This new narrative art often took the form of relief decoration illustrating great military victories – the Colonna Traiana (p74) and Ara Pacis (p112) are stunning examples of the genre.

Dramatically ensconced in a Richard Meier–designed pavilion, the Ara Pacis is a key work of ancient Roman sculpture. The vast marble altar is covered with detailed reliefs, including one showing Augustus at the head of a procession, followed by the entire imperial family.

Early Christian Art

The earliest Christian art in Rome are the traces of biblical frescoes in the Catacombe di Priscilla (p209) and the Catacombe di San Sebastiano (p221). These, and other early works, are full of now iconic images: Lazarus being raised from the dead, Jesus as the good shepherd, and the first Christian saints. Symbols also abound: the dove representing peace and happiness, the anchor or trident symbolising the cross, fish in reference to Jesus Christ.

Mosaics

With the legalisation of Christianity in the 4th century, these images began to move into the public arena, appearing in mosaics across the city. Mosaic work was the principal artistic endeavour of early Christian Rome, and mosaics adorn many of the churches built in this period, including the Mausoleo di Santa Costanza (p209) and the Basilica di Santa Maria Maggiore (p153).

Eastern influences became much more pronounced between the 7th and 9th centuries, when Byzantine styles swept in from the east, leading to a brighter, golden look. The best examples in Rome are in the Basilica di Santa Maria in Trastevere (p174) and the 9th-century Basilica di Santa Prassede (p154).

The Renaissance

Originating in late-14th-century Florence, the Renaissance had already made its mark in Tuscany and Venice before it arrived in Rome in the latter half of the 15th century. But over the next few decades it was to have a profound impact on the city as the top artists of the day were summoned to decorate the many new buildings going up around town.

Michelangelo & the Sistine Chapel

Rome's most celebrated works of Renaissance art are Michelangelo's paintings in the Sistine Chapel (p136) – his cinematic ceiling frescoes, painted between 1508 and 1512, and the *Giudizio universale* (Last Judgment), which he worked on between 1536 and 1541.

Michelangelo Buanarroti (1475–1564), born near Arrezzo in Tuscany, was the embodiment of the Renaissance spirit. A painter, sculptor, architect and occasional poet, he, more than any other artist of the era, left an indelible mark on the Eternal City. The Sistine Chapel, his *Pietà*

Key Renaissance Works

- *Pietà (St Peter's Basilica)*
- *La Scuola di Atene (Vatican Museums)*
- *Deposizione di Cristo (Galleria e Museo Borghese)*
- *Handing over of the Keys (Sistine Chapel)*

ROME'S TOP ART CHURCHES

St Peter's Basilica (p126) Michelangelo's divine *Pietà* is just one of the many masterpieces on display at the Vatican's showcase basilica.

Basilica di San Pietro in Vincoli (p152) Moses stands as the muscular centrepiece of Michelangelo's unfinished tomb of Pope Julius II.

Chiesa di San Luigi dei Francesi (p84) Frescoes by Domenichino are outshone by three Caravaggio canvases depicting the life and death of St Matthew.

Basilica di Santa Maria del Popolo (p107) A veritable gallery with frescoes by Pinturicchio, a Raphael-designed chapel and two paintings by Caravaggio.

Chiesa di Santa Maria della Vittoria (p114) The church's innocuous exterior gives no clues that this is home to Bernini's extraordinary *Santa Teresa traffita dall'amore di Dio* (Ecstasy of St Teresa).

Basilica di Santa Prassede (p152) The Cappella di San Zenone features some of Rome's most brilliant Byzantine mosaics.

in St Peter's Basilica, sculptures in the city's churches – his masterpieces are legion and they remain city highlights to this day.

Raphael, Master of Perspective

Renaissance art, inspired by humanism, which held humans to be central to the God-created universe and beauty to represent a deep inner virtue, focused heavily on the human form. This, in turn, led artists to develop a far greater appreciation of perspective. Early Renaissance painters made great strides in formulating rules of perspective but they still struggled to paint harmonious arrangements of people. And it was this that Raffaello Sanzio (Raphael; 1483–1520) tackled in his great masterpiece *La scuola di Atene* (The School of Athens; 1510–11) in the Vatican Museums.

Originally from Urbino, Raphael arrived in Rome in 1508 and went on to become the most influential painter of his generation. He painted many versions of the Madonna and Child, all of which epitomise the Western model of 'ideal beauty' that perseveres to this day. There are some fine examples at the Museo e Galleria Borghese (p204).

Counter-Reformation & the Baroque

The baroque burst onto Rome's art scene in the early 17th century. Combining an urgent sense of dynamism with highly charged emotion, it was enthusiastically appropriated by the Catholic Church, which used it as a propaganda tool in its persecution of heresy during the Counter-Reformation. The powerful popes and cardinals of the day eagerly championed the likes of Caravaggio, Gian Lorenzo Bernini, Domenichino, Pietro da Cortona and Alessandro Algardi.

Not surprisingly, much baroque art has a religious theme, and you'll often find depictions of martyrdoms, ecstasies and miracles.

Big-Name Baroque Artists

Annibale Carracci (1560–1609)

Caravaggio (1573–1610)

Domenichino (1581–1641)

Pietro da Cortona (1596–1669)

Gian Lorenzo Bernini (1598–1680)

Caravaggio

One of the key painters of the period was Michelangelo Merisi (1573–1610), the *enfant terrible* of the Roman art world better known as Caravaggio. A controversial and often violent character, he arrived in Rome from Milan around 1590 and immediately set about rewriting the artistic rule books. While his peers and Catholic patrons sought to glorify and overwhelm, he painted subjects as he saw them. He had no time for 'ideal beauty' and caused uproar with his lifelike portrayal of hitherto sacrosanct subjects –

his *Madonna dei pellegrini* (Madonna of the Pilgrims) in the Chiesa di Sant'Agostino is typical of his audacious approach.

Gian Lorenzo Bernini

While Caravaggio shocked his patrons, Gian Lorenzo Bernini (1598–1680) delighted them with his stunning sculptures. More than anyone else, Bernini was able to capture a moment, freezing emotions and conveying a sense of dramatic action. His depiction of *Santa Teresa traffita dall'amore di Dio* (Ecstasy of St Teresa) in the Chiesa di Santa Maria della Vittoria (p116) does just that, blending realism, eroticism and theatrical spirituality in a work that is widely considered one of the greatest of the baroque period. For further proof of his genius see his mythical sculptures at the Museo e Galleria Borghese (p204).

Top Galleries & Museums

Vatican Museums (Vatican City, Borgo & Prati)

Museo e Galleria Borghese (Villa Borghese & Northern Rome)

Capitoline Museums (Ancient Rome)

Frescoes

Fresco painting continued to provide work for artists well into the 17th century. Important exponents include Domenichino (1581–1641), whose decorative works adorn Chiesa di San Luigi dei Francesi (p86) and the Chiesa di Sant'Andrea della Valle (p87); Pietro da Cortona (1596–1669), author of the extraordinary *Trionfo della divina provvidenza* (Triumph of Divine Providence) in Palazzo Barberini (p111); and Annibale Carracci (1560–1609), the genius behind the frescoes in Palazzo Farnese (p86), reckoned by some to equal those of the Sistine Chapel.

Futurism

Often associated with fascism, Italian futurism was an ambitious wide-ranging movement, embracing the visual arts, architecture, music, fashion and theatre. The futurists, who first met in 1906 in a studio on Via Margutta, were evangelical advocates of modernism, and their works highlighted dynamism, speed, machinery and technology.

One of the movement's founding fathers, Giacomo Balla (1871–1958) encapsulated the futurist ideals in works such as *Espansione dinamica velocità* (Dynamic Expansion and Speed) and *Forme grido Viva l'Italia* (The Shout Viva l'Italia). Both are on show at La Galleria Nazionale (p207).

Contemporary Scene

Rome's contemporary art scene is centred on the capital's two flagship galleries: the Museo Nazionale delle Arti del XXI Secolo (p207), better known as MAXXI, and the Museo d'Arte Contemporanea di Roma (p208), aka MACRO. Rome also has a thriving gallery scene with a growing number of privately owned galleries across town.

Increasingly, though, you don't have to go to a gallery to see thought-provoking paintings. A recent trend for street art has taken the city by storm, and many suburbs boast colourful wall displays. Providing an impetus for all this is the Outdoor Festival, an urban art event now in its ninth year.

NEOCLASSICISM

Emerging in the late 18th and early 19th centuries, neoclassicism signalled a departure from the emotional abandon of the baroque and a return to the clean, sober lines of classical art. Its major exponent was the sculptor Antonio Canova (1757–1822), whose study of Paolina Bonaparte Borghese as *Venere Vincitrice* (Venus Victrix) in the Museo e Galleria Borghese is typical of the mildly erotic style for which he became known.

Literature

A history of authoritarian rule has given rise to a rich literary tradition, encompassing everything from ancient satires to dialect poetry and anti-fascist prose. As a backdrop, Rome has inspired authors as diverse as Shakespeare, Goethe and Dan Brown.

The Classics

Famous for his blistering oratory, Marcus Tullius Cicero (106–43 BCE) was the Roman Republic's pre-eminent author. A brilliant barrister, he became consul in 63 BCE and subsequently published many philosophical works and speeches. Fancying himself as the senior statesman, he took the young Octavian under his wing and attacked Mark Antony in a series of 14 speeches, the *Philippics*. But these proved fatal, for when Octavian changed sides and joined Mark Antony, he demanded, and got, Cicero's head.

Virgil gave us some of our most famous expressions: 'Fortune favours the bold', 'Love conquers all' and 'Time flies'. However, it was Juvenal who issued the classic warning: *'Quis custodiet ipsos custodes?'* (Who guards the guards?).

Poetry & Satire

A contemporary of Cicero, Catullus (c 84–54 BCE) cut a very different figure. A passionate and influential poet, he is best known for his epigrams and erotic verse.

On becoming emperor, Augustus (aka Octavian) encouraged the arts, and Virgil (70–19 BCE), Ovid, Horace and Tibullus all enjoyed freedom to write. Of the works produced in this period, it's Virgil's rollicking *Aeneid* that stands out. A glorified mix of legend, history and moral instruction, it tells how Aeneas escapes from Troy and after years of mythical mishaps ends up landing in Italy where his descendants Romulus and Remus eventually founded Rome.

Little is known of Decimus Iunius Iuvenalis, better known as Juvenal, but his 16 satires have survived as classics of the genre. Writing in the 1st century CE, he combined an acute mind with a cutting pen, famously scorning the masses as being interested in nothing but 'bread and circuses'.

Ancient Histories

The two major historians of the period were Livy (59 BCE to 17 CE) and Tacitus (c 56–116 CE). Although both wrote in the early days of the empire they displayed very different styles. Livy, whose history of the Roman Republic was probably used as a school textbook, cheerfully mixed myth with fact to produce an entertaining and popular tome. Tacitus, on the other hand, took a decidedly colder approach. His *Annals* and *Histories*, which cover the early years of the Roman Empire, are cutting and often witty, although imbued with an underlying pessimism.

Rome's most influential contribution to literature was the Vulgate Bible. This dates to the 4th century when Pope Damasus (r 366–84) had his secretary Eusebius Hieronymous, aka St Jerome, translate the Bible into accessible Latin. His version is the basis for the Bible currently used by the Catholic Church.

Street Writing & Popular Poetry

Rome's tradition of street writing goes back to the dark days of the 17th-century Counter-Reformation. With the Church systematically suppressing criticism, disgruntled Romans began posting *pasquinades* (anonymous messages; named after the first person who wrote one) on the city's so-called speaking statues. These messages, often archly critical of the authorities, were sensibly posted in the dead of night and then gleefully circulated around town the following day. The most famous speaking statue stands in Piazza Pasquino near Piazza Navona.

Dialect Verse

Poking savage fun at the rich and powerful was one of the favourite themes of Gioacchino Belli (1791–1863), one of a trio of poets who made their names writing poetry in Roman dialect. Belli started his career with conventional verse, but found the colourful dialect of the Roman streets better suited to his attacks on the chattering classes.

Carlo Alberto Salustri (1871–1950), aka Trilussa, is the best known of the trio. He also wrote social and political satire, although not exclusively so, and many of his poems are melancholy reflections on life, love and solitude. One of his most famous works, the anti-fascist poem *All' ombra* (In the Shadow), is etched onto a plaque in Piazza Trilussa, the Trastevere square named in his honour.

The poems of Cesare Pescarella (1858–1940) present a vivid portrait of turn-of-the-century Rome. Gritty and realistic, they pull no punches in their description of the everyday life of Rome's forgotten poor.

In 1559 Pope Paul IV published the *Index Librorum Prohibitorum* (Index of Prohibited Books), a list of books forbidden by the Catholic Church. Over the next 400 years it was revised 20 times, the last edition appearing in 1948. It was officially abolished in 1966.

Rome as Inspiration

With its magical cityscape and historic atmosphere, Rome has provided inspiration for legions of foreign authors from Henry James to Marguerite Yourcenar.

Romantic Visions

In the 18th century the city was a hotbed of literary activity as historians and Grand Tourists poured in from northern Europe. The German author Johann Wolfgang von Goethe captures the elation of discovering ancient Rome and the colours of the modern city in his celebrated travelogue *Italian Journey* (1817).

Rome was also a magnet for the English Romantic poets. John Keats, Lord Byron, Percy Bysshe Shelley, Mary Shelley and other writers all spent time in the city.

Later, in the 19th century, American author Nathaniel Hawthorne took inspiration from a sculpture in the Capitoline Museums to pen his classic *The Marble Faun* (1860).

Rome as Backdrop

In the first decade of the 2000s it became fashionable for novelists to use Rome as a backdrop. Most notably, Dan Brown's thriller *Angels and*

PIER PAOLO PASOLINI, MASTER OF CONTROVERSY

Poet, novelist and film-maker, Pier Paolo Pasolini (1922–75) was one of Italy's most important and controversial 20th-century intellectuals. His works, which are complex, unsentimental and provocative, provide a scathing portrait of Italy's postwar social transformation.

Politically, he was a communist, but he never played a part in Italy's left-wing establishment. In 1949 he was expelled from the Partito Comunista Italiano (PCI; Italian Communist Party) after a gay sex scandal and for the rest of his career he remained a sharp critic of the party. His most famous outburst came in the poem *Il PCI ai giovani*, in which he dismisses left-wing students as bourgeois and sympathises with the police, whom he describes as *'figli di poveri'* (sons of the poor). In the context of 1968 Italy, a year marked by widespread student agitation, this was a highly incendiary position to take.

Pasolini was no stranger to controversy. His first novel *Ragazzi di vita* (The Ragazzi), set in the squalor of Rome's forgotten suburbs, earned him success and a court case for obscenity. Similarly, his early films – *Accattone* (1961) and *Mamma Roma* (1962) – provoked outrage with their relentlessly bleak depiction of life in the Roman underbelly.

True to the scandalous nature of his art, Pasolini was murdered in 1975. A young hustler, Pino Pelosi, was convicted of the crime, but recent revelations have raised doubts that he acted alone, and question marks still hang over the case.

Demons (2001) is set in Rome, as is Jeanne Kalogridis' sumptuous historical novel *The Borgia Bride* (2006).

Robert Harris' accomplished fictional biographies of Cicero, *Imperium* (2006) and *Lustrum* (*Conspirata* in the US; 2010), are just two of many books set in ancient Rome. Other popular books in the genre include the Falco series of ancient murder mysteries by Lindsey Davis.

Roman Reads

Roman Tales (Alberto Moravia)

That Awful Mess on Via Merulana (Carlo Emilio Gadda)

The Secrets of Rome: Love & Death in the Eternal City (Corrado Augias)

Literature & Fascism

A controversial figure, Gabriele D'Annunzio (1863–1938) was the most flamboyant Italian writer of the early 20th century. A WWI fighter pilot and ardent nationalist, he was born in Pescara and settled in Rome in 1881. Forever associated with fascism, he wrote prolifically, both poetry and novels.

The Anti-Fascists

Roman-born Alberto Moravia (1907–90) was banned from writing by Mussolini and, together with his wife, Elsa Morante (1912–85), was forced into hiding for a year. The alienated individual and the emptiness of fascist and bourgeois society are common themes in his writing. In *La Romana* (The Woman of Rome; 1947) he explores the broken dreams of a country girl as she slips into prostitution and theft.

The novels of Elsa Morante are characterised by a subtle psychological appraisal of her characters and can be seen as a personal cry of pity for the sufferings of individuals and society. Her 1974 masterpiece, *La Storia* (History), is a tough tale of a half-Jewish woman's desperate struggle for dignity in the poverty of occupied Rome.

Taking a similarly anti-fascist line, Carlo Emilio Gadda (1893–1973) combines murder and black humour in his classic whodunnit, *Quer pasticciaccio brutto de Via Merulana* (That Awful Mess on Via Merulana; 1957).

Niccolò Ammaniti's 2009 novel *Che la festa cominci* (Let the Games Begin) offers debauchery, laughs and Satanic sects as it gleefully satirises the bizarre excesses of modern society.

Writing Today

Rome-born Niccolò Ammaniti is one of Italy's best-selling authors. In 2007 he won the Premio Strega, Italy's top literary prize, for his novel, *Come Dio comanda* (As God Commands), although he's best known internationally for *Io non ho paura* (I'm Not Scared; 2001), a soulful study of a young boy's realisation that his father is involved in a child kidnapping.

Another Strega winner is Melania Mazzucco, whose acclaimed 2003 novel *Vita* tells of two boys from Campania who emigrate to the US in the early 20th century.

Also of note is Andrea Bajani, the award-winning author of *Ogni promessa* (Every Promise; 2010). Margaret Mazzantini's *Non ti muovere* (Don't Move; 2001) and Francesca Melandri's *Eva dorme* (Eva Sleeps; 2011) were also best-sellers.

Cinema

Rome has a long cinematic tradition, spanning the works of postwar neo-realists and film-makers as diverse as Federico Fellini, Sergio Leone and Paolo Sorrentino, the Oscar-winning director of *La grande belleza* (The Great Beauty). Many Italian film-makers born throughout the country spend time in or work in Rome.

Since its inception in 2006 the Festa del Cinema di Roma has established itself on the European circuit.

The Golden Age

For the golden age of Roman film-making you have to turn the clocks back to the 1940s, when Roberto Rossellini (1906–77) produced a trio

ROME IN THE MOVIES

Rome's monuments, piazzas and atmospheric streets provide the backdrop to many classic, and some not so classic, films.

Roma Città Aperta (*Rome Open City*; 1945) Neo-realist masterpiece shot on the streets of Prenestina.

Roman Holiday (1953) Gregory Peck and Audrey Hepburn scoot around Rome's headline sights.

La Dolce Vita (1960) The Trevi Fountain stars in Fellini's great Roman masterpiece.

The Talented Mr Ripley (1999) Rome sets the stage for this chilling psychological thriller.

To Rome with Love (2012) Rome gets the Woody Allen treatment in this cliché-ridden comedy.

La Grande Belleza (*The Great Beauty*; 2013) Rome's beauty masks cynicism and moral decadence in Sorrentino's Oscar-winner.

of neo-realist masterpieces. The first and most famous was *Roma città aperta* (Rome Open City; 1945), filmed with brutal honesty in the Prenestina district east of the city centre.

Federico Fellini (1920–94) took the creative baton from the neo-realists and carried it into the following decades. His disquieting style demands more of audiences, abandoning realistic shots for pointed images at once laden with humour, pathos and double meaning. Fellini's greatest international hit was *La Dolce Vita* (1960), starring Marcello Mastroianni and Anita Ekberg.

The films of Pier Paolo Pasolini (1922–75) are similarly demanding. A communist Catholic homosexual, he made films such as *Accattone* (The Scrounger; 1961) that not only reflect his ideological and sexual tendencies but also offer a unique portrayal of Rome's urban wasteland.

> Inaugurated in 1937, Rome's Cinecittà studios are part of cinematic folklore. *Ben-Hur*, *Cleopatra*, *La Dolce Vita* and Martin Scorsese's 2002 epic *Gangs of New York* are among the classics that have been shot on the studios' vast 40-hectare site.

Contemporary Directors

Born in Naples but Roman by adoption, Paolo Sorrentino (b 1970) is the big name in Italian cinema. Since winning an Oscar for his 2013 hit *La grande bellezza* (The Great Beauty), he has gone on to direct Michael Caine and Harvey Keitel in *Youth* (2015) and Jude Law in *The Young Pope* (2016) and its follow-up series, *The New Pope*.

In contrast to Sorrentino, a Neapolitan best known for a film about Rome, Matteo Garrone (b 1968) is a Roman famous for a film about Naples. *Gomorra* (Gomorrah; 2008), his hard-hitting exposé of the Neapolitan *camorra* (mafia), enjoyed widespread acclaim. His latest work is *Dogman* (2018), filmed around Rome, Lazio and Campania.

Emanuele Crialese (b 1965) impressed with *Terraferma* (Dry Land; 2011), a thought-provoking study of immigration, and Lamberto Sanfelice won applause at the 2015 Sundance Film Festival for *Cloro* (Chlorine), a slow-burning drama centred on a teenage girl's struggles to keep her dreams alive in the face of family tragedy.

Gabriele Muccino (b 1967), director of the 2001 smash *L'ultimo bacio* (The Last Kiss), has now established himself in Hollywood where he has worked with the likes of Russell Crowe and Will Smith, star of his 2006 hit *The Pursuit of Happyness*.

Going back a generation, Carlo Verdone (b 1950) and Nanni Moretti (b 1953) are two veterans of the Rome scene. Verdone, a comedian in the Roman tradition, specialises in satirising his fellow citizens in bittersweet comedies such as *Viaggi di nozze* (Honeymoons; 1995).

> Throughout the 1960s and '70s Italy was a prolific producer of horror films. Rome's master of terror was, and still is, Dario Argento (b 1940), director of the 1975 cult classic *Profondo rosso* (Deep Red), 1977's *Suspiria* and more than 20 other movies.

SERGIO LEONE, MR SPAGHETTI WESTERN

Best known for virtually single-handedly creating the spaghetti western, Sergio Leone (1929–89) is a hero to many. Astonishingly, though, he only ever directed seven films.

He made his directorial debut on *Il colosso di Rodi* (The Colossus of Rhodes; 1961), but it was with his famous dollar trilogy – *Per un pugno di dollari* (A Fistful of Dollars; 1964), *Per qualche dollari in piu* (For a Few Dollars More; 1965) and *Il buono, il brutto, il cattivo* (The Good, the Bad and the Ugly; 1966) – that he hit the big time. The first, filmed in Spain and based on the 1961 samurai flick *Yojimbo,* set the style for the genre. No longer were clean-cut, morally upright heroes pitted against cartoon-style villains, but characters were complex, often morally ambiguous and driven by self-interest.

Stylistically, Leone introduced a series of innovations that were later to become trademarks. Chief among these was his use of musical themes to identify his characters. And in this he was brilliantly supported by his old schoolmate, the Oscar-winning composer Ennio Morricone (1928–2020).

Moretti, on the other hand, falls into no mainstream tradition. A politically active writer, actor and director, his films are often whimsical and self-indulgent. Arguably his best work, *Caro diario* (Dear Diary; 1994) earned him the Best Director prize at Cannes – an award he topped in 2001 when he won the Palme d'Or for *La stanza del figlio* (The Son's Room).

Focused on a world-weary habitué of Rome's dolce vita society, Paolo Sorrentino's 2013 film *La grande belleza* (The Great Beauty) presents Italy's ancient capital as a complex, suffocating city whose lavish beauty masks a decadent, morally bankrupt heart.

On Location in Rome

Rome itself has featured in a number of recent productions. Villa Borghese and the Terme di Caracalla were among the locations for Ben Stiller's camp fashion romp *Zoolander 2* (2016), while the Tiber riverside and Via della Conciliazione both appeared in the James Bond outing *Spectre* (2015). Down in the city's southern reaches, a remake of *Ben-Hur* was filmed at the Cinecittà film studios, the very same place where the original sword-and-sandal epic was shot in 1959. Television series filmed here include *The Young Pope* and *Baby,* shot in the northern parts of Rome.

Music

Despite austerity-led cutbacks, Rome's music scene is bearing up well. International orchestras perform to sell-out audiences, jazz greats jam in steamy clubs and rappers rage in underground venues.

Choral & Sacred Music

In a city of churches, it's little wonder that choral music has deep roots in Rome. In the 16th and 17th centuries, Rome's great Renaissance popes summoned the top musicians of the day to tutor the papal choir. Two of the most famous were Giovanni Pierluigi da Palestrina (c 1525–94), one of Italy's foremost Renaissance composers, and the Naples-born Domenico Scarlatti (1685–1757).

The papal choirs were originally closed to women and the high parts were taken by *castrati,* boys who had been surgically castrated to preserve their high voices. The use of *castrati* lasted until the early 20th century, when in 1913 Alessandro Moreschi (1858–1922), the last known *castrato,* retired from the Sistine Chapel choir.

To support the pope's musicians, Sixtus V established the Accademia di Santa Cecilia in 1585. Originally this was involved in the publication of sacred music, but it later developed a teaching function, and in 1839 it completely reinvented itself as an academy with wider cultural and academic goals. Today it is a highly respected conservatory with its own world-class orchestra.

Opera

Rome is often snubbed by serious opera buffs, who prefer their Puccini in Milan, Venice or Naples. Exacerbating the situation, the city opera house, the Teatro dell'Opera di Roma (p169), has been plagued by financial crises and labour disputes in recent years. But things took a decided turn for the better in May 2016 when Hollywood director Sofia Coppola's lavish production of *La Traviata* proved to be box-office gold.

The Romans have long been keen opera-goers and in the 19th century a number of important operas were premiered in Rome, including Rossini's *Il barbiere di Siviglia* (The Barber of Seville; 1816), Verdi's *Il trovatore* (The Troubadour; 1853) and Giacomo Puccini's *Tosca* (1900).

Tosca not only premiered in Rome but is also set in the city. The first act takes place in the Chiesa di Sant'Andrea della Valle, the second in Palazzo Farnese, and the final act in Castel Sant'Angelo, the castle from which Tosca jumps to her death.

Jazz, Rap & Hip-Hop

Jazz has long been a mainstay of Rome's music scene. Introduced by US troops during WWII, it grew in popularity during the postwar period and took off in the 1960s. Since then, it has gone from strength to strength and the city now boasts some fabulous jazz clubs, including Alexanderplatz, Big Mama and La Casa del Jazz. Big names to look out for include Roman-born pianist and composer Enrico Pieranunzi, drummer Roberto Gatto, singer Maria Pia De Vito, the acclaimed trio performing as Doctor 3, or the larger band Lingomania.

Rome also has a vibrant underground scene. Rap and hip-hop arrived in the city in the late 1980s and spread via the *centro sociale* (organised squat) network. Originally the scene was highly politicised and many early exponents associated themselves with Rome's alternative left-wing. Since then, exposure and commercialisation have diluted, though not entirely extinguished, this political element. Local names to look out for include Colle der Fomento, Cor Veleno, Jesto, Assalti Fromntali, Achille Lauro, Carl Brave and Franco 126, Gemitaiz, and the ragamuffin outfit Villa Ada Posse.

Theatre & Dance

Surprisingly for a city in which art has always been appreciated, Rome has no great theatrical tradition. That said, theatres such as Teatro India (p230) stage wide-ranging programs offering everything from avant-garde dance to cutting-edge street theatre.

Although not strictly speaking Roman, Dacia Maraini (b 1936) has produced her best work while living in Rome. Considered one of Italy's most important feminist writers, she has more than 30 plays to her name, many of which continue to be translated and performed around the world.

Dance is a major highlight of Rome's big autumn festival, Romaeuropa (p25).

Major ballet performances are staged at the Teatro dell'Opera di Roma (p169), home to Rome's principal ballet company, the Balletto del Teatro dell'Opera.

Architecture

From ancient ruins and Renaissance basilicas to baroque churches and hulking fascist *palazzi* (mansions), Rome's architectural legacy is unparalleled. Michelangelo, Bramante, Borromini and Bernini are among the architects who have stamped their genius on the city's remarkable cityscape, which features some of the Western world's most celebrated buildings. In more recent times, a number of high-profile building projects have drawn the world's top architects to Rome, their futuristic designs provoking discussion, debate and soul-searching among the city's passionate critics.

The Ancients

Architecture was central to the success of the ancient Romans. In building their great capital, they were among the first people to use architecture to tackle problems of infrastructure, urban management and communication. For the first time, architects and engineers designed houses, roads, aqueducts and shopping centres alongside temples, tombs and imperial palaces. To do this, the Romans advanced methods devised by the Etruscans and Greeks, developing construction techniques and building materials that allowed them to build on a massive and hitherto unseen scale.

Etruscan Roots

By the 7th century BCE the Etruscans were the dominant force on the Italian peninsula, with important centres at Tarquinia, Caere (Cerveteri) and Veii (Veio). These city-states were fortified with defensive walls, and although little actually remains – the Etruscans generally built with wood and brick, which don't age well – archaeologists have found evidence of aqueducts, bridges and sewers, as well as sophisticated temples. In Rome, you can still see foundations of an Etruscan temple on the Campidoglio (Capitoline Hill).

Much of what we now know about the Etruscans derives from findings unearthed in their elaborate tombs. Like many ancient peoples, the Etruscans placed great emphasis on their treatment of the dead and they built impressive cemeteries. These were constructed outside the city walls and harboured richly decorated stone vaults covered by mounds of earth. The best examples are to be found in Cerveteri, north of Rome.

ROME'S OBELISKS

More readily associated with ancient Egypt than Rome, obelisks are a distinctive feature of the Roman cityscape. Many were brought over from Egypt after it was conquered by Augustus in 31 CE and used to decorate the *spina* (central spine) of the city's circuses (chariot-racing arenas). Later the Romans began to make obelisks for their elaborate mausoleums. The tallest – and one of the oldest, dating to the 15th century BCE – towers 46m (32m without the base) over Piazza San Giovanni in Laterano. The most curious sits atop Bernini's famous *Elefantino* statue outside the Basilica di Santa Maria Sopra Minerva.

Roman Developments

When Rome was founded sometime around the 8th century BCE, the Etruscans were at the height of their power and Greek colonists were establishing control over southern Italy. In subsequent centuries a three-way battle for domination ensued, with the Romans emerging victorious. Against this background, Roman architects borrowed heavily from Greek and Etruscan traditions.

Ancient Roman architecture was monumental in form and often propagandistic in nature. Huge amphitheatres, aqueducts and temples joined muscular and awe-inspiring basilicas, arches and thermal baths in trumpeting the skill and vision of the city's early rulers and the nameless architects who worked for them.

Temples

Early republican-era temples were based on Etruscan designs, but over time the Romans turned to the Greeks for their inspiration. But whereas Greek temples had steps and colonnades on all sides, the classic Roman temple had a high podium with steps leading up to a deep porch. Good examples include the Tempio di Portunus near Piazza della Bocca della Verità and, though they're not so well preserved, the temples in the Largo di Torre Argentina (p83). These temples also illustrate another important feature of Roman architectural thinking. While Greek temples were designed to stand apart and be viewed from all sides, Roman temples were built into the city's urban fabric, set in busy central locations and positioned to be approached from the front.

The Roman use of columns was also Greek in origin, even if the Romans preferred the more slender and elaborately topped Ionic and Corinthian columns to the plainer Doric pillars. To see how the columns differ, study the exterior of the Colosseum, which incorporates all three styles.

Aqueducts & Sewers

One of the Romans' crowning architectural achievements was the development of a water supply infrastructure, based on a network of aqueducts and underground sewers. In the early days, Rome got its water from the River Tiber and natural underground springs, but as its population grew, demand exceeded supply. To meet this demand, the Romans constructed a complex system of aqueducts to bring water in from the hills of central Italy and distribute it around town.

MAIN ARCHITECTURAL PERIODS

c 8th–3rd centuries BCE

The Etruscans in central Italy and the Greeks in their southern Italian colony, Magna Graecia, lay the groundwork for later Roman developments. Particularly influential are Greek temple designs.

c 4th century BCE–5th century CE

The ancient Romans make huge advances in engineering techniques, constructing monumental public buildings, bridges, aqueducts, housing blocks and an underground sewerage system.

4th–12th centuries

Church building is the focus of architectural activity in the Middle Ages as Rome's early Christian leaders seek to stamp their authority on the city.

15th–16th centuries

Based on humanism and a reappraisal of classical precepts, the Renaissance hits an all-time high in the first two decades of the 16th century, a period known as the High Renaissance.

17th century

Developing out of the Counter-Reformation, the baroque flourishes in Rome, fuelled by Church money and the genius of Gian Lorenzo Bernini and his hated rival Francesco Borromini.

18th century

A short-lived but theatrical style born out of the baroque, the rococo gifts Rome some of its most popular sights.

late 18th–19th centuries

Piazza del Popolo takes on its current form and Villa Torlonia gets a facelift courtesy of Rome's top neoclassical architect, Giuseppe Valadier.

The first aqueduct to serve Rome was the 16.5km Aqua Appia, which became fully operational in 312 BCE. Over the next 700 years or so, up to 800km of aqueducts were built in the city, a network capable of supplying up to one million cubic metres of water a day.

This was no mean feat for a system that depended entirely on gravity. All aqueducts, whether underground pipes, as most were, or vast overland viaducts, were built at a slight gradient to allow the water to flow. There were no pumps to force the water along so this gradient was key to maintaining a continuous and efficient flow.

At the other end of the water cycle, waste water was drained away via an underground sewerage system – the Cloaca Maxima (Great Sewer) – and emptied downstream into the River Tiber. The Cloaca was commissioned by Rome's last king, Tarquin the Proud (r 535–509 BCE), as part of a project to drain the valley where the Roman Forum now stands. It was originally an open ditch, but from the beginning of the 2nd century BCE it was gradually built over.

The Romans used a variety of building materials. Wood and tufa, a soft volcanic rock, were used initially, but travertine, a limestone quarried in Tivoli, later took over as the favoured stone. Marble, imported from across the empire, was used mainly as decorative panelling, attached to brick or concrete walls.

Residential Housing

While Rome's emperors and aristocrats lived in luxurious palaces on the Palatino (Palatine Hill), the city's poor huddled together in large residential blocks called *insulae*. These were huge, poorly built structures, sometimes up to six or seven storeys high, that accommodated hundreds of people in dark, unhealthy conditions. Little remains of the early *palazzi* but near the foot of the Aracoeli staircase – the steps that lead up to the Chiesa di Santa Maria in Aracoeli – you can see a section of what was once a typical city-centre *insula*.

Concrete & Monumental Architecture

Most of the ruins that litter modern Rome are the remains of the ancient city's big, show-stopping monuments – the Colosseum, the Pantheon, the Terme di Caracalla, the Forums. These grandiose constructions are not only reminders of the sophistication and intimidatory scale of ancient Rome – just as they were originally designed to be – they are also monuments to the vision and bravura of the city's ancient architects.

One of the key breakthroughs the Romans made, and one that allowed them to build on an ever-increasing scale, was the invention of concrete in the 1st century BCE. Made by mixing volcanic ash with lime and an aggregate, often tufa rock or brick rubble, concrete was quick to make, easy to use and cheap. Furthermore, it freed architects from their dependence on skilled masonry labour – up to that point construction techniques required stone blocks to be specially cut to fit into each

ALL ROADS LEAD TO ROME

The Romans were the great road builders of the ancient world. Approximately 80,000km of surfaced highways spanned the Roman Empire, providing vital military and communication links. Many of Rome's modern roads retain the names of their ancient forebears and follow almost identical routes.

Via Appia (p218) The 'queen of roads' ran down to Brindisi on the southern Adriatic coast.

Via Aurelia Connected Rome with France by way of Pisa and Genoa.

Via Cassia Led north to Viterbo, Siena and Tuscany.

Via Flaminia Traversed the Apennines to Rimini on the east coast.

Via Salaria The old salt road linked with the Adriatic port of Castrum Truentinum, south of modern-day Ancona.

other. Concrete allowed the Romans to develop vaulted roofing, which they used to span the Pantheon's ceiling and the huge vaults at the Terme di Caracalla.

Concrete wasn't particularly attractive, though, and while it was used for heavy-duty structural work it was usually lined with travertine and coloured marble, imported from Greece and North Africa. Brick was also an important material, used both as a veneer and for construction.

late 19th century

Rome has a major post-unification makeover – roads are built, piazzas are laid and residential quarters spring up to house government bureaucrats.

early 20th century

Muscular and modern, Italian rationalism plays to Mussolini's vision of a fearless, futuristic Rome, a 20th-century *caput mundi* (world capital).

1990s–

Rome provides the historic stage upon which some of the world's top contemporary architects experiment. Criticism and praise are meted out in almost equal measure.

Early Christian Period

The history of early Christianity is one of persecution and martyrdom. Introduced in the 1st century CE, it was legalised by the emperor Constantine in 313 CE and became Rome's state religion in 378. The most startling reminders of early Christian activity are the catacombs, a series of underground burial grounds built under Rome's ancient roads. Christian belief in the resurrection meant that the Christians could not cremate their dead, as was the custom in Roman times, and with burial forbidden inside the city walls, they were forced to go outside the city.

Church Building

The Christians began to abandon the catacombs in the 4th century and increasingly opted to be buried in the churches the emperor Constantine was building in the city. Although Constantine was actually based in Byzantium, which he renamed Constantinople in his own honour, he nevertheless financed an ambitious building program in Rome. The most notable of the many churches he commissioned is the Basilica di San Giovanni in Laterano (p190). Built between 315 and 324 and reworked into its present shape in the 5th century, it was the model on which many subsequent basilicas were based. Other period showstoppers include the Basilica di Santa Maria in Trastevere (p174) and the Basilica di Santa Maria Maggiore (p153).

A second wave of church-building hit Rome in the period between the 8th and 12th centuries. As the early papacy battled for survival against the threatening Lombards, its leaders took to construction to leave some sort of historical imprint, resulting in the Basilica di Santa Sabina (p194), the Basilica di Santa Prassede (p154) and the 8th-century Chiesa di Santa Maria in Cosmedin, home of the Bocca della Verità (Mouth of Truth; p76).

The 13th and 14th centuries were dark days for Rome as internecine fighting raged between the city's noble families. While much of northern Europe and even parts of Italy were revelling in Gothic arches and towering vaults, little of lasting value was being built in Rome. The one great exception is the city's only Gothic church, the Basilica di Santa Maria Sopra Minerva (p83).

Early Basilicas

Basilica di San Giovanni in Laterano (San Giovanni & Testaccio)

Basilica di Santa Sabina (San Giovanni & Testaccio)

Basilica di Santa Maria Maggiore (Monti, Esquilino & San Lorenzo)

Basilica Style

In design terms, these early Christian churches were modelled on, and built over, Rome's great basilicas. In ancient times, a basilica was a large rectangular hall used for public functions, but as Christianity took hold they were increasingly appropriated by the city's church-builders. The main reason for this was that they lent themselves perfectly to the new style of religious ceremonies that the Christians were introducing, rites that required space for worshippers and a central focus for the altar. Rome's pagan temples, in contrast, had been designed as symbolic centres and were not set up to house the faithful – in fact, most pagan ceremonies were held outside, in front of the temple, not inside as the Christian services required.

Over time, basilica design became increasingly standardised. A principal entrance would open onto an atrium, a courtyard surrounded by colonnaded porticoes, which, in turn, would lead to the porch. The interior would be rectangular and divided by rows of columns into a central nave and smaller, side aisles. At the far end, the main altar and bishop's throne (cathedra) would sit in a semicircular apse. In some churches a transept would bisect the central nave to form a Latin cross.

The Renaissance

Florence, rather than Rome, is generally regarded as Italy's great Renaissance city. But while many of the movement's early architects hailed from Tuscany, the city they turned to for inspiration was Rome. The Eternal City might have been in pretty poor nick in the late 15th century, but as the centre of classical antiquity, it was much revered by budding architects. A trip to study the Colosseum and the Pantheon was considered a fundamental part of an architect's training.

One of the key aspects they studied, and which informs much Renaissance architecture, is the concept of harmony. This was achieved through the application of symmetry, order and proportion. To this end many Renaissance buildings incorporated structural features copied from the ancients – columns, pilasters, arches and, most dramatically, domes. The Pantheon's dome, in particular, proved immensely influential, serving as a blueprint for many later works.

Early Years

It's impossible to pinpoint the exact year the Renaissance arrived in Rome, but many claim it was the election of Pope Nicholas V in 1447 that sparked off the artistic and architectural furore that was to sweep through the city over the next century or so. Nicholas believed that as head of the Christian world Rome had a duty to impress, a theory that was eagerly taken up by his successors, and it was at the behest of the great papal dynasties – the Barberini, Farnese and Pamphilj – that the leading artists of the day were summoned to Rome.

The Venetian Pope Paul II (r 1464–71) commissioned many works, including Palazzo Venezia (p76), Rome's first great Renaissance *palazzo*. His successor, Sixtus IV (r 1471–84), had the Sistine Chapel built, and he enlarged the Basilica di Santa Maria del Popolo (p109).

Architecture Reads

Rome: An Oxford Archaeological Guide (Amanda Claridge; 2010)

The Genius in the Design: Bernini, Borromini and the Rivalry that Transformed Rome (Jake Morrissey; 2005)

Rome and Environs: An Archaeological Guide (Filippo Coarelli; 2008)

High Renaissance

It was under Pope Julius II (1503–13) that the Roman Renaissance reached its peak, thanks largely to a classically minded architect from Milan, Donato Bramante (1444–1514).

Considered the high priest of Renaissance architecture, Bramante arrived in Rome in 1499. Here, inspired by the ancient ruins, he developed a refined classical style that was to prove hugely influential. His 1502 Tempietto (p177), for example, perfectly illustrates his innate understanding of proportion. Similarly harmonious is his 1504 cloister at the Chiesa di Santa Maria della Pace (p85) near Piazza Navona.

In 1506 Julius commissioned Bramante to start work on the job that would eventually finish him off – the rebuilding of St Peter's Basilica.

BRAMANTE, THE ARCHITECTS' ARCHITECT

One of the most influential architects of his day, Donato Bramante (1444–1514) was the godfather of Renaissance architecture. His peers, Michelangelo, Raphael and Leonardo da Vinci, considered him the only architect of their era equal to the ancients.

Born near Urbino, he originally trained as a painter before taking up architecture in his mid-30s in Milan. However, it was in Rome that he enjoyed his greatest success. Working for Pope Julius II, he developed a monumental style that while classical in origin was pure Renaissance in its expression of harmony and perspective. The most perfect representation of this is his Tempietto, a small but much-copied temple on Gianicolo hill. His original designs for St Peter's Basilica also revealed a classically inspired symmetry with a Pantheon-like dome envisaged atop a Greek-cross structure.

Rich and influential, Bramante was an adept political operator who was not above badmouthing his competitors. It's said, for example, that he talked Pope Julius II into giving Michelangelo the contract for the Sistine Chapel ceiling in the hope that it would prove to be the undoing of his young Tuscan rival.

The fall of Constantinople's Aya Sofya (Church of the Hagia Sofia) to Islam in the mid-14th century had pricked Nicholas V into ordering an earlier revamp, but the work had never been completed and it wasn't until Julius took the bull by the horns that progress was made. However, Bramante died in 1514 and he never got to see how his original Greek-cross design was developed.

St Peter's Basilica (p128) occupied most of the other notable architects of the High Renaissance, including Giuliano da Sangallo (1445–1516), Baldassarre Peruzzi (1481–1536) and Antonio da Sangallo the Younger (1484–1546). Michelangelo (1475–1564) eventually took over in 1547, modifying the layout and creating the basilica's crowning dome. Modelled on Brunelleschi's cupola for the Duomo in Florence, this is considered the artist's finest architectural achievement and one of the most important works of the Roman Renaissance.

Mannerism

As Rome's architects strove to build a new Jerusalem, the city's leaders struggled to deal with the political tensions arising outside the city walls. These came to a head in 1527 when the city was invaded and savagely routed by the troops of the Holy Roman Emperor, Charles V. This traumatic event forced many of the artists working in Rome to flee the city and ushered in a new style of artistic and architectural expression. Mannerism was a relatively short-lived form but in its emphasis on complexity and decoration, in contrast to the sharp, clean lines of traditional Renaissance styles, it hinted at the more ebullient designs that would arrive with the advent of the 17th-century baroque.

One of mannerism's leading exponents was Baldassarre Peruzzi, whose Palazzo Massimo alle Colonne on Corso Vittorio Emanuele II reveals a number of mannerist elements – a pronounced facade, decorative window mouldings and showy imitation stonework.

The Baroque

As the principal motor of the Roman Renaissance, the Catholic Church became increasingly powerful in the 16th century. But with power came corruption and calls for reform. These culminated in Martin Luther's *95 Theses* and the far-reaching Protestant Reformation. This hit the Church hard and prompted the Counter-Reformation (1560–1648), a vicious and sustained campaign to get people back into the Catholic fold.

Amid this great offensive, baroque art and architecture emerged as a highly effective form of propaganda. Stylistically, baroque architecture aims for a dramatic sense of dynamism, an effect that it often achieves by combining spatial complexity with clever lighting and the use of flamboyant decorative painting and sculpture.

One of the first great Counter-Reformation churches was the Jesuit Chiesa del Gesù (p88), designed by the leading architect of the day, Giacomo della Porta (1533–1602). In a move away from the style of earlier Renaissance churches, the facade has pronounced architectural elements that create a contrast between surfaces and a play of light and shade.

The end of the 16th century and the papacy of Sixtus V (1585–90) marked the beginning of major urban-planning schemes. Domenico Fontana (1543–1607) and other architects created a network of major thoroughfares to connect previously disparate parts of the sprawling city, and obelisks were erected at vantage points across town. Fontana also designed the main facade of Palazzo del Quirinale, the immense palace that served as the pope's summer residence for almost three centuries. His nephew, Carlo Maderno (1556–1629), also worked on the *palazzo* when not amending Bramante's designs for St Peter's Basilica.

Key Bernini Works

St Peter's Square (Vatican City, Borgo & Prati)

Chiesa di Sant'Andrea al Quirinale (Tridente, Trevi & the Quirinale)

Fontana dei Quattro Fiumi (Centro Storico)

Bernini vs Borromini

No two people did more to fashion the face of Rome than the two great figures of the Roman baroque: Gian Lorenzo Bernini (1598–1680) and Francesco Borromini (1599–1667). Two starkly different characters – Naples-born Bernini was suave, self-confident and politically adept; Borromini, from Lombardy, was solitary and peculiar – they led the transition from Counter-Reformation rigour to baroque exuberance.

Bernini is perhaps best known for his work in the Vatican. He designed St Peter's Square (p141), famously styling the colonnade as 'the motherly arms of the Church', and was chief architect at St Peter's Basilica (p128) from 1629. While working on the basilica, he created the baldachin (canopy) over the main altar, using bronze stripped from the Pantheon.

Under the patronage of the Barberini pope Urban VIII, Bernini was given free rein to transform the city, and his churches, *palazzi*, piazzas and fountains remain landmarks to this day. However, his fortunes nose-dived when the pope died in 1644. Urban's successor, Innocent X, wanted as little contact as possible with the favourites of his hated predecessor, and instead turned to Borromini, Alessandro Algardi (1595–1654) and Girolamo and Carlo Rainaldi (1570–1655 and 1611–91, respectively). Bernini later came back into favour with his 1651 Fontana dei Quattro Fiumi (p82) in the centre of Piazza Navona, opposite Borromini's Chiesa di Sant'Agnese in Agone (p82).

Key Borromini Works

Chiesa di San Carlino alle Quattro Fontane (Tridente, Trevi & the Quirinale)

Chiesa di Sant'Agnese in Agone (Centro Storico)

Chiesa di Sant'Ivo alla Sapienza (Centro Storico)

Borromini, the son of an architect and well versed in stonemasonry and construction techniques, created buildings involving complex shapes and exotic geometry. A recurring feature of his designs was the skilful manipulation of light, often obtained by the clever placement of small oval-shaped windows. His most memorable works are the Chiesa di San Carlino alle Quattro Fontane (p114), which has an oval-shaped interior, and the Chiesa di Sant'Ivo alla Sapienza (p84), which combines a complex arrangement of convex and concave surfaces with an innovative spiral tower.

Throughout their careers, the two geniuses were often at each other's throats. Borromini was deeply envious of Bernini's early successes, and Bernini was scathing of Borromini's complex geometrical style.

ROME'S SIGNATURE BUILDINGS

Rome's cityscape is a magical mix of ruins, monuments, palaces, piazzas and churches. Here are some of the city's most significant buildings.

Colosseum (p58) Rome's iconic arena bears the hallmarks of ancient Roman architecture: arches, the use of various building materials, unprecedented scale.

Pantheon (p80) The dome, one of the Romans' most important architectural innovations, finds perfect form atop this revolutionary structure.

Basilica di Santa Maria Maggiore (p153) Although much modified over the centuries, this hulking cathedral exemplifies the Christian basilicas that were built in the early Middle Ages.

Castel Sant'Angelo (p141) Rome's landmark castle started life as a monumental mausoleum before taking on its current form after medieval and Renaissance revamps.

Tempietto di Bramante (p177) A masterpiece of harmonious design, Bramante's 1502 temple beautifully encapsulates High Renaissance ideals.

St Peter's Basilica (p128) Michelangelo's dome and Carlo Maderno's facade are the key architectural features of this, the greatest of Rome's Renaissance churches.

Chiesa del Gesù (p88) One of Rome's finest Counter-Reformation churches with a much-copied facade by Giacomo della Porta and an ornate baroque interior.

Chiesa di San Carlino alle Quattro Fontane (p114) A prized example of baroque architecture, Francesco Borromini's church boasts convex and concave surfaces, hidden windows and a complex elliptical plan.

Palazzo della Civiltà Italiana (p226) Nicknamed the 'Square Colosseum', this EUR landmark is a masterpiece of 1930s Italian rationalism.

Auditorium Parco della Musica (p207) Renzo Piano's audacious arts complex is the most influential contemporary building in Rome.

MAXXI (p207) Zaha Hadid's award-winning 2010 building provides a suitably striking setting for Rome's flagship contemporary-arts museum.

Post-Unification & the 20th Century

Rome's nomination as capital of Italy in 1870 unleashed a wave of urban development that was later to be continued by Mussolini and his fascist regime. Postwar, the focus was on practical concerns as the city worked to house its burgeoning population.

A Capital Makeover

Rome entered the 20th century in good shape. During the last 30 years of the 19th century it had been treated to one of its periodic makeovers – this time after being made capital of the Kingdom of Italy in 1870. Piazzas were built, including Piazza Vittorio Emanuele II, at the centre of a new upmarket residential district, and neoclassical Piazza della Repubblica, over Diocletian's bath complex. And roads were laid: Via Nazionale and Via Cavour were constructed to link the city centre with the new railway station, Stazione Termini, and Corso Vittorio Emanuele II was built to connect Piazza Venezia with the Vatican.

Rationalism & Rebuilding

Influenced by the German Bauhaus movement, architectural rationalism was all the rage in 1920s Europe. In its international form it advocated an emphasis on sharply defined linear forms, but in Italy it took on a slightly different look, thanks to the influence of the Gruppo

ROCOCO FRILLS

In the early days of the 18th century, as baroque fashions began to fade and neoclassicism waited to make its 19th-century entrance, the rococo burst into theatrical life. Drawing on the excesses of the baroque, it was a short-lived fad but one that left a memorable mark.

The Spanish Steps (p108), built between 1723 and 1726 by Francesco de Sanctis, provided a focal point for the many Grand Tourists who were pouring into town in the late 18th century. A short walk to the southwest, Piazza Sant'Ignazio was designed by Filippo Raguzzini (1680–1771) to provide a suitably melodramatic setting for the Chiesa di Sant'Ignazio di Loyola (p90), Rome's second-most important Jesuit church.

Most spectacular of all, however, was the Trevi Fountain (p110), one of the city's most exuberant and enduringly popular monuments. It was designed in 1732 by Nicola Salvi (1697–1751) and completed three decades later.

Sette, its main Italian promoters, and Benito Mussolini, Italy's fascist dictator. Basically, the Gruppo Sette acknowledged the debt Italian architecture owed to its classical past and incorporated elements of that tradition into their modernistic designs. Aesthetically and politically, this tied in perfectly with Mussolini's vision of fascism as the modern bearer of ancient Rome's imperialist ambitions.

> The term *Scuola romana* (Roman School) is used to define a group of architects working in the 1920s and '30s, mainly on large-scale housing projects. Their designs sought to ally modern functionalism with a respect for tradition and a utopian vision of urban development.

Mussolini, a shrewd manipulator of imagery, embarked on a series of grandiose building projects in the 1920s and '30s, including the 1928–31 Foro Italico (p208) sports centre, Via dei Foro Imperiali and the residential quarter of Garbatella (p223). Now a colourful neighbourhood in southern Rome, Garbatella was originally planned as an English-style garden city to house city workers, but in the 1920s the project was hijacked by the fascist regime, which had its own designs. Central to these were innovative housing blocks, known as *alberghi suburbani* (suburban hotels), which were used to accommodate people displaced from the city centre. The most famous of these hotels, the Albergo Rosso, was designed by Innocenzo Sabbatini (1891–1983), the leading light of the Roman School of architecture.

EUR

Mussolini's most famous architectural legacy is the EUR district (p226) in the extreme south of the city. Built for the Esposizione Universale di Roma in 1942, this Orwellian quarter of wide boulevards and huge linear buildings owes its look to the vision of the *razionalisti* (rationalists). In practice, though, only one of their number, Adalberto Libera, actually worked on the project, as by this stage most of the Gruppo Sette had fallen out with the ruling Fascist junta. Libera's Palazzo dei Congressi is a masterpiece of rationalist architecture, but EUR's most iconic building is Palazzo della Civiltà Italiana (p226), known as the Square Colosseum, which was designed by Giovanni Guerrini, Ernesto Bruno La Padula and Mario Romano.

> Via dei Fori Imperiali, the road that divides the Roman Forums from the Imperial Forums, was one of Mussolini's most controversial projects. Inaugurated in 1932, it was conceived to link the Colosseum (ancient power) with Piazza Venezia (fascist power) but in the process tarmacked over much of the ancient forums.

Postwar Developments

For much of the postwar period, architects in Rome were limited to planning cheap housing for the city's ever-growing population. Swaths of apartment blocks were built along the city's main arteries, and grim suburbs sprang up on land claimed from local farmers.

The 1960 Olympics heralded a spate of sporting construction, and both Stadio Flaminio and Stadio Olimpico (p213) date to this period. Pier

Top: Chiesa di Sant'Ignazio di Loyola (p90)

Bottom: Ponte Sant'Angelo leading to Castel Sant'Angelo (p141)

BLUE PLANET STUDIO / SHUTTERSTOCK ©

Luigi Nervi, Italy's master of concrete and a hugely influential innovator, added his contribution in the form of the Palazzo dello Sport (p226).

Modern Rome

The 21st century has witnessed a flurry of architectural activity in Rome. A clutch of 'starchitects' have worked on projects in the city, including Italy's foremost architect Renzo Piano, renowned American Richard Meier, Anglo-Iraqi Zaha Hadid and major French architect Odile Decq.

Controversy & Acclaim

The foundations of this building boom date to the early 1990s, when the then mayor Francesco Rutelli launched a major clean-up of the historic centre. As part of the process, he commissioned Richard Meier to build a new pavilion for the 1st-century-CE Ara Pacis. Predictably, Meier's glass-and-steel Museo dell'Ara Pacis (p102) caused controversy when it was unveiled in 2006. Vittorio Sgarbi, an outspoken art critic and TV celebrity, claimed that the American's design was the first step to globalising Rome's unique classical heritage. The Roman public appreciated the idea of modern architecture in the city centre, but few were entirely convinced by Meier's design.

Meier won far more acclaim for a second project, his striking Chiesa Dio Padre Misericordioso in Tor Tre Teste, a dreary suburb east of the city centre. This was one of a number of churches commissioned by the Vicariate of Rome for the 2000 Jubilee. Another, the Chiesa di Santa Maria della Presentazione, designed by the Rome-based Nemesi studio, sparked interest when it was inaugurated in the outlying Quartaccio neighbourhood in 2002.

Born in Rome in 1944, Massimiliano Fuksas is known for his futuristic vision, and while he has no signature building as such, his 55,000-sq-metre Roma Convention Centre (p226), aka the Nuvola (Cloud), comes as close as any to embodying his style. A rectangular 40m-high glass shell containing a steel-and-Teflon cloud supported by steel ribs and suspended over a vast conference hall, its look is fearlessly modern. Yet it's not without its references to the past: in both scale and form it owes its inspiration to the 1930s rationalist architecture that surrounds it in EUR. Construction started on the €239 million Nuvola in 2007 and was finally completed in 2016.

Other headline buildings from this period include Renzo Piano's Auditorium Parco della Musica (p207; 2002), Zaha Hadid's MAXXI (p207; 2010), Odile Decq's MACRO building (p208; 2010) and, in EUR, the high-rises Eurosky Tower (Franco Purini; 2012) and Europarco Tower (Studio Transit; 2012).

Modern Icons

- *Palazzo della Civiltà Italiana (Southern Rome)*
- *Auditorium Parco della Musica (Villa Borghese & Northern Rome)*
- *MAXXI (Villa Borghese & Northern Rome)*

Rome's Eataly complex is a masterclass in urban regeneration, bringing life back to a derelict train station. Until the complex opened in 2012, the Air Terminal Ostiense, which had originally been designed to serve airport trains arriving for the 1990 football World Cup, had been an abandoned shell.

The Rhinoceros & Future Developments

In the Forum Boarium area, award-winning French architect Jean Nouvel completed a contemporary-arts gallery, hotel and restaurant at Palazzo Rhinoceros in 2018 for the Fondazione Alda Fendi – Esperimenti.

And in the city's southern reaches, much-delayed construction is set to start on a new 52,500-capacity stadium, the Stadio della Roma, which was beset by planning scandals. The €400 million stadium will be the centrepiece of a vast development in the Tor di Valle neighbourhood, comprising a business park, training centre and public parkland.

Architecture Glossary

apse	a semicircular or polygonal recess with a domed roof over a church's altar
architrave	a main beam set atop columns
baldachino (baldachin)	a permanent canopy over an altar or tomb; often supported by columns and free-standing
baroque	style of European art, architecture and music of the 17th and 18th centuries
basilica	an oblong hall with an apse at the end of the nave; used in ancient Rome for public assemblies and later adopted as a blueprint for medieval churches
cloister	enclosed court attached to a church or monastery; consists of a roofed ambulatory surrounding an open area
colonnade	a row of columns supporting a roof or other structure
cornice	a horizontal projection that crowns a building or wall; the upper part of an *entablature*
crypt	an underground room beneath a church used for services and burials
cupola	a rounded dome forming part of a ceiling or roof
entablature	the part of a classical facade that sits on top of the columns; it consists of an architrave, frieze and cornice
forum	in ancient Rome, a public space used for judicial business and commerce
frieze	a horizontal band, often with painted or sculptural decoration, that sits between the architrave and cornice
futurism	Italian early-20th-century artistic movement that embraced modern technology
loggia	a gallery or room with one side open, often facing a garden
nave	the central aisle in a church, often separated from parallel aisles by pillars
neoclassicism	dominant style of art and architecture in the late 18th and early 19th centuries; a return to ancient Roman styles
portico	a porch with a roof supported by columns
rationalism	international architectural style of the 1920s; its Italian form, often associated with fascism, incorporates linear styles and classical references
Renaissance	European revival of art and architecture based on classical precedents, between the 14th and 16th centuries
rococo	ornate 18th-century style of architecture
stucco	wall plaster used for decorative purposes
transept	in a cross-shaped church, the two parts that bisect the nave at right angles, forming the short arms of the cross
trompe l'oeil	a visual illusion tricking the viewer into seeing a painted object as a three-dimensional image

The Roman Way of Life

As a visitor, it is often difficult to see beyond Rome's spectacular veneer to the large, modern city that lies beneath: a living, breathing capital that is home to almost three million people. So how do the Romans live in their city? Where do they work? Who do they live with? How do they let their hair down?

A Day in the Life

Rome's average office worker lives in a small, two-bedroom apartment in the suburbs and works in a government ministry in the city centre. Their working day is typical of the many who crowd *i mezzi* ('the means'; public transport) in the morning rush hour.

Rome is the most congested city in Italy, according to research carried out by traffic analysts Inrix. In 2016 the city's drivers spent an average of 35 hours stuck in traffic. Topping Europe's blacklist were Moscow (91 hours) and London (73 hours).

The morning routine is the same as city dwellers the world over: a quick breakfast – usually nothing more than a sweet, black espresso – followed by a short bus ride to the nearest metro station. On the way they stop at an *edicola* (kiosk) to pick up their local paper *(Il Messaggero)* and share a joke with the kiosk owner. A quick scan of the headlines reveals few surprises – the usual political shenanigans in city hall; the Pope's latest utterances; Roma and Lazio match reports.

Rome's metro is not a particularly pleasant place to be in *l'ora di punta* (the rush hour), especially in summer when it gets unbearably hot, but the regulars are resigned to the discomfort and bear it cheerfully.

Their work, like many in the swollen state bureaucracy, is not the most interesting in the world, nor the best paid, but it's secure, and with a much sought-after *contratto a tempo indeterminato* (permanent contract), they don't have to worry about losing it. In contrast, their younger colleagues work in constant fear that their temporary contracts will not be renewed when they expire.

Lunch, which is typically taken around 1.30pm, is usually a snack or *pizza al taglio* (by the slice) from a nearby takeaway. Before heading back to the office for the afternoon session, there's time for a quick coffee in the usual bar.

Clocking-off time in most ministries is typically from 5pm onwards, and by about 7pm the evening rush hour is in full swing. Once home, there's time to catch the 8pm TV news before sitting down to a pasta supper at about 8.30pm.

According to figures released in late 2016, the average salary in Rome was €30,685. This compared to €34,414 in Milan and €27,302 in Naples. Italy's national average was €29,176.

Work

Employment in the capital is largely based on Italy's bloated state bureaucracy. Every morning, armies of suited civil servants pour into town and disappear into vast ministerial buildings to keep the machinery of government ticking over. Other important employers include the tourist sector, finance, media and culture – Italy's state broadcaster RAI is based in Rome, as is much of the country's film industry, and there are hundreds of museums and galleries across town.

RELIGION IN ROMAN LIFE

Rome is a city of churches. From its great headline basilicas to the hundreds of parish churches dotted around the suburbs, the city is packed with places in which to worship. And with the Vatican in the centre of town, the Church is a constant presence in Roman life.

Yet the role of religion in modern Roman society is an ambiguous one. On the one hand, most people consider themselves Catholic, but on the other, church attendance is in freefall, particularly among the young, and atheism is growing.

But while Romans don't go to mass very often, the Church remains a point of reference for many people. The Vatican's line on ethical and social issues might not always meet with widespread support, but it's always given an airing in the largely sympathetic national press. Similarly, more than half of the people who get married do so in church, and first communions remain an important social occasion.

Catholicism's hold on the Roman psyche is strong, but an increase in the city's immigrant population has led to a noticeable Muslim presence. Friction has flared on occasion, and there were violent scenes in early 2018 when far-right anti-immigration protesters clashed with police.

But as Italy's economy continues to stagnate, it's tough for young people to get a foot on the career ladder. To strike it lucky, it helps to know someone. Official figures are impossible to come by, but it's a widely held belief that personal or political connections are the best way of landing a job. This system of *raccomandazioni* (recommendations) is widespread and, while being tacitly accepted, regularly gives rise to scandal. In recent years controversies have centred on nepotistic appointments to Rome's city council, at La Sapienza University, at the city's public-transport operator and its waste-disposal company.

Like everywhere in Italy, Rome's workplace remains predominantly male. Female unemployment is an ongoing issue, and Italian women continue to earn less than their male counterparts. That said, recent signs have been positive. Half of PM Matteo Renzi's 2014 cabinet were women, and in June 2016 Rome elected its first-ever female mayor. Virginia Raggi, a 37-year-old lawyer and city councillor, swept to a landslide victory in the city's 2016 municipal elections, thus becoming the first Roman able to call herself *sindaca,* as opposed to the more usual (and masculine) form, *sindaco.*

Home Life & the Family

Romans, like most Italians, live in apartments. These are often small – 75 to 100 sq metres is typical – and expensive. House prices in Rome are among the highest in the country and many first-time buyers are forced to move out of town or to distant suburbs outside the GRA (the *grande raccordo anulare*), the busy ring road that marks the city's outer limit.

Almost all apartments are in self-managed *condomini* (blocks of individually owned flats), a fact which gives rise to no end of neighbourly squabbling. Regular *condominio* meetings are often fiery affairs as neighbours argue over everything from communal repairs to noisy dogs and parking spaces.

Italy's single-most successful institution, and the only one in which the Romans continue to trust, is the family. It's still the rule rather than the exception for young Romans to stay at home until they marry, which they typically do at around age 30. Figures report that virtually two thirds of Rome's 18 to 34 year olds still live at home with at least one parent. To foreign observers this seems strange, but there are mitigating factors: up to half of these stay-at-homes are out of work, and

In 2018 the average price for a square metre of residential property was around €3200, with rates topping €8150 in the historic centre. In the suburbs, the going rate ranged from about €2500 to €4055 per square metre.

FASHION & THE BELLA FIGURA

Making a good impression *(fare la bella figura)* is extremely important to Romans. For a style-conscious student that might mean wearing the latest street brands and having the right smartphone. For a middle-aged professional it will involve being impeccably groomed and dressed appropriately for every occasion. This slavish adherence to fashion isn't limited to clothes or accessories: it extends to all walks of life, and trend-conscious Romans will frequent the same bars and restaurants, enjoy the same *aperitivi* (pre-dinner drinks and snacks) and hang out on the same piazzas.

property and rental prices are high. There's also the fact that young Romans are generally reluctant to downgrade and move to a cheaper neighbourhood. Seen from another perspective, it could just mean that Roman families like living together.

English journalist John Hooper examines the contradictions and insecurities that lie beneath the smooth veneer of Italian society in his entertaining 2015 book *The Italians*. Like Luigi Barzini's 1964 classic of the same name, it's an informative read full of obscure details and quirky facts.

But while faith in the family remains, the family is shrinking. Italian women are giving birth later than ever and having fewer children – in 2017 the average number of children per woman was 1.32, a record low. Rome's army of *nonni* (grandparents) berate their children for this, as does Pope Francis, who has criticised married couples for not having children. For their part, Italy's politicians worry that such a perilously low birth rate threatens the future tax returns necessary for funding the country's already over-burdened pension system.

Play

Despite perpetual economic and political crises, and all the trials and tribulations of living in Rome – dodgy public transport, iffy services and sky-high prices – few Romans would swap their city for anywhere else. They know theirs is one of the world's most beautiful cities, and they enjoy it with gusto. You only have to look at the city's pizzerias, trattorias and restaurants to see that eating out is a much-loved local pastime. It's a cliche of Roman life, but food really is central to social pleasure.

Drinking, in contrast, is not a traditional Roman activity. Recent times have seen craft beer and cocktails sweep the city, but the drinks are often little more than accessories to the main business of hanging out and looking cool. Romans are well practised at this – just look at all those photos of *dolce vita* cafe society – and an evening out in Rome is as much about flirting and looking gorgeous as it is about consuming alcohol.

Rome's finest footballing hour came in 2000 and 2001. In 2000, the city turned sky-blue as Lazio fans celebrated their team's *scudetto* (championship). A year later it was the turn of Rome's red-and-yellow fans as their team became Serie A champions.

Clothes shopping is a popular Roman pastime, alongside cinema-going and football. Interest in Rome's two Serie A teams, Roma and Lazio, remains high, and a trip to the Stadio Olimpico to watch the Sunday game is still considered an afternoon well spent. Depending on the result, of course.

Plenty of people play football as well, although sport isn't limited to *calcio* (soccer). The city's gyms and indoor pools are a hive of activity, while joggers take to the parks and groups of impeccably clad cyclists hit the roads out of town.

Romans are inveterate car lovers and on hot summer weekends they will often drive out to the coast or surrounding countryside. Beach bums make for nearby Ostia or more upmarket Fregene, while those in search of a little greenery head to the Castelli Romani, a pocket of green hills just south of town famous for its Frascati wine and casual eateries.

Termini Train Station (p293)

Survival Guide

Transport

ARRIVING IN ROME

Most people arrive in Rome by plane, landing at one of its two airports: Leonardo da Vinci or Ciampino, hub for European low-cost carrier Ryanair. Flights from New York take around nine hours, from London 2¾ hours and from Sydney at least 22 hours. Domestic flights connect Rome with airports across Italy.

As an alternative to short-haul flights, trains serve Rome's main station, Stazione Termini, from a number of European destinations, including Paris (about 15 hours), as well as cities across Italy.

Long-distance domestic and international buses arrive at the Autostazione Tibus near Tiburtina train station.

You can also get to Rome by boat. Ferries serve Civitavecchia, some 80km north of the city, from a number of Mediterranean ports.

Flights, cars and tours can be booked online at lonelyplanet.com/bookings.

Leonardo da Vinci Airport

Rome's main international airport, **Leonardo da Vinci** (☎06 6 59 51; www.adr.it/fiumicino), aka Fiumicino, is 30km west of the city. It currently has two operational terminals, T1 and T3, both within walking distance of each other. The easiest way to get into town is by train, but there are also buses and private shuttles.

Train

Leonardo Express (www.trenitalia.com; one-way €14) Runs to/from Stazione Termini. Departures from the airport every 30 minutes between 6.08am and 11.23pm, and from Termini between 5.20am and 10.35pm. Journey time is approximately 30 minutes.

FL1 (www.trenitalia.com; one-way €8) Connects to Trastevere, Ostiense and Tiburtina stations, but not Termini. Departures from the airport every 15 minutes (half-hourly on Sundays and public holidays) between 5.57am and 10.42pm; from Tiburtina every 15 to 30 minutes between 5.01am and 10.01pm.

Bus

SIT Bus (☎06 591 68 26; www.sitbusshuttle.com; one-way/return €6/11) Regular departures to **Via Marsala** (Map p344; Via Marsala 5) outside Stazione Termini from 7.15am to 12.40am; from Termini between 4.45am and 8.30pm. All buses stop near the Vatican (Via Crescenzio 2) en route. Tickets are available on the bus. Journey time is approximately one hour.

Cotral (☎800 174471, from a mobile 06 7205 7205; www.cotralspa.it; one-way €5, purchased on bus €7) Runs between Fiumicino and Stazione Tiburtina via Termini. Four to six daily departures including night services from the airport at 1.45am, 3.45am and 5.45am, and from Tiburtina at 12.30am, 2.30am and 4.30am. Journey time is one hour.

Schiaffini Rome Airport Bus (☎06 713 05 31; www.romeairportbus.com; Via Giolitti; one-way/return €6.90/9.90) Regular services from the airport to Stazione Termini (Via Giolitti) between 6.05am and midnight; from Termini between 5.10am and 1am. Allow about an hour for the journey.

TAM (Map p344; ☎06 6504 7426; www.tambus.it) Runs buses from the airport to Via Giolitti outside Stazione Termini at least hourly between 12.15am and 11.30pm; to the airport between 12.30am and 11.30pm. Reckon on 40 minutes to one hour journey time.

Private Shuttle

Airport Connection Services (☎338 9876465; www.airportconnection.it) Transfers to/from the city centre start at €22 per person (€28 for two).

Airport Shuttle (☎06 4201 3469; www.airportshuttle.it) Transfers to/from your hotel for €25 for one person, then €6 for each additional passenger up to a maximum of eight.

Taxi

The set fare to/from the city centre is €50, which is valid for up to four passengers including luggage. Note that taxis registered in Fiumicino charge more, so make sure you catch a Comune di Roma taxi – these are white with a taxi sign on the roof and Roma Capitale written on the door along with the taxi's licence number. Journey time is approximately 45 to 60 minutes depending on traffic.

Car

Follow signs for Roma out of the airport and onto the *autostrada* (motorway). Exit at EUR, following signs for the *centro*, to link up with Via Cristoforo Colombo, which will take you directly into the centre.

Ciampino Airport

Ciampino (☎06 6 59 51; www.adr.it/ciampino), 15km southeast of the city centre, is used by Ryanair (www.ryanair.com) for European and Italian destinations. It's not a big airport, but there's a steady flow of traffic, and at peak times it gets extremely busy.

To get into town, the best option is to take one of the dedicated bus services. Alternatively, you can take a bus to Ciampino station and then pick up a train to Termini or get a bus to Anagnina metro station (on line A).

Bus

SIT Bus (☎06 591 68 26; www.sitbusshuttle.com; to/from airport €6/5, return €9) Regular departures from the airport to **Via Marsala** (Map p344; Via Marsala 5) outside Stazione Termini between 7.45am and 12.15am; from Termini between 4.30am and 9.30pm. Get tickets online, on the bus or at the desk at Ciampino. Journey time is 45 minutes.

Terravision (Map p344; www.terravision.eu) Runs from the airport to Stazione Termini between 8.15am and 12.15am; from Termini between 4.30am and 9.20pm. Bank on 45 minutes for the journey.

Atral (www.atral-lazio.com) Runs regular buses between the airport and Anagnina metro station (€1.20) and Ciampino train station (€1.20), from which you can get a train to Termini (€1.50).

Private Shuttle

Airport Connection Services (☎338 9876465; www.airportconnection.it) Transfers to/from the city centre start at €22 per person (€28 for two).

Airport Shuttle (☎06 4201 3469; www.airportshuttle.it) Transfers to/from your hotel for €25 for one person, then €6 for each additional passenger up to a maximum of eight.

Taxi

The set rate to/from the airport is €31. Journey time is approximately 30 minutes depending on traffic.

Car

Exit the station and follow Via Appia Nuova into the centre.

Termini Train Station

Rome's main station and principal transport hub is **Stazione Termini** (www.romatermini.com; Piazza dei Cinquecento). It has regular connections to other European countries, all major Italian cities and smaller towns.

Train information is available from the Customer Service area on the main concourse to the left of the ticket desks. Alternatively, check www.trenitalia.com or phone ☎89 20 21.

From Termini, you can connect with the metro or take a bus from Piazza dei Cinquecento out front. Taxis are outside the main entrance.

Left luggage (1st five hrs €6, 6-12hr per hour €1, 13hr & over per hour €0.50; ⌚6am-11pm) is available by platform 24 on the Via Giolitti side of the station.

CLIMATE CHANGE & TRAVEL

Every form of transport that relies on carbon-based fuel generates CO_2, the main cause of human-induced climate change. Modern travel is dependent on aeroplanes, which might use less fuel per kilometre per person than most cars but travel much greater distances. The altitude at which aircraft emit gases (including CO_2) and particles also contributes to their climate change impact. Many websites offer 'carbon calculators' that allow people to estimate the carbon emissions generated by their journey and, for those who wish to do so, to offset the impact of the greenhouse gases emitted with contributions to portfolios of climate-friendly initiatives throughout the world. Lonely Planet offsets the carbon footprint of all staff and author travel.

Tibertina Bus Station

Long-distance national and international buses use **Autostazione Tibus** (Autostazione Tiburtina; ☎06 44 25 95; www.tibusroma.it; Largo Guido Mazzoni; Ⓜ Tiburtina). Get tickets at the bus station or at travel agencies.

From the bus station, cross under the overpass for the Tiburtina train station, where you can pick up metro line B and connect with Termini for onward buses, trains and metro line A.

Civitavecchia Port

The nearest port to Rome is at Civitavecchia, about 80km north of town. Ferries sail here from Barcelona and Tunis, as well as Sicily and Sardinia. Check www.traghettiweb.it for route details, prices and bookings.

Bookings can also be made at the Termini-based **Agenzie 365** (☎06 4782 5179; www.agenzie365.it; Stazione Termini, Via Giolitti 34; ⏲8am-9pm; Ⓜ Termini), at travel agents or directly at the port.

From Civitavecchia there are half-hourly trains to Stazione Termini (€4.60 to €16, 45 minutes to 1½ hours). Civitavecchia's station is about 700m from the entrance to the port.

GETTING AROUND ROME

Rome is a sprawling city, but the historic centre is relatively compact. Distances are not great and walking is often the best way of getting around.

Public transport includes buses, trams, metro and a suburban train network. The main hub is Stazione Termini.

Metro

- Rome has two main metro lines, A (orange) and B (blue), which cross at Termini. A branch line, 'B1', serves the northern suburbs, while work continues on a third line C, which currently runs through the southeastern outskirts from San Giovanni. However, you're unlikely to need these two lines.
- Trains run between 5.30am and 11.30pm (to 1.30am on Fridays and Saturdays).
- All stations on line B have wheelchair access and lifts except Circo Massimo, Colosseo and Cavour. On line A, Cipro and Termini are equipped with lifts.
- Take line A for the Trevi Fountain (Barberini), Spanish Steps (Spagna) and St Peter's (Ottaviano-San Pietro).
- Take line B for the Colosseum (Colosseo).

Bus

- Rome's public bus service is run by **ATAC** (☎06 5 70 03; www.atac.roma.it).
- The **main bus station** (Map p344; Piazza dei Cinquecento) is in front of Stazione Termini on Piazza dei Cinquecento, where there's an **information booth** (Map p344; Piazza dei Cinquecento; ⏲8am-8pm; Ⓜ Termini).
- Other important hubs are at Largo di Torre Argentina and Piazza Venezia.
- Buses generally run from about 5.30am until midnight, with limited services throughout the night.
- Rome's night bus service comprises more than 25 lines, many of which pass Termini and/or Piazza Venezia. Buses are marked with an 'n' before the number and bus stops have a blue owl symbol. Departures are usually every 15 to 30 minutes, but can be much slower.

The most useful routes:

- **nMA** Follows the route of metro line A.
- **nMB** Follows the route of metro line B.
- **n70** Piazzale Clodio, Piazza Cavour, Via Zanardelli, Corso del Rinascimento, Corso Vittorio Emanuele II, Largo di Torre Argentina, Piazza Venezia, Via Nazionale and Stazione Termini.

For route planning and real-time information, Roma Bus is a useful phone app.

BUSES FROM TERMINI

From Piazza dei Cinquecento outside Stazione Termini buses run to all corners of the city.

DESTINATION	BUS NO
St Peter's Square	40/64
Piazza Venezia	40/64
Piazza Navona	40/64
Campo de' Fiori	40/64
Pantheon	40/64
Colosseum	75
Terme di Caracalla	714
Villa Borghese	910
Trastevere	H

USEFUL BUS & TRAM ROUTES

BUS NO	ROUTE	OPERATING HOURS	FREQUENCY (HOURLY)
H	Termini, Via Nazionale, Piazza Venezia, Viale Trastevere	5.30am-midnight	up to 5
3 (tram)	Trastevere, Testaccio, Viale Aventino, Circo Massimo, Colosseo, San Giovanni, Porta Maggiore, San Lorenzo, Villa Borghese	5.30am-12.30am	up to 6
8 (tram)	Piazza Venezia, Via Arenula, Trastevere	5.10am-midnight	up to 12
23	Piazzale Clodio, Piazza del Risorgimento, Lungotevere, Testaccio, Ostiense, Basilica di San Paolo	5.15am-midnight	up to 5
40	Termini, Via Nazionale, Piazza Venezia, Largo di Torre Argentina, Borgo Sant'Angelo	6am-11.50pm	up to 12
64	Similar route to 40 but slower and with more stops	5.30am-12.30am	up to 12
170	Termini, Via Nazionale, Piazza Venezia, Via del Teatro Marcello, Piazza Bocca della Verità, Testaccio, EUR	5.30am-midnight	up to 7
492	Stazione Tiburtina, San Lorenzo, Piazza Barberini, Largo di Torre Argentina, Corso del Rinascimento, Piazza del Risorgimento, Cipro-Vatican Museums	5.15am-midnight	up to 5
660	Largo Colli Albani to Via Appia Antica	7am-8.45pm	2
714	Termini, Piazza Santa Maria Maggiore, Piazza San Giovanni in Laterano, Viale delle Terme di Caracalla, EUR	5.30am-midnight	up to 6
910	Termini, Piazza della Repubblica, Villa Borghese, Auditorium Parco della Musica, Piazza Mancini	5.30am-midnight	up to 6

Tram

Rome has a limited tram network. For route maps see www.atac.roma.it.

The most useful lines:

- **2** Piazzale Flaminio to/from Piazza Mancini.
- **3** Museo Nazionale Etrusco di Villa Giulia to/from San Lorenzo, San Giovanni, Testaccio and Trastevere.
- **8** Piazza Venezia to/from Trastevere.
- **19** Piazza del Risorgimento to/from Villa Borghese, San Lorenzo and Via Prenestina.

Taxi

- Official licensed taxis are white with a taxi sign on the roof and Roma Capitale written on the front door along with the taxi's licence number.
- Always go with the metered fare, never an arranged price (the set fares to/from the airports are exceptions).
- In town (within the ring road) flag fall is €3 between 6am and 10pm on weekdays, €5 on Sundays and holidays, and €7 between 10pm and 6am. Then it's €1.14–1.66 per kilometre. Official rates are posted in taxis and at https://romamobilita.it/it/media/muoversiaroma/muoversi-taxi.
- You can hail a taxi, but it's often easier to wait at a rank or phone for one. There are taxi ranks at the airports, Stazione Termini, Piazza della Repubblica, Piazza Barberini, Piazza di Spagna, Piazza Venezia, the **Pantheon** (Map p328; Pantheon), the **Colosseum** (Map p324; Piazza del Colosseo, cnr Via Capo d'Africa), **Largo di Torre Argentina** (Map p328; Largo di Torre Argentina), Piazza Belli, **Piazza Pio XII** (Map p336) and **Piazza del Risorgimento** (Map p336).
- To book call the automated **taxi line** (☎in Italian 06 06 09), which sends the nearest car available; a taxi company direct; or use the Chiama Taxi app.
- MyTaxi is another good app. It allows you to order a taxi without having to deal with potentially tricky language problems.
- Note that when you order a cab, the meter is switched on straight away and you pay for the cost of the journey from wherever the driver receives the call.

TICKETS & PASSES

Public-transport tickets are valid on all buses, trams and metro lines, except for routes to Fiumicino airport. Children under 10 travel free. Tickets:

- **BIT** (single ticket valid for 100 minutes; in that time it can be used on all forms of transport but only once on the metro) €1.50
- **10 BIT** (ten 100-minute BIT tickets in one pass) €15
- **Roma 24h** (24 hours) €7
- **Roma 48h** (48 hours) €12.50
- **Roma 72h** (72 hours) €18
- **CIS** (weekly ticket) €24
- **Abbonamento mensile** (a monthly pass) For a single user €35

Buy tickets from *tabacchi* (tobacconist's shops), newsstands and vending machines at main bus stops and metro stations. Validate in machines on buses, at metro entrance gates or at train stations. Ticketless riders risk a fine of at least €50.

The Roma Pass (48/72 hours €35/52) comes with a travel pass valid within the city boundaries.

Travelling Out of Town

For destinations in the surrounding Lazio region, **Cotral** (☎800 174471, from a mobile 06 7205 7205; www.cotralspa.it) buses depart from numerous points throughout the city. The company is linked with Rome's public-transport system, which means that you can buy tickets that cover city buses, trams, metro and train lines, as well as regional buses and trains.

There are a range of tickets including a daily BIRG *(biglietto integrato regionale giornaliero)* ticket, which allows unlimited travel on all city and regional transport until midnight on the day it's activated. It's priced according to zones; tickets range from €3.30 to €14.

Get tickets from *tabacchi* and authorised ATAC sellers.

Pronto Taxi (☎06 66 45; www.6645.it)

Radiotaxi 3570 (☎06 35 70; www.3570.it)

Samarcanda (☎06 55 51; https://065551.it)

Taxi Tevere (☎06 49 94, 06 41 57; www.taxitevere.it)

Train

Apart from connections to Fiumicino airport, you'll probably only need the overground rail network if you head out of town.

- Train information is available from the Customer Service area on the main concourse in **Stazione Termini** (www.romatermini.com; Piazza dei Cinquecento; Ⓜ Termini). Alternatively, check www.trenitalia.com or phone 89 20 21.
- Buy tickets on the main station concourse, from automated machines or authorised travel agencies – look for an FS or *biglietti treni* sign in the window.
- Rome's second train station is Stazione Tiburtina, four stops from Termini on metro line B. Of the capital's other train stations, the most important are Stazione Roma-Ostiense and Stazione Trastevere.

Bicycle

- The centre of Rome doesn't lend itself to cycling: there are steep hills, treacherous cobbled roads and the traffic is terrible.
- Bikes can be transported on certain specified bus and tram routes, and on the metro at weekends and on weekdays from 5.30am to 7am, from 10am to noon and from 8pm until the end of service. However, some line A stations are off-limits to bikes: Spagna, Barberini, Repubblica, Termini, Vittorio Emanuele and San Giovanni.
- Bikes can be carried on the Lido di Ostia train on Saturday and Sunday and on weekdays from the beginning of service to 12.30pm and from 8pm until the end of service. You have to buy a separate ticket for the bike.
- On regional trains marked with a bike icon on the timetable, you can carry a bike if you pay a €3.50 supplement.

Car & Motorcycle

- Driving around Rome is not recommended. Riding a scooter or motorbike is faster and makes parking easier, but Rome is no place for learners, so if you're not an experienced rider, give it a miss. Hiring a car for a day trip out of town is worth considering.

➡ Most of Rome's historic centre is closed to unauthorised traffic from 6.30am to 6pm Monday to Friday, from 2pm to 6pm Saturday, and from 11pm to 3am Friday and Saturday. Restrictions also apply in Tridente, Trastevere and Monti; evening-only Limited Traffic Zones (ZTLs) are operative in San Lorenzo and Testaccio, typically from 9.30pm or 11pm to 3am on Fridays and Saturdays (also Wednesdays and Thursdays in summer).

➡ All streets accessing the ZTL are monitored by electronic-access detection devices. If you're staying in this zone, contact your hotel. For further information, check https://romamobilita.it.

Driving Licence & Road Rules

Photocard UK licences and all EU driving licences are recognised in Italy. Holders of other country's licences should get an International Driving Permit (IDP) to accompany their national licence. Apply to your national motoring association.

When driving you'll need to carry: vehicle registration certificate; valid driving licence; proof of third-party-liability insurance cover.

A licence is required to ride a scooter – a car licence will do for bikes up to 125cc; for anything over 125cc, you'll need a motorcycle licence.

Other rules:

➡ Drive on the right, overtake on the left.

➡ It's obligatory to wear seat belts, to drive with your headlights on outside built-up areas, and to carry a warning triangle and fluorescent vest in case of breakdown.

➡ Wearing a helmet is compulsory on all two-wheeled vehicles.

➡ The blood alcohol limit is 0.05%; for drivers under 21 and those who have had their licence for less than three years, it's zero.

A good source of information is the **Automobile Club d'Italia** (ACI; ☎roadside assistance from Italian phone 803 116, roadside assistance from foreign mobile 800 116800; www.aci.it), Italy's national motoring organisation.

Hire

Car hire is available at both Rome's airports and Stazione Termini. Reckon on from €20 per day for a small car.

Avis (Termini office 06 481 43 73; www.avisautonoleggio.it)

Europcar (Termini office 06 488 28 54; www.europcar.it)

Hertz (Termini office 06 488 39 67; www.hertz.it)

Maggiore National (Termini office 06 488 00 49; www.maggiore.it)

To hire a scooter, prices range from about €30 to €120 depending on the size of the vehicle. Reliable operators:

Eco Move Rent (☎06 4470 4518; www.ecomoverent.com; Via Varese 48-50; bike/scooter/Vespa per day from €11/40/45; ⏲8.30am-7.30pm; Ⓜ Termini)

On Road (☎06 481 56 69; www.scooterhire.it; Via Cavour 80a; scooter rental per day from €44; ⏲9am-7pm; Ⓜ Termini)

Parking

➡ Blue lines denote pay-and-display parking – get tickets from meters (coins only) and *tabacchi* (tobacconist's shops).

➡ Expect to pay up to €1.20 per hour between 8am and 8pm (11pm in some places) in central areas.

➡ If your car gets towed away, call the **traffic police** (☎06 6 76 91).

➡ There's a list of car parks on www.060608.it.

➡ Useful car parks:

Piazzale dei Partigiani (per hr €0.77; ⏲6am-11pm; Ⓜ Piramide)

Stazione Termini (Piazza dei Cinquecento; per hour/day €2.20/18; ⏲6am-midnight; 🚌 Piazza dei Cinquecento)

Villa Borghese (☎06 322 59 34; www.sabait.it; Viale del Galoppatoio 33; per hr/day €2.30/22; ⏲24hr; 🚌 Via Pinciana)

TOURS

Guided Tours

A Friend in Rome (☎340 5019201; www.afriendinrome.it) Silvia Prosperi and her team offer a range of private tours covering the Vatican and main historic centre, plus areas outside the capital. They can also organise kid-friendly tours, food-and-wine itineraries, vintage-car drives and horse rides along Via Appia Antica. Rates start at €165 for a basic three-hour tour (up to eight people); add €55 for every additional hour.

The Tour Guy (☎9480 4747; https://thetourguy.com) A professional setup that organises a wide range of group and private tours. Packages, led by English-speaking experts, include skip-the-line visits to the Vatican Museums and St Peter's Basilica (€60), tours of the Colosseum and Roman Forum (€65), and foodie tours of Trastevere (€90 including dinner). Day trips to Florence and Pompeii are also available.

Through Eternity Cultural Association (☎06 700 93 36; www.througheternity.com) A reliable operator offering private and group tours led by English-speaking experts. Popular packages include a twilight tour of Rome's piazzas and fountains (€33, 2½ hours), and night visits to the Vatican Museums (€69, 3½ hours) and Colosseum (€75, 2½ hours).

Bicycle & Scooter

Red Bicycle (Map p339; ☎327 5387148; www.theredbicycle.org; Via Ostilia 4b; 🚋Via Labicana) A cycle outfit offering bike hire (€10/15 per half/full day) and a range of cycling tours taking in the city's main neighbourhoods and environs. Prices start at €45 for a three-hour sunset tour, rising to €99 for a full-day ride to Ostia Antica.

Bici & Baci (Map p344; ☎06 482 84 43; www.bicibaci.com; Via del Viminale 5; bike tours from €30, Vespa tours from €145; ⊙8am-7pm; Ⓜ Repubblica) Bici & Baci runs a range of daily walking, bike and Segway tours taking in the main historical sites and Via Appia Antica; these are in English or Dutch. Also offers tours on vintage Vespas, classic Fiat 500 cars or funky three-wheeled Ape Calessinos. Bici & Baci also hires bicycles/e-bikes (€12.50/25 per day) and a variety of scooters (from €32 per day).

Rome for You (Map p340; ☎06 4543 3789; www.romeforyou.net; Via dell'Arco di San Calisto 9; bike/scooter rental per day €13/40, tours from €45; ⊙10am-6pm winter, to 8pm summer) Choose from a big range of bikes, mountain bikes, electric bikes and scooters to rent. Or choose from a variety of bike tours that average about 20km in length and four hours in duration and cover sites across the city.

TopBike Rental & Tours (☎06 488 28 93; www.topbikerental.com; Via Labicana 49; ⊙8.30am-8pm summer, to 7pm winter; 🚋Via Labicana) Offers a series of bike tours throughout the city, including a four-hour 14km exploration of the city centre (€45) and an all-day 27km ride through Via Appia Antica and environs (€79). Out-of-town tours take in Castel Gandolfo, Civita di Bagnoregio and Orvieto. Also offers bike hire from €15 per day.

Bus

Open Bus Vatican & Rome (www.omniavaticanrome.org/it/cards/il-servizio-open-bus-vatican-rome; tour €12, 24/48hr ticket €25/28) The Vatican-sponsored Opera Romana Pellegrinaggi runs a hop-on, hop-off bus departing from Piazza Pia and Termini. Stops are situated near main sights, including St Peter's Basilica, Piazza Navona and the Colosseum. Tickets are available on board, online or at the info point just off St Peter's Square.

Directory A–Z

Accessible Travel

Rome isn't an easy city for travellers with disabilities. Cobbled streets, paving stones, blocked pavements and tiny lifts are difficult for wheelchair users, while the relentless traffic can be disorienting for partially sighted travellers or those with hearing difficulties.

If you have an obvious disability and/or appropriate ID, many museums and galleries offer free admission for yourself and a companion.

Arriving in Rome

Airline companies will arrange assistance at airports if you notify them of your needs in advance. Alternatively, contact ADR Assistance (www.adrassistance.it) for help at Fiumicino or Ciampino airports.

To reach the city from Fiumicino, the wheelchair-accessible **Leonardo Express** (www.trenitalia.com; one-way €14) train runs to Stazione Termini. Alternatively, you could organise a private transfer – **Fausta Trasporti** (☎06 540 33 62; http://accessibletransportationrome.com) is one of a number of operators offering transfers in wheelchair-accessible vehicles.

If travelling by train, ring 800 90 60 60 to arrange assistance. At Stazione Termini, the **Sala Blu Assistenza Disabili** (Map p344; ☎800 90 60 60; SalaBlu.ROMA@rfi.it; Stazione Termini; ⏰6.45am-9.30pm; Ⓜ Termini) next to platform 1 can provide information on wheelchair-accessible trains and help with transport in the station. Contact the office 24 hours ahead if you know you're going to need assistance. There are similar offices at Tiburtina and Ostiense stations.

For people with disabilities and reduced mobility, visit the information page of Rete Ferroviaria Italiana (www.rfi.it/rfi-en/For-persons-with-disability) for full details of services offered and barrier-free stations.

Getting Around

Getting around on public transport is difficult. All stations on metro line B have wheelchair access and lifts except Circo Massimo, Colosseo and Cavour. On line A, Cipro and Termini are equipped with lifts. Note, however, that just because a station has a lift doesn't mean it will necessarily be working.

Bus 590 covers the same route as metro line A and is one of 22 bus and tram services with wheelchair access. Routes with disabled access are indicated on bus stops.

Some taxis are equipped to carry passengers in wheelchairs; ask for a taxi for a *sedia a rotelle* (wheelchair). **Fausta Trasporti** (☎06 540 33 62; http://accessibletransportationrome.com) has a fleet of wheelchair-accessible vehicles that can carry up to seven people, including three wheelchair users.

If you are driving, EU disability parking permits are recognised in Rome, giving you the same parking rights that local drivers with disabilities have.

Accessible Travel Online Resources

Village for All (www.villageforall.net/en) Performs on-site audits of tourist facilities in Italy and San Marino. Its listings include three accommodation providers in Rome.

Tourism without Barriers (www.turismosenzabarriere.it) Has a searchable database of accessible accommodation and tourist attractions in several regions of Italy, including Lazio.

Download Lonely Planet's free Accessible Travel guides from https://shop.lonelyplanet.com/categories/accessible-travel.com.

Accessible Travel Agencies

Rome & Italy (☎06 4425 8441; www.romeanditaly.com/tourism-for-disabled; Via

Giuseppe Veronese 50; ⏲9am-8pm) This mainstream travel agency in Rome has a well-developed accessible-tourism arm that offers customised tours, accessible accommodation, and equipment and vehicle hire. Its Wheely Trekky service, which uses a specially designed sedan/rickshaw with sherpas, allows wheelchair users to access many otherwise difficult archaeological sites, including the Colosseum, Castel Sant'Angelo and Terme di Caracalla.

Accessible Italy (www.accessibleitaly.com) San Marino–based, this nonprofit company specialises in holiday services for people with disabilities, including equipment rental, adapted vehicle hire and arranging personal assistants.

Sage Traveling (www.sagetraveling.com) A US-based accessible travel agency, offering tailor-made tours to assist mobility-impaired travellers in Europe. Check out its website for a detailed access guide to Rome.

Customs Regulations

➡ Entering Italy from another EU country you can bring, duty-free: 10L spirits, 90L wine and 800 cigarettes.

➡ If arriving from a non-EU country, the limits are 1L spirits (or 2L fortified wine), 4L still wine, 16L beer, 200 cigarettes and other goods up to a value of €300/430 (travelling by land/sea); anything over this must be declared on arrival and the duty paid.

➡ On leaving the EU, non-EU residents can reclaim value-added tax (VAT) on expensive purchases.

Electricity

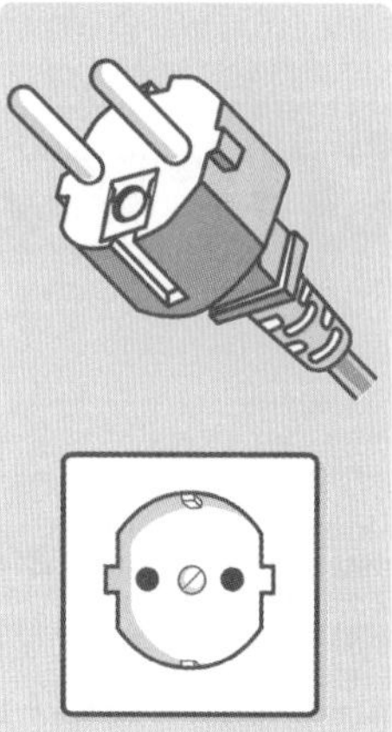

230v/50hz

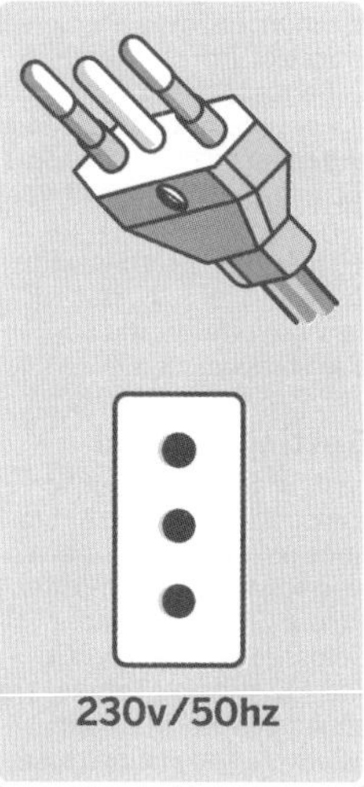

230v/50hz

Emergency

Ambulance	☎118
Fire	☎115
Police	☎112, 113

Health

Non-EU nationals should take out medical insurance before travelling to Rome.

It's also worth finding out if there is a reciprocal arrangement between your country and Italy. If there is, you may be covered for essential medical treatment and some subsidised medications while in Italy.

Tap water is safe to drink in Rome.

Internet Access

➡ Free wi-fi is widely available in hostels, B&Bs and hotels, though signal quality varies. Some places also provide laptops/computers.

➡ Many bars and cafes offer wi-fi.

➡ There are many public wi-fi hotspots across town run by **WiFimetropolitano** (www.cittametropolitanaroma.gov.it/wifimetropolitano). To use these, you'll need to register online using a credit card or Italian mobile phone.

➡ A free smartphone app, wifi.italia.it, is available that allows you to connect to participating networks with a single login. Released in summer 2017, it gets mixed reports.

Legal Matters

The most likely reason for a brush with the law is to report a theft. If you have something stolen and you want to claim it on insurance, you must make a statement to the police. Insurance companies won't pay up without official proof of a crime.

The Italian police is divided into three main bodies: the *polizia*, who wear navy-blue jackets; the *carabinieri*, in a black uniform with a red stripe; and the grey-clad *guardia di finanza* (fiscal police), responsible for fighting tax evasion and drug smuggling. If you run into trouble, you're most likely to end up dealing with the *polizia* or *carabinieri*.

If you're caught with what the police deem to be a dealable quantity of hard or soft drugs, you risk prison sentences of between two and 22 years. Possession for personal use is punishable by administrative sanctions, although first-time offenders might get away with a warning.

ROME'S RULES OF CONDUCT

Sitting on the Spanish Steps is now officially forbidden. The ban, introduced in August 2019, came as part of a package of regulations designed to crack down on anti-social behaviour. Other rules include:

- no wading in the city's fountains;
- no 'messy' outdoor eating near historic monuments;
- no walking around bare-chested;
- no dragging strollers or wheelie suitcases up or down historic staircases;
- when drinking from the public drinking fountains known as nasoni, don't place your lips on the spout, rather drink from your cupped hands.

People caught breaking these rules risk fines of up to €400 or a temporary ban on entering the area in which they caused the offence.

LGBTIQ+ Travellers

Homosexuality is legal and widely accepted, but Rome is fairly conservative in its attitudes and discretion is still wise.

The city has a thriving, if low-key, gay scene. There are relatively few queer-only venues, but the Colosseum end of Via di San Giovanni in Laterano is a favourite hang-out and many clubs host regular gay and lesbian nights. Outside town, there are a couple of popular gay beaches on the Ostia seafront: Settimo Cielo and the nearby Oasi Naturista Capocotta. Both are accessible by bus 061 from Ostia Lido.

Gay Village (☎350 0723346; www.gayvillage.it; Lungotevere Testacci; €3-20; ⏲7.30pm-3.30am Thu-Sat Jun-early Sep; Ⓜ Piramide) This is the big annual event, held between June and September in Testaccio.

Resources include the following:

Arcigay (☎06 6450 1102; www.arcigayroma.it; Via Nicola Zabaglia 14; ⏲4-8pm Mon-Sat) The Roman branch of Arcigay, Italy's national organisation for the LGBTIQ+ community.

Circolo Mario Mieli di Cultura Omosessuale (Map p350; ☎06 541 39 85, Rainbow Help Line 800 110611; www.mariomieli.org; Via Efeso 2a; ⏲11am-6pm Mon-Fri; Ⓜ Basilica San Paolo) Organises debates, cultural events and social functions. Its website has info and listings of forthcoming events.

Coordinamento Lesbiche Italiano (www.clrbp.it; Via San Francesco di Sales 1b; 🚊 Lungotevere della Farnesina) The national organisation for lesbians holds regular conferences, cultural events and literary evenings at the adjoining Casa Internazionale delle Donne in Trastevere.

Medical Services

Italy has a public health system that is legally bound to provide emergency care to everyone. EU nationals are entitled to reduced-cost, sometimes free, medical care with a European Health Insurance Card (EHIC), available from your home health authority; non-EU citizens should take out medical insurance.

For emergency treatment, you can go to the *pronto soccorso* (casualty department) of an *ospedale* (public hospital). For less serious ailments call the **Guardia Medica Turistica** (☎06 7730 6650; Via Emilio Morosini 30; ⏲24hr; 🚊 Viale di Trastevere, 🚊 Viale di Trastevere).

English-speaking doctors are available for house calls or appointments at the private clinic, **Doctors in Italy** (☎370 1359521, 06 679 06 95; www.doctorsinitaly.com; 3rd fl, Via Frattina 48; ⏲10am-8pm Mon-Fri; Ⓜ Spagna).

If you need an ambulance, call ☎118.

Hospitals

Ospedale Fatebenefratelli (☎06 6 83 71; www.fatebenefratelli-isolatiberina.it; Piazza Fatebenefratelli, Isola Tiberina) On the Isola Tiberina.

Ospedale Santo Spirito (☎06 6 83 51; Lungotevere in Sassia 1; ⏲24hr; 🚊 Lungotevere in Sassia) Near the Vatican.

Policlinico Umberto I (☎06 4 99 71; www.policlinicoumberto1.it; Viale del Policlinico 155; Ⓜ Policlinico, Castro Pretorio) Rome's largest hospital, near Stazione Termini.

Pharmacies

Marked by a green cross, *farmacie* (pharmacies) typically open from 8.30am to 7.30pm Monday to Friday and on Saturday mornings. Outside these hours they open on a rotational basis. All are legally required to post a list of places open in the vicinity.

If you think you'll need a prescription while in Rome, make sure you know the drug's generic name rather than the brand name. Regular medications available over the counter – such as antihistamines or paracetamol – tend to be expensive in Italy.

Farmacia Gruppo Farmacrimi (☎06 474 54 21; https://farmacrimi.it; Via Marsala 29; ⏰7am-10pm; Ⓜ Termini) In Stazione Termini, next to platform 1.

Farmacia San Gallicano (☎06 589 57 64; Via di San Gallicano; ⏰24hr; 🚌 Viale di Trastevere, 🚋 Trastevere/Mastai) In Trastevere.

Money

Italy's currency is the euro (€). The seven euro notes come in denominations of €500, €200, €100, €50, €20, €10 and €5. The eight euro coins are in denominations of €2 and €1, while smaller coins run from 50 cents, down to 20, 10, five, two and one.

ATMs

➡ ATMs (known in Italy as *bancomat*) are widely available in Rome, and most will accept cards tied into the Visa, MasterCard, Cirrus and Maestro systems.

➡ Most ATMs have a daily withdrawal limit of €250.

➡ Always let your bank know when you're going abroad to prevent your card being frozen when payments from unusual locations appear.

➡ Beware of transaction fees. Every time you withdraw cash, you'll be hit by charges – typically your home bank will charge a foreign-exchange fee and a transaction fee. These might be a flat rate or a percentage of around 1% to 3%. Check with your bank.

➡ If an ATM rejects your card, try another machine before assuming the problem is with your card.

Changing Money

➡ You can change your money in banks, at post offices or at a *cambio* (exchange office). There are exchange booths at Stazione Termini and at Fiumicino and Ciampino airports.

➡ Take your passport or photo ID when exchanging money.

Credit Cards

➡ Virtually all midrange and top-end hotels accept credit cards, as do most restaurants and large shops. Some cheaper *pensioni* (pensions), trattorias and pizzerias only accept cash. Don't rely on credit cards at smaller museums or galleries.

➡ Major cards such as Visa, MasterCard, Eurocard, Cirrus and Eurocheques are widely accepted. Amex is also recognised, although it's less common than Visa or MasterCard.

➡ Note that using your credit card in ATMs can be costly. On every transaction there's a fee, which can reach US$10 with some credit-card issuers, as well as interest per withdrawal. Check with your issuer before leaving home.

➡ If your card is lost, stolen or swallowed by an ATM, phone to have an immediate stop put on its use.

DISCOUNT CARDS

DISCOUNT CARD	PRICE ADULT/REDUCED	VALIDITY	ADMISSION TO:
Omnia Card	€129/59	72hr	Including fast-track entry to the Vatican Museums & admission to St Peter's Basilica, Basilica di San Giovanni in Laterano, & Carcere Mamertino. Free travel on hop-on, hop-off Open Bus Vatican & Rome, plus unlimited public transport within Rome. Free entry to two sites, then 50% discount to extra sites. A 24-hour version also available (€69/49). Details at www.omniakit.org.
Roma Pass	€52	72hr	Includes free admission to two museums or sites, as well as reduced entry to extra sites, unlimited city transport & discounted entry to other exhibitions & events. The 48-hour Roma Pass (€32) is a more limited version. Details at www.romapass.it.

EU citizens aged between 18 and 25 qualify for discounts at state-run museums; under-18s get in free. City-run museums are free for under-sixes and discounted for six to 25 year olds. In all cases you'll need proof of age, ideally a passport or ID card.

Opening Hours

Banks 8.30am–1.30pm and 2.45pm–4.30pm Monday to Friday

Bars & cafes 7.30am–8pm, sometimes until 1am or 2am

Clubs 10pm–4am or 5am

Restaurants noon–3pm and 7.30pm–11pm (later in summer)

Shops 10am–7.30pm or 8pm Monday to Saturday, some also 11am–7pm Sunday; smaller shops 10am–1.30pm and 3.30pm–7.30pm Monday to Saturday; some shops are closed Monday morning

Public Holidays

Most Romans take their annual holiday in August. This means that many businesses and shops close for at least part of the month, particularly around Ferragosto (Feast of the Assumption) on 15 August.

Public holidays include the following:

Capodanno (New Year's Day) 1 January

Epifania (Epiphany) 6 January

Pasquetta (Easter Monday) March/April

Giorno della Liberazione (Liberation Day) 25 April

Festa del Lavoro (Labour Day) 1 May

Festa della Repubblica (Republic Day) 2 June

Festa dei Santi Pietro e Paolo (Feast of Sts Peter & Paul) 29 June

Ferragosto (Feast of the Assumption) 15 August

Festa di Ognisanti (All Saints' Day) 1 November

Festa dell'Immacolata Concezione (Feast of the Immaculate Conception) 8 December

Natale (Christmas Day) 25 December

Festa di Santo Stefano (Boxing Day) 26 December

PRACTICALITIES

➡ **Newspapers** Key national dailies include centre-left *la Repubblica* (www.repubblica.it) and its conservative rival *Corriere della Sera* (www.corriere.it). For the Vatican's take on affairs, *L'Osservatore Romano* (www.osservatoreromano.va) is the Holy See's official paper.

➡ **Television** The main terrestrial channels are Rai 1, 2 and 3 run by Rai (www.rai.it), Italy's state-owned national broadcaster, and Canale 5, Italia 1 and Rete 4 run by Mediaset (www.mediaset.it), the commercial TV company founded and still partly owned by Silvio Berlusconi.

➡ **Radio** As well as the principal Rai channels (Radiouno, Radiodue, Radiotre), there are hundreds of commercial radio stations operating across the country. Popular Rome-based stations include Radio Capital (www.capital.it) and Radio Città Futura (www.radiocittafutura.it). Vatican Radio (www.radiovaticana.va) broadcasts in Italian, English and other languages.

➡ **Smoking** Smoking is banned in enclosed public spaces, which includes restaurants, bars, shops and public transport. It's also banned in Villa Borghese and other public parks over the summer, from June to September.

➡ **Weights and measures** Italy uses the metric system.

Responsible Travel

COVID Protocols

➡ Masks must be worn in indoor public places and on public transport.

➡ A Green Pass (vaccination certificate) is required for indoor dining at restaurants and to access museums.

➡ Check the latest regulations at www.italia.it/en/useful-info/covid-19-updates-information-for-tourists.html.

Overtourism

➡ Avoid crowds by visiting off-season, between November and March.

➡ Consider staying in less-central neighbourhoods such as Testaccio, Aventino, Prati or San Giovanni.

Lighten Your Footprint

➡ Forget cars or taxis, Rome's centre is best covered on foot.

➡ Don't buy bottled water – fill up on aqua at Rome's *nasoni* (big nose) fountains.

Safe Travel

Rome is a safe city, but petty theft can be a problem. Use common sense and watch your valuables.

➡ Pickpockets and thieves are active in touristy areas such as the Colosseum, Piazza di Spagna, Piazza Venezia and St Peter's Square.

- Be alert around Stazione Termini and on crowded public transport – the 64 Vatican bus is notorious.
- In case of theft or loss, always report the incident to the police within 24 hours and ask for a statement.
- Never drape your bag over an empty chair at a streetside cafe or put it where you can't see it. Also, never leave valuables in coat pockets in restaurants or other places with communal coat hooks.
- Watch your bag during rainstorms when thieves target people concentrating on their umbrellas.
- Beware of gangs of kids or others demanding attention. If you've been targeted, either take evasive action or shout *'Va via!'* ('Go away!').
- Always check your change to see you haven't been short-changed.

Main Police Station (Questura; ☎06 4 68 61; http://questure.poliziadistato.it; Via San Vitale 15; ⏰8.30am-1.30pm Mon-Sat & 3.30-7pm Mon-Fri; 🚌Via Nazionale) Rome's Questura is just off Via Nazionale.

Taxes & Refunds

A value-added tax known as IVA *(Imposta sul Valore Aggiunta)* is included in the price of most goods and services. It currently ranges from 4% to 25%. Tax-free shopping is available at some shops.

All overnight stays in the city are subject to an accommodation tax (p241) – the exact sum depends on the length of your sojourn and type of accommodation.

TAX-FREE SHOPPING

Non-EU residents who spend more than €155 in one shop at a single time can claim a refund when leaving the EU. The refund only applies to purchases from stores that display a 'Tax Free' sign. When making the purchase, ask for a tax-refund voucher, to be filled in with the date of the purchase and its value. When leaving the EU, get this voucher stamped at customs and take it to the nearest tax-refund counter where you'll get an immediate refund, either in cash or charged to your credit card.

Telephone

- Italian mobile phones operate on the GSM 900/1800 network, which is compatible with the rest of Europe and Australia but not always with the North American GSM or CDMA systems – check with your service provider.
- The cheapest way of using your mobile is to buy a prepaid *(prepagato)* Italian SIM card. TIM (Telecom Italia Mobile; www.tim.it), Wind (www.wind.it), Vodafone (www.vodafone.it) and Tre (www.tre.it) all offer SIM cards and have retail outlets across town.
- Note that by Italian law all SIM cards must be registered in Italy, so make sure you have a passport or ID card with you when you buy one.

Time

Italy is in a single time zone, one hour ahead of GMT. Daylight-saving time, when clocks move forward one hour, starts on the last Sunday in March. Clocks are put back an hour on the last Sunday in October.

Italy operates on a 24-hour clock, so 6pm is written as 18:00.

Toilets

Public toilets are not widespread, but you'll find them at St Peter's Square (free) and Stazione Termini (€1). If you're caught short, the best thing to do is to nip into a cafe or bar.

Tourist Information

There are tourist information points at **Fiumicino** (Fiumicino Airport; International Arrivals, Terminal 3; ⏰8am-8.45pm) and **Ciampino** (Arrivals Hall; ⏰8.30am-6pm) airports, as well as locations across the city. Each can provide city maps and sell the Roma Pass.

Information points:

Piazza delle Cinque Lune (Map p328; Piazza delle Cinque Lune; ⏰9.30am-7pm; 🚌Corso del Rinascimento) Near Piazza Navona.

Stazione Termini (Map p344; ☎06 06 08; www.turismoroma.it; Via Giovanni Giolitti 34; ⏰8am-6.45pm; Ⓜ Termini) In the hall adjacent to platform 24.

Imperial Forums (Map p324; Via dei Fori Imperiali; ⏰9.30am-7pm, to 8pm Jul & Aug; 🚌Via dei Fori Imperiali)

Via Marco Minghetti (Map p332; ☎06 06 08; www.turismoroma.it; Via Marco Minghetti; ⏰9.30am-7pm; 🚌Via del Corso) Between Via del Corso and the Trevi Fountain.

Castel Sant'Angelo (Map p336; www.turismoroma.it; Piazza Pia; ⏰9.30am-7pm summer, 8.30am-6pm winter; 🚌Piazza Pia)

Trastevere (Map p340; www.turismoroma.it; Piazza Sonnino; ⌚10.30am-8pm; 🚌Viale di Trastevere, 🚋Belli)

For information about the Vatican, contact the **Ufficio Pellegrini e Turisti** (Map p336; ☎06 6988 1662; www.vatican.va; St Peter's Sq; ⌚8.30am-6.30pm Mon-Sat; 🚌Piazza del Risorgimento, Ⓜ Ottaviano-San Pietro).

Rome's official tourist website, **Turismo Roma** (www.turismoroma.it), has comprehensive information about sights, accommodation and city transport, as well as itineraries and up-to-date listings.

The **Comune di Roma** (☎06 06 08; www.060608.it; ⌚9am-7pm) runs a free multilingual tourist information phone line providing info on culture, shows, hotels, transport etc. Its website is also an excellent resource.

For practical questions such as 'Where's the nearest hospital?' or 'Where can I park?', phone the **ChiamaRoma** (☎06 06 06; ⌚24hr) call centre.

Visas & Passes

➡ Italy is one of the 26 European countries making up the Schengen area. There are no customs controls when travelling between Schengen countries, so the visa rules that apply to Italy apply to all Schengen countries.

➡ EU citizens do not need a visa to enter Italy – a valid ID card or passport is sufficient.

➡ Nationals of some other countries, including Australia, Canada, Israel, Japan, New Zealand, Switzerland, the UK and the USA, do not need a visa for stays of up to 90 days.

➡ Nationals of other countries will need a Schengen tourist visa – to check requirements see www.schengenvisainfo.com/tourist-schengen-visa.

➡ All non-EU and non-Schengen nationals entering Italy for more than 90 days or for any reason other than tourism (such as study or work) may need a specific visa. Check http://vistoperitalia.esteri.it for details.

ETIAS System

In July 2018, the European Parliament approved plans for a visa waiver programme for travellers to the Schengen area.

Under the terms of the European Travel Information & Authorisation System (ETIAS), all non-EU travellers will have to fill in an online form and pay a small fee before they can travel to a Schengen country.

The system is due to be introduced by the end of 2022. For further details, see www.etiasvisa.com.

COVID Requirements

All passengers entering Italy must fill in a digital European Passenger Locator Form (PLF). In addition:

➡ People travelling from the EU and Schengen countries must show a Green Pass (vaccination certificate) or proof of a negative molecular swab test completed within 48 hours of entering Italy.

➡ People travelling from the UK must show a Green Pass (or equivalent certificate) and a negative test result from within 48 hours of entry.

➡ People travelling from Canada, the US or Japan must show a Green Pass (or equivalent certificate) and a negative test result from within 72 hours of entry.

For further details see www.esteri.it.

Permesso di Soggiorno

➡ A *permesso di soggiorno* (permit to stay, also referred to as a residence permit) is required by all non-EU nationals who stay in Italy longer than three months. In theory, you should apply for one within eight days of arriving in Italy.

➡ EU citizens do not require a *permesso di soggiorno* but are required to register with the local registry office *(ufficio anagrafe)* if they stay for more than three months.

➡ Check exact requirements on www.poliziadistato.it – click on the English tab and follow the links.

➡ The main office dealing with permits is the **Ufficio Immigrazione** (☎06 4686 3911; http://questure.poliziadistato.it/it/Roma; Via Teofilo Patini; ⌚8.30-noon Mon-Fri & 3-5pm Tue & Thu; 🚌Via Salviati).

Women Travellers

Sexual harrassment can be an issue in Rome. If you feel yourself being groped on a crowded bus or metro, a loud *'Che schifo!'* (How disgusting!) will draw attention to the incident. Otherwise take all the usual precautions you would in any large city, and as in most places, avoid wandering around alone late at night, especially in the area around Termini station.

Language

When in Rome, you'll find that locals appreciate you trying their language, no matter how muddled you may think you sound. Italian is not difficult to pronounce as the sounds used in spoken Italian can all be found in English.

Note that, in our pronunciation guides, ai is pronounced as in 'aisle', ay as in 'say', ow as in 'how', dz as the 'ds' in 'lids', and that r is a strong and rolled sound. Keep in mind too that Italian consonants can have a stronger, emphatic pronunciation – if the consonant is written as a double letter, it should be pronounced a little stronger. This difference in the pronunciation of single and double consonants can mean a difference in meaning, eg *sonno* *son*·no (sleep) versus *sono* *so*·no (I am). The Italian ch is is usually pronounced as a hard c, so, for example, 'chiesa' is 'key-esa'.

If you read our coloured pronunciation guides as if they were English, you'll be understood. The stressed syllables are indicated with italics.

BASICS

Italian has two words for 'you' – use the polite form *Lei* lay if you're talking to strangers, officials or people older than you. With people familiar to you or younger than you, you can use the informal form *tu* too.

In Italian, all nouns and adjectives are either masculine or feminine, and so are the articles *il/la* eel/la (the) and *un/una* oon/*oo*·na (a) that go with the nouns.

In this chapter the polite/informal and masculine/feminine options are included where necessary, separated with a slash and indicated with 'pol/inf' and 'm/f'.

WANT MORE?

For in-depth language information and handy phrases, check out Lonely Planet's *Italian phrasebook*. You'll find it at **shop.lonelyplanet.com**.

Hello.	*Buongiorno.*	bwon·*jor*·no
Goodbye.	*Arrivederci.*	a·ree·ve·*der*·chee
Yes.	*Sì.*	see
No.	*No.*	no
Excuse me.	*Mi scusi.* (pol) *Scusami.* (inf)	mee *skoo*·zee *skoo*·za·mee
Sorry.	*Mi dispiace.*	mee dees·*pya*·che
Please.	*Per favore.*	per fa·vo·re
Thank you.	*Grazie.*	*gra*·tsye
You're welcome.	*Prego.*	*pre*·go

How are you?
Come sta/stai? (pol/inf) — *ko*·me sta/stai

Fine. And you?
Bene. E Lei/tu? (pol/inf) — *be*·ne e lay/too

What's your name?
Come si chiama? pol — *ko*·me see *kya*·ma
Come ti chiami? inf — *ko*·me tee *kya*·mee

My name is ...
Mi chiamo ... — mee *kya*·mo ...

Do you speak English?
Parla/Parli inglese? (pol/inf) — *par*·la/*par*·lee een·*gle*·ze

I don't understand.
Non capisco. — non ka·*pee*·sko

ACCOMMODATION

Do you have a ... room?	*Avete una camera ...?*	a·*ve*·te *oo*·na *ka*·me·ra ...
double	*doppia con letto matrimoniale*	*do*·pya kon *le*·to ma·tree·mo·*nya*·le
single	*singola*	*seen*·go·la
How much is it per ...?	*Quanto costa per ...?*	*kwan*·to *kos*·ta per ...
night	*una notte*	*oo*·na *no*·te
person	*persona*	per·*so*·na

Is breakfast included?
La colazione è compresa? — la ko·la·*tsyo*·ne e kom·*pre*·sa

air-con	*aria condizionata*	a·rya on·dee·tsyo·*na*·ta
bathroom	*bagno*	*ba*·nyo
campsite	*campeggio*	kam·*pe*·jo
guesthouse	*pensione*	pen·*syo*·ne
hotel	*albergo*	al·*ber*·go
youth hostel	*ostello della gioventù*	os·*te*·lo de·la jo·ven·*too*
window	*finestra*	fee·*nes*·tra

DIRECTIONS

Where's ...?
Dov'è ...? — do·ve ...

What's the address?
Qual'è l'indirizzo? — kwa·*le* leen·dee·*ree*·tso

Could you please write it down?
Può scriverlo, per favore? — pwo *skree*·ver·lo per fa·*vo*·re

Can you show me (on the map)?
Può mostrarmi (sulla pianta)? — pwo mos·*trar*·mee (soo·la *pyan*·ta)

at the corner	*all'angolo*	a·*lan*·go·lo
at the traffic lights	*al semaforo*	al se·*ma*·fo·ro
behind	*dietro*	*dye*·tro
far	*lontano*	lon·*ta*·no
in front of	*davanti a*	da·*van*·tee a
near	*vicino*	vee·*chee*·no
next to	*accanto a*	a·*kan*·to a
opposite	*di fronte a*	dee *fron*·te a
straight ahead	*sempre diritto*	*sem*·pre dee·*ree*·to
to the left	*a sinistra*	a see·*nee*·stra
to the right	*a destra*	a *de*·stra

EATING & DRINKING

What would you recommend?
Cosa mi consiglia? — *ko*·za mee kon·*see*·lya

What's in that dish?
Quali ingredienti ci sono in questo piatto? — *kwa*·li een·gre·*dyen*·tee chee *so*·no een *kwe*·sto *pya*·to

What's the local speciality?
Qual'è la specialità di questa regione? — kwa·*le* la spe·cha·lee·*ta* dee *kwe*·sta re·*jo*·ne

That was delicious!
Era squisito! — e·ra skwee·*zee*·to

Cheers!
Salute! — sa·*loo*·te

KEY PATTERNS

To get by in Italian, mix and match these simple patterns with words of your choice:

When's (the next flight)?
A che ora è (il prossimo volo)? — a ke o·ra e (eel *pro*·see·mo *vo*·lo)

Where's (the station)?
Dov'è (la stazione)? — do·ve (la sta·*tsyo*·ne)

I'm looking for (a hotel).
Sto cercando (un albergo). — sto cher·*kan*·do (oon al·*ber*·go)

Do you have (a map)?
Ha (una pianta)? — a (*oo*·na *pyan*·ta)

Is there (a toilet)?
C'è (un gabinetto)? — che (oon ga·bee·*ne*·to)

I'd like (a coffee).
Vorrei (un caffè). — vo·*ray* (oon ka·*fe*)

I'd like to (hire a car).
Vorrei (noleggiare una macchina). — vo·*ray* (no·le·*ja*·re *oo*·na *ma*·kee·na)

Can I (enter)?
Posso (entrare)? — *po*·so (en·*tra*·re)

Could you please (help me)?
Può (aiutarmi), per favore? — pwo (a·yoo·*tar*·mee) per fa·*vo*·re

Do I have to (book a seat)?
Devo (prenotare un posto)? — *de*·vo (pre·no·*ta*·re oon *po*·sto)

Please bring the bill.
Mi porta il conto, per favore? — mee *por*·ta eel *kon*·to per fa·*vo*·re

I'd like to reserve a table for ...	*Vorrei prenotare un tavolo per ...*	vo·*ray* pre·no·*ta*·re oon *ta*·vo·lo per ...
(two) people	*(due) persone*	(*doo*·e) per·*so*·ne
(eight) o'clock	*le (otto)*	le (*o*·to)

I don't eat ...	*Non mangio ...*	non *man*·jo ...
eggs	*uova*	*wo*·va
fish	*pesce*	*pe*·she
nuts	*noci*	*no*·chee
(red) meat	*carne (rossa)*	*kar*·ne (*ro*·sa)

Key Words

bar	*locale*	lo·*ka*·le
bottle	*bottiglia*	bo·*tee*·lya
breakfast	*prima colazione*	*pree*·ma ko·la·*tsyo*·ne

Signs

Entrata/Ingresso	Entrance
Uscita	Exit
Aperto	Open
Chiuso	Closed
Informazioni	Information
Proibito/Vietato	Prohibited
Gabinetti/Servizi	Toilets
Uomini	Men
Donne	Women

cafe	*bar*	bar
cold	*freddo*	*fre*·do
dinner	*cena*	*che*·na
drink list	*lista delle bevande*	*lee*·sta *de*·le be·*van*·de
fork	*forchetta*	for·*ke*·ta
glass	*bicchiere*	bee·*kye*·re
grocery store	*alimentari*	a·lee·men·*ta*·ree
hot	*caldo*	*kal*·do
knife	*coltello*	kol·*te*·lo
lunch	*pranzo*	*pran*·dzo
market	*mercato*	mer·*ka*·to
menu	*menù*	me·*noo*
plate	*piatto*	*pya*·to
restaurant	*ristorante*	ree·sto·*ran*·te
spicy	*piccante*	pee·*kan*·te
spoon	*cucchiaio*	koo·*kya*·yo
vegetarian (food)	*vegetariano*	ve·je·ta·*rya*·no
with	*con*	kon
without	*senza*	*sen*·tsa

Meat & Fish

beef	*manzo*	*man*·dzo
chicken	*pollo*	*po*·lo
clams	*vongole*	vong-o-lay
duck	*anatra*	*a*·na·tra
fish	*pesce*	*pe*·she
herring	*aringa*	a·*reen*·ga
lamb	*agnello*	a·*nye*·lo
lobster	*aragosta*	a·ra·*gos*·ta
meat	*carne*	*kar*·ne
mussels	*cozze*	*ko*·tse
oysters	*ostriche*	o·stree·ke
pork	*maiale*	ma·*ya*·le
prawn	*gambero*	*gam*·be·ro
salmon	*salmone*	sal·*mo*·ne
scallops	*capasante*	ka·pa·*san*·te
seafood	*frutti di mare*	*froo*·tee dee *ma*·re
shrimp	*gambero*	*gam*·be·ro
squid	*calamari*	ka·la·*ma*·ree
trout	*trota*	*tro*·ta
tuna	*tonno*	*to*·no
turkey	*tacchino*	ta·*kee*·no
veal	*vitello*	vee·*te*·lo

Fruit & Vegetables

apple	*mela*	*me*·la
beans	*fagioli*	fa·*jo*·lee
cabbage	*cavolo*	*ka*·vo·lo
capsicum	*peperone*	pe·pe·*ro*·ne
carrot	*carota*	ka·*ro*·ta
cauliflower	*cavolfiore*	ka·vol·*fyo*·re
cucumber	*cetriolo*	che·tree·*o*·lo
fruit	*frutta*	*froo*·ta
grapes	*uva*	*oo*·va
lemon	*limone*	lee·*mo*·ne
lentils	*lenticchie*	len·*tee*·kye
mushroom	*funghi*	*foon*·gee
nuts	*noci*	*no*·chee
onions	*cipolle*	chee·*po*·le
orange	*arancia*	a·*ran*·cha
peach	*pesca*	*pe*·ska
peas	*piselli*	pee·*ze*·lee
pineapple	*ananas*	*a*·na·nas
plum	*prugna*	*proo*·nya
potatoes	*patate*	pa·*ta*·te
spinach	*spinaci*	spee·*na*·chee
tomatoes	*pomodori*	po·mo·*do*·ree
vegetables	*verdura*	ver·*doo*·ra

Question Words

How?	*Come?*	*ko*·me
What?	*Che cosa?*	ke *ko*·za
When?	*Quando?*	*kwan*·do
Where?	*Dove?*	*do*·ve
Who?	*Chi?*	kee
Why?	*Perché?*	per·*ke*

Other

bread	*pane*	*pa*·ne
butter	*burro*	*boo*·ro
cheese	*formaggio*	for·*ma*·jo
eggs	*uova*	*wo*·va
honey	*miele*	*mye*·le
ice	*ghiaccio*	*gya*·cho
jam	*marmellata*	mar·me·*la*·ta
noodles	*pasta*	*pas*·ta
oil	*olio*	*o*·lyo
pepper	*pepe*	*pe*·pe
rice	*riso*	*ree*·zo
salt	*sale*	*sa*·le
soup	*minestra*	mee·*nes*·tra
soy sauce	*salsa di soia*	*sal*·sa dee *so*·ya
sugar	*zucchero*	*tsoo*·ke·ro
vinegar	*aceto*	a·*che*·to

Drinks

beer	*birra*	*bee*·ra
coffee	*caffè*	ka·*fe*
(orange) juice	*succo (d'arancia)*	*soo*·ko (da·*ran*·cha)
milk	*latte*	*la*·te
red wine	*vino rosso*	*vee*·no *ro*·so
soft drink	*bibita*	*bee*·bee·ta
tea	*tè*	te
(mineral) water	*acqua (minerale)*	*a*·kwa (mee·ne·*ra*·le)
white wine	*vino bianco*	*vee*·no *byan*·ko

EMERGENCIES

Help!
Aiuto! a·*yoo*·to

Leave me alone!
Lasciami in pace! *la*·sha·mee een *pa*·che

I'm lost.
Mi sono perso/a. (m/f) mee *so*·no *per*·so/a

There's been an accident.
C'è stato un incidente. che *sta*·to oon een·chee·*den*·te

Call the police!
Chiami la polizia! *kya*·mee la po·lee·*tsee*·a

Call a doctor!
Chiami un medico! *kya*·mee oon *me*·dee·ko

Where are the toilets?
Dove sono i gabinetti? *do*·ve *so*·no ee ga·bee·*ne*·tee

I'm sick.
Mi sento male. mee *sen*·to *ma*·le

It hurts here.
Mi fa male qui. mee fa *ma*·le kwee

I'm allergic to ...
Sono allergico/a a ... (m/f) *so*·no a·*ler*·jee·ko/a a ...

SHOPPING & SERVICES

I'd like to buy ...
Vorrei comprare ... vo·*ray* kom·*pra*·re ...

I'm just looking.
Sto solo guardando. sto *so*·lo gwar·*dan*·do

Can I look at it?
Posso dare un'occhiata? *po*·so *da*·re oo·no·*kya*·ta

How much is this?
Quanto costa questo? *kwan*·to *kos*·ta *kwe*·sto

It's too expensive.
È troppo caro/a. (m/f) e *tro*·po *ka*·ro/a

Can you lower the price?
Può farmi lo sconto? pwo *far*·mee lo *skon*·to

There's a mistake in the bill.
C'è un errore nel conto. che oo·ne·*ro*·re nel *kon*·to

ATM	*bancomat*	*ban*·ko·mat
post office	*ufficio postale*	oo·*fee*·cho pos·*ta*·le
tourist office	*ufficio del turismo*	oo·*fee*·cho del too·*reez*·mo

TIME & DATES

What time is it?	*Che ora è?*	ke *o*·ra e
It's one o'clock.	*È l'una.*	e *loo*·na
It's (two) o'clock.	*Sono le (due).*	*so*·no le (*doo*·e)
Half past (one).	*(L'una) e mezza.*	(*loo*·na) e *me*·dza

in the morning	*di mattina*	dee ma·*tee*·na
in the afternoon	*di pomeriggio*	dee po·me·*ree*·jo
in the evening	*di sera*	dee *se*·ra

yesterday	*ieri*	*ye*·ree
today	*oggi*	*o*·jee
tomorrow	*domani*	do·*ma*·nee

Monday	*lunedì*	loo·ne·*dee*
Tuesday	*martedì*	mar·te·*dee*
Wednesday	*mercoledì*	mer·ko·le·*dee*
Thursday	*giovedì*	jo·ve·*dee*
Friday	*venerdì*	ve·ner·*dee*
Saturday	*sabato*	*sa*·ba·to
Sunday	*domenica*	do·*me*·nee·ka

January	*gennaio*	je·*na*·yo
February	*febbraio*	fe·*bra*·yo
March	*marzo*	*mar*·tso
April	*aprile*	a·*pree*·le
May	*maggio*	*ma*·jo
June	*giugno*	*joo*·nyo
July	*luglio*	*loo*·lyo
August	*agosto*	a·*gos*·to
September	*settembre*	se·*tem*·bre
October	*ottobre*	o·*to*·bre
November	*novembre*	no·*vem*·bre
December	*dicembre*	dee·*chem*·bre

NUMBERS

1	*uno*	*oo*·no
2	*due*	*doo*·e
3	*tre*	tre
4	*quattro*	*kwa*·tro
5	*cinque*	*cheen*·kwe
6	*sei*	say
7	*sette*	*se*·te
8	*otto*	*o*·to
9	*nove*	*no*·ve
10	*dieci*	*dye*·chee
20	*venti*	*ven*·tee
30	*trenta*	*tren*·ta
40	*quaranta*	kwa·*ran*·ta
50	*cinquanta*	cheen·*kwan*·ta
60	*sessanta*	se·*san*·ta
70	*settanta*	se·*tan*·ta
80	*ottanta*	o·*tan*·ta
90	*novanta*	no·*van*·ta
100	*cento*	*chen*·to
1000	*mille*	*mee*·lel

TRANSPORT

At what time does the ... leave/arrive?
A che ora parte/arriva ...? — a ke *o*·ra *par*·te/a·*ree*·va ...

boat	*la nave*	la *na*·ve
bus	*l'autobus*	*low*·to·boos
ferry	*il traghetto*	eel tra·*ge*·to
metro	*la metropolitana*	la me·tro·po·lee·*ta*·na
plane	*l'aereo*	la·*e*·re·o
train	*il treno*	eel *tre*·no

... ticket	*un biglietto ...*	oon bee·*lye*·to
one-way	*di sola andata*	dee *so*·la an·*da*·ta
return	*di andata e ritorno*	dee an·*da*·ta e ree·*tor*·no

bus stop	*fermata dell'autobus*	fer·*ma*·ta del *ow*·to·boos
platform	*binario*	bee·*na*·ryo
ticket office	*biglietteria*	bee·lye·te·*ree*·a
timetable	*orario*	o·*ra*·ryo
train station	*stazione ferroviaria*	sta·*tsyo*·ne fe·ro·*vyar*·ya

Does it stop at ...?
Si ferma a ...? — see *fer*·ma a ...

Please tell me when we get to ...
Mi dica per favore quando arriviamo a ... — mee *dee*·ka per fa·*vo*·re *kwan*·do a·ree·*vya*·mo a ...

I want to get off here.
Voglio scendere qui. — *vo*·lyo *shen*·de·re kwee

I'd like to hire a bicycle.
Vorrei noleggiare una bicicletta. — vo·*ray* no·le·*ja*·re *oo*·na bee·chee·*kle*·ta

I have a flat tyre.
Ho una gomma bucata. — o *oo*·na *go*·ma boo·*ka*·ta

I'd like to have my bicycle repaired.
Vorrei fare riparare la mia bicicletta. — vo·*ray fa*·re ree·pa·*ra*·re la *mee*·a bee·chee·*kle*·ta

Glossary

abbazia – abbey

(pizza) al taglio – (pizza) by the slice

albergo – hotel

alimentari – grocery shop; delicatessen

anfiteatro – amphitheatre

aperitivo – pre-evening meal drink and snack

arco – arch

autostrada – motorway; highway

biblioteca – library

biglietto – ticket

borgo – archaic name for a small town, village or town sector (often dating to the Middle Ages)

camera – room

campo – field

cappella – chapel

carabinieri – police with military and civil duties

casa – house

castello – castle

catacomba – catacomb

centro sociale –social centre; often a venue for concerts, club nights, cultural events

chiesa – church

chiostro – cloister; covered walkway, usually enclosed by columns, around a quadrangle

città – town; city

colonna – column

comune – equivalent to a municipality or county; a town or city council; historically, a self-governing town or city

corso – boulevard

duomo – cathedral

enoteca – wine bar

espresso – short black coffee

EUR (Esposizione Universale di Roma) – outlying district in south Rome known for its rationalist architecture

ferrovia – railway

festa – feast day; holiday

fiume – river

fontana – fountain

foro – forum

giardino – garden

grattachecca – ice drink flavoured with fruit and syrup

grotta – cave

isola – island

lago – lake

largo – small square

locanda – inn; small hotel

mar, mare – sea

mausoleo – mausoleum; stately and magnificent tomb

mercato – market

necropoli – ancient name for cemetery or burial site

nord – north

osteria – casual tavern or eatery presided over by a host

palio – contest

Papa – Pope

passeggiata – traditional evening stroll

pasticceria – cake/pastry shop

pensione – guesthouse

piazza – square

piazzale – large open square

pietà – literally 'pity' or 'compassion'; sculpture, drawing or painting of the dead Christ supported by the Madonna

pinacoteca – art gallery

PIT (Punto Informativo Turistico) – Tourist Information Point

ponte – bridge

porta – gate; door

porto – port

prenotare – to book or reserve

reale – royal

rocca – fortress

sala – room; hall

salumeria – delicatessen

scalinata – staircase

scavi – excavations

spiaggia – beach

stazione – station

stazione marittima – ferry terminal

sud – south

superstrada – expressway; highway with divided lanes

tartufo – truffle

tavola calda – literally 'hot table'; pre-prepared meat, pasta and vegetable selection, often self-service

teatro – theatre

tempietto – small temple

tempio – temple

terme – thermal baths

tesoro – treasury

Tevere – Tiber

torre – tower

trattoria – simple restaurant

vico – alley; alleyway

Behind the Scenes

SEND US YOUR FEEDBACK

We love to hear from travellers – your comments keep us on our toes and help make our books better. Our well-travelled team reads every word on what you loved or loathed about this book. Although we cannot reply individually to your submissions, we always guarantee that your feedback goes straight to the appropriate authors, in time for the next edition. Each person who sends us information is thanked in the next edition – the most useful submissions are rewarded with a selection of digital PDF chapters.

Visit **lonelyplanet.com/contact** to submit your updates and suggestions or to ask for help. Our award-winning website also features inspirational travel stories, news and discussions.

Note: We may edit, reproduce and incorporate your comments in Lonely Planet products such as guidebooks, websites and digital products, so let us know if you don't want your comments reproduced or your name acknowledged. For a copy of our privacy policy visit lonelyplanet.com/privacy.

WRITER THANKS

Duncan Garwood

A big thank you to fellow authors Virginia Maxwell and Alexis Averbuck for their suggestions and to Anna Tyler at Lonely Planet for all her support. In Rome grazie to Alexandra Bruzzese for her foodie tips and Richard McKenna for his ever-entertaining lunch company. As always, a big, heartfelt hug to Lidia and the boys, Ben and Nick.

Alexis Averbuck

It was a true joy to research Rome, a return to one of my first and most magical travel writing spots – this is thanks in large part to the fabulous company and comradery of my beloved Ryan Ver Berkmoes. And the delightful reunion with our dear Hydriot friends, Sergei and Mina. Many thanks are also due to Anna Tyler who helmed the project with superb attention to detail, guidance and grace.

Virginia Maxwell

I had a number of excellent travelling companions on this research trip who walked, ate and drank their way through the city with me: thanks to Peter Handsaker, Catherine Hannebery and Pat Yale. Thanks also to Anna Tyler for her expert briefing and project guidance, and to Rome-based Duncan Garwood and Alexandra Bruzzese for their tips.

ACKNOWLEDGEMENTS

Cover photograph: Arco di Settimio Severo and Roman Forum, Matteo Colombo/Getty Images ©

Illustration on pp66–7 by Javier Zarracina.

THIS BOOK

This 12th edition of Lonely Planet's *Rome* guidebook was researched and written by Duncan Garwood, Alexis Averbuck and Virginia Maxwell, as was the previous edition. This guidebook was produced by the following:

Destination Editor Anna Tyler

Senior Product Editors Amy Lynch, Elizabeth Jones

Product Editors Kirsten Rawlings, Alison Ridgway

Cartographers Hunor Csutoros, Anthony Phelan, David Connolly

Book Designers Kat Marsh, Wibowo Rusli

Assisting Editors Peter Cruttenden, Emma Gibbs, Jennifer Hattam, Alison Morris, Anne Mulvaney, Simon Williamson

Cover Researcher Brendan Dempsey-Spencer

Thanks to Sonia Kapoor, Gabrielle Stefanos

See also separate subindexes for:
EATING P317
DRINKING & NIGHTLIFE P319
ENTERTAINMENT P319
SHOPPING P319
SLEEPING P320

Index

Sights 000
Map Pages **000**
Photo Pages **000**

D

E

F

G

EATING

Sights 000
Map Pages **000**
Photo Pages **000**

DRINKING & NIGHTLIFE

ENTERTAINMENT

SHOPPING

Rome Maps

Sights
- Beach
- Bird Sanctuary
- Buddhist
- Castle/Palace
- Christian
- Confucian
- Hindu
- Islamic
- Jain
- Jewish
- Monument
- Museum/Gallery/Historic Building
- Ruin
- Shinto
- Sikh
- Taoist
- Winery/Vineyard
- Zoo/Wildlife Sanctuary
- Other Sight

Activities, Courses & Tours
- Bodysurfing
- Diving
- Canoeing/Kayaking
- Course/Tour
- Sento Hot Baths/Onsen
- Skiing
- Snorkelling
- Surfing
- Swimming/Pool
- Walking
- Windsurfing
- Other Activity

Sleeping
- Sleeping
- Camping
- Hut/Shelter

Eating
- Eating

Drinking & Nightlife
- Drinking & Nightlife
- Cafe

Entertainment
- Entertainment

Shopping
- Shopping

Information
- Bank
- Embassy/Consulate
- Hospital/Medical
- Internet
- Police
- Post Office
- Telephone
- Toilet
- Tourist Information
- Other Information

Geographic
- Beach
- Gate
- Hut/Shelter
- Lighthouse
- Lookout
- Mountain/Volcano
- Oasis
- Park
- Pass
- Picnic Area
- Waterfall

Population
- Capital (National)
- Capital (State/Province)
- City/Large Town
- Town/Village

Transport
- Airport
- Border crossing
- Bus
- Cable car/Funicular
- Cycling
- Ferry
- Metro station
- Monorail
- Parking
- Petrol station
- S-Bahn/Subway station
- Taxi
- T-bane/Tunnelbana station
- Train station/Railway
- Tram
- U-Bahn/Underground station
- Other Transport

Routes
- Tollway
- Freeway
- Primary
- Secondary
- Tertiary
- Lane
- Unsealed road
- Road under construction
- Plaza/Mall
- Steps
- Tunnel
- Pedestrian overpass
- Walking Tour
- Walking Tour detour
- Path/Walking Trail

Boundaries
- International
- State/Province
- Disputed
- Regional/Suburb
- Marine Park
- Cliff
- Wall

Hydrography
- River, Creek
- Intermittent River
- Canal
- Water
- Dry/Salt/Intermittent Lake
- Reef

Areas
- Airport/Runway
- Beach/Desert
- Cemetery (Christian)
- Cemetery (Other)
- Glacier
- Mudflat
- Park/Forest
- Sight (Building)
- Sportsground
- Swamp/Mangrove

Note: Not all symbols displayed above appear on the maps in this book

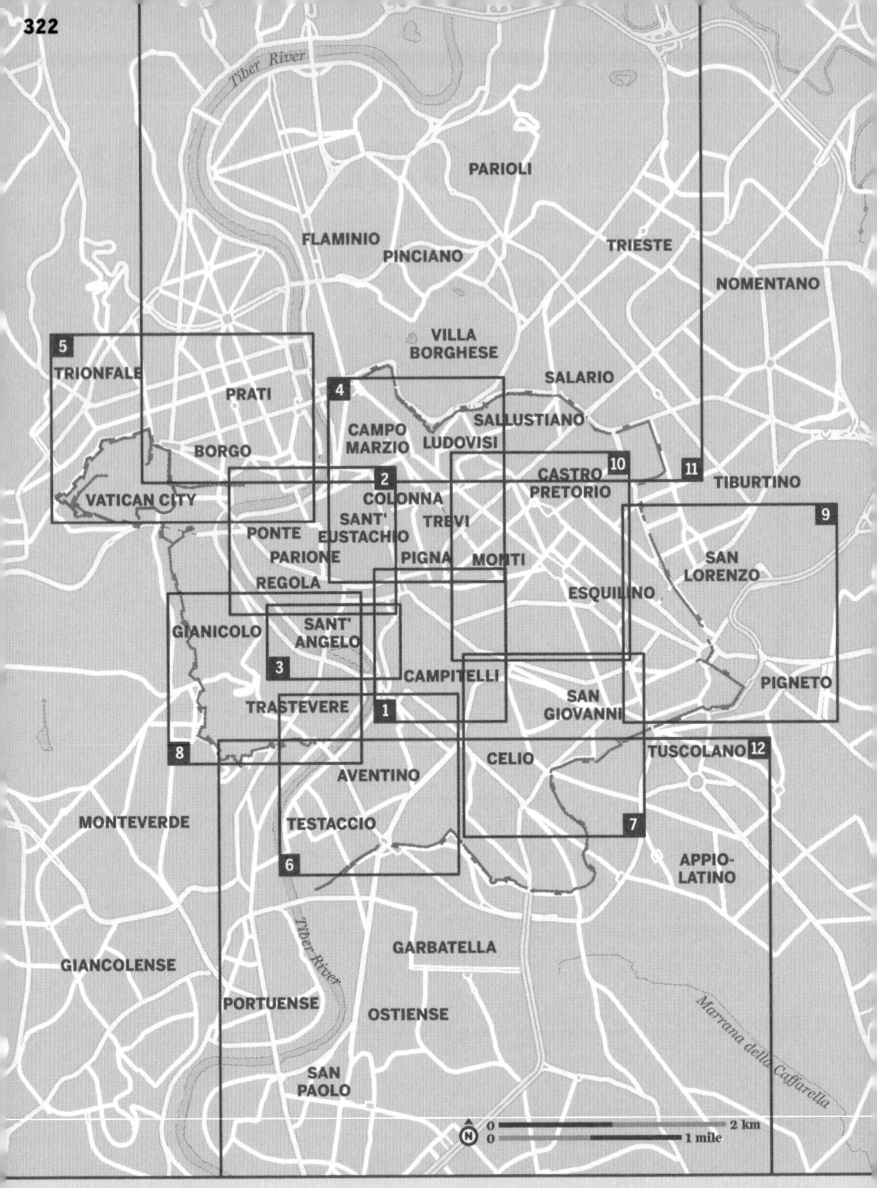
Tiber River
PARIOLI
FLAMINIO
PINCIANO
TRIESTE
NOMENTANO
VILLA BORGHESE
SALARIO
TRIONFALE
PRATI
CAMPO MARZIO
LUDOVISI
SALLUSTIANO
BORGO
CASTRO PRETORIO
TIBURTINO
VATICAN CITY
COLONNA
SANT' EUSTACHIO
TREVI
PONTE
PARIONE
PIGNA
MONTI
SAN LORENZO
REGOLA
ESQUILINO
GIANICOLO
SANT' ANGELO
CAMPITELLI
SAN GIOVANNI
PIGNETO
TRASTEVERE
CELIO
TUSCOLANO
AVENTINO
MONTEVERDE
TESTACCIO
APPIO-LATINO
GARBATELLA
GIANCOLENSE
Tiber River
PORTUENSE
OSTIENSE
Marrana della Caffarella
SAN PAOLO
2 km
1 mile
1
2
3
4
5
6
7
8
9
10
11
12

MAP INDEX

ANCIENT ROME *Map on p324*

Top Experiences **p58**

1 Capitoline Museums ... B3
2 Colosseum ... G6
3 Imperial Forums ... D2
4 Palatino ... D7
5 Roman Forum ... D5

Sights **p72**

6 Arcate Severiane ... D8
7 Arco di Costantino ... F6
8 Arco di Settimio Severo ... C4
9 Arco di Tito ... E5
10 Aula Isiaca ... D7
11 Basilica dei SS Cosma e Damiano ... D4
12 Basilica di Massenzio ... E4
13 Basilica di San Marco ... B2
14 Basilica Fulvia Aemilia ... D4
15 Basilica Giulia ... C4
16 Basilica Ulpia ... C2
17 Bocca della Verità ... A7
18 Capanne Romulee ... C6
19 Carcere Mamertino ... C3
20 Casa delle Vestali ... D5
21 Casa di Augusto ... D7
22 Casa di Livia ... D6
Chiesa di San Lorenzo in Miranda ... (see 56)
23 Chiesa di Santa Maria Antiqua ... C5
24 Chiesa di Santa Maria in Aracoeli ... B3
25 Circo Massimo ... C8
26 Colonna di Foca ... C4
27 Colonna Traiana ... C2
28 Complesso del Vittoriano ... C3
29 Cordonata ... B3
30 Criptoportico Neroniano ... D6
31 Curia ... C4
32 Domus Augustana ... D7
33 Domus Flavia ... D6
34 Domus Severiana ... E8
35 Foro di Augusto ... D3
36 Foro di Cesare ... C3
37 Foro di Nerva ... D3
38 Foro di Traiano ... C2
39 Foro di Vespasiano ... E4
40 Forum Boarium ... A6
41 Lapis Niger ... C4
42 Mercati di Traiano Museo dei Fori Imperiali ... D2
43 Museo Centrale del Risorgimento ... B3
44 Museo Palatino ... D7
45 Orti Farnesiani ... D6
46 Palazzo Venezia ... B1
47 Piazza del Campidoglio ... B3
48 Piazza del Foro ... C4
49 Portico degli Dei Consenti ... C4
50 Rampa di Domiziano ... D5
51 Roma dal Cielo ... B3
52 Roman Insula ... B3
53 Rostri ... C4
54 Stadio ... D7
55 Tempio della Concordia ... C4
56 Tempio di Antonino e Faustina ... D4
57 Tempio di Castore e Polluce ... C5
58 Tempio di Ercole Vincitore ... A6
59 Tempio di Giulio Cesare ... D4
60 Tempio di Portunus ... A6
61 Tempio di Romolo ... D4
62 Tempio di Saturno ... C4
63 Tempio di Vespasiano ... C4
64 Tempio di Vesta ... D5
65 Terme di Settimio Severo ... D8
66 Torre delle Milizie ... D2
67 Via Sacra ... D4
68 Vittoriano ... B2

Eating **p76**

69 47 Circus Roof Garden ... A6
70 Alimentari Pannella Carmela ... B5
71 Terre e Domus ... C1

Drinking & Nightlife **p77**

72 0,75 ... C7
73 Cavour 313 ... E3
74 Terrazza Caffarelli ... B4

Shopping **p77**

75 Colosseum Bookshop ... F5
76 Mercato Campagna Amica al Circo Massimo ... B6

Sleeping **p243**

77 Caesar House ... E3
78 Inn at the Roman Forum ... E3
79 Nerva Boutique Hotel ... D3
80 Residenza Maritti ... D3

ANCIENT ROME

Key on p323

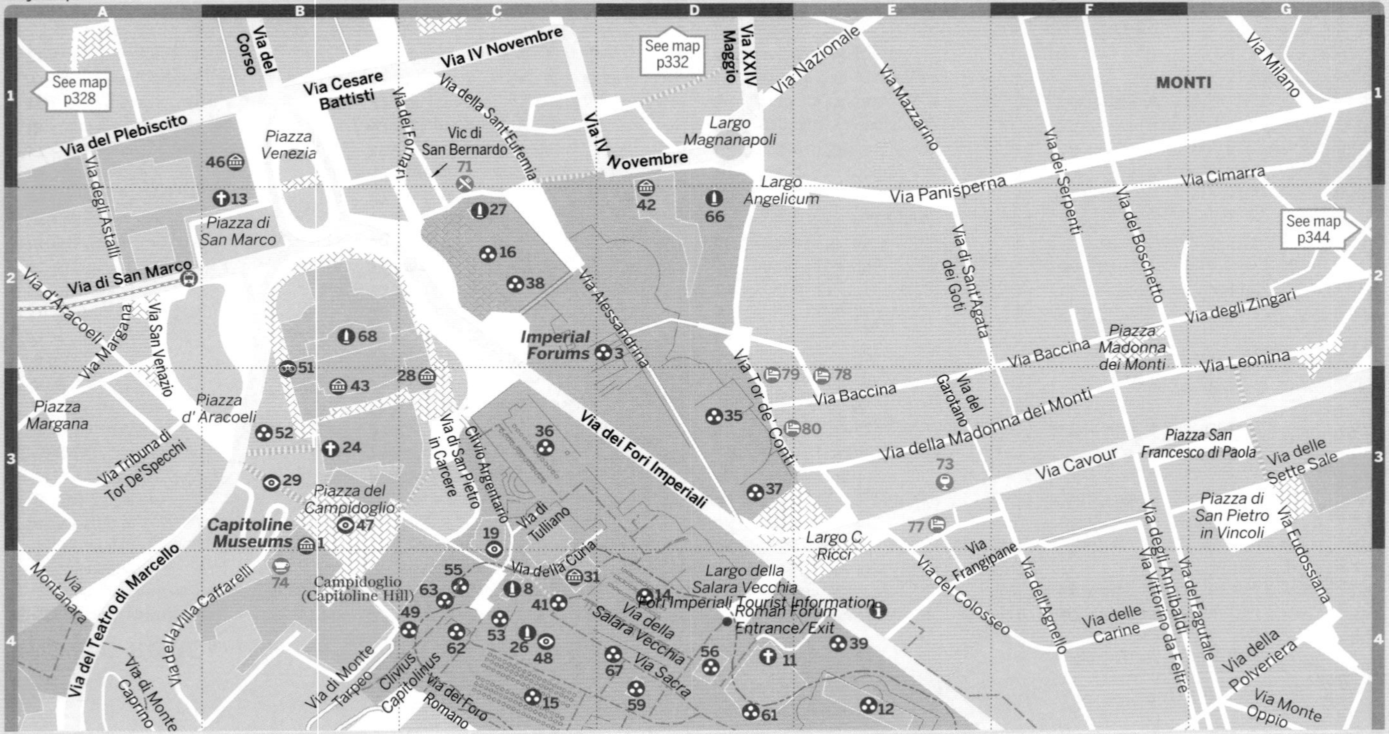

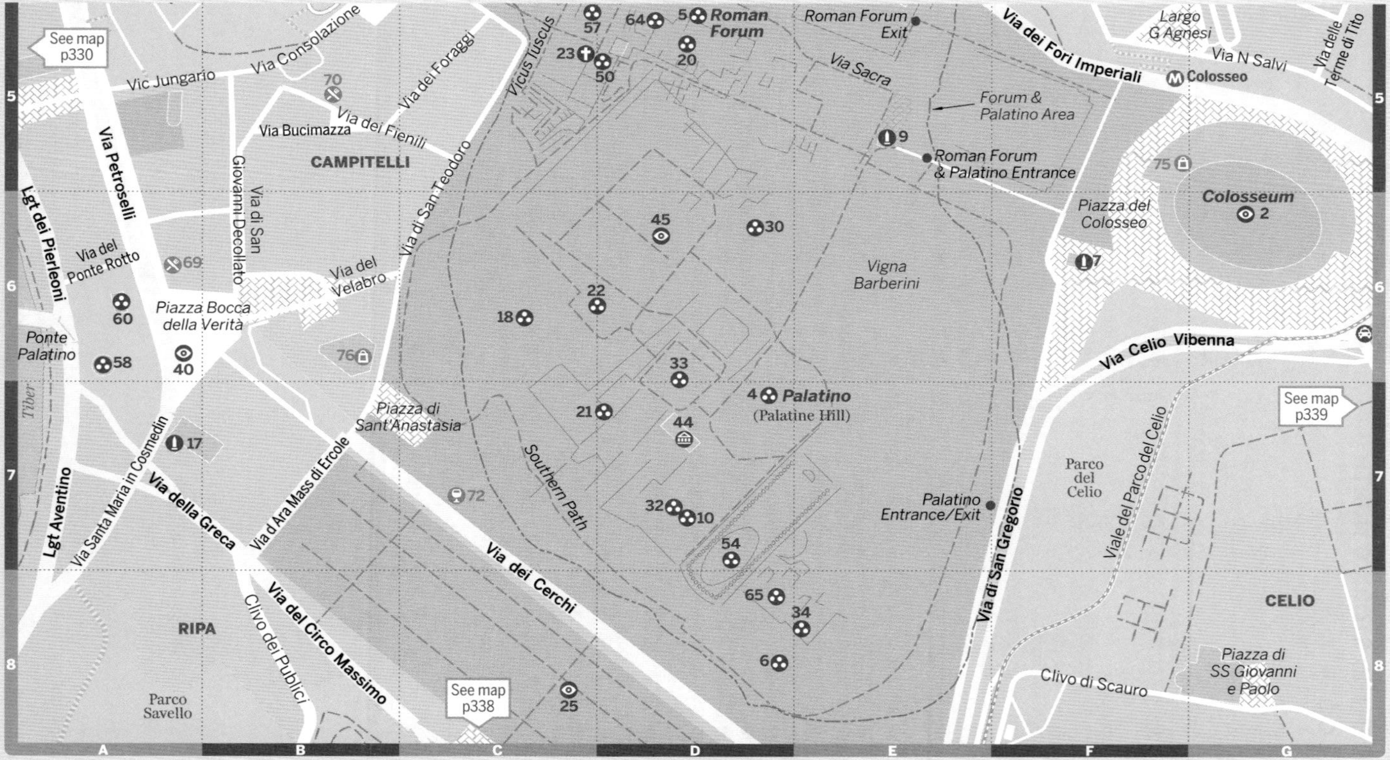
See map p330
Via Consolazione
Vic Jungario
70
Via dei Foraggi
Via dei Fienili
Via Bucimazza
CAMPITELLI
Via Petroselli
Lgt dei Pierleoni
Giovanni Decollato
Via di San
Via di San Teodoro
Vicus Tuscus
57
64
5 Roman Forum
23
50
20
Roman Forum Exit
Via Sacra
Via dei Fori Imperiali
Largo G Agnesi
Via N Salvi
Colosseo
Via delle Terme di Tito
Forum & Palatino Area
9
Roman Forum & Palatino Entrance
75
Colosseum
2
Piazza del Colosseo
7
45
30
Vigna Barberini
Via del Ponte Rotto
69
Via del Velabro
22
18
60
Piazza Bocca della Verità
Ponte Palatino
58
40
76
33
4 Palatino
(Palatine Hill)
Via Celio Vibenna
See map p339
Tiber
Piazza di Sant'Anastasia
21
44
17
Via Santa Maria in Cosmedin
Lgt Aventino
Via della Greca
Via d Ara Mass di Ercole
72
Southern Path
32
10
Palatino Entrance/Exit
Via di San Gregorio
Parco del Celio
Viale del Parco del Celio
54
Via dei Cerchi
65
34
CELIO
RIPA
Clivo dei Publici
Via del Circo Massimo
6
Clivo di Scauro
Piazza di SS Giovanni e Paolo
Parco Savello
See map p338
25

CENTRO STORICO NORTH *Map on p328*

61 Forno Roscioli ... E7
62 Gelateria del Teatro ... C3
63 Ginger ... F5
64 Grappolo D'Oro ... D6
65 Il Pagliaccio ... B5
66 La Campana ... E2
67 La Ciambella ... F6
68 La Focaccia ... D4
69 Matricianella ... G1
70 Mercato di Campo de' Fiori ... D6
71 Osteria del Sostegno ... F4
72 Osteria dell'Ingegno ... G4
73 Renato e Luisa ... F6
74 Retrobottega ... F2
75 Supplizio ... B5
76 Tiramisù Zum ... D6
77 Venchi ... F4
78 Vivi Bistrot ... D5

Drinking & Nightlife **p99**

79 Argot ... C6
80 Barnum Cafe ... C5
81 Caffè Sant'Eustachio ... F5
82 Club Derrière ... F3
83 Ex-Circus ... C4
84 Gin Corner ... F2
85 Il Goccetto ... B5
86 Jerry Thomas Project ... B5
87 La Casa del Caffè Tazza d'Oro ... G4
88 L'Angolo Divino ... D7
89 Salotto 42 ... G4

Entertainment **p100**

90 Teatro Argentina ... F6

Shopping **p101**

91 Alberta Gloves ... G6
92 Aldo Fefè ... F3
93 Bartolucci ... G4
94 Calzoleria Petrocchi ... B4
95 Casali ... B3
96 Chez Dede ... C6
97 Confetteria Moriondo & Gariglio ... G5
98 Ditta Annibale Gammarelli ... F5
99 Ghezzi ... F6
100 I Colori di Dentro ... B5
101 Ibiz – Artigianato in Cuoio ... E7
102 Le Tartarughe ... G5
103 Luna & L'Altra ... D5
104 Marta Ray ... B3
105 Materie ... G5
106 Monocle ... G2
107 namasTèy ... F5
108 Officina Profumo Farmaceutica di Santa Maria Novella ... E4
109 Patrizia Corvaglia Gioielli ... B4
110 Rachele ... D6
111 SBU ... D5

Sleeping **p243**

112 9 Hotel Cesàri ... H4
Argentina Residenza ... (see 113)
113 Argentina Residenza Style Hotel ... F6
114 Dimora degli Dei ... G4
115 Eitch Borromini ... D4
Hotel Barrett ... (see 113)
116 Hotel Campo de' Fiori ... D6
117 Hotel Mimosa ... F5
118 Hotel Navona ... E5
119 Navona Essence ... C6

Key on p326

CENTRO STORICO NORTH

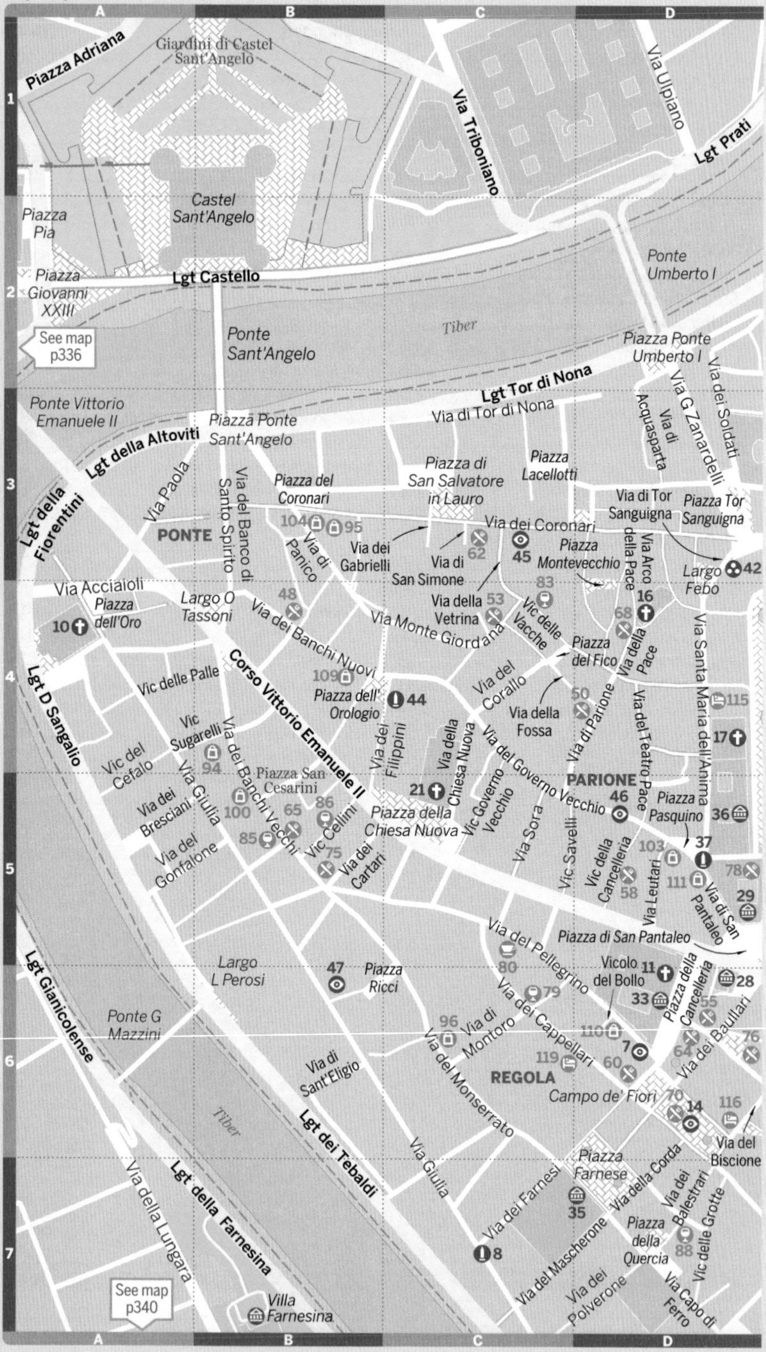
A
B
C
D
1
2
3
4
5
6
7
Piazza Adriana
Giardini di Castel Sant'Angelo
Via Triboniano
Via Ulpiano
Lgt Prati
Castel Sant'Angelo
Piazza Pia
Piazza Giovanni XXIII
Lgt Castello
Ponte Umberto I
See map p336
Ponte Sant'Angelo
Tiber
Piazza Ponte Umberto I
Lgt Tor di Nona
Via di Tor di Nona
Ponte Vittorio Emanuele II
Piazza Ponte Sant'Angelo
Lgt della Altoviti
Via di Acquasparta
Via G Zanardelli
Via dei Soldati
Piazza di San Salvatore in Lauro
Piazza Lacellotti
Piazza del Coronari
Via Paola
Via del Banco di Santo Spirito
Lgt della Fiorentini
Via di Tor Sanguigna
Piazza Tor Sanguigna
PONTE
Via dei Coronari
Via di Panico
Via dei Gabrielli
Via di San Simone
Piazza Montevecchio
Via della Pace
Via Arco della Pace
Largo Febo
Via Acciaioli
Piazza dell'Oro
Largo O Tassoni
Via dei Banchi Nuovi
Via Monte Giordano
Via della Vetrina
Vic delle Vacche
Piazza del Fico
Lgt D Sangalio
Vic delle Palle
Piazza dell' Orologio
Via del Corallo
Via della Fossa
Via di Parione
Via del Teatro Pace
Via Santa Maria dell'Anima
Corso Vittorio Emanuele II
Vic Sugarelli
Vic del Cefalo
Via dei Filippini
Via della Chiesa Nuova
Via del Governo Vecchio
Via Giulia
Via dei Banchi Vecchi
Piazza San Cesarini
PARIONE
Via dei Bresciani
Piazza della Chiesa Nuova
Vic Governo Vecchio
Via Sora
Piazza Pasquino
Via del Gonfalone
Vic Cellini
Via dei Cartari
Vic Savelli
Vic della Cancelleria
Via Leutari
Via di San Pantaleo
Via del Pellegrino
Piazza di San Pantaleo
Lgt Gianicolense
Largo L Perosi
Piazza Ricci
Vicolo del Bollo
Piazza della Cancelleria
Ponte G Mazzini
Via di Montoro
Via dei Cappellari
Via dei Baullari
Via di Sant'Eligio
Via del Monserrato
REGOLA
Campo de' Fiori
Via del Biscione
Lgt dei Tebaldi
Via della Lungara
Lgt della Farnesina
Piazza Farnese
Via della Corda
Via dei Balestrari
Vic delle Grotte
Via dei Farnesi
Piazza della Quercia
Via del Mascherone
Via dei Polverone
Via Capo di Ferro
See map p340
Villa Farnesina

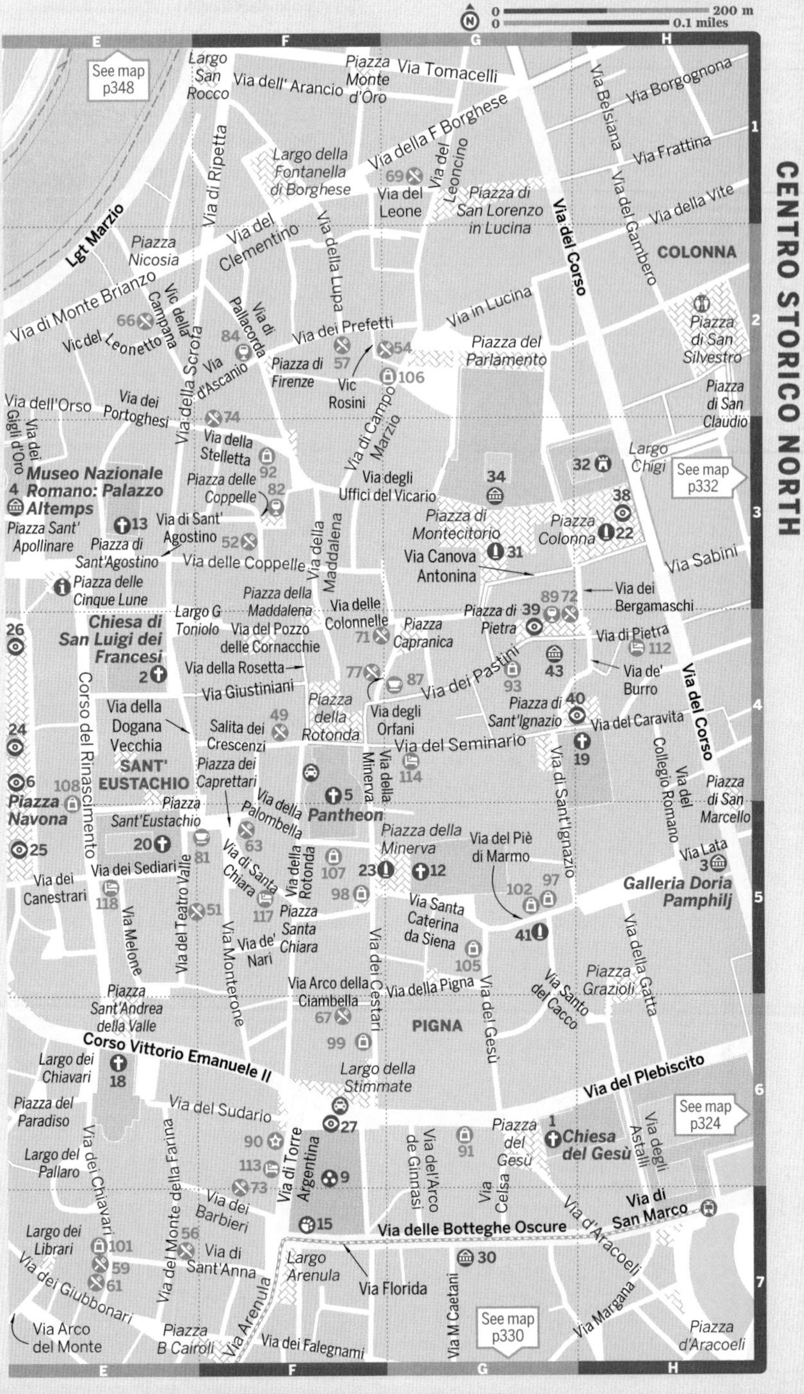
CENTRO STORICO NORTH
200 m
0.1 miles
See map p348
See map p332
See map p324
See map p330
COLONNA
SANT' EUSTACHIO
PIGNA
Museo Nazionale Romano: Palazzo Altemps
Chiesa di San Luigi dei Francesi
Piazza Navona
Pantheon
Galleria Doria Pamphilj
Chiesa del Gesù
Via del Corso
Corso Vittorio Emanuele II
Via del Plebiscito
Via delle Botteghe Oscure
Corso del Rinascimento
Lgt Marzio
Via Tomacelli
Via della Scrofa
Via di Ripetta
Piazza di Montecitorio
Piazza Colonna
Piazza della Rotonda
Piazza della Minerva
Largo di Torre Argentina
Via dei Giubbonari
Piazza B Cairoli

CENTRO STORICO SOUTH

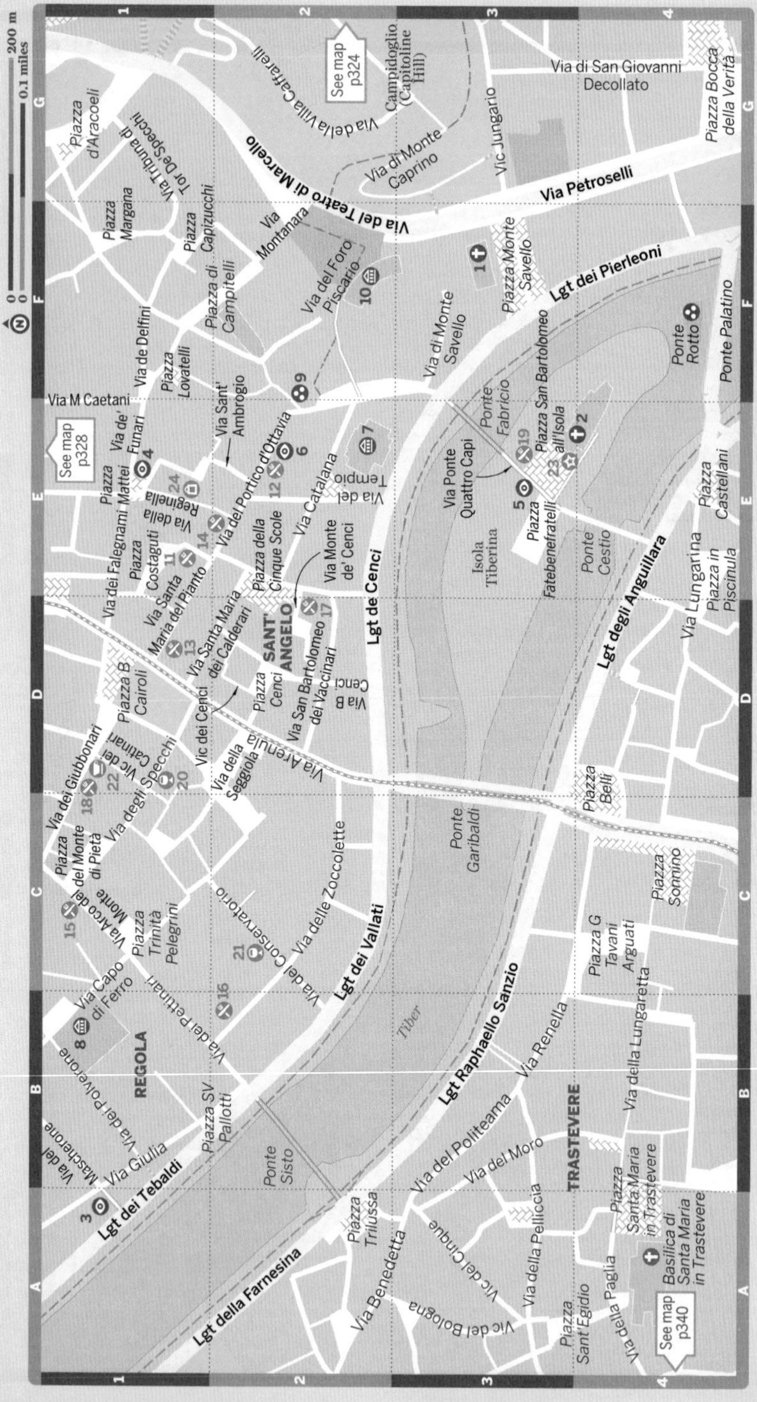

CENTRO STORICO SOUTH

Sights **p83**

1 Basilica di San Nicola in Carcere ... F3
2 Chiesa di San Bartolomeo ... E4
3 Fontana del Mascherone ... A1
4 Fontana delle Tartarughe ... E1
5 Isola Tiberina ... E3
6 Jewish Ghetto ... E2
7 Museo Ebraico di Roma ... E2
8 Palazzo Spada ... B1
9 Portico d'Ottavia ... F2
10 Teatro di Marcello ... F2

Eating **p91**

11 Antico Forno Urbani ... E1
12 Ba'Ghetto ... E2
13 Beppe e i suoi Formaggi ... D1
14 Cremeria Romana ... E2
15 I Dolci di Nonna Vincenza ... C1
16 Pianostrada ... B2
17 Piperno ... D2
18 Salumeria Roscioli ... D1
19 Sora Lella ... E3

Drinking & Nightlife **p99**

20 Open Baladin ... D1
21 Rimessa Roscioli ... C2
22 Roscioli Caffè ... D1

Entertainment **p100**

23 Isola del Cinema ... E3

Shopping **p101**

24 Il Museo del Louvre ... E1
Salumeria Roscioli ... (see 18)

TRIDENTE, TREVI & THE QUIRINALE

Key on p334

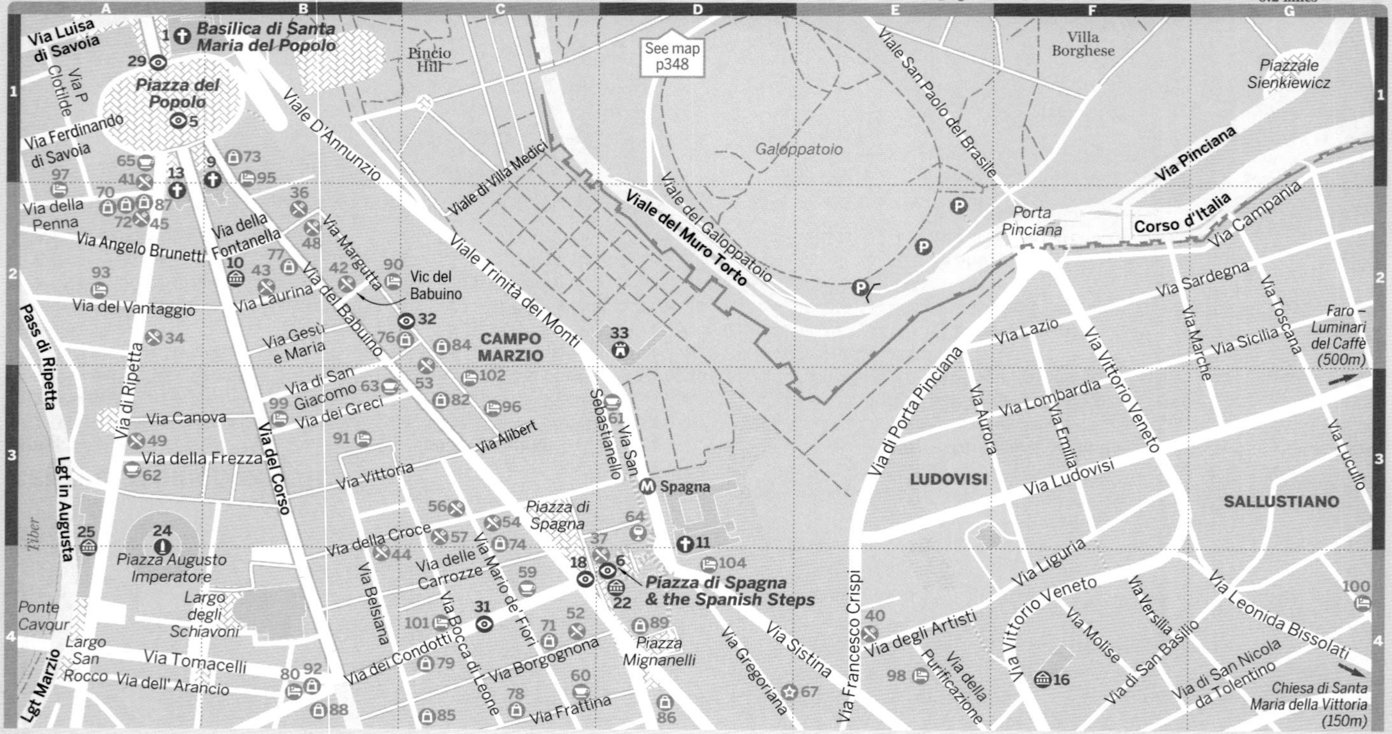

TRIDENTE, TREVI & THE QUIRINALE

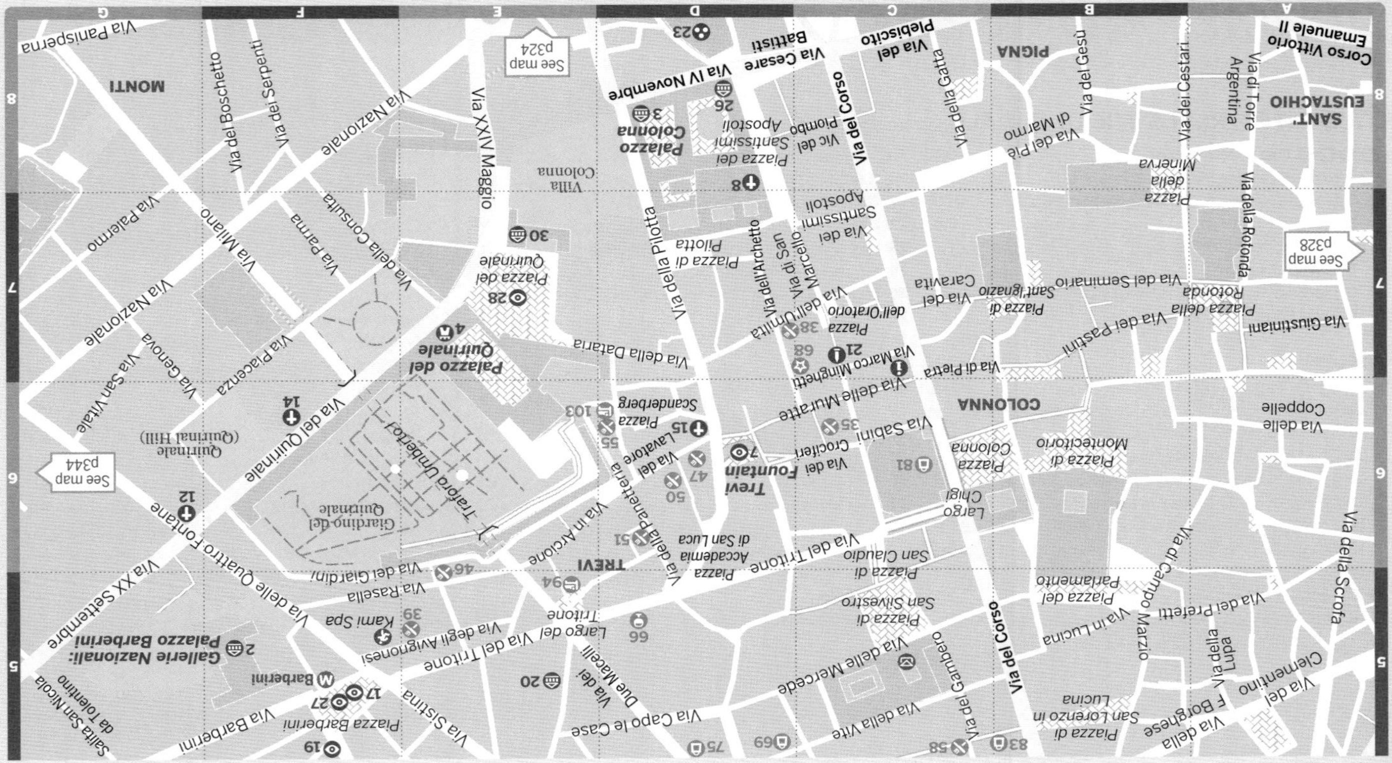

TRIDENTE, TREVI & THE QUIRINALE *Map on p332*

Top Experiences **p108**

1 Basilica di Santa Maria del Popolo ... A1
2 Gallerie Nazionali: Palazzo Barberini ... F5
3 Palazzo Colonna ... D8
4 Palazzo del Quirinale ... E7
5 Piazza del Popolo ... A1
6 Piazza di Spagna & the Spanish Steps ... D4
7 Trevi Fountain ... D6

Sights **p112**

8 Basilica dei Santi Apostoli ... D8
9 Basilica di Santa Maria in Montesanto ... B1
10 Casa di Goethe ... B2
11 Chiesa della Trinità dei Monti ... D3
12 Chiesa di San Carlino alle Quattro Fontane ... G6
13 Chiesa di Santa Maria dei Miracoli ... A2
14 Chiesa di Sant'Andrea al Quirinale ... F6
15 Chiesa di Santi Vincenzo e Anastasio ... D6
16 Convento dei Cappuccini ... F4
17 Fontana del Tritone ... F5
18 Fontana della Barcaccia ... C4
19 Fontana delle Api ... F5
20 Gagosian Gallery ... E5
21 Galleria Sciarra ... C7
22 Keats-Shelley House ... D4
23 Le Domus Romane di Palazzo Valentini ... D8
24 Mausoleo di Augusto ... A4
25 Museo dell'Ara Pacis ... A4
26 Museo delle Cere ... D8
Obelisk ... (see 5)
27 Piazza Barberini ... F5
28 Piazza del Quirinale ... E7
29 Porta del Popolo ... A1
30 Scuderie al Quirinale ... E7
31 Via dei Condotti ... C4
32 Via Margutta ... C2
33 Villa Medici ... D2

Eating **p116**

34 Al Gran Sasso ... A2
35 Al Moro ... C6
36 Babette ... B2
37 Babington's Tea Rooms ... D4
38 Bistrot del Quirino ... D7
39 Colline Emiliane ... E5
40 Crispy ... E4
41 Dal Bolognese ... A1
42 Edy Ristorante ... B2
43 Fatamorgana Corso ... B2
44 Fiaschetteria Beltramme ... B4
45 Gelateria Dei Gracchi ... A2
46 Hostaria Romana ... E5
47 Il Chianti ... D6
48 Il Margutta ... B2
Imàgo ... (see 104)
49 La Buca di Ripetta ... A3
50 Le Tamerici ... D6
51 Nanà Vini e Cucina ... D6
52 Nino ... C4
53 Osteria Margutta ... C2
54 Pastificio Guerra ... C3
55 Piccolo Arancio ... D6
56 Pompi ... C3

57 Venchi ... C3
58 VyTA Enoteca Regionale del Lazio ... C5

Drinking & Nightlife **p120**

59 Antico Caffè Greco ... C4
60 Bar Frattina ... C4
61 Caffè Ciampini ... D3
62 Caffè Ripetta ... A3
63 Canova Tadolini ... B3
64 Il Palazzetto ... D3
Locarno Bar ... (see 97)
65 Rosati ... A1
Stravinskij Bar ... (see 95)
66 Up Sunset Bar ... D5
Zuma Bar ... (see 92)

Entertainment **p122**

67 Gregory's Jazz Club ... D4
68 Teatro Quirino ... C7

Shopping **p123**

69 Anglo American Bookshop ... D5
70 Artisanal Cornucopia ... A2
71 Balenciaga ... C4
72 Bomba ... A2
73 Borsalino ... B1
74 c.u.c.i.n.a. ... C3
75 Catello d'Auria ... D5
76 Chiara Baschieri ... C2
77 Fabriano ... B2
78 Fausto Santini ... C4
79 Federico Buccellati ... C4
80 Fendi ... B4
81 Galleria Alberto Sordi ... C6
82 Gente ... C3
83 Gente ... B5
84 La Bottega del Marmoraro ... C2
85 Laura Biagiotti ... C4
86 Mandarina Duck ... D4
87 Patrizia Fabri ... A2
88 Tod's ... B4
89 Valentino ... D4

Sleeping **p244**

90 BDB Luxury Rooms ... B2
91 Casa Fabbrini: Campo Marzio ... B3
92 Fendi Private Suites ... B4
93 First Roma ... A2
94 Giuturna Boutique Hotel ... E5
95 Hotel de Russie ... B1
96 Hotel Forte ... C3
97 Hotel Locarno ... A2
98 Hotel Modigliani ... E4
99 Hotel Mozart ... B3
Il Palazzetto ... (see 64)
100 La Controra ... G4
101 Lungarno Collection: Portrait Roma ... C4
102 Margutta 54 ... C3
103 Palazzo Scanderbeg ... D6
104 Roma Hassler ... D4

VATICAN CITY, BORGO & PRATI

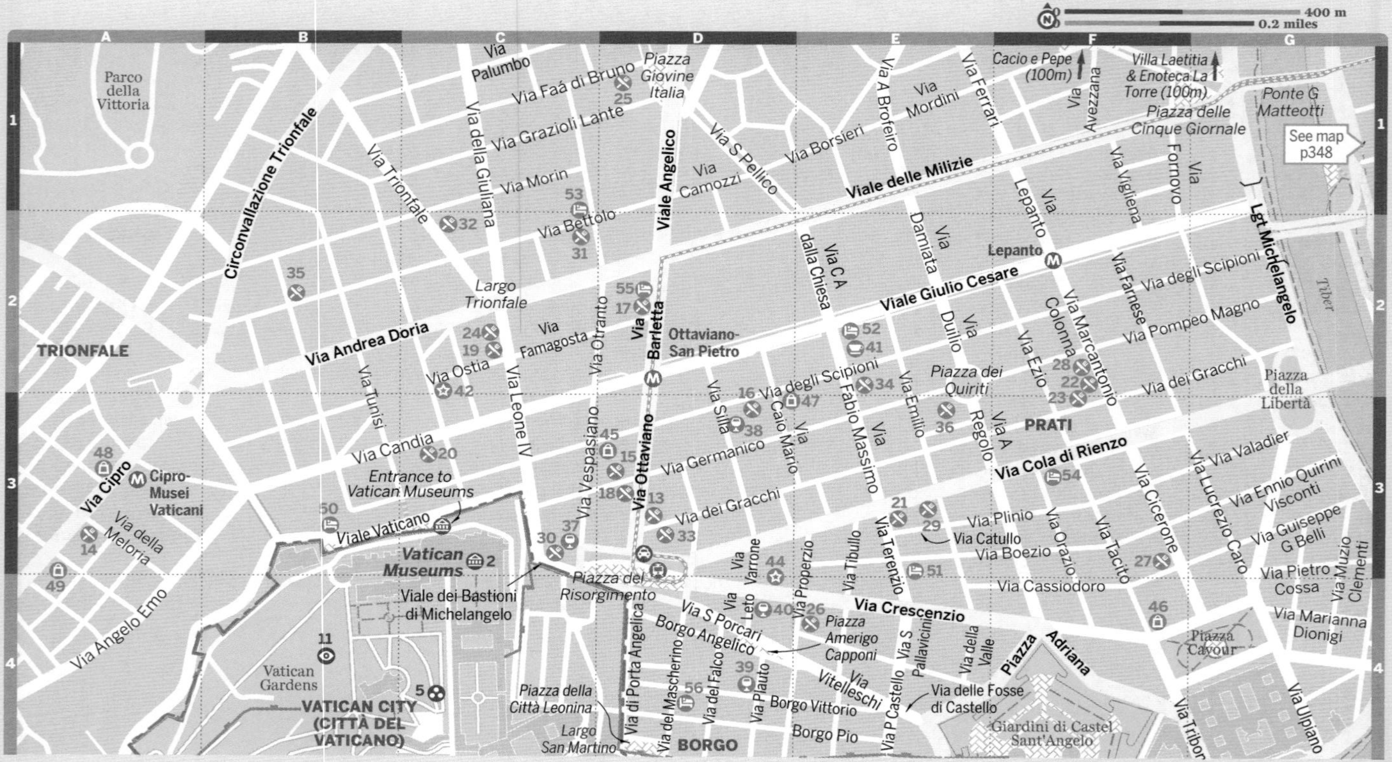

Top Experiences p128

1 St Peter's Basilica ... C5
2 Vatican Museums ... C3

Sights p141

3 Castel Sant'Angelo ... F5
4 Museo Storico Artistico ... C5
5 Necropoli Via Triumphalis ... C4
6 Ponte Sant'Angelo ... F5
7 Sistine Chapel ... C5
8 St Peter's Basilica Dome ... C5
9 St Peter's Square ... D5
10 Tomb of St Peter ... B5
11 Vatican Gardens ... B4
12 Vatican Grottoes ... C5

Eating p142

13 Amalfi ... D3
14 Bonci Pizzarium ... A3
15 Dal Toscano ... D3
16 Del Frate ... D3
17 Dolce Maniera ... D2
18 Fa-Bìo ... D3
19 Fatamorgana ... C2
20 Forno Feliziani ... C3
21 Franchi ... E3
22 Gelarmony ... F2
23 Gelateria dei Gracchi ... F3
24 Hostaria Dino e Toni ... C2
25 Hostaria-Pizzeria Giacomelli ... D1
26 Il Sorpasso ... E4
27 L'Arcangelo ... F3
28 Mondo Arancina ... F2
29 Mo's Gelaterie ... E3
30 Old Bridge ... C3
31 Osteria dell'Angelo ... C2
32 Panificio Bonci ... C2
33 Panino Divino ... D3
34 Stilelibero ... E2
35 Tordomatto ... B2
36 Velavevodetto Ai Quiriti ... E3

Drinking & Nightlife p145

37 Be.Re. ... C3
38 L'Osteria di Birra del Borgo Roma ... D3
39 Makasar Bistrot ... D4
40 Passaguai ... D4
41 Sciascia Caffè ... E2

Entertainment p146

42 Alexanderplatz ... C2
43 Auditorium Conciliazione ... E5
44 Fonclea ... D4

Shopping p146

45 Antica Manifattura Cappelli ... D3
46 Enoteca Costantini ... F4
47 Il Sellaio ... D3
48 La Tradizione ... A3
49 Paciotti Salumeria ... A3

Sleeping p246

50 Casa di Accoglienza Paolo VI ... B3
51 Colors Hotel ... E3
52 Fabio Massimo Design Hotel ... E2
53 Hotel San Pietrino ... C1
54 Le Stanze di Orazio ... F3
55 Quod Libet ... D2
56 Vatican Style ... D4

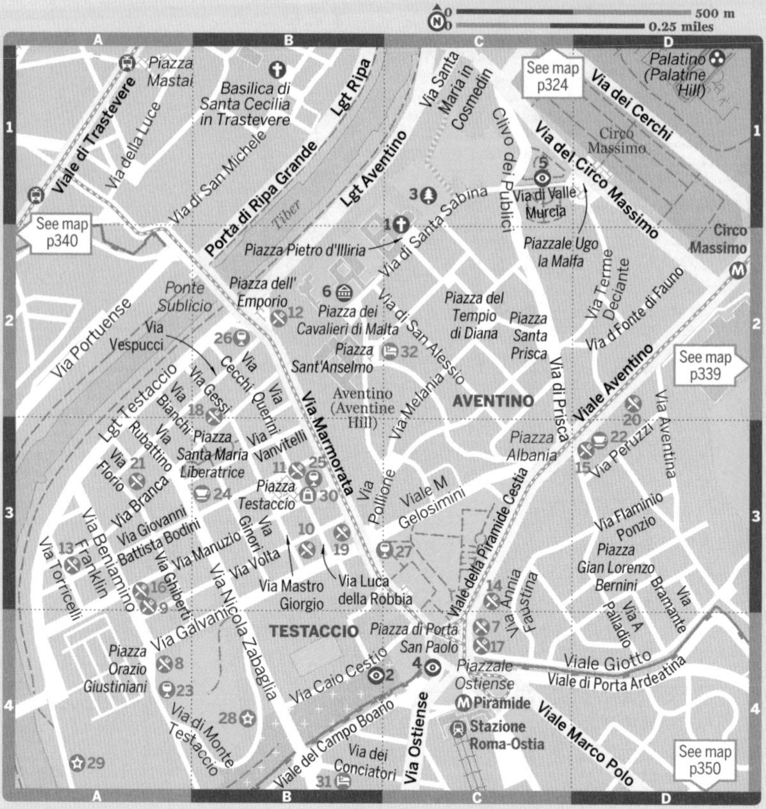

Sights **p192**

1 Basilica di Santa Sabina C1
2 Cimitero Acattolico per gli Stranieri B4
3 Parco Savello C1
4 Piramide di Caio Cestio C4
5 Roseto Comunale C1
6 Villa del Priorato di Malta B2

Eating **p195**

7 100% Bio C4
8 Checchino dal 1887 .... A4
9 Cups A3
10 Da Felice B3
11 Foodie Fresh Market B3
12 Giulietta B2
13 La Torricella A3
14 La Villetta C3
15 Marco Martini Restaurant D3
16 Mordi e Vai A3
17 Paraponzipò C4
18 Pizzeria Da Remo B2
19 Taverna Volpetti B3
20 Torcè D2
21 Trapizzino A3

Drinking & Nightlife **p199**

22 Casa Manfredi D3
23 L'Alibi A4
24 Linari B3
25 L'Oasi della Birra B3
26 Rec 23 .... B2
27 Tram Depot C3

Entertainment **p201**

28 ConteStaccio B4
29 Villaggio Globale A4

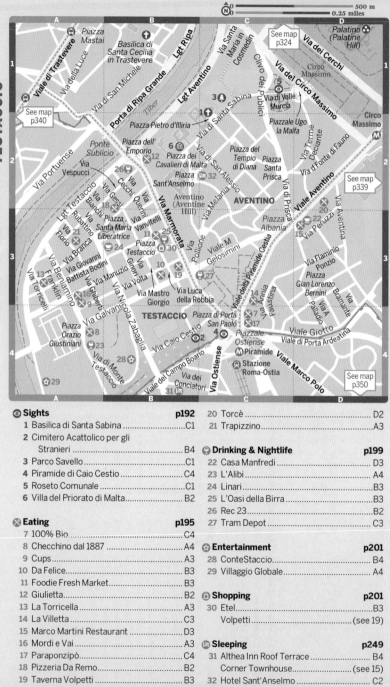

Shopping **p201**

30 Etel B3
Volpetti .... (see 19)

Sleeping **p249**

31 Althea Inn Roof Terrace B4
Corner Townhouse .... (see 15)
32 Hotel Sant'Anselmo C2

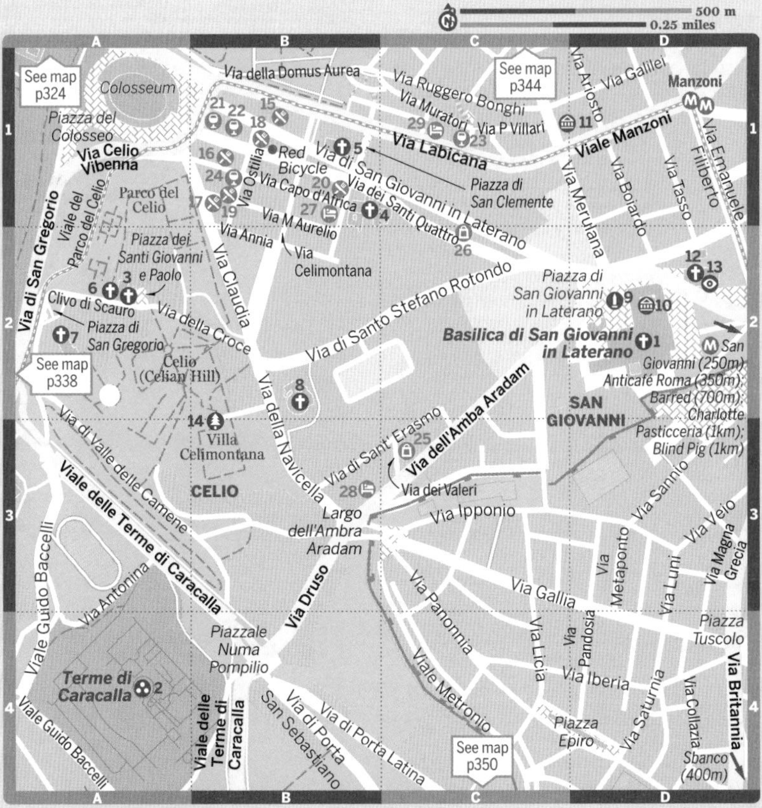

Top Experiences p190

1 Basilica di San Giovanni in Laterano D2
2 Terme di Caracalla A4

Sights p192

3 Basilica dei SS Giovanni e Paolo al Celio A2
4 Basilica dei SS Quattro Coronati B1
5 Basilica di San Clemente B1
6 Case Romane A2
7 Chiesa di San Gregorio al Celio A2
8 Chiesa di Santo Stefano Rotondo B2
9 Obelisk D2
10 Palazzo Laterano D2
11 Palazzo Merulana C1
12 Santuario della Scala Santa & Sancta Sanctorum D2
13 Triclinium Leoninum D2
14 Villa Celimontana B3

Eating p195

15 Aroma B1
16 Cafè Cafè B1
17 Caffè Propaganda B1
18 Divin Ostilia B1
19 Il Bocconcino B1
20 Li Rioni B1

Drinking & Nightlife p199

21 Coming Out B1
22 My Bar B1
23 Race Club Speakeasy C1
24 Wine Concept B1

Entertainment p201

Terme di Caracalla .... (see 2)

Shopping p201

25 Pifebo C3
26 Soul Food C2

Sleeping p249

27 Hotel Lancelot B1
28 Hotel Valeri B3
29 Top Floor Colosseo C1

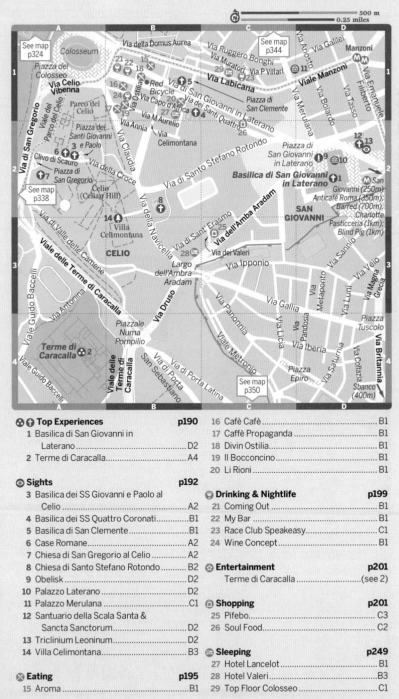

Key on p342

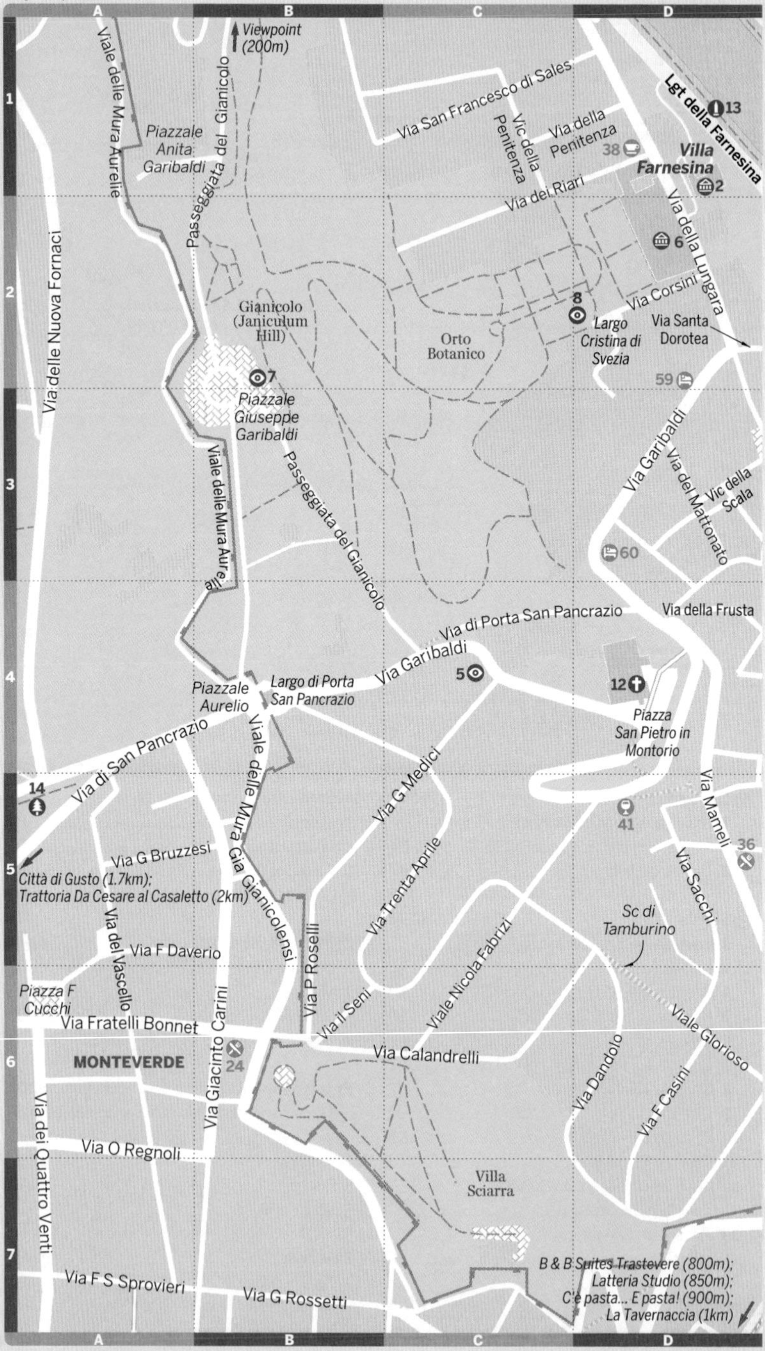
Viewpoint (200m)
Viale delle Mura Aurelie
Piazzale Anita Garibaldi
Passeggiata del Gianicolo
Via San Francesco di Sales
Vic della Penitenza
Via della Penitenza
Lgt della Farnesina
13
38
Villa Farnesina
2
Via dei Riari
Via della Lungara
6
Via delle Nuova Fornaci
Via Corsini
8
Gianicolo (Janiculum Hill)
Orto Botanico
Largo Cristina di Svezia
Via Santa Dorotea
59
7
Piazzale Giuseppe Garibaldi
Via Garibaldi
Via del Mattonato
Vic della Scala
60
Via della Frusta
Via di Porta San Pancrazio
5
12
Piazzale Aurelio
Largo di Porta San Pancrazio
Via di San Pancrazio
Piazza San Pietro in Montorio
14
Via G Medici
Via Mameli
41
36
Via G Bruzzesi
Via Trenta Aprile
Via Sacchi
Città di Gusto (1.7km); Trattoria Da Cesare al Casaletto (2km)
Viale delle Mura Gianicolensi
Sc di Tamburino
Via del Vascello
Via F Daverio
Via P Roselli
Viale Nicola Fabrizi
Piazza F Cucchi
Via Giacinto Carini
Via il Seni
Via Fratelli Bonnet
Viale Glorioso
MONTEVERDE
24
Via Calandrelli
Via Dandolo
Via F Casini
Via dei Quattro Venti
Via O Regnoli
Villa Sciarra
B & B Suites Trastevere (800m); Latteria Studio (850m); C'è pasta... E pasta! (900m); La Tavernaccia (1km)
Via F S Sprovieri
Via G Rossetti

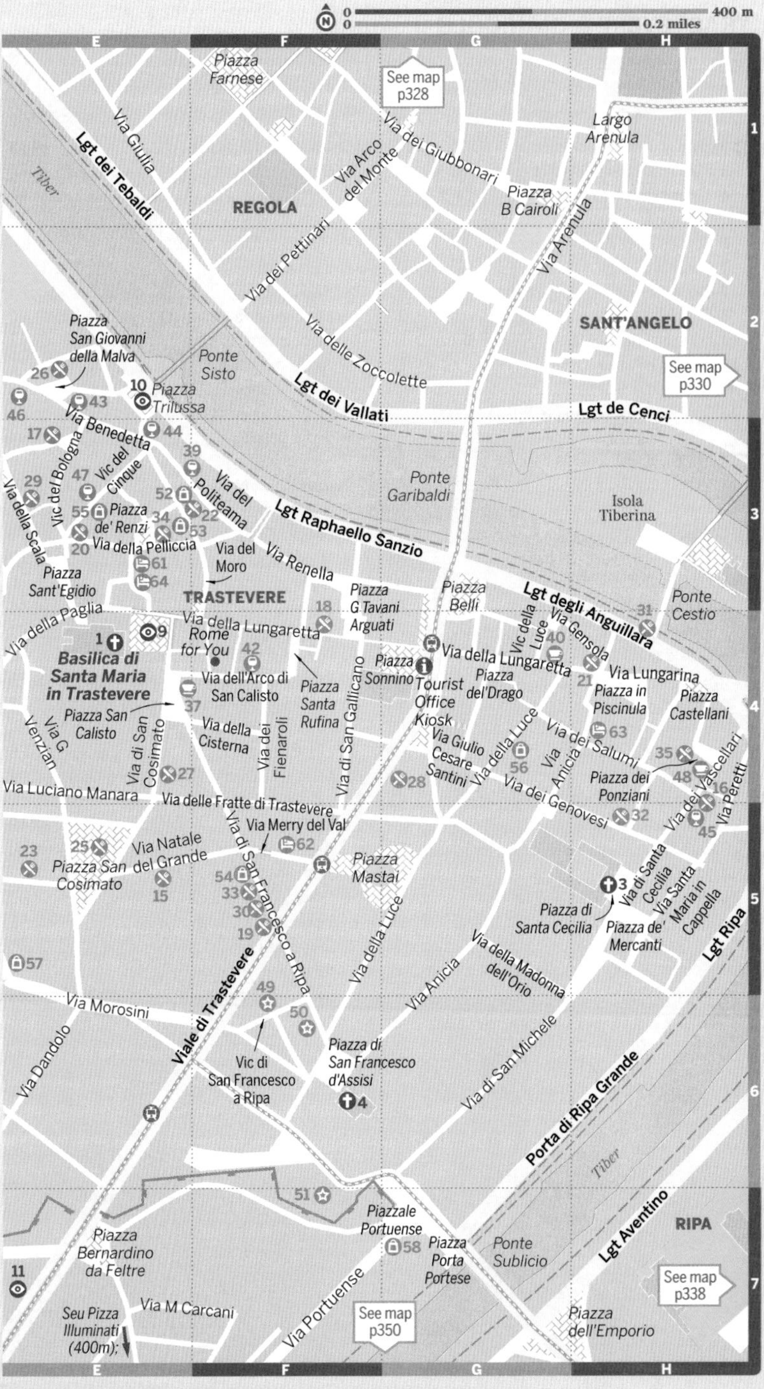

0 400 m
0 0.2 miles
E
F
G
H
Piazza Farnese
See map p328
Via Giulia
Lgt dei Tebaldi
Tiber
Via Arco del Monte
Via dei Giubbonari
Largo Arenula
Piazza B Cairoli
REGOLA
Via dei Pettinari
Via Arenula
SANT'ANGELO
Via delle Zoccolette
Piazza San Giovanni della Malva
Ponte Sisto
See map p330
Lgt dei Vallati
Lgt de Cenci
10 Piazza Trilussa
Via Benedetta
Vic del Bologna
Vic del Cinque
Via del Politeama
Ponte Garibaldi
Isola Tiberina
Via della Scala
Piazza de' Renzi
Lgt Raphaello Sanzio
Via della Pelliccia
Via del Moro
Via Renella
Piazza Sant'Egidio
TRASTEVERE
Piazza G Tavani Arguati
Piazza Belli
Lgt degli Anguillara
Ponte Cestio
Via della Paglia
Via della Lungaretta
Rome for You
Vic della Luce
Via Gensola
1 Basilica di Santa Maria in Trastevere
9
Via dell'Arco di San Calisto
Piazza Sonnino
Tourist Office Kiosk
Via della Lungaretta
Piazza del'Drago
Via Lungarina
Piazza in Piscinula
Piazza Castellani
Piazza Santa Rufina
Via di San Gallicano
Piazza San Calisto
Via G Venzian
Via di San Cosimato
Via della Cisterna
Via dei Fienaroli
Via Giulio Cesare Santini
Via della Luce
Via Anicia
Via dei Salumi
Piazza dei Ponziani
Via dei Vascellari
Via Peretti
Via Luciano Manara
Via delle Fratte di Trastevere
Via dei Genovesi
Via Merry del Val
Via Natale del Grande
Piazza San Cosimato
Via di San Francesco a Ripa
Piazza Mastai
3
Via di Santa Cecilia
Via Santa Maria in Cappella
Piazza di Santa Cecilia
Piazza de' Mercanti
Lgt Ripa
Via della Luce
Via della Madonna dell'Orio
Via Anicia
Via Morosini
Viale di Trastevere
Via Dandolo
Vic di San Francesco a Ripa
Piazza di San Francesco d'Assisi
4
Via di San Michele
Porta di Ripa Grande
Tiber
Piazzale Portuense
RIPA
Lgt Aventino
Piazza Bernardino da Feltre
Piazza Porta Portese
Ponte Sublicio
See map p338
Via M Carcani
Via Portuense
See map p350
Piazza dell'Emporio
Seu Pizza Illuminati (400m);

TRASTEVERE & GIANICOLO *Map on p340*

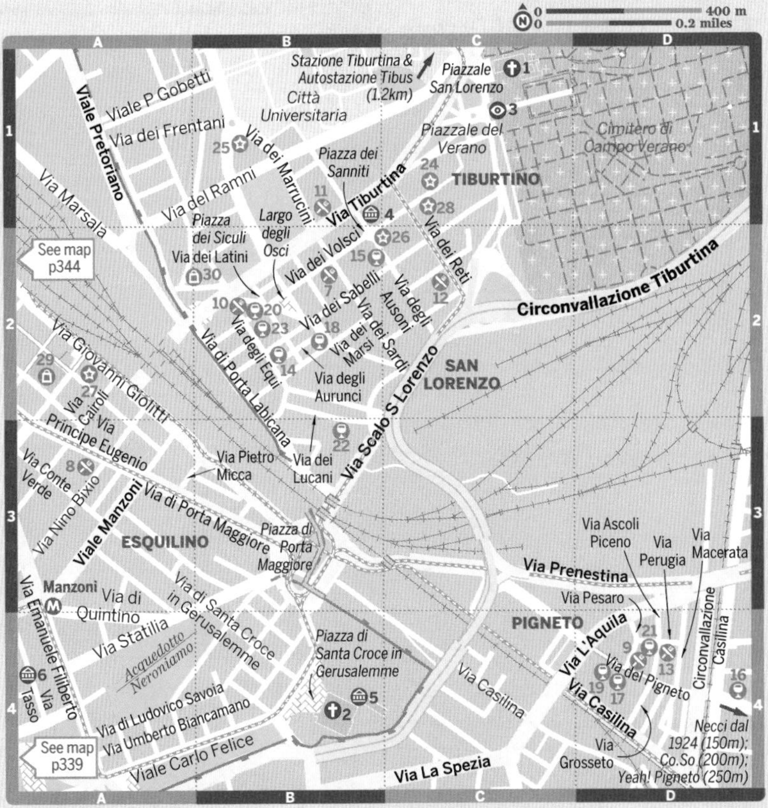

Sights p154

1 Basilica di San Lorenzo Fuori le Mura C1
2 Chiesa di Santa Croce in Gerusalemme B4
3 Cimitero di Campo Verano C1
4 Fondazione Pastificio Cerere B1
5 Museo Nazionale degli Strumenti B4
6 Museo Storico della Liberazione A4

Eating p159

Ex Pastificio .... (see 4)
7 Mozzico B2
8 Palazzo del Freddo di Giovanni Fassi A3
9 Pigneto Quarantuno D4
10 Pizzeria Formula 1 .... B2
11 Said B1
12 Tram Tram C2
13 Vitaminas 24 .... D4

Drinking & Nightlife p164

14 Artisan B2
15 Bar Celestino B2
16 Birra Più D4
17 Cargo D4
18 Gente di San Lorenzo B2
19 Guerra al Pigneto D4
20 Il Sorì B2
21 Il Tiaso D4
22 Locanda Atlantide B3
23 Officina Beat B2

Entertainment p169

24 Esc Atelier C1
25 Istituzione Universitaria dei Concerti B1
26 Nuovo Cinema Palazzo C2
27 Teatro Ambra Jovinelli A2
28 Wishlist C1

Shopping p169

29 Nuovo Mercato Esquilino A2
30 Transmission B2

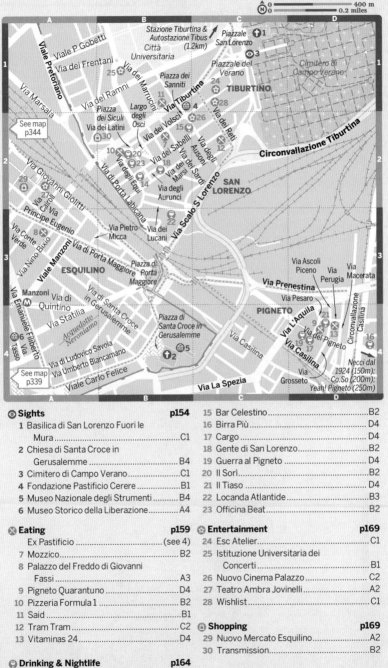

MONTI & ESQUILINO

Key on p346

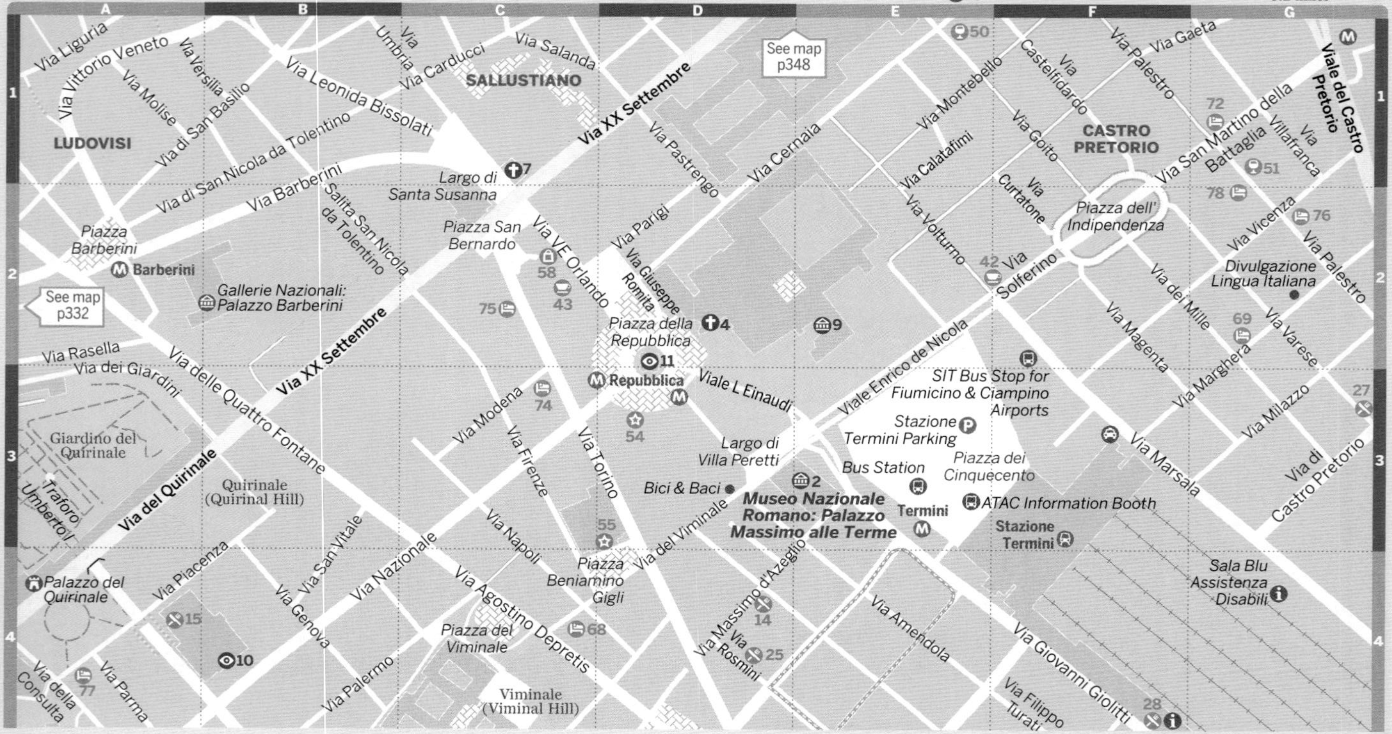

MONTI & ESQUILINO

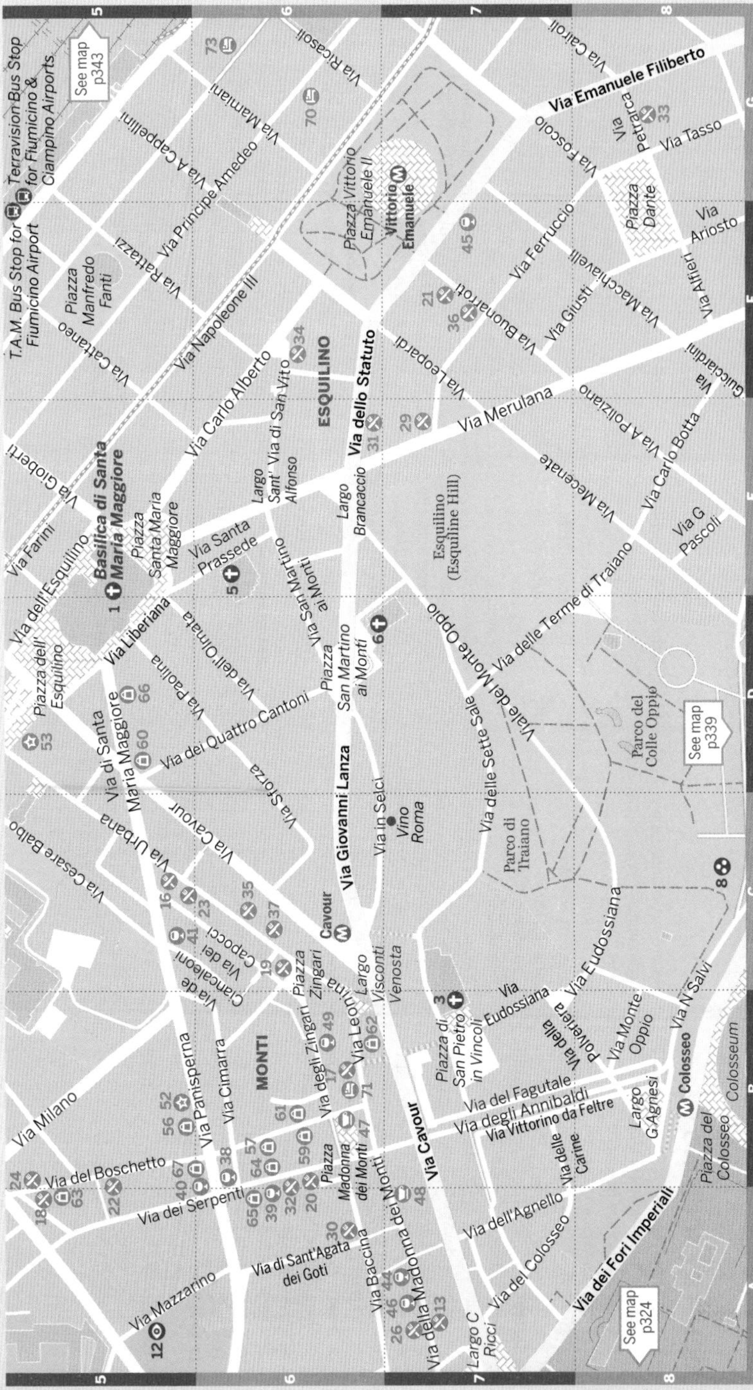

MONTI & ESQUILINO *Map on p344*

Top Experiences p152
1 Basilica di Santa Maria Maggiore.. E5
2 Museo Nazionale Romano: Palazzo Massimo alle Terme ... E3

Sights p154
3 Basilica di San Pietro in Vincoli B7
4 Basilica di Santa Maria degli Angeli e dei Martiri ... D2
5 Basilica di Santa Prassede ... E6
6 Chiesa di San Martino ai Monti ... D6
7 Chiesa di Santa Maria della Vittoria ... C1
8 Domus Aurea ... C8
Fontana delle Naiadi ... (see 11)
9 Museo Nazionale Romano: Terme di Diocleziano ... E2
10 Palazzo delle Esposizioni ... B4
11 Piazza della Repubblica ... D2
12 Villa Aldobrandini ... A5

Eating p159
13 Alle Carrette ... A7
14 Amodei Banco e Bottega ... D4
15 Antonello Colonna Open ... A4
16 Aromaticus ... C5
17 Ciuri Ciuri ... B6
18 Da Valentino ... A5
19 Fatamorgana Monti ... C6
20 Forno da Milvio ... B6
21 Forno Roscioli Pietro ... F7
22 Green & Go ... B5
23 Grezzo ... C5
24 La Barrique ... B5
25 La Gallina Bianca ... D4
26 La Taverna dei Fori Imperiali ... A7
27 Meid in Nepols ... G3
28 Mercato Centrale ... F4
29 Panella ... E7
30 Pasta Chef ... A6
31 Pasticceria Regoli ... E6
32 Temakinho ... B6
33 Trattoria Da Danilo ... G8
34 Trattoria Monti ... F6
35 Urbana 47 ... C6
36 Vecchia Roma ... F7
37 Zia Rosetta ... C6

Drinking & Nightlife p164
38 Ai Tre Scalini ... B6
39 Al Vino al Vino ... A6
40 Barzilai Bistro ... B6
41 Blackmarket Hall ... C5
42 Caffè e Pasticceria U. Giuliani ... F2
43 Dagnino ... C2
44 Fafiuché ... A7
45 Gatsby Café ... F7
46 Ice Club ... A7
47 La Bottega del Caffè ... B6
48 La Casetta a Monti ... A7
49 Libreria Caffè Bohemien ... B6
50 Trimani ... E1
51 Yellow Bar ... G1
Zest Bar ... (see 73)

Entertainment p169
52 Charity Café ... B5
53 Orbis Servizi ... D5
54 Space Cinema Moderno ... D3
55 Teatro dell'Opera di Roma ... D3

Shopping p169
56 Abito ... B5
57 Centoventisette ... B6
58 Feltrinelli International ... C2
59 Flamingo Vintage ... B6
60 Giacomo Santini ... D5
61 Le Nou ... B6
62 Mercato Monti Urban Market ... B6
63 Perlei ... A5
64 Pifebo ... B6
65 Podere Vecciano ... A6
66 Roma Liuteria di Mathias Menanteau ... D5
67 Tina Sondergaard ... B5

Sleeping p247
68 66 Imperial Inn ... C4
69 Beehive ... G2
70 Generator Hostel ... G6
71 Hotel Duca d'Alba ... B6
72 Meininger Roma Hostel ... G1
73 Radisson Blu es. ... G6
74 Residenza Cellini ... C3
75 RomeHello ... C2
76 The Liberty ... G2
77 Villa Spalletti Trivelli ... A4
78 Yellow Hostel ... G2

VILLA BORGHESE & NORTHERN ROME *Map on p348*

Key on p347

VILLA BORGHESE & NORTHERN ROME

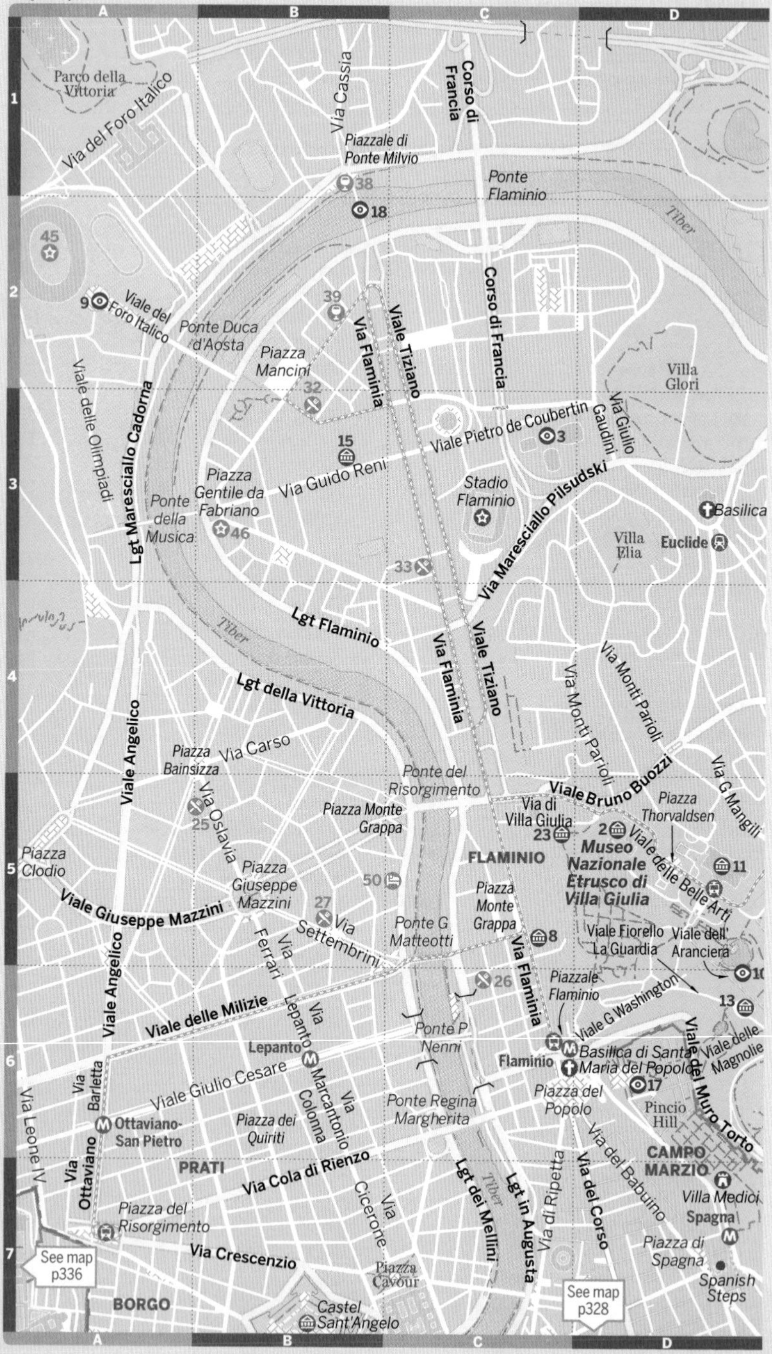

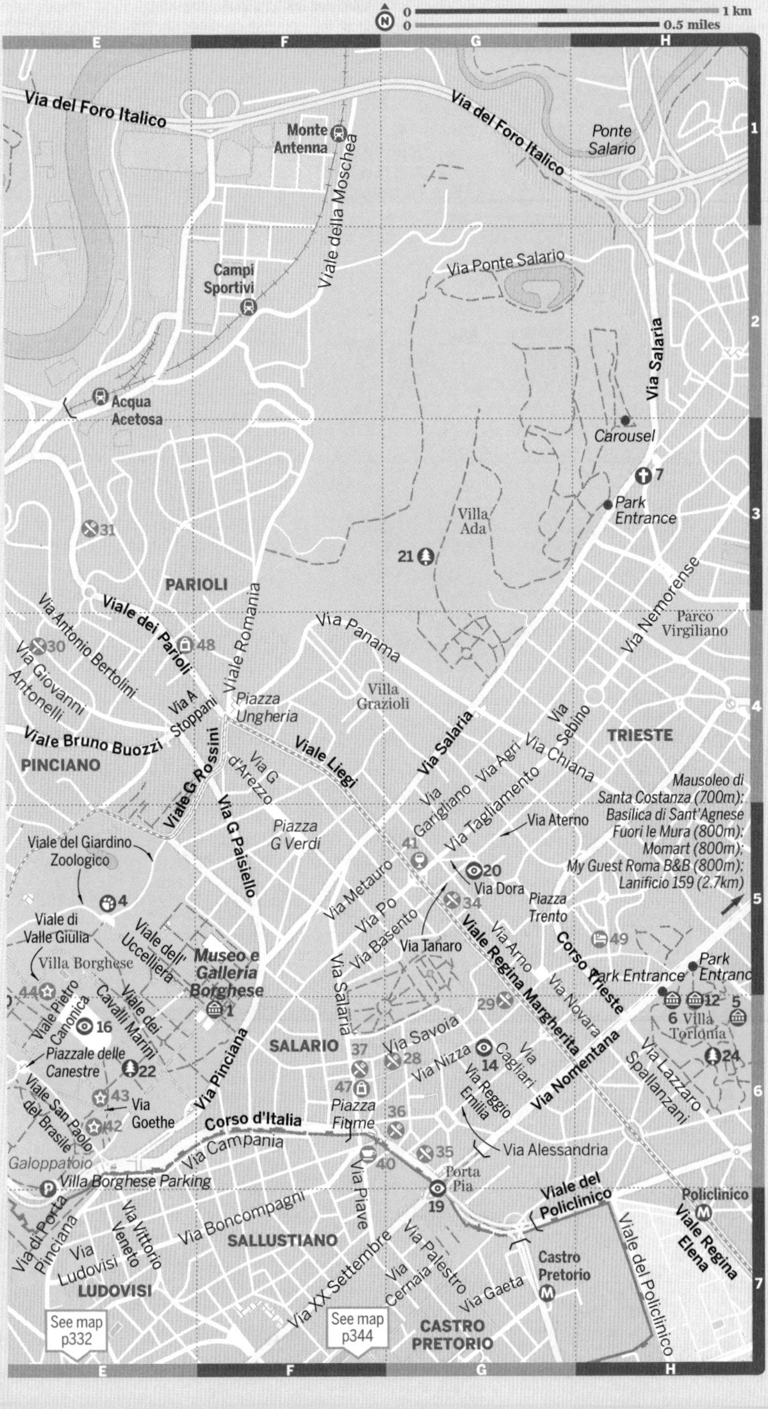

VILLA BORGHESE & NORTHERN ROME
0
1 km
0.5 miles
Via del Foro Italico
Monte Antenna
Viale della Moschea
Ponte Salario
Campi Sportivi
Via Ponte Salario
Via Salaria
Acqua Acetosa
Carousel
7
Park Entrance
Villa Ada
21
31
PARIOLI
Viale Romania
Via Nemorense
Parco Virgiliano
Via Panama
Via Antonio Bertolini
Viale dei Parioli
48
30
Via Giovanni Antonelli
Piazza Ungheria
Villa Grazioli
Via A Stoppani
Via Sebino
Via Chiana
Via Agri
TRIESTE
Viale Bruno Buozzi
PINCIANO
Viale G Rossini
Via G d'Arezzo
Viale Liegi
Via Garigliano
Via Tagliamento
Mausoleo di Santa Costanza (700m); Basilica di Sant'Agnese Fuori le Mura (800m); Momart (800m); My Guest Roma B&B (800m); Lanificio 159 (2.7km)
Via G Paisiello
Piazza G Verdi
Via Aterno
Viale del Giardino Zoologico
41
20
Via Metauro
Via Dora
Piazza Trento
4
Via Po
34
Viale di Valle Giulia
Viale dell' Uccelliera
Via Basento
Via Tanaro
Via Arno
Corso Trieste
49
Villa Borghese
Museo e Galleria Borghese
Via Salaria
Viale Regina Margherita
Park Entrance
Park Entrance
44
Viale Pietro Canonica
Viale dei Cavalli Marini
1
Via Novara
29
6
12
5
Villa Torlonia
16
SALARIO
37
Via Savoia
14
Via Cagliari
Via Nomentana
Via Lazzaro Spallanzani
24
Piazzale delle Canestre
22
28
Via Nizza
Via Reggio Emilia
Via Pinciana
47
43
Via Goethe
Piazza Fiume
36
Viale San Paolo del Brasile
42
Corso d'Italia
Via Alessandria
Galoppatoio
Via Campania
35
40
Via Piave
Porta Pia
Villa Borghese Parking
19
Viale del Policlinico
Policlinico
Via di Porta Pinciana
Via Vittorio Veneto
Via Boncompagni
Viale Regina Elena
Via Ludovisi
SALLUSTIANO
Via XX Settembre
Via Palestro
Castro Pretorio
Viale del Policlinico
LUDOVISI
Via Cernaia
Via Gaeta
See map p332
See map p344
CASTRO PRETORIO
E
F
G
H
1
2
3
4
5
6
7

SOUTHERN ROME

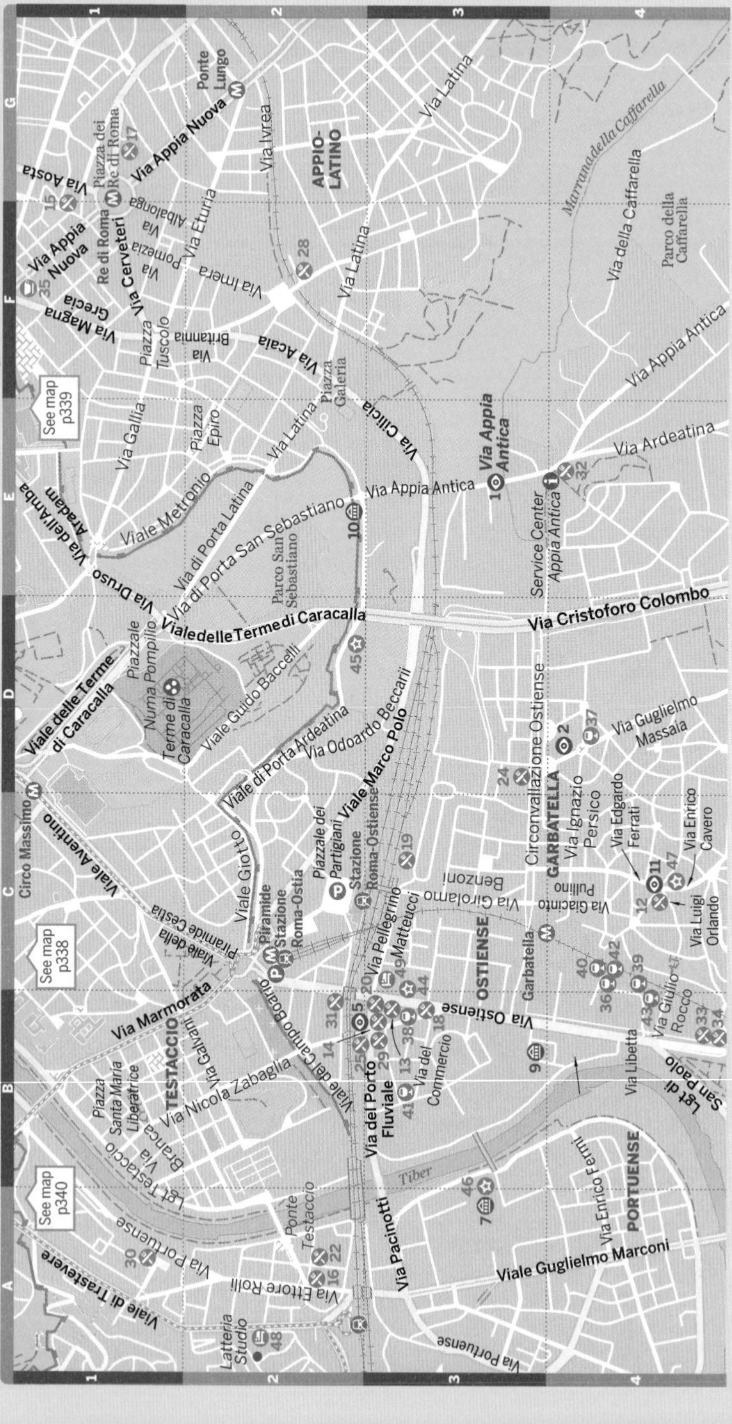

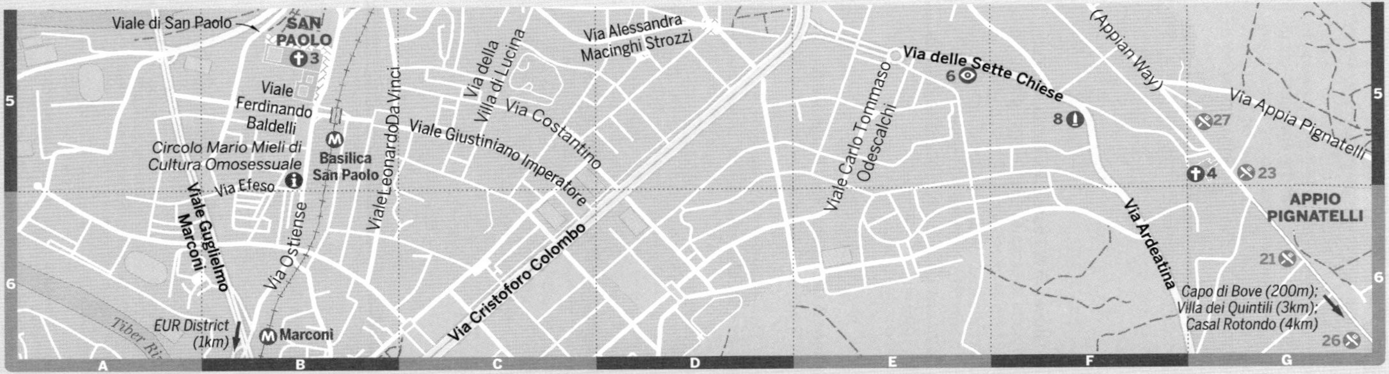

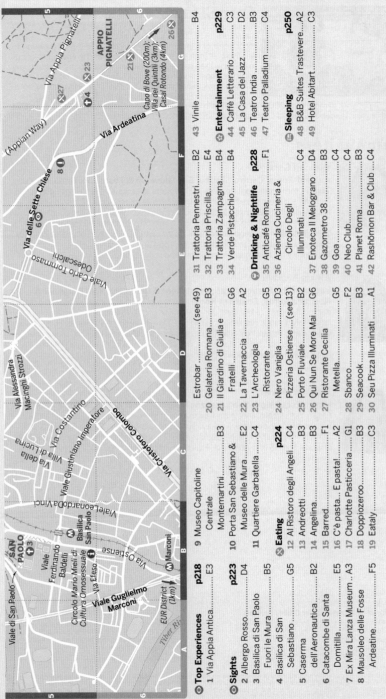

Top Experiences p218
1 Via Appia Antica........E3

Sights p223
2 Albergo Rosso........D4
3 Basilica di San Paolo Fuori le Mura........B5
4 Basilica di San Sebastiano........G5
5 Caserma dell'Aeronautica........B2
6 Catacombe di Santa Domitilla........E5
7 Ex Mira Lanza Museum..A3
8 Mausoleo delle Fosse Ardeatine........F5
9 Museo Capitoline Centrale Montemartini........B3
10 Porta San Sebastiano & Museo delle Mura........E2
11 Quartiere Garbatella........C4

Eating p224
12 Al Ristoro degli Angeli.....C4
13 Andreotti........B3
14 Angelina........B3
15 Barred........F1
16 C'è pasta... E pasta!........A2
17 Charlotte Pasticceria........G1
18 Doppiozeroo........B3
19 Eataly........C3
Estrobar........(see 49)
20 Gelateria Romana........B3
21 Il Giardino di Giulia e Fratelli........G6
22 La Tavernaccia........A2
23 L'Archeologia Ristorante........G5
24 Nero Vaniglia........D3
Pizzeria Ostiense....(see 13)
25 Porto Fluviale........B2
26 Qui Nun Se More Mai........G6
27 Ristorante Cecilia Metella........G5
28 Sbanco........F2
29 Seacook........B3
30 Seu Pizza Illuminati........A1
31 Trattoria Pennestri........B2
32 Trattoria Priscilla........E4
33 Trattoria Zampagna........B4
34 Verde Pistacchio........B4

Drinking & Nightlife p228
35 Anticafé Roma........F1
36 Azienda Cucineria & Circolo Degli Illuminati........C4
37 Enoteca Il Melograno........D4
38 Gazometro 38........B3
39 Goa........C4
40 Neo Club........C4
41 Planet Roma........B3
42 Rashōmon Bar & Club....C4
43 Vinile........B4

Entertainment p229
44 Caffè Letterario........C3
45 La Casa del Jazz........D2
46 Teatro India........B3
47 Teatro Palladium........C4

Sleeping p250
48 B&B Suites Trastevere....A2
49 Hotel Abitart........C3

Our Stor

A beat-up old car, a few dollars in the pocket and a sense of adventure. In 1972 that's all Tony and Maureen Wheeler needed for the trip of a lifetime – across Europe and Asia overland to Australia. It took several months, and at the end – broke but inspired – they sat at their kitchen table writing and stapling together their first travel guide, *Across Asia on the Cheap*. Within a week they'd sold 1500 copies. Lonely Planet was born.

Today, Lonely Planet has offices in the US, Ireland and China, with a network of more than 2000 contributors in every corner of the globe. We share Tony's belief that 'a great guidebook should do three things: inform, educate and amuse'.

Our Writers

Duncan Garwood

Ancient Rome; Centro Storico; San Giovanni & Testaccio; Ostia Antica; Tivoli From facing fast bowlers in Barbados to sidestepping hungry pigs in Goa, Duncan's travels have thrown up many unique experiences. These days he largely dedicates himself to the Mediterranean and Italy, his adopted homeland where he's been living since 1997. He's worked on around 50 Lonely Planet titles, including guidebooks to Italy, Rome, Sardinia, Sicily, Spain and Portugal, and has contributed to books on world food and epic drives. He's also written about Italy for newspapers, websites and magazines.

Alexis Averbuck

Vatican City, Borgo & Prati; Trastevere & Gianicolo; Villa Borghese & Northern Rome; Southern Rome Alexis was born in Oakland, California, and earned a degree at Harvard University. For Lonely Planet, she specialises in Iceland, Italy, France (especially Provence, Dordogne, Brittany and the Loire Valley), Greece and Antarctica. She also writes for the BBC, international magazines and newspapers and online platforms; exhibits her oil paintings and watercolours; and starred in a television program on Catalunya.

Virginia Maxwell

Monti, Esquilino & San Lorenzo; Tridente, Trevi & the Quirinale Although based in Australia, Virginia's major area of interest is the Mediterranean. She has covered Spain, Italy, Turkey, Syria, Lebanon, Israel, Egypt, Morocco and Tunisia for Lonely Planet – but she also covers Finland, Bali, Armenia, the Netherlands, the US and Australia. Follow her @maxwellvirginia on Instagram and Twitter.

Published by Lonely Planet Global Limited
CRN 554 153
12th edition – Apr 2022
ISBN 978 1 78868 409 5

10 9 8 7 6 5 4 3 2 1
Printed in China